Pl. XII.

Drawn by R. B. Price. L. Gast & Bro. lith., St. Louis.

View of Quincy and the Mississippi bottom,
from Col. Mays in Marion County Mo.

THE

FIRST AND SECOND

ANNUAL REPORTS

OF THE

GEOLOGICAL SURVEY

OF

MISSOURI,

BY

G. C. SWALLOW,

STATE GEOLOGIST.

BY ORDER OF THE LEGISLATURE:

JAMES LUSK, PUBLIC PRINTER,

JEFFERSON CITY.

1855.

PREFACE.

A REPORT, professing to give the Geology of a State, so extensive and possessing so many geological features as Missouri, after the labors of eighteen months only, may seem to be premature; but the law under which the Survey was organized, and a universal anxiety to learn the general features of our Geology, have made it necessary and expedient.

A Survey may gain temporary popularity by exaggerating the mineral and agricultural wealth of the region examined; but the results must prove alike fatal to the Geologist and those who credit his statements. It has, therefore, been our aim to give no opinion, which is not based upon the very best evidence; and to place our estimates below, rather than above the reality. Some may be disappointed by this course, but the truth of science, and the general and permanent utility of the work, must be preferred to the personal interests of the few.

Justice to the different members of the Geological corps, seems to demand a few words of explanation as to the manner in which the labors of the Survey have been performed and the Reports made. Particular duties and fields of labor have been assigned to each member, with the understanding that he is to be particularly responsible for the discharge of those duties, and to report upon the results of his own labors. Consequently, every one has, by his own examinations, and independent of others, arrived at the results reported. By thus laboring in different localities, we have been able to accomplish much more than by any other system of operations; * and by a comparison

* The experience and skill of the various members of the corps have rendered this course entirely safe.

of the results of the examinations made by different individuals in distant parts of the State, the accuracy of our conclusions respecting its geological features, could be tested in the most satisfactory manner. Since each Report was made, without a knowledge of what would be submitted by others, and as some of the same geological features appear in the different districts examined, some repetition of the facts and conclusions, must be expected in the various Reports.

Circumstances have compelled us to omit the Reports upon the Missouri River Section, the Section from Providence to Hannibal, that from St. Louis to the Iron Mountain; and the chapter explaining the principles of the science has been replaced by the Vocabulary of Scientific Terms; while the Reports on Economical Geology, Cooper County and the South-West, have been very much abridged and condensed.

Such has been the anxiety to push forward our field operations that but very little time has been devoted to the preparation of Reports; this, together with the hasty manner in which the work has been carried through the press, has, doubtless, caused many violations of elegance and accuracy of style; but for errors in matters of fact and scientific deductions, we ask no indulgence. Our object has been to give a true and unvarnished statement of the facts observed, and the deductions which may be legitimately derived from them; those, therefore, who correct our errors, either in matters of fact or scientific deduction, will aid us in our labors and be entitled to our gratitude. All errors will be most cheerfully corrected when they are made known. Great care has been taken to get all the names and localities, which are mentioned in the Report, or laid down on the maps, correct; still, where so many thousands occur and are passed so rapidly through the press, it is almost certain that some are wrong. If so, they will be corrected hereafter. The numerous Geological Maps and Sections contain so many details of our Geology, that a large amount of letter-press explanation respecting the locality, dip, relative position and range of the strata, has been rendered unnecessary.

Justice and grateful memories prompt us to mention our numerous obligations to the citizens of Missouri for the sympathy and aid everywhere bestowed upon us while prosecuting our labors. The Survey is particularly indebted to his Excellency, STERLING PRICE, the Governor of Missouri, for the prompt manner, in which he has rendered the Survey all the coöperation necessary to secure its progress and success. The Curators and Faculty of the State University have greatly facilitated our labors by inviting us to occupy its spacious apartments, with free access to its Library, Laboratory and Apparatus. We are, also, under like obligations to Dr. POPE and other members of the Faculty for similar facilities in the St. Louis Medical College, where the Chemical Department is located. General LOUGHBOROUGH has rendered essential service in granting us free access to the maps and charts of the General Land Office. The Officers and Engineers of the various Railroad Companies in the State, have greatly facilitated our labors by their courtesies in furnishing the Survey with maps and profiles of the roads surveyed; but we are particularly indebted to the Hannibal and St. Joseph Railroad Company for placing Maj. HAWN under our direction to make the Survey along the line of that road, and to Professor G. C. PRATT, and Mr. GEO. C. BROADHEAD, for sections and specimens collected.

Gen. T. E. THOMPSON, Col. W. C. BAYLEY, Dr. A. F. JETER, Capt. F. WHALEY, Mr. J. W. LEAR, and Dr. L. S. BANKS, of Marion; Messrs. BROWN & BROTHER, at Dallas; Col. R. MIDDLETON, and Capt. L. J. EASTIN, of St. Joseph; Messrs. BRANHAM & NORRIS, and H. M. MORE,. Esq., of Weston; Mr. GEO. S. PARK, of Parkville; Hon. CHARLES SIMS, of Cass; Prof. JAMES LOVE, of Liberty; WM. MUSGROVE, Esq., W. ANDERSON, ESQ., and Dr. ALEXANDER, of Lexington; Gen. STRINGFELLOW, of Brunswick; CLARK H. GREEN, Esq., and Dr. TALBOT, of Howard; A. W. SIMPSON, Esq., Mr. B. S. WILSON, Prof. LOOMIS, Mr. JOSEPH STAPLES, Mr. WM. L. SCOTT, Mr. H. C. LEVENS and Mr. Z. P. VANDIVEER, of Cooper; Judge WRIGHT, and JAMES ATKISSON, Esq., of Warsaw; Hon. W. J. MAYO and Dr. LAWRENCE LEWIS, of Oscola; Judge G. W. MOULDER and Capt. W.

D. MURPHY, of Camden; Hon. R. G. ROBERTS, of Frémont; Messrs. HARKLERODE & BROTHER, E. B. JAMES, Esq., and Mr. J. R. CHENAULT, of Jasper; Judge M. H. RITCHIE and Mr. GEO. W. MOSELEY, of Newton; Dr. SNEIDER, Col. J. I. TILTON, and Dr. B. M. JEWETT, of Bolivar; Capt. JOHN G. SCOTT, at Iron Mountain; Col. C. C. ZEIGLER and Col. L. V. BOGY, of Ste. Genevieve; Col. A. H. GLASBY and Mr. JOHN B. VALLE, at Pilot Knob; Col. JOHN HINTON and Mr. J. W. HARRIS, of Rocheport; ELI E. BASS, Esq., Maj. ROLLINS and Mr. JOHN H. CHAFFEY, of Boone; Mr. H. COBB, of St. Louis, and many others in various parts of the State, have rendered the Survey important services, by which its progress has been very much facilitated. We are, also, under many obligations to the lamented Col. ADAM B. CHAMBERS, for much information respecting the topography and mineral wealth of the State.

The excellent illustrations of this Report show how much we are indebted to the skill and taste of Mr. R. B. PRICE, the indefatigable Draughtsman of the Survey, and of those gentlemen, who have made the engravings; and the beautiful letter-press is of itself sufficient praise to the gentlemen who have executed it.

JEFFERSON CITY, *Sept.*, 1855.

TABLE OF CONTENTS.

CHAPTER II.

CHAPTER III.

CHAPTER IV.

CHAPTER V.

PART II.

DR. LITTON'S REPORT.

MR. MEEK'S REPORT ON MONITEAU COUNTY.

MR. HAWN'S REPORT.

PAGE.

DR. SHUMARD'S REPORT.

APPENDIX.

LIST OF ILLUSTRATIONS.

PART I.

PART I.

THE FIRST ANNUAL

REPORT,

1853.

HON. JOHN M. RICHARDSON,

Secretary of State of Missouri.

IN making the First Annual Report on the Geology of Missouri, according to the law providing for the Survey, it is not deemed advisable to enter upon a detailed description of the geological features thus far observed, for the following reasons: —

1st. Such a report can not be printed, and will consequently be of no possible service to any one, until the meeting of the next Legislature, or the time for making the Second Annual Report.

2d. The facts developed by our researches can be stated at the end of the second year, in one report, with much less labor than by compiling a part for the first, and the remainder for the second.

3d. In order to make out a full report, before the 1st of December, it would have been necessary to suspend our field operations for several months, at a season the best adapted to such work; whereas, by postponing all details until the next year, much of it can be prepared when field work will be impracticable.

For these reasons, I have thought it expedient to report progress merely, at this time, and continue our field operations as far into the winter as possible.

The specimens of Rocks, Minerals and Fossils, thus far collected, have not been distributed, as we shall need them at the Geological Rooms for reference, in making out our future reports.

Hoping the progress of our labors will meet the approbation of the Citizens of Missouri, I herewith submit my First Annual Report.

Very respectfully,

Your Ob't Serv't,

G. C. SWALLOW,

STATE GEOLOGIST.

Geological Rooms, State University,
Columbia, Mo., Nov. 10, 1853.

B

REPORT OF PROGRESS.

On the 12th day of April last, I had the honor of receiving a Commission from the Governor of Missouri, directing me to make a

"*Thorough Geological and Mineralogical Survey of this State, with a view to determine the order, succession, arrangement, relative position, dip or inclination, and comparative magnitude of the several strata, or geological formations within the State; and to discover and examine all beds or deposits of ore, coal, marls and such other mineral substances, and mineral waters, as may be useful or valuable; and to perform such other duties as may be necessary to make a full and complete Geological and Mineralogical Survey of the State.*"

Under the direction and with the advice of His Excellency, the Governor, I forthwith set about such arrangements as seemed best adapted to secure an early completion of this great work, in the best possible manner.

The necessary instruments and outfit were immediately ordered; and every effort was made to secure the assistance of able and experienced men.

On the 15th of April, A. Litton, M.D., of St. Louis, was appointed "Chemist," and R. B. Price, Esq., of Brunswick, "Draughtsman" of the Survey.

Early in May I visited St. Louis, to procure another Assistant and make the necessary arrangements for the Chemist to enter upon his duties. While there, it was ascertained that B. F. Shumard, M.D., of Louisville, then employed in the United States Geological Survey of Oregon, could be obtained early in the Autumn.

He was subsequently appointed "Palæontologist and Assistant Geologist."

As the cost of outfit for the different companies, and the necessary instruments, would come out of the sum appropriated for the first year, it was deemed advisable to appoint only three first-class Assistants for that season.

On the 24th of May I appointed Mr. Frederic Bass, of Columbia, subordinate Assistant, and entered upon the field work of the Survey. The remainder of May, and the June following, were spent in making examinations in Boone and Howard counties; and particularly in collecting the fossils so abundant in the Carboniferous rocks of those counties. By making these examinations and collections near the Depôt, we avoided the necessity of collecting and transporting the same specimens from distant parts of the State.

On the 21st of June, Dr. Litton visited Ste. Genevieve, Farmington, Mine la Motte, Pilot Knob, Shepherd Mountain, Caledonia, Potosi, Old Mines, Shibboleth, Tarpley's Mines, Vallé's and Perry's Mines, and collected, besides much valuable information, the ores, minerals and rocks found in those various localities.

A part of this collection was forwarded to the "World's Fair," at New York, and the remainder was reserved for analyses and the cabinets to be made up.

After completing this tour, Dr. Litton entered upon his duties in the Laboratory, where he remained making analyses of the minerals collected until the 12th of September, when he again took the field in company with Dr. Shumard.

As the success of the Survey would depend somewhat upon the accuracy of the instruments used, it was thought advisable to visit New York, make our own selections, and superintend their transportation.

I accordingly visited that city in July; purchased barometers, thermometers, compasses, hydrometers, theodolite, blow-pipes, chemicals, etc., and reached St. Louis on my return, on the 11th of August, with an excellent outfit of instruments in good condition.

In order to reap the earliest possible advantages of an Official Report on our mineral resources, Drs. Litton and Shumard were detailed to make an examination of the mineral lands in Franklin, Washington, St. François and Madison counties, and such other localities, as they might deem important to accomplish the objects of the Survey.

After making all necessary preparation, they entered upon that work on the 12th of September, and, during its prosecution, made several excursions: —

1st. Starting from St. Louis, they visited Union, Washington and Franklin, and returned thence to St. Louis.

2d. They traversed the line of the Pacific Railroad to Franklin county, and thence along the Springfield road to the Lead and Iron district, in Towns. 41 and 42 N., R. 1 W. They then visited Stanton Copper Mine, and continued their examinations along the Springfield road to the boundary of Franklin county, and back to St. Louis by the way of Union.

3d. On the 12th of October they again left St. Louis for the

Iron Mountain, which they reached by way of Jefferson county, Potosi and Caledonia, on the 20th of October. From Iron Mountain they passed over the plank road to Ste. Genevieve, and thence through the northern parts of Ste. Genevieve and St. François counties, to French Village, Perry's Mines, Hillsboro and Fenton, to St. Louis.

During these several excursions they made Geological Sections, visited mines, collected statistics, ores, minerals and fossils, and made barometrical observations. All of which will be reported in detail in our future communications.

Mr. Price spent the months of July and August drawing Township Maps from those in the General Land Office in St. Louis.

As the detailed and careful examinations demanded by the Bill providing for the Geological Survey, could be much more advantageously made after the Geological character of the whole State is better known, it was determined to make a somewhat rapid though careful reconnoissance of those parts, whose Geological features were not known; to make Geological Sections along the Mississippi and Missouri rivers; along the line of the Hannibal and St. Joseph Railroad, and from the mouth of the Kansas, or some point on the Missouri, to the South-Western counties, and thence East to the Mississippi.

After obtaining a life-boat and other necessary out-fit, and engaging Capt. M. Carson for pilot, and the necessary boatmen, we left for Bluff City,* August 20th, on the *Robert Campbell.*

We arrived at our destination on September 9th; when an unexpected difficulty opposed our progress. Our boatmen had failed to meet us according to agreement, and our pilot was on the sick list. But no aid could be obtained, and we resolved to perform extra duty, and proceed, with what force we had, to make our examinations along the Missouri river.

Matters thus arranged, we left our camp, near Bluff City, on October 14th, and reached Rocheport on the 5th of November, running 600 miles in forty-five days.

The Missouri river has made so many and so great changes in its position since the lineal surveys were made, that we found all the

* We passed up thus high that we might see the Upper Carboniferous rocks, where they are supposed to be the best developed, between Bluff City and the mouth of the Kansas; as the commercial value of a large portion of our coal-beds depends upon the position and thickness of these strata, which rest upon them in large portions of the State.

existing maps of it very inaccurate. This fact led us to the determination of collecting the data for a correct one, while we were making the necessary Geological examinations and observations. To this end we took the bearings and distances from bend to bend of the river, as we descended, comparing and correcting each day's work by the township plats of the lineal surveys. Besides, we made careful and minute Geological examinations wherever the rocks showed themselves along the bluffs, and constructed eighty-two measured sections, with lithological descriptions of the rocks, together with a catalogue of minerals and fossils found in them. We, also, collected several thousand fossils and specimens of rocks, minerals and soils, for analyses and the cabinets; made many barometrical observations to obtain the general level of the country and the height of the bluffs; and meteorological tables, and catalogues of the plants and trees, to ascertain the agricultural capacities of the region.

Though these various duties, added to the perplexities and anxieties of such a voyage, upon such a river, were somewhat onerous, still the sublime views of the boundless prairies of Nebraska and Kansas; the broad luxuriant savannas of the Missouri bottom and its magnificent forests; the unequalled soils of the "Rolling Prairie," of the "Timber," and of the "Oak Openings" of the Platte Purchase; and the hundred species of extinct beings, now for the first time exhumed to advance the cause of science, all conspired to render our labors a pastime, and fill us with the highest anticipations of the future wealth and power of our State.

In conclusion, it gives me great pleasure to say, the Survey, thus far, has been eminently successful. Drs. Litton and Shumard have been indefatigable in their efforts to push the work forward to a successful completion. Mr. Price has not only most skillfully discharged his duties in sketching maps and Geological scenery, but has been ever ready to lend a helping hand to the other departments of the Survey. In short, all have appeared to feel that they are employed in a work of the highest importance; that the mining, agricultural and commercial interests of our State, are in a considerable degree placed in their hands; and that our reputation and future prospects will, in no small degree, depend upon the successful completion of this great work.

THE

SECOND ANNUAL

REPORT.

1854.

HON. JOHN M. RICHARDSON,

Secretary of State of Missouri.

SINCE my last Report, the labors of the Survey have progressed without interruption. We have spent the time, when out-door operations were impracticable, in examining collections and notes, and in arranging materials for the Reports.

DR. LITTON has been engaged in the Laboratory during the year, except a few weeks devoted to explorations in some of the Eastern mines. For the result of his labors, so valuable to our Economical Geology, and especially to our mining interests, I must refer to his able Report.

DR. SHUMARD spent the winter examining and arranging collections of fossils; the summer and autumn were devoted to examinations on the Mississippi, and in the counties of Franklin, Jefferson, Washington and St. Louis. His Report gives a detailed account of his efficient labors, and some of the additions made to our Palæontology.

MR. PRICE has divided his time between copying township plats for our field notes, and preparing maps, sketches and sections of the country examined. These maps, sketches and sections, are scarcely inferior to any published in the country, and will add much to the interest and utility of our Reports.

In December last, MR. F. HAWN, Assistant Engineer on the Hannibal and St. Joseph Railroad, was commissioned as Assistant Geologist, and directed to examine the country along the line of that road, and to make sections of the strata therein exposed. His Report gives an account of his explorations, which were very successful in developing the agricultural and mineral wealth of that part of the State.

On the 1st of July, Mr. F. B. Meek, of Owensboro, Kentucky, was commissioned as Assistant Geologist. After a few weeks devoted to making out catalogues of the fossils in the Geological rooms, he entered upon and has now completed a minute and accurate Survey of Moniteau county. His Report gives a detailed and excellent view of the Geology and mineral deposits of that part of the State.

This Report gives the results of my own labors during the year.

WHAT WE HAVE ATTEMPTED TO ACCOMPLISH.

It has been our aim to make out: —

1*st*. *An Outline of the Geology of the Whole State.*

2*d*. *A General View of the Mineral Wealth of the Mining Districts.*

3*d*. *An Exposition of the Agricultural and Manufacturing Resources of the State.*

4*th*. *Reports in Detail upon as many Counties as possible.*

WHAT HAS BEEN ACCOMPLISHED.

In making out an Outline of the Geology of Missouri, I have made careful examinations and sections, through various parts of the State: —

1. *From Council Bluffs, along the Missouri river, to Providence* — 600 *miles.*

2. *From Providence, through Paris and Hannibal, to the mouth of the Des Moines* — 165 *miles.*

3. *From Boonville, through Calhoun, Clinton, Papinsville and Carthage, to Grand Falls and Shoal Creek* — 220 *miles.*

4. *From Grand Falls, through Neosho, Jollification and Mt. Vernon, to Springfield* — 94 *miles.*

5. *From Springfield, through Bolivar, Warsaw and Versailles, to Rocheport* — 160 *miles.*

6. *From Boonville to Frémont, by the way of Warsaw and Oseola* — 138 *miles.*

7. *From Frémont, through Bolivar and Buffalo, to the Niangua —48 miles.*

8. *From Buffalo, along the Niangua to Erie, and thence up the Gravois through Versailles, California and Pisgah, to Columbia— 169 miles.*

9. *From Fayette, through Columbia to Fulton—50 miles.*

10. *Dr. Shumard has made a section along the Mississippi, from our northern boundary to Commerce—350 miles.*

11. *Mr. Hawn has made a section from Hannibal along the Railroad line to St. Joseph—210 miles.*

12. *Drs. Litton and Shumard made the various sections and examinations mentioned in my last Annual Report.*

Three other Sections would have completed our General Examination of the State; one from Providence to the mouth of the Missouri; another, along the South-West Branch of the Pacific Railroad to Springfield; and a third, from Cassville, through the southern tier of counties, to New Madrid.

During the progress of these examinations we have made detailed sections wherever the rocks are exposed—measured the thickness and observed the dip and superposition of the strata, and collected specimens of all the Rocks, Ores and other Minerals, Fossils, Mineral Waters and Soils. We, also, made such meteorological observations as our circumstances would permit, and noted the trees and plants, water power, and other indications of the Agricultural and Manufacturing resources of the regions visited.

From the specimens and facts thus collected we have been able to determine for the regions examined,—

The Formations developed;

The lithological characters and mineral contents of each;

Their thickness, dip and geographical range;

The geological and geographical position of the ores and other minerals useful in the productive arts;

The different kinds of soils and subsoils;

And the probable amount of lumber, and water power, available for manufacturing purposes.

We have thus completed for those regions examined,* that part of the requisitions of the Bill providing for a Geological Survey, which directs me to —

"*Determine the order, succession, arrangement, relative position, dip or inclination, and comparative magnitude of the several strata or geological formations within the State.*"

And we have endeavored so to develop and arrange the facts collected as to enable the possessors of the land to derive the greatest possible benefit from its mineral and agricultural resources; to attract foreign capitalists to our unequalled mineral wealth; and induce farmers to make their homes upon our virgin soils, which are now selling at mere nominal prices, though their fertility and mineral wealth has, probably, no parallel on this continent.

But in making these general surveys, where the wide areas to be examined in so short a time compelled us to travel twenty-five and thirty miles per day, it was impossible to trace out all the localities of rocks, ores, coal and other minerals, and to determine the exact areas occupied by them, and estimate the amount of each in the space occupied by it; yet, these explorations, besides giving us a general view of our mineral and agricultural wealth, have prepared the way for making the more detailed examinations necessary to determine the facts above mentioned, and to carry out those instructions of the Bill requiring us —

"*To discover and examine all beds or deposits of ore, coal, marl and such other mineral substances and mineral waters, as may be useful or valuable; and to perform such other duties as may be necessary to make a full and complete geological and mineralogical survey of the State.*" * * * * "*To make full and complete examinations, assays and analyses of all such rocks, ores, soils or other substances,*" *etc., etc.*

In accordance with these instructions, we have commenced detailed examinations in several parts of the State, directing our labors, so far as geological formations† would permit, in such a manner as to

* These comprise the whole State, save the counties along the Missouri from Providence to its mouth, along the South-Western Branch of the Pacific Railroad, and the southern and south-eastern counties.

† It may not be improper to state that our examinations can often be made much more successfully by following geological boundaries rather than political ones, and hence one advantage of those preliminary surveys which gave us a general outline of the Geology of the State.

complete as many counties as possible. But the political and geological boundaries so widely differ, that we have completed but few entire counties; though portions of a great many have been examined.

I have finished Marion and Cooper, and a large part of Boone, Howard, Ralls, Jasper, Bates and Newton; besides some considerable portions of all the other thirty-five counties, lying along the preliminary surveys above mentioned.

Dr. Shumard has completed the surveys of St. Louis and Franklin counties; and made some considerable progress with the other counties bordering upon his Mississippi section.

Mr. Hawn has made partial examinations of the twelve counties upon and near the Hannibal and St. Joseph Railroad. Mr. Meek has completed the survey of Moniteau.

We thus have five counties finished, eight advanced towards completion, and some fifty others* commenced.

In these detailed examinations we have, in addition to what was done by the preliminary surveys, as above stated, determined—

The areas occupied by each geological formation;

What formations contain ores, coal, marble, clay or other valuable minerals;

The quality and probable quantity of such ores and minerals.

Their probable value, and the facilities for working them;

The varieties of soils, and the areas occupied by each;

The modes of culture and crops adapted to them;

The amount of prairie, timber and swamp lands;

The quantity and quality of timber, and facilities for manufacturing it;

The saline and fresh-water springs;

And the streams, and the water power they furnish.

---

* The requirements of the bill providing for the Survey, and particularly our plan of operations, have compelled us to examine parts of many counties; but this will not retard the final completion of the Survey.

We have, also, made accurate maps of the counties completed. In addition to the usual geographical features (all of which are from actual observation on the ground), they represent the bottom and upland, prairie and timber, the soils and geological formations, furnaces, mineral deposits and mineral springs, and all the important topographical and geological features. These maps are very accurate in all their varied representations; and will be useful not only to the inhabitants of the counties themselves, for the common uses of Geographical and Topographical and Geological maps, but will also be exceedingly valuable to them and others, both here and elsewhere, who may desire to buy or sell agricultural or mineral lands.

We have, so far as possible, without retarding the legitimate labors of the Survey, collected materials for making out catalogues of the trees, shrubs and herbaceous plants growing upon the various soils, and of the different classes of animals inhabiting our domain.

OUR COLLECTIONS.

During the progress of the Survey a vast number of specimens of rocks and minerals, and fossils,* have accumulated at the Geological rooms. These collections cannot fail to impress all with a firm belief in our great mineral wealth; and, when properly arranged in cabinets, they will attract attention to our mineral deposits, facilitate the progress of science, and be a source of pride to every Missourian.

DIFFICULTIES ENCOUNTERED IN OUR WORK.

Several circumstances have rendered our labors unusually difficult: —

1st. The consolidated strata are buried so deep beneath the vast

---

* A large number of new fossils have been discovered, which will make a very important addition to our Palæontology.

Quaternary deposits, that it is difficult to find them sufficiently exposed for Geological examinations. These superincumbent beds are often one hundred and two hundred feet thick; and are of so loose a texture, that even where streams have cut through them into the underlying rocks, they have usually fallen down and covered up the beds thus exposed.

2d. The strata are so undulating, some of them so thin, and so extensively and irregularly denuded, that the beds of many adjacent formations come to the surface and again disappear several successive times in a few miles.

3d. There are numerous local deposits of some of the upper Formations, in the valleys and ravines of denudation in the older rocks, which deposits can scarcely be outliers, in the usual acceptation of the term. We frequently find excellent beds of coal, some of great thickness, in ravines, whose side walls are Encrinital Limestone (Fig. 3, of Mr. Meek's Report), Chouteau Limestone (see Drafton's Coal Mine), on magnesian limestone (Fig. 4, Mr. Meek's Report). And these beds of coal are usually different from any in the regular coal series. They are often very thick, and contain strata of both the bituminous and cannel varieties, resting upon each other. These beds are, also, in places, far removed from any strata of the Coal Measures; as in Cooper and Moniteau and Cole counties.

4th. Many of our rocks, particularly those between the Carboniferous and Magnesian Limestones, are but the thin Western representatives of well-developed and well-marked Eastern Formations. Ours were evidently deposited in a part of the ancient ocean much deeper and farther from the land; and they consequently present more uniform lithological characters, and fewer organic remains, and those few of more permanent types, making it much more difficult to identify and distinguish the various Formations.

5th. We have a series of seven Formations, four Magnesian Limestones and three Sandstones, occupying large areas in the State, whose lithological characters are so similar, and fossils so rare, that it is almost impossible to distinguish them, except by their superposition.

These facts make it extremely difficult to identify our strata, and a very tedious, complicated business, to trace out the exact area occupied by each. It is especially so with those abnormal coal-beds, since their formation and position are indicated by none of the established principles of science, and they are generally covered deep beneath the Quaternary deposits.

We have, also, felt the want of Scientific Libraries and Cabinets of Foreign Specimens for consultation and comparison; and the members of the corps have been compelled to supply this desideratum. Still it is believed, the results exhibit such a progress of the work, minutia of detail, accuracy in all departments, and such an amount of useful information, as will meet the approbation not only of scientific men but also of those engaged in the industrial pursuits.

Very respectfully,

Your Ob't Serv't,

G. C. SWALLOW,

STATE GEOLOGIST.

Geological Rooms, State University,
Columbia, Mo., Dec. 1, 1854.

INTRODUCTION.

THE ADVANTAGES TO BE DERIVED FROM OUR GEOLOGICAL SURVEY.

We everywhere meet the inquiry, "What good is to result from the Survey?" Many men devoted to the industrial pursuits of life, do not seem to understand how the sciences can aid them in their particular callings. And yet it would be easy to show that science has been of essential service to every economical pursuit in life. There is not a trade or profession, now in my mind, in which man earns his bread by the sweat of his brow, or by the exercise of his mental energies, that has not had the means of facilitating its operations doubled, and in many instances quadrupled, by the direct application of science. Still, men who admit this fact, are faithless respecting any future benefits from that source. Various causes have led practical men to this state of feeling. A few of the most important may well be examined.

1st. Many shallow men, incapable of success in any pursuit, who would be scientific, have become scientific quacks, and have, by a kind of brazen science, won their way to temporary favor. The contempt, which all sensible and practical men must feel for such pretenders, has, to some extent, been exercised towards science itself.

2d. Many distinguished scientific men have never made any apparent practical use of the vast fund of scientific knowledge which they have acquired. Nor is it strange that men successful in interrogating Nature, should become so absorbed in the delightful pursuit, as to forget the many applications of their scientific knowledge by which human industry, wealth and happiness, might be promoted.

3d. But the most prominent cause is, that science has not been rightly understood. Many have supposed it the mere theories, fine-spun from the imaginations of learned men, without any foundation in fact or experience: whereas, science properly understood, is but a classification of all known facts—all the experience of all the past, so arranged and classified, as to manifest all those great principles, which lie at the foundation of the practical pursuits of life.

We often hear that "Experience is more valuable than science." But science is the *very essence of all experience.*

The science of Agriculture concentrates all the known experience of all farmers, from Adam to the present moment. And yet, even unskillful farmers say, We want no scientific farming; *i. e.*, We want none of the experience of the Egyptians, whose agriculture fed the world; none of the experience of the venerable Cincinnatus, who loved the plow better than the scepter; none of the experience of those men, whose agricultural science has doubled the products of Western Europe.

Again, the science of Mining and Metallurgy, contains all the known experience of all miners and workers of metals from Tubal Cain to our day. And yet it is not uncommon to hear the miner, who has never seen but one coal-pit or one lead-vein, ridicule book mining. We know how to dig better than the Geologist. We know more than all the miners of Siberia, Saxony, Prussia, France, England, Golconda and California combined.

The science of Geology comprises all that is known of the earth and its formation. Men skilled in all professions, in all sciences, have brought all their knowledge into its vast treasury. A thousand eyes have examined every nook and crevice of the earth's crust. Such men as Humboldt and Cuvier, have explored every continent and island, have scaled the Alps and the Andes; they have traversed the burning sands of the Equator and the frozen shores of either Pole.

They have interrogated Nature in the deep pit of the miner, and in the smoking crater of the volcano. They have examined the strata, the shells, the bones, the stems, the leaves, and every impression of the animate and inanimate, left upon the rocks of the Pre-Adamite earth. With Chemistry and Philosophy in one hand, and Botany and Zoology in the other, they have interpreted those wonderful records impressed by Nature's hand upon Earth's everlasting strata; and presented to our wondering gaze those gigantic animals, huge monsters, and tiny fishes, which stalked through the forests and gamboled in the waters of the primeval world.

So fixed are the laws of Nature, so minute has been this examination, that, from the leaf of a plant, the scale of a fish or the hoof and teeth of an animal, the size, habits and food of each can be determined.

The rocks which contain the ores and useful minerals are definitely indicated by the same unerring laws of Geological science.

In short, Geology comprehends all the facts ever known respecting the rocks and minerals of the Earth, and all the uses to which they have been applied. It has treasured up the agricultural capacities of every soil, and the best means of developing those capacities. And yet some doubt whether such a science can aid in developing the unparalleled resources of our State.

But fortunately our farmers, mechanics, miners and legislators are beginning to see what it has done for other States and countries, and to appreciate what it can do for our own.

Nature has given us one of the richest, if not the very richest domain in the world. Let her Agricultural and Mineral, Mechanical and Mercantile resources be developed, and she will soon be among the most progressive of the States.

As yet we have done but little; Nature has done so much, we have been content with her gifts. While the practical deductions of science have given a new impulse, have infused new life, and new energy, into almost every department of human industry, we are cultivating our farms as did our sires and grandsires before us.

While by the applications of science the farmers of New York and Massachusetts, led by such men as Norton and Webster, have doubled the products of their soil; while Watt and Fulton have given us steamships to spurn the winds and stem the currents of our mighty rivers; while the steam-horse is puffing his way along the iron track to our rich prairies; while the lightning speeds to us the last changes in stocks and merchandise, and every move upon the political chess-board; while, in short, progress is stamped upon every department of business, our farmers and mechanics, to a great extent, are plodding on "In the good old way of our fathers."

The result is, we, in this land of mighty forests, are importing and paying three prices for our lumber. Our houses, plank-roads, and fences, cost twice their usual value. We "go East" for our agricultural and mechanical implements of every grade, from the plow to the butter-stamp. With iron-mountains and a vast area of rich coal-beds, we import every article of Iron, from the anvil to the ten-penny nail. Our mineral veins contain nearly every paint from the costly smalt blue, to the yellow ochre; and yet all we use, with, perhaps, a single exception, comes from a foreign market. While we are exhausting the richest soil the sun shines upon, some of our crops are no better than those harvested from the once barren hills of New England.

But you may say "We are doing very well as we are." Perhaps "We are doing well enough," yet, if we listen to that Siren song, we may be aroused from our pleasant dreams to the humiliating reality, that our neighbors, with fewer natural advantages, are reaping richer harvests, and supplying our markets with their domestic manufactures.

While the planters of Virginia were *doing well enough*, many of them were surprised to find their soils exhausted and their plantations unproductive. Many are *doing well enough* with mule-wagons and mud-roads, but the steam-horse, with his iron sinews, proclaims their thriftless folly. While the "jolly flat-boat man" was doing *almost too well*, the steam-whistle startled him from his easy jollity, and gave a hundred-fold energy to the commerce of our western rivers. When perfection is reached, then, and not till then, should an Anglo-Saxon let *well enough alone.*

The Divine Economy wisely provides that we shall eat our bread by the sweat of the brow; yet no divine or human wisdom demands that we shall toil and sweat, and sweat and toil on, from year to year, simply for the corn cake and bacon, our appetites demand. We can do better — we can become better farmers and better mechanics. Then, like men, let us go about it.

But how will the Geological Survey aid us in this matter?

If properly conducted, it cannot fail to develop the mineral resources of our State, and place our mining interests on a more permanent basis, by inviting capital, and by securing systematic and profitable operations.

It will increase our mechanical and manufacturing interests, by pointing out the raw materials and the facilities for converting them into articles of domestic and foreign trade.

Agriculture will be advanced by investigating the structure and the chemical properties of the soils, as the results will enable us to determine the modes of culture necessary to sustain and even increase their productive energies.

Commerce will also receive a new impulse, from the increased products of the farm, the mine, and the work-shop.

Should the Survey be made with sufficient minuteness to point out the soils of each township, the facilities for settling, and the great prosperity of our agricultural communities, the reports would attract thousands of those who are yearly seeking homes in this great valley. The increase of our yeoman population and tax-payers thus secured, would soon be felt in the financial and political resources of the State.

The development of the mineral and agricultural resources, will so enhance the value of land in the State, as to make an aggregate increase of a vast amount.

The Survey will, in no small degree, promote the interests of our Railroads, by showing the existence of vast mineral deposits along their lines, awaiting the means of transportation to some good market.

But let us examine these subjects a little more in detail.

MINES AND MINING.

A few considerations will illustrate the advantages of a Geological Survey in developing our mineral wealth, and in extending and directing our mining operations.

It is a well-known principle of science that the various ores, coal, and minerals, are found in certain strata, and in those only. Now when the Geologist has pointed out the position and extent of each stratum, and has indicated what minerals may be found in each, he will have done much to aid the explorer. Thousands will be saved, which are spent in searching, where nothing can be found; and the field of search will be so limited to the proper localities that the chances of success will be greatly increased.

When the report has pointed out the quality and locality of a coal-bed, its extent and thickness, the nature and thickness of the superincumbent strata, and the facilities for draining, the capitalist will have all needed data to determine whether a profitable investment can be made. It will thus prevent the investment of capital where profit is doubtful, and encourage it where success is certain.

Mining will thus be rendered more profitable and permanent; and more capital will seek investment in it.

Several companies are now ready to invest large amounts in mining and manufacturing, so soon as it shall be ascertained that a sufficient quantity of coal and iron can be obtained convenient to certain localities. We shall prove the existence of the coal and iron desired, and prove the practicability of establishing profitable works in several parts of the State where none have yet been started. Capital is sure to follow where profitable investment is made certain.

These principles are not a matter of theory merely, but have often been realized in practice. In Pennsylvania this truth has been triumphantly vindicated.

Before the Geological Survey of that State, coal mining was uncertain and vacillating; sometimes profitable, often ruinous. In some years, according to the census reports, the quantity raised would greatly increase, in others, decrease as much. In 1837 the increase in the Anthracite mines alone, was 189,000 tons; but in the next year there was a decrease of 141,000 tons. But, since the accurate surveys of the Geologists demonstrated the abundance of the coal, and the sure profits of systematic mining, capital has been freely invested, and the amount raised has constantly and rapidly increased. The increase from the Anthracite mines alone is about 4,000,000 tons. From 1850 to 1851 it was more than 1,000,000 tons.

The same happy results have been realized in the Lehigh and other mines. Now nothing but a Geological Survey by State or individual enterprise, could have secured the confidence necessary to accomplish these results, and enabled Pennsylvania to supply the coal markets of the Union. And this is but one of the many happy results of that Survey.

But England, perhaps, affords the best illustration of wealth and power resulting from a scientific development of mineral resources. England, though less than Missouri in extent, has spent millions in Geological Surveys; and yet, the capital invested has returned a thousand fold from her mines alone. Our mineral wealth is probably as great as hers. She depends mostly upon her iron and coal; and still, we have more and better iron, and our Coal Measures will prove as extensive. Yet, while England annually raises from her mines $100,000,000 worth of raw materials, we raise but a few thousands. *This difference is not because Nature has done less for us, but that Science has done more for her.*

What, then, shall prevent us from attaining to an equal development of our mineral wealth, when this Survey shall have proved, as it will, that we have more and better iron than England, and good coal sufficient for many generations to come?

Some of us, doubtless, envy California her golden destiny; but our Cobalt and Zinc, and Lead, and Iron, and Coal, and Soil, are a better foundation for national wealth and greatness, than her golden *sands*. The latter may give temporary prosperity, but the former will ensure permanent greatness.

Scarcely three centuries have elapsed since the united thrones of Castile and Arragon swayed as powerful a scepter as the combined crowns of Albion and Scotia. Spain extended her sway over the best and largest portions of this Western World, and held the commerce of both hemispheres. Galleon after galleon, deeply laden with the precious metals from the mines of Mexico and Peru, poured them, in unparalleled profusion, into the treasury of the home government. England on the other hand was pushing her mining and manufacturing interests by all possible applications of science and capital.

England was digging for iron and coal, while Spain was mining for gold and silver. Spain squandered her gold, and has become a mere pensioner upon Cuba. But England holds the commerce of both Indies, and the world pays a *golden* tribute to her *iron* and *coal.*

To come nearer home, Massachusetts, according to the census of 1840, has derived more wealth from her granite quarries, than Alabama, Georgia, South Carolina, North Carolina and Virginia, have from all their gold mines.

We shall show the existence of many inexhaustible quarries of excellent marble in various parts of the State. If then, Massachusetts makes money by transporting her granite to New Orleans, cannot Missouri make more by bringing her marbles into western markets?

In addition to this, we shall show that capital and systematic mining alone, are wanting to render our copper and lead mines sources of vast wealth.

The Survey, besides pointing out the quantities and properties of the mineral deposits already known, will bring to light many unknown deposits of the same minerals, and, perhaps, other valuable ores not known to exist in the State.

Our miners may be at the present throwing away minerals even more valuable than those for which they are mining. Such an event would not be unprecedented in Missouri.

Nothing is more probable, than that our vast territory, still unexplored, will furnish some minerals hitherto not known to exist in our State. But, besides the metals, we have already discovered large deposits of Hydraulic Limestone, Fire Clay, Lithographic Limestone, Mineral Paints, and Coal in vast quantities.

Since, then, we have so many and so abundant sources of mineral wealth whose development is unattended by those exciting and demoralizing influences, that ever accompany the mining of the precious metals, why should we prefer the destiny of California? None have more and better natural resources than Missouri; and, if true to herself, none will surpass her in wealth and population.

MECHANICS AND MANUFACTURES.

A passing notice must suffice to illustrate the advantages of such a Survey to the mechanical and manufacturing interests of the State.

There is every reason to believe from the Geological formations of the State, that a Survey would prove the existence of abundant materials of the very best quality for glass and porcelain manufactures, and thus secure the establishment of manufactories of those wares, to such an extent, that Missouri would not only supply her own markets, but have a surplus for exportation.

If Surveys already made are correct, we have a very excellent coal-bed for the manufacture of iron; and in a few feet of the coal, a deposit of good iron ore, and all the needed fluxes. Should an accurate Survey prove this coal-bed as abundant as appearances indicate, and also the iron, iron-works there could compete with the world. Such a combination of favorable circumstances seldom, if ever, occur.

At all events, when our railroads are prepared to take the ore of our *iron-mountains*, and the vast coal-beds of the north-western parts of the State, to St. Louis, our proud city must inevitably become the great iron mart of our Continent.

Missouri can, then, and should make her own railroad iron. The present high prices of iron in England, caused by the miners and workmen leaving in such numbers for Australia, and America, will greatly encourage such an enterprise. It has already led to the formation of large companies in Pennsylvania and other States, for the express purpose of making railroad iron.

Is it not wisdom, then, for us to show capitalists our superior advantages for such manufactures? Let Missouri make the iron for her thousand miles of railroad, and she will save, according to the present rates of iron, some more than $8,000,000 in her own pockets, which would make a difference in the balance sheet of our trade, of $16,000,000.

And this can be done, if we are true to our own interests; yea, and much more. We can supply the demands of this great valley. Does not a manifest destiny point to those iron-mountains as the source whence the Iron-Horse is to get his shoes for his long race across the plains to the Pacific? That he will go, no one can doubt. Go he must, and pay $40,000,000 in California gold, to the smith who shoes him.

Our yearly imports of lumber of various kinds amount to some 50,000,000 feet, and yet our soil is actually groaning beneath the enormous load of the very best living lumber. Our Geological Survey will point out the best lumbering regions and mill-sites, and the various facilities for the lumber business, as they are now known to exist. Not many years will elapse before those men, before whom the forests of Maine have fallen, and been distributed to all the cities along the Atlantic coast, to New Orleans, the West Indies, South America, Europe, the Sandwich Islands, and California; who have sent companies of lumber-men into the forests of the Carolinas, Georgia and Florida; on to the head waters of the Delaware, the Susquehanna, and the Ohio, the Illinois and the Mississippi; not many years, before those men will fill our forests with indomitable lumber-men, and make our streams dance to the music of a thousand saws. And what is still better, they will furnish our lumber at half its present prices. Companies have already expressed a desire to invest capital in this business as soon as the most desirable localities shall be made known.

These and many similar facts show, that the Survey will benefit our manufacturing and mechanical interests more than sufficient to repay all the outlay of labor.

AGRICULTURAL IMPROVEMENTS.

But your attention is particularly and earnestly invited to the advantages of such a Survey to the Agriculture of the State.

Agriculture is the true basis of all national greatness. For the farmers, then, we ask the aid and sympathy of all professions; not for their benefit only, but that in their success we all may be prospered. They are the great heart of the body politic; if its pulsations are languid, the life blood will flow feebly in every department of human industry. We do not ask it as a favor, but demand it as a debt of long standing, one so just, that all have frankly confessed the obligation, whenever and wherever its claims have been presented.

Since man was driven from Eden, they have fed and clothed the world, and filled its dwellings with plenty and luxury. They have been freely taxed for the support of public schools, and have contributed liberally for the endowment of Colleges and Universities, for the education of Physicians and Lawyers, Clergymen and Gentlemen; and yet we look in vain for a school where the science of agriculture is practically taught.

They have also been taxed to give manufactures and commerce

the aid of science; but have themselves been scarcely permitted to know there is any genuine, valuable, science for Agriculture.

Some object to the science of agriculture, because its principles do not succeed in all cases. But this want of success is owing to a neglect of a part of the principles of the science. A single illustration will show what kind of science fails in agriculture.

One day while walking along the sea-shore, I came upon a farmer sowing salt over a field of young wheat. I asked his object. "Why, sir, last year you told me to sow salt upon my onions and asparagus, which I did, and obtained admirable results; and I am determined to do the same for all my crops this year."

Here was science with a vengeance; and it resulted in the entire failure of the wheat thus treated, according to what he supposed "*scientific farming.*"

Onions and asparagus are natives of the salt beach, and need a large quantity of salt; but the wheat needed but little, and the field, often wet by the spray of the ocean, had too much salt, already, for that crop.

Chemistry teaches us that plants contain a large portion of the four organic elements; viz., Carbon, Oxygen, Hydrogen and Nitrogen; that they also have more or less of some twenty inorganic elements, such as Lime, Silica, Potash, Phosphorous, Alumina, Soda, etc. These substances are found in different proportions in different species of plants; but it is to be kept constantly in mind, that a perfect plant of any given species contains the same elements, and those elements in the same proportions as every other perfect plant of that species. Upon this uniform law* of the vegetable kingdom is based the whole structure of Agricultural Chemistry, or the adaptation of the soil to any particular crop.

---

* There are one or two apparent exceptions to this rule. The alkaline bases of plants cultivated on different soils, may vary somewhat; still the whole amount of such alkalies in each plant, will be about the same. Under certain circumstances lime and magnesia will replace soda and potassa, and *vice versa.*

Botany, or Vegetable Physiology, teaches us that plants draw a portion of their organic elements from the air, through their leaves, and the remainder of the organic, together with their inorganic elements, from the water and the soil through their roots.

By analysis we learn that an acre of wheat assimilates besides the sap, which evaporates on drying, some 3,000 pounds of organic, and 200 pounds of inorganic matter, about a ton and a half per acre for each crop of wheat. Now all of the inorganic matter and a large portion of the organic, must come from the soil; and such a yearly draft upon its fertilizing portions, which always exist in small quantities, must eventually exhaust them. And this has been the sad result in some of the most fertile counties of New York, Maryland and Virginia.

But it is said our soil is rich and we need not fear its exhaustion. The farmers of Dutchess, one of the most fertile counties of New York, once thought so, but a late average crop of five bushels of wheat per acre, shows how false their theory and how desolating its results.

But we need not go out of Missouri to find examples of exhausted lands. Many of our farmers have seen their crops grow gradually less from year to year until exhausted lands are a sad reality.

In the minds of many, *large crops* and a ready market, are the only conditions necessary to the prosperity of a rural community. Could these conditions be maintained *in perpetuum*, all might assent to the proposition. But with the present exhausting mode of culture, the *large crop* must soon fail, and then the ready market will avail nothing. Under such a system, the larger the crop and the nearer the market, the more certain and rapid will be the deterioration of the soil.

This proposition may appear strange, yet the short history of our own country furnishes many sad examples to prove its truth. If we inquire in New York, Maryland, and Virginia, what lands were most effectually exhausted, we shall find them to be the rich bottom lands along their navigable waters, which were at once the most fertile and accessible to market.

There, greedy of present gain, and unmindful of the future, the husbandman taxed the generous soil to its utmost powers. Cargo after cargo of its fertilizing ingredients, in corn, wheat, and tobacco, went to feed and fumigate the busy city; and the golden return was invested in stocks and merchandise.

Thus the unwary fathers robbed their sons of *good farms, God's richest gifts*, and laid the strongest of all temptations for them to leave the moral, happy influences of a rural community, for the exciting bustle and tempting pleasures of the city.

Dutchess and Schoharie counties, in New York, are a good illustration of this principle. Both were settled early, both among the most fertile, and both easily harvested thirty or forty bushels of wheat per acre. But within a few years the average crop in Dutchess, was but five bushels per acre, while the harvests of the beautiful Schoharie, were almost as abundant as ever. And yet, no superior culture has produced this difference in favor of Schoharie; for even to the present day her farmers haul their manure to the creek, or remove their stables to get rid of the accumulated heaps.

The true secret is, Dutchess had had a ready market down the Hudson, while the mountain barriers of the Helderberg range have shielded the other from the grasp of the great commercial emporium.

What New York had done for Dutchess, as good a market would do for Platte. Continue the exhausting system, and give one dollar per bushel for corn, and fifty years would make Platte a desert, where the prairie-fowl and the deer would disdain to grub a scanty living. Our railroads, so nobly begun, will only hasten the evil, by giving a better market; unless some speedy remedy be applied to meet the present and prospective demands upon the soil.

"How shall we preserve and increase the fertility of our soils," has become the great question in our political economy.

Agricultural Science alone can answer this great question. Give us an Agricultural School, where our sons can acquire a thorough practical knowledge of Agricultural Science, and we will have men prepared to do this great work.

But it may be said, we have good schools now. This is true; and it is doubtless true, that they answer all the purposes of the learned professions; yet, something should be done to make *Farming and the Mechanical Arts, learned professions.* Farmers and Mechanics should be so educated, that they could bring all the treasures of science to the improvements of the farm and the work-shop.

Our sons are taught to trace the root of a word up through the French, Italian, Latin, Greek, and Sanscrit, to discover its meaning; but who of them can trace the root of a potato beneath the soil and discover the food it seeks there?

It is not expected that an Agricultural School will educate the *present* race of farmers. But the Geological Survey is the best possible arrangement to supply their present wants, to give them such information as will enable them to adopt the best modes of culture to prevent the exhaustion of their rich soils.

Let us make careful examinations of the subsoils, and underlying strata; let us thoroughly analyse the soils; let us examine all the mineral deposits suited to sustain or improve the fertility of these soils, such as humus, green sand, and marl, and we shall be able to give such a report, as would enable every farmer, not only to preserve, but even to increase, the productive energies of his lands. This will greatly increase the profits of agriculture, and preserve and increase the intrinsic value of cultivated lands.

Several of our best farmers have estimated the annual decrease of fertility in our cultivated lands, to be sufficient to lessen the profits of cultivation, *fifty cents* per acre; some higher than that, and others still lower. To bring it within the limits of deterioration, beyond all doubt, let us set it down at *twenty* cents per acre. That would give us an annual loss, upon our 3,000,000 acres in cultivation, of $600,000; which is the interest, at six per cent., on $10,000,000. This, then, is the actual yearly loss, by decrease of production, in the intrinsic value of the farms of our State.

Thus farmers, by the exhausting system, have annually placed a mortgage of $10,000,000 upon their farms. And this mortgage must be removed, or scanty crops will publish its foreclosure, and send us westward for new lands.

That our Geological Survey will point out the means of redeeming these farms and preventing such a calamity, is morally certain. When the expenditure of a few thousands will save such sums, shall we hesitate even on the score of economy?

Should we be able to make such improvements as would increase the products of cultivated lands *one cent* per acre, it would give an annual increase of $30,000 in the income from our farms. But there would be no difficulty in increasing the products *one dollar* per acre, as many of our farmers have done the two past years; and that would give us an annual return of $3,000,000, equal in all beneficial results to individuals and the State, to an investment of $50,000,000 in new farms.

Here again we are not left with nothing but theory and logic to rely upon. We have the facts to sustain us. We have the proof in the results of the Surveys and other means of agricultural improvement, in New York, Massachusetts, South Carolina, North Carolina, and other States.

New York is an old State, and large portions of her soil were much exhausted; and she had comparatively little new land to come into cultivation; so that nearly all increase of products must arise from improved culture.

She spent $130,000 in a most thorough Survey. The reports, which are an imperishable monument to her far-sighted liberality, gave every department of business a fresh impulse. Her Agriculturalists commenced an improved system of culture, which has resulted in increasing the annual products of her farms some $50,000-000. The increase in corn and hay alone is over ten millions for the last ten years, say one million per annum; which would be from two staples only, the interest, at six per cent., on more than sixteen and a half millions.

Provided that only one-tenth of this increase was the result of the Geological Survey, still, it has annually repaid the whole outlay for the most liberal survey ever made in this country, with enough left to sustain several such surveys as that contemplated by the law under which we are acting.

But we already have results in our own State still more surprising. The State Geologist, on examining the soils of the State several years since, at once saw the benefits which would result from subsoil-plowing. Those conclusions were made known to many of our farmers, who have adopted the system with wonderful success.

Says Major Rollins,* who plowed from fourteen to sixteen inches deep, "The increase of each crop, I should estimate, amounted to twenty-five per cent.," and "The increased profit of cultivation by the system of deep plowing, at from twenty to thirty per cent.

Eli E. Bass, Esq., who subsoiled his land, says, his "Crops were *doubled* and the profits doubled" by this system of cultivation.

Now, these results are most satisfactory; but still more surprising effects would have resulted, had the subsoil-plow reached a greater depth. Several fields thus subsoiled did not even wilt beneath the unprecedented drought of last season, while those adjoining were very badly burned.

Now, three-fourths of the land in Missouri would be equally benefitted by deep plowing. When this fact is proved, for all the counties of the State, as this Report does prove it for Boone, Marion, Monroe and Cooper counties, and when our farmers shall

---

* See Letters, Chap. II. of this Report.

adopt the system, two millions at least, of our three million acres of cultivated lands, will give an increased annual profit of from one to five dollars per acre.

Such a result is as certain as any future event in political economy can be; and who will estimate the pecuniary advantages resulting from such an improvement?

THE INCREASED VALUE OF LAND

Is a matter of no small importance to the State, or to individuals. That our Survey will greatly increase the value of land in many parts of the State, is placed beyond a doubt. We expect not to add any thing to the intrinsic value of our domain; but it is certain we shall make known vast treasures not before supposed to exist.

With but few exceptions, the coal-beds of our State have exerted but little influence upon the price of the lands in which they exist. In Boone county, for an example, it is known that the coal crops out in many places, and in some few, is worked for local use; but nothing was known of the amount or value of this mineral upon a single acre in the county. Since it is proved that a large portion of this county is underlaid by from two to five beds of this mineral, whose average aggregate thickness varies from six to ten feet; that every acre contains 5,000 or 8,000 tons, whose *value in the pit* is not less than twenty cents* per ton, or $1,000 per acre; that farms of a thousand acres, now selling at $10,000, $20,000 and $30,000, actually have beneath their rich soil $1,000,000 worth *of coal;* since all this is proved, will not the price of these lands increase? Who will estimate the increased value of land in the State, when we have collected the statistics of the forty other counties, in which we have ascertained the existence of this valuable mineral; since many of them are known to have much more than Boone? We might show the same necessary result from the discovery of Iron, Lead, Copper, Cobalt, Zinc and other minerals. The results in

---

* This is much less than the present price, five cents per bushel, in the pit, equal to $1.35 per ton, allowing twenty-six and a half bushels per ton.

States, where surveys have been made, fully justify our expectations in this.

The following extract, from a Tennessee paper, shows how the matter stands there: —

"Within the last two years, lands in Polk county, East Tennessee, have advanced in value almost incredibly. It is now asserted by those who profess to know how the fact is, that within the time, minerals have been developed in that region, which make the land worth *ten millions* of dollars more than before."

An Ohio journal makes the following statement: —

"In several counties where it is supposed coal existed to the extent of a few rods or hundred yards at most, the geologist informed them that they might consider their supply inexhaustible. The rise in real estate in different counties was variously estimated at from $100,000 to $500,000, when it was known that manufacturing means were possessed in unexpected abundance."

A more general, though not less satisfactory account of the results in North Carolina, is thus given: —

"Three years ago, the Legislature of North Carolina made a small appropriation for a Geological Survey of that State. The discoveries of the first year, developed the existence of copper and gold ores, drew to them the attention of capitalists, and have already increased the revenues of the State, to five times the cost of the whole survey. In the second year, seams of the purest bituminous coal, some of them fifteen feet in thickness, extending through a region of some forty-five square miles, rewarded their investigations. It is estimated that every thousand acres of these seams will yield thirty millions of tons of bituminous coal, of the best quality."

The effects of the surveys in Pennsylvania and Virginia, have been still more encouraging.

BENEFIT TO OUR RAILROADS.

To secure the building of a railroad at this day, it is only necessary to show the existence of an abundance of merchandise, seeking transportation, and a population to supply the travel.

The Survey will do much towards showing the existence of these conditions, for at least six of our projected railroads. We already have data, which will settle these facts for some of those roads.

Mr. Hawn's examinations and report, show the existence of at least five workable beds of good coal in the counties of Macon, Linn, Livingston and Chariton.

The thickest of these beds varies from five to six feet, and altogether, they will furnish twelve or fourteen feet of good coal. These beds extend over an area, all within fifteen miles of the Hannibal and St. Joseph Railroad, of at least 500 square miles in Macon, 400 in Linn, 400 in Livingston, and 200 in Chariton, making in all, 1,500 square miles, within fifteen miles of the road, in those four counties alone. It is estimated by the best mining engineers of England, that every foot of workable coal will furnish 1,000,000 tons per square mile, which would give us for those four counties 1,500,000,000 tons for every foot in these beds. If we deduct one-half of the thickness for waste, and for the areas where some of these beds may run out, we shall have 9,000,000,000 tons of workable coal, within the limits above mentioned, seeking transportation to the Mississippi and Missouri rivers. Should the road be able to transport 100,000 tons per day, it would supply freight for 90,000 days. Allowing 300 running days per annum, it would occupy it 300 years. At 50,000 tons per day, it would freight the road 600 years, which is quite as long as the stockholders need provide for themselves and their heirs; as by that time *Young America* will have no use for railroads.

Shelby county will, also, furnish small quantities; and all the counties on the line, west of Livingston, have still more coal, but its depth below the surface may prevent profitable mining at the present prices of coal and labor.

But few, if any, railroads run through so good a body of land as the Hannibal and St. Joseph. The facilities afforded by the road will bring this land into market, and settle it with a stirring agricultural population, unless speculators place its price above that of other lands possessing similar qualities and advantages.

Coal mining will, also, bring in an increase of population to swell the travel over this road.

Should the North Missouri Road be finally located over the western route, every county through which it will pass has more or less coal. The north-eastern part of Boone alone, will furnish many million tons of coal, available for that road. This, too, would pass through a rich agricultural region, capable of sustaining a dense population.

The *St. Louis and Weston Road* would run through a series of counties sustaining a numerous population — counties rich in agricultural resources and coal deposits. But we are not prepared to speak with certainty of the quantity in any one county; yet we know it would be immense in some; as in Boone, Callaway and Howard.

We shall, also, show a vast quantity of coal, lead and marble, in the central and western counties on the line of the Pacific Railroad; and that the agricultural resources of some of these counties are unsurpassed in the West. But we are not prepared to enter upon any statistical account of the mineral or agricultural wealth of these counties until we have completed our detailed examinations of them. Our general examinations have proved the presence of Coal, Iron, Lead and Marble in large quantities, and the existence of vast areas of the very best soil.

The South-Western Branch will have no small amount of freight from the mining community of the South-West. Some of the counties will sustain a dense agricultural population, and furnish large quantities of beef, pork and grain, for the St. Louis market. Others present unequalled prospects of mineral wealth. But future examinations must determine the amount of resources in the central counties on the line of this road. It has long since been proved, without our aid, that the Iron Mountain Road will not lack freight for the want of vast mineral deposits along its line.

But without enlarging upon the advantages that such a Survey would confer upon Commerce; how it would draw settlers to our rich acres; how aid the cause of Education, by furnishing materials and facts for the practical application of the principles of Chemistry, Geology and Mineralogy to mining, farming and mechanics; it is hoped the considerations already presented, will be thought sufficient to prove the economy of a liberal Survey.

Such are some of the advantages to be derived from the Survey. They have been mentioned to satisfy the anxiety of those who have not had an opportunity of giving the subject a careful consideration. It may be supposed by some, that these advantages have been magnified and exaggerated; but they have been made after a general examination of the State, and a careful consideration of the whole subject, in view of the fact that a watchful community will hold us responsible for the accomplishment of them all. Still the truth must be told, though it compel us to assume that responsibility. Should the Survey, however, be carefully completed by skillful, practical men, and should the citizens of Missouri manifest their wonted zeal in carrying out the improvements suggested, there can be no reasonable doubt that all, and more than all, of these advantages will be realized.

SCIENTIFIC TERMS.

Many object to the use of scientific terms in Geological Reports. "Why not write in plain English, so that all can understand?" As far as possible we shall comply with this request. But it is both absurd and impossible to write a Geological Report and use no scientific terms. No Geologist can do it; and were it possible, no one could understand it. Every science, every profession, and every trade, has its appropriate terms and names peculiar to itself.

The sailor's *buoy;* the printer's *pi;* the carpenter's *rabbet;* the saddler's *tree;* the *mandrel* of the smith; the warrior's *mangonel;*

the merchant's *bocasine*, and the thousand and one undefined, outlandish names; and the politician's *Hards*, *Softs*, *Rottens*, etc., are as peculiar and limited to those departments, as *Pentremite* and *Muschelkalk* are in Geology. Why not ask these trades and professions to drop the use of all terms peculiar to them, and employ *plain English?* There is just as much reason in asking the lawyer to plead without using the names of the crimes on the statute-book; the clergyman to preach without employing the names of Deity and of the virtues, which adorn the Christian character; or the politician to make a stump speech without using Whig, Democrat, Abolitionist, and Nullifier, as in expecting the Geologist to write a report without using the names of the particular rocks and fossils he is compelled to describe.

But it may be said every one understands these political terms. True, for all of us understand something of politics. Should an Englishman listen to our stump orators, he would need something besides the *Queen's English* to aid him in understanding its force. Take this example of Canadian politics from a newspaper: —

"The *Toronto Globe* divides the thirty-four Members of Parliament returned from Upper Canada as follows: Six are *Secularizationists*; seven are *Conservatives;* sixteen are *Reformers;* four are *Ministerialists;* and one is a *Corruptionist.*" Who can tell what these terms mean? or what is the particular platform of each of these parties? And yet, we do not blame every party for having a name, notwithstanding their rapid increase.

We give names to all objects of conversation and use. Geologists must talk about rocks and fossils, to make them useful; and hence the necessity of giving them names. But why not give *English names?* We do as much as possible, for rocks discovered here; and for the same reasons the Germans gave German names to such rocks as they found; and, to save the confusion of many names, we of course use theirs for those rocks. Thus the German and other Geologists, by following this "*very reasonable*" request, to use vernacular terms, and not the *barbarous Latin*, have placed in the Geological vocabulary such beautiful, euphonious names as *Graywacke*, *Muschelkalk* and *Roth-todt-liegendes*—all good *English* to Germans, but *High Dutch*, I presume, to all who clamor against scientific terms. Is it not evident, that good, euphonic names from the Latin, read by all scientific nations, would be better?

Again, it is said, "Use common names." Well, Muschelkalk and Roth-todt-liegendes are common names in Germany, where they were first used in Geology. But there is a more serious objection to common names: they must, of necessity, be more or less ambiguous, as every such name has, at least, one *common* meaning, and, if used in science, it would have another—a scientific meaning. Take, for example, *Black-Jack:* as a common name it means, "a leathern cup;" scientifically applied to Zoology, it means, a *Black Negro;* in Botany, a *Scrub Oak;* and in Mineralogy, *Sulphuret of Zinc.* Thus this *common* name has one common and three scientific meanings, which render it too ambiguous for scientific purposes.

But let us give it a fair trial. Take the following sentence from a scientific paper: "We saw the two *crystalline masses* of *sulphuret of zinc* lying at the Duke of Sutherland's front entrance." Now, *crystalline masses* and *sulphuret of zinc*, are scientific terms, which have one meaning, and one only; so that we know precisely *what* was seen at that Duke's front entrance; but if the learned author had used two very common names instead of those scientific terms, the sentence would read thus: "We saw the two *Dornicks of Black-Jack* lying at the Duke of Sutherland's front entrance;" and no one could have told what did lie there; as Dornicks and Black-Jack are both ambiguous, common terms.

It is perfectly obvious, that we can have no definite science, no accurate science, *no science at all*, without definite terms; that we must have an old term with a new meaning, or a new term for every new object discovered; that it is just as easy to learn the meaning of a new word, as a new meaning for an old one; and that old words would of necessity be ambiguous, while new ones would be definite.

For these and other reasons, scientific men have made and used scientific terms; and for the same reasons, we have given scientific names to many of the numerous new fossils we have discovered.

In concluding this subject, it may be proper to repeat, that we shall use as few scientific terms as possible without sacrificing accuracy. Those used, save some *names* of fossils and plants, are explained in Webster's Quarto Dictionary, and the Elementary works on Geology.

WHAT SHOULD BE EXPECTED IN THIS REPORT.

A Geological Survey proposes to accomplish various objects by the application of scientific principles: —

1*st.* *To point out the Mineral Wealth of the State.* — To do this, the Geologist must first determine the Formations in the State, the areas covered by each, and what valuable minerals it contains. When these facts are ascertained he is prepared to enter upon the detailed examinations, which will enable him to show the probable value of the useful minerals in the State. And the scientific explorations for determining the Geological Structure of the country to be examined, must precede and lay the foundation for the economical and utilitarian labors of the Laboratory and the Office.

2*d.* *To develop the Agricultural capacities of the Soils of the State.* — In order to determine the productive powers of the soils, it is necessary to know the rocks, which have or which may, enter into their composition; to know their mechanical properties; their chemical composition and the trees and plants they produce.

Now, to analyze the soil of every man's farm, would be impracticable, and the same results must be obtained in some other way. Large tracts are found to possess soils, derived from the same rocks, having the same mechanical structure and chemical composition, and sustaining the same plants. The whole State, even, will furnish but few varieties of soils.

Economy, then, requires us to make careful examinations to determine these varieties, and the area occupied by each, so that when we have analyzed one or two specimens of each variety, and determined its agricultural capacities, what crops, and what modes of culture are adapted to it, we can at once point out the kind of soil, to which these results are applicable, and that part of the State occupied by it.

With this plan in view we have carefully examined the soils and collected specimens from various parts of the State, but have analyzed none, as we have not yet collected all the facts necessary to guide us in the classification so much needed to secure the desired results, in the most economical manner.

So it is with other departments of the Survey. The facts and specimens must first be collected and the specimens analyzed; and, in some cases, submitted to experimental tests, and all the results classified and compared, before we can make any general and practical applications of our labors to the industrial pursuits. Hence in the present Reports we should not be expected to do much more than state the facts collected in our explorations, together with the results indicated by the phenomena observed.

Some have even deemed it hazardous for us to give, at this early day, a classification of the rocks of a field so extensive, and possessing so many and so variable Geological Formations.

It has, it is true, required a vast amount of labor to collect the fossils of so many Formations; to determine the point where one terminates and another commences, and to make the comparisons necessary to refer them to their true position in the classification adopted by Geologists; yet such has been the anxiety to learn the Geology of the State, I have classified our rocks, and given the results in Chapter I. of this Report, even at the risk of making some slight mistakes.*

---

* In that chapter I have not only given our opinion of the rocks, but also the *facts* on which that opinion is founded. The *lithological characters*, the *fossils*, and the *stratigraphical position* of each Formation, are given, so that all can judge of the accuracy of our conclusions. The specimens collected for the Cabinets, will enable any one to judge of the descriptions and fossils mentioned.

SECOND REPORT.

CHAPTER I.

GEOLOGY OF MISSOURI.

It has long been known, that a large portion of Missouri is occupied by a series of marine deposits, extending, in the Geological Scale, from the Coal Measures down through all the great divisions to near the base of the Lower Silurian. There has, however, for various reasons, existed some doubt as to the precise location of many of these rocks in the Geological System; but, so far as they have come under our observation, we have been able, with a few unimportant exceptions, to refer them to their positions in the series. It is true, we have found but few fossils in some of the lower sandstones and magnesian limestones by which we can determine their exact equivalents, if, indeed, all of them have such equivalents.

So far as practicable, we have adopted the Nomenclature of those Geologists, who have thoroughly investigated the rocks, where they are the best developed and well characterized, as the Nomenclature of the New York Reports, for the older Palæozoic rocks. But there are a few minor divisions, whose exact representatives in other localities, we have not yet determined, to which we have given provisional names, until future investigation shall more fully develop their range, structure and organic remains. The *Chouteau Limestone* and *Vermicular Sandstone* are provisional terms thus used.

In the general section, a space is left between the Systems I. and III. for another, System II., the Cretaceous, which may be found in the south-eastern counties. I have a specimen of *Catenipora escharoides* * from Lewis county, indicating the presence of the Clinton or Niagara Group. It is, also, expected that an equivalent of the

---

* This Coral was given me by a gentleman, who said he obtained it in Lewis county, near Monticello; but I suspect there must be some mistake, as I have several fossils from that region, which are characteristic of the St. Louis Limestone.

Potsdam Sandstone will be added to the section when the lower strata, skirting our igneous rocks, shall have been more thoroughly examined.

Though Section I. is not given as a perfect exposition of all the rocks of Missouri, yet we trust it will be found as accurate as could be expected from the time (eighteen months) spent upon the work.

It represents the strata in their natural order, from the surface downward, commencing with the Alluvium, and terminating with the 4th Magnesian Limestone.

The first column contains the names and numbers of the *Geological Systems*; the third, the *letters* used to represent the Formations in the text, in other Sections, and on the Maps; the fourth, the names of the *Formations*; the fifth, their observed *thickness*; the sixth, the *colors* and *shading* used to represent them; and seventh, some of the *localities* where they have been observed.

It is deemed advisable to give a short description of these Formations, to present a general and condensed view of the Geology of Missouri, so far as determined, that the reader may be better prepared to enter upon the more detailed examinations of the districts reported upon in the following pages.

SYSTEM I. — QUATERNARY.

This System includes the *Drift* and all the strata above it, all the deposits included in the Alluvion and Diluvion of former authors. There are within this period, four distinct and well-marked Formations in this State: —

F. *a* — ALLUVIUM.
F. *b* — BOTTOM PRAIRIE.
F. *c* — BLUFF OR LOESS.
F. *d* — DRIFT.

These comprise all of our surface deposits, all the loose clays, marls, sands, soils, humus and mould, found upon the surface of our State; all of which have been formed in a period very recent in the geological cycles. All of the latest deposits, all that have been formed since the present order of things commenced upon our Continent, are included in —

F. *a* — ALLUVIUM.

All the deposits observed in the State, belonging to this formation, are: —

1*st.* — *Soils.*
2*d.* — *Pebbles and Sand.*
3*d.* — *Clays.*
4*th.* — *Vegetable Mould or Humus.*
5*th.* — *Bog Iron Ore.*
6*th.* — *Calcareous Tufa.*
7*th.* — *Stalactites and Stalagmites.*

1st. *Soils* are a well-known mixture of various comminuted and decomposed mineral substances, combined and mingled with decayed vegetable and animal remains, all comprising those ingredients peculiarly adapted to the nourishment of the vegetable kingdom. They are formed by the action of water, particularly in the form of rain and dews, cold, heat and other atmospheric influences, together with the coöperation of the vegetable and animal kingdoms.

The process by which soils are formed is one of the most beautiful and wonderful in Nature. By a careful examination of what is transpiring in this great laboratory of Nature, we may easily detect that process. If a rock, fresh from the quarry, be exposed, its surface will soon present a dull, earthy appearance, which is caused by a disintegration of its surface by atmospheric influences. Fine particles have been separated from the mass, and this meager coating of decomposing mineral matter will soon become the resting place of numerous microscopic germs, which will be developed into a minute growth of lichens. These in turn will decay and add their remains to the pulverized particles, and prepare them to sustain a more vigorous growth of herbs, and to become the abode of the small insects and worms, which will burrow in their recesses, feed upon the increasing vegetation, and swell the mass both by their mechanical agency, and by adding their exuviæ to the accumulating soil. Larger plants and animals will accelerate the process by their more powerful agencies, and by the greater amount contributed by their decaying remains. Thus by almost imperceptible increments our rich deep soils have been accumulated.

These facts clearly show the influence of the rocks upon the characters of the soils formed by their disintegration. Hence soils resting upon sandstones are light and sandy, those upon limestone, are calcareous, and those on shales, wet and clayey. But the varieties of soils will be more fully noticed under the head of Economical Geology.

2*d*. *Pebbles and Sand.*—Many of our streams abound in water-worn pebbles, which constitute their beds, and form bars along their margins and across their channels. These pebbles were derived from the Drift and the harder portions of the adjacent rocks. They vary in size according to the transporting power of the stream in which they are found.

The economical value of these pebbles for roads and streets, and the obstruction they often present to navigation, as in the Osage, give them unusual importance in our Geology. The Osage, Gasconade, Niangua, Marais des Cygnes, Sac and Spring Rivers of the

South; and the Salt, South, North, Fabius and Chariton of the North, all furnish good and abundant examples of these deposits, which have been formed by the action of those streams.

Sand is the most abundant material in the Alluvial bottoms of the great rivers in the State. Vast quantities of it are constantly borne along by the irresistible current of the Missouri.* Its whirling, rolling, turbulent waters, form of it extensive bars in incredibly short periods, which they again wear away, often, still more rapidly than they were formed.

These sand-bars, so common in this stream, frequently extend along its bed several miles, with a breadth varying from one to five or six furlongs, and limited in thickness only by the depth of the water. A slight fall in the river leaves these vast sand-beds dry, when their surfaces are soon covered by a growth of weeds, interspersed with young willows and cotton-wood. The fickle stream, however, seldom leaves these sand-beds to a long repose; but returns to its old channel by a rapid removal of their loose materials.

A former disaster of the ill-fated *Timour No.* 2 presents a good illustration of the rapidity with which the Missouri forms and destroys these extensive deposits of sand. This steamer ran upon a sand-bar, and was soon left high and dry some seventy-five or one hundred yards from the water, with a fair prospect of leaving her timbers to decay in a young cotton-wood forest. But the current changed and cut its way through the sandy stratum upon which the boat rested, and floated her away uninjured to the great City of the West. And all this transpired in a few weeks.

As these sand-bars are cut away, their perpendicular faces present beautiful illustrations of their stratification, which is usually very irregular and complicated, as might be expected from the changeable character of the current.

Fig. 2, sketched from a sand-bar in the Missouri river, two miles above Wayne City, presents a good example of their stratification.

At high stages of water, both the Missouri and Mississippi overflow their low bottoms, and leave deposits of a grayish brown, or a grayish yellow sand, similar to that in the sand-bars mentioned above. The thickness of these beds depends upon the height and

---

* The sand of the Missouri, usually grayish brown and fine-grained, contains a considerable quantity of lime and clay and vegetable matter, which render it so productive.

Sec. 2.

Dr. by R. B. Price. On the Lithog. [illegible] Limestone Ill. Lith. by Schaerff & Bro., St. Louis.

JUNCTION OF WACONDA PRAIRIE AND THE TIMRERED BOTTOM BELOW.

continuance of the overflowing waters, varying from a mere perceptible stratum to several feet.

That from the flood of 1844 is very conspicuous throughout the length of the Missouri bottom in this State. It is sometimes six or eight feet thick, particularly in low bottoms, so heavily timbered as to obstruct the current.

At the lower end of Waconda Prairie, this deposit is very evenly distributed over its surface; but it increases in thickness as the prairie descends to the low timbered bottom, where it is six or seven feet, and its surface becomes very irregular, like the surface of a lake, when disturbed by a high wind, or a *chopped sea.*

Fig. 2.

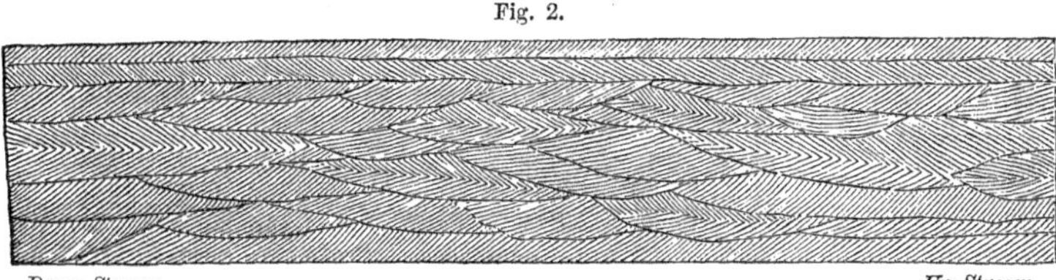

SECTION OF A MISSOURI SAND-BAR, REPRESENTING A PORTION, 20 FEET BY 4.

Sec. 2, showing the lower extremity of Waconda Prairie and the cotton-wood bottom below, finely illustrates these phenomena. Nos. 6, 7, 8, 9 and 10 represent older strata, and No. 5, that left by the flood of 1844. The small timber in the middle is a young growth of cotton-wood, which has sprung up subsequent to that event, and the larger trees just below is the older growth, where the deposit is so thick and uneven. Similar appearances are exhibited by the same formation in the bottom, nearly opposite Jefferson City.

These sands were doubtless derived from those extensive sandstone formations on the Platte* and other tributaries of the Missouri. It is nearly all silex, but contains enough calcareous and argillaceous matter to render it fertile; as is abundantly proved by the growth of weeds and willows, cotton-wood and sycamores, which immediately spring up on these sand-bars whenever they are exposed above the water. There are many points on the Missouri, as in the bottom opposite St. Charles, where a thrifty growth of young timber may be seen on the sand deposits of 1844.

* The Platte is a rapid stream, and brings down large quantities of sand, though its waters are not so turbid as those of the Missouri, either above or below their junction.

3*d*. *Clays.*—These are dark, bluish gray, argillaceous strata, rendered more or less impure by fine silicious, calcareous, and decomposed organic matter. When the floods of the Mississippi and the Missouri subside, the lagoons, sloughs and lakes are left full of turbid water. The coarser materials soon settle into a stratum of sand, but the finer particles more gradually subside and form the silico-calcareous clays of those Alluvial bottoms. Thus after each flood, new strata of sand and clay are deposited, until the lakes and sloughs are silted up.

The thickness of each stratum of sand depends upon the height and continuation of the floods, but that of the clay-beds is governed more by the time between the overflows.

These alternations of sand and clay may be observed in nearly all the Alluvial bottoms of our two great rivers; Section 3, from the Mississippi bottom above Tully, and Section 4, below the mouth of the Kansas, in the Missouri bottom, present good examples of the deposits under consideration.

The thickness of these beds of clay is very variable, from the tenth of an inch to ten feet. The argillaceous materials which formed them, were doubtless derived from the Cretaceous Clays of the Upper Missouri, whence, as from Mauvaises Terres, such a vast quantity of a similar material has been removed by denudation.

4th. *Vegetable Mould, or Humus*, is a dark brown or black deposit of decayed vegetable matter, containing variable, though small, quantities of fine silicious and argillaceous particles. When wet, it is very soft and plastic and quite black; but when dry, it separates into angular cuboidal fragments, which readily crumble into a dark brown, very light, impalpable powder.

The process by which these strata of humus are deposited is very obvious. When the lakes and sloughs of these bottoms are so far filled up as to sustain vegetable life, the decay of the annual growth, and of the foreign matter which falls or floats into these waters, forms a stratum of humus at the bottom, over the beds of clay and sand, previously deposited by the floods and still waters. Another overflow gives another succession of sand and clay; and the succeeding annual crop of vegetable matter, another stratum of humus.

These changes have often continued until several series of these deposits were formed. But when the bottoms of those bodies of water had been thus raised so high above the river, that the floods less frequently flowed into them, the deposits of sand diminished, and the long, quiet intervals, favored the deposition of clay and

Section 4.

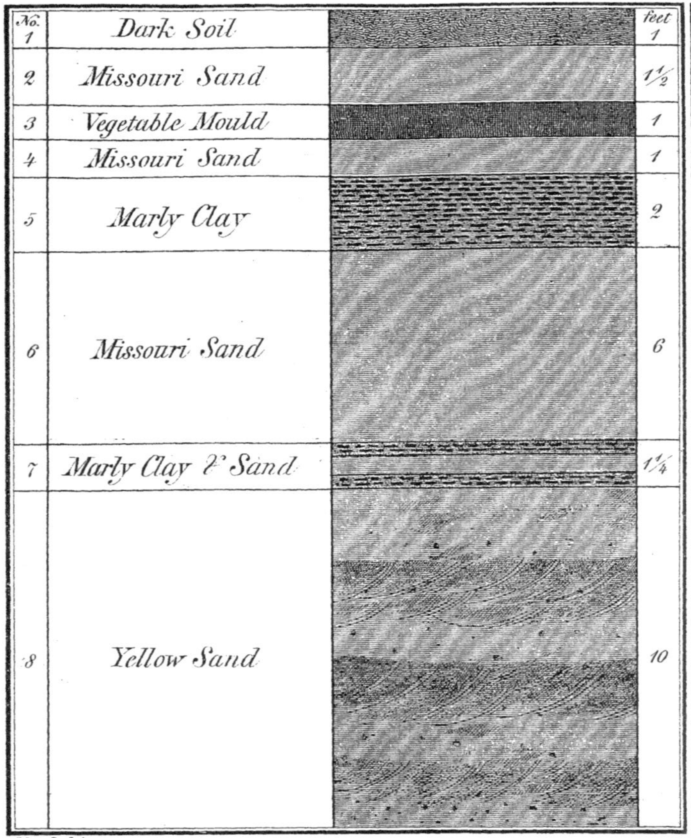

No.		feet
1	Dark Soil	1
2	Missouri Sand	1½
3	Vegetable Mould	1
4	Missouri Sand	1
5	Marly Clay	2
6	Missouri Sand	6
7	Marly Clay & Sand	1¼
8	Yellow Sand	10

Mrs S. del.

Missouri Bottom below Mouth of Kansas.

Section 3.

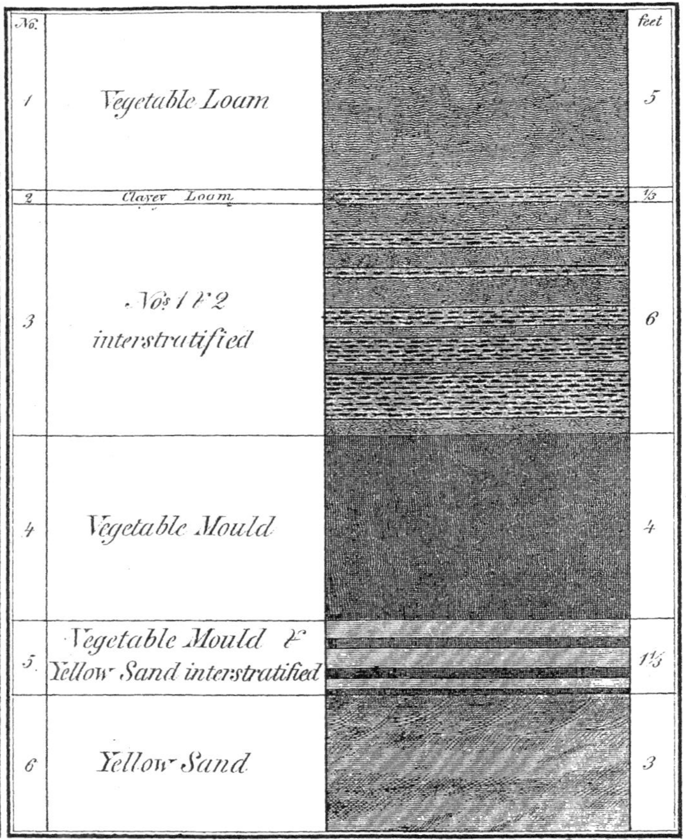

No.		feet
1	Vegetable Loam	5
2	Clayey Loam	⅓
3	Nos 1 & 2 interstratified	6
4	Vegetable Mould	4
5	Vegetable Mould & Yellow Sand interstratified	1⅓
6	Yellow Sand	3

L. Gast & Bro lith St Louis

Mississippi Bottom above Tully.

Humus. In time these shallow waters became mere marshes, where a rank vegetation rapidly formed thick beds of vegetable mould for the support of the magnificent forests which now occupy the sites of those former lakes and sloughs.

Such is the process by which the succession of Sands, Clays, and Humus in those alluvial bottoms, has been deposited; whence it is easy to see why the Sands are most abundant at the bottom, when the waters from the river floods would more frequently overflow them; the Clays in the middle, when the waters would be rarely disturbed by overflows; and the Humus or Vegetable Mould at the top, when a rank vegetation prevailed and inundations were rare.

Sections 3 and 4 are good illustrations of the manner in which these strata of Sand, Clay and Vegetable Mould succeed each other in the Alluvial bottoms of our two great rivers.

Such is the structure of the vast Alluvial plains bordering the Missouri and Mississippi rivers. The bottom of the former stream extending from the Iowa line to its mouth, is about 700 miles long and five broad, presenting an area of 3,500 square miles. More than half of this, say 1,800, we may set down as Alluvium, while the river, bottom prairies, and lakes occupy the remainder. This 1,800 square miles is equivalent to 1,152,000 acres. If we allow two-thirds as much more for the Mississippi bottom, we shall have on these two streams alone about 2,000,000 acres of the most productive and inexhaustible lands in the world, based upon these Alluvial strata of Sand, Clay, Marl and Humus. And besides, this quantity is constantly increasing by the silting up of the lakes and sloughs, as above described.

The rich productive power of this formation is abundantly proved by the immense burden of timber growing upon it, and by the unparalleled crops of corn and hemp harvested from its cultivated fields.

There are numerous shallow lakes in these bottoms, in which vast quantities of Marly Humus are accumulating, which will eventually become very valuable for the improvement of poor or exhausted soils.

5th. *Bog-Iron Ore* is deposited from several Chalybeate Springs. Large quantities of the Hydrated Oxide have accumulated near a fine spring, some two miles West of Oseola; and a smaller amount from another near Sharpsburg, in Marion county. Small quantities of Bog Ore are very common, but of little economical value in a State so bountifully supplied with excellent ores of this useful metal.

6th. *Calcareous Tufa* has been found in many places in the State.

In a ravine south of Parkville is a mass, in which several species of moss are well preserved; and another similar deposit was observed under the bluffs of magnesian limestone, near Bryce's Spring, on the Niangua.

7th. *Stalactites* and *Stalagmites* are abundant in some parts of the State. Some very beautiful specimens were found in the extensive caves of Boone county.

Such are the Alluvial Deposits, so far as observed, in Missouri. Future investigations may bring to light others belonging to this Formation.

Range and Thickness. — Our Alluvium is, as a matter of course, diffused throughout the entire State, as it comprises all the soils and other deposits now forming. It is, however, much more abundant in the valleys of our great streams. The thickness is often thirty or forty feet, though generally much less.

Organic Remains. — Many fossils have been observed in these rocks; but a catalogue of them would be useless, as all belong to living species.

F. *b* — BOTTOM PRAIRIE.

This important Formation in many respects resembles that of the *alluvial bottoms* above described, with which it has usually been confounded by Geologists; though Agriculturists have made a distinction.

There are, however, important differences: —

1st. The stratification in the Prairie is much more uniform, and more regularly extended over wide areas.

2d. In the Prairie Formation, the strata are not so distinct, nor are they so purely silicious or argillaceous.

3d. It was evidently formed by agencies operating over the entire bottoms, whose action was more uniform and quiet, and continued uninterrupted through longer periods, than those now forming the Alluvial deposits in the same bottoms.

4th. Where these two Formations meet, one can usually trace out the line of demarcation. Either the strata of the Prairie pass under those of the Alluvium, or are cut off and replaced by them. Instances of both of these changes may be observed at the lower end of Waconda Prairie, as shown in Sec. 2. The upper stratum of the Prairie No. 1 passes under No. 5 of the Alluvial Bottom, and continues in that position several hundred yards; while Nos. 1, 2, 3 and 4 of the former are cut off at *b*, and are replaced by Nos. 6, 7, 8, 9 and 10 of the latter.

5th. The Alluvial Bottom is continually increased at the expense of the Prairie, through the action of the rivers. The current is constantly cutting away the Prairie, forming new channels and filling up the old ones with drift and silt. This explains the fact that the strata of the Prairie are frequently cut off, and others quite different set in, as we pass from it to the timbered bottoms, as illustrated in Sec. 2. The part of that section under the large timber was once the channel of the river, and has been filled up by the process explained above, in describing the last Formation. At high stages of water the lower portions of the Prairie are overflowed, and deposits of sand are left on its surface, which are soon covered with willows, sycamores, or cotton-wood, as in the middle of Sec. 2, where a young growth of cotton-wood has sprung up on the deposits from the flood of 1844.

6th. No causes now in operation could, at the present level of the country, produce a formation of such extent and uniform structure as the Bottom Prairies. *

Such are some of the facts which have convinced me that this is an older formation, and one entirely distinct from the Alluvial Bottoms. Several facts show it to be distinct from and newer than the Bluff or Loess. Its composition, structure and position, are entirely different; and in many places the former rests non-conformably upon the latter, as at St. Joseph, and at the mouth of the Big Nemaha. See Fig. 4.

Fig. 4.

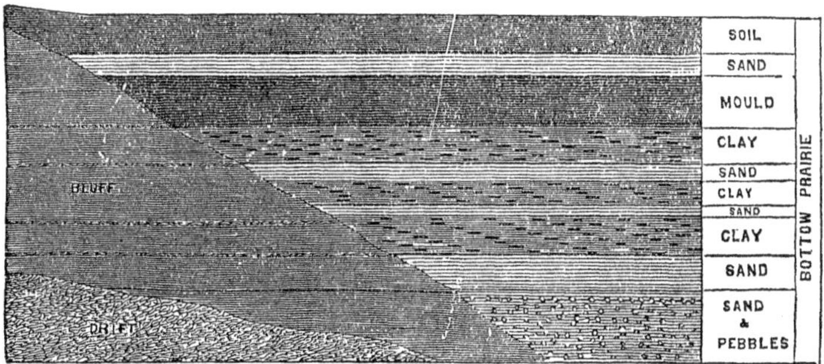

BELOW THE MOUTH OF BIG NEMAHA.

* Some of the Bottom Prairies of the Missouri are, at least, thirty miles long, and from ten to twenty broad, as the Huppan-Kuty of Nicollet, above the mouth of the Sioux River, and the Waconda, in Carrol county. And these are probably only fragments of one which was once continuous from the former to the mouth of the Missouri.

This Formation, like the last, is made up of Sands, Clays and Vegetable Mould, variously interstratified, as in Fig. 4.

The *Sand* in the upper part is fine and yellowish brown, like that of the Missouri sand-bars, but the lower beds are more purely silicious.

The *Clays* are usually dark, bluish brown and marly, with more or less sand and humus intermingled.

The *Humus* or *Vegetable Mould*,* has a brownish black color; when wet, it is somewhat plastic, and slightly tenacious; when dry, brittle, breaks into angular fragments, and can be easily reduced to an impalpable powder.

It has evidently been formed, by the growth and decay of plants, where it is found. Sec. 5 represents the thickness and super-position of these strata in the bottom prairie, below St. Joseph; and Sec. 6, the same Formation, on the Mississippi, near Marion City.

These sections show a greater proportion of clay in this Formation on the Missouri than on the Mississippi. This greater abundance is doubtless derived from the denuded Cretaceous clays, high up the former river.

I have proposed the term "*Bottom Prairie*" for this Formation, as these beautiful Savannas are usually designated by that title.

Range and Thickness.—The Bottom Prairie is, so far as my observations have extended, limited to the valleys of our two great rivers, and is about half as extensive as the *Alluvial Bottom* on the same streams.

This estimate will give us about 1,000,000 acres of these vastly rich Savannas, all prepared by Nature for the plow. Their agricultural capacities are scarcely inferior to any in the world, as is abundantly demonstrated by the mineral contents of the strata and the products of the numerous flourishing farms located upon it. I have observed not more than thirty-five feet of this formation.

Organic Remains of this Formation are very numerous and well preserved. All the mollusks of Catalogue I., found in the Bluff, excepting *Helicina occulta*, and perhaps one or two others, have been detected in it. Numerous species of trees, shrubs and

* This substance differs from peat in having no vegetable fibres, or partially decomposed plants. It is identical with the "*Vegetable Mould, or Humus,*" of Liebig's Agricultural Chemistry, and Colman's European Agriculture; the "*Vegetable Mould*" of Johnston's Lectures on Agriculture, and the "Humus" of Rogers' Scientific Agriculture.

Section 5.

Nº		Thickness in feet
1	Soil	3
2	Sandy Loam	5
3	Vegetable Mould Marly Clay & Sand interstratified	8
4	Marly blue Clay with ferruginous Stains	5
5	Fine gray Sand	1½
6	Marly blue Clay	3

Dr. by Mrs. S.

MISSOURI BOTTOM PRAIRIE, AT ST. JOSEPH.

Section 6.

Nº		Thickness in feet
1	Soil	3
2	Vegetable Mould	1
3	Yellow Sand & Clayey Mould	4
4	Clayey Mould	2
5	Yellow Sand	5

Lith. by Schaerff & Bro.

MISSISSIPPI BOTTOM PRAIRIE, NEAR MARION CITY.

vines have been collected from it, but they have not yet been examined.

The scenery of the Alluvial Bottoms and the Bottom Prairie is well represented in Sec. 2, and Plate XII. The timber shows the former, and the Prairie the latter.

F. c—BLUFF, OR LOESS.

The Geological position of this Formation in the series of Missouri rocks is easily determined. That it is newer than the Drift, is satisfactorily proved by the fact, that it rests upon the latter Formation, when both are present and undisturbed.

This is obvious wherever both of these deposits are exposed in the bluffs of the Missouri.

Section 7, taken at St. Joseph, shows their relative position; figure 4, also, shows the Drift underlying the Bluff, and at the same time, the Bottom Prairie resting upon it. Sections 11, 14 and 15, show this Formation occupying the same intermediate position. It caps nearly all the bluffs of the Missouri and Mississippi within our State, forming the very highest deposits skirting their valleys. Thus, while the Bottom Prairie occupies a higher geological horizon, the Bluff is usually several hundred feet above it in the topographical.

This Formation, when well developed, usually presents a fine, pulverulent, obsoletely stratified mass of light grayish buff, silicious and slightly indurated marl. Its color is usually variegated with deeper brown stains of oxide of iron. Section 7, taken at the Bluff above St. Joseph, exhibits an exposure of it 140 feet thick, presenting its usual characteristic features.

When but sparingly developed, it generally becomes more argillaceous and assumes a deeper brown or red color; as on the railroad south of Palmyra, where it is a dark brick red, tinged with purple. In some places the ferruginous and calcareous matter increases, and we find concretions of marl and iron-stone, either disseminated through the mass or arranged in horizontal belts, as in Section 7. At other places it has more arenaceous matter, and is much more decidedly stratified, as at a point one mile above Wellington, and in the bluff at St. Joseph.

These are the only places seen where the stratification assumed the irregular appearance so often presented by sand-bars. It is barely possible that this stratified sand is a portion of *Altered Drift;* but the beds between it and the Drift, having the usual appearance of the bluff, militates against such a supposition.

The Bluff Formation is often penetrated by numerous tubes or cylinders, about the size or thickness of pipe stems, some larger and others smaller. They are composed of clay, carbonate of lime and oxide of iron, being argillo-calcareous oxide of iron, or calcareous clay-ironstone. But it is not so easy to say how they were formed. Several facts may aid us in determining this matter. These tubes penetrate the formation in all directions, and are most abundant near the surface; though some extend to the depth of twenty feet. The space for some half-inch around each tube, more or less, according to its size, is of a much lighter color; as if the coloring matter (oxide of iron) had been extracted.

The same appearances were observed around the green and dry roots of the white oak (*Quercus alba*), which had penetrated the same formation. Qualitative analyses proved these same roots to contain a large portion of oxide of iron. And besides, oak-wood always contains a large portion of that metal and manganese. An analysis of its ashes, by Saussure, gave 2.25 per cent. of the oxides of those metals; while the analysis of "oak-wood mould," or the decayed wood, by the same chemist, gave 14 per cent. of the same oxides.

It is thus made manifest that oak-wood contains iron, which must have been absorbed through the roots from the earth. This fact readily explains the loss of the iron from the marl around the roots, and around the tubes, provided they were once oak-roots. But the question naturally arises, how these roots became tubular. But they were seen in the various stages of decay, and the woody fibers of some had disappeared and left the bark, in the form of a tube, still retaining its organic structure, though strongly impregnated with the oxide of iron and aluminum and carbonate of lime.

It may, also, be objected that oak-roots do not penetrate to the depth of twenty feet, where these tubes appear numerous; as represented in Section 8, taken in the city of Lexington, where a street or passage had been cut through this deposit, and in Fig. 5, which gives a good view of these tubes and holes in this Bluff, and at many other points in the State.

But it must be remembered that this Bluff Formation is very light and mellow; that it is filled with the food suited to nourish the iron vigor of the sturdy oak, and that this tree sends its roots deeper into the sustaining soil than any other of our forests. This fact enables it to stand before the blasts, which hurl other trees from their foundations, and makes it, everywhere, an emblem of strength. It is, also, sustained by the concurrent testimony of past ages.

Fig. 5.

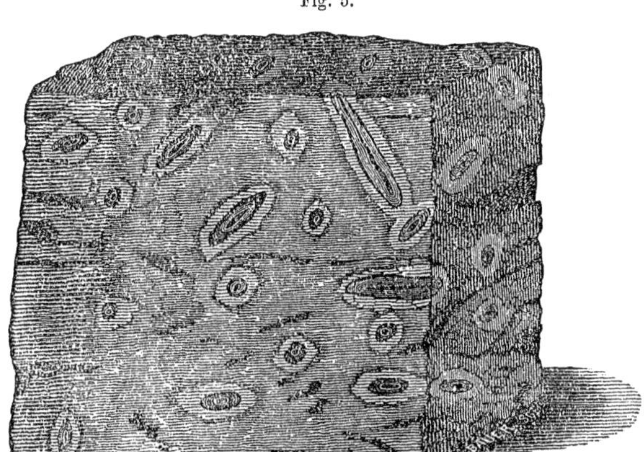

BLOCK OF BLUFF, ONE FOOT SQUARE, FROM NUMBER 4, OF SECTION 3.
Showing the perforations or tubes, so numerous in this formation.

Virgil incorporates the idea in Georgica, Lib. II., li. 291, in these beautiful lines:—

> "Aesculus in primis; quae quantum vertice ad auras,
> Aetheras, tantum radice in Tartara tendit."

Dryden thus translates:—

> "High as his topmost boughs to heaven ascend,
> So low his roots to hell's dominion tend."

And, besides, green roots, both of the white oak (*Quercus alba*) and the poke-weed (*Phytolacca decandra*), were found seventeen feet below the surface, in the perpendicular cut at section 8.

These facts have led to the conclusion, that these tubes of calcareous clay-ironstone are the decayed roots of oaks and other plants. Small holes, also, without any tubes of different material, penetrate this formation in great numbers, and are probably caused by similar agencies.

These phenomena have been thus minutely investigated, not merely as interesting scientific facts, but, also, as one of the most useful agricultural features of this preëminently valuable formation; for upon it, and sustained by its absolutely inexhaustible fertilizing resources, rest the very best farms of the Mississippi and Missouri valleys. These tubes and holes, also, constitute the *most thorough system of drainage* imaginable.

The marlites of the Bluff at St. Joseph, Section 7, yield, by the analysis of Dr. Litton, from 100 parts—

Insoluble in hydrochloric acid,	35.08
Oxides of alumina and iron,	5 22
Carbonate of lime,	58.33
Carbonate of magnesia,	0.77
	99.40

A specimen of this deposit, possessing its usual characters, collected at Hannibal, Section 7 of the schedule, gave, by two analyses of Dr. Litton, the following results:—

In one hundred parts, dried at 212° F., there were of—

	1	2
Silica,	76.98	77.02
Alumina and peroxide of iron,	11.54	12.10
Lime,	3.87	3.25
Magnesia,	1.68	1.63
Carbonic acid	not determined,	2.83
Water,	2.01	2.43
	96.17	99.26

Brick, made from this formation, at the above locality, gave—

Silica,	79.52
Alumina and peroxide of iron,	12.80
Lime,	3.45
Magnesia,	1.95
Carbonic acid	1.11
	98.83

A specimen from the Big Mound, St. Louis, gave—

Silica,	76.19
Alumina and peroxide of iron,	16.88
Lime,	2.50
Magnesia,	0.73
Carbonic acid and water,	2.68
	98.98

According to Bischoff's Chemical Geology, the Loess of the Rhine, supposed by some to be identical with our Bluff, gives the following results from five analyses:—

Section 7.

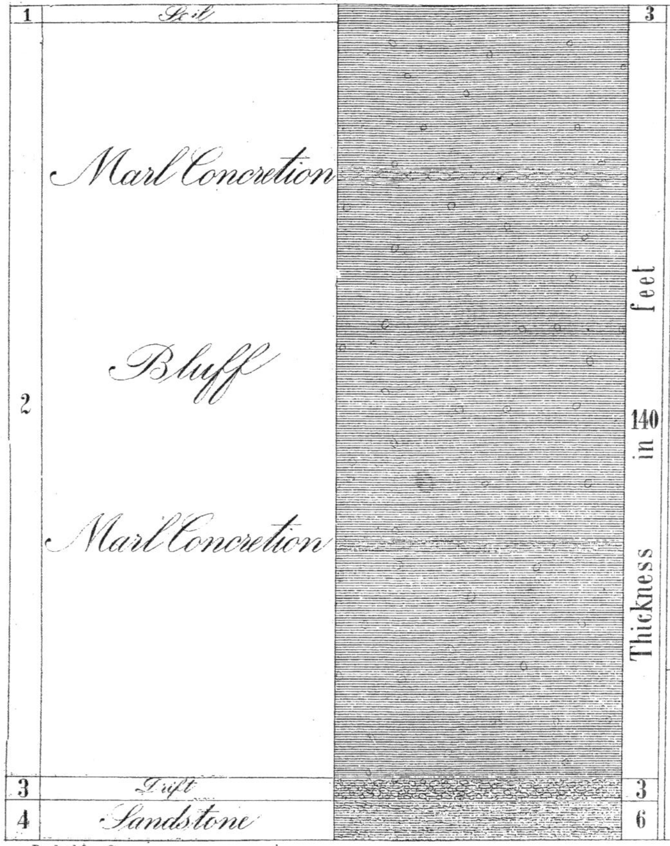

No.	Stratum	Thickness in feet
1	Soil	3
2	Marl Concretion Bluff Marl Concretion	140
3	Drift	3
4	Sandstone	6

Dr. by Mrs. S.

SECTION OF BLUFF ABOVE ST. JOSEPH.

Section 8.

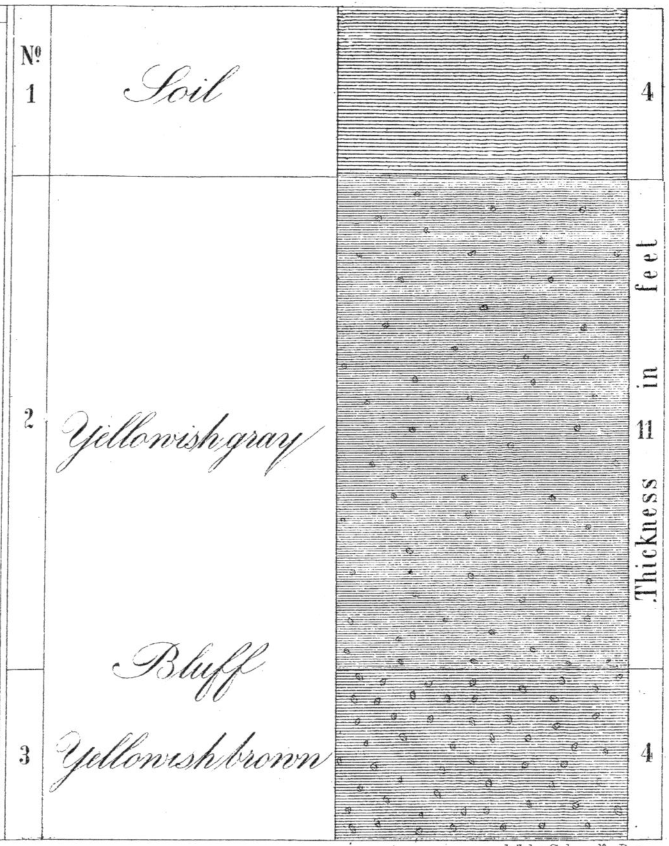

No.	Stratum	Thickness in feet
1	Soil	4
2	Yellowish gray Bluff	11
3	Yellowish brown	4

Lith. by Schaerff & Bro.

BLUFF FORMATION AT LEXINGTON.

PLATE I.

Drawn by R. B. Price.

E. Robyn Lithr St. Louis Mo.

BLUFFS IN NEBRASKA JUST BELOW THE MOUTH OF PLATTE RIVER.

NUMBER OF ANALYSIS.	* 1st.	* 2d.	* 3d.	* 4th.	* 5th.
Silicic acid	58.97	79.53	78.61	62.43	81.04
Alumina	9.97	13.45	15.26	7.51	9.75
Peroxide of iron,	4.25	4.81		5.14	6.67
Lime,	0.02	0.02	....	....	....
Magnesia	0.04	0.06	0.91	0.21	0.27
Potash	0.11	1.05	3.31	1.75	2.27
Soda	0.84	1.14			
Carbonate of lime	20.16	....	....	11.63	....
Carbonate of magnesia	4.21	....	....	3.02	....
Loss by ignition	1.37	....	1.89	2.31	....

The first specimen was obtained on the road from Oberdollendorff to Heisterbach, and the fourth on the road from Bonn to Ippendorf. The Loess of Pitten, in Lower Austria, contains 30.68 per cent. carbonate of lime, and 12.33 carbonate of magnesia, according to Hauer.

According to Krocker's analyses of the Loess, from seven places on the left bank of the Rhine, between Magnesia and Worms, the quantity of carbonate of lime varies from 12.03 to 36.00 per cent., and carbonate of magnesia from a trace to 3.02 per cent.†

These analyses show a striking coincidence in the composition of these widely-separated Formations.

Range and Thickness.—So far as my own observations extend, this formation caps all the bluffs of the Missouri, from Council Bluffs to its mouth, and those of the Mississippi, from the mouth of the Des Moines to that of the Ohio, and forms the upper stratum beneath the soil of all the high-lands, both timbers and prairie, of all the counties north of the Osage and Missouri, and also St. Louis, and the other Mississippi counties on the south.

According to Mr. Meek, its western or north-western limit is probably a few miles below Fort Pierre; Lyell traces a similar formation up the Ohio and further down the Mississippi; Dr. Owen mentions its existence on the Wabash River; and Dr. G. G. Shumard saw a similar deposit on Red River.‡

The identity of the deposits at Council Bluffs, at St. Joseph, at

* This analysis was made after ignition and the extraction of the carbonates.

† For these interesting chemical facts, I am indebted to Dr. Litton.

‡ Capt. Marcy's Report on Red River of Louisiana, p. 182.

Lexington, at Boonville, and at St. Louis, is placed beyond all doubt, by the following facts; —

1st. They occupy the same Geological position.

2d. They have the same topographical position on the tops of the bluffs.

3d. They present the same Lithological and Chemical characters.

4th. Nearly all the fossils (see Catalogue I.) are found at all those places.

5th. These localities are connected by an unbroken continuity of the same deposit.

Its greatest development in this State is in the counties on the Missouri, from the Iowa line to the Boonville; but thence to St. Louis it is not so thick. In some places it is two hundred feet thick. At St. Joseph, it is one hundred and forty; at Boonville one hundred; and at St. Louis, in St. George's quarry, and the Big Mound, it is about fifty feet; while its greatest thickness observed in Marion county was only thirty.

Organic Remains. — The fossils of the Bluff Formation are very numerous and interesting. Those I have had time to identify are mentioned in Catalogue I. of Appendix B. I have collected from it, of the Mammalia, two teeth of the *Elephas primigenius*, the jaw-bone of the *Castor fiber Americana*, the molar of a *Ruminant*, and the Incisor of a *Rodent*; of the Mollusca, seventeen species of the genus Helix, eight *Limnea*, eight *Physa*, three *Pupa*, four *Planorbis*, six *Succinea*, and one each of the genera *Valvata*, *Amnicola*, *Helicina* and *Cyclas*, besides some others not determined. These *lacustrine*, *fluviatile*, *amphibious* and *land* specias, indicate a deposit formed in a fresh-water lake, surrounded by land and fed by rivers. These facts carry back the mind to a time when a large portion of this great valley was covered by a vast lake, into which, from the surrounding land, flowed various rivers and smaller streams. We see the waters peopled with numerous Mollusks; the industrious beaver building his habitation, the nimble squirrel, the fleet deer, the sedate elephant and huge mastodon, lords of the soil. There must have been land to sustain the elephant and mastodon and Helices; fresh water and land for the beaver; and fresh water for the Cyclas and Limneas.

I have proposed the title *Bluff Formation* for this deposit, as it forms a large portion of, and gives the peculiar characters to, the bluffs so conspicuous and unique in the scenery about Council Bluffs and other portions of the Missouri valley, and as it forms the tops of the bluffs wherever it is developed.

PLATE 11

BOB CAMPBELL

R. B. PRICE, DEL.

J. M. KERSHAW, SC.

BLUFFS OF THE BLUFF FORMATION, ON THE MISSOURI RIVER, ABOVE ST. JOSEPH.

Plate I. is a view of these bluffs below the mouth of the Platte, as they appear from the Iowa side; and Plate II. gives the appearance of the bluffs of the same formation, just above St. Joseph.

Loess, the name of a similar formation on the Rhine, has been given to this by some geologists. But this would imply that these two formations are identical, when they may or may not be, so far as any proof has been given. It is true they are both fresh-water deposits, both have recent shells of the same genera, and in lithological and chemical characters, they are somewhat similar. But there are other deposits, whose Fauna, and lithological and chemical properties, are quite as similar to the Bluff, and some of them more so, and yet they are more recent.

There is just as much evidence of the identity of the Loess and the Bottom Prairie, as there is of the Loess and the Bluff; and still we know the Bluff was formed long before the Bottom Prairie, and under a very different condition of this part of the continent. It may, also, be stated, that there is just as much evidence of the identity of the Bluff and the Bottom Prairie, as of the Bluff and Loess, and yet the Bluff and Bottom Prairie are not identical. The fossils of all three Formations only prove they belong to the Quaternary System, or were formed since some of the present Fauna came into being.

There is, indeed, but little probability that two such vast fresh-water lakes existed at the same time on the two continents, with the ocean rolling between.

But it would seem impossible to identify Formations so recent on separate continents, whose recent Faunas are so widely different; as the deposits on these continents, though cotemporaneous, would of necessity present Faunas very distinct. Hence, if we make fossils our only guide in identifying them, it will be impossible to distinguish deposits formed since the present genera of animals and plants came into existence, and we should be compelled to omit all distinctions between formations of the recent period, and to make all of our recent deposits identical with each other, and with all belonging to the same system in Europe and Asia; and this would deprive us of distinctions recognized in Scientific, and almost indispensable in Economical Geology. I have been thus minute in my examinations of the Bluff, the Bottom Prairie, and the Alluvial Formations, both on account of their vast importance to our agricultural interest, and the comparatively little attention geologists have given to them.

The scenery presented by the Bluff Formation is at once unique and beautiful, and gives character to nearly all the best landscapes on the Lower Missouri. Plates I. and II. give views characteristic of the scenery where this Formation is well developed.

F. *d*—DRIFT.

This Formation lies directly beneath the Bluff, as seen at St. Joseph, Sec. 7; near Hannibal, Sec. 15; at the mouth of the Des Moines, Sec. 14; above Weston, Sec. 11; and in many other places in Northern Missouri. It rests upon the various members of the Palæozoic series, as they successively come to the surface of that system. At the mouth of the Platte, and thence along the Missouri to Miami, it rests upon the Coal Measures; at Hannibal, Sec. 15, upon the Encrinital Limestone; at the Railroad, two miles west of Hannibal, on the Vermicular Sandstone and Shales, Plate III.; at Salt River, on the Trenton Limestone; and in the south of Cooper, on the Devonian and Silurian Limestones.

In this Formation there appears to be three distinct deposits:—

1st. What might be called an *Altered Drift* frequently appears in the banks of the Missouri river, as at the mouth of the Kansas, Sec. 4, No. 8, and in the Bottom Prairie below Brunswick, and at Waconda Prairie, Sec. 2, No. 4. These strata of sand and pebbles appear to be the finer materials of the Drift, removed and reärranged by aqueous agencies subsequent to the Drift period and prior to the formation of the Bluff. The pebbles are from all the varieties of rocks found in the true Drift, but are comparatively small.

2d. The Boulder Formation, as it was left distributed by those powerful and widely-extended agencies, which formed that deposit of the Northern Hemisphere. It is a heterogeneous stratum of sand, gravel and boulders, all water-worn fragments of the older rocks. The larger part are from the Igneous and Metamorphic rocks, in place at the North, and the remainder from the Palæozoic strata, upon which they rest. The Metamorphic and Igneous rocks must have come from the northern localities of those strata, the nearest of which according to Dr. Owen's Report, is on the St. Peter's river, about 300 miles north of St. Joseph. But the Palæozoic fragments are usually from localities near where they rest, as shown by the fossils they contain, and are as *completely rounded** as those from the more distant points.

The largest boulders observed in Missouri are five or six feet in

* This subject was particularly investigated, as it has an important bearing upon the theories respecting the agencies which produced the Drift.

PL. III.

R. B. Price Del

Lith by Schaerff & Bro. St. Louis.

BLUFFS OF DRIFT NEAR THE PLANK AND RAIL-ROADS WEST OF HANNIBAL IN MARION COUNTY

diameter; they are Granite and Metamorphic Sandstone. These, though large for this latitude, sink into insignificance when compared with those huge rounded masses so abundant in the North-Eastern States, and particularly along the coast of Maine.*

3d. The *Pipe Clay*† lies directly below the Boulder deposit, wherever it has been observed; and boulders are more or less dispersed through the upper part of it, as seen in the railroad cut, one mile south of Palmyra. This deposit is abundant in Marion, Boone and Cooper counties, and has been seen in Moniteau, Howard and Monroe. Its thickness varies from one to six feet. This clay may possibly belong to an older formation. It is not fossiliferous.

Range and Thickness.—Drift abounds in all parts of the State north of the Missouri, and exists in small quantities as far south as the Osage and Meramec. Its thickness is very variable, from one to forty-five feet. Its development is greater, the boulders larger, and those of a foreign origin more numerous, towards the North. At the mouth of the Platte its thickness is twenty feet; at Wellington, two feet; and two miles west of Hannibal, forty-five feet; see Plate III., which gives a view of the Drift bluffs so conspicuous at that place; also, a small outlier of the same deposit in the Alluvial Bottom.

In places, the sand or the Drift is sufficiently sharp and pure for the best of mortars and cements; the pebbles make the most approved materials for roads and walks; and the clay is a superior article for all the uses to which such clays are adapted.

Organic Remains.—I have seen no fossils in this deposit, save a few logs in the Altered Drift of the Missouri. These are still sound, and burn quite well when dry, as we proved by building our camp fires with them on several occasions. The species to which they belong are not yet determined.

There are other deposits, particularly in the middle and southern parts of this State, which are not genuine Drift, and yet they

---

* Granite boulders often occur, on the islands of Penobscot Bay, thirty-five and forty feet in diameter.

† A specimen from Mr. White's land, in Town. 58, R. 7 W., Sec. 10, in Marion county, gave, by Dr. Litton's analysis, in 100 parts:—

Silica,	63.01
Alumina, nearly pure,	28.24
Lime,	a trace.
Water,	8.62
	99.87

bear a greater resemblance to that than any other Formation, and occupy precisely the same stratigraphical position.

Beneath the Alluvium of the bottoms we often find deposits of pebbles similar to the genuine or altered Drift of the Missouri, but all the materials came from the neighboring rocks, and appear like the beds of ancient streams.

On the high-lands there are, in the same position, numerous beds of angular fragments of the adjacent rocks, somewhat worn, and in discriminately commingled with sands and clays.

Whether these deposits were formed by the same agencies which produced the Drift, or by a part of them only, or by other causes, has scarcely been determined. Our future examinations may throw some light upon this subject. But as we advance in our investigations of the lower strata, those formed in the more distant cycles of the Geological History of our State, we may expect to find phenomena still more inexplicable, as they were produced by agencies which have, perhaps, long since ceased to exist.

The Pebbles and Gravel of this Formation have a great economical value for roads and streets; while the Clay is well adapted to the manufacture of first quality of brick and pottery. No better materials exist for making a beautiful and durable brick than a proper mixture of this clay and the fine sharp sands of this Formation.

SYSTEM III.—CARBONIFEROUS.

Both divisions of the Carboniferous rocks are well developed in Missouri.

1st.—COAL MEASURES, OR UPPER CARBONIFEROUS.
2d.—MOUNTAIN, OR CARBONIFEROUS LIMESTONE—LOWER CARBONIFEROUS.

F. e—COAL MEASURES.

So far as the coal strata of Missouri have come under my observation, they appear to be separated into three divisions, by two very important sandstones. These divisions have, for convenience, been called the *Upper, Middle and Lower Coal Series.* The *Upper Coal Series*, so far as it has been observed, comprises, where best developed the following strata:—

No. 1.—10 feet of hard, bluish gray, ferruginous, sub-crystalline, silicious limestone in regular beds, interstratified with brown clay. This is the highest rock of the Coal Measures seen on the Missouri, and is exposed in the top of the Bluffs, back of Fort Leavenworth, and furnishes the beautiful building stone at that station. The upper quarries near the graveyard, back of Parkville, are in this rock. It is, also, exposed in the bluffs two miles above Weston, near Mr. Elliford's residence, and at Dallas and Elizabethtown. The most abundant fossils are *Fusulina cylindrica, Productus costatus, P. aequicostatus*, and *Orthis umbraculum.*

No. 2.—3 feet of yellow and blue shale, which decomposes on exposure, and forms a plastic clay. It crops out under No. 1, at the localities given for that rock. No fossils were seen in it.

No. 3.—3 feet of bituminous shale. It underlies the last stratum at the localities mentioned. We observed no organic remains in it.

No. 4.—3 feet of coarse, grayish white crystalline limestone. It burns into an excellent lime, and is much used for that purpose at Parkville. Its common fossils are *Terebratula subtilita* and *Productus costatus.*

No. 5.—15 feet of bituminous and blue shale, which is usually covered by debris, as at Weston and Leavenworth.

No. 6.—20 feet of fine blue, buff and gray silicious cherty, limestone, interstratified with a few thin laminae of shale. This rock crops out at the water's edge at Bellevue and the mouth of the Platte, and some 200 feet above the water at Dallas, King's Hill, below St. Joseph, Weston and Parkville. At the last place, the upper strata are very hard, silicious, even-bedded, and interstratified with brown clay. The more silicious strata make a most excellent fire-rock. It furnishes the famous building stone of that town. It usually forms a conspicuous bench near the top of the bluff, in this part of the Missouri valley. *Fusulina cylindrica, Spirifer Meusebachanus, S. lineatus, S. plano-convexa, Productus Wabashensis, P. costatus, P. aequicostatus, Chonetes granulifera,* and *Terebratula subtilita,* are the most abundant fossils.

No. 7.—12 feet of bituminous and blue shale. It underlies the last rock at the above-named localities, and, in places, contains a thin stratum of coal. *

No. 8.—7 feet of red, yellow and gray friable sandstone; at the mouth of the Big Nemaha. No fossils were observed.

No. 9.—4 feet of dark buff and ferruginous gray argillaceous limestone, as seen at Parkville, Weston, Fort Leavenworth, King's Hill, Fort Kearney, and at the mouth of the Little Nemaha. But few fossils were seen; among them were *Fusulina cylindrica, Orthis umbraculum, Productus Wabashensis, P. costatus, P. semireticulatus*, and *Terebratula subtilita.*

No. 10.—20 feet of purple, green and blue shales. These beautiful strata are exposed in the bluffs of Nebraska, opposite to Bethlehem; at Fort Kearney; in the bluff ten miles below that station, opposite Sonora; at the mouth of the Little Nemaha; at Dallas, Weston and Parkville. The purple beds are an excellent fire-proof paint for out-side work.

No. 11.—5 feet of dark gray, coarse calcareous sandstone.

No. 12.—16 feet of blue calcareous and bituminous shales in thick beds, with a conchoidal fracture. It sometimes contains thin seams of coal and *Terebratula subtilita, Orthis umbraculum*, and *Spirifer Kentuckensis.*

---

* This stratum of shale often presents the appearance of a hard, impure cannel-coal; as in the bluffs of Little Tarkeo, four miles above Dallas, where it has been opened for coal. It burns freely, and some have mistaken it for cannel-coal. It has a very fine texture, is susceptible of a beautiful polish, and, when wrought, it very much resembles jet. It will answer very well for some ornaments usually made of that mineral.

A specimen from the bluff below Weston gave, by analysis, in 100 parts—

Silica,	28.47
Alumina and peroxide of iron,	17.96
Carbonate of lime,	46.52
Carbonate of magnesia,	2.91
Water,	3.04

It may make a good hydraulic cement.

No. 13.—6 feet of soft shaly sandstone, of a brown color. It crops out above Weston.

No. 14.—18 feet of fine-grained, light gray, cherty limestone, containing numerous small cavities filled with oxide of iron; some beds are very white and pure. This rock crops out at the top of the bluff above Wayne City, and forms a prominent bench in the bluffs below Weston, and for some two miles above. The quarries in the bluff just below that town are in these strata. It is the lowest rock exposed in King's Hill, and forms a bench at Whitehead's Ferry, some 100 feet above the water. Fossils are very abundant in this limestone; *Fusulina cylindrica, Terebratula subtilita* (very abundant,) *Orthis umbraculum, Spirifer Kentuckensis, Productus punctatus*, and *P. costatus* were obtained.

A specimen from Weston gave, by analysis, in 100 parts—

Insoluble in hydrochloric acid,	2.82
Alumina and peroxide of iron,	4.03
Carbonate of lime,	87 86
Carbonate of magnesia,	4.82
	99.53

Another specimen from Bondtown gave, in 100 parts—

Insoluble in nitric acid,	3.24
Alumina and peroxide of iron,	1.46
Carbonate of lime,	93.10
Carbonate of magnesia,	a trace.
Water,	1.33
	99.13

The purest portions make excellent lime.

No. 15.—17 feet of bituminous and blue shale. This is exposed at Weston, below the last rock described, where it is a bluish shale; but four miles north, on Bear Creek, near Mr. N. W. Asbury's residence, it contains a bed of coal six inches thick, some bituminous shale and several thin strata of marlite.

No. 16.—3 feet dark buff, ferruginous limestone. In the bluffs, at Weston, and Parkville, and Wayne City.

No. 17.—20 feet of blue shales, which are exposed at Weston and Wayne City.

No. 18.—10 feet of fine blue and coarse gray limestone, which on exposure, breaks into small angular fragments. It was observed at Parkville and Wayne City, where it contains *Fusulina cylindrica, Productus costatus, Terebratula subtilita* and *Campophyllum torquium.*

Pl. IV.

Lith. by Schaerff & Bro. St. Louis

BLUFF & STEAM MILL BELOW WESTON. THE LIMESTONES & SHALES OF THE UPPER COAL SERIES CROP OUT ON THE SLOPE

No. 19. — 24 feet of blue calcareous shale, in thick beds, with a conchoidal fracture. It contains many impressions of plants, like the leaves of the Iris — at Wayne City and Liberty Landing — probably hydraulic.

No. 20. — 8 feet of argillaceous shaly limestone — Wayne City and Parkville.

No. 21. — 3 feet of thin-bedded ripple-marked sandstone — Weston.

No. 22. — 4 feet of bituminous and blue shales. This bed was observed at the mouth of Weeping Water, Elizabethtown, Weston and Fort Leavenworth.

No. 23. — 20 feet of hard, fine-grained, bluish gray and buff, somewhat ferruginous limestone, in regular strata, which are often much curved, as in the bluff at Kickapoo village. This limestone forms the perpendicular walls that rise from the water, both above and below the landing at Fort Leavenworth, and the lower terrace at Dallas, Weston and Kansas. It abounds in fossils: *Fusulina cylindrica, Spirifer Kentuckensis, S. lineatus, S. hemiplicatus, S. Meusebachanus, Productus costatus, P. punctatus, P. aequicostatus, P. Nebrascensis, Allorisma terminalis, A. regularis, Orthis umbraculum, Bellerophon hiulcus, Chaetetes milleporaceus* and *Terebratula subtilita.*

A specimen of this limestone from Kickapoo gave, in 100 parts —

Insoluble in nitric acid,	5.27
Alumina and peroxide of iron,	2.57
Carbonate of lime,	90.48
Water,	0.74
	99.06

It is generally sufficiently pure to make a good lime; but the iron is sometimes so abundant as to give it a dark color.

No. 24. — 5 feet of bituminous shale. This rock is exposed at Fort Leavenworth, beneath No. 23, just below the landing; at Weston, below the Steam Mill; and at a little higher level, at Kansas and at Liberty and Owen's Landings.

No. 25. — 2 feet of hard, compact dark blue limestone. It contains *Fusulina cylindrica*, and many Fucoidal impressions. It crops out near the water at Weston, Parkville and Kansas, and at a higher level, near Liberty and Owen's Landings.

A specimen from Liberty Landing gave, in 100 parts —

Insoluble in nitric acid,	3.25
Alumina and peroxide of iron,	1.92
Carbonate of lime,	91.94
Carbonate of magnesia,	1.05
Water,	1.60
	99.76

No. 26. — 3 feet of blue and purple shales.

No. 27. — 1 foot of bituminous shale.

These beds* of the Upper Coal Series are exposed in the bluffs

* These rocks have been, by Verneuil and other geologists, referred to the Lower Carboniferous age, but there can be no question that they belong to the Coal Measures, and are above the principal coal-beds in this State.

of the Missouri from Bellevue to Lexington. It will be observed that No. 6 is but little above the common water level at Bellevue and the mouth of the Platte, while at Weston, Parkville and Kansas, it is about 250 feet above the surface of the river. The fall of the Missouri river, has been estimated at one foot per mile. If this be correct, the rise of the strata above the water from Bellevue to Kansas, is about equal to the fall of the stream, the distance being 260 miles. There are, however, many undulations of the strata between the two points; though none are of sufficient magnitude to bring many of the lower strata above the water. There are several places between the mouths of the Platte and the Kansas, where nearly all the strata of the Upper Coal Series are exposed; as at Parkville, Fort Leavenworth, Weston, Elizabethtown and Dallas. Section 11 gives the strata as developed at Weston.

Thin strata of coal were observed in the bituminous shales of Nos. 7, 15, 24 and 27. In No. 7 it was noticed five miles below the mouth of the Platte, at the Big Nemaha and on the Little Tarkio, four miles above its mouth. Four miles north of Weston on Bear Creek, the coal was six inches thick in No. 15; and below that city, a thin stratum was seen in No. 24; but no bed of sufficient thickness to pay for working, was discovered in the bluffs of the Missouri, until we reached Sibley. It should not be understood, however, that there is no coal until we reach Sibley, but, that none was observed in the bluffs. We know there are beds beneath the water level; and that those beds do crop out in many places, as the strata rise to the surface, on the east and south, and perhaps in some places on the west of the river. It may also be observed that several fossils range through nearly all the limestones of this series. The *Fusulina cylindrica* was found in Nos. 1, 6, 9, 14, 18, 23 and 25; *Terebratula subtilita*, in Nos. 4, 6, 9, 12, 14 and 18; *Productus costatus*, in Nos. 1, 4, 6, 14, 18 and 23; and *Spirifer Meusebachanus*, in Nos. 6, 9, 14 and 23; *Productus punctatus*, *P. aequicostatus*, *P. Wabashensis*, *Orthis umbraculum* and *Chonetes granulifera* are also found in nearly all the limestones.

The Middle Coal Series, on the Missouri, is made up of the following strata:—

No. 28.—5 feet of fine calcareous, bluish gray, ripple-marked sandstone in thin strata. This rock crops out near the medium water level at Weston, Leavenworth and Kansas.

No. 29.—30 feet of blue silico-argillaceous shale with some vegetable impressions. These beds are well exposed in the base of the bluff at Owen's Landing, where their curious structure proves a deposition in shoal water, or that

Section 11.

No.	Strata	Thickness
	Bluff	
	Drift	6
6	Fine blue bluff and gray Limestone	10
7	Bituminous & blue Shale	12
9	Dark buff & grey Marly Limestone	4
10	Purple blue & green Shales.	20
11	Dark coarse gray Calcareous Sandstone.	5
12	Blue & bituminous Shale Thin seams of coal	20
13	Soft shaly Sandstone	6
14	Fine gray ferruginous Limestone quarried below Weston	14
15	Blue Shale and Marlite Coal Blue Shale	10 1/2 7
16	Dark buff ferruginous Limestone	3
17	Blue Shale	21
18	Fine blue & coarse gray Limestone	10
19	Blue Shale	20
20	Shaly argillaceous Limestone.	8
21	Shaly calcareous Sandstone.	3
22	Bituminous & blue Shale	3
23	Hard gray & buff Limestone interstratified	10
24	Bituminous Shale	3
25	Fine hard blue Limestone	3
26	Blue & purple Shale	2
27	Bituminous Shale	1
28	Fine calcareous ripple marked Sandstone.	6

R. B. Price del.

SECTION OF STRATA IN BLUFFS AT WESTON

they were alternately submerged and exposed above the waters in which they were formed. Many of its strata were exposed and sun-cracked while soft, and afterwards submerged until those cracks were filled with the same material, and other beds formed above them. These shales, also, show that they were very rapidly deposited in turbid waters; for, after the beds were cracked and again submerged, the fissures were filled with sediment before the mass was sufficiently saturated with water to expand and close the cracks. Thus we have preserved, in the rock itself, the history of its formation — that away back in the middle ages of the geological cycles, this shale was formed in turbid waters, so shoal that they were frequently exposed above its surface, and as often submerged and increased by new strata.

No. 30. — 3 feet of bituminous sandy shale. This bed is exposed at Lexington and three miles below Sibley.

No. 31. — 8 feet of purple and blue shale, green clay and Septaria.* This stratum may be seen at the steam mill above Lexington and above Wellington.

No. 32. — ½ foot of bituminous coal, containing large concretions of Septaria of silicious and argillaceous matter, traversed by veins of iron pyrites, is exposed at Wellington and Lexington, and above the former place it is one foot thick.

No. 33. — 6 feet of blue clay and marlite, charged with fossils: *Fusulina cylindrica*, *Terebratula subtilita*, *Orthis umbraculum*, and *Chonetes granulifera*, are most abundant, at Wellington and Lexington.

No. 34. — 10 feet of indurated brownish sandstone in thick beds, with white particles of pure silex disseminated through it. It is a good building stone, and has been used for grindstones. Large angular blocks of this rock are lying under the bluff above the landing at Lexington.

No. 35. — 6 feet of purple, blue and green shales and clays.

No. 36. — 4 feet of buff and gray ferruginous magnesian limestone; the upper part is shaly and full of *Fusulina*, *Chonetes*, *Producti* and *Crinoidea;* but the lower is hard, compact and silicious, and contains huge lenticular masses of *Chaetetes milleporaceus*. This limestone can be identified at all places, and is the best guide in this part of the coal series. It forms the lowest bench a little above the water at Sibley and Poston's Landing, is eighty or ninety feet above the river at Lexington, and about forty above the Lexington coal-bed. At Poston's Landing and Sibley huge lenticular masses of the characteristic coral (Chaetetes) are strown along the bank of the river. Seams in the rock are often filled with beautiful specimens of carbonate of iron, and sometimes the coralline portions contain masses of oxide of iron.

Two analyses of the more compact beds of this rock, gave —

---

* Analyses of two specimens of the Septaria of this stratum, gave —

	For the 1st.	For the 2d.
Res. insoluble in nitric acid,	8.45	17.24
Alumina and peroxide of iron,	1.87	5.25
Carbonate of lime,	87.70	75.82
Carbonate of magnesia and loss,	2.72	1.69
	100.74	100.00

	1.	2.
Residuum insoluble in hydrochloric acid, ...	3.11	3.04
Alumina and peroxide of iron, ...	9.01	9.00
Carbonate of lime, ...	60.18	61.18
Carbonate of magnesia, ...	26.53	25.70
Water, ...	0.29	......
	99.12	98.92

The composition indicates good hydraulic properties. It makes an excellent building stone, when free from corals.

No. 37. — 10 feet of bluish green clay.

No. 38. — 8 feet of bluish gray calcareous sandstone, sometimes passing into a calcareous shale; as at Lexington.

No. 39. — 12 feet of blue, green and yellow shales.

No. 40. — 3 feet of buff ferruginous shaly hydraulic limestone, which gives, by analysis —

Res. insoluble in nitric acid, ...	3.55
Alumina and peroxide of iron, ...	4.47
Carbonate of lime, ...	82 85
Carbonate of magnesia, ...	8.90
	99.77

No. 41. — 4 feet of hard, gray semi-crystalline limestone. This rock is a very pure limestone, giving 98.56 per cent. of carbonate of lime, will burn to an excellent quicklime, and is much used for building at Lexington. It contains *Chaetetes milleporaceus* and *Fusulina cylindrica.*

No. 42. — 7 feet blue and black shales and dark brown limestone, irregularly interstratified. It is exposed in the bluffs at Lexington, about twelve feet above the principal coal-bed at that place.

The limestone gives, by analysis, in 100 parts —

Insoluble in hydrochloric acid, ...	7.26
Alumina and peroxide of iron, ...	1.77
Carbonate of lime, ...	90.12
	99.15

Its fossils are *Orthis umbraculum, Chonetes variolata, C. mesoloba, Terebratula subtilita*, and *Productus costatus.*

No. 43. — 4 feet of bituminous shale.

No. 44. — 5 feet of hard blue and gray compact limestone, in irregular beds, which are intersected by numerous fissures and veins of light and dark brown calcareous spar, and carbonate of iron. *Terebratula subtilita, Spirifer lineatus, Fusulina cylindrica,* and many other shells are found in it.

It gave by analysis, in 100 parts —

Silica, ...	16.31
Alumina and peroxide of iron, ...	4.01
Carbonate of lime, ...	69.77
Carbonate of magnesia, ...	8.94
	99.03

No. 45. — 2 feet of bituminous shale, filled with light gray globular concretions of argillo-calcareous and silicious matter. This stratum readily breaks

Section 12.

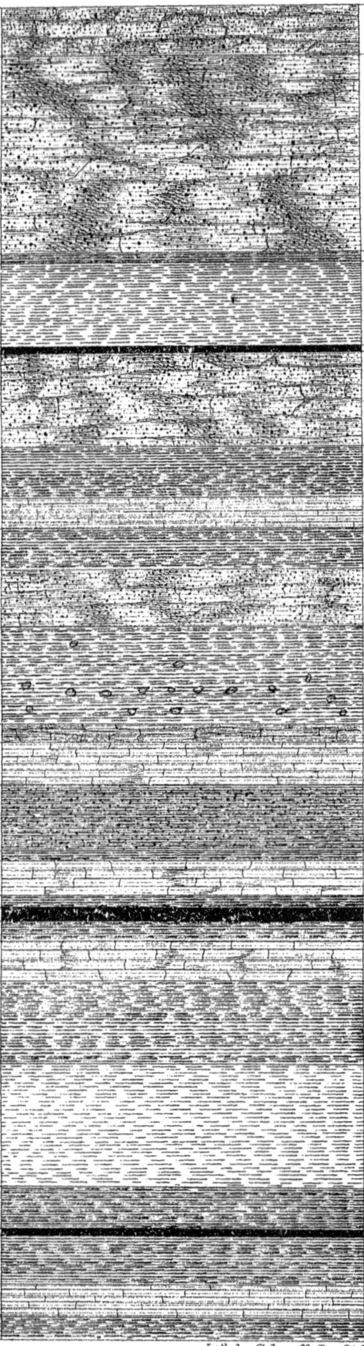

No.	Description	Ft.
28	Fine calcareous ripple marked Sandstone	5
29	Brown & gray argillaceous shaly Sandstone	23
30	Bituminous Shale	1
31	Blue & purple argillaceous Shale Green Clay & Septaria	9
32	Bituminous Coal	1/2
33	Brown ferruginous Sandstone	10
34	Bluish purple green argillaceous Shale with marlites	6
35	Hard blue silicious Limestone Choetetes	4
36	Bluish green argillaceous Shale	5
37	Gray & blue argillo Ferruginous Sandstone	8
38	Blue green & yellow argillaceous Shales with calcareous Concretions	12
39	Buff ferruginous slaty Limestone	2
40	Hard gray semicrystalline Limestone — Choetetes	5
41	Blue & black argillaceous Shale with dark Marlite	8
42	Bituminous Shale	1/2
43	Hard blue compact Limestone	4
44	Bituminous Shale	1½
45	Bituminous Coal	1⅝
46	Bituminous & yellow Shales	2¼
47	Hard bluish gray compact Limestone	5
48	Yellow & blue argillaceous Shales	9
49	Blue & purple Shales	16
50	Bituminous Shale	5
51	Bituminous Coal	¼
52	Yellowish & blue argillaceous Shales	6
53	Hard blue compact Limestone	4
54	Argillaceous Shale	2½

Dr. by R. B. Price. Lith. by Schaerff & Bro. St. Louis.

SECTION OF THE MIDDLE COAL SERIES EXPOSED IN BLUFF AT LEXINGTON.

into very regular blocks, which are extensively used by the miners for supporting the cap-rock in the coal-mines.

No. 46. — 2 feet of bituminous coal of excellent quality. This is the bed worked at Wellington, Lexington, near Dover Landing, and at various points between those localities. Its thickness is somewhat variable.

No. 47. — 2 feet of bituminous shale, and blue and yellow clay. This may be seen at all places under the coal-bed, No. 46.

No. 48. — 6 feet of hard, compact, bluish gray limestone, with cavities, containing silico-argillaceous matter, stained with iron. It often passes into a marlite, and contains *Fusulina cylindrica.*

One hundred parts dried at 100° C, gave —

Silica,	4.02
Alumina and peroxide of iron,	3.02
Carbonate of lime,	87.73
Carbonate of magnesia,	1.87
Water,	2.99
	99.63

No. 49. — 8 feet of blue and yellowish argillaceous shaly sandstone.

No. 50. — 16 feet of purple and blue shales, interstratified. These beds are in the bluff, both above and below the Levee at Lexington. Some portions of the purple beds would make a good paint for outside work.

No. 51. — 5 feet of bituminous shale.

No. 52. — ½ foot of coal.

No. 53. — 6 feet of blue and yellowish shales, interstratified.

No. 54. — 4 feet of hard, blue, compact limestone. The upper and lower parts are argillaceous. It probably forms the low bench, three miles below Lexington, and contains *Allorisma terminalis*, *A. regularis*, *Productus costatus*, *Spirifer Meusebachanus* and *Bellerophon hiulcus.*

No. 55. — 1 foot of clay.

No. 56. — 6 feet of buff-gray and ferruginous limestone and clay interstratified.

No. 57. — 12 feet of bluish gray shale, with ferruginous sandy laminæ intercalated.

No. 58. — ⅔ of a foot of coal.

No. 59. — 4 feet of shale and ferruginous, sandy laminæ, interstratified.

Besides the three permanent beds of coal in this series, thin beds of that mineral are frequently found in the various strata of bituminous shale. Fossils are not so abundant as in the Upper Coal Series.

The *Fusulina cylindrica* was found in five of the limestones and shales of this series; *Chaetetes milleporaceus*, in three; while *Terebratula subtilita*, *Productus costatus*, *Chonetes granulifera*, and several other shells, have a range quite as extensive.

The rocks of this series are exposed in the bluffs of the Missouri, from the mouth of the Kansas to Glasgow. The best section of them was obtained at Lexington, as shown in Section 12.

These strata extend southward from Lexington into Henry

county, and north to the valleys of Grand, Nodaway and Chariton Rivers.

The *Lower Coal Series* is made up of—

No. 60.—75 feet of soft, brown, heavy-bedded, irregularly stratified micaceous sandstone, often passing, towards the base, into a more compact, gray variety. It contains many ferruginous concretions in the middle and upper portions; while the lower strata abound in vegetable remains. Several species of *Calamites*, *Sigillaria* and *Lepidodendron*, together with many water-worn fragments of wood, were observed. This sandstone occurs in Marion, Boone, Howard, Cooper, Lafayette, Henry, Bates and St. Louis counties. It appears in the bluffs of the Missouri at Dover Landing, at Glasgow, and below the mouth of the La Mine. When exposed to atmospheric agencies, it readily decomposes and forms a bed of loose sterile sand.

No. 61.—3 feet of sandy shale. This bed is not persistent.

No. 62.—1 foot of coal, which often abounds in silico-argillaceous concretions, filled with *Leda arata*, *Goniatites planorbiformis*, and other new species. These concretions are abundant above Dover Landing, and in the coal mines, south of Boonville.

No. 63.—4 feet of bituminous and sandy shale, which often runs out.

No. 64.—6 feet of coal. This bed is variable in thickness and quality. At the mouth of the La Mine it is six feet thick, but contains some sulphuret of iron; on the Hinkston, it is only three feet thick, but of an excellent quality; while in St. Louis county, its thickness is much less. In some places it thins out entirely, and is replaced by shale, as in the bluff near Mr. Haas', above Boonville.

No. 65.—1 foot of argillaceous and sandy shale.

No. 66.—8 feet of fine compact hard blue and gray hydraulic limestone. It is frequently interstratified with clay, and variegated with blue and gray spots. The beds are generally divided into irregular blocks by seams filled with calcareous spar. They are often made up of detached masses lying in regular order in the clay. The fossils are abundant, and often most perfectly replaced by calcareous spar, *Chaetetes milleporaceus*, *Chonetes mesoloba*, *Productus splendens*, *Spirifer lineatus*, *S. Meusebachanus*, *Fusulina cylindrica*, *Terebratula subtilita*, and several undescribed species were observed. The first four of these fossils have been found associated in no other rock of a similar character, and this limestone may, consequently, be easily identified and made a sure guide in exploring this part of the Coal Measures.

Dr. Litton has analyzed specimens of this rock from two localities, the first from Cooper and the second from Boone county, with the following results:—

	1.	2.
Res., insoluble in hydrochloric acid,	5.04	31.40
Alumina and peroxide of iron,	2.19	3.42
Carbonate of lime,	89.96	64.45
Carbonate of magnesia,	2.29	......
	99.48	99.27

Section 13.

	Nº		Ft.
Coal Measures Lower Series.	1	Micaceous Sandstone	65
	2	Sandy Shale	3
	3	Coal	1
	4	Bituminous Shale	4
	5	Coal	6
	6	Bituminous Shale	1
	7	Hydraulic Limestone	6
	8	Bituminous Shale	6
	9	Coal	1½
	10	Shale	7
	11	Coal	½
	12	Bituminous Shale	7
	13	Coal	1
	14	Bituminous Shale	4
	15	Coal	3
	16	Shales Fire Clay	23
	17	Ferruginous Sandstone	10
Carboniferous Limestone.	18	Archimedes Limestone	65

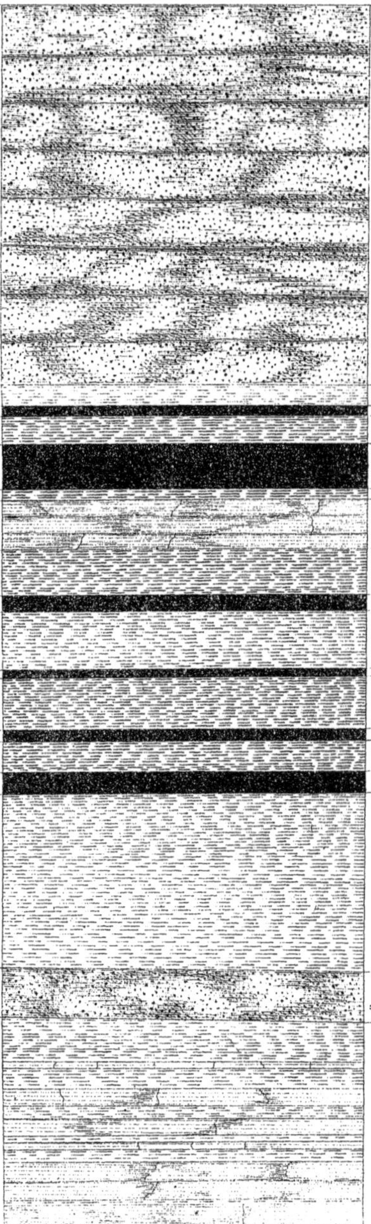

Dr. by Mrs S. Lith. by Schaerff & Bro. St. L.

BETWEEN BOONEVILLE & THE MOUTH OF THE LA MINE.

It was tested in Cooper county, and found to possess good hydraulic qualities. Other experiments are necessary before we can decide with absolute certainty upon the value of this and several other limestones for hydraulic cements. We expect to give all that indicate such properties, a thorough trial.

No. 67. — 6 feet of bituminous and blue shales. Near Mr. Wilson's coal-bed, in Boone county, this shale is so thoroughly impregnated with sulphate of alumina that a few dry days will cover the surface with a thick crust of the white salt. It is probably produced by the oxidation of sulphuret of iron, and the union of the sulphuric acid thus formed with the alumina of the shales.

No. 68. — 1½ feet of coal. This bed is worked in Boone, Cooper and Howard counties.

No. 69. — 7 feet of dark shales and fire clay.

No. 70. — ½ foot of coal. This bed is not constant.

No. 71. — 7 feet of bituminous or blue shales.

No. 72. — 1 foot of coal.

No. 73. — 4 feet of bituminous shale.

No. 74. — 3 feet of coal. This coal is good, and is worked in Cooper and Boone counties.

No. 75. — 23 feet of shales and fire clay. This bed is widely extended through the State and gives every indication of a good article for fire-brick. Experiment alone can prove whether the bricks made from it at all localities will be of the first quality. Those made from it in St. Louis county, have a high reputation.

The beds of the Lower Coal Series are well developed in Cooper county, between the mouth of the La Mine and Boonville, as shown in Section 13, Nos. 1–16, and on the Hinkston, in Boone, as shown in Fig. 1.

They are also met with in Marion, Monroe, Pike, Clark, Lewis, Shelby, Audrain, Callaway, St. Charles, St. Louis, Howard, Saline, Henry, St. Clair, Bates and Jasper; and they underlie the upper coal rocks in nearly all the counties north-west of these. The strata of this series are very irregular in their thickness and lithological characters. The coal-beds can not be identified or distinguished except by their position relative to the hydraulic limestone, No. 66, which is the only sure guide in exploring this part of the Coal Measures. The coal-beds, Nos. 62 and 64, appear to be wanting in many places. They are found, as represented in Sec. 13, Nos. 1—9, in Howard's bluff at the mouth of the La Mine. The coal in St. Louis county comes from one or more of the lower beds; as the upper beds, with the exception of a thin stratum, seem to be wanting there. At a point near Sharpsburg, in Marion county, all the strata below No. 60, are wanting, as that sandstone rests directly upon the Encrinital Limestone.

Organic Remains.—Fossils are not so numerous in this Lower Series as in the beds above; they appear to become more and more abundant as we ascend from the lowest to the highest. It may be observed, however, that the *Fusulina** *cylindrica*, *Terebratula subtilita*, and *Spirifer Meusebachanus*, which have been found in all parts of the Middle and Upper Series, continue down into these lower beds.

So far as our observations extend, in Missouri, the *Fusulina cylindrica*, *Spirifer Meusebachanus*, *S. planoconvexa*, *S. hemiplicata*, *S. Kentuckensis*, *Productus splendens*, *P. aequicostatus*, *P. Nebrascensis*, *P. costatus*, *P. Wabashensis*, *Terebratula subtilita* (?) *Chonetes mesoloba*, *C. parva*, *C. Smithi*, *Myalina subquadrata*, *Allorisma regularis*, *A. terminalis*, *Leda arata*, *Pleurotomaria sphaerulata*, *Campophyllum torquium*, *and Chaetetes milleporaceus*, are confined to, and very characteristic of, the Coal Measures. Many fossils are common to the Coal Measures and the Carboniferous Limestone, as *Productus punctatus*, *P. cora*, *P. muricatus*, *P. semireticulatus*, *Spirifer lineatus* and *Orthis umbraculum*.

The Organic Remains of the Coal Measures, so far as identified, are in Catalogue II., of Appendix B.

Range and Thickness.—From the Section given above, it may be seen that—

The Upper Coal Series are,	about 300	feet thick.
The Middle Coal Series are,	about 200	" "
The Lower Coal Series are,	about 150	" "
Making the whole thickness on the Missouri river,	650	feet.

But Mr. Hawn makes the total thickness of the Coal Measures on the line of the Hannibal and St. Joseph Railroad, 739 feet. (See his Section, p. 135, Part II.)

It is probable we shall find the coal strata much thicker in some parts of the State.

The extent of the Coal Measures of the State, has already been indicated while mentioning the range of the different series. Perhaps we may get a more definite idea of the area covered by these

---

* Some have supposed the *Fusulina cylindrica* marks a very definite horizon in the Carboniferous System of this country as well as in that of Russia; but the fact, that we have found it in *thirteen* strata, ranging from the very highest in the Coal Measures down to near the base of the Lower Series, proves it useless for identifying any particular bed or part of the Upper Carboniferous rocks.

rocks, if a line be drawn from the north-east corner of Marion county to the middle of the western boundary of Jasper; as that would run near the line between the upper Carboniferous rocks on the north-west, and the older strata on the south-east. It is said, this line is *near* that boundary; for the older rocks come to the surface in many places on the north-western side of this line: as in the valleys of the Mississippi and Salt River, and of the Missouri, as high up as Miami, in Saline county; while the coal strata are known to cover large areas in St. Louis, St. Charles, Callaway, Montgomery, Audrain and Ralls counties, on the south-east of it. It is safe to estimate the area covered by Coal Measures in the State equal to all on the north-west of the boundary indicated above, which will give 26,887 square miles of coal-beds. This estimate is below the truth, for there are more square miles occupied by coal-rock to the south-east of the line, than there are to the north-west, where those rocks are wanting. For we ourselves, have either seen coal, or have heard, from good authority, of its existence, in nearly every county* of the area d signated.

There are, also, in this State, many very remarkable and important deposits of coal and shales, which are referred to the regular Coal Measures with some degree of hesitation, as we have as yet found no positive evidence of their true geological position. These formations are made up of beds of cannel and common bituminous coal (the same bed often containing both varieties), and a few unimportant strata of shales. These coal strata vary in thickness from one to thirty-six feet; † while the accompanying shales are very

---

*The strata of the Upper Coal Series, exposed in the bluffs of the Missouri, between Bluff City and Wayne City, have generally been considered *Lower Carboniferous;* but their lithological characters, their stratigraphical position, and, above all, their organic remains, do, beyond all doubt, prove them to be members of the Coal Measures. The strata under consideration are limestones, sandstones, shales, clays and coals, which have all the characteristics pertaining to the genuine Coal Measures; they overlie the rocks at Lexington, which all geologists have placed in that Formation; and all the fossils, known to be characteristic of the Coal Measures in this State, and indeed all the fossils found in the well-marked coal-rocks of the State, with one or two unimportant exceptions, are known to exist, in still greater abundance, in these beds. Nor have we found any of the Lower Carboniferous fossils in them, which have not been observed in rocks admitted by all to belong to the Coal Measures. If these facts do not prove these beds, members of the Coal Measures, it would be difficult to say what would.

† The famous bed in Callaway, near Cote Sans Dessein, is said to be over eighty feet thick, but we speak of the beds which have come under our observation.

thin. These abnormal deposits are found in ravines and cavities of denudation, in the rocks of all ages, from the Archimedes Limestone down to the Calciferous Sandrock.

Staples' Coal-bed, in Cooper, is in a ravine in the Archimedes Limestone; Stephens' Coal-bed, in Cooper, is in a ravine in the Encrinital Limestone; Robertson's Coal-bed, in Moniteau, is in a ravine in the Encrinital Limestone; Drafton's Coal-bed, in Cooper, is in a ravine in the Chemung Group; Farley's Coal-bed, in Cooper, is in a cavity in the Saccharoidal Sandstone. Some others have been seen in lower beds of this formation. For a more detailed notice of these beds, see the reports of Cooper and Moniteau.

All the cannel-coal observed in the State, belongs to these irregular deposits. They, also, contain bituminous coal of the very best quality, and varieties of various shades between the two. When one variety rests upon the other, the transition is usually very abrupt, a mere line separating them; but the change is sometimes gradual. These beds exist in Cooper, Moniteau, Cole and Callaway. They are usually limited in extent.

The surface of the Coal Measures have, in many parts of the State, been denuded, doubtless, by the agencies which produced the Drift; as in may places the Drift is mostly made up of rounded fragments of the harder members of the Coal Measures.

The following section from Boone county shows the denuded surface of the coal strata, dipping to the south, and the Quaternary deposits resting nonconformably upon them.

Fig. 6.

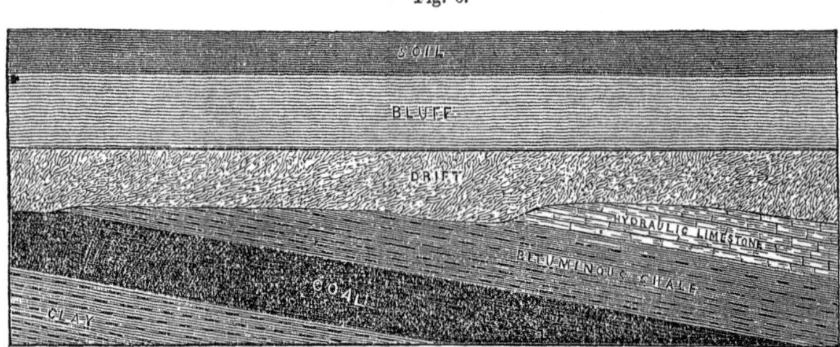

ON THE HINKSTON, ABOVE THE MEXICO ROAD.

The Scenery produced by the Coal Measures is somewhat peculiar, as seen in the lower parts of the bluffs of the Missouri, between Miami and Iowa line. The bluffs usually ascend from the water in gentle declivities, covered with soil and debris, which is interrupted by the out-crops of the more durable limestones, that present continuous low terraces with precipitous mural faces, rising above each other like steps.

Minerals.—But little iron ore, usually so abundant in the Coal Measures, has been seen in the State. Some clay-ironstone, carbonate and the oxides have been found, but none of any practical value. The sulphurets of lead and zinc have been observed in several of the limestones. These ores were, also, observed by Mr. Meek and myself in the coal-beds of Cooper and Moniteau counties. For further particulars respecting this singular fact, see reports on Cooper and Moniteau.

MOUNTAIN, OR CARBONIFEROUS LIMESTONE.

There are four very important and well characterized divisions of this Group—

F. *f*—FERRUGINOUS SANDSTONE. F. *g*—ST. LOUIS LIMESTONE.
F. *h*—ARCHIMEDES LIMESTONE. F. *i*—ENCRINITAL LIMESTONE.

F. *f*—FERRUGINOUS SANDSTONE,

Is quite variable in its lithological characters. In some places it is very white and Saccharoidal; in others, fine impure particles are disseminated through the mass, and the color becomes a dirty brown; and in a few localities, as near Fulton, Callaway county, it is a coarse conglomerate. But generally, where well developed, it is a coarse-grained, heavy-bedded, friable sandstone, colored with various shades of brown, red and purple; as it appears in the bluffs near Salt-Creek Sulphur Springs, some two miles west of Oseola, in Town. 38, R. 26, Sec. 27; or clouded with yellow and red, as on Turkey Creek, in Cedar county. (See Plate V.) The upper part is more regularly stratified and finer grained, contains more argillo-calcareous matter, and has a lighter brown, yellowish gray or cream color. It is very soft when quarried, and may then be easily dressed for building purposes; but exposure renders it much harder and more durable. These upper beds are very abundant in St. Clair county, west of Oseola, and are exposed in Newton, near Judge Ritchie's, who uses them very extensively in fencing his prairie-farm. These beds, when nearly white, are often called *Cotton Rock*, from their resemblance to that variety of the magnesian limestone.

The lower beds are thick, and often present the regular stratification of sands deposited in running water.

The face of the mural bluff at the Salt-Creek Sulphur Springs has been weather-worn, until the softer parts have been so removed as to present a most beautifully furrowed and honey-combed appearance.

This sandstone contains large quantities of Oxides of Iron, Brown and Red Hematites, which in many places form extensive beds of excellent Ore. In Cooper county, in the N. E. quarter of Sec. 3, Town. 48, R. 19, this Sandstone, in the bluffs of the Black-Water, contains a good bed of Ore, three feet thick.* The same bed again shows itself in several places in Sec. 33, Town. 48, R. 19, and in various other places in the county. It was also observed in large masses on Grand River, in Henry county; in Sec. 28, Town. 39, R. 24, in St. Clair county; and in Bates and Hickory; in short, wherever this Formation appears, Iron is more or less abundant. But this Ore will be more particularly noticed in the Special Reports of the counties.

The stratigraphical position of this sandstone is between the Lower Coal Series and the St. Louis Limestone. Below the mouth of the La Mine, in the bluff near Mr. Howard's, the Lower Coal Series is seen resting directly upon it and the Archimedes Limestone underlying it. (See Sec. 13.) Its position is shown in Sec. 14, at the mouth of the Des Moines; it also rests upon the St. Louis Limestone, near the Cheltenham Sulphur Spring, in St. Louis county.

Thus it will appear that this sandstone occupies the place of the Mill-stone Grit of the English Geologists; and in some localities, as in Callaway county, its lithological characters resemble those of that Formation.

Thickness and Range.—Its thickness is as variable as its lithological characters, ranging from five to two hundred feet. In the northern counties it is quite thin and purely silicious, while in the central it is thick, ferruginous and argillaceous. This formation has a wide range through the State, and, as a matter of course, is very abundant along the line above mentioned as separating the Coal Measures from the Carboniferous Limestone. It is seen at intervals

---

* The following is a section of the bluff at that place:—

No. 1.—12 feet of reddish sandy Bluff.
No. 2.— 5 " of coarse reddish brown Ferruginous Sandstone.
No. 3.— 3 " of iron ore—Hematite.
No. 4.—10 " of Ferruginous Sandstone.
No. 5.—95 " of Encrinital Limestone.

Section 14

	No		Thickness in feet
Quarternary.	1	Bluff	40
	2	Drift	5
Carboniferous.	3	Coal Measures	30
	4	Ferruginous Sandstone	35
	5	St. Louis Limestone	15
	6	Archimedes Limestone (Shale)	135
	7	Encrinital Limestone	25

Dr. by Mrs. S. Lith by Schaerff & Bro

NEAR THE MOUTH OF THE DES MOINES.

PLATE V.

R. B. PRICE, DEL. J. M. KERSHAW Sc.

Bluffs of Ferruginous Sandstone, highly colored, on Turkey Creek, North of Fremont.

from the mouth of the Des Moines, along the bluffs of the Mississippi to La Grange, and thence through Marion, Monroe, Boone, Howard, Cooper, Pettis, Henry, St. Clair, Cedar and Jasper, to the Indian Territory. It again appears in St. Louis county, and on the Mississippi below. (See Dr. Shumard's section.) The large quantity of iron in this Formation, both as a coloring material and in thick beds of valuable ore, has induced me to give it the provisional name, *Ferruginous Sandstone.* It doubtless occupies the position of the *Mill-Stone Grit* of the English Geologists, the Conglomerates of Ohio and Tennessee, and the "Conglomerates and Ferruginous Grits" of Iowa (Owen); but I have not yet felt at liberty to give it either of those names, and thereby decide the question of identity. We need more definite information respecting the exact position of those Formations.

The Scenery produced by this Formation, when well developed, is wild and grand, beautiful and unique; it produces the wild, rugged, mural, castellated, and gaudy-colored bluffs on the Osage and its tributaries, in St. Clair, Cedar, Polk and Hickory counties. Plate V. presents a very characteristic view of this Sandstone on the Pomme de Terre, in Polk county, where the road from Bolivar to Buffalo crosses that stream. This bluff is beautifully variegated with the brilliant yellows, reds and purples, so common in this rock.

As a general rule, the Ferruginous Sandstone is too friable to make a good building stone. But the upper, fine-grained, impure, light-colored beds, are very valuable where great strength is not required. It occurs in regular beds of convenient thickness; is easily quarried and dressed; becomes harder and more durable by exposure; withstands the action of fire quite well; is very abundant in some neighborhoods where other rocks cannot be obtained; and is much used for foundations, chimneys, walls, and all ordinary purposes, in St. Clair, Jasper, Newton and other counties. It is also used for fencing prairie. Judge Ritchie, of Newton, has employed it extensively for this purpose; and, according to his experience, fences made from it, are at once durable and economical, and in other respects inferior to none in use.

In many places this sandstone renders the soil too light and sandy; but where the soil is naturally too clayey, a portion of it improves the quality.

F. g—ST. LOUIS LIMESTONE.

This important Formation is made up of beds of hard, crystalline, gray and bluish gray cherty limestone, interstratified with thin layers of argillaceous shale. Some of the strata are impure silico-magnesian limestone, with a dull earthy fracture, as in St. George's quarry, St. Louis; others are silico-argillaceous and compact, with a conchoidal fracture and drab or yellowish gray color, as on the river bank east of the Arsenal quarry; and others still at the same locality, are silicious. Many of the strata have a peculiar jointed structure, resembling the sutures of the cranium.

The silico-magnesian strata present every appearance of hydraulic properties, while the calcareous and silico-calcareous beds make excellent building materials, and are surpassed by none but the primary slates for flags and curbstones; the silicious are also much used for macadamizing. Many of the pure calcareous strata* make lime of the very best quality, as would some of the silicious, if burned with care; otherwise the silica might cause it to melt in the kiln. This excellent limestone is very extensively quarried and used for all ordinary purposes in and about St. Louis. Some *of its beds* appear like a good lithographic stone; but practical tests have proved it defective.†

Its stratigraphical position is between the Ferruginous Sandstone and the Archimedes Limestone, as seen near the Des Moines, Sec. 14; and near the 1st Tunnel on the Pacific Railroad, southwest of Kirkwood. (See Dr. Shumard's section along that road.)

A more detailed account of this formation may be found in Dr. Shumard's Report on St. Louis county; he has had better opportunities of observing it.

Range and Thickness. — I have seen but two localities of this Formation out of St. Louis county — one in Marion, and the other in Clark. In both places it was imperfectly represented by a few thin beds, resting upon the Archimedes Limestone, having the *Palaechinus multipora*, together with a few other fossils. I have the *Lithostrotion Canadense* from Lewis county, but did not see the locality.

The St. Louis Limestone is about 250 feet thick.

---

* Analysis by Dr. Litton, gave —

Insoluble residue,	0.50
Carbonate of lime,	99.40
Alumina,	a trace.
	99.90

† Dr. Litton's analysis of it gives —

Insoluble residue,	1.12
Alumina,	a trace.
Carbonate of lime,	97.99
Water,	0.21
	99.32

Organic Remains. — The fossils are given in Catalogue III. The most characteristic are *Palaechinus multipora*, *Lithostrotion Canadense*, *Echinocrinus Nerei*, *Poteriocrinus longidactylus*, and *Atrypa lingulata.*

F. *h* — ARCHIMEDES LIMESTONE.

This member of the Carboniferous System is usually made up of hard gray, bluish and brownish gray, and drab crystalline and compact limestones, interstratified with blue shales. The beds of shale are thicker at the top, and decrease downwards until they are scarcely perceptible at the bottom; while the converse is true of the limestone. See Sec. 14 of the rocks on the Des Moines river and near Keokuk.

In some places this formation is made up of thin strata of brownish drab, impure silico-argillaceous limestone; as they appear at Miami and below the mouth of the La Mine (see Sec. 13), on the Missouri, and in many places in Marion county.

The shales are sometimes much indurated, and do not readily decompose on exposure; but they usually disintegrate and form soft clays. They contain numerous corals, of which the *Archimedipora Archimedes* is very abundant and gives name to the Formation. There are also some ten or fifteen undetermined species of the genera *Fenestella*, *Zaphrentis*, *Chaetetes*, *etc.* These corals often constitute almost all of the entire mass of the argillo-calcareous beds.

This Formation in the South-West presents characters quite different from those seen in other parts of the State.

I obtained the following Section on Shoal Creek, one mile above Grand Falls: —

No. 1. — 105 feet of white, bluish white and buff, compact, thick-bedded chert, in regular layers, interstratified with irregular beds of brown, impure, ferruginous, porous varieties of the same rock, which very much resembles the Wool-Rock of the miners.

No. 2. — 15 feet of blue and gray, crystalline and cherty heavy-bedded limestone, separated by thin laminæ of blue and brown shale.

In a bluff, one half mile below the Falls, the following strata were seen: —

No. 1. — 40 feet slope, covered with soil and loose chert.

No. 2. — 45 feet of whitish gray and brown, crystalline and thick-bedded cherty limestone, containing large varieties of *Orthis umbraculum* and *Productus punctatus*, *P. semireticulatus*, *Spirifer cuspidatus?* and *S. incrassatus?*

No. 3. — 30 feet slope.

No. 4. — 70 feet chert, like No. 1 of the last Section, and is a part of the same bed.

The water at the falls runs over beds of this chert; which also form the bluffs above and below the mill, on both sides of the stream. Lead has been found in it, in many places in this region. This chert resembles that of the magnesian limestones more than what is usually found in the Carboniferous Series.

The well-known oolite found at Ste. Genevieve, called Ste. Genevieve Marble, belongs to the Archimedes Limestone; it is a very superior building stone, at once economical, durable and beautiful.

Organic Remains. — The limestone strata abound in very large varieties of *Orthis umbraculum*, and *Productus punctatus;* but the most characteristic fossils are *Spirifer incrassatus*,* *S. spinosus*, *Productus elegans*, *Pentremites florealis* and *P. pyriformis*.

The other fossils are in Catalogue IV.

Mineral Contents. — There are many nodules of chert and silicious geodes disseminated through these beds. These geodes are filled with a great variety of crystals of calcareous spar, quartz, lead, zinc and copper. I have observed the following varieties: —

1st. Geodes whose drusy cavities are set with crystals of nail-head spar.

2d. Geodes whose drusy cavities are set with crystals of dog's-tooth spar.

3d. Geodes set with crystals of rhombic spar.

4th. Geodes set with crystals of calcareous spar, bespangled with small crystals of galena.

5th. Geodes set with crystals of calcareous spar, bespangled with small crystals of iron pyrites.

6th. Geodes set with crystals of calcareous spar, bespangled with small crystals of iron pyrites.

7th. Geodes set with prismatic crystals of quartz.

8th. Geodes set with silicious crystals, bespangled with crystals of galena.

9th. Geodes whose drusy cavities of prismatic quartz are bespangled with crystals of iron pyrites.

10th. Geodes lined with mammillated chalcedony.

11th. Geodes lined with coatings of red and milky agate.

Several ores have been found in this Formation. Sulphurets of copper and iron, the oxides of iron and cobalt in small portions;

---

* This variety is found in no other Formation in this State, and is the most abundant characteristic fossil in the absence of the *Archimedipora*.

R. B. Price Del.

Lith. by Schaerff & Bro, St. Louis.

GRAND FALLS AND SCOTT & STEWART'S MILL, ON SHOAL CREEK IN NEWTON COUNTY.
THE ROCK AT THE FALLS IS A CHERT BED OF THE CARBONIFEROUS LIME-STONE.

while the sulphurets of lead and zinc, and the silicate of zinc, exist in great abundance in the South-Western Mines, which are in this rock. At Scott's Mine, in Cooper county, large beds of heavy spar were found in it.

Range and Thickness. — This Formation extends from the north-eastern part of the State to the south-west, in an irregular zone, skirting the eastern border of the Ferruginous Sandstone, through Clark, Lewis, Marion, Monroe, Howard, Cooper, Pettis, St. Clair, Jasper, Newton, McDonald, Barry, Lawrence and Green counties; and in several other counties to the east of this range, where the Upper Carboniferous rocks are exposed; and in St. Louis and Ste. Genevieve counties. The Limestones are, in general, most excellent building materials.

Its thickness varies from fifty to two hundred feet. See Dr. Shumard's Sections on the Mississippi, and Sec. 14, at the mouth of the Des Moines, and the Schedule of Sections for Marion county.

Its Stratigraphical position is between the St. Louis and Encrinital Limestones, as seen in Sec. 14 and in the Section of the Pacific Railroad, in Dr. Shumard's Report.

F. *i* — ENCRINITAL LIMESTONE.

This is at once the most extensive and best characterized of the divisions of the Carboniferous Limestone. It is made up of brown, buff, gray and white, coarse crystalline heavy-bedded limestones. The darker-colored impure varieties prevail near the base, while the lighter and more purely calcareous strata abound in the upper part. It everywhere contains globular, ovoid and lenticular masses of chert, disseminated or arranged in beds parallel to the lines of stratification. These masses of chert are more abundant in the upper divisions.

The beds of this Formation are frequently intersected by joints resembling the sutures of the cranium, which I have ventured to call *suture-joints.** The remains of Corals and Mollusks are very abundant; some of the strata are made up, almost entirely, of their exuviæ, especially of the joints and plates of *Crinoideans.* The lower beds are more impure, darker colored, and contain fewer fossils than other portions.

Many *caves* have been observed in these limestones; several in

---

* The necessity for a term to designate these joints without the usual circumlocution, seems to justify this use of the word.

Boone county were explored; one for the distance of some two miles. They abound in beautiful stalactites and stalagmites. Some have streams running along their beds, and constitute a natural system of drainage for a considerable extent of country. "*Sink-holes*," funnel-shaped depressions, are common, in all places where this Formation is well developed, and form the natural channels by which much of the surface water reaches the caverns below. Small streams sometimes enter them and again appear at the mouth of the cavern. These "Sink-holes" frequently become ponds by the closing up of the passages, to the caverns below, with clays impervious to water. There are several such in the western part of Boone county.

Mineral Contents.—Its mineral contents are varied and important. Flint and calcareous spar are found in all parts of it. Heavy spar and quartz abound in some localities; as at Scott's Mine, in Cooper, and in the mines of the South-West;* while various ores of lead and zinc are found in large quantities at the latter, and lead at the former locality. Copper and cobalt were also observed in the South-Western Mines.

Ancient Diggings.—There are several ancient diggings in this Formation, which have excited the curiosity of many; while some have spent no small amount of labor, exploring them, with the vain hope of finding valuable ores.

All seem to admit, that no set of men would make such extensive excavations, unless some valuable mineral rewarded their labors. Some think they were made by the early Spanish or French explorers; while others are equally confident they are the work of the Indians. The latter are, doubtless, correct; as we could find no mark of any instrument of iron or steel, upon, in or about these "diggings," save those made by late adventurers.

We made careful examinations of several of these "ancient diggings;" one of the most important is in Town. 34, R. 22, Sec. 34, S. ½, N. W. ¼.

After spending some time at this locality we were convinced that these "diggings" were made by the Indians, in search of Flint—the most valuable mineral in an economical point of view, known to them. A more detailed account of these diggings may be found in Chap. III., Notes on the South-West.

---

* The shaft at Scott's Mine and many of those of the South-West, seem to pass down into the upper beds of the Encrinital Limestone.

Range and Thickness.—The thickness of this Formation is quite variable; on the Osage it is about 200 feet; on the Mississippi, above Hannibal, 175; and on the Hinkston, in Boone county, about 400 or 500.

Stratigraphical Position.—Its position is below the Archimedes Limestone, as in Sections 14 and 29, and above the Chouteau Limestone, as in Sections 15, 17 and 19, and numerous others in the Schedule of sections for Marion county.

This Formation extends from Marion county to Green, forming an irregular zone on the east of the Archimedes Limestone. It is also exposed in Callaway, and in some of the eastern counties south of the Missouri.

The Organic Remains of the Encrinital Limestone are very numerous, and many of the species very abundant. Entire strata are sometimes made up almost exclusively of fragments of crinoidal columns, with a few other fossils interspersed. But the most of the fossils are changed to an opaque whitish calcareous spar, so crystalline as to break easily in the direction of the cleavage-joint, making it very difficult to obtain perfect specimens of many species.

There are eight divisions of this limestone in Missouri, each quite well marked by its fossils.

1st. At the top, we generally find some eight or ten feet of chert in regular strata, or in lenticular masses more or less regularly arranged, having the interstices between the masses and strata filled with red ferruginous clay. (See Sec. 15, No. 3.) These beds are often exposed in Marion county, as at Palmyra; and in the southwestern counties they are much thicker.

2d. Below the chert we usually find beds of coarse gray and white, crystalline, thin-bedded cherty and crinoidal limestones. The most abundant fossils are *Spirifer striatus*, *Productus punctatus*, *Orthis Michelini*, *Pentremites melo* and *Terebratula Roissyi.*

These beds abound in Benton, St. Clair, Cedar, Polk and Green counties, Sec. 19, No. 1.

3d. The middle portions of the Encrinital Limestone are made up of thick-bedded, gray and buff and brown, crystalline, crinoidal cherty limestones, marked with many suture-joints. Its fossils are *Spirifer striatus*, very large, *Orthis Michelini*, *Terebratula Roissyi*, *Platycrinus planus* and *Chonetes Shumardiana?* This part of the Formation is conspicuous in the bluffs of the Missouri, both above and below Rocheport, in Boone and Howard county; also, on Salt River, in Monroe, where it furnishes an abundance of good building material. The foundations and columns of the State University, are from these beds, as are those of the beautiful Court House, in Boone county.*

4th. This division is a bed of coarse white crystalline marble, some eighteen feet thick. It contains but few fossils; a large thick variety of *Spirifer striatus* is sometimes observed. It is exposed in Marion county, in the bluffs of the Mississippi, between McFarlin's branch and the Fabius.

5th. Brown, buff and gray, earthy or crystalline limestones, with some chert and suture-joints. But few fossils have been observed in it — *Spirifer striatus, Orthis Michelini, Terebratula lamellosa* and *Productus punctatus.* These beds are exposed in the castellated bluffs at Lovers' Leap, near Hannibal, Sec. 15, No. 3.

6th. Brown, earthy crinoidal limestones, which readily decompose and leave most perfect specimens of *Actinocrinus rotundus, A. Christyi, A. pyriformis, A. concinnus,* and *A. Missouriensis.* On North River, in Marion county, these beds are exposed, where I first found most beautiful specimens of these new Crinoids.

7th. In the bluffs at Hannibal, and south of Palmyra, is a stratum of white crystalline limestone, which makes a most beautiful and durable building stone, and quicklime of the best quality. The calaboose, at Hannibal, is built of it. The *Spirifer Burlingtonensis* is the characteristic fossil; as I have seen it in no other part of this Formation, save in the upper beds of the next division.

8th. The lowest beds of the Encrinital Limestone are thick, hard, crystalline, earthy and brown. They contain but few fossils; a large flat variety of *Spirifer striatus, S. Burlingtonensis, Pentremites melo* and *Pentremites Norwoodi; Terebratula lamellosa* are most common. These beds are exposed at Palmyra and Hannibal. This division is represented in Sec. 15. The fossils of this Formation are in Catalogue V.

---

* The composition, according to Dr. Litton, is —

Insoluble residue,	0.14
Alumina and peroxide of iron,	0.60
Carbonate of lime,	99.01
	99.75

A specimen of same rock from Callaway, at Jenkins' lime kiln —

Res. insoluble in acid, alumina and peroxide of iron,	0.51
Carbonate of lime,	98.93
Carbonate of magnesia,	a trace.
	99.44

CHEMUNG.*

This group presents three Formations, very distinct in lithological characters, though scarcely distinguishable by their organic remains. And even the lithological characters of the Chouteau and Lithographic Limestones, are sometimes quite similar; but they are separated by the Vermicular Sandstone and Shales, which always present well marked characteristic features, and at least one Fucoid peculiar to them.

There appears to be some difference of opinion respecting the precise age of these Formations and those of the New York series, to which I have referred them. Many of our fossils are, either identical with, or very similar to, those of the Chemung of New York. Among these are a species of those remarkable forms of the New York Reports, called *Fucoides caudá-galli?* and *Filicites gracilis;* also, *Avicula subduplicata* and *Nucula bellatula.*

I have given the three Formations of this group the following provisional names:—

F. j—CHOUTEAU LIMESTONE.
F. k—VERMICULAR SANDSTONE AND SHALES.
F. l—LITHOGRAPHIC LIMESTONE.

F. j—CHOUTEAU LIMESTONE.

This Formation, when fully developed, is made up of two quite distinct divisions.

1st. At the top, immediately under the Encrinital Limestone, we find some forty or fifty feet of brownish gray, earthy, silico-magnesian limestone in thick beds, which contain disseminated masses of white or limpid calcareous spar. This rock is very uniform in character, and contains but few fossils. Reticulated corals, and Fucoidal markings like the Cauda-galli, are most abundant.

In the quarry it is quite soft, but becomes very hard on exposure, and forms a very firm and durable building rock.

It presents every appearance of a hydraulic limestone; and gives by analysis, in 100 parts—

---

* There is some difference of opinion respecting the System to which this Group belongs; but if we make a division of the Missouri rocks into Devonian and Carboniferous, the line of separation, the most distinctly marked, is between the Encrinital and Chouteau Limestones.

Insoluble in hydrochloric acid,	13.90
Alumina and peroxide of iron,	2.01
Carbonate of lime,	48.23
Carbonate of magnesia,	34.93
	99.07

The specimen analyzed was from Chouteau Springs, Cooper county.

This rock ranges through the western part of Boone and Moniteau; and is very common on the La Mine, in Cooper, and in Polk and Green counties.

2d. The upper division passes down into a fine compact blue, or drab thin-bedded limestone, whose strata are quite irregular and broken. Its fracture is conchoidal, and its structure, somewhat concretionary. A specimen from Chouteau Springs, gave by analysis, in 100 parts —

Insoluble in hydrochloric acid,	1.51
Alumina and peroxide of iron,	0.38
Carbonate of lime,	96.38
Water,	0.76
	98.93

Another specimen from the same locality gave, in 100 parts —

Insoluble in hydrochloric acid,	1.44
Alumina and peroxide of iron,	1.68
Carbonate of lime,	95.51
Water,	0.47
	99.10

Some beds are filled with a great profusion of most beautiful fossils. In many the organic substance has been replaced by calcareous spar. The most characteristic are *Spirifer Marionensis*, *Productus Murchisonianus*, *Chonetes ornata*, *Atrypa gregaria*, *A. occidentalis*, *A. obscuraplicata*, *Leptaena depressa*, *Avicula Cooperensis*, *Mytilus elongatus*, and several new species of Trilobites. (Catalogue VI. gives the fossils so far as determined.)

These beds are very common on the La Mine, in Cooper, where the fossils are very numerous and well preserved.

Chouteau Limestone has been applied to these rocks, as they are well developed at the Chouteau Springs, in Cooper; where I first found large quantities of its new, beautiful, and characteristic fossils.

In the north-eastern part of the State the Chouteau Limestone is represented by a few feet of coarse, earthy, crystalline calcareous

Section 17.

Group	No.	Formation	Thickness in feet
Carboniferous.	No 1	Encrinital Limestone	45
Chemung	2	Chouteau Limestone	
	3	Vermicular Sandstone and Shales	30
	4	Lithographic Limestone	20
	5	Devonian ? Cooper Marble	55
Calciferous Sandrock	6	Saccharoidal Sandstone	25
	7	2d Magnesian Limestone	30

Dr. by Mrs. S. Lith. by Schaerff & Bro

SOUTH OF MARSTON'S BRIDGE IN BLUFFS OF THE LA MINE.

rock, like the lower division of the Encrinital Limestone. There is, indeed, in that part of the State, no change of lithological characters as you pass from the Encrinital Limestone to this Formation; but the change in the organic remains is both sudden and great. This remarkable change in organic forms, while the lithological characters remain the same, taken in connection with the fact that some fifteen feet below, the limestone passes rapidly into a dull, earthy, soft calcareous sandstone, while the fossils are unchanged, is very remarkable.

Range and Thickness. — This Formation is seventy feet thick in Cooper (see Sec. 17), and from ten to thirty in Marion. (See Sec. 15.) It has been observed in Marion, Cooper, Boone, Moniteau, Benton, St. Clair, Cedar and Polk counties.

Its Geological position is between the Encrinital Limestone and Vermicular Sandstone and Shales; as seen in Secs. 15 and 17.

F. *h*—VERMICULAR SANDSTONE AND SHALES.

The upper part of this Formation is usually a buff, or yellowish brown, fine-grained, pulverulent, argillo-calcareous sandstone. It is usually perforated in all directions with pores, filled with the same materials more highly colored and less indurated. This portion, when exposed to atmospheric agencies, often disintegrates, and leaves the rock full of winding passages, as if it were worm-eaten. In the South-West the harder part is much more silicious and indurated. The middle portion is a bluish brown and gray silico-calcareous magnesian shale. It has a conchoidal fracture, the peculiar markings of the upper part, together with those of a curious undescribed *Fucoid.*

These beds often pass into an impure magnesian limestone, which has every external appearance of good *hydraulic limestone;* as in the south-west of Cooper, and on North River, in Marion. Two specimens — 1st from the bluffs of the La Mine, near Marston's Bridge, Sec. 17; and 2d, from North River, Marion county — gave, by analyses, in 100 parts: —

	1.	2.
Insoluble in hydrochloric acid, ...	10.99	8.47
Alumina and peroxide of iron, ...	1.32	2.09
Carbonate of lime, ...	60.49	51.02
Carbonate of magnesia, ...	25.93	38.63
	98.73	100.21

This bed sometimes becomes more calcareous and makes a fine

clouded marble, when sufficiently indurated to receive a polish, as some of the beds passed through in the well of Mr. Winston Walker, of Cooper. A specimen from his well gave, by analysis:—

Insoluble in hydrochloric acid,	14.02
Alumina,	2.17
Cabonate of lime,	53.93
Carbonate of magnesia,	28.94
	99.06

Of the insoluble portion 11.89 was silica; and the remainder principally alumina.

The lower part of this Formation is usually a blue, sometimes brown, argillaceous Shale or Fire-Clay, in regular thin strata. It contains many elliptical, globular and irregular masses of iron pyrites, whose surfaces are set with numerous minute cubic crystals; their facets are tarnished, and present all the varying colors of changeable dove-colored silks. The golden or purple colors of these masses have led some to suppose them valuable metals. Masses of white chalcedonic quartz, either globular, botryoidal or semi-crystalline, are disseminated through these shales in the South-West, where they have a yellowish brown color, and, on exposure, form a semi-plastic clay. These minerals are abundant at Cedar Gap, east of Frémont, and in the mounds in the neighborhood of Bolivar. A specimen from North River, Marion county, gave:—

Silica,	73.11
Alumina and peroxide of iron,	10.66
Carbonate of lime,	8.70
Carbonate of magnesia,	6.11
Water,	1.16
	99.74

Organic Remains.—This Formation contains but few fossils, and those are in the upper portions. *Spirifer Marionensis*, *Productus Murchisonianus*, *Chonetes ornata*, *Avicula circula*, the Fucoids above named, and the *cauda-galli*, are most numerous. These beds can always be detected by the lithological characters and its peculiar *Fucoids*.

Range and Thickness.—Its thickness is variable, from thirty to one hundred feet, as in Secs. 15 and 17; and it extends from Marion, through Boone, Cooper, Benton and Polk, to Green.

Its stratigraphical position is between the Chouteau and the Lithographic Limestones; as in Secs. 15 and 17.

F. *l*—LITHOGRAPHIC LIMESTONE.

It is a pure, fine, compact, even-textured silicious limestone,* breaking rather easily, with a conchoidal fracture, into sharp angular fragments. Its color varies from a light drab to the lighter shades of buff and blue. It gives a sharp ringing sound under the hammer, from which it is called "pot-metal" in some parts of the State. It is regularly stratified in beds varying from two to sixteen inches in thickness, often presenting, in mural bluffs, all the regularity of masonry; as at Louisiana, on the Mississippi. The beds are intersected by numerous fractures, leaving surfaces covered with beautiful dendritic markings of oxide of iron. The strata are much thinner towards the top, where they often become silicious, and sometimes pass into an impure, thin-bedded oolitic limestone; as in the bluffs, south-east of Elk Springs, in Pike county.

Mineral Contents. — These strata contain numerous large masses of Iceland spar, so limpid as to show the beautiful phenomena of double refraction. Small quantities of the sulphurets of lead and zinc and iron were observed in it on South River in Marion county, at Sec. 3 of the Marion Schedule, and other localities.

The lower strata are thicker, darker colored and a pure carbonate of lime; while the upper parts are more magnesian, and present the various shades of drab and buff, as at the mouth of McDowell's Cave, in the north-eastern part of Ralls county. But towards the south its lithological characters so change, that it cannot be recognized except by its fossils and stratigraphical position. It there appears as a thick-bedded, impure, earthy, brownish magnesian limestone.

Thickness. — The thickness varies from sixty or seventy feet, as at Hannibal, to two or three, as on South River, some thirteen miles west of that place. (See Sections 6 and 126 of the Marion Schedule.)

Its Stratigraphical Position is between the Vermicular Sandstone and Shales and the Hamilton Group; as seen north of Ashley, in Pike county, and Section 15, at Hannibal.

---

* An analysis by Dr. Litton of a specimen from Cooper county gave, in 100 parts: —

Silica,	6.22
Alumina and oxide of iron,	0.93
Carbonate of lime,	89.66
Carbonate of magnesia,	1.55
Water,	1.63
	99.99

Range.—It is exposed at numerous localities, from Marion, along the eastern border of the belt occupied by the upper members of this system, to Green county.

Organic Remains.—It has but few fossils, and it is very difficult to separate them from the rock. The most abundant are *Spirifer Marionensis*, *S. cuspidatus*, *Productus Murchisonianus*, *P. minutus*, *Proetus Missouriensis*, *Filicites gracilis*, a *Conularia* and *Fucoides cauda-galli?* and several large-chambered shells. (See Catalogue VI.) This Formation has been called Lithographic Limestone, from its evident adaptation to Lithographic purposes.

The Sulphur and Salt Springs of Cooper county come to the surface in valleys of denudation in the various members of the Chemung Group. These rocks are represented in Benton and St. Clair counties by a few feet of pure blue compact limestone; as at Sec. 19, above Warsaw, and Fig. 8, on Bear Creek; but farther south, in Polk and Green, all of the divisions of the group are again developed and easily distinguished.

The *Scenery* produced by the Chemung rocks is, in many instances, very marked and peculiar. Where all the members of the Group are developed, the bluffs present two terraces with a slope between, covering the Vermicular Sandstone and Shales. Where the Shales are argillaceous, as in Marion county, this slope is covered with a cold wet soil, saturated by the numerous bold springs which break out between it and the limestone above; but where they are magnesian, as in Cooper, it is usually a barren glade sustaining a few dwarf sumacs, cacti and mulleins. The bluffs of the La Mine abound in these glades; while the bluffs of North River have the wet slopes covered with heavy timber. The bluffs of the Mississippi, both above and below Hannibal, show the lower terrace, of Lithographic Limestone, at the water's edge, and the upper one, of Chouteau and Encrinital Limestones, near the top.

SYSTEM IV.—DEVONIAN.

Two Formations of this System exist in Missouri—

F. *p*—HAMILTON GROUP. F. *m*—ONONDAGA LIMESTONE.

F. *p*—HAMILTON GROUP.

I have seen well marked fossils of this Group, in but one place in the State. Three-fourths of a mile north of Ashley, in Pike county, I found the following section:—

No. 1. — 8 feet of gray, sub-crystalline, concretionary, irregularly-stratified Limestone, with thin partings of brown clay.
No. 2. — 20 feet of blue argillaceous shale.

No. 1 contains *Terebratula reticularis*, and a *Spirifer* found in the Hamilton * Group, at the Falls of the Ohio; and No. 2 contains a *Cyathophyllum*, very characteristic of the same rocks.

In Marion county we found forty-five feet of blue shales immediately below the Lithographic Limestone, and at Louisiana, four feet of dark purple and brown shales in the same position; but no fossils could be discovered in any of the localities. Still, the great similarity of the shales and the same stratigraphical position, lead to the conclusion that they are identical, and belong, with the above described rocks in Pike county, to the Hamilton Group.

F. m—ONONDAGA LIMESTONE.

This Formation, so far as observed, is usually a coarse gray or buff, crystalline, thick-bedded and cherty limestone, abounding in *Terebratula reticularis, Spirifer cuspidatus*, and a small *Pentamerus*, like *galeatus*.

Dr. Shumard has observed it where more fully developed, and gives the following description: —

"Gray compact, and ash-colored earthy limestone, with intercalations of chert, and cherty concretions in places, and sometimes seams of sandstone. The fossils are *Terebratula reticularis, Orthis resupinata, Chonetes nana, Productus subaculeatus, Spirifer eurutcines* (Owen), *Phacops bufo, Cyathophyllum rugosum, Emmonsia hemispherica*, and remains of *Crinoidea*."

On the Cedar in Callaway, this formation is principally made up of fine compact, hard, bluish gray heavy-bedded limestone; some beds have small particles of calcareous spar disseminated. Beds of Saccharoidal Sandstone, filled with masses of *Zaphrentis cornicula, Acervularia Davidsoni?* and *Cyathophyllum rugosum*, are intercalated with the upper strata.

At Louisiana, in Ralls county, the Onondaga Limestone is represented by ten feet of white hard Oolitic Limestone in one stratum, overlaid by three feet of brown impure arenaceous limestone. The Oolitic bed abounds in *Zaphrentis cornicula*, and large portions of the rock consist of *Acervularia Davidsoni?* Three miles west

* I am indebted to Dr. Shumard for comparing these fossils with those of his collection from the Falls of the Ohio.

of Louisiana, on the plank-road, this Formation is represented by a bed of Oolite only ten inches thick.

In Marion county, is a hard compact bluish and gray limestone, filled with particles of limpid spar, underlaid by bluish drab, fine-grained argillaceous limestone, in thin strata. No fossils were found in these rocks, save a coral very similar to, if not identical with, *Acervularia Davidsoni?* These rocks underlie the Shales of the Hamilton Group, and are doubtless *Onondaga.* On the plank-road, in the bluffs of Salt River, these same beds occur, and beneath them, three feet of calcareous sandstone, like the upper bed at Louisiana, and below it thirty feet of soft brown sandstone, in which no fossils were observed. This Sandstone occupies the same stratigraphical position as the Oolite at Louisiana, and is doubtless Onondaga.

Dr. Shumard saw a similar sandstone on the Mississippi, near Rattlesnake Creek, which he thinks is Onondaga. Thick beds of a fine-grained, nearly compact silicious rock, occupy the same position in the bluffs at Providence, in Boone county. Nearly opposite the last locality, in Moniteau, this Formation is made up of beds, which Mr. Meek calls, "arenaceous limestone, or a calcareous sandstone." In places, he thinks, "it passes into a pure quartzose sandstone." At this locality, *Terebratula reticularis, Favosites polymorpha,* and a *Pentamerus like galeatus,* were obtained. In Cooper county, this Formation consists of a few thin beds of bluish gray semi-crystalline limestone, containing *Terebratula reticularis, Leptaena depressa, etc.* Under these strata are some sixty feet of a bluish drab compact limestone, in thick beds, containing cavities filled with bluish green talcose matter; but the lower beds are darker and more compact, and contain numerous small crystals of calcareous spar, disseminated, as in Sec. 17. This limestone, which is called "Cooper Marble," has afforded us no fossils; but, its stratigraphical position and lithological characters being the same as those of this Formation in Marion, I have placed it here until fossils are found to decide its true position with more certainty.

No formation in Missouri presents such variable and widely different lithological characters as the Onondaga. It is, generally, a coarse gray crystalline limestone; often, a somewhat compact bluish concretionary limestone, with shale partings; in many instances a drab compact limestone, containing cavities filled with green matter, or calc-spar; in a few places, a white Saccharoidal Sandstone; in two or three localities, a soft brown sandstone; and, at Louisiana, a pure white Oolite. Will those who would have us follow lithological characters exclusively, tell us how we are to identify this Formation without its fossils, at these various localities?

Range and Thickness. — The most important localities have been already given, in Marion, Ralls, Callaway, Saline, Moniteau, Cooper, Perry and Scott counties. Its thickness ranges from ten inches to seventy-five feet.

The Organic Remains of Catalogue VIII. belong to this Formation.

SYSTEM V. — SILURIAN.

UPPER SILURIAN.

We have thus far made out but two divisions of this group; and they are of but little importance, save the scientific interest connected with them, as western representatives of Formations well developed elsewhere.

F. *n* — DELTHYRIS SHALY LIMESTONE. F. *o* — CAPE GIRARDEAU LIMESTONE.

F. *n* — DELTHYRIS SHALY LIMESTONE.

This Formation has not come under my own observation; and I am indebted to Dr. Shumard for the following description of it: —

"It is a light gray magnesio-calcareous rock, sometimes clouded with yellowish gray, assuming, on exposure to the air, a light buff color. It occurs in thin layers, generally close textured, and often contains a great many fossils, some of them closely allied to species of the Niagara Group of New York. In lithological characters it resembles very closely the Upper Silurian strata of the glades of Decatur county, Tennessee. The fossils are: *Leptaena depressa,* (small var.); *Leptaena,* several species undetermined; *Orthis,* two species very similar to *O. hybrida* and *O. elegantula, Atrypa camura? Platyostoma,* several species; *Capulus, Dalmania tridentifera* (Shumard); *Phacops, Cheirurus,* species? *Haplocrinus,* a species identical with one I have from Decatur county, Tennessee. Locality, one mile below Bailey's Landing, on the Mississippi river, in Perry county. About thirty feet of these strata are exposed at the base of hills from 120 to 130 feet high." Its fossils are named in Catalogue IX.

For a more detailed account of its properties and geological position, see Dr. Shumard's Report.

F. *a* — CAPE GIRARDEAU LIMESTONE.

I am also indebted to Dr. Shumard for a description of this

Formation. It is, according to him, a "compact bluish gray, brittle limestone, with a smooth fracture, in layers from two to six inches in thickness, with thin argillaceous partings. These strata contain a great many fossils, principally Trilobites and Crinoids. In a small slab, not more than three by three inches, I have counted four genera of Trilobites, viz: *Cyphaspis Girardeauensis; Acidaspis Halli, Proetus depressus, Asaphus Nov. sp.* None of these Trilobites have been before noticed in this country; and, so far as I can ascertain, the species are distinct from European forms. According to Barande, the first three genera occur in the greatest numbers in the Upper Silurian period, and are very sparingly represented in the Lower Silurian groups. The Crinoids belong mostly to the genera Glyptocrinus, Homocrinus and Tentaculites and Palaeaster? and the shells to Orthis, Leptaena, and Turbo—all being of undescribed species.

"These strata occur on the Mississippi river, about one mile and a half above Cape Girardeau. Thickness, forty to fifty feet." Catalogue X. gives its fossils.

Dr. Shumard's Report gives a more extended description of this Formation. I have not seen it.

LOWER SILURIAN.

We have thus far observed ten Formations belonging to this series.

F. q—HUDSON RIVER GROUP.
F. r—TRENTON LIMESTONE.
F. s—BLACK RIVER AND BIRD'S-EYE LIMESTONE.
F. t—1ST. MAGNESIAN LIMESTONE.
F. u—SACCHAROIDAL SANDSTONE.
F. v—2D. MAGNESIAN LIMESTONE.
F. w—2D. SANDSTONE.
F. x—3D. MAGNESIAN LIMESTONE.
F. y—3D. SANDSTONE.
F. z—4TH. MAGNESIAN LIMESTONE.

F. q—HUDSON RIVER GROUP.

There are three Formations, which we have referred to this Group.

1st. Immediately below the Oolite, of the Onondaga Limestone, in the bluffs both above and below Louisiana, we find some forty feet of blue, gray and brown, argillaceous magnesian limestone.*

* Dr. Litton's analysis of this rock gave—

Silica,	30.54
Alumina and peroxide of iron,	17.07
Carbonate of lime,	30.90
Carbonate of magnesia,	20.02
Water,	0.70
	99.23

The upper part of these shales is in thick beds, presenting a dull conchoidal fracture, and containing *Asaphus megistos* and *Calymene senaria*. The lower part of this division becomes more argillaceous, and has several thin beds of bluish gray crystalline limestone, intercalated, which contain many fossils of the following species: — *Leptaena sericea*, *L. alternata*, *L. planumbona*, *Orthis jugosa* and *O. subquadrata*.

There are, also, strata of calcareo-arenaceous slate, in the same position, filled with remains, which I am unable to distinguish from Prof. Hall's *Palaeophycus virgatus*, and another contorted species, smaller than No. 2, pl. 70 of Prof. Hall's Report. There are, also, beds of slate, similar to those above mentioned, at the base of these shales, whose surfaces are covered with great numbers of the *Lingula ancyloidea*.

Dr. Shumard thus describes these beds at another locality: —

"On the shore of the Mississippi, five miles below Louisiana, a bluish gray earthy limestone occurs in thin layers, with conchoidal fracture. These rocks, from the fossils, I am disposed to regard as identical with the Blue Limestone of Cincinnati, and Madison, Indiana, which are now considered as being the equivalents of the Hudson River Group of New York. The fossils are *Asaphus Megistos* (Locke), some specimens of which were found ten inches in length, *Calymene senaria*, *Dalmania callicephala ? Leptaena sericea*, *Lep. planumbona* and *Rhynconella capax*."

2d. On the Grassy, three and a half miles north-west of Louisiana, about sixty feet of blue and purple shales are exposed, below the beds above described. They contain three species of *Lingula*: *Lingula quadrata*, *L. fragilis*, and still another not named. The first resembles the *L. quadrata* of Hall, but is destitute of the "radiating striae" of that species, and is larger; it is more like the variety from the Trenton Limestone than that from the Hudson River Group.

3d. Under the 2d division, are some twenty feet of argillo-magnesian limestone, similar to that in the 1st division, interstratified with blue shales. *Orthis subquadrata*, *O. jugosa*, *Leptaena alternata*, *Rhynconella capax* and *Asaphus megistos* are abundant.

Range and Thickness. — These rocks have been seen only in Ralls and Pike counties. On the Grassy, a thickness of 120 feet is exposed; and they extend below the surface, to an unknown depth. The following section gives the strata at that locality: —

No. 1. — 25 feet of Lithographic Limestone — Chemung Group.
No. 2. — 2 feet of brown arenaceous limestone — } Onondaga Limestone.
No. 3. — 1 foot of grayish white oolitic limestone — }
No. 4. — 40 feet of argillo-magnesian limestone — }
No. 5. — 62 feet of dark blue and purple shales — } Hudson River Group.
No. 6. — 18 feet of argillo-magnesian limestone — }

The Onondaga beds are perfectly well defined at this locality, though they are but three feet thick. The top and bottom divisions of the Hudson River Group have some beds, whose lithological and chemical characters indicate hydraulic qualities.

Where this Formation is the surface rock, the shales disintegrate so rapidly that the country is characterized by gentle slopes and a heavy wet soil, as in places on the plank-road between Louisiana and Frankfort.

Its stratigraphical position is below the oolite of the Onondaga Limestone, as is shown in the above section, and there is no doubt of its resting upon the Trenton Limestone.

The Organic Remains are recorded in Catalogue XI.

F. *t*—TRENTON LIMESTONE.

The upper part of this Formation is made up of thick beds of hard compact bluish gray and drab limestone, variegated with irregular cavities filled with greenish materials; while the beds below are filled with irregular cylindrical portions, which readily decompose on exposure, and leave the rock perforated with numerous irregular passages, that somewhat resemble those made in timber by the *Teredo navalis.*

The appearance of the rock, when thus decomposed, is very singular, and is a well-marked character of this part of the Formation.

The decomposed, honey-combed portions are most admirably adapted to ornamental rock-work, in gardens and yards. These beds are exposed on the plank-road, from Hannibal to New London, north of Salt River, and are seventy-five feet thick. Below them are thick strata of impure, coarse, gray and buff crystalline magnesian limestones, with many brown earthy portions, which rapidly disintegrate on exposure to atmospheric influences. This part may be seen in the bluff of Salt River, near the plank-road, 150 feet thick. The lower part is made up of hard blue and bluish gray, semi-compact silico-magnesian limestone, interstratified with light buff and drab, soft and earthy magnesian beds. Fifty feet of these strata crop out at the quarries south of the plank-road bridge over Salt River, and on Spencer's Creek, in Ralls county.

In the bluffs of Salt River, near the crossing of the Hannibal and New London Plank-road, the following section of the Trenton Limestone was observed: —

No. 1. — 25 feet of bluish white compact limestone, variegated with irregular cavities, filled with a softer bluish green substance. It contains *Murchisonia bellicincta* and other fossils.

No. 2. — 200 feet of buff and gray crystalline limestone, filled with irregular masses of softer materials, which decompose on exposure and leave the beds full of winding passages. Sometimes nearly half of the rock is gone, leaving a mere skeleton of the harder parts, which, in general appearance, somewhat resembles a coarse sponge. These beds abound in the characteristic fossils of the Trenton Limestone.

On the south side of the river, on the same road, the lower beds are exposed as follows: —

No. 3. — 55 feet of dark blue fine-grained limestone, interstratified with buff and drab magnesian beds: the layers are separated by thin partings of blue shale, filled with Trenton fossils.

The upper and lower divisions of this rock make excellent building materials; but the middle beds disintegrate rapidly, and are not sufficiently uniform in texture for such purposes.

The Scenery connected with this Formation is characterized by bold mural bluffs, which are often castellated in appearance, as in the bluffs of Salt River and the Mississippi. (See view on page 147, Part II.)

Organic Remains. — Fossils are abundant in all parts of the Formation. *Leptaena deltoidea*, *L. sericea*, *L. alternata*, *Orthis pectinella*, *O. testudinaria*, *O. tricenaria*, *Rhynconella capax*, *Murchisonia gracilis*, *M. bellicincta*, *Receptaculites Sulcata*, and *Chaetetes lycoperdon*, are most common.

Catalogue XII. gives the fossils of the Trenton Limestone in Missouri, so far as they have been identified.

Range and Thickness. — It has been noticed in Ralls, Pike, Franklin, St. Louis and Jefferson counties, and at several places below on the Mississippi. The greatest thickness observed is 375 feet. Dr. Shumard gives the following description of it, and the Black-River and Bird's-eye Limestones in Jefferson county: —

"Bluish gray and light drab compact limestone, with a smooth conchoidal fracture, in thin and heavy beds, frequently presenting a castellated appearance. Near the base of the Formation the rock is frequently traversed in all directions by vermicular cavities and cells. The superior layers represent the Trenton Limestone, and are usually highly fossiliferous. The following species are most characteristic:

Leptaena fillitexta, L. sericea, Orthis tricenaria, O. subaequata, Illaenus crassicauda and *Chaetetes lycoperdon.* Towards the base we find fossils of the "Black-River," and, perhaps, of the "Birds-eye Limestone" of the New York System. Those representing the former group are, *Orthoceras fusiforme, Ormoceras tenuifilum, Gonioceras anceps, etc.*, and of the latter group *Orthoceras multicameratum ?* and *Modiola obtusa.* Thus far, we have not been able to separate these different groups by any well-marked changes in lithological characters."

There is a mere possibility that the lower beds of the Cooper Marble of Marion and Cooper counties (see Reports on those counties) belong to this Formation. And, though no fossils have been found in that part of them, it has the lithological characters of the upper division of this limestone, and may occupy the same stratigraphical position; but this can not be ascertained with certainty, as the 1st Magnesian Limestone and the Hudson River Group are wanting at those localities.

No valuable minerals have been observed in it. The upper and lower beds furnish very superior building stones; but the columns of the Court-House in St. Louis, were from the middle strata, that much more readily disintegrate, and, consequently, fail to produce so happy an effect as those rocks which carry the impress of durability. The Cape Girardeau Marble, and McPherson's, are in the upper beds.

F. s — BLACK-RIVER AND BIRD'S-EYE LIMESTONES.

I have not had an opportunity of examining these rocks; but, according to Dr. Shumard —

"They are bluish gray or dove-colored, compact, brittle limestones, with a smooth conchoidal fracture. The beds vary in thickness from a few inches to several feet." "Near the base, the rock is frequently traversed in all directions by vermicular cavities and cells."

They may be used for building purposes and for quicklime, where no better limestones are found.

Range and Thickness. — They crop out under the Trenton Limestone at St. Albans, and in other localities in Franklin county, and at Selma and several other places on the Mississippi river. Their thickness is fifty or sixty feet.

The Organic Remains are mentioned in Catalogue XIII.

CALCIFEROUS SANDROCK.

We have referred seven very important formations to this division of the New York System. Future investigations may prove those, in which we have found no characteristic fossils, distinct from the Calciferous Sandrock. The seven divisions are as follows:—

F. *t*— 1st MAGNESIAN LIMESTONE.

This Formation is developed in many parts of the State. It is usually a gray or buff, crystalline, cherty, silico-magnesian limestone, filled with small irregular masses of a soft white or greenish yellow silicious substance, which rapidly decomposes when exposed, and leaves the rock full of irregular cavities, and covered with rough projecting points. These rugged weather-worn strata crop out in the prairies, and cap the picturesque bluffs of the Osage in Benton and the neighboring counties.

These beds often pass into a homogeneous buff or gray crystalline magnesian limestone, which is frequently clouded with blue or pink, and would make a good fire-rock and building stone.

At other places the strata become compact, hard, and clouded as above, forming a still more beautiful and durable marble.

Some of the upper beds are silicious, presenting a porous, semi-transparent vitreous mass, in which are disseminated numerous small globular, white, enamelar oolitic particles. They are sometimes in regular and continuous strata, at others in irregular masses, presenting mammillated and botryoidal and drusy forms of this beautiful mineral. In some parts of Benton and the neighboring counties, these masses, left by the denuded strata, literally cover the surface and render the soil almost valueless for ordinary cultivation.

Other strata abound in concretions, or organic forms, which resemble wooden button-moulds, with a central aperture and one convex surface. Masses of calcareous spar are quite abundant in the upper beds. But the lower part of this Formation is made up of thin regular strata, of a soft earthy, light drab or cream-colored silico-argillaceous magnesian limestone.*

Above the beds already described, we find, in several places in the State, a succession of hard silicious, dark bluish gray semi-crystalline limestones, interstratified with grayish drab earthy magnesian varieties, all in regular layers destitute of chert. These strata have been joined to the 1st Magnesian Limestone, with the expectation that they may prove distinct from the Calciferous Sandrock and the 1st Magnesian Limestone, and be identified with the Chazy Limestone or some other formation.

---

* This variety of Magnesian Limestone is generally called "*Cotton Rock*" in many parts of the State. (See 2d Magnesian Limestone.)

The following section on Spencer's Creek gives the position of these beds: —

No. 1. — 250 feet of Trenton Limestone.

No. 2. — 50 feet of grayish drab argillo-magnesian limestone, in regular beds, interstratified with harder blue semi-crystalline layers. A very large *Orthoceratite* was found at the junction of this and the Trenton Limestone, and *Cythere sublaevis* is abundant in the dark-colored beds.

No. 3. — 5 feet of grayish buff crystalline limestone, containing numerous particles of calcareous spar.

No. 4. — 12 feet of grayish drab argillo-magnesian limestone, in beds from four to ten inches thick. It has an earthy dull conchoidal fracture — Cotton Rock.

No. 5. — 15 feet of buff crystalline magnesian limestone, containing numerous cells or cavities of light-colored pulverulent silicious matter.

No. 6. — 12 feet of magnesian limestone, like No. 4.

No. 7. — 15 feet of Saccharoidal Sandstone.

Nos. 3, 4, 5 and 6 are, doubtless, identical with the strata described above, from localities in Benton county, and belong, without doubt, to the Calciferous Sandrock; but No. 2 is probably a distinct formation. Dr. Shumard gives the following description of this Formation: —

"1st. Light buff and gray magnesian limestone, in layers from an inch to a foot in thickness, passing downwards into more compact close-textured magnesian limestone, with thin partings of bluish argillaceous shale. These beds often contain cavities filled with crystals of calc spar, and the newly-fractured surfaces present a shining appearance from the presence of spar. This group contains a small species of *Cythere sublaevis*, which we have found in great numbers near its junction with the sandstone on the Pacific Railroad, near Hamilton's Creek, and at the "White Sand Cave," on the old Potosi road, seven and a half miles from Ste. Genevieve.

"Greatest thickness observed, two miles below Plattin Rock, is 152 feet.

"2d. Alternation of buff and gray magnesian limestone and bluish gray compact, fine-textured limestone, in layers from an inch to two feet thick. Thickness, thirty to fifty feet."

The 1st division described by Dr. Shumard, is identical with the beds No. 2 of the above section, on Spencer's Creek. Dr. Shumard, also, found the *Cythere* in the beds by him described. The 2d division may be the same as the rocks overlying the Saccharoidal Sandstone in Benton and Ralls.

Thickness and Range. — The lower division of this formation varies from ten to fifty feet in thickness; while the upper division ranges from 75 to 150 feet. It crops out along the bluffs of the Osage in Benton and St. Clair counties, on the Missouri in Boone, and on Brush Creek, in Sec. 18 of Town. 36, R. 25, and on Spencer's Creek in Ralls.

Minerals.—It contains calcareous spar, heavy spar, and the Sulphurets of Iron, Lead and Zinc, in small quantities. Its stratigraphical position is between the Trenton Limestone and the Saccharoidal Sandstone; as shown in section 19, and in the above section from Spencer's Creek.

Organic Remains.—Only two described species have been detected in the 1st Magnesian Limestone; *Cythere sublaevis* in the upper division, and *Straparollus* (*Ophileta*) *laevata?* was found in the lower division, only twelve feet above the Saccharoidal Sandstone, in the bluff above Warsaw.

Economical Value.—Some of the magnesian beds furnish a good fire-rock; the compact clouded layers, a beautiful and durable marble; and the *Cotton Rock* is much used for building purposes. It is soft and easily wrought when fresh from the quarries, but becomes harder on exposure; though it is scarcely compact enough to endure our climate, or strong enough to sustain heavy masonry without crushing. The porous silicious strata promise to make good mill-stones. The decomposition of these rocks forms a productive soil; but the almost indestructible cherty portions cover the land in many places, and render it almost useless for cultivation.

F. *u*—SACCHAROIDAL SANDSTONE.

This Formation is usually a bed of white friable sandstone, slightly tinged with red and brown, which is made up of globular concretions and angular fragments of limpid quartz. It presents very imperfect strata, but somewhat more distinct lines of deposition, variously inclined to the planes of stratification. When separated at the lines of stratification or deposition, the surface presents larger globular particles of quartz and water-worn fragments of chert, apparently from the inferior limestone; while still larger fragments of decomposing chert are frequently disseminated through the whole stratum. Sometimes it becomes a pure white homogeneous mass of slightly coherent particles of silex, which very much resembles loaf-sugar.

A portion of this gave, by Dr. Litton's analyses, in 100 parts—

	1	2
Silica,	98.81	99.02
Lime,	0.92	0.98
	99.73	99.90

This sandstone is so friable, that specimens are broken off with great difficulty, and when separated from the mass, can be crumbled with ease between the fingers. And yet, it withstands the action of atmospheric and aqueous agencies as long as almost any rock in the State.

The projecting mass, represented in Fig. 8, is an illustration of its abilities to endure the action of the weather; and the numerous instances where it extends into the bed of the Missouri and other streams, and their strong currents sweep over and against it, show its power to withstand the abrading force of running water.

At places, the whole, or a part of it, becomes vitreous, semi-transparent, and oolitic. This change seems to be produced by a deposition of white opaque chalcedonic silex, in the interstices between the original particles of the sandstone, perhaps from an aqueous solution percolating through the bed.

These vitreous portions are most abundant where the formation is thin and the unaltered parts most distinctly stratified; but the lines separating the vitreous from the unchanged parts do not correspond with the lines of stratification, as may be seen in many localities, and even in hand specimens. A horizontal line often separates the common varieties from the vitrified, as if waters had stood on a level with the line, and deposited the silex in sufficient quantities to fill all the interstices of the part of the sandstone covered by it.

On the road from Bolivar to Springfield, fifteen miles from the former town, in Sec. 16, Town. 31, R. 22, I saw fine specimens of this rock, thus changed, and the whole more distinctly stratified than at any other place observed. We there get the following Section : —

No. 1. — 65 feet of *Ferruginous Sandstone.*
No. 2. — 150 feet of *Encrinital Limestone.*
No. 3. — 30 feet of *Chouteau Limestone.*
No. 4. — 75 feet of *Vermicular Sandstone and Shales.*
No. 5. — 10 feet of *Lithographic Limestone.*
No. 6. — 12 feet of *Saccharoidal Sandstone.*

In some places this sandstone is highly colored with various shades of red and brown. At Versailles it is brown, with some strata tinged with purple, and peach-blossom, and red; at Bolivar it is brown, red and ash-colored; and a yellowish brown at several places between Bolivar and Springfield.

These colors are due to various substances, mostly oxides of iron, which have infiltrated and filled up the interstices between the original particles of the sandstone. This is obvious when the rock is examined with the microscope; for the colorless particles of quartz are as abundant as ever in the portions most highly colored, while the shades of color are caused by the matter between them, which forms a cement, and renders these colored parts of this rock much more tenacious and durable.

Range and Thickness. — This interesting Formation has a wide range over the State. I have seen it in Ralls, Boone, Saline, Cooper, Moniteau, Pettis, Benton, Morgan, Hickory, St. Clair, Cedar, Polk and Dallas; and Drs. Shumard and Litton observed it in Perry, Franklin, Ste. Genevieve and other counties.

Its thickness is very variable, from one to seventy feet. At times it thickens very rapidly; so much so, as to increase thirty or forty feet in a few hundred yards.

In a bluff about two miles north-east of Warsaw, is a very striking illustration of this change of thickness. This sandstone crops out along the bluff, between the 1st and 2d Magnesian Limestone, and in a few yards decreases in thickness from twenty feet to one. Where thinnest it is semi-vitreous, and the line of demarcation between it and the limestones is very distinct.

Near the same place is a locality where the sandstone thickens so rapidly as to present the appearance of a dyke, cutting off the strata of limestone above and below that Formation. I have hand specimens broken from the junction of this dyke-like mass with the wall of the adjacent limestone, which are half sandstone and half limestone, showing the two rocks firmly cemented together.

On Bear Creek, south-west of Warsaw, is another instance of the same phenomenon, still more remarkable. Fig. 8 is a hasty sketch made upon the spot.

In this section the highest rock exposed is the Chouteau Limestone; the highest in the lower exposure is the 1st Magnesian Limestone; the thick white stratum in the middle is the Saccharoidal Sandstone; and the large mass, in front is the same, suddenly increasing in thickness from one and a half to twenty feet, cutting off the strata of limestone both above and below it, like a dyke of trap, or greenstone. The rock below the Saccharoidal Sandstone is the 2d Magnesian Limestone. The projecting thick mass is a homogeneous friable white sandstone, while the regular bed, on each side, shows lines of stratification and is more vitreous.

Such are the facts here; and similar phenomena were observed in the railroad cut above Hermann, in Moniteau, and elsewhere, by myself and Mr. Meek; but I must admit that such a freak among sedimentary rocks, I have never observed in any other formation.

One might give a satisfactory reason for its penetrating the strata above, but by what process of Nature it was made to cut off the beds below, is not so obvious. There is, perhaps, a possibility, that after the deposition of the 2d Magnesian Limestone, the waters, which deposited the silicious matter of the sandstone, first cut a channel in the upper strata of the limestone. But future investigations may enable us to solve the difficulty more satisfactorily.

Fig. 8.

VIEW OF THE SACCHAROIDAL SANDSTONE ON BEAR CREEK, ST. CLAIR COUNTY.

Organic Remains. — A few imperfect shells, probably of the genus *Murchisonia*, discovered by Mr. Meek, are the only organic remains yet observed in this sandstone. Those fossils were in small concretionary masses, which may have contained them previous to the deposition of the sandstone.

Stratigraphical Position. — Sections 19 and Nos. 4 and 5, of Pl. XIV., show its place between the 1st and 2d Magnesian Limestones. See, also, Fig. 8.

Economical Value. — The purer portions of this rock furnish the best sand for glass manufacture, cements and mortars; and, in short, for all purposes for which similar material is used. It sometimes renders the soil too sandy; as may be observed south of Bolivar and many other places.

Mineral Contents. — Fragments of chert, and the infiltrated oxides of iron, carbonate of lime and silex, are the only mineral substances seen in it.

F. v—2D MAGNESIAN LIMESTONE.

The Lithological characters of this Formation are very much like those of the 1st Magnesian Limestone above described. The following section from the bluffs of the Osage, above Warsaw, will give an idea of its general character: —

No. 1. — 12 feet 1st Magnesian Limestone.
No. 2. — 4 feet Saccharoidal Sandstone.
No. 3. — 15 feet of soft, earthy, fine-grained, yellowish white or drab silico-magnesian limestone, with a conchoidal earthy fracture, in beds from half of an inch to one foot thick, interstratified with thin layers of bluish silico-argillaceous Magnesian Limestone. It is called "*Cotton Rock.*"
No. 4. — 1 foot of coarse-grained crystalline greenish brown limestone, in thin laminæ. The crystals are as large as buck-shot, and give the rock a brecciated appearance.
No. 5. — 8 feet of limestone, like No. 3, interstratified with chert.
No. 6. — 10 feet of compact buff silicious limestone, filled with heavy spar and iron pyrites, some parts so variegated with flesh-colored spots as to present the appearance of a breccia — a beautiful and durable marble.
No. 7. — 3 feet coarse gray brown and buff crystalline magnesian limestone, filled with masses and veins of calcareous spar.
No. 8. — 1 foot, like No. 3.
No. 9. — 5 feet, like No. 7.
No. 10. — 5 feet of hard compact gray silicious limestone, interstratified with chert and "Cotton Rock."
No. 11. — 1 foot of yellowish gray Saccharoidal Sandstone.
No. 12. — 4 feet, like No. 10.
No. 13. — 10 feet, like No. 3.
No. 14. — 5 feet semi-oolitic sub-crystalline hard gray silicious limestone, interstratified with compact flesh-colored silicious beds.
No. 15. — 6 feet of soft buff fine-grained Magnesian Limestone, interstratified with chert and a compact flesh-colored silicious limestone.

No. 16. — 25 feet of coarse gray and buff silico-magnesian limestone, variegated by cavities filled with a white or yellowish pulverulent silicious substance, which decomposes on exposure and leaves the rock porous. It is an excellent fire-rock.

No. 17. — 4 feet, like No. 14.

No. 18. — 10 feet, like No. 15. Strata undulating.

No. 19. — 2 feet of fine compact flesh-colored silicious limestone.

No. 20. — 8 feet of hard gray crystalline semi-vitreous calcareous sandstone, with chert interspersed.

No. 21. — 20 feet slope to water.

A specimen from No. 3 of this section, from Mr. Atkisson's well at Warsaw, gave, by Dr. Litton's analysis, in 100 parts —

Silica,	13.27
Alumina and peroxide of iron,	0.52
Carbonate of lime,	47.01
Carbonate of magnesia,	38.86
	99.66

A specimen from the bluish silico-argillaceous* beds of No. 3 gave, in 100 parts —

Silica,	63.44
Alumina and peroxide of iron,	10.72
Carbonate of lime,	13.59
Carbonate of magnesia,	10.75
Water,	0.41
	98.91

A specimen from No. 16 gave, in 100 parts —

Insoluble in hydrochloric acid,	6.08
Alumina and peroxide of iron,	0.60
Carbonate of lime,	52.16
Carbonate of magnesia,	40.39
	99.23

The white and yellowish part of the same rock gave, in 100 parts —

Silica,	91.14
Alumina and a trace of peroxide of iron,	1.63
Lime,	2.60
Magnesia,	1.56
Carbonic acid and water,	3.07
	100.00

---

* Very thin strata of bluish white silico-argillaceous magnesian limestone, abound in the upper part of the formation.

A specimen of semi-oolitic, gray and buff, porous silico-magnesian limestone, from the prairie north-east of Warsaw, gave, in 100 parts—

Insoluble in nitric acid,	6.67
Alumina and peroxide of iron,	0.98
Carbonate of lime,	49.35
Carbonate of magnesia,	41.98
Water,	0.90
	99.88

In many places, this Formation contains thin beds of white pulverulent argillo-silicious mineral, which is frequently called Chalk, and is often used as a substitute for that mineral.

A specimen of it from the land of Mr. Ruby Walker, of Cooper, gave, in 100 parts—

Silica,	89.18
Alumina,	7.37
Lime,	0.52
Water,	2.21
	99.28

These results prove it entirely different from chalk, which is a very pure carbonate of lime.

Range and Thickness.—I have observed this limestone in Boone, Cooper, Moniteau, Cole, Callaway, Morgan, Benton, Pettis, St. Clair, Cedar, Green, Camden, Ste. Genevieve, Gasconade, Franklin, Polk and Dallas. It forms many of the bluffs of the Osage, Pomme de Terre, Sac, Grand and Tebo rivers, and of the Missouri, from Providence to Washington.

Its thickness above Warsaw is more than 180 feet; and on the Moniteau, in Sec. 18, Town. 46, R. 15, it is 156 feet. See the following, taken by Mr. Meek at that place:—

No. 1.—Saccharoidal Sandstone,	4 feet.
No. 2.—2d. Magnesian Limestone,	156 feet.
No. 3.—2d. Sandstone,	5 feet.

Its stratigraphical position is between the Saccharoidal and 2d. Sandstone, as seen in the section above, and in Nos. 6 and 7 of Pl. XIV.

Organic Remains.—But few fossils have been observed in this Formation. Mr. Meek discovered some imperfect specimens of the genera *Straparollus*, *Murchisonia* and *Pleurotomaria.*

Dr. Shumard has observed two species of *Straparollus* and *Murchisonia melaniaformis*. I saw a *Straparollus* near Warsaw, and a *Murchisonia melaniaformis* and *Crinoidal* columns at Jefferson City.

Economical Value.—The so called "Cotton Rock" of this Formation is very soft when fresh from the quarry, and can be easily wrought for building purposes. It is much used for chimneys and all ordinary structures, and is more durable than its lithological characters would at first indicate, as it hardens on exposure; but it seldom becomes sufficiently strong to sustain the pressure of heavy masonry, or so compact as to endure our climate without disintegration, unless care be taken to select the harder beds where free from joints and seams, as the most of those used in the Capitol at Jefferson City. Many of the compact silicious beds, afford a very durable building rock. Some beds make an excellent fire-rock. Soils produced by its decomposition are good; but the almost indestructible masses of chert left on the surface, are very troublesome to the cultivators of the soil, as many in the counties of Benton, Morgan and Moniteau can well testify.

Mineral Contents.—The *chert* of this Formation is often beautifully agatized. *Heavy Spar,** *Calcareous Spar,*† and *Iron Pyrites*‡ are abundant. At a locality, in the prairie north-east of Warsaw, there is a large bed of *heavy spar* or *sulphate* of *baryta*, which is penetrated by numerous long cylindrical columns of *iron pyrites*. The *iron pyrites* often decomposes and leaves the spar full of parallel holes.

Sulphate of *Magnesia* frequently forms incrustations in the crevices and caves; *sulphate* of *iron*, also, exists as an incrustation in many places.

Sulphurets of *Copper* and *Zinc* occur in small quantities. I am indebted to Judge Wright, of Warsaw, for one locality of those minerals, north-east of that town.

Galena, the *mineral* of our miners, is found in large quantities in this limestone, in Moniteau,|| Benton and Morgan counties; and has been seen in St. Clair, Hickory, Dallas and Polk. Several mines have

---

* *Heavy Spar, Sulphate* of *Baryta*, is the well-known *Tiff* of the miners.

† *Calcareous Spar* is called "*Blossom*," or "*Glass Tiff*," by miners.

‡ Called Sulphur by coal miners, and *Mundic* by others.

|| For an account of the Lead Mines of Moniteau, see Mr. Meek's Report; and for those of Franklin, Dr. Litton's and Dr. Shumard's Report.

been opened on Cole-Camp Creek, in Benton, which promise an abundant yield. There is much lead in that region.

A specimen of galena from a mine opened by Mr. James Glenn, near this creek, in Town. 42, R. 21, gave, in 100 parts—

Sulphur,	13.86
Lead,	85.43
	99.29

A specimen from this locality, was reported as yielding 90 per cent. of Lead; but I saw none *quite* so rich in that metal.

Good *Iron Ore*, *Hematite*, was observed in Dallas, west of Buffalo. That ore was, also, seen in the bluff above Warsaw; but in this locality, it contains too much sulphuret of iron, as the following analysis shows: —

Sulphur,	1.05
Silica,	2.11
Peroxide of iron,	89.85
Alumina,	0.87
Water,	10.01

Contrary to the expectation of many, the 2d Magnesian Limestone is proved to be rich in mineral deposits.

Clark's Sulphur Spring, on the north of Grand River, rises from a valley of denudation in this Formation.

The scenery connected with the 2d Magnesian Limestone is well represented in Pl. VII.

F. *w* — 2ND. SANDSTONE.

This is usually a brown or yellowish brown fine-grained sandstone, distinctly stratified in regular beds, varying from two to eighteen inches in thickness. The surfaces are often ripple-marked and micaceous. It is sometimes quite friable, though generally sufficiently indurated for building purposes. The upper part is often made up of thin strata of light, soft and porous, semi-pulverulent sandy chert or horn-stone, whose cavities are usually lined with limpid crystals of quartz. Fragments of these strata are very abundant in the soil and on the ridges where this sandstone forms the surface rock. It sometimes becomes a pure white fine-grained soft sandstone, as on Cedar Creek in Washington county, in Franklin and other localities.

Range and Thickness. — This rock was observed on the bluffs of the Niangua, Osage and Gravois, in the counties of Camden and

Morgan, where it is seventy feet thick. Nos. 6 and 7, Pl. XIV. Its *stratigraphical position* is between the 2d and 3d *Magnesian Limestones*, as seen on the Niangua and Gravois. (See Nos. 6 and 7, Pl. XIV.)

Organic Remains. * — Some very imperfect shells of the genera *Orthis*, *Leptaena* and *Straparollus*, and a *Trilobite*, were found in the cherty portions of this Formation, on the Niangua. Dr. Shumard, also, observed a *Pleurotomaria* and *Orthoceratite* in this rock, in Franklin county.

Economical Value. — Some of the strata are so true and even, present surfaces so smooth, and break so easily into any desirable shape, that it furnishes excellent building material and flagstones at a very moderate expense. When fine-grained and purely silicious, it makes a very refractory fire-rock, as experience has abundantly proved. The excellent hearth-stones used in the iron furnaces at Pilot Knob and Iron Mountain, and at the Moselle Iron Furnace, in Franklin county, are from this Formation.

It has a deleterious effect upon the soils over it, save where they are so clayey as to need sand to render them light and porous.

At Cove Mine the lode of galena extends into this sandstone. (See Dr. Litton's Report, p. 18, Part II.)

F. *x* — 3D MAGNESIAN LIMESTONE.

This limestone is exposed in the high and picturesque bluffs of the Niangua, in the neighborhood of Bryce's Spring, where the following strata were observed: —

No. 1. — 50 feet of the 2d Sandstone.

No. 2. — 80 feet of gray and buff crystalline silico-magnesian limestone, somewhat clouded with flesh-colored spots and bluish bands. It is regularly stratified in thick beds, some of which have many cells filled with a white pulverulent silicious substance; while others are ferruginous and semi-oolitic. It contains very little chert.

No. 3. — 50 feet of blue and white ferruginous chert, interstratified with hard, compact and flesh-colored silicious limestone.

No. 4. — 190 feet, like No. 2, save some beds are hard, compact, buff or flesh-colored and silicious.

No. 5. — 20 feet of light drab fine-grained crystalline silico-magnesian limestone, often slightly tinged with peach-blossom and beautifully clouded with darker spots and bands of the same hue or flesh color. It is distinctly stratified in beds of medium thickness.

No. 6. — 50 feet, like No. 2.

No. 7. — 30 feet of the 3*d Sandstone* crops out lower down.

---

* Mr. Meek has lately found, in the chert-bed of this Formation, a *Trilobite*, of the *genus Arionellus*, which he and Dr. Shumard consider identical with one that occurs in the Potsdam Sandstone of the N. W.

A specimen from No. 5 gave, by analysis, from 100 parts —

Insoluble in nitric acid,	6.21
Alumina and peroxide of iron,	1.07
Carbonate of lime,	50.80
Carbonate of magnesia,	40.56
Water,	0.21
	98.85

Range and Thickness. — It is exposed in the bluffs of the Niangua nearly all the way from Edwards' Mill to its mouth, and thence in the bluffs of the Osage to the mouth of the Gravois, and several miles up that stream. Throughout this whole distance there is scarcely any change in its lithological characters. Its thickness, where fully developed, is more than 390 feet, as that much was seen in the Section near Bryce's Spring, where the whole is not exposed. It is, doubtless, 500 or 600 feet thick.

Its stratigraphical position is between the 2d and 3d Sandstones; as in Nos. 6 and 7 of Pl. XIV.

Organic Remains. — I saw but one fossil, an *Orthis*, in this Formation; but Dr. Shumard has observed some species of *Pleurotomaria*, and *Turbo;* also, *Straparollus* (*Ophileta*) *complanata* and *S. laevata.*

Economical Value. — Nearly all the limestone of this Formation will make good building materials. The hard, compact, clouded varieties, from Nos. 3 and 4 of the last section, are fine and durable marble; while the even-textured beds of No. 5, will furnish an inexhaustible supply of material, inferior to none in Missouri, for beauty, durability, and the ease with which it may be wrought.

Mineral Contents. — *Iron Ore* of good quality, occurs in this limestone. But the most important locality is on the ridge in the forks of the Little and the Big Niangua, extending from the mouth of the former to Sec. 12, Town. 38, R. 18. (See Analysis 46, p. 94, Part II.) *Lead* was found in this rock in many parts of the State. The mines at Erie and on the Gravois, are in it, as are nearly all of the Eastern mines. *Copper*, *Zinc* and *Cobalt* abound in this limestone, in the eastern counties. This, in short, has been considered *the metalliferous* rock of the State; and, doubtless, contains more valuable ores than any other Formation in our territory.

Calcareous Spar abounds in this limestone; and always, so far as my observation has extended, accompanies the lead ore; while *Sulphate of Baryta* has generally been found with that mineral in the 2d *Magnesian Limestone.*

Some of the grandest scenery in the State is produced by the high castellated and mural bluffs of this Formation, on the Niangua and the Osage.

There is, in the right bank of the Niangua, one mile south of Morris', a very singular disturbance of the beds of this limestone. A kind of dyke, seventy feet thick, cuts off the strata, the entire height of the nearly perpendicular face, which is about 100 feet. This immense fissure is filled with the fragments of the original strata, cemented with calcareous spar. Disseminated through this, I saw small masses of the sulphurets of iron, lead, zinc and copper. The following sketch shows the appearance of the bluff at that place.

Fig. 9.

DYKE IN THE MAGNESIAN LIMESTONE ON THE NIANGUA RIVER.

Bryce's, or the Upper Big Spring, probably the largest in the State, rises from this limestone.

F. *y* — 3D SANDSTONE.

This is a white Saccharoidal Sandstone, made up of slightly cohering, transparent, globular and angular particles of silex. It shows but little appearance of stratification, yet the well-marked lines of deposition, like those of a Missouri sand-bar, indicate its formation in moving water. This is the least changeable of all our sandstones. It was partly stratified and colored light brown, in one or two places on the Niangua; and these are the only changes observed in it.

Range and Thickness. — This sandstone has been observed only on the Gravois, and the lower portions of the Niangua. Its greatest thickness observed is thirty feet.

Stratigraphical Position. — Nos. 6 and 7, of Pl. XIV., shows its true position between the 3d and 4th Magnesian Limestones. But its position below the 3d Magnesian Limestone, makes it as old, at least, as the Calciferous Sandrock, and there is great probability that it will prove to be Potsdam Sandstone. *

Organic Remains. — No fossils were seen in this sandstone.

Economical Value. — It would furnish the very best materials, in inexhaustible quantities, for the manufacture of glass, cement and other articles, for which pure sand or silex is used.

F. z — 4TH MAGNESIAN LIMESTONE.

This presents more permanent and uniform lithological characters than any of the Magnesian Limestones. It is usually a grayish buff, coarse-grained, crystalline magnesian limestone, containing a few cavities filled with less indurated silicious matter. Its thick uniform beds contain but little chert.

Range and Thickness. — It forms the base of the bluffs of the Niangua, from a point some ten miles below Bryce's Spring to the mouth of that river. At the upper place mentioned it emerges from the water, and rises gradually until it reaches an elevation of 300 feet, about three miles below Gunter's Big Spring, as shown in Pl. XIV. It has been observed on the Niangua River and on the Osage.

Stratigraphical Position. — This limestone underlies the 3d Sandstone, as shown in Nos. 6 and 7 of Pl. XIV., on the Niangua.

Mineral Contents. — Calcareous spar, heavy spar, and iron ores are the only minerals seen in this limestone. The brown hematite is quite abundant at some localities on the Niangua.

Organic Remains. — No fossils of any description have been observed in this Formation; yet we are not to conclude none will be found, when it shall be more carefully examined. It is, doubtless, as old as the Potsdam Sandstone.

Economical Value. — The beds of this rock will furnish any amount of limestone suitable for all the ordinary uses to which such

* Since this Report was written, Mr. Meek has discovered a *Trilobite* in the 3d Magnesian Limestone, which he and Dr. Shumard consider identical with one in the Potsdam Sandstone of the North-West.

material is applied in the useful arts. The soil, from its decomposition, is very productive and comparatively free from the chert, so common in those derived from the other Magnesian Limestones.

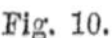

Fig. 10.

VIEW OF A NATURAL BRIDGE IN THE 4TH MAGNESIAN LIMESTONE, ON THE NIANGUA.

Several caves and the bridge sketched above, were observed in this rock. The scenery produced by this Formation is peculiar and interesting. Plate VIII. exhibits its characteristic features. The bluffs usually rise from the bottom in a perpendicular wall to the height of 100 feet, and then in a gentle slope by terraces to the top of the Formation. The rise in each of these terraces varies from one to three feet, according to the thickness of the stratum which forms it. Each presents a surface from five to ten feet wide, covered with a luxuriant growth of grass, shrubs and vines. The bluffs thus formed rise by gentle slopes into rounded knobs, surrounded by the terraces above mentioned. The whole reminds one of the vine-clad hills of the Eastern world; while the rich soil, the natural terraces, and the salubrious climate, all adapted to the growth of the grape, invite vine-growers to occupy the beautiful and picturesque valleys of the Niangua and the Osage.

SECTION OF MR. BELCHER'S ARTESIAN WELL.

As some may be desirous of comparing our section with that obtained from the borings of Mr. Belcher's Artesian well, at St. Louis, I insert the latter, together with notes, as copied from the journal of borings, kept at the Refinery. It will be somewhat difficult to make out the parallelism between this and our section. This difficulty may arise from the absence of some one or more of the formations, at the well, which are found elsewhere.

No.		THICKNESS IN FEET.	BELOW THE TOP.
1.........	Sandstone, ...	28	28
2.........	Shale and Clay, ...	2	30
3.........	Sandstone, ...	231	261
4.........	Cherty Rock, ...	15	276
5.........	Limestone, ...	74	350
6.........	Blue Slate or Shale, ...	30	380
7.........	Sandstone, ...	75	455
8.........	Shale or blue Slate, ...	1½	456½
9.........	Limestone, ...	38½	495
10.........	Sandy Shale or blue Sandrock, ...	6½	501½
11.........	Limestone with Sand, ...	128½	630
12.........	Red Marl or soft red Sandstone, ...	15	645
13.........	Shale or soft blue Slate, ...	30	675
14.........	Red Marl or soft red Slate, ...	50	725
15.........	Shale or blue Slate, ...	30	755
16.........	Limestone, lower part mixed with sand............	119	874
17.........	Shale or blue Slate, ...	66	940
18.........	Bituminous Marl or brown Slate, ...	15	955
19.........	Shale or blue Slate, ...	80	1025
20.........	Limestone, ...	134	1169
21.........	Cherty Rock, ...	62	1221
22.........	Limestone, ...	128	1369
23.........	Slate or Shale, ...	17	1376
24.........	Limestone, ...	20	1396
25.........	Shale or Slate, ...	56	1452
26.........	Magnesian Limestone, ...	34	1486
27.........	White soft Sandstone, interstratified with layers of Limestone, and in some parts Clay, ...	690	2176

"At 460 feet below the surface Carburetted Hydrogen first made its appearance; and at 750 feet much more gas evolved.

"At 610 feet, water was salty.

"At 858 feet, it contained 1⅞ per cent. of common salt.

"At 1,027 feet, the water contained 2¼ per cent.; and the evolution of gas was more abundant.

"At 1,090 feet, the quantity of gas evolved began to diminish, and continued to do so until reaching the depth of 1,183 feet, when it began to increase.

"At 1,190 feet, there was more gas, and the water contained less salt — one pound contained 148 grains.

"At 1,231 feet, the water contained 3 per cent. of salt."

TABULAR VIEW OF GEOLOGICAL FORMATIONS.

It may be interesting to compare the formations already discovered in Missouri with those known to exist elsewhere in the world. For this purpose we have compiled a table, from standard authors, of all known Formations, and placed them in the first column; and in the last column, each of those observed in Missouri, opposite its known equivalent.

GENERAL.	MISSOURI.
SYSTEM I. — QUATERNARY.	SYSTEM I. — QUATERNARY.
Alluvium.	Alluvium.
Newer Pleistocene.	Bottom Prairie.*
Older Pleistocene.	Bluff or Loess.*
Drift.	Drift.
SYSTEM II. — TERTIARY.	
Pleiocene.	
Meiocene.	
Eocene.	
SYSTEM III. — CRETACEOUS.	
Chalk.	
Green Sand.	
SYSTEM IV. — WEALDEN.	
Weald Clay.	
Hastings' Sand.	
Purbeck Beds.	
SYSTEM V. — OOLITIC.	
Upper.	
Middle.	
Lower.	
SYSTEM VI. — LIASSIC.	
Upper Lias.	
Marlstone.	
Lower Lias.	
SYSYEM VII. — TRIASSIC.	
Upper Trias.	
Muschelkalk.	
Lower Trias.	
SYSTEM VIII. — PERMIAN.	
Upper Permian.	
Lower Permian.	

* This may not be the exact equivalent of the corresponding Formation.

GENERAL.	MISSOURI.
SYSTEM IX. — CARBONIFEROUS.	SYSTEM IX. — CARBONIFEROUS.
Coal Measures.	Coal Measures.
Mountain Limestone.	Mountain Limestone.
SYSTEM X. — DEVONIAN.	SYSTEM X. — DEVONIAN.
Old Red Sandstone.	
Chemung Group.	Chemung Group.
Portage Group.	
Hamilton Group.	Hamilton Group.
Upper Helderberg Group.	Upper Helderberg.
Oriskany Sandstone.	
SYSTEM XI. — SILURIAN.	SYSTEM XI. — SILURIAN.
Upper Silurian.	*Upper Silurian.*
Lower Helderberg Group.	Lower Helderberg Group.
Onondaga Salt Group.	
Niagara Group.	Niagara?
Clinton Group.	
Medina Sandstone.	
Oneida Conglomerate.	
Lower Silurian.	*Lower Silurian.*
Hudson River Group.	Hudson River Group.
Utica Slate.	Utica Slate?
Trenton Limestone.	Trenton Limestone.
Black-River & Bird's-eye Limestone.	Black-River & Bird's-eye Limestone.
Chazy Limestone.	
Calciferous Sandrock.	Calciferous Sandrock.
Potsdam Sandstone.	Potsdam Sandstone?

METAMORPHIC ROCKS.

The only place where rocks, apparently metamorphic, have been observed, is at Pilot Knob. The upper part of this mountain is made up of beds of Iron Ore interstratified with metamorphic slates, more or less impregnated with iron. Some of these slates are silicious; others appear like metamorphosed conglomerates; while a few thin strata are talcose or argillaceous. These beds often contain a very large per cent. of iron; the less compact varieties, which occur towards the summit, have more of that metal than the lower beds.

They are very distinctly stratified and divided by joints into rhomboidal masses, which, in the iron beds, are often very regular. This jointed structure of the ore greatly facilitates the operation of the miners in excavating it. These strata occupy the top and south-western slope, dipping in that direction at an angle of thirty or thirty-five degrees.

These rocks, though limited in extent to a very small space, acquire an unusual importance from their association with one of the most extensive iron deposits of the State. The base of Pilot Knob, on the north-east, appears to be made up of Porphyry and Iron Ore.

IGNEOUS ROCKS.

Besides the stratified formations already described, there are in Missouri several varieties of *Igneous Rocks*. *Granite*, *Greenstone* and *Porphyry*, are the most important yet observed.

GRANITE.

In Town. 34, R. 3 E., Sec. 15, N. W. ¼, is an exposure of good red granite. The feldspar is in coarse grains or crystals of a red or flesh color; the quartz is transparent, nearly colorless, and not so coarse or abundant as the feldspar; while the mica occurs sparingly in small irregular crystalline particles of a silvery gray color.

On the west, this granite rises above the surface, at an angle of thirty or forty degrees, in a rounded dome-shaped hill, to the height of 110 feet. On the surface and at the base, there are numerous rounded masses, varying in size from four to forty feet in diameter. These boulder-like masses were produced by joints, which separated the surface of the Granite Knob into huge blocks, whose angles and edges have been removed by atmospheric and aqueous agencies, acting upon them during the long period since their upheaval. Many of them have rolled down to the base, while others remain in their original position on the Knob. Some rest upon very narrow bases; and one, about five feet in diameter, is so exactly poised on a small base that it can be moved with a very slight pressure of the finger, and is a very fine *Rocking Stone.*

The Granite is easily split into regular blocks of any desirable size and dimensions, and appears to be very durable; as the blocks at the quarry, which were split out eight years ago, show no signs whatever of disintegration. It is an excellent building material, and would, rough-hewn, produce the finest effect in all large structures and heavy masonry. It can scarcely be surpassed for city use, where strength and durability are desirable.

In other places this rock has no mica, and becomes a coarse-grained Granulite, which decomposes much more readily, and is, generally, of but little value for building purposes.

GREENSTONE.

Some four miles north-east of Pilot Knob, masses of greenish black sub-crystalline Greenstone, rest upon the slope of a Porphyritic ridge. These fragments, though not in place, came, without doubt, from localities in the neigborhood, as we saw no indication of Drift, or the agencies which produced it, in this part of the State.

PORPHYRY.

This is a compact reddish purple feldspathic rock, which breaks with a smooth conchoidal fracture, and contains crystals or fragments of different shades, usually lighter, but sometimes darker than the mass. Nearly all the hills and ridges in the neigborhood of Iron Mountain and Pilot Knob are, wholly or in part, formed of this rock. The base of Pilot Knob, near the lower part of the north-eastern slope, appears to be made up of it and iron ore. It is very variable in appearance, often resembling breccia, and at other times presenting the characteristics of metamorphosed conglomerate; and is usually separated by joints into rhombic or cuboidal blocks.

In many places it would furnish an abundance of material well adapted to all purposes where a hard beautiful surface and a fine polish is desirable; such as window-sills, hearths, jambs, mantelpieces and tables; for it is so hard, no ordinary accident or use would injure the polish or scratch its surface.

This Porphyry is one of the oldest rocks in the State. No opportunity occurred for determining whether it be older than the Granite; but there can be no doubt that it was formed before the Greenstone, and the Iron Ore of Shepherd Mountain, and the Shut-In, and probably before that of Iron Mountain, as the ore at Shepherd Mountain and the Shut-In is found filling regular fissures, like dykes, in the Porphyry of those localities. The Greenstone is said to occur in dykes in this rock. It must be older than the stratified rocks of this region, as they are usually found resting upon the knobs and ridges of the Porphyry, in a position so nearly horizontal as to preclude the idea that they were deposited before the upheaval of the principal masses which form the hills. Whether the slates interstratified with the iron, near the top of Pilot Knob, be older, is not so easily determined.

The Iron Ore of this rock gives it an unusual importance in a scientific and economical point of view; for the most important deposits of that metal in the State, are in it. The ore at Iron Mountain, Shepherd Mountain and the Shut-In, is in the Porphyry. No other minerals of any importance were seen in it.

Such are the rocks of Missouri, as they have been observed during the progress of the Survey. Several features described have appeared to us somewhat striking and peculiar. This is particularly true of the abnormal coal-beds, and the dyke-like character often assumed by the Saccharoidal Sandstone. A few of the facts stated may challenge a doubt in the minds of some; but the evidence, upon which they rest, appears perfectly conclusive.

By an examination of the sections and maps accompanying this Report, it will appear that the stratified rocks of the State lie in a position nearly horizontal. There are, however, a few important variations. The strata rise and form a Geological ridge, which commences on Salt River, in Ralls county, and extend through Pike, Callaway, Franklin and Washington to the Iron Mountain. Springfield, is also, on an elevation of the strata, which, probably, extends to the Iron Mountain. There is another elevation in the valleys of the Osage and the Niangua. Depressions, also, exist; one in the strata at St. Louis, and another, doubtless, still more important, in the South-East. But there are numerous undulations, which produce axes of elevation and depression in various parts of the State.

After passing the mouth of the Osage, in ascending the Missouri river, the strata are found dipping gradually beneath the surface, until, at the Iowa line, a part only of the upper Coal Series remains above the surface; the Silurian, Devonian and nearly all of the Carboniferous rocks having disappeared below the river. On the Osage, also, the Silurian, Devonian and Lower Carboniferous rocks successively dip below the surface, and leave the Coal Measures only exposed, in the western part of Henry county.

CHAPTER II.

ECONOMICAL GEOLOGY.

The Soil* of a country is the great source of national power, and individual wealth and happiness; it should, therefore, receive the fostering care of the State. And, besides, there is no department of human industry, whose profits have been more advanced by science, than those of agriculture, and none upon which the future prosperity of our State so much depends. The Law providing for a Geological Survey has, consequently, made it the duty of the State Geologist to give special attention to the Soils and Agricultural Resources of the State.

In order to secure for the farming interests the best possible results from the Survey, we have directed our attention to the following subjects: —

1st. To the classification of the Soils † of the State, according to their physical and chemical properties.

2d. To the determination of the amount of mineral and organic elements which enter into the composition of each variety.

3d. To the examination of their physical properties, with the design of determining the capacity of each variety for absorbing moisture from the atmosphere, and its disposition to dry on exposure to the sun; its power to absorb and retain the heat of the sun, oxygen, ammonia and other fertilizing gases.

4th. To making meteorological observations, with the view of determining the *temperature* and the *moisture* of the *atmosphere*, the *amount of rain*, the *prevailing storms* and *winds*, and, in short, to ascertain the adaptation of our climate to the various staple crops.

5th. To examine the *chemical* and *physiological properties* of the various plants cultivated, and determine their adaptation to our *soils* and *climates*.

6th. To ascertain the best systems of culture, to improve and develop the resources of our soils, and adapt them to the crops cultivated.

7th. To collect and publish all the important information respecting the experiments made for agricultural improvements.

CLASSIFICATION OF SOILS.

No department of Agricultural Science is more defective than that governing the classification of soils. No classification has, as

---

* For an account of the formation of Soils, see page 61.

† In what is said upon our soils, I have been guided by their physical properties, the rocks from which they are derived, and the trees and other plants which grow upon them. For many purposes these give indications sufficient; but a vast amount of labor must be done in the analyses of the soils, of the crops to be cultivated, and of the strata supposed to contain fertilizing properties, before we can deduce conclusion so definite and positive as to give practical cultivators the most valuable and legitimate fruits of the Agricultural Department of the Survey.

yet, been adopted, by which the many varieties of soils can be so arranged and described, that all can be easily identified. This is in some degree due to the fact, that farmers have been so averse to the use of scientific names, which are definite, that all writers upon the subject, have used the indefinite terms in common use, often, too, in a sense entirely different from their common signification among farmers. The words *loam, clay* and *mould*, having various meanings both in books and among farmers, are good illustrations of the indefinite use of agricultural terms.

The best classification of soils* yet proposed, is based upon the proportion of *Silica*, *Alumina* and *Lime*, the three earths which enter more largely than any others into the composition of soils. When *Silica* or *Sand*, is most abundant, the soil is called *Silicious* or *Sandy;* where the *Alumina* or *Clay* prevails, the soil is *Argillaceous* or *Clayey;* but when *Lime* abounds, it is *Calcareous* or *Limy*. The *Argillaceous* soils may contain an unusual quantity of *Silica*, when it would be called a *Silico-Argillaceous Soil*, or, a *Somewhat Sandy Clayey Soil.* The same principles govern the varieties of the other classes.

But a large portion of the soils of Missouri are composed of these three earths in such proportions that it is difficult to say which prevails, or to which class they properly belong. This is the case with nearly all of those founded upon the Bluff Formation.

As no analyses of soils have yet been made, it will not be possible to speak with absolute certainty respecting some of them; but their physical properties and geological relations enable us to assign many of them their proper position, and to speak with tolerable certainty of their productive powers. The soils derived from the various Formations are very materially different, yet it should not be understood that those derived from the same Formation always have the same properties; for a Formation does not always and in all parts, present the same structure and composition. The various soils derived from the Bluff fully illustrate this principle. All the

* It may not be improper to state the relations sustained by the soil to the vegetable kingdom, as it will greatly aid us in determining its value: —

1st. It serves as a foundation for, and gives mechanical support to, the plant.

2d. It supplies the plant with the inorganic and a part of the organic elements, which its nature demands.

3d. It absorbs heat, air and moisture, which are essential to healthy vegetation.

4th. It is the laboratory in which the food of the vegetable is prepared to be taken up by its roots.

pure limestones have very similar effects upon the soil, as they increase its calcareous matter, but often in different degrees.

The Alluvium of our river bottoms generally produces a light rich silicious soil, which sustains a larger growth of timber than any other in the State. This growth is Cotton Wood; * Sycamore; White and Sugar Maple; Box-Elder; Slippery and American Elm; Red Birch; Black, White and Blue Ash; Coffee Tree; Wild Cherry; Buckeye; Honey Locust; Bur, White, Swamp White, Rock Chestnut, Yellow, Laurel, Pin, Red and Scarlet Oaks; Common, Shellbark, Thick Shellbark and Pignut Hickories; Hack-Berry; Papaw; Red Bud; Black and White Walnuts; Linden; Wild Plum; Several Willows; Pecan; Mulberry, and Red Birch. The Trumpet Creeper, Poison Ivy, and several species of Grape, almost cover with their graceful foliage many of the largest trees.

This variety of soil occupies the bottoms of all our large streams, covering an area of some four or five millions of acres. It is not surpassed in fertility by any in the State, and is particularly adapted to corn and hemp. It is usually so light and porous and deep, that in wet weather the superabundance of water readily passes off; while, in drought, the roots sink deep, and the water below easily ascends by capillary attraction and keeps the surface moist. These scientific deductions are abundantly sustained by the experience of the unprecedented drought of the present season; as the corn fields, on this soil, suffered comparatively little injury from it.

The Bluff, where well developed, produces a light deep calcareo-silicious soil, of the very best quality. The alumina, silex and lime are mingled in such proportions with the other fertilizing properties in this Formation (p. 72), as to adapt it, in an admirable degree, to the formation of soils and subsoils. And, as might be expected, the soils formed upon it, under favorable circumstances, are equal to any in the country. It is usually covered with a growth of American and Slippery Elms; Wild Cherry; Coffee Tree; Honey Locust; Mulberry; Bur, Swamp White, Rock Chestnut, White, Chestnut, Black, Scarlet and Laurel Oaks; Sugar Tree; White and Blue Ashes; Hack-Berry; Common, Shellbark and Pignut Hickories; Red Bud; Red Haw; Linden; Papaw; and Black and White Walnuts.

The soil is the best where the Bluff is well developed, pulverulent and of a brownish ash color. In such localities, the American Elm; Wild Cherry; Honey Locust; Common and Pignut Hickories; Coffee Tree; White, Bur, Swamp White and Chestnut Oaks; Black Walnut, and Mulberry, are most abundant. The area covered by this, the best of all soils, is very large. It includes the greater part of Lafayette, Jackson, Clay, Platte and Andrew; and some portions of Howard, Marion, Saline, Buchanan, Holt and Atchison, and probably of several other counties, which I have not yet visited. Hemp and Corn are the favorite crops. The Bluff, when not fully developed, becomes more argillaceous and forms a soil somewhat inferior on account of the impervious nature of the subsoil. In such localities, the Common, Shellbark, Thick Shellbark and Pignut Hickories; White and Black and Scarlet Oaks; White and Black Walnuts; Sugar Tree; and White and Blue Ashes; Papaw; Hack-Berry; Red and Black Haws; and Summer, Fox and Frost Grapes, become more abundant. This variety of soil prevails in Monroe, Marion, Pike, Callaway, Audrain, Boone, Cooper, St. Louis, Chariton and St. Charles, and in parts of Cole, Moniteau and Pettis. It is well adapted to Corn, Wheat, Oats and Tobacco, and is vastly improved by subsoiling.

---

* For the scientific names of the trees and shrubs mentioned in this report, see Appendix C.

In some few high prairies and timbered ridges, the waters have washed away the finer materials of this Formation and left a poor sandy soil, which sustains a small growth of Post, White, Black and Black-Jack Oaks; Black Hickory; and Dwarf Sumachs. This variety is common in the north-west corner of Marion and in other localities. It will produce good crops of Corn and Wheat by deep and careful cultivation. Nothing, save manuring, can so much benefit it as the subsoil plow. Subsoiling and green manures would soon render it highly productive.

There is in the southern counties a reddish marly clay, probably of the same age as the Bluff, which is the foundation of a very productive and durable chocolate-colored soil. This soil when not affected by the subjacent rocks is very good, and sustains a fine growth of American, Slippery and Wahoo Elms; Honey Locust; Black Cherry; Mulberry; Black Gum; Hack-Berry; White, Red, Black, Bur, Chestnut, Rock Chestnut and Laurel Oaks; Common, Shellbark, Thick Shellbark and Pignut Hickories; Crab Apple; Black and Red Haws; Papaw; White and Blue Ashes; White and Black Walnuts. This variety of soil abounds in many of the southern counties. It is well represented in the neighborhood of Farmington, St. François county, in the beautiful valley of Arcadia, south of Pilot Knob, and in the valleys and on the slopes of that whole region. This variety, somewhat deteriorated by the small fragments of chert and sands from the underlying rocks, prevails in the south-western counties. It is well adapted to wheat, corn, oats and tobacco.*

But, where this soil is thin and filled with the chert and sand of the subjacent limestones and sandstones, it becomes very poor, useless for ordinary cultivation, and sustains a scattered growth of Black, White, Post and Black-Jack Oaks; Black Hickory; Yellow Pine; Sumachs, and Hazels. Only a stunted growth of Post Oak, Black-Jack, Black Hickory, Dwarf Sumachs and American Hazel, is found on the poorest ridges. These cherty hills and ridges are prevalent in all the southern counties, except those on the western, eastern and south-eastern borders of the State.

The *Drift* furnishes a sandy soil, more or less filled with small boulders and pebbles, which is not very productive. But the Bluff covers it so deep that it has but little influence on the soil, except in the few localities where it comes to the surface. (See Pl. III.)

The Coal Measures produce a variety of effects upon the soil, according to the character of the rocks which come to the surface. The soft micaceous sandstones render the soil arenaceous; as at Sharpsburgh, and a few localities in Henry and Bates; while the shales and clays form a very argillaceous, cold and wet soil. But the deleterious effects, usually produced by the Coal Measures, are prevented by the thick Bluff deposit, which covers nearly all the coal strata in the State. And, indeed, the very best soils of the State overlie the Coal Measures.

The *Ferruginous Sandstone* is usually so thin as to have a very little influence upon the soil; but, where it is well developed in St. Clair, Cedar and Newton counties, its decomposition renders it arenaceous and dry.

The St. Louis Limestone is of such a character as to render the soils calcareous; but it decomposes so slowly, and is generally so deep beneath the Bluff, that it has scarcely any effect upon them.

The Archimedes Limestone has a more extensive range than the formation last

---

* The prevailing winds of this part of the State very much injure tobacco grown on exposed localities; but by planting it in rows (running at right angles to the usual direction of the winds), alternating with corn, these injurious effects can be, in a good degree, avoided.

mentioned. The shales, so abundant in the upper part of it, render the soils argillaceous and consequently heavy, wet and cold; but the limestone strata yield calcareous matter, and also cherty geodes, which are often so abundant as to be very troublesome.

The Encrinital Limestone more readily decomposes and renders the soil calcareous, light and productive. The chert of the upper beds, is very frequently so abundant as to render it useless for cultivation; as may be observed in many of the bluffs of Boone, Cooper, Monroe; and, in short, wherever this formation prevails. White, Red, Black, Rock Chestnut and Chestnut Oaks; Black and White Walnuts; American and Slippery Elms; Sugar Tree; Papaw; and Red Bud, are common on it.

The Chouteau Limestone decomposes so slowly as to have but little influence over the soil. The upper part is so magnesian (see p. 102) as to exert a deleterious effect, were it not for the almost indestructible nature of these beds.

Vermicular Sandstone and *Shales.* — The upper part of this formation decomposes very rapidly and renders the soil silicious; but the shale beds exert a contrary effect, and produce a cold, wet and clayey soil; as on many of the slopes in Marion county where this rock prevails. The growth upon these wet slopes and valleys consists of Bur, Swamp White, Red, Pin and Laurel Oaks; Buckeye; Sugar Tree; American Elm; Hack-Berry; Thick Shellbark Hickory, and Linden.

In the central counties, where this formation becomes very magnesian, its decomposition so injures the soil as to render it nearly barren; as may be seen in the glades, on the bluffs and slopes of the La Mine, in Cooper. These glades produce a few stunted Crab Apples, Mulleins, Sumachs and Cacti.

Lithographic Limestone. — This rock decomposes so very slowly that its effects upon the soil, are not perceptible.

Hamilton Group. — The shales of this Formation crumble very rapidly, and produce a very wet, clayey soil, which is usually productive and covered by a heavy growth of Bur, Red, Swamp White, Pin and Laurel Oaks; Sugar Tree; Honey Locust; Box Elder; American Elm; Hack-Berry, and Buckeye; as may be seen in Marion, Town. 57, R. 6.

The Onondaga Limestone is so sparingly developed and decomposes so slowly, that it has but little influence on the soils over it, except where it becomes arenaceous, and is more easily disintegrated.

The Delthyris Shaly Limestone is but sparingly developed in the State, but it would naturally render the soil calcareous.

Cape Girardeau Limestone. — The county where this rock is found, has not been sufficiently examined to enable us to state what effects it has on the soils.

Hudson River Group. — The calcareo-magnesian shales of this Formation decompose very rapidly and form a heavy, damp and clayey, but productive soil, which sustains a heavy growth of Bur, Swamp White (called Bur Oak in Marion, Ralls and Pike), Red, Pin, Chestnut and Laurel Oaks; American and Slippery Elms; Honey Locust; Linden; Sugar Tree; Black and White Walnuts; Coffee Tree; Cherry; Hack-Berry; Buckeye; Dogwood; Red Bud; Black, White and Blue Ashes; Red Birch; Papaw; common Shellbark and Pignut Hickories.

Trenton Limestone. — Some parts of this Limestone decompose very rapidly and form a light, rich calcareous soil. It is usually covered with a fine growth of White, Bur, Rock Chestnut, Yellow, Laurel and Black Oaks; Sugar Tree; Linden; American and Slippery Elms; Red Mulberry; Papaw; common, Shellbark and Pignut Hickories; Red Bud, and Red Haw; as may be seen on North River, in Pike county.

The Black-River and Bird's-eye Limestones have nearly the same influences upon the soil as the Trenton.

Calciferous Sandrock. — The different limestone members of this Formation produce light magnesio-calcareous soils, which are very productive. The large quantity of magnesia in these soils, gives them great absorbent powers, and enables them to endure dry seasons, with comparatively little injury. The timber upon it is Black, Red, White, Laurel, Chestnut and Rock Chestnut Oaks; common Shellbark, Black and Pignut Hickory; American and Slippery Elms; Persimmon; Papaw; Red Mulberry; Red Haw; Red Bud; White and Black Walnuts; and several varieties of Grapes. Grapes, corn, wheat and oats will do well on this soil.

But, in places where the 1st, 2d and 3d Magnesian Limestones prevail, the chert from the decomposed strata is so abundant as to render the soil useless for common cultivation. These places are usually covered with a stunted growth of Black-Jack, Black, Laurel and Post Oaks; Black Hickory; American Hazel, and Dwarf Sumach. The sandstones of this Formation usually render the soil light and arenaceous.

When we have collected all the plants and trees, and carefully compared and arranged them according to the quality of the soils, much more perfect catalogues can be made out, and such ones as will well characterize each important variety of soil.

CHEMICAL PROPERTIES AND ANALYSIS OF SOILS.

To make useful Analyses of Soils, requires all the ability* of the skillful and experienced analyst, the most delicate and perfect apparatus, and reagents chemically pure. The process is long and complicated. This will be very obvious, when we take into consideration the fact, that the presence or absence of some ingredients of the soil, in proportions as small as one or two grains in a thousand, often renders it productive or sterile; while those ingredients are detected and separated with the greatest difficulty.

As has been stated (page 44), every plant must obtain from the soil certain inorganic elements, such as silica, lime, etc., and from the atmosphere and water a portion, at least, of their organic ingredients, as oxygen, hydrogen, carbon and nitrogen. As the air, in all places and at all times, has about the same composition, plants do not usually suffer for the ingredients which come from that source. But as the quantity of water, and the quantity and quality of the soil, are variable, the elements derived from those sources may be too abundant, deficient, or entirely wanting.

If water be deficient, the sap fails and the plant dries up. If it be too abundant, the roots are drowned, and decay. When the soil is too dry, subsoiling will often obviate the difficulty by loosening

---

* Many practical men have been led into fatal errors by those pretenders, who have advertised cheap sets of apparatus and chemicals for sale, and who have represented it as an easy matter for intelligent farmers to analyze their own soils.

the earth for the roots to penetrate below the action of the sun, and for the water to find a more ready passage to the surface by capillary attraction.

When the water is too abundant it can be drawn off by ditching and subsoiling, so that under ordinary circumstances a crop need not suffer from a superabundance or a dearth of water.

In order that any given plant, as wheat, may come to perfection, all of its inorganic elements must be in the soil within range of its roots. If silicate of potassa be wanting, the stock will be weak and the grain lodge; if Carbon, Lime or Phosphorus be deficient, the kernel will not fill. If too much vegetable matter be present, the stock will grow large and succulent, rust will strike it and the wind will prostrate it.

As Chemical Analysis gives us the elements and their exact proportions in every plant, so by an analysis of a soil, we can tell whether it is adapted to any given crop, and what elements, if any, are deficient.

When these facts are ascertained, the farmer will be able to add to his soils the ingredients needed, in the most economical manner.

When our soils are all collected, analyzed and classified, we shall be able to give a large amount of information, which will prove very valuable to our farming community.

PHYSICAL PROPERTIES OF SOILS.

Though the fertility of a soil mainly depends upon its composition, there are other qualities which exert an important influence over the growth of the plant. It is true the physical properties depend mainly upon the elements of which the soil is composed, and they, consequently, give very correct indications of its fertility. A knowledge of the physical properties, which indicate and promote fertility, is of the highest importance to the farmer, as it will enable him to select those most productive and to improve the defective. The following are the most important physical properties of soils: —

1st. The *Specific Gravity or Density* of a soil depends upon the elements which enter into its composition and their mechanical arrangement.

According to Johnston —

" A cubic foot of dry Silicious or Calcareous Sand, weighs				180 lbs.	
"	"	" half sand and half clay,	.	" 95	"
"	"	" common arable land, .	.	" 80 to 90	"
"	"	" rich garden mould,	.	" 75	"
"	"	" peaty or vegetable soil,	.	" 39 to 50	"

The density of soils can be increased or diminished by adding other ingredients, or by mechanical means. When soils are very loose and light, they are borne away by winds and water, and do not give sufficient support to the plants growing upon them. This quality often proves injurious to winter grain in dry seasons, when the soil is not protected by frost or snow. The *roller* is often used with success in such cases. Soils too dense, are best improved by deep and thorough plowing, and by the addition of vegetable matter in the form of straw or mould, or by *green manuring*.

2d. *Firmness and Adhesiveness.* — Argillaceous soils are usually rendered too firm and adhesive by an abundance of water. This, for many reasons, is a very serious defect, and should be remedied, when practicable, by *subsoiling* or *trenching*, or by the addition of lime and vegetable mould or green manures; as vegetable matter tends to render a soil light and porous.

3d. *Power of Imbibing Moisture.* — This is a very necessary quality of a soil in a climate like ours, where the summers are long and dry, as by it the moisture, carried off by evaporation from soil and plant during the day, may be restored by absorption from the dews and humidity of the night.

The following table shows the comparative absorbing power of the various ingredients of soils: —

Silicious Sand, . .	0	Pure Clay, . . .	48
Gypsum, . .	1	Carbonate of Lime, .	35
Calcareous Sand, . .	3	Carbonate of Magnesia,	80
Common Soil, . . .	23	Humus, . . .	110
Sandy Clay, . . .	28	Garden Mould, . .	50
Loamy Clay, . . .	34	Slaty Marl, . . .	32

From this table it will be seen that silex absorbs nothing; and that while gypsum absorbs one grain, humus absorbs one hundred and ten. It also indicates the means of giving soils absorbent powers. The addition of vegetable matter and carbonate of magnesia and thorough cultivation, are the best means of increasing this very essential quality of all good soils.

4th. *Power of Containing and Retaining Water.* — A moderate degree of these properties is very important. Loose sandy soils are rendered barren for a want of the power to contain water.

If the power of pure sand to contain water be represented by 25 —

Pure Clay will be, .	70	Carbonate of Magnesia, .	256
Carbonate of Lime will be,	85	Gypsum, . . .	27
Garden Mould, " "	89	Slaty marl, . . .	34
Humus, . . " "	181	Common Soil, . . .	52

The power of retaining water exists in these substances in nearly the same ratio as that of containing it; it is greatest in magnesia and least in sand. Water will evaporate much more rapidly from sandy than from magnesian, calcareous or vegetable soils.

5th. *Contractibility on Drying.* — As a general rule, those soils which contain the greatest amount of water, contract the most on drying. An excess of this property is much more injurious to clayey soils, which crack and bake hard, than to those which are so friable that they become pulverulent on drying.

6th. *The Power of Absorbing and Retaining Heat.* — The color and texture of the soil, in an eminent degree, govern its powers of absorbing the heat of the sun. The dark soils absorb much more than the light-colored ones. Sandy soils, also, absorb more than clayey. It might be supposed that those soils which absorb heat the most rapidly would, also, lose it with greater facility; but this is far from the truth. For while clays and vegetable mould are heated slowly, they give off their caloric with great facility.

7th. *Power of Absorbing Gases.* — Soils possess the power of absorbing oxygen, ammonia and carbonic acid from the air, and conveying them, properly prepared, to the roots of plants. Vegetable mould absorbs oxygen and converts it into carbonic acid. Argillaceous soils, well tempered with vegetable mould, possess the ability to absorb gases in an eminent degree. When soils are light, porous and moist, they are in the best condition to exercise this power.

While these principles, which apply to soils in general, may be of great service to us, the examination of the physical properties of our own soils, will enable us to give more detailed information for their improvement and adaptation to climate and crops. A soil may be adapted to one climate, which would not be fertile in another, possessing more or less of rain and heat.

According to the principles above stated, the calcareo-magnesian and vegetable soils, so prevalent in Cedar, Moniteau, Cole, Gasconade, Franklin, Osage, Camden, Morgan, Benton, Polk, Dallas, St. Clair, Miller and other counties, must be warm, capable of sustaining severe droughts, and are eminently adapted to the culture of the grape; as is abundantly indicated by the luxuriance of the wild vines growing upon it. These facts, together with the high and salubrious character of the country, and the long, dry and temperate summers, offer inducements to vine-growers scarcely to be met with elsewhere.

The profits of grape culture are very great in proportion to the capital required; and with our adaptation of soil and climate, it can be easily made one of our principal sources of wealth and luxury.

Mr. Buffum, in a speech in the California Assembly, makes the following statement: —

"In Los Angelos, the number of bearing vines amounts to 800,000; the number of acres under grape culture is 1,500; the quantity of wine which can be made to the acre is 400 gallons; the amount of capital invested in the grape culture is $1,000,000; and the number of persons engaged in the various branches of the trade is 4,000. Thus, these 1,500 acres only under grape culture can produce 600,000 gallons of wine annually, which, at two dollars per gallon, will yield, in this single district, the annual income of $1,200,000."

This shows a very large profit for the capital invested.

Now, in Southern Missouri, there are at least 1,000,000 acres which give every indication of being eminently adapted to the vine culture. Were only half of these in cultivation, and the yield 100 gallons per acre, but one-fourth the above estimate, the price of the wine, at one dollar per gallon, would be $50,000,000.

IMPROVEMENT OF SOILS.

All operations for the improvement of soils, may be classed under *Manuring* and *Tillage:* the first, to change the *chemical composition* of soils, or add the ingredients needed for the nourishment of the crops; and the second, to change the *physical properties* of the soils, or adapt them to the climate and the crops.

In a country so new as ours, whose virgin soils are rich in all needed fertilizing ingredients, but little thought is usually given to manuring; yet, both science and observation warn us against a mode of cultivation which must eventually leave us the poor heritage of exhausted lands. It has already been stated that every plant takes its inorganic ingredients from the soils; if these be removed from year to year and nothing restored, the process of exhaustion is surely progressing, and will be completed in a time proportionate to the richness of the lands and the modes of cultivation. By weighing and analyzing the crop, we can determine what and how much, is yearly removed from the soil. By analyzing the soil and considering the mode of cultivation, an approximation may be made to the time it will remain fertile.

Farms, where the crops are fed to stock, are much more slowly exhausted than those whose products are removed to market; as animals return to the earth nearly all the matter taken from it by the growth of their food. By the cultivation of wheat and tobacco, the rich soils of Virginia were exhausted in one hundred years; and in that time, these crops, according to Liebig's estimate, removed from each acre 12,000 pounds of alkalies in leaves, grain and straw. An approximation to the amount taken from the soil by the different crops can be obtained from the following tables: Table I. is from Whitley's Geology of Agriculture, and Table II. is compiled from Liebig's Chemistry of Agriculture.

TABLE I.

According to SPRENGEL.	Potassa.	Soda.	Lime.	Magnesia.	Alumina.	Oxide of Iron.	Oxide of Manganese.	Silica.	Sulphuric Acid.	Phosphoric Acid.	Chlorine.	Total of fixed* Ingredients.	Fixed* Ingredients.	Azote.	Water and Carbon.
	FIXED* INGREDIENTS IN 100,000 lbs. EACH OF THE FOLLOWING VEGETABLES.												FIXED AND VOLATILE INGREDIENTS, According to BOUSSAINGAULT.	Volatile Ingred's.	
Wheat,	225	240	96	69	26			400	50	400	10	2137	2430	3510	94,060
Wheat straw,	20	29	240	32	90 (Alumina and Oxide of Iron together)			2870	37	170	30	3518	6970	350	92,680
Barley,	278	290	106	180	25			1182	59	210	19	2349		2020	95,631
Barley straw,	180	48	554	76	146	14	20	3856	118	160	72	5244		260	94,498
Oats,	150	132	86	67	14	40		1976	35	70	10	2580	3980	2240	93,780
Oat straw,	870	2	152	22	6	2	2	4588	79	12	5	5740	5090	380	94,530
Rye,	532 (Potassa and Soda together)		122	44	24	42	34	164	23	46	9	1040	2370	1690	95,340
Rye straw,	32	11	178	12	25 (Alumina and Oxide of Iron together)			2297	170	51	17	2793	3680	300	96,020
Beans,	415	816	165	158	34			126	89	292	41	2136		5130	92,734
Bean straw, dry,	1656	50	624	209	10	7	5	220	34	226	80	3121		1000	95,879
Vetches,	897	622	160	142	22	9	5	200	50	140	43	2290			
Straw of vetches, dry,	1810	52	1955	324	15	9	8	442	122	280	84	5101		1570	98,329
Peas,	810	739	58	136	20	10		410	53	190	38	2464	3140	4180	92,680
Pea straw, *green*,	235		2730	342	60	20	7	996	337	240	4	4971	(11000 dry)	1000	94,029
Lucerne, do.,	362	166	1304	94	8	8		90	109	353	86	2580		300	97,120
Sainfoin, do.,	494	105	527	69	16			120	82	220	38	1671		500	97,829
Red clover, do.,	419	111	584	70	3			76	94	138	76	1571	(7760 dry)	500	97,929
Potatoes, *fresh*,	390	234	33	32	5	2¾		8½	54	40	15½	814	(3900 do.)	500	98,686
Turnips, do.,	73	110	127	22	8	2	2	40	41	73	23	556	(7580 do.)	168	99,276
Swedes, dry,	2651	1164	835	282	40	35		475	890	408	266	7046			
Carrots, do.,	2718	709	505	295	30	25	46	105	208	395	54	5090		2400	92,510
Beet-root, do.,	1481	3178	285	139	20	58	50	105	123	167	380	5986	6240	1660	92,100
Cabbage, do.,	1847	578	1822	202	11	151	40	529	774	436	518	6908		5550	88,542

* Those which will not burn away, but remain in the ashes.

The bulk of the plant consists, as the table shows, of "water (or its ingredients) and carbon."

The nutritive power is nearly in proportion to the "azote."

The "fixed or mineral ingredients" are the guides for appropriating the manure to the crop.

The distinction between "dry," and "fresh or green," must be particularly attended to; lucerne, etc., often losing three-fourths of their weight in drying; so that 100,000 lbs. "dry" would contain four times as much fixed ingredients as the same weight "green." And turnips lose from four-fifths to nine-tenths their weight; so that 100,000 lbs. of "fresh" may be only 10,000 lbs. when "dry."

RECENT ANALYSES OF THE ASHES OF PLANTS.—TABLE II.

Plants, or Parts of Plants.	Ashes per cent.	Potash.	Soda.	Magnesia.	Lime.	Phosphoric Acid.	Sulphuric Acid.	Silica.	Peroxide of Iron.	Chloride of Sodium.	Chloride of Potassium.	Locality of the Plant.	Analyst.
Wheat, grain,		6.43	27.79	12.98	3.91	46.14	0.27	0.42	0.50			Holland,	Bichon.
Wheat, grain,		24.17	10.34	13.57	3.01	45.53		1.91	0.52			Solz,	Thon.
White Wheat, grain,		33.84		13.54	3.09	49.21			0.31			Giessen,	Will and Fresenius.
Red Wheat, grain,		21.87	15.75	9.60	1.93	49.32	0.17		1.36			Giessen,	Will and Fresenius.
Barley, grain,		3.91	16.79	10.05	3.36	40.63	0.26	21.99	1.93			Cleves,	Bichon.
Rye, grain,		32.76	4.45	10.13	2.92	47.29	1.46	0.17	0.82			Giessen,	Will and Fresenius.
Rye, grain,		11.43	18.89	10.57	7.05	51.81	0.51	0.69	1.90			Cleves,	Bichon.
Rye, straw,		17.19		2.41	9.06	3.82	0.83	64.50	1.36	0.57	0.26	Giessen,	Will and Fresenius.
Oats, grain,		12.3		7.7	3.7	14.9	1.0	53.3	1.3		1.0	Alsace,	Boussingault.
Oats, straw,		12.18	13.01	4,58	7.29	1.94	2.15	54.25	1.41	2.48		Giessen,	Levi.
Maize, straw,	6.5	14.46	39.92	1.84	5.35	11.76	0.59	18.89	0.90	6.29		Styria,	Hruschauer.
Maize, straw,	2.3	4.00	10.57	9.58	9.68	18.76	0.68	29.36	0.61	0.46		Styria,	Hruschauer.
Buckwheat, grain,		8.74	20.10	10.38	6.66	50.07	2.16	0.69	1.05			Cleves,	Bichon.
Hempseed,	5.60	21.67	0.66	1.00	26.71	34.96	0.10	14.04	0.77	00.9		Giessen,	Leuchtweiss.
Linseed,	4.63	25.85	0.71	0.22	25.98	40.11	0.99	0.92	3.67	1.55		Giessen,	Leuchtweiss.
Phaseolus Vulg., or common bean,		21.71	21.07	7.35	5.38	35.33	2.28	1.48	0.34	3.32		Hesse Cassel,	Thon.
		51.23		12.03	6.07	28.53	1.36	1.05			0.21	Alsace,	Boussingault.
Clover, Red,	11.17	16.10	40.71	8.28	21.91	4.12	1.06	2.60	0.46	4,73		Giessen,	Horsford.
Vine,	2.25	24.93	7.00	8.79	35.94	19.55	2.35	0.62	0.24	0.58		Styria,	Hruschauer.
Vine,	2.83	17.55	26.76	9.17	30.33	2.85	2.01	1.61	6.63	3.05		Worms,	Levi.
Quercus Robur, Wood,		5.65	3.77	3.01	50.58	2.32	0.78	0.52	0.38	0.02		Giessen,	Denninger.
Quercus Robur, Seeds,		64.64		5.57	6.86	19.19		0.96	1.89	0.98		Giessen,	Kleinschmidt.
Ulmus Campestris, Wood,		21.92	13.72	7.71	47.80	3.33	1.28	3.07	1.17			Giessen;	Wrighton.
Ulmus Campestris, Bark,		2.22	10.09	3.19	72.70	1.59	0.62	8.77	0.82			Giessen,	Wrighton.
Tilia Europea, Bark,		16.14	4.53	8.03	60.81	4.02	0.75	2.27	1.24	2.21		Giessen,	L. Hofmann.
Tilia Europea, Wood,		35.80	5.23	4.15	29.93	4.85	5.30	5.26	7.97	1.49		Giessen,	L. Hofmann.
Tobacco,		30.67		8.57	27.12	1.88	3.27		4.15	5.95		Debreczyn,	Will and Fresenius.
Tobacco,		27.88		7.31	33.84	1.99	3.75		4.40	9.34	4.90	Debreczyn,	Will and Fresenius.
Tobacco,		18.20		15.73	32.06	2.12	5.91		4.68	11.41	3.92	Banat,	Will and Fresenius.
Tobacco,		19.55	0.27	11.07	48.68	3.66	3.29		2.99	3.54		Funfkirchen	Will and Fresenius.
Tobacco,		11.21		12.77	49.16	1 97	2.98		4.33	2.58	2.97	Funfkirchen	Will and Fresenius.
Hops, entire plant,	9.87	25.18		5.77	15 98	12.13	5.41	21.50	5.12	7.24	1.67	England,	Nesbit.
Hops, leaves,	13.6	14.95	0.39	2.39	49.67	3.52	5.04	12.14	2.41	9.49		England,	Nesbit.
Hops, stalks and tendrils,	3.74	24.35		4.10	38.73	6.92	3.44	6.07	0.28	6.47	9.64	England,	Nesbit.
Hemp, entire plant { Leaves, Stalks,	22.00 / 4.54	5.45	0.72	4.88	42.05	3.22	1.10	6.75			3.22	England,	Kane. { Carded hemp c'ntain'd only ¼ per cent. ashes.
Flax, entire plant,	5.00	0.57	9.82	7.79	12.33	10.84	2.65	21.35			5.07	England,	Kane.

But how shall the exhaustion of the soil be prevented? Simply by restoring to it the ingredients found to be deficient, which, in the cultivation of wheat, are usually phosphoric acid and the alkalies, substances needed in small quantities only. When soils, exhausted by wheat, are analyzed, phosphoric acid and lime are usually deficient. Now, an acre of wheat needs but seventeen pounds of phosphoric acid and sixteen pounds of lime, both of which would be supplied by sixty-eight pounds of bone-ashes, sowed with the wheat; whereas, it would require many tons of stable manure to supply that quantity of lime and phosphoric acid, while the other ingredients of that dressing might prove injurious; as they certainly would, in a soil rich in vegetable matter, as are the most of those in Missouri.

We are now prepared to judge of the value of those quack fertilizers, called composts, which are said to cure all diseases of all soils, and of "the good old way of our fathers," which cured all defects of soil by stable manure. The latter, it is true, is much preferable to the former, as stable manure contains nearly all the ingredients of the staple crops. But it is often attended with great waste, and sometimes with positive injury. And he who follows it should well understand the constituents of his soil and the elements conveyed to it by the manures. This is especially true in Missouri, where the ingredients, always abundant in stable manure, often exist in the soils in such quantities as to prove injurious to some crops.

The comparative merits of the three methods of farming alluded to, which I may call the *good old way*, the *compost method* and the *scientific*, were happily illustrated by an experiment of a progressive farmer. He sowed a field of rich clayey loam with wheat. The straw was luxuriant and healthy; but the kernel was badly filled, and the crop almost a failure.

The next year he was resolved to remedy the evil, and discover the cause of failure. A gray-headed old farmer told him he must give it a good dressing of stable manure; for he had tried it forty years without failure. An agent told him, he must use his Patent Compost, for it had never failed. An agricultural chemist advised him to use green sand from a bank in another part of his field. He resolved to give five acres to an experiment according to the advice of each. Upon the first five acres, he spread twenty cords of manure, at an expense of seven dollars per acre. The second five he treated with the compost (of ashes, lime and some vegetable matter), at an expense of ten dollars per acre. But upon the last five he spread ten tons of the green sand, at a cost of two dollars per acre.

On the first five acres the straw was large and thrifty, but succulent and weak; the rust struck it, and portions of it lodged badly; it was poorly filled, and yielded but ten bushels per acre. The second portion was much like the first, except the straw was not so large; it was less injured by rust, and remained erect till harvest; but was poorly filled and yielded but five bushels to the acre. The third was not so large; but the straw was firm, clean and yellow; it was well filled, and gave twenty-five bushels per acre.

The soil possessed enough organic matter, but was deficient in phosphoric acid, which was supplied by the sand and not by the compost. The stable manure gave the phosphoric acid and such an excess of vegetable matter as to render the stalk succulent and predisposed to rust. The compost, also, injuriously for wheat, increased the vegetable matter. For corn, the stable manure might have been best. Stable manure is, also, admirably adapted to restore the soils, from which the feed of stock is derived, as it will contain the elements removed by the crop consumed. Composts, too, may be used with great profit when the composition is adapted to the wants of the soil.

But *green manure*, or crops plowed in while green, is best adapted to most of the deteriorated lands of our State, particularly those exhausted by corn; as they will be found deficient in potassa, soda and phosphoric acid and vegetable matter, which the clover would restore. The long tap-roots of the clover* will obtain the acid and alkalies from the subsoil; and the leaves, other needed elements from the air; and all will be restored to the soil. Many of our farmers have used clover with great success. Buckwheat may be used to better advantage on lands exhaused by wheat, as it contains many times as much phosphoric acid as clover. In short, the crop used should be adapted to the wants of the soil. Clover will return to the soil four times as much organic matter as it extracts from it; it also supplies large quantities of the alkalies; and is well adapted to the restoration of corn lands.

TILLAGE.

But many of the soils of Missouri can be greatly improved by a change of their physical properties through a judicious system of deep and thorough tillage. Some of these changes can be accomplished in the best manner by the combined use of the common and the subsoil plows. A furrow should be cut some eight or ten inches deep with the common plow, then the subsoil plow should follow at a depth of twelve or fourteen inches, making, in all, twenty to twenty-four inches of loosened soil. Whether the subsoil should be thrown up to the top or suffered to remain below, depends upon the character of the soil and subsoil, and what crops are to be cultivated.

The second variety of soil formed upon the bluff deposit (see p. 139), is greatly improved by subsoil plowing. The subsoil is dense, clayey and almost impervious to water, in its undisturbed state, and can exert no beneficial effects upon the crop; but when it is thoroughly subsoiled, the water and air, with the accompanying fertilizing gases, and heat penetrate and prepare it to receive the roots of the plants and to yield them food.

---

* Clover should be plowed in before full bloom, as the flowers give off nitrogen, which ought to be retained in the soil.

Subsoiling confers many advantages. It furnishes an additional amount of soil to receive the roots and prepare food for their nourishment; it permits the water to percolate through the soil and deposit the fertilizing gases absorbed by it from the air; it so loosens the subsoil that air and heat may permeate through it and elaborate the elements needed by plants; by it the excess of water passes through the soil, instead of running over its surface and removing the fertilizing properties; by its influence the soil dries much quicker after a rain and can be worked much earlier in the spring; it, also, provides against the injurious effects of a drought, by enabling the roots to penetrate the moist earth below the influence of the sun's rays, and by so loosening the soil that the water will more rapidly rise to the surface by capillary attraction; and by it the crops will ripen some two weeks earlier and escape the early frosts. Thus, subsoiling furnishes more food to the crop, prevents the injurious effects of a superabundance of water, and provides a reservoir of that element to counteract the influences of droughts. These beneficial results have been fully realized by several of our farmers during the past two years, and particularly during the excessive drought of the present season. For, while the other fields were very much burned, scarcely a leaf curled on some that were subsoiled.

The following letter was addressed to several gentlemen, who had used the subsoil plow, in order to obtain the results of their experiments: —

COLUMBIA, MO., *August 24th*, 1854.

MY DEAR SIR —

I take the liberty to address you for information on the following subjects; that I may publish it in my Geological Report, and give others the benefit of your experience in subsoiling: —

1st. — Have you subsoiled any of your land?
2d. — How deep did you stir the soil?
3d. — What was the character of the subsoil?
4th. — Is it Prairie or Timber Land?
5th. — When was it subsoiled?
6th. — In what crops was it cultivated?
7th. — What was the increase of the crop from deep plowing?
8th. — Was the good effect perceptible after the first year?
9th. — Were the crops injured by the drought of this or the past seasons?
10th. — At what would you estimate the increased profit of cultivation per acre, by the system of deep plowing?

An early reply will greatly oblige,

Your obedient serv't,

G. C. SWALLOW,
State Geologist.

ELI E. BASS, ESQ.,
Boone Co., Mo.

The following answers only were received: —

COLUMBIA, *September 9th*, 1854.

PROF. G. C. SWALLOW.

Dear Sir, — Your favor of August 24th, was not taken from the office for several days after it was written, and I have to apologize to you for delaying my reply so long.

I proceed to answer the questions, contained in your letter, *seriatim*: —

1st. — I have, during the last year or two, subsoiled a small portion of my land.

2d. — It was double plowed; the subsoil plow, which followed a large Carey, attaining a depth, below the surface, of from fourteen to sixteen inches.

3d. — The subsoil was chiefly clay, of a dark yellow color.

4th. — Mine is timbered land.

5th. — It was subsoiled in the spring (April), and in September.

6th. — The field subsoiled in the spring was cultivated in corn; that in September, in wheat.

7th. — The increase of each crop, I should estimate, amounted to twenty-five per cent.

8th. — The good effect of subsoiling, both in breaking the ground, and in increased product, was very perceptible after the first year.

9th. — On one of my subsoiled fields I have raised a crop of corn this year. It is a poor crop. Calculating largely upon the deep plowing, I drilled the corn and left it very thick, instead of planting it in the usual way. This, connected with the continued drought, caused the failure. If it had been planted three and a half feet apart each way, leaving two stalks in the hill, I would have raised, even this *unprecedented dry year*, a fine crop.

10th. — I would estimate the increased profit of cultivation, by the system of deep plowing, at from twenty to thirty per cent. per acre.

I am, most respectfully,
Your obedient servant,
JAMES S. ROLLINS.

FOREST HILL, BOONE COUNTY, *September 5th*, 1854.

SIR, —

Yours of the 24th ult. came to hand a few days since. I herewith submit the answers to your interrogatories in the order in which they were propounded: —

1st. — I have subsoiled the two past years.

2d. — My plows run to the depth of ten or twelve inches.

4th. — The land double plowed is prairie.

5th. — It was subsoiled in the spring of 1853.

6th. — It was cultivated in corn.

7th. — The crop was, at least, double.

8th. — Cannot tell, on account of the drought.

9th. — It was injured seriously this year, but not last.

10th. — The profits of cultivation are doubled.

I have, occasionally, double plowed for wheat, and found it of considerable benefit. My crop of corn is greatly injured by drought this season, but it is in part owing to its being planted too thick. So far as I have observed through the county, the only tolerable crops produced this year, are the results of deep plowing.

Yours, very respectfully,
ELI E. BASS.

PROF. G. C. SWALLOW,
State Geologist.

Results equally beneficial might be obtained on a very large portion of the soils of Cooper, Howard, Moniteau, Boone, Audrain, Monroe, Marion, Pike, Callaway and St. Louis counties, and, doubtless, in four-fifths of all the land in the State; which would give an increased profit from farming, far exceeding all of our most sanguine expectations.

It may be proper to state that some have not obtained such beneficial results; but, in all cases of apparent failure, the stiff clayey subsoil was brought to the top, whereas it should have remained in its original position, unless the soil was too light and sandy, when a portion, sufficient to give it the proper consistency, should have been raised to the surface.

COAL.

Mineral Coal has done much to promote the rapid progress of the present century; commerce and manufactures could not have reached their present unprecedented prosperity without its aid. And no people can expect success in those departments of human industry, unless their territory furnishes an abundance of this useful mineral. Previous to the present Survey, it was known that coal existed in many counties of the State; but there was no definite knowledge of the continuation of workable beds over any considerable areas. But since the Survey commenced, the south-eastern outcrop of the Coal Measures, has been traced from the mouth of the Des Moines, through Clark, Lewis, Marion, Monroe, Audrain, Boone, Cooper, Pettis, Henry, St. Clair, Bates and Jasper, into the Indian Territory; from Glasgow up the Missouri river to the Iowa line; and from St. Joseph along the line of the Hannibal and St. Joseph Railroad, to Shelby, showing the existence of the Coal Measures over an area of more than 26,000 square miles, in the Northern and Western parts of the State. Regular Coal Measures, also, exist in Ralls, Montgomery, Callaway, St. Charles and St. Louis; and local deposits of cannel and bituminous coal in Moniteau, Cole, Morgan and probably other counties.

Workable beds of good coal exist in nearly all places where the Coal Measures are developed, as some of the best beds are near the base, and must crop out on the borders of the coal-field. This is found to be the fact where examinations have been made. All of the little outliers along the borders contain more or less coal, though the strata are not more than ten or fifteen feet thick.

But exclusive of these outliers and local deposits, we have an area of 26,887 square miles (see p. 89) of the regular Coal Measures. If the average thickness of workable coal be one foot only, it will give 26,887,000,000* tons for the whole

* The Mining Engineers of England, allow 1,000,000 tons per square mile for every foot of workable coal.

area occupied by coal rocks. But in many places, the thickness of the workable beds, is over fifteen feet; and the least estimate that can be made for the whole area, is five feet. This will give 134,435,000,000 tons of good available coal in our State. In our efforts to estimate the economical value of so vast a deposit of this most useful mineral, we should constantly bear in mind the position of these beds, beneath the soil of one of the richest agricultural regions on the Continent, within a State whose manufacturing and commercial facilities and resources are scarely inferior to any, and adjacent to the Missouri river, and the Pacific, the North Missouri and the Hannibal and St. Joseph Railroads. With all these advantages of location, the certainty that these coal-beds can furnish 100,000,000 tons per annum for the next 1,300 years, and then have enough left for a few succeeding generations, is a fact of no small importance to the State. All of the counties in the Platte Purchase, except Nodaway, have been set down heretofore, as belonging to the Lower Carboniferous rocks, and destitute of coal; but my first excursion in the Survey, proved, beyond a possibility of doubt, the existence of Coal Measures throughout their whole extent, and that, if the lower coal-beds do not thin out, Atchison, Holt, Andrew, Buchanan and Platte are underlaid by all the workable coal-beds of the State. There are, then, more than 20,000 square miles in those counties which, at least, have an average thickness of ten feet of workable coal,* which will yield 20,000,000,000 tons.

The local deposits of Cannel and Common Bituminous varieties, furnish some of the best coal in the State, and, though many of these beds will not yield sufficient quantities for exportation or extensive manufacturing purposes, they are of great value for supplying the local demand. But some of the beds of the Cannel varieties could furnish a very large supply of an excellent article for gas and those manufacturing purposes, where a light pure coal, producing an abundance of flame, is desirable. A more detailed account of these coals will be given in the reports of Callaway, Cooper, Moniteau, Morgan and Cole counties, where they are most abundant.

When our coals are all collected, and have been subjected to analyses and practical tests, we shall be prepared to speak with more certainty of their qualities and adaptation to the various manufacturing purposes. As yet, we can judge of them only by their physical properties and the manner in which they burn on the grate. But there can be no reasonable doubt that our various beds will furnish any desirable quantities adapted to all the uses, to which bituminous coals are applied.

IRON.

Among minerals, Iron stands preëminent in its influence upon the power and prosperity of a nation. Nations, who possess it in large quantities, and by whom it is extensively manufactured, seem to partake of its hardy nature and sterling qualities. Missouri possesses an inexhaustible supply of the very best ores of this metal.

* There can be no mistake about the existence of this vast amount of coal, only on the supposition that in these counties the several coal-beds thin out, a supposition scarcely in the limits of possibility; as nearly all of the beds have appeared wherever the whole of the Lower Coal Measures have been observed. They, also, grow thicker towards the west, until they dip beneath the Middle and Upper Coal Series. And besides, coal strata are more permanent away from the borders of a coal basin, and where buried beneath superincumbent strata.

She, also, has all desirable facilities for becoming the great Iron Mart of the Western Continent.

Specular Oxide. — This is, probably, the most abundant and valuable ore in the State. Iron Mountain is the largest mass observed, and is made up almost exclusively of this ore in its purest form; as it contains no perceptible quantity of other mineral, save some less than one per cent. of silica,* which improves rather than injures its quality.

But little need be said of this Mountain of Iron, as there is no room for speculation or doubt as to the quantity or quality — one is inexhaustible, and the other can not be improved for many purposes. The quantity above the level of the valley is easily estimated. The height of the Mountain is 228 feet, and its base covers an area of 500 acres, which gives, according to Dr. Litton,* 1,655,280,000 cubic feet, or 230,187,375 tons of ore. But this is only a fraction of the ore at this locality. The nature of the ore, the plutonic character of the associated rocks and the position † of the ore beneath the level of the valley, and the sedimentary rocks skirting the base of the mountain, all indicate its igneous origin, and that it extends downwards indefinitely, enlarging as it descends. But, on the supposition that it continues of the same size, every foot of descent will give over 3,000,000 tons of ore. Each one can judge for himself, how deep he will be compelled to go to get *enough.*

Several veins of this ore, of good quality, are found intersecting the Porphyry at the Shut-in, in Town. 33, R. 4, N. ½ Sec. 2. The largest vein exposed is nearly vertical, ranging north and south, and is one foot thick. One of the first iron furnaces in this part of the country, was erected at this place. There are other important localities of this ore in the neighborhood of Pilot Knob, which I have not seen. The Bogy or Buford ‡ Ore Bed, in Town. 33, R. 3 E., N. E. ¼ Sec. 24; the Big Bogy ‡ Mountain, in Town. 33, R. 3 E., S. E. ¼ Sec. 13, and the Russell ‡ Mountain, in Town. 33, R. 3 E., E. ½ Sec. 3, are the most noted.

The Specular and Magnetic Oxides. — At Shepherd Mountain the ore is usually a mixture of these varieties (the magnetic being the least abundant), in a very pure state; as they yield less than two per cent. of silex and alumina, which are the only substances perceptible

* See Dr. Litton's Report, pp. 77 and 78.

† See Sec. 20, p. 77, Dr. Litton's Report.

‡ See Dr. Litton's Report, p. 83.

in the most of the ore; and they do not injure its quality. The ore at this mountain exists in vertical veins, ranging in different directions through the porphyry of which the mountain is composed. They vary in thickness from one foot to fourteen. Three of these veins have been partially explored.* They will yield an enormous amount of ore, as they, doubtless, continue downward indefinitely; for they have every appearance of an igneous origin. They exist in nearly perpendicular fissures in a plutonic rock; the walls of these fissures appear to be striated in places; the purple porphyry on each side has lost its color and become very soft and somewhat friable, as might be expected from such a rock, after exposure to heat and the action of atmospheric influences; and fragments of the porphyry, were detected in the ore and changed in the same manner as the wall rocks. Such facts, it seems to me, indicate an igneous origin, and the indefinite continuation of the veins in a downward direction.

Silicious Specular Oxide.—The ore of the Pilot Knob, is somewhat different from the other iron ore of this neighborhood, both in appearance and composition.† It is more compact and breaks with a gray steel-like fracture, and contains ten or twenty per cent. of silica. The silica should make the ore no less valuable, as the presence of that mineral usually renders it more fusible, and better adapted to some uses. Pilot Knob is 581 feet high (its base, 537 feet above St. Louis), and it covers an area of 360 acres. A large portion of this mountain is pure ore; but it is not so easy to estimate the quantity, as it is interstratified with the slates, which, together with the ore, form the greater portion of the mountain. At any rate, the quantity is enormous, and may be considered inexhaustible. The amount above the surface can not be less than 13,972,773 tons.† But it evidently far exceeds this estimate; for the thick stratum, from which the most of the ore has been obtained, will give nearly 10,000,000 tons. There are several strata above, and, at least, one below. Whether this ore had an igneous origin, is not so certain; still, the metamorphosed character of the slates with which it is interstratified, the relative position of the plutonic rocks below and around it, and its similarity to the ores in Shepherd Mountain, Iron Mountain and the Shut-in, all go to show its igneous origin. If this be true, the main stratum is, probably, connected with the fissure through which it was ejected. This fissure or vein is to be

---

* Dr. Litton's Report, p. 81. † Dr. Litton's Report, pp. 79 and 80.

PATE XIII

R.B. PRICE DEL.

J.M. KERSHAW ENGRAVER, ST. LOUIS.

VIEW OF THE PILOT KNOB.

sought on the south-western side, where the dip of this stratum brings it near the base of the mountain, or within its base.

There is no probability that this valuable ore can be exhausted within any time, sufficiently short, to affect the market value of the deposit.

There is ore enough of the very best quality within a few miles of Pilot Knob and Iron Mountain, above the surface of the valleys, to furnish 1,000,000 tons per annum, of manufactured iron, for the next two hundred years.

All of these ores are well adapted to the manufacture of pig-metal;* and those of Iron Mountain and Shepherd Mountain, are used for making blooms by the Catalan process, in the Bloomeries, at Pilot Knob and at Vallé Forge.

Hematite.—This ore is very generally diffused through the southern part of the State wherever the Ferruginous Sandstone,† or the 2d† and 3d† Magnesian Limestones are developed, as it is most abundant in those formations. The Hematite of the Ferruginous Sandstone is not generally so uniform in texture, and so pure as that found in the Calciferous Sandrock. There are three important localities of it in Cooper county. One is immediately on the bluffs of the Blackwater, in Town. 48, R. 19 W., N. E. ¼ Sec. 3. The ore at this place forms a stratum in the sandstone some three feet thick (see p. 92), which promises an abundant yield. The same ore again shows itself in the same geological position, in Sec. 33 of the same Township, where it covers a large area, and will furnish much more ore than the last locality. Loose masses were, also, seen in Town. 47, R. 19, Sec. 35. which had evidently fallen down from this sandstone in the hill above. The same ore was, also, observed on the eastern bluffs of the La Mine, above the mouth of Clear Creek. Large blocks of Hematite were discovered resting on the surface of the Encrinital Limestone, on the brow of a bluff in Town. 39, R. 24, Sec. 28, in St. Clair county. The ore at this place has been derived from the sandstone, which had disintegrated and left

---

* At the time of my visit, two furnaces were in blast at Iron Mountain, one* of which was making about fifteen tons of pig-metal per diem. At Pilot Knob only one was in blast, which was making from ten to twelve tons per diem, and was increasing its yield every week. Another furnace will soon be started at Pilot Knob.

* This is a cold-blast furnace, thirty-eight feet high and nine feet boshes. It receives 140 charges per diem, each charge contains seventeen bushels of coal, and from 400 to 450 pounds of ore.

† See this formation in the description of the general section.

the iron. In Town. 38, R. 26, some half mile south-east of the Salt-Creek Sulphur Springs, which are in Sec. 27, I saw a great many large blocks of this ore from the same sandstone. There are, also, localities on Grand River, in Henry county, in the bluffs of the Missouri, just above Miami, and on a Branch near Siloam church, in Pike county. At the last place, the ore is a fine red hematite. That on the Missouri and in Pike county had fallen down from the banks above. The Ferruginous Sandstone and the Coal Measures were exposed in the bluff at Siloam Church, and it is difficult to say, from which the ore came. Whether iron exists in quantity at these localities, can not be determined without further examination. The places, where small quantities of the ore were observed in this rock, are too numerous to be mentioned.

The Hematite of the Magnesian Limestones, is of better quality and quite as extensively diffused. The most important localities in the 2d Magnesian Limestone are in Franklin county, in Towns. 41 and 42, R. 1 E. For a notice of these beds, see Dr. Litton's Report, pp. 74 and 75, and Dr. Shumard's Report on this county. These beds will yield a large amount of excellent ore. There is, also, a quantity of this ore a short distance above Warsaw, and several localities west of Buffalo, which will be more fully noticed in the report on Dallas county. Many localities of it were observed in the 3d Magnesian Limestone. But the most important is in the ridge, in the forks of the Big and the Little Niangua, extending from the mouth of the latter to Sec. 12, Town. 38, R. 18. The slopes of this ridge and the ravines skirting it, are covered with fragments of the ore in such quantities as seem to indicate a vast deposit. The Hematite, in Town. 34, R. 3, Sec. 21, is probably in this limestone. The ore is good; but I cannot speak with certainty of the amount or geological position, as I have not seen the locality.

The 4th Magnesian Limestone, also, contains several important deposits of this ore in Camden, which will be noticed in the report of that county.

We had reason to expect the existence of considerable quantities of iron in the Coal Measures; but it has not been observed, in workable quantities, in a single locality in these rocks.

LEAD.

But two ores of this metal have been found in Missouri, in sufficient quantity to be of any economical value; the *Sulphuret* and

Carbonate. The former is called *Mineral,* while the latter is sometimes named *Wool-Mineral,* in the South-Western Mines.

These ores of Lead occur in the Coal Measures, Archimedes Limestone, Encrinital Limestone, 2d Magnesian Limestone, 2d Sandstone and 3d Magnesian Limestone. But the Archimedes Limestone and the 2d and 3d Magnesian Limestones are the only rocks in which any considerable quantity has been observed. The most of the Eastern Mines and those in the Osage valley and in Moniteau, are in these two Magnesian Limestones; but the mines of the South-West, and Scott's Mine, in Cooper, are in the Archimedes Limestone; but many of them pass down into the Encrinital Limestone.

Dr. Litton gives a detailed account of the Eastern Mines. For those of Moniteau, see Mr. Meek's Report.*

The other mines of the State have been worked but little, save some few on the Gravois and near Linn Creek; but when visited, the working was suspended in the most of these. It is not deemed advisable to enter upon any detailed account of the mines of the Osage valley, as a more minute examination of them is now in progress, and when it is completed, we can speak with more certainty of their value. Still, the examinations already made show very flattering indications of an abundance of Lead in several places on the Gravois, Cole Camp and near Erie. The mines at Cole Camp are in the 2d Magnesian Limestone; while those at Erie and several of those on the Gravois are in the 3d Magnesian Limestone. For an account of Scott's Mine, see Report of Cooper county.

The Mines of the South-West were examined very hastily, more with a view to learn the character of the deposits and the area over which they extend, than with a design to judge of, and report upon the particular lodes or diggings. The extent of country over which the lead has been discovered, may be best understood by pointing out the various localities where it was seen.

The first locality visited was in the prairie south-west of Carthage, in Town. 28, R. 31, Sec. 8, where some little digging had been done; and the following section was exposed: —

No. 1. — 5 feet of Chert and Soil — *Quaternary.*
No. 2. — 6 feet of fine brown stratified Sandstone — *Ferruginous Sandstone?*
No. 3. — 3 feet of blue Shale. } *Archimedes Limestone.*
No. 4. — 4 feet of blue Limestone. }

---

* Since the water has been removed from High-Point Lead Mine, I have satisfied myself by a recent careful examination, that the disturbance of the strata observed there is, beyond a doubt, due to a powerful elevating force acting from beneath. The evidence of this is the distinct and well-marked vertical striæ to be seen at various places on the surrounding wall-rock, as it is impossible that these striæ could have been made by a settling down of the broken-up strata forming the central mass. Whether the lead ore was brought up from a lower position along with the broken rock, or has been subsequently deposited there by some other agency, I am unable to say. I saw no evidences that it has been deposited there by sublimation or any other direct igneous agency. — MEEK.

Several hundred pounds of Sulphuret of Lead were found in the chert and soil; but none in the rocks below. In section 31 of the same township, is another locality which I did not visit. Lead has been found in several other places in this neighborhood; but they had not yielded much mineral. The next locality visited, was the Center-Creek Mines, which are situated in Town. 29, R. 33, Sec. 36, and Town. 29, R. 32, Sec. 31. These mines are on the border of the prairie, which extends from Carthage on towards the Territory, in the slopes on both sides of a small run. The following section will give an idea of the Geological features: —

No. 1. — 10 to 30 feet of chert, limestone and clay, broken and mingled promiscuously, and more or less cemented into a solid mass. The limestone is not so abundant as the clay, and the chert predominates over both.

No. 2. — 5 feet of regularly stratified bluish crystalline limestone.

No. 3. — 10 feet same as No. 1, save the limestone is more abundant.

No. 4. — ? of limestone, same as No. 2.

On the east side of the run, the conglomerate of No. 1 is overlaid by eight or ten feet of brown stratified sandstone, which is the same as that at the first locality named. Irregular viens of galena, very variable in thickness, cut through this conglomerate of chert, etc., and through the limestone, in directions approaching an east and west line, and varying from a perpendicular to a horizontal. The galena usually fills the fissure, when it is small, without any vein rock or gang; but when the opening is large, the sheet of mineral runs through the middle, the space on each side being filled with clay and crystals of calcareous spar. There are several diggings at this place on the west side, on White and Conovy's land, at some of which numerous shafts have been sunk from ten to forty feet, and some drifting done. The more important are, Old Diggings, Burnine's, Sunday's, Howard's, Harker's, and Thorp's Diggings. On the east side of the run, on Mr. Chenault's land, several shafts have been sunk.

From what I could see of the veins and learn of the amount of mineral raised, and from the general satisfaction of the miners, I would judge that mining at the Center-Creek Diggings has been very profitable.

Of the mineral raised at these mines, 270,000 pounds were sold to Harklerode's furnace, and 99,074 pounds, to Moseley & Co.'s furnace; about 5,000 pounds, still at the mines, making 419,074 pounds raised.

Turkey-Creek Mines. — Several localities are included in this term: —

Mineral-Point or Shake-rag Mines, in Town. 28, R. 33, Sec. 33;

Duff's Mines, in Town. 28, R. 32, Sec. 31, S. E. ¼;

Orchard's Mines, in center of Town. 27, R. 33;

Cox's Mines or Nigger Diggings, Town. 27, R. 33, two miles south-east of Mineral Point.

At Mineral Point are several diggings. Harklerode's, so far as I could judge from the miners and the mineral thrown out (for the shaft was full of water), gives great promise of a fine yield. There are two lodes or sheets of mineral lying nearly horizontal in the Carboniferous Limestone. The upper one is made up of galena and carbonate of lead and chert and clay mingled together and cemented, and is about one foot thick. The lower is pure galena, from twelve to eighteen inches thick. These lodes have been explored but a short distance.

At Messrs. Fraser and Cavenar's, one shaft, sunk thirty feet, reached a horizontal lode. The fissure in the conglomerate of chert, etc., is four feet, filled with soft clay and galena. Through the middle runs a sheet of galena ten inches thick, and the space on each side is filled with clay and large masses of cog-mineral. This lode had been explored only some fifteen feet. Other diggings at Mineral Point are quite as much esteemed by the miners. The other localities on Turkey Creek were not visited.

From these mines, 95,530 pounds had been sold to Moseley's furnace, and 110,000 pounds, to Harklerode's furnace; 55,000 pounds were still at the mines, making in all 260,530 pounds.

Moseley & Co.'s Mines are located in Town. 26, R. 32, Sec. 35. More systematic mining has been done at this place than at any other locality visited in the South-West. Three shafts have been sunk; Main Shaft 48 feet, Pump Shaft 68, and Third Shaft 50, besides about 400 feet of drifting. All the shafts and driftings are very large and the mines are kept dry and well ventilated. The efficient conductor of these mines, Mr. John Ryan, accompanied me through the mines, and gave much valuable information, as to the location and thickness of the veins worked out. These mines were opened in 1850. From February, 1854, to November of the same year, he worked, on an average, three hands, and raised from 140,000 to 150,000 pounds of mineral, of a very superior quality. The whole amount raised at these mines is estimated at 562,875 pounds; the workmen estimated it as high as 800,000.

These mines are opened in the side of a bluff, of Carboniferous Limestone, which crops out on both sides of them; but the shafts do not strike the limestone, as they commence in and pass downward in the cherty conglomerate above described. Large veins of reddish and white clay, which, in appearance, very much resembles tallow,* cut this conglomerate in various directions; and they sometimes accompany the lead.

Oliver's Prairie Mines are located on Oliver's Prairie. There are numerous diggings on and near this prairie, in the same character of rocks, cherty conglomerate and Carboniferous Limestone.

At *Richardson & Brock's Diggings*, three hands have worked eighteen months, and raised 70,000 pounds.

At *Davis & Cole's Diggings*, three hands worked two months, and two hands, two months, and raised 15,000 pounds.

At *Richardson & Foster's*, four hands worked three months, and raised 24,000 pounds.

At *Vickory & Johnson's*, two hands worked three months, and raised 3,500 pounds.

There are a great number of shafts sunk in many places in this neighborhood, and the produce of all the mines here, has been estimated at 208,000 pounds.

Spurgeon's Prairie Mines, three miles from Moseley's Furnace, were not visited; but they are represented as very productive, and in the same geological position as the other mines. Their produce is estimated at 276,000 pounds.

Baxter's Lead Mines are about one mile south of Grand Falls, and have produced some 3,000 pounds.

Strickland's Mines. — The ore raised and smelted on a log furnace sold for some $2,500.

There are several other localities which were not visited. The produce of all the mines in Newton and Jasper counties, is estimated at 1,721,679† pounds. This estimate is made up from the data in Mr. Moseley's letter, on page 163, and the opinion of others well acquainted with the whole or a part of these mines. So far as I could judge, they are not much above the reality, in any case, and in some, they must be far below it.

---

* This clay, probably, contains large quantities of silicate of zinc.

† This is higher than Mr. Moseley's estimate. He sets down 300,000 pounds as the supposed quantity smelted at Harklerode's furnace; but the estimate of Mr. Harklerode is 470,000 pounds.

Besides the Galena at these mines, there are large quantities of the Sulphate and Carbonate of Lead, which are somewhat indiscriminately called *Ash Mineral*, *Dry Bones* and *Wool Mineral.* The Carbonate is most abundant and is successfully smelted on the log furnaces; 3,000 pounds were smelted at Strickland's log furnace during the last winter.

Sulphuret of Zinc. — Zinc Blende, called Black-Jack by the miners, is almost as abundant as the galena in many of the mines. At Mineral Point and the Center-Creek Mines, many thousand pounds have been thrown out with the rubbish. The great abundance of this ore, and the increasing demand for Zinc in the useful arts, must make the working of it profitable, notwithstanding the difficulty of reducing the ore, as soon as a cheap mode of transportation be secured.

In one or two places in the mines of Oliver's Prairie, we saw very small portions (existing as a mere coating) of a mineral which gave the characters of cobalt by the blowpipe; but no opportunity has occurred for testing it in solution.

At first, the lead of the South-West was smelted on log-heaps and in log furnaces; but at present nearly all the galena is reduced in blast furnaces. There are two excellent furnaces of this description; Harklerode's and Moseley's.

Harklerode's furnace is situated on a small spring branch, in Town. 28, R. 33, Sec. 10, N. E. of S. E. ¼. The blast is produced by water-power, derived from a large spring near the furnace. Fig. 11 gives a fine view of the internal structure of the furnace.

Fig. 11.

HARKLERODE'S FURNACE.

The charcoal used for smelting the lead costs about $0,033 per bushel; according to the following estimate of expenditures for making 1,600 bushels:—

25 cords of wood, at $0,75 per cord, gives,	$18,75
One hand, one month, at $25,	25,00
Team for hauling the wood,	10,00
	$5,375

Ten bushels make a ton of lead. The mineral costs about $20 per thousand pounds.

Since this furnace started, on the first of March, 1854, they have smelted from—

Center-Creek Mines,	270,000	pounds.
Turkey-Creek Mines,	110,000	"
Oliver's Prairie Mines,	90,000	"
In all,	470,000	"

An account of the furnace of G. W. Moseley & Co., may be seen in the following letter of Mr. Moseley, to whom the Survey is much indebted for valuable aid:—

NEWTON COUNTY, MISSOURI, *November 25th,* 1854.

DEAR SIR,—By your request, I give you the information desired, in regard to the mineral operations in this part of the State.

The first smelting of Lead Ore in this county, was on the rude log furnace, by Mr. A. Spurgeon and others, in the years 1850 and 1851. The ore, raised on Spurgeon's Prairie, Newton county, was dug from Sec. 32, Town. 26, R. 32. The amount smelted from this section on log furnaces, was 226,000 pounds.

Second.—The next furnace, generally known as the Drummond, was erected by Moseley & Co., of Neosho, in 1850, on G. W. Moseley & Co.'s lands, near their mines. On this furnace they smelted, in 1850 and 1851, from Moseley's Mines, situated in Sec. 35, Town. 26, R. 32, Newton county, 259,875 pounds of the ore; 25,000 pounds from Spurgeon's and Turkey-Creek Mines.

Third.—In the fall of 1851, G. W. Moseley & Co. commenced building a blast furnace (double-eyed), and on the 9th day of February, 1852, lead was run from the first ore ever smelted on a blast furnace in the South-West. On this furnace we smelted ore raised from our own mines, in Sec. 35, Town. 26, R. 32, 142,500 pounds; from Center-Creek Diggings, in Jasper county, 99,074 pounds, and from Turkey-Creek Mines, in Jasper county, 95,073 pounds.

Fourth.—The Moseley Lead Manufacturing Company commenced operations in October, 1853, and smelted, on the blast furnace erected by G. W. Moseley & Co., and situated on Sec. 22, Town. 26, R. 32; ore raised from the Moseley Mines, on Sec. 35, Town. 26, R. 32, 110,500 pounds; from Oliver's Prairie, Newton county, and from Center and Turkey-Creek Mines, 93,000 pounds.

From the best information that I can get from the blast furnace in Jasper county, built by Mr. Harklerode in 1853, they have smelted from the different mines, Oliver's Prairie, Newton county, Center and Turkey-Creek, in Jasper county, about 300,000 pounds.

From the best information, sought by me amongst the miners, I have set down 200,000 pounds as the amount of ore, at the different mines, ready for delivery and that may be delivered by the miners up to the 20th day of December next.

Total amount raised at the different mines:—	lbs.	lbs.
Spurgeon's Mines, in 1850 and 1851, and smelted on log furnace,	226,000	226,000
Amount on the Drummond furnace, by Moseley & Co., and from Moseley's Mines,	259,875	
From other mines,	25,000	
		284,875
Smelted on the blast furnaces, up to the present time:—		
From Moseley's Mines, by Gwin & Co.,	142,500	
" " " and Lead Manufacturing Company,	110,500	
		253,000
From Center-Creek,	99,074	
From Turkey-Creek,	95,073	
From Oliver's Prairie, Center and Turkey-Creek,	93,000	
		287,147
Supposed amount smelted by Harklerode,	300,000	
Supposed amount ready for delivery and up to 20th December,	200,000	
		500,000
		1,551,022

Until this last spring, all the lead made in this county was sent to New York and Boston by Grand River and Arkansas, and through the Indian country to Fort Smith, and thence, by steamboat, to New Orleans.

Respectfully, yours, &c.,
G. W. MOSELEY.

PROF. G. C. SWALLOW,
State Geologist.

There are, at least, 400 square miles in the south-west of Jasper, and the north-west and central and eastern portions of Newton, which give every indication of being very valuable mineral lands. Mines have been already opened and successfully worked in ten townships; and there are several others which give indications just as promising as those already worked. Mineral is found over this whole region; scarcely a shaft has been sunk, however carelessly the spot was chosen, without obtaining mineral sufficient to render the labor profitable. One may get a good view of this mineral region by starting from Carthage and traveling a little north of west, ten miles, to the Center-Creek Mines; thence, a little west of south, seven miles, to Mineral Point; from there, south-east, eleven miles, to Moseley's Mines; and from there, a little south of east, nine or ten miles, to Oliver's Prairie Mines, and then eastward some six miles. The country along this whole route, and for several miles on either side, presents the same geological features, and the same indications of great mineral wealth; and the day is not far distant when this will prove to be one of the richest mineral districts in the country.

There are several experienced miners, who have worked in the mines of Iowa and Wisconsin, and of the eastern counties of Missouri, who say they can make more money in these mines, raising mineral at $20* per thousand, than they could in any other mines they have seen, at double that price; and this seemed to be the universal opinion among the miners.

This country has every facility for sustaining a large population. The climate is salubrious; the country is well watered with bold springs and limpid streams. Timber is abundant; and much of the soil is very productive, particularly that in the bottoms. It is, probably, increasing in wealth† and population as rapidly as the other parts of the State.

Could this part of the State have some cheap and certain communication with such a market as St. Louis, its progress would be very rapid, and the State would soon feel the advantages in the increase of wealth and population.

COPPER.

There are several important localities of copper ore in the State; but, as I have not seen them, I must refer to Dr. Litton's Report (p. 67, Part II.), for what information can be given respecting them.

ZINC.

All valuable deposits of zinc which have come under my observation are mentioned above, while speaking of the South-Western Mines. Dr. Litton's Report describes other localities. (See p. 84, Part II.)

SILVER.

It is not known that silver occurs in the State, save the small quantities found with lead in the galena. (See p. 13, Part II.)

GOLD, NICKEL AND COBALT.

These metals occur in Missouri, but none of the localities have been visited.

MANGANESE.

The oxides of manganese have been observed in Stephens' coal-bed, in Cooper

---

* The miners of the South-West generally lease the mines, and pay for rent one-eighth of the mineral raised. They sell the remainder at about $20 per thousand, the difficulty of transportation reducing its value about one-half.

† The taxable property in Newton county increased from $390,000 in 1853, to $700,000 in 1854.

county, in the sandstone of the Calciferous Sandrock on the plank-road, west of Ste. Genevieve, and at the Buford Ore Bank, in Town. 33, R. 3 E., Sec. 34.

BUILDING MATERIALS.

The possession of materials for the construction of habitations, is one of the first necessities of the human race. And, as the race advances in civilization and wealth, the demand for the more beautiful and durable qualities, constantly increases ; and it becomes a matter of no small importance to determine whether we are prepared to supply the demand, which our advancement will create for dwellings, warehouses and public edifices. Our examinations in Missouri, prove the existence of such materials in nearly every formation in the State. (See Chap. I.)

Limestones, suitable for building purposes, are abundant in the Upper and Middle Coal Series, in the St. Louis Limestone, the Archimedes Limestone, the Encrinital Limestone, the Chouteau Limestone, the Onondaga Limestone, the Cape Girardeau Limestone, the Trenton Limestone, and the 2d, 3d and 4th Magnesian Limestones. All of these formations are, more or less, employed in the places where they are exposed. Nos. 1 and 6 of the Upper Coal Series furnish the rock used in the Presbyterian Church and the public-house, erected by Mr. Park at Parkville, and in the public buildings at Fort Leavenworth, all of which indicate their durability and beauty; and the ease with which it is wrought into any desirable form, renders it a very economical building material. No. 41, of the Middle Coal Series, is a light gray semi-crystalline limestone, which is both durable and beautiful. It is used at Lexington.

The St. Louis Limestone has many beds of excellent rock, which are extensively quarried and employed for various purposes in St. Louis county. The Archimedes beds furnish a great amount of very durable limestone. It is used for the Custom-house in St. Louis. The Encrinital strata are more extensively employed for economical purposes than any other limestone in the State. The State University, and the Court-house at Columbia, furnish abundant proof of its adaptation to building purposes. The upper beds of the Trenton Limestone, and the dark compact and the light magnesian strata in the lower part, are very desirable building stones ; but the middle beds are not so durable; still, they are sometimes used. The Court-house in St. Louis, presents good examples of the Trenton Limestone.

The strata of Cotton-Rock, so abundant in the Magnesian Limestones, are much used. The State-house, Court-house, and many other buildings at Jefferson City, show the adaptation of this limestone to such purposes. These formations, also, contain numerous beds of the silicious and the magnesian crystalline varieties, which are much stronger and more durable than the Cotton-Rock.

Marbles. — There are several beds of excellent marble in the State. The beautiful and durable oolite in the Archimedes Limestone, near Ste. Genevieve, is well worthy the attention of those who desire a light-colored marble. The residence of the Hon. L. M. Kennett, in St. Louis, is built of it. The 4th division of the Encrinital Limestone (see p. 100) is a white, coarse-grained crystalline marble, of great durability. It crops out in several places in Marion county. One of the best localities is in the bluffs of the Mississippi, between McFarlin's Branch and the Fabius. The Lithographic Limestone would furnish a hard, fine-grained bluish drab marble, that would contrast finely with white varieties in tesselated pavements for halls and courts.

The Cooper Marble of the Onondaga Limestone, has numerous pellucid crystals of calcareous spar disseminated through a drab or bluish drab, fine compact base.

It exists in great quantities on the La Mine, in Cooper, and on See's Creek, and in other places in Marion; and it is admirably adapted to many ornamental uses.

McPherson's Marble, a bed of the Trenton Limestone, situated in the vicinity of Rattlesnake Creek, is a hard, light-colored, compact limestone, intersected with numerous thin veins of transparent calcareous spar, which give it a beautifully variegated surface, when well polished. It appears to be strong and durable. McPherson's marble block, on Fourth-street, St. Louis, is constructed of it.

Cape Girardeau Marble is, also, a part of the Trenton Limestone, located near Cape Girardeau. I have not seen it, and must refer to Dr. Shumard's Report, page 155, for a description of its properties.

There are several beds of very excellent marble in the Magnesian Limestone Series. In Secs. 34 and 35 of Town. 34, R. 3 E., are several beds of semi-crystalline light-colored marbles, beautifully clouded with buff and flesh colors. They receive a fine polish, are durable, and well fitted for many varieties of ornamental work and building purposes. But one of the most desirable of the Missouri marbles, is in the 3d Magnesian Limestone, on the Niangua. It is a fine-grained, crystalline, silico-magnesian limestone of a light drab, slightly tinged with peach-blossom, and beautifully clouded with the same hue or flesh color. It is twenty feet thick (see p. 126), and crops out in the bluffs of the Niangua, where the 3d Magnesian Limestone prevails, as seen in No. 6, Pl. XIV. This marble is rarely surpassed in the qualities which fit it for ornamental architecture.

There are, also, several other beds in this and the other magnesian limestones, which are excellent marbles. Some are plain, while others are so clouded as to present the appearance of breccias.

Granite. — Granite Knob* will furnish any amount of a superior coarse granite, admirably adapted to all structures where durability and strength are desirable. Its introduction to general use, in St. Louis, would add much to the architectural effects produced by her public and private edifices.

Brick. — The pipe-clay and sands of the Drift will furnish a large amount of the very best materials suitable for manufacturing the most durable and beautiful brick. The argillaceous portions of the Bluff, make a very good article. It is generally diffused, and is almost universally employed for that purpose. Nearly every township, in those parts of the State, thus far examined, has an abundance of these clays.

Fire-Bricks are manufactured from the fire-clays of the Lower Coal Series, in St. Louis county. These bricks have the reputation of possessing fine refractory properties. There are many beds of fire-clay in the Coal Measures; and, besides, some beds of the Hudson River Group, in Ralls and Pike counties, of the Hamilton Group, in Pike and Marion, and of the Vermicular Sandstone and Shales on North River, seem to possess all the qualities of the very best fire-clays. The quantity of these clays is great, almost beyond computation. No possible demand could exhaust them.

Fire-Rock has often been observed, and a few localities were mentioned in Chapter I. Some of the more silicious beds of No. 6 of the Coal Measures, are very refractory, as many have discovered in attempting to burn them to lime. The sandstones of Nos. 28 and 34 are, also, good fire-rocks. The upper strata of the Ferruginous Sandstone, some arenaceous beds of the Encrinital Limestone, the upper part of the Chouteau Limestone, and the fine-grained impure beds of the Magnesian Limestones, all possess qualities which will enable them to withstand the

---

* See a description of this rock on page 134.

action of fire. But the 2d * and 3d Sandstones are the most refractory rocks yet examined, and are well adapted to use where great strength and firmness are not demanded.

Paints. — There are several beds of purple shales in the Coal Measures, which seem to possess the properties requisite for paints used in outside work. Nos. 10, 31 and 50 of this Formation, have shales of a bright purple color and firm texture. But No. 10 possesses the best qualities. It has a more uniform texture and color, and is much more abundant than either of the others. This bed is exposed in the bluff opposite to Bethlehem; at Fort Kearney; in a bluff, ten miles below that station, opposite Sonora; at the mouth of Little Nemaha, and at Dallas, Weston and Parkville. Mr. Park, of the last place, has used it with oil, both alone and mixed with white lead, for outside work; and several years' exposure have proved it very durable. Its color is more brilliant when prepared with oil; but when mixed with white lead, it produces a dark, dull peach-blossom color, which is very agreeable and appropriate for some purposes. Its properties as a fire-proof paint, were also tested by Mr. Park.† An inch board was covered with a thick coat, when coals were burned upon the painted side, until the whole thickness of the board was charred; but the paint remained firm and uncracked. He has, also, compared it in use, with the famous Ohio paint, and thinks ours the best. At several of the above localities, thousands of tons could be thrown from the beds into a boat lying in the river beneath.

Cements. — All of the limestone formations in the State, from the Coal Measures to the 4th Magnesian, have more or less strata of very nearly pure carbonate of lime, which will, consequently, make good quick lime. But few, if any, of the States have such an abundance, and so general a distribution of this important article of domestic use.

Hydraulic Cements. — It is well known that limestones containing considerable quantities of silex, alumina, magnesia and iron, often make good hydraulic cements; but we know but little of the exact proportion there should be of each ingredient, what order of combination should exist among them, or what changes take place in the hardening of the cement. It is, therefore, impossible to tell, with certainty, from the physical or chemical properties of a limestone, whether it will form a good hydraulic cement. And, hence, arises the necessity for practical experiment upon the rock by making it into a cement, before we decide upon its merits as a hydraulic lime. A press of other duties has prevented us from making these experiments. Still, we know that a limestone must have certain ingredients to render it hydraulic. By the appearance of the stone, we can tell with tolerable certainty, whether it contain the necessary elements; and an analysis will show whether those elements exist in such proportions as will probably render the lime hydraulic.

All the limestones, whose physical characters indicated hydraulic properties, have been collected, and some of them subjected to analysis. So far as can be judged from the results obtained, we have many beds of hydraulic limestone.

From all the experiments made upon this subject, Burnell, in his work on Cements, deduces the following principles: —

1st. "When the limestones contain silex in combination with alumina (common clay), magnesia, the oxides of iron and of manganese, in various respective proportions, but limited to eight or twelve per cent. of the whole mass, they yield moderately hydraulic limes."

---

* A description of this rock is given on page 125.

† The Survey is much indebted to Mr. Park for information and aid, while exploring the neighborhood of Parkville.

2d. "Where the above ingredients are present in the proportion of from fifteen to eighteen per cent., but the silex always predominating, the limestones yield an hydraulic lime."

3d. "When the limestones contain more than twenty and up to thirty per cent. of the above ingredients, but with the silex in proportion of, at least, one half of them, they yield eminently hydraulic limes."

According to these principles, we have, as indicated by analysis, eight limestones, which come under the 1st class, and six. under the 3d class, or those eminently hydraulic.

Those beds which come under the 1st class, belong to the following formations:

Middle Coal Series. — No. 36 comes in this class of cements. For description and analysis, see pages 83 and 84.

Middle Coal Series — No. 48, also, belongs here. Its description and analysis are given on page 85.

Lower Coal Series. — No. 66 belongs to the same class. Its description and analysis are given on page 86.

Vermicular Sandstone and Shales. — The middle beds are hydraulic, as indicated by the analysis and description, on page 103.

Lithographic Limestone. — The upper beds come in this class. Its analysis and description are on page 105.

Cape Girardeau Limestone. — The analysis and description may be seen in Dr. Shumard's Report, on page 154.

Magnesian Limestones. — Several beds in these formations belong in this class. See the description of these rocks in this and Dr. Shumard's Report.

The following come under the 3d class: —

Upper Coal Series. — No. 12 shows strong indications of being an excellent cement. The description is given on pages 79 and 80.

Middle Coal Series. — The septaria of No. 31, which is exposed in the bluff at Lexington, give good evidence of hydraulic properties. The analysis and description are on page 83.

Middle Coal Series. — No. 44 of this Series comes in this class. Page 84 gives its analysis and geological position.

The Chouteau Limestone. — The upper division of this formation, as it is developed in Boone, Cooper and Moniteau counties, gives the best indications of excellent hydraulic properties. The beds are about thirty feet thick, and have a uniform texture and composition. These very much resemble the hydraulic strata at Louisville; and can furnish any desirable quantity. The analysis and description are on pages 101 and 102.

Vermicular Sandstone and Shales. — The middle beds of this formation, both in Marion and Cooper, have superior hydraulic properties. This is especially indicated by the dark-clouded beds, which were passed through, in sinking the well of Mr. Winston Walker, in Cooper. The analyses and description may be seen on pages 103 and 104. These strata are developed over a large area in the counties mentioned.

Hudson River Group. — The upper and lower beds of this formation give good evidence of being hydraulic. The description of the rock and its analysis are on pages 110 and 111.

From present indications, the hydraulic limestones of our State may be expected to supply the home demand, and furnish large quantities for exportation.

ROAD MATERIALS.

In a country where the superficial deposits make such bad roads, it is a matter of no small importance to have an abundance of good materials for highways. The limestones, so abundant in the country, are much used for macadamized roads. But the rapid pulverization of limerock, and the consequent mud and dust, particularly in towns and cities, render it very desirable to point out a more durable and economical substitute. The coarse gravels of the Boulder Formation, and of the river-beds, furnish an abundance of the best possible substitute. These deposits contain gravels of any degree of fineness, from the sand, suited to the formation of footpaths, to the pebbles best adapted for carriage-ways. Any amount, of any given coarseness, may be obtained by screening, in all parts of the country, either from the Drift or the river-beds. These pebbles have the advantage of limestone in several particulars: —

1*st.* They are more durable, being fragments of chert and the harder igneous and crystalline rocks, which have withstood the action of those unknown but all-powerful causes, which have worn away and ground to dust so large a portion of our superficial rocks, and transported to our territory such quantities of the rocks *in situ*, several hundred miles to the north. Those from the river-beds, also, have been exposed to aqueous action for unknown ages.

2*d.* They are less injurious to animals and carriages, as all the pebbles are water-worn and rounded.

3*d.* By their use we should avoid the impalpable dust of the limestone, so injurious to health and property in our cities. We should, also, escape much of the mud, which is scarcely less objectionable.

Should St. Louis but pave a single street with these pebbles, every person living or doing business upon it, would at once see the difference in comfort and health. The impalpable dust of the dry weather and the *liquid* mud of the wet, would no longer soil the furniture and goods of the houses and shops, and clog the lungs and disfigure the garments of those passing over it. Material could be obtained from various parts of the State. Good pebbles are abundant in the streams of Marion, Boone, Cooper and Moniteau. The Osage and its tributaries can supply any needed quantity. And there can be no doubt that the Gasconade and the Meramec have a good supply of them in localities nearer to St. Louis. Small steamers could easily reach bars, made up of good pebbles, on the Osage, the La Mine and other streams, and obtain a supply sufficient to meet all demands.

LITHOGRAPHIC LIMESTONE.

This is a very fine compact even-textured rock, which resembles the best lithographic stones so closely that hand-specimens of them can scarcely be distinguished. The following analyses show them to be similar in composition. The first specimen was from Hannibal, and the second from Solenhofen, Germany *: —

	1.	2.
Residuum, insoluble in acid,	1.53	1.90
Alumina,	a trace.	a trace.
Carbonate of Lime,	97.86	96.34
Carbonate of Magnesia,	0.51	......
Water,	......	1.23
	99.90	99.47

Messrs. Schaerff & Brother, of St. Louis, have tested this rock and pronounced some parts of it good. Excellent slabs, large enough for small engravings, can be

* The Survey is indebted to Messrs. Schaerff & Brother for a specimen of a good stone used by them for engraving.

obtained with ease; but the jointed structure of the strata and an occasional particle of iron pyrites, will make it difficult to get large slabs of suitable quality.

LUMBER, AND WATER-POWER.

It may be a matter of surprise to some to learn that Missouri, notwithstanding our heavy importations of lumber (see p. 42), has a great abundance of almost every desirable variety, most advantageously situated. Indeed, with the exception of White Pine, Cedar and Live Oak, our supply seems to be all that could be desired. (See Appendix C.) On the borders of our navigable streams (see page 139) and their large tributaries, Oak, Hickory, Walnut, Maple, Ash, Linden, Cherry, Locust and Birch, grow in the greatest abundance, and in magnificent dimensions. There is no physical reason why St. Louis should not export several times as much lumber as she now imports. Though Bangor, in Maine, exports more lumber than any city on this continent, and, perhaps, more than any in the world, the forests which supply it are located at a greater distance and on streams much more impracticable than ours in Missouri.

It seems unnecessary to specify where good localities exist, for there is scarcely a stream in the State which is not bordered by forests of excellent lumber. The Missouri, the Osage and all its tributaries, Spring River, Gasconade, Grand, Chariton, La Mine, South, North, Salt and Fabius rivers, are bordered with magnificent forests of the trees peculiar to the Alluvium.

All of these streams, save the Missouri, furnish water-power and good mill-sites; and even the large springs of the Niangua, afford the best water-power and mill-sites observed in the State. But steam has usually proved the most economical power for the manufacture of lumber, as the site can be selected with greater advantage.

SPRINGS.

We have a great abundance of Springs, both fresh and mineral. The fresh springs are very numerous in all parts examined, and some of them are very large.

Bryce's Spring, on the Niangua, is the largest observed. The quantity discharged was carefully measured; and it was ascertained that 455,328 cubic feet of water were discharged per hour, and 10,927,872 cubic feet per diem. The Gunter and Sweet Springs are not quite so large. And what increases their value, the quantity and temperature of the water scarcely changes during the year. We have several varieties of Mineral Springs; Chalybeate, Sulphur and Brine. The most important Chalybeate Spring observed, is in or beneath the Ferruginous Sandstone, west of Oseola. Salt Springs are very generally diffused, and will be mentioned in the County Reports. The Sulphur Springs are, also, very abundant; and a few have acquired some considerable reputation for their sanitary qualities. Those most popular are the Chouteau Springs, in Cooper; the Elk Springs, in Pike; and the Monagaw Springs, in St. Clair. We have seen Sulphur Springs in Marion, Pike, Howard, Cooper, Saline, Benton, St. Clair and St. Louis counties.

Petroleum Springs.—I am indebted to the Hon. Charles Sims for a bottle of Petroleum, from what is commonly called *Tar Spring*, situated about five miles west of Cold-water Grove, which is near the middle of the western boundary of Cass county. The Petroleum usually rises with the water and forms a stratum on its surface; but, in drought, when the spring does not discharge water, it comes up in a pure state and fills the basin.

CHAPTER III.

SCIENTIFIC GEOLOGY OF MARION COUNTY.

SYSTEM I.

F. *a*—ALLUVIUM.

THIS Formation in Marion county presents its usual characteristic features. It everywhere presents evidences of its being the result of agencies now in operation. It has been formed since the present order of things commenced. These deposits have been accumulated by the combined action of frost, air and water upon the mineral, animal and vegetable kingdoms. It is found in small quantities in all places, but, as usual, most abundant in ponds, marshes and river bottoms.

The rocks of this formation found in Marion, are—

1*st*. *Soils*. 2*d*. *Sands and Pebbles*.
3*d*. *Clays*. 4*th*. *Vegetable Mould or Humus*.
5*th*. *Calcareous Tufa*. 6*th*. *Bog Iron*.
7*th*. *Stalactites and Stalagmites*.

1st. The *Soil* is, as usual, made up of the debris of the underlying rocks commingled with vegetable and animal remains. (See Economical Geology of Marion county, and pp. 61 and 137.)

2d. *Sands and Pebbles* are abundant in the bottoms and beds of the streams. In the Mississippi bottom, the sands abound where they were deposited by the river at high stages of water. In the beds of the other streams are found numerous bars of a coarse water-worn gravel or pebbles, like shingle. The materials are derived from the Drift and the chert of the Carboniferous Limestones.

3d. *Clays* are fine deposits formed in the more tranquil waters of sloughs and ponds. They are common in the Mississippi Alluvium.

4th. *Dark Vegetable Mould or Humus*, variable in character from pure vegetable matter to a clayey vegetable mould, is abundant in the swamps, ponds and sloughs, particularly in those bottoms which support a rank vegetation.

5th. *Calcareous Tufa* was found in small quantities in caves and under bluffs, where it is deposited by the evaporation of limestone water.

6th. *Bog Iron* exists in small quantities. It is deposited from the waters of the Chalybeate Spring, near Sharpsburg.

7th. *Stalactites and Stalagmites* are seen in a few localities only, in this county.

The fossils of the Alluvial strata are numerous, and all belong to living species, save those found in the fragments of the older rocks.

We may get a good idea of the Alluvium of the Mississippi bottom from Sec. 3 of Chap. I., taken above the City of Hannibal, in Sec. 5 of Town. 57, R. 4.

A more complete description of this Formation may be found under Alluvium, in Chap. I. of this Report.

F. *b* — BOTTOM PRAIRIE.

There is an extensive area of this Formation in the Mississippi bottom. Its thickness varies from fifteen to thirty feet, and is made up of alternate layers of sands, clays and vegetable deposits. As usual, the vegetable deposits are most abundant at the top, the clays in the middle, and the sands at the bottom. Section 6 of Chap. I. gives a good representation of this Formation in Marion county. It was taken near Marion City, which stands upon it.

A more extended account of this Formation is given in Chap. I. of this Report. Its properties and fossils are the same here, and need not be repeated.

F. *c* — BLUFF OR LOESS.

This Formation is not so well developed here as in some of the western and central counties; yet it is so thick and so universally distributed, as to exert its happy influences upon the soils of Marion. This is especially true of the Elm and Hickory Lands.

This deposit is, as usual, a rich silico-argillaceous marl, furnishing at once the materials for an invaluable subsoil and an excellent brick.* In some places it becomes more argillaceous and furnishes a subsoil too retentive of water; in other positions, and particularly over the micaceous sandstone of No. 1, Sys. III., it becomes too arenaceous to furnish a first-rate soil. A small portion only, in the south-western part of the county, is thus affected.

In the central parts of the county, the lower part of this deposit is highly charged with the red oxide of iron, and presents a very bright red color.

In other respects, this Formation has its usual composition and brown ash color, and furnishes some of the best lands in the county. But few fossils were found in it in Marion. All found, however, were identical with those already given. Its thickness is variable; in some places, thirty feet. See Secs.† 6, 7 and 118.

F. *d* — DRIFT.

In this Formation we find two important divisions: —

1*st*. *Boulder*. — This deposit is more abundant in this county than in any yet examined. It is seen everywhere under the Bluff Formation, and the materials are much finer than usual in the

---

* See analysis of specimen from Hannibal, p. 72.

† Sections not otherwise designated, refer to the Schedule of Sections for Marion county appended to this Report.

northern part of the State. On Hopkins' Branch, Sec. 18 of Marion county Schedule, it is highly charged with red oxide of iron. It furnishes an excellent gravel for roads and walks, and a fine sand for cements and mortars.

Its thickness varies from one to fifty feet. See Secs. 26 and 18 of the Schedule, and the bluffs near the Plank-road, two miles from Hannibal. (See Pl. III.)

2*d*. *Pipe Clay.* — This is a bluish white plastic clay. Its color seldom varies to a yellowish tinge. It contains little, if any, foreign matter, and furnishes a most excellent material for pottery, and the other uses for which such clays are employed. It is not so abundant as the two last Formations, but is found in sufficient quantities, in the various parts of the county, to supply all demands for its use.

Its thickness is often four feet. See Secs. 31 and 92. No fossils have been found in it, and it is doubtful whether it belongs to the Drift period; but, since it is everywhere associated with the Boulder deposit, I have ventured to place it here until further investigation enables us to say positively where it belongs.

SYSTEM III. — CARBONIFEROUS.

F. *e*—COAL MEASURES.

The Coal Measures of Marion county are made up of: —

No. 1. *Micaceous Sandstone.** — This rock is a dark brown micaceous sandstone, containing concretions of the oxides of iron, alumina and silica, or impure sandy concretions of the oxides of iron. It is usually found in thick irregular beds, but sometimes regularly stratified; when the surfaces of the strata are much more abundantly studded with particles of mica. It frequently passes into a conglomerate, which contains water-worn fragments of wood. The pebbles, the wood, and all the other ingredients of this rock, have every appearance of a deposit formed near a shore, at the mouth of a stream.

This sandstone is very variable in thickness, and frequently decreases many feet in a hundred yards. At Sec. 140 it is twenty-five feet thick. It is most abundant in the south-western portion of the county.

No. 2. *Bituminous Shales.* — These deposits are thin-bedded argillo-arenaceous shales, colored black by bituminous matter. Their range is very limited, and they seldom crop out. In appearance they resemble, in a slight degree, some varieties of coal, for which they are sometimes mistaken, as they burn freely until the bitumen is exhausted. Secs. 30, 62 and 139.

No. 3. *Coal.* — This bed is a very pure light Bituminous Coal, which appears to be made up of innumerable small plants. In many places it presents the appearance of charcoal.

It varies in thickness from twelve to fourteen inches. (See Secs. 30 and 62.)

---

* See No. 60 of the Lower Coal Series, p. 86.

At Sec. 139, we have another bed of Coal in a ravine, whose sides are mural bluffs of Encrinital Limestone. The coal in this bed is very poor, being highly charged with the sulphuret of iron, so injurious to the health of those who use it, and the metals worked with it.

No. 5. Fire-Clay. — This deposit is more argillaceous than the Fire-Clays underlying the coal, usually are. It was seen in a few places only. No fossils were found in it.

Its thickness varies from one to two feet. (See Secs. 84 and 141.)

LOWER CARBONIFEROUS.

F. f—FERRUGINOUS SANDSTONE.

This deposit is a brown or white saccharoidal sandstone. It is generally indurated and regularly stratified; but it sometimes becomes more massive, friable and saccharoidal. When indurated, it furnishes a good building material, and is sometimes used for grindstones. When saccharoidal, it readily crumbles, and affords the best possible sand for cement, mortars and glass.

No fossils have been found in it.

Its thickness is about eight feet. (See Secs. 80, 82, 84 and 135.)

F. g—ST. LOUIS LIMESTONE.

This formation was recognized in but one place in Marion, and the only proof seen of its existence there, is a few imperfect plates of *Palæchinus multipora.* Sec. 61 gives the locality on Troublesome Creek.

F. h—ARCHIMEDES LIMESTONE.

This is well developed in the county. It is composed of bluish gray crystalline limestones, interstratified with blue argillaceous shales. These shales, when exposed, readily decompose and form a bluish gray clay. It is most abundant in the upper part of the formation. (See Sec. 14, p. 92.) In places, the limestone assumes an impure argillo-arenaceous character, with a light brown color.

This rock abounds in silicious geodes, varying in size from one to fourteen inches in diameter. The crust is silicious, and the drusy cavity set with crystals of quartz, or calcareous spar, whose surfaces are often bespangled with small brilliant crystals of Galena, Pyrites or Zinc Blende. (See p. 96.)

This rock furnishes an excellent material for building, and for lime. We saw no large quarries in it in this county; but those at Keokuk show the fine qualities of this limestone.

When fully developed, it is about one hundred feet thick. (See Secs. 35, 53, 94 and 108.)

Zinc and Lead were found in this rock, in small quantities only, in this county.

F. i—ENCRINITAL LIMESTONE.

This important Formation is found in nearly every highland township in the county. It is (if we have any) the equivalent of the Scar Limestone of England.

It is usually a coarse-grained, crystalline, grayish white limestone. Some strata are reddish or brown, and arenaceous. Some few thin strata are argillaceous. It is everywhere characterized by lenticular masses of chert disseminated, or arranged in beds parallel to the lines of stratification. It, also, has a peculiar jointed structure, resembling in general appearance the sutures of the cranium.

Many strata are mostly made up of fragments of Crinoideans. (See p. 97 — Fossils, pp. 99 and 100.)

Marion county presents seven of the eight distinct and permanent divisions of this Formation; *i. e.*, all but the 2d. (See p. 99.)

1st. The upper and cherty portion, whose characteristics are given in Chap. I.

4th. This part of the Encrinital Limestone is exhibited in the bluffs above Hannibal. (See description in Chap. I.)

6th. Impure, arenaceous, coarse-grained limestones. The arenaceous portions are stained with iron, and decompose rapidly, leaving the fossils in a very perfect condition.

These beds are about twenty feet thick, at Sec. 27, on North River, below Palmyra; Sec. 85, near Hick's Mill; and Sec. 77, below Marshall's Mill.

7th. A bed of coarse-grained, white crystalline Limestone or Marble, very uniform in structure, and containing but few fossils.

It is well characterized by the *Spirifer Burlingtonensis.* Its thickness is ten or fifteen feet, at Sec. 13, at McClintock's Hill, south of Palmyra; and Sec. 12, above Hannibal. The Calaboose, at Hannibal, is built of this beautiful and durable rock.

8th. This is the lowest member of this Formation, and is an impure, crystalline, brownish gray limestone, in thick beds.

Its thickness is fifteen or twenty feet, at Sec. 97, Price's Branch, near Philadelphia; Sec. 119, at McClintock's Hill; and Sec. 12, above Hannibal. Some of these divisions of the Encrinital Limestone, though obvious and persistent in this county, have not appeared so distinct in other parts of the State.

This rock sustains an important relation to the useful arts. It furnishes a large portion of the lime and building materials in various parts of the State. The quarries at Hannibal, Palmyra, Sharpsburg and Philadelphia, are in this rock. In the bluffs of the Mississippi, between the Fabius and McFarlin's Branch, it presents some strata of pure white granular marble, suitable for ornamental buildings and monuments.

This formation is not so well developed in this county as in some other parts of the State. Here its greatest thickness is not more than one hundred and eighty-five feet. (See Secs. 6, 10, 44, 94, 110 and 136.)

CHEMUNG.

F. j—CHOUTEAU LIMESTONE.

This rock, in its lithological characters, very nearly resembles that above it, but its fossils are very different. The change in fossils is very abrupt. Scarcely a species, from either rock, passes the line of demarcation.

It is a gray crystalline limestone, interstratified with impure, brown ferruginous beds of very hard, massive and durable limestones, from which it gradually passes into the impure sandstones beneath.

Its greatest thickness is forty feet. (See Secs. 97, 103 and 115.)

This formation is so thin, and so similar to that above it, and the lithological change is so great immediately below it, that one would scarcely expect so many fossils entirely distinct from all in the rocks above. (See p. 101.)

F. k—VERMICULAR SANDSTONE AND SHALES.

The upper part of this formation is usually a buff or brown, fine-grained, pulverulent, argillo-calcareous sandstone. It is usually perforated in every direction by vermicular pores, filled with the same material in a softer state, and more highly colored by iron.

When exposed to atmospheric agencies, this portion often disintegrates, and leaves the rock full of vermicular passages, as if worm-eaten.

The middle portion is a silico-calcareous argillite, of a grayish blue color. It has the peculiar markings of the upper part, together with those of a curious Fucoid. It often passes into a hydraulic limestone.

The lower part is usually a blue argillaceous shale or fine clay, in regular thin strata. It contains numerous cylindrical, elliptical and globular masses of Iron Pyrites, whose surfaces are set with myriads of minute cubic crystals, the faces of which are tarnished and present all the varying colors of changeable silks.

This shale, on exposure to atmospheric influences, disintegrates and forms a semi-plastic clay.

The middle portion has very interesting fucoidal markings. On North River, the upper strata show some markings like those which give name to the Cauda-Galli Grit of New York.

The thickness of this formation is about seventy-five feet. (See Secs. 12, 88, 114, 115, 122 and 128.) It is well exposed on the Mississippi, South, North and

Fabius rivers; on See's, Lick and Clear Creeks; and on Tyrrill's and Price's Branch.

The upper part of these strata is sometimes used for foundations, and in one instance, at least, for a culvert on the Railroad.

It is not sufficiently indurated to prove a strong and durable stone, or it would be exposed in the bluffs like other durable rocks, instead of being covered by its own disintegrated particles. It has never been seen, except where its surface had been recently exposed.

F. *l*—LITHOGRAPHIC LIMESTONE.

This rock presents very constant and well-marked lithological characters. It is a pure compact limestone, breaking rather easily, with a smooth conchoidal fracture, into sharp angular fragments. Its color varies from a light drab to the lighter shades of buff and blue. It gives a sharp ringing sound under the hammer, from which it is called "pot-metal" in some parts of the county.

It is very regularly stratified, in beds varying from four to fifteen inches in thickness, often presenting, in mural bluffs, all the regularity of masonry. In the bluffs above Louisiana, on the Mississippi is a fine example of this characteristic feature.

This rock contains much calcareous spar in large crystalline masses, and in drusy cavities. Fine specimens of Iceland spar, showing the beautiful phenomenon of double refraction, are found at Hannibal and other places.

Small quantities of Lead and Zinc were found in it, on South River, near the county line, Sec. 3.

The lower strata are thicker, darker colored and a purer carbonate of lime; while the upper are magnesian, and present various shades of drab and buff, as at the mouth of McDowell's cave, in the north-east corner of Ralls county.

It is very variable in thickness. At Hannibal, Sec. 11, it is fifty-six feet, while at Sec. 126, on South River, thirteen miles west, it is but two feet. (See Secs. 6, 2, 127 and 135.

Its fossils are scarce, and are rarely obtained in a perfect state. The most characteristic are *Spirifer Marionensis*, *S. cupidatus*, *Productus Murchisonianus*, *Phillipsia Missouriensis* and *Filicites gracilis*.

It burns to an excellent lime, and furnishes a rock for rough walls, both durable and cheap. The lower beds are a very good lithographic stone, and a future demand may make it very valuable for that purpose. (See p. 169.)

It may be proper to state here that there is, just below this rock, some two feet of soft, brown argillo-calcareous sandstone, which contains the same fossils as the Lithographic Limestone above, together with a beautiful species of *Conularia*.

SYSTEM IV.

F. *p*—HAMILTON GROUP.

In Marion county this rock is very constant in its lithological characters. It is an argillaceous shale or fire-clay, somewhat arenaceous and very uniformly and thinly stratified. On exposure to the air, it crumbles and forms a semi-plastic clay.

It is so similar to the lower portion of the *Vermicular Sandstones and Shales*, as seen at Sec. 114, on North River, that it is impossible to distinguish them, except by their stratigraphical relations to the other rocks. It is about fifty feet thick, though often much thinner. (See Schedule of Secs. 6, 125, 127 and 135.)

No fossils but a *Canularia* have been observed in these shales in Marion county, but the few found in Pike are characteristic of the Hamilton Group. (See p. 107 and Catalogue VII.)

It is doubtless, identical with the shales near Ashley, in Pike county, which contain fossils common in the Hamilton Group of the West. It occupies the same position, or one very near it, and presents nearly the same lithological characters. The absence of the Oolitic Limestone of Louisiana, and the overlying shales, produces the uncertainty of the position of this Group in Marion. Still, all the evidence places it in the Hamilton age.

This rock gives every indication of a good Fire-Clay. Analysis and experiment will soon determine the matter. The quantity on the South River alone is sufficient to supply the world.

F. *m*—ONONDAGA LIMESTONE—COOPER MARBLE.

This marble is easily distinguished by its lithological characters. It is a hard, compact, blue limestone, which has disseminated through it, numerous small angular masses of pellucid calcareous spar. These particles of spar often present the appearance of Arabic characters, like the quartz in graphite granite. This marble is hard and durable, and receives a fine polish.

It passes down into a light-colored, thin-bedded, argillaceous limestone, which is, probably, the upper part of the *Hudson River Group*. A single filiform coral, *Acervularia Davidsoni?* is the only fossil found in this rock.

ECONOMICAL GEOLOGY OF MARION COUNTY.

BUILDING MATERIALS.

Limestones.—The Archimedes and the Encrinital Limestones and the Cooper Marble, all furnish building materials, at once cheap, durable and beautiful. The quarries at Hannibal, Palmyra, Philadelphia and Sharpsburg, and the beds of those Formations exposed in all the bluffs of the county, afford ample evidence of a vast quantity of excellent limestones for building purposes. The Calaboose at Hannibal presents a fine specimen of the Encrinital Limestone.

Marble.—Some beds of the Encrinital Limestone in the bluffs of the Mississippi, between the Fabius and McFarlin's Branch, and in several other places in the county, would furnish an abundance of durable white crystalline marble. The Cooper Marble, F. *m*, on North and South Rivers, and See's Creek, presents many beds of a fine blue marble, bespangled with numerous pellucid crystalline particles of calcareous spar. This rock receives a fine polish, and is well adapted to ornamental marble work, where dark varieties are appropriate.

The Lower beds of the Lithographic Limestone, exposed near the water at Hannibal, are, also, well adapted to the same varieties of work, though the color is not so dark, it being a bluish drab.

These marbles are admirably fitted for use in tessellated pavements. Squares of the latter varieties, alternating with the white, would present a fine effect.

Freestone. — The sandstone, F. *f*, contains, in many places, beds of excellent freestone for building purposes; as in the quarry near Mr. Pond's and in the bluffs of North River and the Fabius. The micaceous Sandstone, F. *e*, is sometimes used, but it disintegrates too rapidly to be durable.

The upper strata of the Vermicular Sandstone, are used for the Eastern abutment of the bridge over the South Fork of North River, near the mouth of See's Creek, and for a culvert of the Railroad, near Sec. 124. It is not sufficiently firm for durable masonry.

Bricks. — The clays of the Bluff Formation furnish an abundance of excellent material for bricks. The sand and clay are often mixed in the requisite proportions for use, while there is enough of the oxide of iron to give the burnt brick a fine red color. (See page 72.)

The red clay in the Railroad cut at Palmyra, with a small mixture of clean sand, would make superior, hard, durable and deep red brick. In short, materials for this use, are abundant in all parts of the county.

Cements and Mortars.—The Limestones, Fs. *h*, *i*, *l* and *m*, all contain strata which will burn into lime of the very best quality. The Boulder Deposit and the Alluvium of the river bottoms, abound in good sands for mortars and cements.

Hydraulic Cement.—The upper part of the Lithographic Limestone and the middle portions of the Vermicular Sandstones and Shales, afford some Hydraulic Limestones, but the quality of the cements formed from them has not yet been examined. We shall test their value by experiment. (See pp. 167 and 168.)

ROAD MATERIALS.

Materials of the very best quality for roads are found in the greatest abundance in the Drift and the rivers and creeks, in various parts of the county. The gravel of the Drift, when well selected, can not be surpassed for roads; as roads made of it, are smoother and many times more durable than those made of plank.

The Gravel Road, leading westward from Hannibal, is a good illustration of the fitness of this material for such purposes. And yet the best of it was not used on this road.

Long experience in England, has proved the chert pebbles to be the best material ever used there for highways.

USEFUL MINERALS.

Silicious Marl.—This marl is at once the most abundant and most valuable of all the minerals of Marion. It abounds in every section and quarter section of the county, save those in the river bottoms, where its presence is not needed to make a good soil. It varies in depth from two to thirty feet, and lies directly under the soil, into which it enters as its largest ingredient. Almost all of the subsoils are made up of it, and subsoil plowing will give the crops the advantages of its fertilizing properties.

This marl forms almost the entire mass of the Bluff or Loess, as described above. Its quantity in the county is immense, and should become an inexhaustible bank, upon which the farmer may draw for ages to come.

For the agricultural value of this marl, see Economical Geology, Chapter I.

Pipe-Clay.—A most excellent quality of this useful mineral is abundant in the county. It is found on the lands of Mr. James Maddox and Mr. White, south of North River; on Mrs. Brown's and Mr. Pond's, east of Cedar Creek; at the coal-bank of Hays & Muldrow, in Sec. 20, of Town. 57, R. 7; and Sec. 10, of Town. 58, R. 7, south of Sharpsburg, and north of Judge Gore's, where it was obtained for the pottery of Oldham & Davis. It exists in many other places, sufficiently abundant for all the purposes to which such clays are applied. We have a fine specimen from Mr. Enoch Griffith.

This clay is much used for white-washing; and some think it preferable to lime, for that purpose. It is as white, more tenacious, and does not soil so easily.

Fire-Clay.—No. 5, S. III., is, in many places a good fire-clay, and the Formations *p* and *k* furnish inexhaustible beds of this material.

The two beds mentioned are each from thirty to fifty feet thick, and they crop out in the bluffs of North River, Fabius, South River and the Mississippi. The quantity is unlimited, but experiments and analyses, which will be made, alone can prove its quality. Should it make good fire-bricks, the manufacturing of them would make these beds a source of great wealth.

Gritstone.—Mr. A. Pond has a fine grindstone of coarse sharp grit, made from a sandstone, F. *f*, on his farm.

Marble, Hydraulic Limestone, Limestone and Sandstone, are mentioned under the head of building materials.

Lithographic Limestone.—The lower beds of F. *l*, present every appearance of a fine lithographic stone. The jointed structure will render it somewhat difficult to obtain slabs for the larger lithographs, but any quantity suitable for smaller sizes can be procured.

Coal—This useful mineral, so abundant in some of the neighboring counties, was found in small quantities only in this; as the Coal Measures exist merely as outliers of limited extent. The largest area covered by them, is in the south-western part of the county, where the micaceous sandstone is so abundant. Whether any coal exists there, is a problem yet to be solved, though the probabilities are, that it will be found under the sandstone; for in several places, as below the mouth of the La Mine in Cooper county, three coal-beds exist under this sandstone. But, in several places in the vicinity of Sharpsburg we saw this sandstone resting directly upon the Encrinital Limestone, with no intervening strata of any description whatever. But two beds of coal have been discovered in this county. The one is seen at Keller's, and at Hays & Muldrow's bed; the other, at Mr. Pinkston's pit, in Town. 57, R. 8, Sec. 29. These coal strata, and, doubtless, the coal also, crop out on the land of Capt Carson,* Town. 58, R. 7, Sec. 1. The former bed is variable in thickness, according to the testimony of those who saw the mines opened; the pits are now filled up. Its depth may be set down at eighteen inches, near Mr. Keller's,

* Since this Report was written, Capt. Carson has discovered the coal on his land in the south-east quarter of Sec. 1. The bed is one foot thick.

and at one foot, north of Houston. The quality of the specimens seen, was good; yet, the limited extent of these beds, renders it probable that they will be worked for home demand only. The latter bed is a narrow valley, excavated in the Encrinital Limestone, whose mural bluffs must have been the shores of the estuary in which this deposit of coal was found. It contains so much sulphuret of iron as to render it valueless for all ordinary purposes.

A considerable sum of money has been spent in sinking shafts for coal in the shales at Hannibal, and in the bluffs, a few miles south of that town; but without the least possibility of success. No workable beds of this mineral have been found in, or below the Archimedes and the Encrinital Limestones, both of which are above the shales just mentioned. These shales are so similar to those of the Coal Measures, it is not surprising that one unacquainted with Geology, should mistake them for the same, and deem them good indications of coal. But a Geologist could at once detect their difference, and show the impossibility of finding coal so low in the series.

No coal of any extent will be found in Marion county, save in or near the localities indicated as occupied by the Coal Measures; and all money spent exploring these lower shales will be thrown away.

Carbonate of Lime exists in great abundance in this county; as *Limestones* fit for common building purposes, *Marble* for ornamental work, *Lithographic Stone*, *Hydraulic Limestone* and those suitable for mortars, besides the numerous varieties of Calcareous Spar, so beautiful in structure and appearance.

These spars are found in cavities of all the Limestones mentioned above, but more particularly in the Lithographic and Archimedes beds. They are most abundant in the numerous Geodes of the latter, where we found the varieties mentioned in Chapter I., under the head of Archimedes Limestone.

ORES.

Iron is abundantly disseminated through the rocks of Marion, but it nowhere furnishes a sufficient quantity of good ores to justify manufacturing operations.

Oxides of Iron constitute a large part of the coloring matter in the brown sandstones, limestones, shales and clays. In many places the boulder and bluff deposits are so charged with it as to present the brilliant colors of the red and yellow ochres.

Iron Pyrites is quite common in the Shales of the Coal Measures and the Vermicular Sandstone and Shales. When exposed to the air it readily decomposes, and the sulphur unites with oxygen, forming sulphuric acid, which réunites with the iron and forms sulphate of iron, or with the alumina and potassa of the Shales, and forms the Alum so often present in the water percolating through those rocks.

Sulphuret of Iron is, also, found in the coal in greater or less abundance. It produces those sulphurous fumes, so annoying and injurious to those who use such coal either in the house or work-shop. Its sulphur, also, unites with the iron and steel worked with the coal, and renders them brittle and worthless for many purposes.

The Limestones, Fs. *h* and *i*, contain more or less of this mineral in small particles and crystals, which renders some beds unfit for outer walls where beauty is an object; for a very small fragment will, on exposure to the air and water, produce an iron stain, several feet in length. The Lithographic Limestone often contains brilliant cubic crystals of it.

In the blue shales of the Hamilton Group, it is found in cylindrical or globular masses set with myriads of minute crystals, whose splendent tarnished facets present all the brilliant hues of the dove-colored changeable silks. These worthless masses are often mistaken for valuable ores.

Zinc. — The *Sulphuret* of *Zinc*, *Blende*, or the *Black-Jack* of miners, exists in small quantities in the Archimedes Limestone at Sec. 106, and in the Lithographic Limestone, Sec. 2.

Lead. —Small portions only, of *Galena*, or the sulphuret, were found in the Encrinital Limestone, and in the geodes of the Archimedes Limestone.

Manganese. —The oxide of manganese forms most perfect dendritic markings on the conchoidal fractures of the Lithographic Limestone. These markings are as delicate as frost work, and far more beautiful than the most perfect productions of the Lithographic art.

Quartz, in the form of a Saccharoidal Sandstone, fit for glass manufacture, is not uncommon in the Ferruginous Sandstone. Granular, smoky, milky and limpid quartzose pebbles, are found in the Drift.

Chalcedony. —Many of the geodes above mentioned, have internal coatings of this beautiful mineral.

Agates of a very fine quality are found encrusting the drusy cavities of the silicious geodes so common in the Archimedes Limestone.

Jasper and *Touchstone* exist in the Drift.

SOILS.

A good soil is the most useful and enduring wealth of a country. We elsewhere stated, without the fear of contradiction, that Missouri possesses one of the best soils upon the Continent, for the cultivation of our great staples, *Hemp*, *Corn*, *Wheat* and *Tobacco*.

There are five distinct varieties of soil in Marion county: —

1st. The *Elm Land*, so called from the heavy growth of the American Elm, *Ulmus Americana*, which it produces, is scarcely inferior to the very best in the State. It is based upon a deep, light and rich deposit of the silicious marls of the Bluff Formation, which has a large admixture of vegetable mould, from the rank vegetation it has sustained for many a bygone age. It produces the finest crops of Hemp and Corn; and, after the superabundance of vegetable matter has been exhausted by several successive crops, it brings most excellent wheat. The country occupied by this soil presents a surface gently rolling, well watered, well drained, and heavily timbered.

The principal growth is American Elm,* Hack-Berry, Red Mulberry, Honey Locust, Black Walnut, Black Oak, Wild Cherry, Blue Ash, Red Bud and Papaw. These lands are marked on the map by dotted lines.

2d. The *Hickory* and the best *Prairie Lands*† occupy the next grade, and, in fact, are often but little inferior to the *Elm Lands* just described. This soil, also, rests upon the same marl deposit of the Bluff, contains less vegetable matter, and is more argillaceous and less porous.

It produces good wheat, corn, tobacco, etc., etc. The surface of these Prairies is gently rolling; but the Hickory Lands are more broken, and the slopes more abrupt. The timber most abundant is Common Shellbark, Thick Shellbark and Pignut Hickories, White, Red, Black and Scarlet Oaks; White and Black Walnuts; Sugar Tree; and White and Blue Ashes; Sassafras; ‡ Papaw; Hack-Berry; Red and Black Haws; and Summer, Fox and Frost Grapes.

---

* The scientific names of trees are given in Appendix C.

† This is the same as the 2d grade of soil from the Bluff, mentioned on p. 139.

‡ On the Mississippi bluffs, between the North and South Fabius, the Sassafras is very abundant and large, often one and a half or two feet in diameter. It is much used for rails in that region.

3d. The *White Oak Lands* and the poorer Prairies possess the least productive soil in the county. It is, also, based upon the Bluff marls; but it is more argillaceous and silicious, contains less vegetable matter than either of the soils above mentioned, and appears to have lost the finer and lighter portions, by the constant action of rains. In most cases, the subsoil is better than the surface. It occupies the ridges in the north-western part of the county, and is but sparingly timbered with White Oak (*Quercus alba*), Laurel Oak* (*Quercus imbricaria*, Mx), Black-Jack Oak (*Quercus ferruginea*), Crab Apple (*Malus caronaria*), Black Hickory (*Juglans microcarpa*), and the dwarf variety of Post Oak (*Quercus obtusiloba*).

4th. Under the bluffs, where the shales of the Vermicular Sandstone and Shales and of the Hamilton Group, are exposed, we find a wet, heavy, clayey soil, rich in vegetable matter. It sustains a growth of rank weeds and heavy timber. Thorough draining and subsoiling alone, can fit this soil for common agricultural purposes; but when once reclaimed, it will be very permanent and productive for oats, grasses and all kindred crops. The timber is a growth of Bur, Red, Swamp White, Pin and Laurel Oaks; Honey Locust; Box-Elder; Buckeye; Sugar Tree; White Maple; American Elm; Hack-Berry; Thick Shellbark Hickory; Linden; Red Birch; Black Walnut, and Papaw.

5th. The *Alluvial Bottoms* and *Bottom Prairies* along the Mississippi, present a rich, loose vegetable soil, well adapted to hemp and corn; only a small portion of them is sufficiently safe from inundations to warrant cultivation at the present prices of land. The timber of the alluvial bottoms, is mentioned on page 139.

6th. The *Swamp Land* of the Mississippi Bottom is more or less covered with water, and sustains a rank growth of vegetation, which, together with the fine sediment of the waters, adds yearly to the vast amount of fertilizing matter in the soil. When these lands are eventually reclaimed, they will be very productive and well nigh inexhaustible.

So universal is the Bluff Deposit in this county, that the older rocks have but little effect upon the soils, save in two instances, where these rocks readily decompose. The Micaceous Sandstone of S. III. renders the soil sandy in the south-western part of the county, where it is so well developed; and the shales of S. IV. make the soils clayey and wet, as described in the 4th variety above. This effect of these shales, is obvious wherever they crop out in the bluffs of the South, North and the Mississippi rivers, and of See's, Lick and Cedar Creeks. The numerous springs, which break out at the top of these shales, overflow their impervious soils and render them extremely wet.

This description of the soils of Marion county must be imperfect from the nature of the case. In order to have a full knowledge of a soil and its agricultural capacities, we need an analysis of its ingredients, the rocks upon which it rests, the herbs and trees it supports, the topography of the country and meteorological tables, giving the amount of rain, the dew point and the temperature of the climate.

We collected soils, but the analyses have not yet been made; we made imperfect collections of the plants and trees, and such meteorological observations as our stay of four weeks would permit; but no time has yet been found for arranging the plants and observations for use. I have, however, appended to each variety of soil a list of some of the most important and abundant trees growing upon it.

When these analyses are completed and full catalogues of the plants made out, a more detailed account of the soils will be given, together with the crops and modes of culture best adapted to each. One thing, at least, is very certain, that nothing could so much benefit the soils of Marion, and particularly the 2d, 3d and 4th varie-

* This species is called Water Oak in Marion county.

ties, as subsoiling with a plow, that would stir the soil to a depth of eighteen or twenty inches. Had this been done, not even the severe drought of the present season would have burned the crops. Several fields in Boone county, where this was tried, prove this position beyond a cavil. (See p. 151.)

A glance at the map of this county will show how admirably the timber and prairie lands are arranged to meet the wants of an agricultural community. There is scarcely a township without its quantum of each, and that so arranged that every farm may have its due proportion.

SPRINGS.

Fresh-water Springs rise, bold and limpid from the limestones in all parts of the county. But they are particularly abundant along the line of separation between the Encrinital Limestone and Vermicular Sandstone and Shales. The strata of the latter are impervious to the waters, which percolate through the superincumbent limestones; and they are forced along the dividing plane until they find an exit, where that plane reaches the surface. A large portion of the springs in the bluffs of the Fabius, South and North Rivers, break out along the line of separation between these rocks.

A small creek comes rushing out of the eastern bluff of South River, just above the Railroad crossing, which, in all probability, has the same origin as the springs above mentioned.

Salt Spring.—I saw but one in the county. It is called North-River Lick; and is situated in Town. 58, R. 7, Sec. 25. The water is said to be a strong brine; but we have not yet analyzed it, and cannot speak positively of its qualities.

Chalybeate Springs.—A chalybeate spring rises in the bed of the creek west of Sharpsburg; but its waters were so mingled with those of the creek, and its passage so choked up, that I could not judge of its medicinal properties. The large amount of iron deposited, indicates that it is strongly impregnated with that metal in the form of a Carbonate.

On the land of Mr. Gelaspie, a spring strongly impregnated with the sulphate of iron, rises from the chert beds above the Encrinital Limestone. Four or five yards below, a fresh spring breaks out of the limestone itself. The ferruginous clay, interstratified with the chert, is, probably, the source of the iron in the former.

Sulphur Springs. — A bold sulphur spring rises from the Blue Shales of S. IV., on Lick Creek, east of Mrs. Shannon's. This, so far as we could judge, from the gas, the deposite, the taste, and the testimony of those who have used it, is a most excellent sulphur water. A quantity was collected for analysis, which will, doubtless, prove it to be a valuable medicinal water, and worthy of the reputation it sustains. It is located in a beautiful valley, and could easily be made a desirable watering place.

STREAMS.

But few counties are so well watered as Marion. A glance at the map will show how admirably every portion of it is intersected by river, creeks and branches. The North and South Fabius, the North and South Rivers, the Troublesome, the Grassy, See's and Lick Creeks, besides numerous Branches, intersect every township in the county. Water-power and mill-sites are abundant. These streams abound in fish, particularly the sloughs and bayous, as Bay de Charles, in the Mississippi Bottom, where large quantities are caught for market.

Thus much we have thought it best to say of Marion county, without waiting for more definite conclusions respecting the soils, waters, limes and clays, to be derived from the labors of the chemist.

Now, the question naturally arises, "What good will result from this Survey?" The amount of good depends, in the main, upon those who own the soils and minerals of the county. Will the farmers develop the full wealth of their rich soils by working some twenty inches, instead of the five or six heretofore loosened? I have shown that the subsoil in the White Oak and prairie lands is as good, or better than the surface, while that of the Hickory and the Elm lands, is almost as good; and, in short, that subsoiling would benefit every acre cultivated. If the farmer still chooses to occupy but five inches of his soil, and let every drought burn up his crops, it is not our fault; we have pointed out a more perfect way. If deep plowing be adopted, the increased profits in farming in this county alone, would more than pay the annual expenses of the Survey.

But we have pointed out extensive beds of three varieties of *Marble*, suited to ornamental architecture, one bed of *good Lithographic Limestone*, two vast beds of *Fire Clays*, numerous beds of first-rate *Pipe-Clay*, besides *Building* and *Road Materials* without limit. These are better sources of national wealth than Gold or Silver Mines But few men would prefer, when dying, to leave their sons on a golden placer in California, rather than upon one of the rich farms of Marion, with its *inexhaustible* soil and beds of *Marl*, *Marble*, *Fire-Clay*, *Pipe-Clay* and *Lithographic Limestone*, all imperishable sources of wealth.

Again, we have proved that no coal can be found in the limestones and shales of the central and south-eastern parts of the county. This may prevent the expenditure of thousands in searching for that mineral. Had the fact been known a few years sooner, it would have saved more than the survey of the county cost.

We have, also, made an accurate topographical map of the county, with all the streams, prairies, Elm Lands, bluffs and towns laid down, together with the Geology. This map must be of great service to all; and when similar maps are completed for all the counties, much will have been added to the geographical knowledge of the State.

The bluffs along the streams are most beautiful when clothed with the rich foliage, and numerous flowers, which adorn them. In the months of April, May, and June, these bluffs are beautiful by a gaudy and delicate flora. The snowy *Spirea opulifolia*, *Mespilus arborea*, Anemone, Violets, Geraniums, Hepaticas, Sanguinarias, purple and white Anomias, the gaudy purple and yellow Rudbeckias, the graceful Canadian Aquilegia, the magnificent pink, purple and orange Asclepias, the fairy-like Sensitive Briar, and numerous others of the lovely sisterhood, profusely adorn the bluffs and broken grounds along the streams.

The Flora of the prairies is still more gaudy and magnificent. Baptisias, Coreopses, Larkspurs, Lillies, and numerous other showy flowers, gem the green carpet of those vast meadows.

EXPLANATION OF MAP AND SCHEDULE.

On the map of this county, besides the usual geographical features, the bluffs, the bottom, and prairie and timber and Elm lands, are laid down. The Geological Formations are marked by colors and boundaries; and the localities of the sections on the Schedule, are marked S 1, S 2, S 3, etc , etc. If any one wishes to know what rocks occur at any of these localities, the section of the same number on the Schedule will give them. In the same manner, the locality of any section on the Schedule, can be found on the map by the corresponding number.

CHAPTER IV.

COOPER COUNTY.

Cooper county is situated on the south side of the Missouri river, near the center of the State. It contains about fifteen and a half townships, or an area of 558 square miles. The face of the country is nearly level, but agreeably undulating, and diversified with timber and prairie. It is watered by several streams, which have cut their beds much below the general level of the country, so that on their borders the strata have been so denuded as to present many ridges and rounded knobs, varying in height from 100 to 300 feet. The highest bluffs in the county, are on the La Mine, below Corum's Mill.

SCIENTIFIC GEOLOGY.

The strata of Cooper county range from the Alluvium to the 2d Sandstone, or near the base of the Calciferous Sandrock.

SYSTEM I.—QUATERNARY.

F. *a*—ALLUVIUM.

The alluvium of this county presents the same features as it does in other parts of the State; these are fully described * in Chapter I., page 60–66. Besides the soil, which, as a matter of course, is cöextensive with the county, and a few unimportant localities, this Formation is confined to the bottoms of the Missouri, La Mine, the Little Saline and other streams. The largest part of the Missouri bottom is located in Towns. 48 and 49, R. 15, and in Town. 49, Rs. 16 and 18. These alluvial deposits are very fertile, and sustain a heavy growth of the usual timber. (See page 139.) The bottoms of the La Mine extend from its mouth to the southern boundary of the county, presenting everywhere a growth of large timber.

F. *c*—BLUFF.

This Formation is well developed in Cooper, and presents its usual physical characters, and contains the most of its fossils. (See

* It is not deemed necessary to repeat descriptions of Formations in the County Reports, unless they present some new features.

Catalogue I., Appendix B.) It shows its usual characteristic features, and is thickest on the bluffs of the Missouri, and gives to them their rounded contour and fertility. Under some parts of the city of Boonville, the Bluff is 100 feet thick, as shown by the following section:—

No. 1.—100 feet of brown and ash-colored silico-argillaceous marl of the Bluff. It contains many delicate land and fluviatile shells. *Helix electrina*, *H. alternata*, *H. minuta*, *Helicina occulta*, *Succinea campestris*, etc.

No. 2.—3 feet of Drift, which is mostly pebbles and sand.

No. 3.—3 feet of chert in irregular beds, interstratified with clay. } Archimedes Limestone.

No. 4.—30 feet of gray crystalline limestone, containing beds of shale. } Archimedes Limestone.

Near Mr. Haas', above Boonville, it is only fifty feet thick, and about forty near Mr. Howard's, below the mouth of the La Mine. In the south part of the county, it is not so thick, and is more argillaceous, and contains more foreign matter.

F. *d*—DRIFT.

This deposit is very sparingly developed in Cooper. Boulders of metamorphic and igneous rocks are often seen in the beds of the small streams, and those places from which the superincumbent Bluff has been removed; but the undisturbed beds of pebbles and sands, so common in this Formation farther north, are seldom seen in the county.

Beds of water-worn pebbles and sand frequently appear where the streams have cut through the strata in the valleys of denudation. But these strata are made up almost entirely of fragments of the adjacent rocks; and were, doubtless, formed by causes more limited than those which produced the Drift, and still more recent, as pebbles from the drift are sometimes found in them. (See page 78.)

SYSTEM III.—CARBONIFEROUS.

F. *e*—COAL MEASURES.

The beds of the Lower Coal Series, only, were observed in Cooper. The strata, from No. 60 to No. 75, (see pp. 86 and 87), of the Coal Measures are exposed in the Bluffs of the Missouri, between Boonville and the mouth of the La Mine. These strata are, also, represented in Sec. 13; No. 1 of this section being the same as No. 60 of the Coal Measures, and No. 16 of the former corresponding with No. 75 of the latter. But all of these strata are not permanent in these bluffs. This is particularly the case with the coal-beds, Nos. 3 and 5 of Sec. 13. This want of permanency in some of the beds, and the frequent slips of the upper strata, caused by the wearing away of the underlying shales, make it very difficult to trace out the coal-beds in these bluffs. But after examining and comparing the strata in some forty or fifty places, the number and arrangement of the beds were found to be as represented in Sec. 13. Still, it may be proper to say that all of these beds were not seen at any one place. This, however, is no proof that all do not exist at some localities; for the loose materials are so abundant that a part were covered up by them, at every locality observed.

The best exposure of these beds, is in Mr. Howard's bluff, three-fourths of a mile below the mouth of the La Mine, in Town. 49, R. 18, Sec. 36, where we get the following section:

No. 1.—50 feet slope, which is nearly all Bluff.
No. 2.—35 feet of brown friable Micaceous Sandstone.—No. 1 of Sec. 13.
No. 3.—3 feet of gray sandy shale —No. 2 of Sec. 13.
No. 4.—1 foot of poor bituminous coal.—No. 3 of Sec. 13.
No. 5.—4 feet of grayish blue sandy shale.—No. 4 of Sec. 13.
No. 6.—6 feet of bituminous coal.—No. 5 of Sec. 13. This bed is ten or fifteen feet above the river, and the strata dip to the north-east, at an angle of twenty-five degrees.

In the bluff, 100 yards below, and nearly east of the last section, we get—

No. 1.—30 feet slope—nearly all bluff.
No. 2.—45 feet of brown friable Micaceous Sandstone.—No. 1 of Sec. 13.
No. 3.—2½ feet of coal.
No. 4.—10 feet slope, covered by debris.
No. 5.—3 feet of compact gray and blue hydraulic limestone.—No. 7 of Sec. 13.
No. 6.—5 feet of bituminous shale.—No. 8 of section 13.
No. 7.—3? feet of coal.—No. 9 of Sec. 13.
No. 8.—1 foot of bituminous shale.—No. 10 of Sec. 13.
No. 9.—45 feet slope.—Probably Nos. 10, 11, 12, 13, 14, 15 and 16 of Sec. 13.
No. 10.—10 feet of coarse brown and white thick-bedded sandstone.—No. 17 of Sec. 13, or Ferruginous Sandstone.
No. 11.—6 feet slope, covered with debris. This is, probably, the upper shales of the Archimedes Limestone.
No. 12.—40 feet of Archimedes Limestone.

No. 2 of the first locality, is the same as No. 2 in the second, but is eighty-five or ninety feet below it. This difference of level, and the great dip of the first section, show that they can have slidden down. On Sec. 1, Town. 48, R. 18, we get the following:—

No. 1.—55 feet slope—mostly bluff.

No. 2.—35 feet of brown Micaceous Sandstone.—No. 1 of Sec. 13.
No. 3.—3 feet slope.
No. 4—4 feet of hydraulic limestone.—No. 7 of Sec. 13.
No. 5.—4 feet of bituminous shale?
No. 6.—1½ feet of coal of the best quality.—No. 9 of section 13.

On Sec. 31 of Town. 49, R. 17, the land of Mr. David Griffith, we get the following section:—

No. 1.—12 feet of clay and shale.
No. 2.—1 foot of pure coal.
No. 3.—2 inches of shale.
No. 4.—2½ feet of good coal.

At Mr. James R. Payne's coal-bed, in Town. 49, R. 17, Sec. 31, the strata were—

No. 1.—5 feet of hydraulic limestone.—No. 7 of Sec. 13.
No. 2.—8 feet of bituminous shale.—No. 8 of Sec. 13.
No. 3.—3 inches of coal.—No. 9 of Sec. 13.
No. 4.—7 feet of shale.—No. 10 of Sec. 13.
No. 5.—3 inches of coal.—No. 11 of Sec. 13.
No. 6.—7½ feet of bituminous shale.—No. 12 of Sec. 13.
No. 7.—8 inches of coal.—No. 13 of Sec. 13.
No. 8.—4 feet of red shale.—No. 14. of Sec. 13.

At this place I saw on the surface, dark concretions which contained *Leda arata* and *Goniatites planorbiformis*. They evidently came from the decomposed strata above, probably from No. 3 of Sec. 13. At Mr. Holman's coal-bed, south of Boonville, we get—

No. 1.—6 feet of Bluff.
No. 2.—3 feet of Drift.
No. 3.—2 feet of Micaceous Sandstone.—No. 1 of Sec. 13.
No. 4.—2 feet of soft sandy shale.
No. 5.—3 feet of Hydraulic limestone,
No. 6.—3 feet of brown and yellow shale,
No. 7.—4 inches of hydraulic limestone,
No. 8.—1½ feet of blue and yellow shale,
No. 9.—10 inches of hydraulic limestone,
No. 10.—15 inches of bituminous shale,
No. 11.—6 inches of hydraulic limestone,
}Hydraulic limestone, interstratified with shales, as it often appears. It contains *Productus splendens*, *Spirifer lineatus*, *Chonetes mesoloba*. It is No. 7 of Sec. 13.
No. 12.—4 feet of bituminous and blue shale.—No. 8 of Sec. 13.
No. 19.—1½ feet of good coal.—No. 9 of Sec. 13.

In the bluff above Mr. Haas', the strata were as follows:—

No. 1.—Bluff.
No. 2.—4 feet of Micaceous Sandstone.—No. 1. of Sec. 13.
No. 3.—4 feet of blue shale.
No. 4.—2 feet of bituminous shale.

No. 5.—4 feet slope.
No. 6.—8 feet of hydraulic limestone.—No. 7 of Sec. 13.
No. 8.—7 feet of bituminous shale.—No. 8 of Sec. 13.
No. 9.—50 feet slope.—Probably Nos. 9, 10, 11, 12, 13, 14, 15 and 16 of Sec. 13.
No. 10.—25 feet of Archimedes Limestone.

One mile above the last, we get—

No. 1.—Bluff.
No. 2.—40 feet of micaceous Sandstone.
No. 3.—1 foot of coal.
No. 4.—20 feet of slope.
No. 5.—3 feet of hydraulic limestone.—No. 7 of Sec. 13.
No. 6.—7 feet of bituminous shale.—No. 8 of Sec. 13.
No. 7.—50 feet slope.—Probably Nos. 9–16 of Sec. 13.

One half of a mile above Boonville:—

No. 1.—30 feet of Bluff.
No. 2.—30 feet of brown friable micaceous Sandstone.—No. 1 of Sec. 13.
No. 3.—2 feet of hydraulic limestone.—No. 7 of Sec. 13; Nos. 2, 3, 4, 5, and 6 are wanting.
No. 4.—30 feet of slope.—Probably Nos. 8–15 of Sec. 13.
No. 5.—20 feet of blue and yellow shales, fire-clay.—No. 16 of Sec. 13.

Though all of the beds in Sec. 13 are not exposed in any one of these sections, yet all can be seen by visiting different localities.

Organic Remains.—But few fossils were seen; only those of the Lower Coal Series, which are mentioned on page 86.

Economical Value.—The Micaceous Sandstone, No. 1 of Sec. 13. is sometimes used at Boonville, as a foundation stone, and for other building purposes; but it is so friable and crushes so easily, that it cannot endure a great weight or a long exposure.

The *Hydraulic Limestone*, No. 7 of Sec. 13, has been tested and found to possess hydraulic properties; and, besides, Dr. Litton's analysis shows that it belongs to the cements of the first class. (See pages 86 and 168.) If, on trial, this should prove a valuable cement, as we have reason to expect, it can be found in great abundance. It crops out in all the bluffs between Boonville and the mouth of the La Mine; and, in short, it extends over the whole region marked on the map as Coal Measures or F. *e.*

The Fire-Clay, No. 16 of Sec. 13, possesses good qualities, and bricks made from it, will be very refractory. Fire-bricks are made of it in St. Louis county.

An adit has been opened into the bituminous shales of No. 8 of Sec. 13, near Mr. Haas', in such a manner as to follow that stratum in a horizontal direction, with the expectation that coal would be reached. But a shaft, sunk at the same place, would have reached coal much sooner. The extent of country covered by these coal-rocks may be seen by a reference to the accompanying map of Cooper county. The part colored purple, or that marked F. *e*, represents the area of the Coal Measures. They extend some three miles south of Boonville, and seven west to the La Mine, giving an area of about twenty square miles, which will yield for every foot of workable coal 20,000,000 tons of that valuable mineral. Should the whole area average three feet, which is certainly the lowest figure, after allowing for the denudation of strata in some places and for the thinning out of beds in others, the whole amount in this area of the regular Coal Measures, will be 60,000,000 tons, of workable coal. And it is very probable that the quantity is even double this amount.

Every foot of workable coal will give over 1,500 tons per acre; and three feet, 4,500 tons per acre. At Howard's Bluff there are, at least, six feet of workable beds, which will give over 9,000 tons per acre, for that region. On the southern and eastern borders of this area, the strata are not so thick. Besides these beds of the regular Coal Measures, there are many other local deposits of the very best coal, which often occurs in beds of great thickness and purity.

Col. James Staples' Coal-Bed is located on the south of the 16th Sec. of Town. 49, R. 19.

On the south side of the opening to this valuable bed, the following section was measured: —

No. 1.—6 feet of soil and local Drift.
No. 2.—6 feet of good cannel-coal, in regular strata.
No. 3.—20 feet of very good common bituminous coal.
No. 4.—4 feet of calcareous shale.

This bed seems to be in a ravine in the Carboniferous Limestone. The stratum of soil and local Drift, No. 1, rests in a horizontal position, and non-conformably upon the coal, which dips to the south at an angle of fifteen or twenty degrees. It has been so denuded, that the whole of No. 2 is worn away on the north side, where the common bituminous variety of No. 3 comes to the surface of the deposit. A few feet to the east, a thick concretionary mass of No. 4 projects up into the lower part of the bed, and forms what some miners, call a *horse-back*, which causes a dip of the strata on each side, one to the east and the other to the west. This is a very valuable bed; but its character is of such a nature, the quantity cannot be determined until it is worked out.

Paxton's Coal-bed is located about one mile south of Chouteau Springs, in a ravine in the Encrinital Limestone. The following section was measured in the shaft, which was partially filled with water at the time it was visited: —

No. 1.—2 feet of soil.
No. 2.—2 feet of local Drift.
No. 3.—2 feet of yellow aluminous earth.
No. 4.—6 feet of bituminous shale, containing large quantities of iron pyrites in thin lamina.
No. 5.—4? feet of coal. This coal is said to be four feet thick, and of good quality.

The quantity of coal at this bed cannot be determined by the principles which usually govern such estimates; as it is an irregular deposit. It cannot, however, extend beyond the bluffs on each side of the valley, as no coal exists under the Encrinital Limestone, which forms them.

Stiger's Coal-bed is situated about half a mile south of Paxton's. Some considerable area had been worked over, at this locality; but the shafts, or diggings, were filled up, and we could only determine its geological position, which is the same as Paxton's Coal-bed.

Stephens' Coal-bed is in Town. 47, R. 17, Secs. 27 and 28,* in a valley cut in the Encrinital Limestone. The principal bed is seven feet thick and has an irregular dip to the west. This is a very excellent quality of common bituminous coal. It breaks with a clean shining conchoidal fracture, and burns with a free white flame. The surfaces of the coal are often covered with brilliant irised colors. A second stratum is said to exist below the principal bed above named. On Town. 46, R. 17, Sec. 10, is a bed of cannel-coal, in a ravine cut in the Chouteau Limestone. The strata dip at an angle of fifty-five or sixty degrees, and are covered by a bed of local Drift resting upon the edges of the strata. The following section will give the associated rocks:—

No. 1.—2 feet of bituminous shale.
No. 2.—4 feet of cannel-coal, of medium quality.
No. 3.—1 foot of bituminous shale.
No. 4.—1 foot of common bituminous coal.
No. 5.—3 feet of bituminous shale.

Col. Thos. Russell's Coal-bank is located in Town. 47, R. 16, Sec. 19? This bed is in a ravine of the Encrinital Limestone. When visited, the diggings were full of water and the position of the bed could not be seen; but the specimens thrown out were a good cannel-coal, of a dull conchoidal fracture and an even firm texture.

J. T. Johnson & Co. and Wash. Adams' Coal-bed, in Town 47, R. 16, Sec. 17, is in a valley on a level with the lower part of the Encrinital Limestone, or the top of the Chouteau, which form the low bluffs on either side. Shafts have been sunk in two places into this bed, one near the branch and another about seventy feet to the east on a higher level. At the first the following strata were passed through:—

No. 1.—6 feet of local Drift.
No. 2.—1 foot of bituminous shale.
No. 3.—18 inches of bituminous coal, of good quality.
No. 4.—12 feet of cannel-coal. The water in the shaft, covered a part of this bed; but I was informed by a miner that they had passed into the bed twelve feet without reaching the bottom. In the eastern shaft the coal is not so thick.

The cannel-coal of this bed is an excellent article.

It presents an even, dull, conchoidal fracture and a firm homogeneous texture; burns freely with a brilliant white flame, and is well suited to form cheerful fires for the domestic circle. For reasons before stated, it is impossible to estimate the quantity of coal in this bed. Still, the valley is so wide and the bed so thick, that the amount of coal cannot be very small, and it may be very large. Every acre of this bed, should its thickness be only thirteen feet, will give 20,000 tons.

Farley's Coal-bed, in Town. 46, R. 18, Sec. 31, N. E. ¼, is in a small basin in the Saccharoidal Sandstone. At the time of my visit, the excavation was filled with water; but, judging from the specimens thrown out, and the statements of Mr. Farley, the coal was about five feet thick, of an impure slaty variety. At the bottom of the excavation a circular cavity passed down into the sandstone, which was filled with the coal to the depth of seven feet, or as far as the drill was sunk into it. Sheets of Sulphuret of Zinc, about one inch thick, were thrown out with the coal. They came from a vertical vein, which cut through the whole extent of the coal-bed.

Drafton's Coal-bed, on Town. 46, R. 16, Sec. 18, S. W. ¼, † has the same geological position as the last. The stratum dips to the east at an angle of some forty

* I am indebted to Mr. H. C. Levens and Mr. Barton S. Wilson, of Boonville, for the Township and Section, in many of the localities given in this county.

† I am indebted to Mr. Meek for the examination of this and the three following beds.

degrees, and is, at least, eighteen feet thick. It has been worked in an open pit, forty feet by thirty, to the depth of sixteen feet. This coal has a greater specific gravity than the other cannel varieties above described, and, though it burns freely, a large amount of ashes is left. It has a dull conchoidal fracture, and is divided into cubic or rhomboidal masses by joints, which separate, on exposure, into thin lamina. The quantity at this locality is large.

Mrs. Fryer's Coal-bed contains a very impure cannel-coal or bituminous shale. It is in Town. 46, R. 17, Sec. 18, N. E. ¼.

Moody's Coal-bank is on Clark's Fork. The coal is similar to that at Drafton's bed; and the bluffs on each side are Encrinital Limestone.

Mr. Jenkin Rob'nson's Coal-bed, in Town. 48, R. 16, Sec. 22, S. W. ¼, is in a ravine in the Encrinital Limestone.

This coal is similar to Drafton's, above described, and is six or eight feet thick. The pit was filled with water when it was visited.

Mr. Son's coal-bed, in Town. 47, R. 18, Sec. 13, N. W. ¼, is situated in a ravine in the Encrinital Limestone. No specimens of the coal were seen; and the pit was filled up when visited.

There are several other small deposits of coal in various parts of the county. One in Sec. 16, Town. 47, R. 18, and another in Town. 46, R. 19, one-half mile south-west of Corum's Mill, in a ravine in the 2d Magnesian Limestone, and, probably, others which we did not see. These beds, so far as we can judge from their structure and the associated rocks, may not be members of the regular Coal Measures. * Whether they be outliers of the coal formation, or mere abnormal deposits, science gives us no clue to their position, save that they may be found in any of the ravines or valleys of denudation in the older rocks, provided such valleys and ravines are not above the level of those beds already mentioned; and, should others exist, the Geologist cannot be held responsible for not pointing out their locality.

CARBONIFEROUS LIMESTONE.

The following divisions of this group, are found in the county:—

F. *f* — FERRUGINOUS SANDSTONE.

This Formation is but sparingly developed in Cooper. Its thickness varies from one to twenty feet. In the section at Howard's Bluff, on page 188, it is ten feet thick; in the bluff east of Chouteau Springs, it is only four feet; and in the following section, in the bluff of the La Mine, opposite to the mouth of the Blackwater, it is six feet:—

No. 1. — 10 feet of Bluff — more argillaceous and darker colored than at Boonville.
No. 2. — 6 feet of brown and yellowish semi-saccharoidal Ferruginous Sandstone.
No. 3. — 50 feet of Encrinital Limestone, in thick beds.

In the bluffs of the Blackwater, in Sec. 3, Town. 48, R. 19, the thickness is 15 feet, and in the bluff of the La Mine, one mile south south-west of the last locality, we saw the following section:—

* For an account of these deposits, see pages 89 and 154.

No. 1. — 20 feet of brown Ferruginous Sandstone; the upper beds pass into a hornstone in thin layers.
No. 2. — 180 feet of Encrinital Limestone.
No. 3. — 175 feet of the Chemung Group.

This Sandstone is very generally diffused over that part of the county occupied by the Carboniferous Limestone; and is very often seen in blocks or masses near the tops of the bluffs formed of the Encrinital Limestone. It so much resembles the Saccharoidal Sandstone, that it may be mistaken for that rock, unless care be taken to examine its position, whether above or below the Encrinital Limestone and Chemung Group.

Economical Value. — This variable Formation, when well stratified, will make a good building-stone; but when massive and saccharoidal, it is too friable, and is well adapted to the formation of mortars and cements.

F. *h* — ARCHIMEDES LIMESTONE.

It is well exposed and exhibits its characteristic features, as described on page 95, in the bluffs of the Missouri, from Boonville to the mouth of the La Mine.

Range and Thickness. — It underlies all the Coal Measures of the county, extends eastward several miles below Boonville, and occupies nearly all that part of the county west of the La Mine and north of the Blackwater. It is marked F. *h*, on the map. Its greatest thickness observed, is seventy-five feet.

Economical Value. — The dark crystalline beds, make a firm and durable building material. Some of the shales appear like good fire-clays. Scott's Lead Mine is in this rock. (See Economical Geology, p. 199.)

Organic Remains. — Some of the beds are made up, almost entirely of corals and shells; as may be seen in the thin strata at the quarries above Boonville. The *Archimedipora Archimedes* and *Spirifer incrassatus?* are the most characteristic. (For other fossils, see Catalogue IV., Appendix B.)

F. *i* — ENCRINITAL LIMESTONE.

This valuable limestone presents its usual features — a coarse crystalline, nearly pure limestone, of brown, white and gray colors, as described in Chapter I., page 97.

Range and Thickness. — It underlies the Archimedes Limestone, and occupies nearly all the higher parts of the county where that rock is not developed, save some parts of the south. It is marked F. *i*, and colored blue on the map. Its thickness varies from 100 to 200 feet. It is 180 feet in the section above from the Blackwater, 105 at Chouteau Springs, and 45 at Marston's Bridge, Sec. 17.

Economical Value. — It is extensively used for quicklime and other building purposes, for which it is admirably adapted.

Its Organic Remains are very abundant, as shown in Catalogue V.

CHEMUNG GROUP.

F. *j* — CHOUTEAU LIMESTONE.

This Formation, with its numerous and beautiful fossils, was first observed at the Chouteau Springs, from which its name is derived.

There are two divisions, very distinct both in lithological and palæontological characters, as described on pages 101 and 102.

The Upper Chouteau Limestone is a brownish gray, earthy, silico-magnesian limestone, in heavy beds, which contain masses of calcareous spar, a few *reticulated corals* and *Fucoides cauda-galli?*

The Lower Chouteau Limestone is a blue or gray compact limestone, irregularly stratified in thin beds, which contain the new and characteristic fossils of the Formation. The *Spirifer Marionensis*, *S. peculiaris*, *Atrypa gregaria*, *A. Cooperensis*, *A. obscuraplicata*, *Avicula Cooperensis*, *A. circulus*, *A. tenuilineata*, *Chemnitzia tenuilineata*, and *Chonetes ornata*, are all new and described in this Report.

Range and Thickness. — The Chouteau Limestone underlies the Encrinital Limestone, and crops out in all parts of the county where the streams have cut through the latter Formation; as may be seen in the bluff of the La Mine, the Little Saline and the Moniteau. It is colored green and marked F. *j*, on the map. Its thickness is seventy feet at Marston's Bridge (see Sec. 17), and fifty at Chouteau Springs; as in the following section at that place: —

No. 1. — 15 feet of Bluff.
No. 2. — 4 feet of Ferruginous Sandstone.
No. 3. — 105 feet of Encrinital Limestone.
No. 4 — 30 feet of the Upper Chouteau Limestone.
No. 5. — 20 feet of the Lower Chouteau Limestone.

Economical Value. — The upper division gives the very best evidence of possessing good hydraulic properties, as is indicated by the analyses on page 103, and by the principles laid down on pages 167 and 168.

F. *k* — VERMICULAR SANDSTONE AND SHALES.

This Formation is not so well developed in Cooper, as it is in Marion or Green county; nor are its lithological characters the same. The *Upper Part* is usually a yellowish gray, earthy, silico-magnesian limerock in thin beds, with a few intercalated strata of blue and brown compact limestone; while the *Lower Part* is a darker compact variety, with a dull conchoidal fracture, containing small dark fucoidal markings. This passes down into buff, compact strata, which have a smooth fracture.

Range and Thickness. — These beds are from twenty to fifty feet thick in Cooper. (See Sec. 17.) One mile above Marston's Bridge, on the La Mine, it is fifty feet, as shown by the following section: —

No. 1. — 50 feet of impure yellowish silico-magnesian limestone. — *Vermicular Sandstone and Shales,*
No. 2. — 30 feet of gray, buff or blue compact strata. — *Lithographic Limestone.*
No. 3. — 60 feet of compact buff limestone, containing crystals of calcareous spar. — *Cooper Marble, Onondaga?*
No. 4. — 25 feet of the *Saccharoidal Sandstone.*
No. 5. — 70 feet of the 2d *Magnesian Limestone.*

The *Upper Part* may be seen in the barren glades so common on the bluffs of the La Mine, and in the road above Mr. Ruby Walker's, whose well passes through the *Lower Part.*

Economical Value. — The lower part, particularly the beds exposed in Mr. Walker's well, give indications of a superior hydraulic limerock.

F. *l*—LITHOGRAPHIC LIMESTONE.*

This Formation is but sparingly developed in Cooper. It is usually a bluish gray semi-crystalline limestone; but near Harriman's Lick it possesses its usual color and texture. (See p. 105.) The fresh-water spring at this lick, rises from the base of these beds.

Range and Thickness.— Its thickness varies from fifteen to thirty feet, as in Sec. 17, and the one above from the La Mine.

Economical Value. — It is a pure limestone, and may be employed to good advantage for quicklime, where the Encrinital Limestone is wanting.

These members of the Chemung Group become much thinner towards the southern and eastern parts of the county, and so homogeneous in structure that they cannot be distinguished.

The Organic Remains are mentioned in Catalogue VI.

F. *m*—ONONDAGA LIMESTONE—COOPER MARBLE.

The upper part is a bluish drab compact limestone, containing cavities filled with a yellowish green substance, which gives the rock a fine mottled appearance; but it passes down into bluish compact beds, which contain numerous small crystals of calcareous spar.

Range and Thickness. — Its thickness varies from twenty to sixty feet, as may be seen in Sec. 17, and the one above from the La Mine, and the following from Clear Creek, some two miles above its mouth: —

No. 1.— 6 feet of *Bluff.*
No. 2.— 20 feet of *Ferruginous Sandstone.*
No. 3.— 100 feet of *Encrinital Limestone.*
No. 4.— 30 feet of *Chouteau Limestone.*
No. 5.— 50 feet of *Vermicular Sandstone and Shales.*
No. 6.— 30 feet of *Lithographic Limestone.*
No. 7.— 20 feet of *Cooper Marble.*

It is best developed on Clear Creek, and on the La Mine, between the mouth of Clear Creek and Otter Creek, and on Little Saline, in Town. 47, R. 18, Sec. 34. It becomes much thinner, and passes into dull bluish gray semi-crystalline beds, towards the southern and eastern parts of the county, where it is often entirely wanting. On the map it is colored green, and marked F. *m*.

Organic Remains. — No organic remains have been found in the *Cooper Marble* proper, but the beds into which it passes to the south and east, contain the characteristic fossils of the Onondaga Limestone. (See Catalogue VIII.)

CALCIFEROUS SANDROCK.†

Three divisions of this rock have been observed in Cooper.

---

* The beautiful plate, Sec. 2, facing page 63, was engraved on a slab of this Formation from Marion county.

† The St. Louis Limestone, the Hamilton Group, and all the Formations of the Silurian System above the Saccharoidal Sandstone, are wanting in Cooper.

F. *u*—SACCHAROIDAL SANDSTONE.

This sandstone exhibits all of its peculiar and interesting features in the county, under consideration. Its thickness is quite as variable as usual, ranging from one foot to fifty. At Marston's Bridge, it is twenty-five feet thick; at Cox's Bluff, one mile below Corum's Mill, one foot; and in Town. 46, R. 19, Sec. 35, it is fifty feet. At the last locality, the sandstone strata, from five to ten feet thick, are seen, for some distance, resting horizontally upon the 2d Magnesian Limestone, when its lower surface curves down in the form of a semicircle to the depth of fifty feet, it then rises on the same curve to the former level, and continues on in the same position as before; while the upper surface of the sandstone remains horizontal, the thickness of the whole being increased in proportion to the downward curvature of the lower beds. The Limestone Strata appear to be depressed a very little on both sides, and below this enlargement of the sandstone, but show no other signs of disturbance. It appears as if one-half of a cylinder of sandstone, ninety feet in diameter, and lying perpendicular to the face of the bluff, had been pressed down into the limestone.

Its upper surface is, also, very uneven, as is shown by the numerous projecting knobs, which rise above the soil, where it is the surface rock. It is found capping, or cropping out of the bluffs of all the streams in the south part of the county.

Economical Value. — It can furnish any quantity of the purest sand for glass and cements; but it is usually too friable for building purposes. (See pp. 117–121.)

F. *v*—2D MAGNESIAN LIMESTONE.

The description of this Formation in Chapter I., p. 121, is applicable to it, as developed in this county.

Range and Thickness. — This limestone first rises above the surface, on the La Mine, near Marston's Bridge, and two miles above, in Cox's Bluff, it reaches an elevation of 160 feet, which is the greatest thickness observed in the county. In the bluffs of Wilkinson's Branch, we get the following section: —

No. 1. — 50 feet of *Chemung Group.*
No. 2. — 60 feet of *Onondaga Limestone.*
No. 3. — 20 feet of *Saccharoidal Sandstone.*
No. 4. — 150 feet of *2d Magnesian Limestone.*
No. 5. — 22 feet of *2d Sandstone.*

It crops out in the bluffs of all the streams in the south part of the county. (See Sec. 20, p. 123.)

F. *w*—2D SANDSTONE.

This rock was observed in but two places in the county — on Wilkinson's Branch and in Town. 46, R. 15, Sec. 18. It is a regularly stratified brown sandstone, which may serve as a fire-rock, or for some building purposes, where great strength is not needed.

Organic Remains of the Calciferous Sandrock, are in Catalogue XIV.

ECONOMICAL GEOLOGY OF COOPER.

SOILS.

It is not necessary to enter upon any details respecting the agriculture of this county, as the principles stated in Chapter I., on pages 137 – 153, are applicable to the soils of Cooper.

The *Alluvial Soil* (see page 139) occupies a large area in the bottoms of the Missouri, the La Mine and the Little Saline, and is covered with a heavy growth of Cotton-Wood; Sycamore; Slippery and American Elms; Box-Elder; Sugar Tree; White Maple; Red Birch; White, Black and Blue Ashes; Coffee Tree; Honey Locust; Bur, White, Swamp White, Chestnut, Rock Chestnut, Laurel, Pin, Red and Scarlet Oaks; Pignut, Mockernut, Shellbark and Thick Shellbark Hickories; Red-Bud; Linden; Papaw; Plum; Hack-Berry, and several varieties of the Willow and the Grape.

There are about 7,000 acres of the very best alluvial soil in the Missouri bottom, and a much larger quantity on the other streams, which is not, perhaps, quite so good, but it has the advantage of being placed beyond the abrading power of the Missouri.

The soil of the timber and prairie lands in nearly all of the northern and central parts of the county, is based upon the Bluff, and possesses all the excellent qualities of the second variety, derived from that formation. (See page 139.) It sustains a heavy growth of White, Bur, Swamp White, Chestnut, Rock Chestnut, Black, Red, Scarlet, Laurel and Bartram's* Oak; Linden; Slippery and American Elm; Common, Pignut and Shellbark Hickories; Blue and White Ashes; Buckeye; Sassafras; Box-Elder; Mulberry; Cherry; Plum; Crab-Apple; Hack-Berry; Black and White Walnut; Red and Black Haws; Hornbeam; Red-Bud; Papaw, and Grapes; and it is well adapted to corn, oats and tobacco, and to wheat also, where the vegetable matter has been partially exhausted by other crops.

It is susceptible of vast improvement by subsoiling (see pp. 150 and 151); as a large part of the prairie in Cooper, is similar to that subsoiled by Mr. Bass, and the timber like that cultivated by Maj. Rollins, and referred to in his letter. In the southern part of the county, and on the bluffs of the streams, where the Bluff deposit is thin, and where the Magnesian Limestones and Sandstones of the Calciferous Sandrock, come to the surface, the soil is much injured by the chert and sand of those formations. But still it is strong, and produces good corn, wheat, oats and a luxuriant growth of wild grapes. (See p. 142.) In some places, however, the chert is so abundant as to render the soil useless for ordinary cultivation; but the area

---

* This rare species was observed in two places in Cooper; south of Round Hill, and at Pleasant Green.

thus injured is very small. There are, also, small tracts of the other varieties of soils described on pages 139-142.

The physical properties of the soils, the rocks from which they are derived, and the crops produced, all prove the agricultural resources of Cooper county to be very great. *Deep and thorough tillage* should be her motto.

COAL.

This mineral exists in such quantities as will meet all the demands of the county for domestic and manufacturing purposes. In the regular Coal Measures, colored purple on the map, without including what have been considered the best beds in the county, there are, at least, 60,000,000 tons of good available coal. And besides, the local deposits promise to furnish a large amount of the very best quality for all ordinary uses.

IRON.

Brown Hematite is the only iron ore of economical value observed in the county. There are two localities which can furnish a sufficient supply of good ore to justify manufacturing operations; though there may be some doubt whether iron-works on a small scale, will be able to compete successfully with the extensive establishments, which will eventually spring up in other parts of the State. These beds are in the Ferruginous Sandstone, as shown in the section on page 92, from the bluffs of the Blackwater, in Sec. 3, Town. 48, R. 19, and in Sec. 33 of the same township. The stratum of iron ore at these localities, varies in thickness from one to three feet, and extends over a large area in the last locality. Some of this Hematite is too sandy for use, but a large portion of it is an excellent ore; it will melt easily and make good iron. This ore could be taken in boats to the mouth of the La Mine, where an abundance of coal can be obtained for working it.

Iron ore was, also, seen resting on the slopes of the bluffs, above the mouth of Clear Creek on the La Mine, and east of Mr. Winston Walker's, which had, doubtless, fallen down from the disintegrated sandstone above, now covered with soil and debris.

LEAD.

The only valuable locality of lead observed in Cooper, was at Scott's Lead Mine, in Town. 49, R. 19, Sec. 26, N. E. ¼. This, like the mines of the South-West, is in the Archimedes Limestone, passing down into what appears to be the upper beds of the Encrinital Limestone; but, instead of the calcareous spar, which occurs in the mines of the South-West, heavy spar or tiff is very abundant in this and at various other localities in the neighborhood. A shaft had been sunk twenty-six feet, passing down through the superficial deposits, and penetrating the limestone twenty feet to the pocket where the most of the mineral was found. An adit had, also, been opened twenty feet to the base of the shaft, and a drift continued thirty feet in the direction of the lode to the north-east, with a downward inclination of twenty-five degrees. About 6,000 pounds of galena were obtained. There is another locality, 300 feet north north-east of the last, where some work has been done, and a small quantity of mineral raised.

The work done at these places is scarcely sufficient to test the character and value of these deposits; but the indications are such as would seem to justify a more careful exploration of the lodes. The formation is one that may be expected to contain lead, and the associated minerals are such as most usually accompany that ore.

The sulphate of baryta at this mine, is often penetrated by numerous small cylinders of iron pyrites, as was observed in the tiff of the 2d Magnesian Limestone, near

Warsaw. Lead may, also, be found in the 2d Magnesian Limestone, marked *v* and colored yellow, on the map; as the mines of Moniteau, those on the Cole Camp, and in other localities, are in this limestone.

Thin veins of Lead were found cutting through the coal, at Drafton's bed. These veins have inclinations, varying from a vertical to nearly a horizontal position.

MANGANESE.

Small quantities of this metal were observed at Stephen's coal-bed, though not in sufficient quantity to be of any economical value. But it is said, a stratum exists below, which the workings had not reached when the mine was visited.

ZINC.

Thin veins of zinc blende were, also, observed intersecting the coal at several of the abnormal deposits above described; at Drafton's and at Farley's bed, they were the most abundant.

BUILDING MATERIALS.

Limestones. — The Archimedes Limestone, the Encrinital Limestone, the Chouteau Limestone, the Vermicular Sandstone and Shales, the Cooper Marble and the 2d Magnesian Limestone, all have strata adapted to the various building purposes to which limestones are applied. But the first three contain beds of the most durable and economical building stones in this part of the State; and these rocks are so generally diffused, that every part of the county is well supplied. The lower beds of the Vermicular Sandstone and Shales, can, also, furnish an abundance of clouded limestone, adapted to fine work.

Sandstones. — The Ferruginous and 2d Sandstone are, in some localities, suitable for building purposes; but the sandstones of Cooper are, usually, too friable to endure exposure and sustain the weight of heavy masonry; and this is particularly true of the micaceous sandstone of the Coal Measures so much used at Boonville.

Marble. — Some portions of the Cooper Marble, particularly the lower beds, which contain the small crystals of calcareous spar, are very beautiful and receive a fine polish. This rock will become very valuable, as the country advances, and a demand is created for the more expensive and durable styles of architecture.

Cements and Mortars. — Formations *h*, *i* and *v*, some of the lower beds of the Lithographic Limestone and the Chouteau Limestone, and the Onondaga, all contain beds of the best quality for quicklime. The Encrinital Limestone is used at the kiln some three miles east of Boonville, and the Archimedes, at that on Thompson's Branch, in Town. 48, R. 17, Sec. 9.

Hydraulic Cements. — The lower part of the Vermicular Sandstone and Shales, and the upper part of the Chouteau Limestone, give the very best evidence of superior hydraulic properties. These beds of the former, crop out at the Chouteau Springs; in nearly all the bluffs of the La Mine, between these springs and Corum's Mill; and on the Little Saline, in Town. 46, R. 18; and at Conner's Mill. At all of these localities the quantity is inexhaustible. The lower beds of the Vermicular Sandstone and Shales, crop out below the last in the bluff at Fink's Mill, and in the neighborhood of Pleasant Grove. The well of Mr. Winston Walker passes through those which give the best evidence of hydraulic properties. (See pp. 167 and 168.)

The Hydraulic Limestone, No. 66 of the Coal Measures, will make a good cement, if the more impure portions are selected.

Fire-Brick. — No. 75 of the Coal Measures, or No. 16 of Sec. 13, which crops out in the bluffs of the Missouri, from Boonville to the mouth of the La Mine, is the bed which furnishes the fire-clay used in St. Louis county, and will, so far as we can judge from the physical properties and geological relations, make good fire-brick. The quantity can be easily estimated, as the bed is twenty-three feet thick, and extends over an area of twenty square miles, that occupied by the Coal Measures.

Fire-Rock.—The Ferruginous Sandstone and the 2d Sandstone contain some beds of a very refractory nature; while the more impure strata of the Encrinital Limestone and the 2d Magnesian Limestone, are well adapted to common use, as they are able to withstand the action of ordinary fires.

ROAD MATERIALS.

Sands, gravel and pebbles are abundant in the beds of the La Mine, the Little Saline, and in nearly all the smaller streams in the county; and it has already been shown (see page 169), that these are the best materials for good and durable roads.

LUMBER, AND WATER-POWER.

Timber, of the best varieties found in the State, exists in great abundance on all the streams; it also covers the bluffs of the streams and a large part of the north-eastern division of the county. Oak, Walnut, Ash, Hickory, Linden, Cherry, Maple, Mulberry, Locust and Elm, can be obtained in sufficient quantities to supply the home demand, both present and prospective.

Water-Power is not so available as in some other parts of the State. There are, however, a few mill-sites on the La Mine and the Little Saline. But experience has proved steam to be quite as economical as ordinary water-power, for the manufacturing of lumber.

SPRINGS.

Cooper abounds in springs, both fresh and mineral. The mineral springs are very numerous, and may be classed as *Brine* and *Sulphur;* but it should be borne in mind that all the *brine* springs discharge sulphuretted hydrogen in greater or less abundance, and that all the *sulphur* springs contain more or less of common salt (*chloride of sodium*). And besides, the two varieties frequently come to the surface within a few yards of each other. Nearly all of the mineral springs in the county are situated in valleys of denudation in the Chemung Rocks, and much the larger number are in Town. 48, extending from Sec. 16 of R. 18, westward along the La Mine through R. 19, to the county line; but some exist in Town. 49, R. 19, on the Black-Water; and in Town. 48, R. 15, near Gooche's Mill, on the Little Saline.

The most important of the brine springs are Harriman's, Bailey's, Howard's, Heath's and Hugh's. Water was collected from these for analysis; but a variety of accidents, has prevented us from getting an analysis of more than one.

Dr. Harriman's Salt Springs were visited June 28th, 1854. The weather was warm and clear, and the sun shining directly upon the springs and the surface of the earth for some distance around them. The temperature of the atmosphere at the springs, in the sun, was 98° F., and that of the salt springs, 58° F.; while a fresh spring rising from the base of the bluff, in the shade, 100 yards to the south, gave, 54° F. There are four places where the brine is discharged, which are from forty to forty-five feet apart; and hydrosulphuric acid escapes from all. The following is the result of Dr. Litton's analysis:—

Specific gravity at Temp. 66° F., ... 1.0155

In 1,000 grains of the water were found the following constituents:—

Silica,	.00984	Lime,	1.39577
Carbonic Acid,	.38207	Magnesia,	-62964
Sulphuric Acid,	.93471	Potassa,	.08665
Chlorine,	11.50487	Soda,	8.33619
Peroxide of iron,	.00393		

The ingredients may be combined to give the following composition of 1,000 parts of the water: —

Silica,	.00984	Chloride of sodium,	15.75677
Carbonate of the protoxide of iron,*	.00571	Carbonic acid,	.29798
Carbonate of lime,	.12210		
Carbonate of magnesia,	.05514	Total weight of salts and carbonic acid,	20.58167
Sulphate of lime,	1.59094	Water,	979.41833
Chloride of calcium,	1.32624		
Chloride of magnesium,	1.40325		1000,00000
Chloride of potassium,	.01370		

There are several sulphur springs in Cooper.

Chouteau Springs justly enjoy a fine reputation as a watering place. The water is good, the buildings neat and commodious, and the scenery beautiful. They are situated in the 16th section of Town. 48, R. 18, about ten miles from the city of Boonville.

The water comes to the surface in four places, located but a short distance from each other, in a line nearly east and west. The water from the easterly spring contains the most common salt; but the one farthest west is most esteemed and generally used. Large quantities of hydrosulphuric acid, and perhaps other gases escape. All the gas would yield, at least, two gallons per minute; while the water is discharged at the rate of ten gallons per minute, 600 per hour, or 14,400 per day. The water gives an acid reäction and a temperature of 58° F.

Dr. Litton's analysis † gave the following results: —

Water from Chouteau Springs—

Specific gravity at 66° F., ... 1.0064

In 1,000 grains of the water were found the following constituents: —

Silica,	.00794	Lime,	.65783
Sulphuric Acid,	.39088	Magnesia,	.29535
Carbonic Acid,	.26069	Potassa,	.05382
Chlorine,	4.90237	Soda,	3.51659
Peroxide of iron,*	.00496		

The ingredients may be combined to give the following composition of 1,000 parts of the water: —

Carbonate of the protoxide of iron,	.00862	Carbonic acid,	.18453
Carbonate of lime,	.17339	Silica,	.00794
Carbonate of magnesia,	.03615		
Sulphate of lime,	.66538	Total weight of salts, silica &c.,	9.00696
Chloride of calcium,	.56567	Water,	990.99304
Chloride of magnesium,	.64790		
Chloride of potassium,	.08501		1000.00000
Chloride of sodium,	6.63237		

For reasons stated above, the gases could not be determined at the laboratory, but the abundance discharged at the spring, shows their existence in quantities sufficient to render the water light and agreeable; while the other ingredients must render it a healthful alterative.

---

* This does not represent all the iron contained in the water, as a portion had fallen as a sediment before it was analyzed.

† The water and gas of this, and the water of several other springs of Cooper, were carefully collected, sealed and shipped to the Laboratory in St. Louis, where they arrived some three months after. Meanwhile the gases had escaped, and some of the demijohns had been tested in a practical way, which rendered them useless for analysis.

But the healthful properties of the Chouteau Water, have been abundantly proved by the numerous individuals, who have been greatly relieved or entirely cured by resorting to these springs. The locality is very desirable for the invalid, who would give his native powers an opportunity to recuperate in a quiet healthful retreat, where he may enjoy all the rational amusements of a country life.

It is very obvious that Cooper county possesses very many and superior natural advantages. Her agricultural resources are indeed very great, but little inferior to those of Lafayette and Platte, for many of our staple crops. There are, at least, 30,000 acres of the richest alluvial soil, a large part of which, still sustains an immense burden of the timber characteristic of our rich bottoms (p. 198), not less than 200,000 acres of excellent high timber land, based upon the rich marls of the Bluff Formation, the most of which retains its native growth (p. 198), and about 80,000 acres of fine prairie, resting upon the same marls.

Place but half of this in a good state of cultivation, and it would easily give an annual yield of 5,000,000 bushels of wheat, 10,000,000 of corn, or a similar proportion of other crops; while the remaining 50,000 acres of inferior soil, is well adapted to the cultivation of grapes or grass for grazing.

Mineral coal and timber suitable for charcoal, are sufficiently abundant for all domestic and manufacturing purposes. Building materials, marbles, limestones, sandstones, clay, sand, timber and iron, exist in great abundance; while fire-clays and hydraulic limestones are found in inexhaustible quantities.

And, besides, Cooper occupies a central position in the State, with the navigable waters of the Missouri on the north, and the Pacific Railroad on the south, to transport her surplus produce to the best market of the West, and return the merchandise to supply her domestic traffic, and a large flourishing trade with the South-West.

These natural advantages and the characteristic energy of her citizens, will soon develop these agricultural and manufacturing resources and quadruple her population.

The Map of Cooper has been prepared with great care. It exhibits the timber, prairie, bottom, level and broken lands, the mines, springs, streams, congressional townships, and sections and towns, and the various Geological Formations, by the appropriate symbols and colors. The geological boundaries are laid down with as much accuracy as possible; but the older strata are so completely covered with the Quaternary deposits, that it is often impossible to tell the exact point where one formation ends and another commences. Still the boundaries given can not be far from their true position.

CHAPTER V.

GEOLOGY OF THE SOUTH-WEST.

After preparing the Sections on Plate XIV., but little need be said to give a good understanding of the Geology of the country through which they pass.

Secs. Nos. 1 and 2 give the strata from Boonville through Cooper into Pettis, in Town. 46, R. 20, and thence to the north-east corner of Henry, and through Calhoun and Clinton to Papinsville, and from there south to Neosho. No. 3 gives the formations developed between Neosho and Springfield. On the road from Springfield to Bolivar the strata of the Carboniferous, Chemung and Calciferous Rocks, successively rise to the surface. The Saccharoidal Sandstone is highly colored, and renders the soil sandy south of the latter town.

Section No. 4 gives the rocks and their relative position between Warsaw and Frémont; and No. 5 exhibits the position of the strata from Frémont, on the road through Bolivar and Buffalo, to the Niangua, near Edwards' Mill. No. 6 gives a section of the formations on the Niangua from Edwards' Mill to the Osage; while No. 7 gives a view of the strata on the line from the Osage, at Erie, up the Gravois, through Versailles, to the Missouri opposite Rocheport. The line of Nos. 1 and 2, from Boonville to Carthage, through Cooper, Pettis, Henry, Bates and Jasper, runs through a country beautifully diversified with timber and prairie. Though in some portions the streams and timber are not so abundant as might be desirable for agricultural purposes, still the soil is good, and hedges and cisterns may obviate all the difficulties which might be experienced from a scarcity of timber and water, at a few localities. The timber skirting all the streams on this route is very fine, and consists of nearly all the varieties mentioned in Appendix C. In the region occupied by the Coal Measures, the sandstones have an unusual development, and, in localities where the superficial deposits are thin, they often render the soil light and sandy.

The prairie of this region is characterized by what are called Knobs or Mounds; they are somewhat variable in size and form, but usually present the appearance of a truncated cone. The tops of these mounds are usually flat, and covered by a thin soil, underlaid by a durable stratum of sandstone or limestone, which crops out on all sides near the top, prevents the wearing away of the upper edges, and preserves the well defined angle between the top and side; while the stratum of shale or clay, which forms the lower part, is easily decomposed and carried away by aqueous agencies. The sides rise with a gentle declivity, at first, but become more and more abrupt until they are nearly perpendicular at the top. The most of these mounds belong to the Coal Measures; but those near Bolivar are in the Chemung Group, the upper beds of the Vermicular Sandstone and Shales forming the top, and the underlying Shales, the lower part of them. The country on the Niangua and Osage is characterized by high mural or castellated bluffs, rich alluvial bottoms and broad undulating prairies. The bottoms produce a growth of timber equal in size* and quality to any in the State; the bluffs are often covered with flint, and sustain a stunted growth of Post and Black-Jack Oaks, Black Hickory, Sumachs and Hazels; while the prairies are usually fertile, and clothed in a rank growth of native grass. No country is better watered. Its streams are numerous, limpid and filled with a great variety and abundance of fish; and the springs are pure and wonderfully large.

---

* Several trees were measured in the Pomme de Terre bottom: a Sycamore, whose circumference was twenty-eight feet; Bur Oak, twenty-six feet; Black Walnut, twenty-three; and thick Shellbark Hickory, sixteen feet.

PL. XIV.

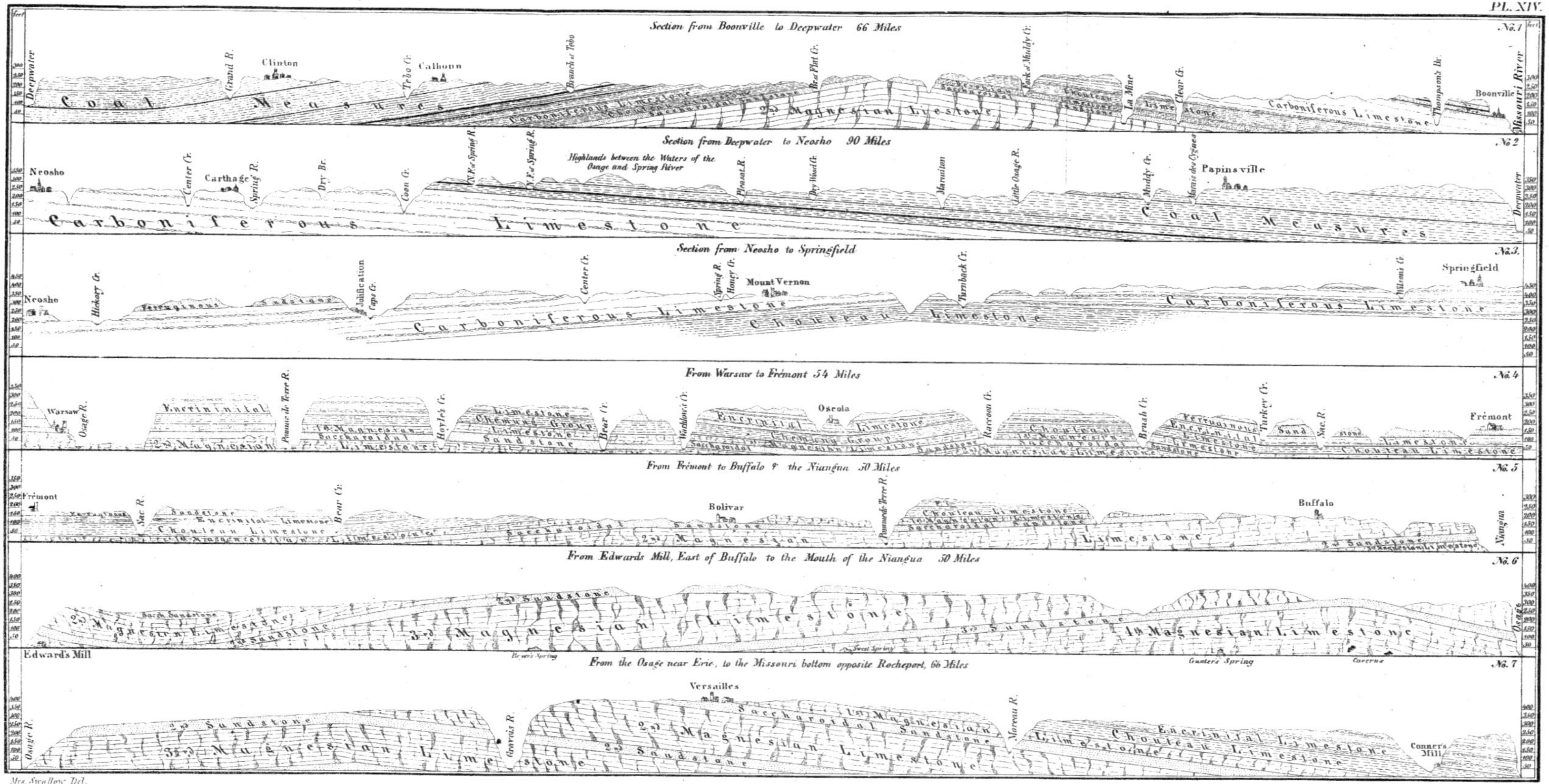

No. 1
Section from Boonville to Deepwater 66 Miles

Deepwater, Grand R., Clinton, Tebo Cr., Calhoun, Branch of Tebo, Brai Flat Cr., Fork of Muddy Cr., La Mine, Clear Cr., Thompson's Br., Boonville, Missouri River

Coal Measures
Carboniferous Limestone
2d Magnesian Limestone
Lime stone
Carboniferous Limestone

No. 2
Section from Deepwater to Neosho 90 Miles

Neosho, Center Cr., Carthage, Spring R., Dry Br., Coon Cr., N. F. of Spring R., N. F. of Spring R., Highlands between the Waters of the Osage and Spring River, Pleasat. R., Dry Wood Cr., Marmiton, Little Osage R., Muddy Cr., Marais des Cygnes, Papinsville, Deepwater

Carboniferous Limestone
Coal Measures

No. 3.
Section from Neosho to Springfield

Neosho, Hickory Cr., Jolification, Caps Cr., Center Cr., Spring R., Honey Cr., Mount Vernon, Turnback Cr., Wilson's Cr., Springfield

Ferruginous Sandstone
Carboniferous Limestone
Chouteau Limestone
Carboniferous Limestone

No. 4
From Warsaw to Frémont 54 Miles

Warsaw, Osage R., Pomme de Terre R., Hoyle's Cr., Bear Cr., Wachlow's Cr., Osceola, Raccoon Cr., Brush Cr., Turkey Cr., Sac. R., Frémont

Encrinital
2d Magnesian
Limestone
Chemung Group
Sand stone
Chouteau Limestone
Ferruginous
Sand

No. 5
From Frémont to Buffalo & the Niangua 50 Miles

Frémont, Sac R., Bear Cr., Bolivar, Pomme de Terre R., Buffalo, Niangua

Sandstone
Encrinital Limestone
Chouteau Limestone
Saccharoidal Sandstone
2d Magnesian
Limestone

No. 6
From Edwards Mill, East of Buffalo to the Mouth of the Niangua 50 Miles

Edward's Mill, Bryer's Spring, Sweet Spring, Gunter's Spring, Caverns, Osage

2d Sandstone
3d Magnesian Limestone
3d Sandstone
4th Magnesian Limestone

No. 7
From the Osage near Erie, to the Missouri bottom opposite Rocheport, 66 Miles

Osage R., Gravois R., Versailles, Moreau R., Conner's Mill

2d Sandstone
3d Magnesian Limestone
Saccharoidal Sandstone
1st Magnesian
2d Magnesian Limestone
Encrinital Limestone
Chouteau Limestone

Mrs. Swallow Del.

L. Gast & Bro. lith. St. Louis.

Sections in South Western Missouri.

The largest observed is the Upper Niangua, or Bryce's Spring, which is situated in Town. 34, R. 18, Sec. 1. It was visited on the 24th of December, 1853; when the minimum temperature, at night, was 22° F., and the maximum, by day, 60° F.; the temperature of the water was 58° F., about 100 feet from the place where it rises to the surface. The stream formed by the spring was carefully measured, and found to be 136 feet wide and to give an average depth of 0.93; so that every foot in length of this stream would give 126.48 cubic feet. The velocity of the current was measured at five places: at six feet from each shore, at forty-five feet from each, and in the middle. The sums set down are an average of several trials: —

At 6 feet from the right bank, it ran 80 feet in 73 seconds.
At 6 feet from the left bank, it ran 80 feet in 110 seconds.
At 45 feet from the left bank, it ran 80 feet in 73 seconds.
At 45 feet from the right bank, it ran 80 feet in 58 seconds.
And in the middle it ran 80 feet in . . 53 seconds.
Making an average of 80 feet in . . . 73 seconds.

If we allow seven seconds for what the friction at the bottom and sides would retard the water, the rapidity will be one foot per second, which will give 126.48 cubic feet per second, 455,328 per hour, or 10,927,872 cubic feet per day, which is less than the actual quantity.

This immense spring rises in a low secluded valley, where it forms a small pond and a fine mill-site, and then flows away, a river. The water is nearly pure, sustains about the same temperature at all seasons, and shows no perceptible fluctuation in volume, either in the dryest or wettest season.

The spring and stream, flowing from it, abound in a great variety of fish and fluviatile mollusks of the genera, *Paludina Malania, Planorbis Physa*, and *Limnea*. Numerous species of *Algae* were very abundant; and swans, geese, brants and ducks, came in thousands to rest and feed in its waters by night.

Gunter's and Sweet Spring are, also, on the Niangua, but they are not so large as Bryce's.

Caves, natural bridges and subterranean streams occur in the valley of the Osage and its tributaries.

There is, in the counties of Benton, St. Clair, Cedar, Polk, Dallas, Hickory and Camden, a general belief that a "white metal," resembling silver, has been melted from ore that is very similar to brown hematite; and, though several localities are given, it is generally supposed the ore came from a place west of Buffalo, from which specimens were obtained, as well as from individuals who declared them identical with those which had yielded the "white metal;" but the following analysis of one specimen, by Dr. Litton, gives no indication of any such metal, and the others obtained were essentially the same: —

Silica,	2.88
Alumina,	0.64
Peroxide of iron,	84.80
Water,	11.62
Sulphur,	0.12
	100.06

An alloy, found in a cave, once occupied by counterfeiters, was given me at Warsaw, which, it was surmised, might be the same "white metal;" but the alloy contains bismuth, arsenic, copper and nickel, none of which was found in the hematite supposed to contain the "white metal."

It was, also, surmised by some that the alloy and the "white metal" had been obtained from the *Old Diggings*, so frequent in the Encrinital Limestone of this region; but after a careful examination of several of these diggings (see page 98), no evidence could be found that they were made for metals, as no ore, except very small particles of the oxides and sulphuret of iron, was discovered.

In Town. 34, R. 22, Sec. 34, a large area has been dug over, and the surface left in ridges and knolls; and in some places, the loose materials have been removed from the fissures and cavities of the rock.

The following facts lead to the conclusion that these diggings were made by the Indians in search of flint: —

1st. They were made over 100 years ago, as is shown by the age of the trees on the rubbish thrown out.

2d. They are in the rock, and soil derived from the rock, which contains the best flint in the State.

3d. At all the diggings, chips of flint and broken arrow-heads, were abundant; as if arrow-heads and other implements had been manufactured on the spot.

4th. Flint was the most useful and valuable of all minerals to the Indians of that day.

5th. No marks of the usual mining implements of civilized nations, were observed in the diggings.

6th. Not a particle of any mineral valuable to civilized nations, was observed at these localities.

But why should they *dig* for flint when so much is exposed on the surface? All workers of this mineral are fully aware that it cannot be wrought into the desirable shapes, after long exposure to the atmosphere; hence manufacturers of gun-flints keep this rock, after it is quarried, in tanks of water until it is needed for use.

The agricultural resources of the South-West have been vastly underrated. The alluvial bottoms of the Osage, Niangua, Pomme de Terre, Sac, Marais des Sygnes, Grand and Spring Rivers, Turkey, Horse, Deep-Water, Dry Wood, Muddy, Center, Shoal Oliver's, Cap's, Hickory and Sugar Creeks, are but little inferior in fertility to the Missouri bottom, and all covered by a heavy growth of the characteristic timber. All of these bottoms produce superior corn, and many of them are adapted to the production of hemp. Vast areas of the high timber land and prairie, also, possess strong, durable and productive soils, admirably adapted to the culture of wheat, corn, oats, tobacco and grass; while the remainder is suitable for grazing purposes and the production of timber.

But the South-West is doubtless better adapted to the culture of the grape than any other part of this or the neighboring States. Nature has endowed this part of the country with a temperate, dry and salubrious climate, and a light, rich, calcareous and vegetable soil, which produces a vigorous growth of the native vines. And besides, the high bluffs of magnesian limestone of the Calciferous and Potsdam age, on the Osage, Niangua, Pomme de Terre, Sac and Grand Rivers, usually present natural terraces covered by a rich soil, all wonderfully prepared by nature for the planting of vineyards. This character of the bluffs is well represented in plate VIII., page 130. It is quite certain, in short, that the cultivation of the grape in the South-West can be made a source of great profit and national wealth. But there is another and higher consideration, which should lead us to encourage the production of native wines; as the vigor and sobriety of the nation would be greatly promoted by substituting the pure healthful juice of the grape for the drugged and poisonous liquors so abundantly manufactured and consumed at the present day.

Stock. — The South-West possesses many advantages for raising stock, particularly neat cattle, horses, mules and sheep. The broad prairies furnish excellent grazing for the long salubrious summers; and the winters are so short and mild that but little feeding is necessary. Indeed, the drovers of this part of the State, have been able to compete most successfully with those from the other divisions of this and the adjoining States in the St. Louis market.

Wheat, corn and tobacco might be produced in any desirable quantity; but the price of transportation is such that but little is grown, save what is needed for domestic consumption.

Timber. — The alluvial bottoms, on the streams of this part of the State, sustain a very heavy growth of White, Blue and Prickly Ashes; Linden; Red Birch; Buckeye; Box-Elder; Sycamore; Coffee-Tree; Cotton-Wood; American, Slippery and Wahoo Elms; Honey Locust; Hack-Berry; Common, Thick Shellbark and Pignut Hickories; Pecan; Black and White Walnuts; Red Bud; Sugar and White Maples; Mulberry, Bur, Swamp-white, Chestnut-white, Laurel, Red and Pin Oaks; Papaw; Red Plum, and the Summer and Fox Grapes; while a large area of the high land is timbered with Yellow Pine; White, Post, Chestnut, Black, Laurel and Black-Jack Oaks; Common and Black Hickories; Hornbeam; Iron-Wood; Red Bud; Persimon and Dog-Wood. Timber exists in sufficient quantities to supply all the necessary demands for its consumption, particularly in a country where hedges of the Osage Orange* can be so successfully cultivated, and where stone fences† can be made at so small a cost.

---

* This plant was found growing, apparently native, in the Spring River bottom, above Carthage.

† Judge Ritchie, who has fenced large portions of his prairie farm in Newton with Sandstone, assured me it made a very economical and durable fence.

Water-Power is very abundant in this part of the State; good mill sites may be obtained on nearly all of the larger streams and on many of the springs. Bryce's Spring, above mentioned, furnishes the best mill site observed in the State. The large and constant quantity of water and its even temperature render it most desirable; as no ice ever forms in it to obstruct the machinery, as no drought makes a scarcity of water, and no flood ever endangers the safety of dam or mill. One can estimate with precision how strong a dam must be to raise and retain the water at any given height, and how much machinery can be driven by the constant discharge of 11,000,000 cubic feet of water per diem. A fine flouring mill now occupies this site.

Gunter's Spring, below Bryce's on the same stream, discharges about half as much water, and in other respects, affords the same advantages as the latter. It drives a saw-mill and perhaps other machinery.

Grand Falls, on Shoal Creek, furnishes a superior mill site, now occupied by Scott & Stewart's mill. Plate VI., page 96, gives a fine view of the Falls and mill.

Mineral Wealth. — A condensed view of what is known of the mineral wealth of the South-West, has already been given on pages 159–164.

The Climate is mild and salubrious; the summers are long and temperate; and the winters warm and short, and not subject to the sudden and extreme changes so prevalent in some parts of the West.

This part of the State is filling up very rapidly with an enterprising population; new dwellings meet our view one very side; while, on one hand, the forests are disappearing before the axe of the pioneer — the prairie, on the other, is yielding to the plow.

Wealth and all its attendant comforts and luxuries are also rapidly increasing, as is shown by the assessors' books in the various counties. The taxable property of Newton increased from $390,000 in 1853, to $700,000 in 1854.

Still, with all these sources of wealth and permanent prosperity and actual progress, the enterprise of this beautiful country is greatly paralyzed by the want of a good market. The farmer finds no sale for his surplus produce, and the miner is compelled to sell his mineral at half price.

Complete the South-Western Branch of the Pacific Railroad, and the value of the farm and the mine, the timber and the water-power, will be vastly increased; and the farmer will grow his wheat and corn to feed the millions of Europe and be exchanged for their gold and merchandize.

PART II.

A
PRELIMINARY REPORT

ON SOME OF THE

PRINCIPAL MINES

IN

FRANKLIN, JEFFERSON, WASHINGTON, ST. FRANCOIS
AND MADISON COUNTIES, MISSOURI,

BY

A. LITTON, M. D.,
CHEMIST.

INTRODUCTION.

St. Louis, Mo., *December 27th*, 1854.

G. C. Swallow,
State Geologist.

Sir: I herewith send you a preliminary report on some of the Mines of Missouri. That it is imperfect and incomplete, I am fully sensible. At present it would be premature to attempt to give a complete sketch of the mines and mineral wealth of this State. Before this can be done, the geological formations must be accurately defined and their thickness known. This demands more minute, more general and extensive explorations. Nor am I unconscious that the details and unavoidable repetitions in the description of the mines will be excessively dry and uninteresting. But I knew not how to communicate to you the minute knowledge of each of these localities, which it was evidently the design of the Geological Survey to obtain, without entering into these details of length and breadth and height, and frequently of almost repeating the same things of many localities.

To enter many of the mines, at the time of my visits, was impossible; and though I could not speak from a personal examination, I thought it better to give such details of them as could be obtained from those who were familiar with them, than to omit them entirely. In such cases I have endeavored scrupulously to avoid misrepresentations, and have rejected such information as seemed to me improbable or doubtful. That in the description of these, as also of other localities, I have made no mistakes, would be to claim something that belongs not to mortality, and when satisfied of my errors I shall most cheerfully confess and correct them, having nothing in view save the attainment of truth; but until thus convinced, what has been reported shall, by me, be regarded as facts. Nor have I, excepting in some few instances, where the evidence was so legible that he who runs may read, given an expression of opinion as to the value and continued productiveness of particular mines; for in most instances this can be nothing more than a speculation, only natural when based upon and restricted by the observations and teachings of other mining regions; and such opinion, if at all proper, should most certainly be reserved until all the facts furnished by our mines shall have been collected, when alone an expression of opinion on this point can with justice and propriety be given.

At every point I have endeavored to collect reliable statistics of our mineral wealth. The numbers of those given might have been considerably increased, but I preferred to under rather than overrate the produce of our mines, knowing with how little discrimination estimates are often made, and fully conscious that nothing, at home and abroad, is so injurious to mining interests as false and exaggerated estimates. Their influence is to create doubt and scepticism; or, if perchance they should gain credence for a time, it is almost invariably to the great detriment of individuals, and ultimately, by reäction in public confidence, to the great injury of all mining interests.

To enumerate all the kindness and assistance, I have received in the prosecution of my labors, would be impossible. Everywhere I have found persons ready to communicate and willing to assist. To Mr. A. F. Evans, Mr. Wm. Skewes, Mr. Vivian, Dr. Reed, Rev. Mr. Clarke, Mr. I. Nash Inge, of Franklin co.; and Mr. S. T. Dunklin, Col. Jesse McIlvaine, Dr. McCallion, Mr. Halfner, and Mr. O'Mara, of Washington co.; to Mr. Daly, to Mr. Fulton, of St. François county, and to Col. Bogy, Mr. Zeigler, Mr. Felix Valle and Julius Valle, I am indebted for much kind attention and valuable information.

To my colleague, Dr. B. F. Shumard, I am under obligations for assistance in the examination of many mines in Franklin county.

To Mr. A. H. ULFFERS, I am indebted for the drawing of the accompanying maps and sections, and for making the necessary surveys for the construction of the topographical maps of the Iron Mountain and the Pilot Knob.

To Dr. HOFFMEISTER I am indebted for assistance when engaged in the cupellation of the lead ores.

Finally, to JOHN BRUERE I am indebted for daily, constant and uninterrupted assistance in the laboratory since September, 1853. He has worked with a patience, a fidelity and a perseverance worthy of the highest commendation, and by his assistance I am enabled to report far more work than would have been possible by my own unassisted labor.

Hoping, Sir, that the following pages may be of some service to you in the execution of the important commission confided to you, I remain,

Respectfully,

Yours, &c.,

A. LITTON.

DR. LITTON'S REPORT.

Of Missouri, that portion designated the mining region, is, most probably, of all others the most widely known. Its wonderful deposits of iron and lead have for many years been attracting the attention of the capitalist, and exciting the curiosity of men of science. The story of its inexhaustible treasures of iron ore, was abroad for a long time only considered either as the baseless credulity of ignorance, or the wily scheming of reckless and unscrupulous speculators. Within the last few years, however, by the increased facilities for transportation, and by the aid of capital, these once barren and unproductive treasures are beginning to give up their buried wealth, and eradicate the suspicion which was generally excited abroad by the first attempts to obtain an investment of capital.

It was in this region that was made one of the earliest attempts at mining on the North American continent. The first discovery of the mines of Missouri, was made about the year 1720; and the credit of it is due to La Motte and Renault, who were acting under the Company of the West, that had been chartered during the minority of Louis XV., of France. To this Company had been granted the exclusive privilege of mining in all that region of country bordering on the Mississippi and its tributaries, and extending from the Gulf of Mexico to the Wabash and Illinois rivers.

The moving spirit or the guiding genius of this Company was the notorious John Law, whose claim to the very first rank among knaves or visionaries there is none to dispute, though there may be some difference of opinion as to which of the two classes he more properly belongs. By his representations and his influence, the prince and the peasant, the nobleman and the laborer, the capitalist and the artisan, were alike deluded and persuaded to invest their capital and labor, with the hope of obtaining the most extravagant returns for their investments, from mining the gold and silver which were reported to exist so abundantly in this region.

Acting under this Company, Renault, accompanied by two hundred miners and laborers, left France in 1719, and came to the Valley of the West in search of the silver and the gold which were so confidently believed to exist here in the greatest abundance. Selecting for his head-quarters a place in the vicinity of Kaskaskia, he sent out exploring parties in different directions; and, though disappointed in their cherished expectations of finding gold and silver, among the first fruits of their earliest explorations, was the discovery of the lead mines at Mine la Motte and in the neighborhood of Potosi, the names of which have served as monuments to record and perpetuate the names and memory of their discoverers.

Renault, having been disappointed in discovering gold and silver, began to turn his attention to the mining of the lead ore, the existence of which his exploring parties had made known. As to the extent of his explorations we have but few and imperfect accounts; and of his mining operations, almost the only record left was in the upturned earth, and the lost and deserted mining utensils, discovered after the occupation of the country by the Anglo-Saxon race. His mining operations were, however, checked by the Company of the West having been united to the Royal Company of the Indies; and though he remained several years longer in the country after this union, he finally returned in 1742 to his native country, when almost all mining operations ceased so long as the country belonged to France.

Thus they remained, until the country was ceded to Spain, when the mines again attracted some attention; and among the first discoveries was that of Mine à Burton, made accidentally by Le Breton, who was still living in 1818, near Ste. Genevieve, having then reached his 109th year.

In 1798, Moses Austin, of Virginia, obtained a grant of land in the neighborhood of Potosi, from the Spanish Government, sunk the first regular shaft, and erected a reverberatory furnace. Soon, other Americans immigrated and settled in this mining region; but as to the extent of their mining operations, or the richness of the mines, or the profits of their labor, we have but few, if any, reliable statistics; and when we remember that almost the only means of getting the lead to market, was by packing on mules, we cannot suppose that the amount made was very great, or that the mining was very extensive.

After the purchase and possession of the country by the United States, this mineral region attracted more attention, and since then what is denominated (with us) mining, has been carried on at some point or other. The points, however, are very few at which it has been pursued, for a series of years, without cessation and plied with that constancy and perseverance which is customary in transatlantic mining countries. With us, the number of persons is very small, whose sole occupation is mining, but in general this is united with the cultivation of the soil. Though there may have been in the earliest settlement of the country, many who made mining their sole business and pursued it as their only avocation, the number of such, since the purchase of the country by the United States, has been but very few, and it is in general only an occupation for the leisure and unemployed time of the farmer.

This mining region, of the South-East, is principally confined to Jefferson, Franklin, Crawford, Washington, St. François and Madison counties. The geological formations that present themselves in approaching this part of the State from St. Louis, or from Ste. Genevieve, are, first, the members of the Carboniferous, and then the Silurian, in the lower beds of which, and in the igneous rocks around which, at some points, these beds lie, are found all the metallic ores of any economical value that have as yet been discovered. As to the particular beds composing this formation, their lithological and palaeontological characters, I refer you to Dr. Shumard's sections from St. Louis to Franklin county, and to the Iron Mountain, and to that from Ste. Genevieve to the Iron Mountain.

This region is broken and hilly, though not what could with propriety be denominated mountainous. It is interspersed with hills and ridges and knobs, most of which are composed of magnesian limestone, and which sometimes attain an elevation of 200 or 300 feet above the adjacent valleys. Though in Franklin no igneous rocks have yet been found in place, in the southern part of Washington, and more particularly in St. François and in Madison counties, these igneous ridges are frequently met with. As to their relative age, whether they were ejected anterior or posterior to the deposition of the magnesian limestones, is a question to be settled by farther and more minute observations; though all the facts, gathered by me during my visits to Washington, Madison and St. François counties, incline me to the opinion that they are older than the stratified rocks, for wherever these last are found exposed, they are lying almost perfectly horizontal, with little if any dip, and presenting scarcely an indication of violent disturbance or metamorphic action.

This mineral region is well watered. Through it flows, in part, the Meramec, the Bourbeuse, the Big and St. François rivers, with their almost numberless and their many never-failing tributaries, which furnish an abundance of water for all agricultural purposes, and at most points where required for mining operations. The land is well timbered, and much of it highly suitable for agricultural purposes. In the innumerable valleys that lie secluded in it, the soil in general is good and highly productive, and would, with proper culture, amply supply provisions for the thousands who might find constant and profitable occupation in the mines. Though in other parts, the soil seems shallow and but little endowed with fertility, it has ever been found, when tried, productive and yielding beyond expectation.

In this mineral region the only minerals as yet found, of economical value, are those of lead, iron, copper, nickel, cobalt, zinc and manganese; and this preliminary report shall be principally confined to the localities of each of these, so far as is yet known to me, in Franklin, Jefferson and Washington counties.

LEAD AND ITS ORES.

Native, or metallic lead, has been but rarely discovered in the mineral kingdom. But three localities are reported at which it is thus found: viz., in the county of Kerry, in Ireland; Carthagena, in Spain; and at Alston-Moor, in England: and as it occurs so sparingly in this form, it has no economical value. Its ores, however, are very numerous, and more abundantly distributed. Many of them have only a scientific value, for most of the lead which is found in commerce, is obtained almost entirely from its sulphuret and carbonate. Of all these ores, by far the most important, on account of its general distribution, its abundance and the facility with which it is smelted, is the

Sulphuret of Lead, frequently denominated galena, and in this state most generally called, *blue mineral*, or *mineral*. It is often found crystallized in regular cubes, and sometimes, though not often, in Missouri, in some of the derived forms of this regular system. It is also found in granular masses. Its lustre is metallic, and its color a lead gray, though often it is externally tarnished. It always contains more or less of the isomorphous compound, the sulphuret of silver; but in general this impurity is most abundantly found in the galena obtained from the Azoic formations. It is also frequently accompanied by antimony, which imparts to the specimens a bright steely fracture and causes the laminæ of it to be curved.

When perfectly pure, the galena contains—

Sulphur, ...	13.34 per cent.
Lead, ...	86.66 "

The galena of Missouri is, in general, remarkably pure, occurring sometimes well crystallized, most generally massive and sometimes inclining to granular.

In most of the specimens examined qualitatively, I found no other impurity than iron and a mere trace of silver, but some very few gave indications of traces of nickel and copper.

Many different specimens of lead from different furnaces, and of galena from a variety of localities, were cupelled with the view of seeing whether they were sufficiently argentiferous to justify the separation of the silver.

Galena from Mine la Motte gave, ...	00.0027 per cent. of silver.
" " " " by another cupellation, .	00.0025 " "
" " " " from a greater depth, .	00.0012 " "
" " Perry's Mine, intermixed with zinc ores, .	00.0009 " "
" " " " well crystallized, . .	00.0007 " "
" " Shaft Diggings of Potosi Mining Company,	00.0012 " "
" " Tarpley's Mine, ...	00.0021 " "
" " Cove Mine, ...	00.0010 " "
" " Mt. Hope gave a button of silver scarcely visible.	
" " Short Lode, " " " " "	
" " Hill near Virginia Mines, " " "	
" " Lynn Creek, " " " "	
" " Brinker's field, near Potosi, " " "	
" " Kendall's Diggings, " " "	
" " Cole Camp Spring gave, ...	00.0000
" " Elliot Mines, Franklin county, gave, .	00.0000
" " McCormack's, ...	00.0000
Lead from Vallé's Furnace (Slag Lead), . . .	00.0020 per cent. of silver.
" " Casey & Clancy's Furnace, . . .	00.0022 " "
" " " " " " by a second cupellation,	00.0019 " "
" " Vallé's Furnace, (Soft Lead) gave, . .	00.0029 " "
" " Vallé & Skewes', ...	00.0029 " "
" " Long's Furnace gave less than, . . .	00.0016 " "
" " Virginia Furnace gave less than, . .	00.0016 " "
" " Center Creek gave less than, . . .	00.0016 " "
" " Moseley's gave a button of silver scarcely visible.	

In England, ores containing from 00.02 to 00.03 per cent. of silver or lead which contains from seven to eight ounces of it in each ton can be desilverized with profit; but taking the highest per centage obtained by the cupellation of any of the above specimens of either galena or metallic lead at 0.003 per cent., it would give for the quantity of silver in one ton of our lead only sixteen pennyweights and two grains, a quantity the one-ninth of that in the English lead, and which is too small to justify its separation by the methods at present in use.

It is not improbable that veins of lead ore may be discovered in the igneous rocks of our State; and should they be, there is a probability that the ore may be so rich in silver as to justify desilverization.

Two analyses of a specimen of galena obtained by you from Mr. Glenn's Mine, at Cole Camp Spring, gave the following results: —

	1	2
Sulphur, ...	13.76	13.86
Lead, ...	Not determined.	85.43

A specimen of uncrystallized galena from Mine la Motte gave —

Sulphur, ...	13.50
Lead, ...	84.50
Iron, ...	A trace.
Copper, ...	A trace.
Nickel, ...	A trace.

Another specimen from the same locality, accompanied by carbonate of lead, which it was impossible entirely to separate, gave 82.93 per cent. of lead and 00.63 of iron.

Carbonate of Lead, in Missouri known by the name of white mineral, and at Mine la Motte called dry bones, is another of the ores of lead of some economical importance. Wherever found it has, doubtless, resulted from the decomposition of the galena, effected by water holding in solution oxygen and carbonic acid.

At Mine la Motte quantities of it were formerly found beautifully crystallized. When pure its color is white, though sometimes specimens have been found nearly black (doubtless, from the presence of a small quantity of the sulphuret); its lustre is adamantine, and when broken its fracture is conchoidal; and when pure it yields 77.7 per cent. of metallic lead. In Missouri, when crystallized, it is generally found coating the galena, or in crevices of it; when massive, it has an earthy, grayish white appearance, and can be readily distinguished by its greater specific weight. It is readily soluble in nitric and even acetic acid. It is an ore which is easily smelted, and will frequently yield as high as sixty per cent. of lead.

For a long time this ore was considered valueless, and large quantities of it, both in this State and in Spain, were thrown out with the rubbish from the mines. In Spain they are now excavating from the rubbish this once rejected ore, and sending into market large quantities of lead obtained by the smelting of it. In former years large quantities of it were found on the Mine la Motte tract, but the miners, not knowing its value, threw it aside as so much worthless earth. Afterwards, however, it was bought up and smelted with great profit.

A specimen of the dry bones from Mine la Motte, that was impure, earthy, massive, and that still was somewhat intermixed with a small quantity of galena, gave upon analysis 57.39 per cent. of lead.

Sulphate of Lead, another of the ores resulting from the decomposition of the galena, has been found still more sparsely in Missouri than the last. The only crystallized specimen I have seen was from Massey's Diggings. It is generally found as an earthy, grayish white mass, with a considerable specific gravity, and is designated, by the miners, rotten or ash mineral. The interior of the mass generally contains some of the galena. Though it often retains the cubic form of the galena, it is very pulverulent and crumbles readily under the fingers. When pure, it contains 68.28 per cent. of lead.

Besides the above, a great variety of other ores of lead are sometimes found in the mineral kingdom; but as they are not found, so far as my knowledge extends, in Missouri, and have but little economical value, I shall not attempt an examination or description of them.

Of all the lead found in commerce, according to Mr. Whitney —

Great Britain	furnishes	45.9	per cent.
Spain	"	22.5	"
United States	"	11.3	"
Prussia	"	6.0	"
Austria	"	5.2	"
Hartz	"	3.8	"

That furnished by Great Britain is obtained principally from the sulphurets, and by far the greater portion of these is found in the Carboniferous formation. In Spain, the lead deposits are in calcareous beds belonging to the lower Silurian. The greater portion of the lead from Prussia is obtained from a bed, not over twelve feet thick (of which the galena forms only a part), that lies between the

Muschelkalk and the dolomite, and which, most probably, belongs to the Triassic formation. It is from the same formation that a great part of the lead furnished by Austria comes, while all of that from the Hartz is obtained from the Azoic and Palaeozoic rocks.

The principal deposits of lead ore in the United States are found in the lower series of the lower Silurian. In Iowa and Wisconsin, the galeniferous beds are magnesian, and form a sub-division of the lower Silurian, that, in all probability, directly overlies the Trenton Limestone of the New York system.

In Missouri, however, our lead deposits have a more extensive range; for your examinations of the South-West will show that the mines there are in the Carboniferous, while in the South-East, and Franklin county, the galena is, so far as my knowledge extends, confined to the magnesian members of the lower Silurian formation. These magnesian limestones are not, however, of the same age as the galeniferous beds of Wisconsin; but, as may be seen in Dr. Shumard's sections, they all lie below the Trenton limestone, and are, doubtless, the equivalent of the Calciferous sandrock of the New York system.

In the south-eastern and Franklin counties, the galena is found either in the gravel, when in general it shows evidences of attrition, or in the heavy beds of a plastic ferruginous clay that overlie the magnesian limestones, or in the rock. When in this last, it is deposited either in fissures that are almost vertical, that, with walls well defined, preserve a nearly uniform course, and though varying in their width, seldom exceed four feet, or in what are called openings, which, doubtless, were once cavities and caves communicating one with another, but are now filled with clay, mineral and loose tumbling rock. These openings vary much in size, sometimes being scarcely one foot, and sometimes ten or twelve feet square. When very small, they are called pockets. They do not preserve an uniform course, but are found communicating one with another, by passages, filled with material, different from the wall rock, and extending out to every point of the compass.

Of all the localities, at which lead ore has been found, I do not intend to speak, but only of those which have been visited, and of those, of which such information, as shall be given, has been obtained from what is deemed a reliable source.

GOLCONDA MINES,

Lie in town. 43, N., R. 1 E., sec. 8, W. ½ of S. E. ¼.

The first digging was done here probably in 1830. The mineral was found here at first in the clay, and for the first two years most of the mining was limited to this. In sinking down, a fissure was discovered; the course of which is N. 10° or 15° E. The greatest width of this fissure is three feet. At a point, south from the shafts, and distant 400 yards, the fissure is visible, and has at that point a width of two or three inches. Seven shafts have been sunk on this fissure, the deepest of which is eighteen, and the shallowest twelve feet. The fissure is filled with clay, mineral and calc spar.

To the east of this fissure, and distant from it but a few feet, is another, with nearly the same course, and having, in some points a, width of four feet. From it, also, has been obtained galena. These fissures are in the second magnesian limestone.

Under a new lease, parties again commenced working here last May, and with two hands and a working time of not over four months, they report to have obtained 12,000 pounds of mineral. It is to be hoped that the party now engaged will sink their shafts deeper, and properly explore, by drifting and stopping, this deposit, for it presents strong indications of a perpendicular lode.

VALLE AND SKEWES' MINES.

These are the Cove Mine and Short Lode, on the north, and the Mount Hope Mine, on the south side of the Meramec.

The Cove Mine and the Short Lode are in town. 42 N., R. 1 E., sec. 22, N. W. ¼. They are on the side of a high ridge, the height of which is about 200 feet above the level of the valley. This ridge is capped with about fifty feet of sandstone, the lower portion of which is interstratified with magnesian limestone, and beneath which, so far as explored, are heavy-bedded magnesian limestones, intermixed with chert and quartz.

At the Cove Mine, the galena is found in a vertical fissure, whose average width is not over six inches, the course of which is N. 5° E., and with a slight inclination of seven inches to the fathom to the east. This fissure has never yet been found to widen out much over the above average width, but preserves a nearly uniform course and width, so far as explored. This fissure is sometimes filled entirely with galena; at other points, this is accompanied by heavy spar and calc spar; and sometimes these last, with clay, fill it completely.

The main shaft is about 150 feet deep, at the head of which is a fine exposure of sandstone that extends up to the top of the ridge. South of this, sixty feet, is the bluff shaft, 132 feet deep; and south of this are three other shafts, varying from eighty-eight to fifty feet in depth, and distant from each other from thirty to fifty-eight feet.

South of main shaft, three levels have been run, connecting with the different shafts; and north, but two have been cut, at a depth from each other of 101 feet into the hill, and extending northwardly to a distance from the main shaft of over 200 feet. Much of the ground has been stopped away from main shaft, south to the ladder shaft, between the first and second levels, and also between the same levels, north of the main shaft. Above the first level, and north of the main shaft, the fissure has been followed up into the sandstone, and has been found well filled with mineral, which, at the time of my visit, was yielding a large quantity of galena. This is a not unimportant part, for though the results of observation in other mining countries would teach us to anticipate a change in the character and productiveness of a vein, in passing from one rock into another of a totally different character, here, at least, is one fact tending to show that the presence of sandstone was not incompatible with the deposition of the galena, and that, perhaps, it is a too hasty generalization to conclude that our lead deposits are only productive within the limits of the magnesian limestones.

Plate 1.

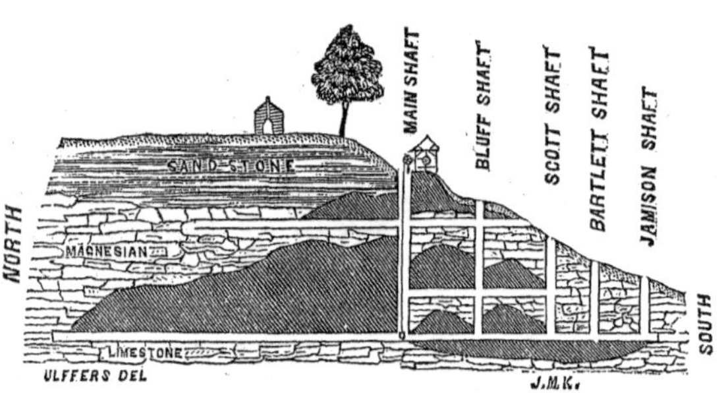

COVE MINE, FRANKLIN COUNTY.
Scale—200 feet to inch.

On plate 1 is a vertical section of Cove Mine, with all the shafts and levels according to measurements, and with the stoppings from my observations and the corrections made by Mr. Skewes. From this can be obtained a better idea of the amount of work and the character of the mining than from any written description. The mineral is remarkably pure, and among the many specimens examined I found no intermixture with other ores.

East of Cove Mine 120 yards, and on the same ridge, is another fissure called the negro lode. On it have been sunk, on the south side, three or four shafts, the deepest of which is fifty or sixty feet. Its course is nearly N. 10° W. But little work has been done by the present proprietors.

Two hundred feet east of the negro lode is, apparently, another fissure, and running nearly parallel with it. Nothing has been done towards exploring it, excepting to dig some few shallow shafts on the hill side. It is called the Scott lode.

SHORT LODE.

This lode is 300 feet east of the Scott, about 280 yards east of the Cove Mine, and on the same hill with them. The lead is found here in fissure, that varies from one inch to two and a half feet in width. Its course is nearly north and south, being nearly parallel with the preceding. The fissure is vertical, and contains, in addition to the ore, the heavy spar, which most frequently accompanies the galena in this fissure. The lead ore is accompanied, sometimes, by sulphuret of zinc. Frequently, cubes of the galena are found encrusted with crystals of the carbonate of lead.

A vertical section of this mine is represented on plate 2, and from this it will be seen that a considerable amount of systematic mining has been done here. Three shafts—one, ninety feet; one, eighty-five feet; and another seventy-seven feet—have been sunk: levels at three different depths have been run, and the quantity of stopping has been considerable. It has been, and is still, worked with profit.

Plate 2.

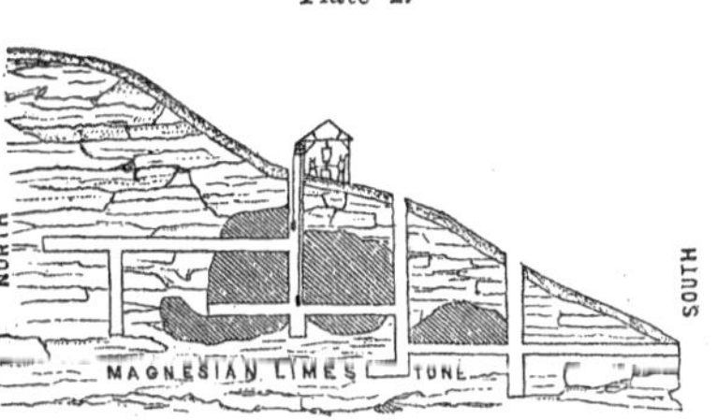

SHORT LODE, FRANKLIN COUNTY.
Scale—200 feet to inch.

On this ridge, which belongs to the third magnesian limestone, are three or four fissures passing down perpendicularly, with a course varying but little from a due north and south, and containing galena as far down as they have been explored. They cover a belt of about 300 yards east and west, and though neither on the top nor on the side of the ridge is there scarcely any natural indication of their existence, they are found, under ground, preserving a uniform course to the north, and one has been traced and worked in this direction nearly 300 feet.

As we pass directly south from the Cove Mine we travel through the valley of the Meramec, and at a distance of about half a mile we come to a lone, isolated hill, which, from its total disconnection with all others, and its solitary appearance, has been denominated the Lost Hill. This has a height nearly equal to that of the ridge in which the above mines are situated, and in this it is reported that galena has also been found. After leaving the Lost Hill, and traveling nearly due south, we cross the Meramec, and in the bluffs on the south side we again find explorations for lead ore, nearly on a due south line and about two and a half or three miles from Cove Mine.

EVANS' LODE.

The first point we reach on this ridge, at which mining has been carried on, is what is known by the name of Evâns' Lode. The galena is found here, also, in vertical fissure, which has a width at some points of two feet. Its course is nearly north and south. It is filled with clay, sulphate of baryta and mineral, and the galena is frequently intermixed with sulphuret and carbonate of zinc. The mining here extends over a distance of 400 feet north and south, and seven shafts, varying from thirty-eight to one hundred and twenty feet, have been sunk, but three of which, however, are connected with levels. The work has not been so systematical nor so regular as at the preceding mines, and this it is reasonable to suppose would be the case, inasmuch as it has not been worked by the proprietor, but has been leased to different parties.

Plate 3.

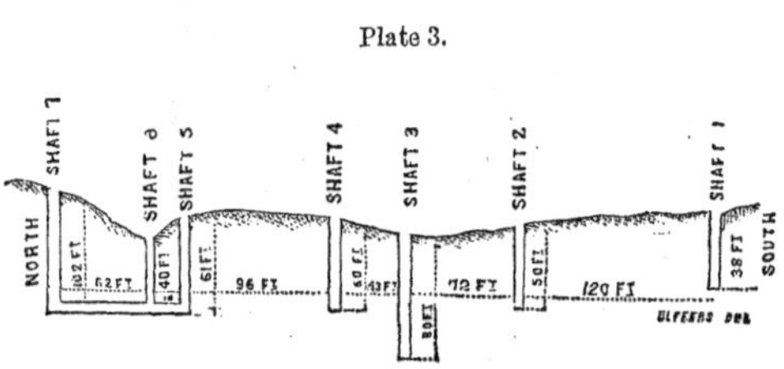

A. F. EVANS' LODE, FRANKLIN COUNTY.
Scale—200 feet to inch.

By Mr. Evans I am informed that it has yielded about 200,000 pounds of mineral.

The accompanying plate 3, represents a section of this mine.

MOUNT HOPE MINE.

Farther south and almost joining the above, and not improbably a continuation of it, is the Mount Hope Mine. They are both in the same ridge, the geological character of which is the same as that of the Cove Mine.

The lead ore is here also found in a vertical fissure, the width of which varies from one inch to two feet. Its course is a little east of north and west of south, with a very slight inclination to the east. Sometimes it is filled entirely with a sheet of galena, and at other points it is found to contain, with lead ore, clay and heavy spar. The ore is sometimes accompanied with the carbonate and the sulphuret of zinc.

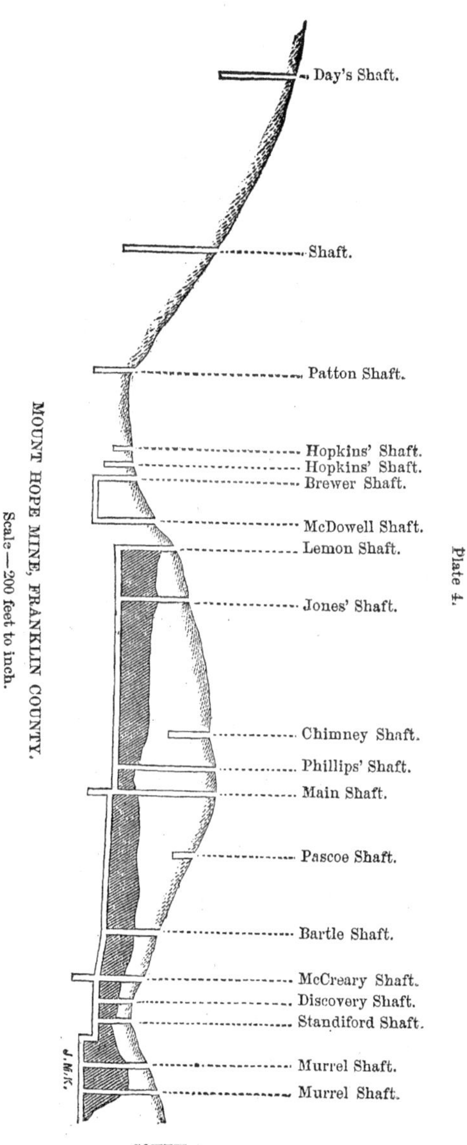

MOUNT HOPE MINE, FRANKLIN COUNTY.
Scale—200 feet to inch.

Plate 4.

Plate 4 represents a vertical section of this mine, with its shafts, levels and stoppings. About thirteen shafts have been sunk, varying from twenty feet to one hundred and thirty-three feet in depth. Most of them have been connected by levels, and the mining has extended over a line of nearly 800 feet, north and south.

Among the debris brought up from the lowest levels at Mount Hope and Cove Mines were some few well-preserved Pleurotomaria and Euomphalus, and one of the most perfect of these last was almost directly in contact with galena.

The galena found in this mine is accompanied, at some points, with the carbonate and sulphuret of zinc.

The ore obtained from the Mount Hope, the Short, and the Cove Mines has been all smelted, since the commencement of operations by the present Company in 1849, in a rude reverberatory furnace in the neighborhood of the Cove, and no separate account has been kept of the yield of each mine. The quantity of lead made from 1849 to October of the present year (1854), according to the statement furnished me by Mr. Wm. Skewes, has been 1,947,780 pounds, all the ore having been obtained from the above mines of the Company, and the greater part from Mount Hope Mine. The average number of hands employed has been between twenty and twenty-five.

A blast furnace is now being erected, with which it is intended to smelt the very large quantity of slag, that has been accumulating since the Company obtained possession of the mines, and which will increase considerably the total amount of lead obtained from these mines during the last five years.

VIRGINIA MINE.

Some two or three miles nearly due south of Mount Hope is the famous Virginia Mine, on the 16th section, in township 41 and range 1, east. This mine was discovered in 1834 or 1835, by Bartlett Brundage, and the fame of it soon attracted to it a number of miners, who obtained the privilege of working lots of twenty-four feet in diameter; and during the first year of its discovery the number engaged in mining is supposed to have been between 200 and 300. The School Commissioners (for it was on the public school land), in order to secure the rent on the mineral obtained, determined to appoint a single smelter, who should be responsible for it; and the number of applicants was so great, that they decided to make the selection by the drawing of lots, when it fell to John

Williamson, who, having held it for a short time, sold to C. B. and I. Inge for $7,000. They having retained this office until the autumn of 1835 or '36, disposed of their right for $14,000 to Mr. Clendennin. He held it for about one year, when the mineral having accumulated in such quantities that he could not or did not smelt as fast as it was brought in by the miners, great dissatisfaction was excited, and the miners having rebelled and refused to furnish him the mineral, suit was commenced, the final termination of which was that the lease granted to him was broken. Soon after a number of smelters were appointed by the Trustees of the Public Schools, and at one time there were as many as ten log and three ash furnaces in operation.

In 1844, the Meramec Company obtained a lease for working the mine and smelting the mineral, with the understanding that they were to buy the miners' rights to the tracts on the lode. They commenced operations actively and energetically, putting up a steam engine and pump, sinking the shafts deeper, running levels, and erecting a furnace; when one of the parties becoming embarrassed in his mercantile business, and another dying, operations were suspended, in 1846, for the want of funds; and since that time little or nothing has been done, while the machinery has been rusting, the buildings decaying, and the shafts and levels been caving in.

The ore is found more in a vertical fissure, whose course is nearly due north and south, and has been traced by diggings from a short distance north of the Meramec, over a line, extending northwardly into the Bennett tract, of not less than one mile in length. The fissure varies in width from one to fifteen feet; and at one point, at which it is still visible from the top of the shaft, is not less than two feet wide. The rock is covered with a thick, heavy bed of ferruginous clay, the average thickness of which is fifty feet, beneath which is some ten or twelve feet of a cherty limestone, and below this is the magnesian limestone. The fissure is filled with clay, heavy spar (some of which was well crystallized, mostly, however, amorphous, with a light sky-blue color), and with galena.

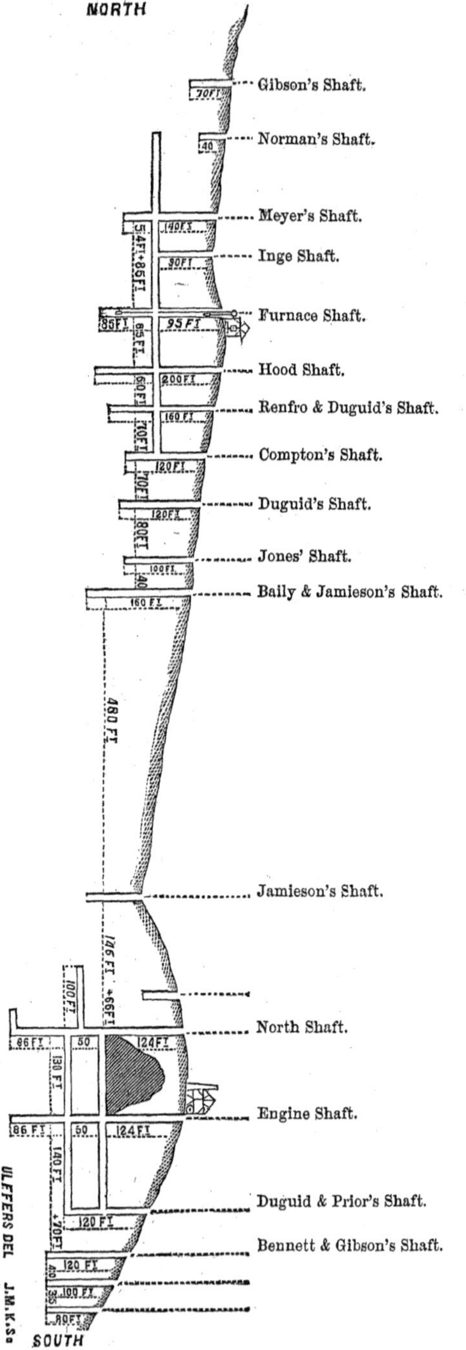

VIRGINIA MINES, FRANKLIN COUNTY.
Scale—300 feet to inch.

Plate 5.

Plate 5 gives a vertical section of this mine, from the best information I could get. At the time of my visits it was impossible, on account of the presence of water and the decayed state of the timbers, to enter more than one shaft. I measured the distances from one shaft to another, and am indebted to Mr. I. N. Inge for the names and depths of these, with the distances of the levels beneath the surface of the ground, excepting that of the lowest level, between Duguid's and Prior's shaft, which I take from a lately published report of Dr. King, who had an opportunity of examining this mine when it was worked by the Meramec Company.

From this section it will be seen that the shafts sunk were very numerous; but, doubtless, before the possession of the mine by the Meramec Company, most of them were sunk without regard to any system or regular mining operations. After the Company took possession, the mining was more systematic, and most of their labor was confined to the neighborhood of the engine and north shafts, each of which was sunk to a depth of about 260 feet. Levels were cut from north shaft, both north and south, the latter communicating with Duguid and Prior's shaft. Dr. King, in his report, says that between engine and north shaft there was a vast cavern, extending from the first level connecting these two shafts, almost to the surface of the ground, with an average breadth of nearly five feet, and from fifty to one hundred feet in height, nearly filled with pure galena; and that in the engine shaft, at the depth of 260 feet, the lode was as large and distinct as it generally was throughout the shaft.

Before the operations of the Meramec Company, the mining was carried on at different points by different parties, acting without regular system, and the one independently of the other. Most of the mineral, I doubt not, was then obtained from comparatively shallow depths. How much of this fissure has been worked out along its course, so far as yet explored, and to the depth of the deepest shafts, I have no sufficient data to enable me to judge; but from the best information I have been enabled to obtain of the levels and the stopping, I should deem it an exaggerated estimate to place it at one-half.

Of the total amount of mineral obtained here, it is, perhaps, impossible, at present, to obtain any true and accurate statement. Dr. King, who had an opportunity, about ten years ago, of examining the books of the School Trustees, found the total amount on which rent had been charged and paid, to be 4,610,158 pounds; but neither he nor any one else supposes that this was all that, up to that time, had been obtained.

Among all the estimates I have obtained from those who were familiar with the operations at this mine, there is none less than 8,000,000 pounds; some, 15,000,000 pounds; but the majority of them place it at 10,000,000 pounds of ore.

However great may seem the above estimate, I do not doubt, had shafts been sunk systematically, levels been run at suitable and required depths, machinery been erected to keep the mine dry, and the ground been stopped away with any thing like scientific and practical skill, that the Virginia Mine would have been more productive than it has been, and instead of lying idle, would be still yielding a handsome interest on the investment.

For many of the above facts, in regard to the Virginia Mine, I am indebted to the Rev. Mr. Clarke and Mr. I. Nash Inge.

DARBY'S MINE.

Town. 41 N., R. 1 W., sec. 20, S. E ¼.

This mine was worked some four or five years ago, and, according to all reports, with considerable profit. Operations were suspended on account of the water, but lately a new lease has been obtained by Mr. Giles, who is now engaged in working it.

This mine is in the spur of a magnesian limestone hill. A shaft has been sunk fifty-two feet deep, and an adit cut, for the purpose of drainage. At the bottom of this shaft a level has been run thirty feet, nearly east and west, and near this was found a large cave (denominated by the miners, chimney), extending nearly to the surface of the hill, and which was found filled with clay, tumbling rock, and a considerable quantity of mineral.

The quantity of water (which is removed by pump, worked by horse power) is so great, that it is necessary to keep the present pump in constant operation, night and day; and, this having been intermitted for several days previous to my visit, I found the shaft filled with water to nearly the adit level.

Specimens of the mineral seen from this mine were tolerably massive, much of it crystallized in cubes, the sides of many of which were coated with crystals of the carbonate of lead. At the bottom of the shaft were found considerable quantities of the yellow iron pyrites, intermixed with sulphuret of zinc.

Mr. Giles reports, that during the seven months he has been working, with the assistance of seven hands, more than half the time, and during the remainder, with that of only four hands, he has obtained 3,000 pounds of mineral. The estimated amounts of mineral, obtained from this mine, anterior to Mr. Giles' lease, varies from 100,000 to 126,000 pounds of mineral.

ELLIOT MINE.

Town. 41 N., R. 1 W., sec. 6.

This mine lies on the south-western extremity of a ridge, the course of which is a little west of north, and east of south. According to Dr. Shumard, the top of the hill is sandstone, beneath which is the third magnesian limestone.

The only mineral obtained here has been from the clay, on the side of the hill, one acre of which is almost entirely covered with shallow shafts, the deepest I found open being twenty-one feet. The mineral obtained has been principally from three ranges, the general course of which was N. E. and S. W., running parallel with one another, and distant fifteen to twenty feet from each other. The exposure in the shafts was a reddish ferruginous clay, varying from twelve to twenty feet, below chert, and beneath this the tumbling magnesian limestone. The average depth of the shafts is not over twelve feet, and the deepest ever sunk was forty feet.

The mineral is a very pure galena, accompanied by neither calc spar nor heavy spar, and exhibits not the least intermixture with either iron or zinc ores. As yet, it has been found only in the clay and chert. Work was commenced here in June, 1853; and since then, with six hands, it is reported that 70,000 pounds of mineral has been obtained.

Besides the above, there are quite a number of points in Franklin county at which galena has been obtained, and, at some of them, in considerable quantities, but which were not worked during the times of my visits to that county in 1853 and 1854. Most of them were not visited; and I subjoin a list of them, with the amounts of mineral which were reported to me as having been obtained.

On the school section, in town. 42 N., R. 1 W., in 1827 and '28, there had been considerable digging. The mineral was found in the clay. The deepest shafts were about fifty feet. The diggings extended over an area of nearly ten acres, but did not extend down into the rock. Mr. A. Chambers, who worked these, obtained and smelted during the above years, 40,000 pounds of mineral, and estimates the amount obtained at other times, and hauled to other furnaces, at 25,000 pounds.

The Hamilton Mines, town. 42 N., R. 1 W., sec. 31, have not been worked for the last six years. The digging was confined to the clay, and the amount of mineral reported to have been obtained was 100,000 pounds.

At Massey's Mine, town. 41 N., R. 1 W., sec. 14, one shaft had been sunk sixty feet, but most of the other shafts were not over twelve feet. Up to October, 1853, Mr. Massey estimated the amount of mineral obtained at from 2,000 to 3,000 pounds. They are much incommoded by water at these diggings.

Berthold and Generally's diggings are near Mitchel's creek, in sec. 13, town. 41 N., R. 1 W. They are principally on the side of a hill. The deepest shaft was fifty-four feet, and which was filled with water at the time of my visit, in October, 1853. Mr. Generally gave, as the total amount of mineral obtained here, 100,000 pounds.

REPORTED AMOUNT OF MINERAL OBTAINED.

Silver Hollow Mines,	town. 40 N., R. 1 W., sec. 8,	140,000 lbs.
Thomas' "	town. 41 N., R. 1 W., sec. 32,	100,000 "
Lolla "	town. 41 N., R. 2 W., sec. 15,	50 to 100,000 "
Wheeler "	town. 40 N., R. 1 W., sec. 6 and 7,	50,000 "
Nick Frank's "	town. 42 N., R. 1 W., sec. 8, S. W ¼ of S. E. ¼.	
Whitmire "	town. 41 N., R. 1 W., sec. 28,	60,000 "

LEAD FURNACES IN FRANKLIN.

Formerly, not only in Franklin, but also in other counties in the mining region of Missouri, only the log and ash furnaces were used. These have been gradually replaced every-where, excepting at one locality in Washington county, by either the Scotch hearth or the reverberatory furnaces. The Scotch hearth requires a blast, hence sometimes called the blast furnace, and this is produced either by water or horse-power, or by steam.

The old log furnace was simple in its construction, and easily built. After the smelting of one charge, about 5,000 pounds of ore, the furnace was cooled, and after the removal of the ashes, which were rich in lead, it was again charged.

When, after repeated smeltings with the log furnace, a sufficient quantity of ashes had been accumulated, these were washed to separate the wood from the mineral ashes, when these last were smelted in an ash furnace.

The slag, from both the reverberatory furnace and Scotch hearth, is washed and cleaned, and re-smelted in a slag furnace.

At present, there are but three lead furnaces in operation in Franklin county.

GALLAHER'S FURNACE.

Town. 41 N., R. 1 W., sec. 19.

It is the Scotch hearth, and the blast is produced by water-power. This furnace has been in operation but two years. All the mineral and slag smelted here came from Franklin county, excepting a lot of 1,900 pounds. Most of the slag came from the Virginia Mine, and Hebbler and Chapman's Furnace.

Amount of lead made at this furnace, according to the statement furnished me by Mr. Gallaher, was, for—

1853, . .	700 pigs, average of 72 lbs. each, . .	50,400
1854, . .	600 " " " " . .	36,000

At the Virginia Mines are two furnaces; only one, however, has, I believe, been in operation since the Meramec Company ceased operations, and this has been under the control of I. Nash Inge.

INGE'S FURNACE.

According to the statement, furnished me by Messrs. Patridge & Co., the agents of Mr. Inge, the following amounts of lead were made at this furnace, from 1849 to 1854:—

	PIGS.		POUNDS.
1849, from 20th June, . .	202,	weighed . .	13,574
1850, " " . .	3,237,	" . .	196,744
1851, " " . .	1,229,	" . .	80,606
1852, " " . .	277,	" . .	18,630
1853, " " . .	613,	" . .	39,989
1854, " " . .	85,	" . .	5,557

VALLE AND SKEWES' FURNACE, AT COVE MINE.

At this furnace has been smelted only the ore obtained from the mines of the Company. I am indebted to Mr. Wm. Skewes for the following statement of lead made at this furnace:—

1850, . .	5,000 pigs, average weight of each, 61 lbs., . .	300,000
1851, . .	5,000 " " " " . .	300.000
1852, . .	6,000 " " " " . .	360,000
1853, . .	9,463 " " " " . .	567,780
1854, to Oct.,	7,000 " " " " . .	420,000

Mr. Skewes believes that the amount that will be made this year will fully equal that of 1853.

Statement of the total amount of lead made at the furnaces in Franklin county, from commencement of 1850 to October, 1854:—

	1850.	1851.	1852.	1853.	1854.
Gallaher's Furnace,				50,400	36,000
Inge's "	196,744	80,606	18,630	39,989	5,557
Vallé and Skewes' Furnace,	300,000	300,000	360,000	567,780	420,000
	496,744	380,606	378,630	658,169	461,557

LEAD MINES OF JEFFERSON.

The points at which mining has been carried on in Jefferson county are comparatively few; but, from the geological formations prevailing here, there is every reason to believe that these will be considerably increased. Among the best known may be enumerated Sandy, Tarpley, and Mammoth Mines.

SANDY MINES,

Town. 41 N., R. 5 E., Sec. 18.

These mines have been worked, at intervals, for a number of years. The diggings extend over a line nearly one mile in length, the course of which is a little east of north and west of south; though the principal part of the work has been done on some 500 feet at the south end.

The ground is covered with clay, the thickness of which varies from fourteen to thirty feet. Below this, judging from the debris thrown out, are some beds of impure, blueish, argillaceous limestone. Plate 6 represents a vertical section of the more important works at this mine, and in the construction of which I am indebted to Mr. Coolidge, the present proprietor, for considerable aid, for at the time of my visit it was filled with water, and all underground examinations were impossible.

Plate 6.

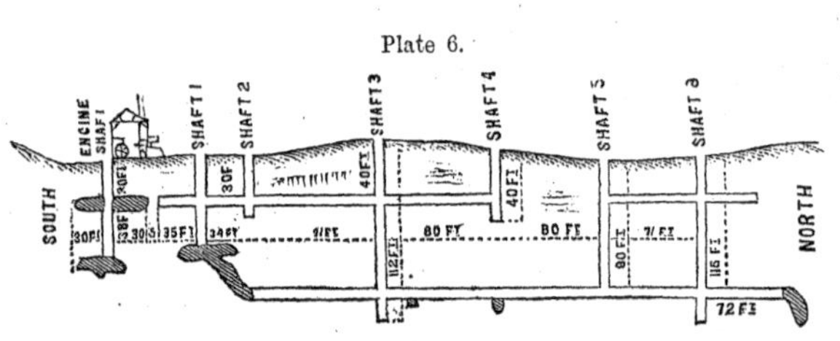

H. A. ULFFERS, *Del.*

SANDY MINES, JEFFERSON COUNTY.

Scale—200 feet to inch.

The deepest shaft has been sunk 115 feet; drifts have been run between some of them at two different levels. A short time ago a pump and engine were put up to drain the mine; but at the time of my visit, operations had been intermitted by the person who now has a lease and has been working it for some year and a half.

Above the rock considerable quantities of mineral were obtained, some twenty years ago, but all on the same north and south line, and even extending into the rock. In the rock the mineral seems to exist in a vertical fissure, and, so far as I can learn, not continuous from top to bottom, but principally accumulated at three different levels.

At the first point, at which mineral is found, in the rock it is represented as having a vertical range of six or eight feet, below which the fissure partially closes to a depth of from six to ten feet, when it is again found to widen out and contain mineral, in a vertical range of ten or twelve feet. Below this the fissure again partially closes for a depth of ten or fifteen feet, and at this point mineral is again found, with a vertical range of from fourteen to twenty-five feet. I am assured that the fissure is well defined and distinct from one level of mineral to the other. Of the yield of this mine since 1840, Mr. Coolidge is unable to give any definite and accurate statement, as the furnace in the neighborhood has, during this period, belonged to different persons. By one who was working for the present lessee, I was informed that, during the present year, about 30,000 pounds of mineral had been obtained; and from Mr. Coolidge I learn that, in 1842 and '43, several thousand pounds of mineral were raised; and, in 1846 and '47, some 300,000 pounds; and at other times considerable amounts, of which we can give no accurate account.

The ore is the sulphuret, with small quantities of the carbonate, and sometimes accompanied by yellow iron pyrites and zinc blende.

MAMMOTH MINE,

Town. 39 N., R. 3 E., sec. 12, N. W. ½ of N. W. ¼.

This mine was discovered by Mr. Higgins in 1843, and, being on government land, was entered by Messrs. Boldur and Higginbotham. It lies in a hill, the height of which is not over 150 feet, and the entrance to it is on the north-west side. The hill is covered with a reddish clay, varying in depth, having a thickness of nineteen feet in the main shaft. Below this is the magnesian limestone, and through which one shaft has been sunk sixty-two feet.

On plate 7 is represented a vertical section of this mine, with the courses and distances of the driftings, from a survey of them made in 1848, by Mr. O'Mara.

The lead was deposited here in a series of irregular caves, varying in size from four to nine feet in height, and in width from four to twelve feet. These caves communicated one with another by openings, varying in size, and which were never found closed entirely, excepting twice, in the 533 feet through which they have been explored. These caves were sometimes found partially filled with clay and loose tumbling rock, accompanied by mineral, while oftentimes immense quantities of massive mineral were found adhering to the sides and top of the caves. In passing from the entrance of the mine, south of the pump shaft, there are two points at which the descent is considerable, and south of the main shaft there is again another descent. Beyond this point there have been but few explorations, for here water rises up, and, when the pump is not in operation, attains such a height as to flow out through the adit level. A former Company attempted to remove this body of water with a pump of an eight-inch bore and a four-feet stroke, but found it inefficient to keep the mine dry.

Plate 7.

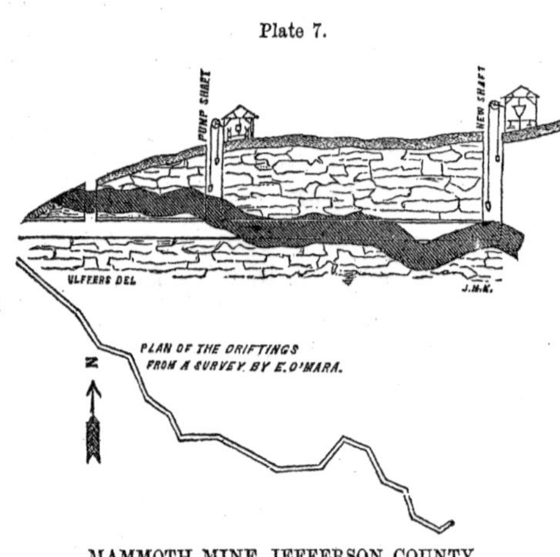

MAMMOTH MINE, JEFFERSON COUNTY.
Scale—200 feet to inch.

Nothing has been done here since 1852.

The reported amount of mineral obtained here is almost incredible. From the best information, obtained from different parties engaged at different times in working this mine, I estimated in 1852 the total amount obtained at 5,000,000 pounds of ore; and since, no facts have come to my knowledge to induce me to alter this estimate. In 1851 and 1852, Col. J. N. Reading, President of the former Company, reported that 21,692 pounds of ore had been obtained in tracing out some lateral arms from the caves.

Belonging to the same Company as the Mammoth, and six miles north of it, is the Edging Lead. It is near a branch of Cedar creek, and on the side of a hill that is covered with clay, the average depth of which is twelve feet, while below is the magnesian limestone.

The lead is found here in a vertical fissure, the course of which is nearly north and south, and the width usually varying from eighteen inches to two and a half feet. Five shafts have been sunk on this fissure: the deepest is about thirty feet. The ore, where visible, was from one to four inches thick. The only difficulty to contend with here, is water; and as the drainage of this is not impossible, it is to be hoped that the present Company, with so good a prospect, will test, by still farther explorations, the character of this deposit.

TARPLEY MINES.

Town. 38 N., R. 4 E., Sec. 11.

At this point much work has been done; but, at the time of my visit, none of those then engaged in mining were present, so that it was impossible for me to enter any of the shafts; and for most of my information I am indebted to Mr. Hale, superintendent of the Vallé Mines, who had the kindness to accompany me, and who had spent several years in working there. The deepest shaft ever sunk was 180 feet; the average depth of the shafts is, however, from seventy-five to eighty feet. In digging, a red ferruginous clay is passed through, the average thickness of which is forty feet; beneath it is the solid magnesian limestone. After passing into this, when successful openings or cavities are reached (from which almost all the mineral has been obtained, and which are filled with clay, mineral and tiff), there have been found two series of caves or openings, at different levels, the depth of the lower being some fifteen feet beneath that of the first. These two series are reported to have been nearly equally productive.

The mineral obtained here is a very pure massive galena, and the mines have been quite productive. One-half of the mineral obtained was smelted at White's, and the other half at Perry's furnace. The following is the statement of mineral received at Perry's furnace, as furnished by the kindness of Mr. Daly, and which should be doubled, to show the true yield of this mine, during the annexed years:

YEAR.	PERRY'S SHARE.	TOTAL AMOUNT.
1845,	50,365	100,730
1846,	100,650	201,300
1847,	125,625	251,250
1848,	42,184	84,368
1849.	45,560	91,120
1850,	158,750	317,500

YEARS.	PERRY'S SHARE.	TOTAL AMOUNT.
1851,	55,685	111,370
1852,	62,800	125,600
1853,	65,150	130,300
1854, to Oct.	25,000	50,000
Total	731,769	1,463,538

In addition to the above, there has, also, been some mining in Jefferson county, in town. 41 N., R. 5 E., sec. 34, S. part of S. W. ¼, at what are denominated the Gopher, or Herculaneum Mining Company's Diggings, and at the Plattin or Howe's Diggings, on Plattin creek, but of these I cannot speak from personal observation.

FURNACES OF JEFFERSON COUNTY.

In this county, there are three furnaces—the Sandy, the Mammoth and the Vallé.

At Vallé's is smelted, principally, the mineral that comes from Vallé's Mines, in St. François county, and the amount of lead made here belongs properly to that county. There is, at this place, both a Scotch hearth and a slag furnace, the blast for both being produced by steam.

The Mammoth furnace is a Scotch hearth; blast produced by steam; and here is smelted the lead obtained from the mines of the Company: viz., Mammoth, Edging Lode, Prairie, Elliot, Becquette and Wet Diggings, the first two of which, only, are in Jefferson, the others in Washington.

Of the amount of lead made at these last two furnaces (Sandy and Mammoth), I have not been able to obtain any full statement, and, consequently, have no certain and accurate data to show the amount of lead obtained annually from this county.

MINES OF ST. FRANCOIS COUNTY.

Near the boundary line of Jefferson and St. François, in Town. 38 N., R. 5 E., is a hilly and broken country; and here is a small section of country, probably not extending over an area of more than fifty acres, that has been proved by explorations, long carried on and vigorously pursued, to have been one of the richest localities in the State. On it are the mines of Bisch, of Perry and of Vallé, the last two of which are more generally known than any other lead mines in Missouri; known, not only on account of the length of time during which mining has been here carried on, but also by the large amount of ore which has been obtained.

By reference to plate 8, will be seen a topographical map of these two mines, and for the drafting of which I am indebted to the kindness of Mr. A. H. Ulffers. From this, it will be seen they are contiguous, lying on opposite sides of the main ridge, the course of which, at this point, is nearly north-west and south-east. From this main ridge, other hills run off north and south. These two mines being in the same main ridge, the Vallé on the north and the Perry mine on the south side of it, the driftings of the two communicate with each other at several points.

VALLE'S MINE, OR BIG LODE.

Town. 38 N., R. 5 E., Sec. 7 and 8.

This mine was discovered, in 1824, by Joseph Schuts, since which it has, I believe, been worked without interruption. The mining has been limited almost entirely to the West Hill, and the number of shafts sunk, since the commencement of operations, has been very considerable. The deepest is the Wilkinson shaft, 170 feet in depth, and which was sunk from near the summit of the ridge. The depths of the other principal shafts are as follows: —

Evans' Shaft,	115 ft.	Tippet's	80 ft.	Harris'	65 ft.	Murdock's	55 ft.	Discovery	37 ft.
Joe's "	110 "	Ben's	75 "	Old lad'r	64 "	James'	45 "		
Marsh's "	110 "	Carron	72 "	Pernot	55 "	Ladder	50 "		

The ore was found here in openings or caves, which, on the same level, communicated the one with the other, and which were found filled with clay, tumbling rock and mineral. Of these caves, there seem to be three series, at different depths. The depth at which the first series is reached, is dependent upon the point of the hill side from which the shaft is sunk. The second series is eighteen or twenty feet below the first, and the third series is about eight feet below the second. All the work done in this mine has been confined to the second, and little or nothing has been done towards exploring the first and third series of caves.

Plate 9 represents the driftings through this series of caves, in 1842. I am indebted to Mr. Wm. Skewes for the original of it, which was drafted (from actual surveys, made by himself in that year) by Mr. A. E. St. Gemme. Since then, however, the driftings have been greatly extended, but to obtain a more complete survey of the works is now impossible. From this, it will be seen that these caves run out in every direction, while, probably, the general course of the whole body may be considered as nearly north-west and south-east.

It is not improbable that this hill is pretty well worked out on the level of the second series of caves; but it is well worthy of being tested, by explorations, whether the first and third series are not not sufficiently rich in mineral to justify the mining of them.

For the last year, or more, the Company has been engaged in exploring entirely new ground—the East, or Madden Hill. On this hill, one shaft, the Madden, had been sunk 110 feet, the first sixty of which was through clay and gravel, and the remainder through a silicious magnesian limestone. They have here found two series of caves, the second being eighteen feet below the first.

Of the total amount of mineral obtained from this mine, it is now, perhaps, impossible to obtain a perfectly accurate statement. Of much of the mineral, no record was ever kept. The old books, so far as they have been preserved, were examined by Mr. Felix Vallé and Mr. Felix Rozier, and to their kind labors I am indebted for the following statement of the yield of this mine, as the most minute and accurate that can now be obtained:—

From 1824 to 1830,	5,229,146	lbs. of lead.
" 1830 to 1834,	5,000,000	" "
" 1834 to 1839,	2,890,959	" "
" 1839 to 1845,	2,227,495	" "
" 1845 to 1850,	1,559,040	" "
" 1850 to 1854,	2,577,137	" "
Total amount,	19,483,777	

PERRY'S MINE.

Town. 38 N., R. 5 E., Sec. 18, E ½ of N. E. ¼.

This mine was discovered after Vallé's. It lies just south of Vallé's, and in the same main ridge. This southern declivity is divided by a slight depression, making on this, also, a west and an east hill. It is in the first that most of the work has been done, up to this period.

The number of the principal shafts is about eight, the names and depths of which are as follows:—

Taylor's, 80 feet.	McGuire's, 165 feet.	New Shaft, 85 feet.
Stoney, 95 "	Tyler's, 85 "	Water Shaft, ——
Deloney, 85 "	Fulton, 130 "	

Taylor, Stoney, McGuire and Deloney shafts are on the west hill, while on the east hill are the New, the Water, the Hale and

Harris shafts; and in or near the ravine, between these two hills, lie the Tyler and Fulton shafts. On plate 8 are represented the relative distances and courses of these shafts.

The mineral is found here, also, in caves or openings, of which, in the deepest shaft, four series have been found.

The average depth of the 2nd series, below the 1st, is 18 or 20 feet.
" " " of the 3rd " " " 2nd, is 40 or 45 feet.
" " " of the 4th " " " 3rd, is 40 or 45 feet.

The lowest two series have only been reached by one shaft: viz., the McGuire; all of the other shafts extending down only to the second series. It is on the level of this second series of caves that most of the work has been done; and, by drifts through them, all the shafts on the west hill have been connected with one another, while there has been little drifting from the shafts on the east hill, this being entirely new ground.

During the present year, the first series of caves, near the Fulton shaft, have been worked, and with considerable profit. They are found, now and then, communicating with the series below, by openings or "chimneys."

These caves and chimneys are filled with clay, loose rock and mineral, which is accompanied by carbonate and silicates of zinc, and so thoroughly intermixed with them, that they can not well be separated by hand. In these caves are frequently found beds and seams of what the miners denominate slate. It is soft, plastic, sometimes perfectly white, and sometimes of a reddish brown color. When exposed to the air, it crumbles and falls into powder. It has the appearance of tallow. Specimens of it, exposed in my laboratory, became covered with small delicate crystals. These were found to be a hydrated silicate of zinc; and they are, doubtless, the same substance that is frequently found coating with crystals the galena taken from the mine. The reddish brown variety is the same substance, essentially a hydrated silicate of zinc, with some oxide of iron.

Much of the ore obtained here is what is locally denominated dry bones. It is an intermixture of the galena with silicates and the carbonate of zinc. This impure ore is first roasted, then washed, and afterwards smelted, the average yield of which being seventy per cent. The smelting has all been done at Perry's furnace, which is a Scotch hearth, with slag furnace; the blast is produced by steam.

To Mr. Daly I am indebted for the following statement of mineral, obtained from the Perry Mine, from 1839 to November, 1854:—

	MINERAL.
1839,	1,176,502 lbs.
1840,	1,899,011 "
1841,	1,865,746 "
1842,	1,212,989 "
1843,	992,686 "
1844,	1,307,223 "
1845,	1,217,875 "
1846,	998,350 "
1847,	1,014,444 "
1848,	1,223,158 "
1849,	948,833 "
1850,	907,097 "
1851,	792,724 "
1852,	808,059 "
1853,	851,211 "
1854, to November,	902,673 "
	18,118,673

BISCH'S MINES.

Town. 38 N., R. 5 E., Sec. 18, W. ½ of N. E. ¼, adjoining Perry's.

The principal work has been done on the side of a hill. Ten shafts have been sunk, the deepest of which is 105 feet, and the average depth of the others is about seventy feet. In these have also been found two series of caves, the second being twenty feet below the first. There are, sometimes, found chimneys, connecting the upper and lower caves. The caves are found running out in every direction; and it has, in general, been found, that when the one series of caves, at any point, is rich in mineral, the corresponding upper or lower series is poor.

Here, as at Vallé & Perry's Mines, in sinking shafts, they first pass through gravel and clay, varying in depth from ten to thirty feet; then, a light-colored, heavy-bedded silicious magnesian limestone, which passes into a harder, more compact, fine-grained magnesian limestone, that is denominated, by the miners, the cast-steel rock.

The ore obtained here is very similar to that from Perry's Mines. These mines have been, probably, worked since 1825, but not with the same constancy, nor with the same number of hands, as the Perry & Vallé Mines. Most of the mining done here has been by Mr. Bisch's negroes, the average number of which was not over eight; but, at times, other miners have been engaged.

The ore obtained here was all smelted by Messrs. A. Bisch & Co.; and their furnace, which is the reverberatory, is in Town. 38 N., R. 5 E., Sec. 18, S. W. ¼; and I am indebted to them for the total amount of lead made here from 1825 to 1854, which was 6,000,000 pounds, which would be an average of 200,000 pounds per annum, obtained from their mine.

On the lands of Vallé, Perry and Bisch, there are many other points at which mineral has been obtained; but at all these, with the exception of the above three mines, all the mineral found has been in the clay, below which the explorations, at these points, have not been extended. There are many other points in St. François county at which mineral has been discovered, and where there has been mining, though, at present, but little or nothing is done. Among them may be mentioned —

THE McCORMACK DIGGINGS.
Town. 38 N., R. 5 E., Sec. 11, N. E. ¼.

At this point two shafts have been sunk; one, eighty-five feet in depth, and the other, sixty-five feet. At the bottom of this last was found a series of openings, which, though but little explored, have, so far as mined, yielded handsomely.

THE HAZEL-RUN DIGGINGS.
Town. 38 N., R. 5 E., Sec. 33, S. W. ¼.

These diggings lie mostly in low ground, near Hazel-Run creek. These mines were in operation in 1806, and worked, at various times, up to 1823; since which but little has been done; the great obstacle to mining here, is the labor necessary for drainage. The mineral is represented as being found in fissures, running nearly east and west, and varying in width from six inches to two feet. The fissures are filled with clay and galena, which is found in sheets; the thickest I saw not being over two and a half inches.

Mineral has also been obtained near the St. François river, close to the Ste. Genevieve plank-road, on Luzane's claim; and, at the time of my visit, in October, 1853, was worked by Mr. Murphy. He had sunk one shaft twenty-eight feet; the first ten feet through a light gray, banded silicious limestone, beneath which was ten feet of clay, and the lower eight feet was through a grayish limestone. The driftings, at the bottom of the shaft, were, south-east, fourteen feet, and north-west, twelve feet. The mineral was found in pockets, and Mr. Murphy reported that he had obtained 35,000 pounds.

Mineral has also been found in this county, at the Dogget Diggings, Town. 38 N., R. 4 and 5 E., Secs. 36 and 31; at the Manchester, Town. 38 N., R. 5 E., Sec. 31, E. $\frac{1}{2}$ of S. E. $\frac{1}{4}$.; at the Potosi, Town. 38 N., R. 5 E., Sec. 21, S. E. $\frac{1}{4}$; and at several other points, none of which I had time to visit.

I subjoin the following estimate of lead, made annually, from 1839 to 1854, at the furnaces of Bisch, Perry and Vallé, based upon the above reports. That it is not perfectly accurate, I am fully aware, but the data upon which it is founded are the most minute and accurate that can now be obtained; and though not showing the total amount produced, annually, by St. François county, it will, at least, serve to give some idea of the minimum quantity of lead that has been sent to market from the mines of this county:—

AMOUNT OF LEAD, MADE AT

YEAR.	BISCH'S FUR'E.	VALLE'S FUR'E.	PERRY'S FUR'E.	TOTAL AM'T.
1839,	200,000	371,246	823,552	1,394,798
1840,	200,000	371,246	1,329,308	1,900,554
1841,	200,000	371,246	1,306,022	1,877,268
1842,	200,000	371,246	849,092	1,420,338
1843,	200,000	371,246	694,880	1,266,126
1844,	200,000	371,246	915,056	1,486,302
1845,	200,000	311,808	852,513	1,364,321
1846,	200,000	311,808	698,845	1,210,653
1847,	200,000	311,808	710,111	1,221,919
1848,	200,000	311,808	856,211	1,368,019
1849,	200,000	311,808	664,183	1,175,991
1850,	200,000	515,427	634,968	1,350,395
1851,	200,000	515,427	554,907	1,270,334
1852,	200,000	515,427	565,641	1,281,068
1853,	200,000	515,427	595,848	1,311,275
1854,	200,000	515,427	631,936	1,347,363

LEAD MINES OF WASHINGTON COUNTY.

It was in this county that the first mining of the lead ore, in Missouri, was commenced; and since the purchase of Louisiana, by the General Government, it has been almost uninterruptedly continued (though not at the same point) during this period. To enumerate every point at which there have been diggings, and, still farther, to give an accurate account of the mining at each, would now be impossible, for the actors have disappeared, leaving, most frequently, only to false and exaggerated tradition the story of their failures and successes; and though the upturned earth and the caved-in shafts remain to tell us of their labors, they are but dumb memorials, only reminding us of their mining, but giving no information as to its extent, nor to the success with which it was crowned.

Washington county embraces not less than 680 square miles; and this area may be considered as one extensive lead digging, for there is scarcely a township on which there has not been, at some period, more or less mining, and, perhaps, scarcely a section on which mineral has not been actually found. Many of the points, that, during the earlier periods of mining, were most worked and most productive, have now been almost deserted; not that they have been exhausted, but that others became known, that seemed to offer a more abundant supply, and with less labor; and these last have, in their turn, been deserted for others, when the surface and clay mineral has been exhausted. In truth, our mining population, if such can be said to exist, is, as a general rule, a nomadic race, flocking from diggings to diggings, attracted by the rumors of greater success, that sometimes have no other foundation than the sanguine hopes of misguided credulity, or the quixotic schemes of selfish avarice and of reckless speculation.

MINES ON THE OLD MINES CONCESSION.

These are principally near the Old Mine creek. The names of the principal of them are as follows: — Block, Prairie, Mud-Town, Horse-Battle, Argnait and Crawfish Diggings. The number of shafts now open is not over twenty, and the deepest is about sixty feet.

The mineral found here has, in general, been in the gravel and clay that overlie the rock. In the rock, the mineral is found with clay in openings or caves; and but little work has been done in the rock at the majority of the diggings.

At Horse-Battle, there are but three shafts: one, thirty-two feet; one, twenty-five feet; and the other, fifteen feet. The deepest shaft reaches only to the rock, and there has been no drifting. The mineral is frequently accompanied by heavy spar. It is reported, that, with four hands, they have obtained, in one month, 4,000 pounds of mineral.

Mud-Town Diggings have been worked, at intervals, for twenty years, and were, after having remained idle for some time, again opened, about five years ago; and, according to Mr. Thomas White, have since then yielded about 500,000 pounds of mineral per annum.

The Block Diggings cover, probably, an area of ten acres. At this point there are now six shafts open. In sinking these, there was found, first, four to six feet of soil, flint and gravel; then, a bed of red, ferruginous clay, of variable thickness, was passed through; and beneath this was the magnesian limestone. The mineral has been found here, both in the clay and the rock. In the clay, it is frequently accompanied by heavy spar; and in the rock, it is found in openings, with clay and heavy spar. Three of these shafts are now worked by Mr. Summers, and are, respectively, fifty-four, twenty-eight and twenty-four feet deep. He found but little mineral until reaching the above depths. From the bottom of these shafts he has drifted some little, but in no direction over fifty feet. During the three months he has been working, with an average of three hands, and he has obtained 8,000 pounds of mineral.

On the Block tract, a little west of south, are the Briscoe Diggings, covering about ten acres; and north of the Block Diggings lie the Guibourd, at neither of which are there any deep shafts; for the mining has been confined to the clay, in which the mineral is found, accompanied by sulphate of baryta.

SHIBBOLETH MINES.

Town. 38 N., R. 3 E., sec. 22, S. W. ¼.

These have been, more or less, worked for the last forty-four years, and have been very productive, having, according to Schoolcraft, yielded, in 1811, 3,125,000 pounds of ore. They extend south of east, and north of west, for about three-fourths of a mile, and are about one-quarter of a mile wide. The mineral obtained has been almost entirely from the clay, at depths of from sixteen to forty feet. The deepest shaft is about fifty feet. There is one point on the tract, which is denominated the Rock Diggings, where the mineral is found in the rock. This point is more elevated, and the rock is, in all probability, not in place, but loose and tumbling. The number engaged in mining here, latterly, has been very small. Those, however, who have been, though their labor was confined to the mineral in the clay, have been well repaid. The average number of hands employed, during the last few years, has not, probably, exceeded twenty, and their average working time has not been over one month during the year.

BELLEFONTAINE MINES.

Town. 38 N., R. 3 E., sec. 9, S. E. ¼.

The total area over which mining has, at different times, been carried on here, is probably not less than forty acres. The deepest shafts ever sunk, were from sixty to seventy-five feet; the deepest, however, that I measured, was forty-five feet; the average depth of the shafts was about fifteen feet.

The digging has been almost entirely confined to the clay. The average depth of the rock, below the surface, is from thirty to thirty-five feet. The mineral, in general, is accompanied by heavy spar, and has been but little searched for in the rock.

That portion of the tract, known by the name of Picayune Diggings, covers, probably, thirty acres, and at which the mining has been much the same as at the Bellefontaine.

Mr. Burrus, of Bellefontaine, informed me, that, from November, 1853, to October, 1854, there had been obtained from Bellefontaine 95,000 pounds, and from the Picayune, 15,000 pounds of mineral: the average number of hands employed at the two being about twelve.

CANNON MINES.

These extend one and a half miles north and south, and three-quarters of a mile east and west. The deepest shafts have not been sunk lower than fifty feet. The deepest shaft measured was twenty-one feet. Most of the mineral obtained here has been from the clay, and at depths from twelve to fifteen feet. A space of ground, near Mr. Higginbotham's, half a mile east and west, and one-quarter of a mile north and south, is thickly covered with shafts. Mr. Higginbotham, who has been working here thirteen years, estimates the amount of mineral obtained from this mine at three millions. Some iron pyrites is found here with the mineral.

SCOTT AND BEE DIGGINGS.

Town. 38 N., R. 2 E., Sec. 22.

These diggings are on the same tract of 160 acres. At the Scott, almost every part of three acres is literally covered with shallow shafts, the deepest of which is forty feet; and the mineral obtained has been principally taken from the clay.

The Bee Diggings are a little west of south from the Scott, and are situated on the spur of the hill. The deepest shaft sunk was sixty-five feet, but the average depths of the shafts are not over forty feet. The mineral is found here in caves or openings, communicating one with the other; and of these, in some of the shafts, are three different series, running nearly horizontally, at different levels. The average depth of the first series, beneath the surface, is twenty feet; the second series is about ten feet below the first, and the third is about ten feet below the second series.

These openings are filled with clay, mineral, accompanied by heavy spar, and sometimes with tumbling rock, the character of which is similar to that of the rock in place: viz., the light gray, sub-crystalline, silicious magnesian limestone.

The drifting is limited, almost entirely, to the course of the openings, which, in the western part of the diggings, is, in general, north and south, while, in the eastern part, they have nearly an east and west course. In general, there are but few openings between the upper and lower series of caves, and these preserve nearly a horizontal course.

On this tract, but at a more easterly point than either of the above diggings, the mineral is found in chimneys, or perpendicular openings, filled in the same manner as the above; but these have no communication, the one with the other. They extend from six to eight feet beneath the surface of the ground, to a depth of forty feet. In excavating one of these, to a depth of forty feet, I was informed, by Mr. Thomas White, that 40,000 pounds of mineral has been obtained.

In the immediate vicinity of Potosi, once the busy scene of mining, and the head-quarters of almost all mining and smelting operations, but comparatively little is now done. The old citadel, though completely burrowed with shallow shafts, the signs of the labor and activity of former times, is now almost deserted, and but little mining is there carried on. One reason for this may be found in the fact, that, at about the depth of eighteen feet, water is encountered; and no one is willing to erect the necessary machinery to remove this, while opportunities for mining are abundantly found in dry, rich clay diggings. Some few, however, were found scratching the ground, apparently picking up what, in former days, had been spurned as unworthy of being gathered.

A little west of Potosi, was the field of Austin's labors, and at which, mining had, at intervals, been carried on, since the first discovery of the lead region.

It was here, in February, 1853, that the Potosi Lead Company commenced mining operations. An open cut, with a course of N. 67½° E., was made on the hill side, from the valley, for the distance of 156 feet. From the termination of this, a level was run, sixty-seven feet into the hill, on the same course. On the head of this level, a shaft, fifty-seven feet, was sunk. From the bottom of this shaft, a level was run N. E. 160 feet, on the termination of which, another shaft, ninety-seven feet, was sunk. Another shaft, fifty-seven feet deep, was sunk at a point north-west from the head of main level, and distant 140 feet. The Company, for reasons best known to the stockholders, have, for the present, ceased operations.

From February to September, of 1853, sixteen hands were employed; after which, for two months, eighty hands were employed. The average number of hands engaged, during the whole period of operations, was about forty.

Of the actual amount of mineral obtained, from the sinking of these shafts, and the running of the levels, I can obtain no reliable information.

Plate 10 represents a vertical and ground plan of the works of this Company.

Plate 10.

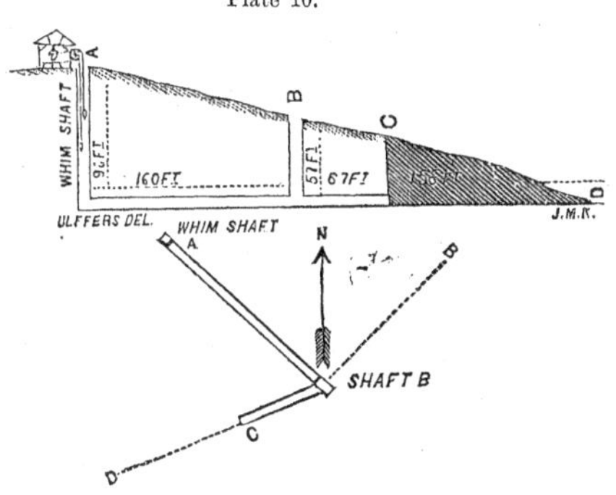

WORKS OF THE POTOSI LEAD MINING COMPANY, WASHINGTON COUNTY.
Scale—200 ft. to inch.

BURT'S DIGGINGS.

These diggings are west of Potosi, and in the Austin survey. They are principally confined to two hills and an intervening hollow. The ground is here literally covered with holes. Of the number of shafts sunk, at different times, it is impossible to form any opinion. Formerly, they were much worked; but, at the time of my visit, I found but two persons engaged in mining; one, in a shaft forty feet, and the other, in a shaft fifty-five feet deep. For the last three or four years but little has been done here, for the land belonged to the estate of Mr. Perry; and, as it was soon to be sold, miners were uncertain into whose hands it would fall, and, consequently, being uncertain whether they could retain the benefit of any discovery they might make, were loth to expend their labor.

The rock is covered here with a bed of ferruginous clay. The mineral is found in the rock, in caves or openings, filled with clay, mineral and heavy spar. All shafts sunk in the hollow are liable to be filled with water, and most of the digging has been confined to the hill sides. Most of the mineral has been obtained here at depths from fifteen to sixty feet.

PIERCE AND WILLOUGHBY'S DIGGINGS.
Town. 37 N., R. 2 E., Sec. 15.

A short distance nearly south-west of Potosi, and on a part of the Austin grant, are considerable diggings, on land now belonging to Mr. Desloge. These cover, in all probability, ten acres of ground, and have been worked, at different times, by different persons. Of these, that part now worked by Messrs. Pierce & Willoughby is the best known, and has been the most extensively mined. This portion is on a high hill. A shaft, 110 feet deep, has been sunk. For the first twenty feet, this passed through gravel, clay and tumbling rock, when a perpendicular sheet of mineral, the average thickness of which was ten inches, was reached. This was followed down to a depth of 110 feet, when it was found running out horizontally in every direction, and with an average thickness of eight inches. In general, the mineral was accompanied, sometimes on both sides, with the heavy spar, or sulphate of baryta. The mineral is represented as being found here in openings, that vary in size from that of "the fist to that of a barrel," and filled alone with mineral and heavy spar. Seventy feet below the surface, they drifted west about twenty feet, and found the mineral passing downwards to a lower level, but did not follow it further.

At the time of my visit (October 18, 1854), they had just commenced cleaning out for the winter's operations, and it was impossible for me to enter their shafts. Judging from the debris thrown out from the shafts, the rock here is a compact, semi-crystalline magnesian limestone, being, apparently, less silicious, and of a harder and more compact character, than that usually found near the surface. The specimens of mineral seen were very pure, and not accompanied by other minerals.

Messrs. Pierce & Willoughby commenced mining here in 1846, and their labor has been principally during the winter months. With an average of not over four hands (the greatest number at any time having been six), they have, I was informed by Mr. Desloge, obtained a half-million pounds of mineral.

NEW DIGGINGS.

These diggings are south-east of Potosi, some three or four miles. They extend east and west about a quarter, and north and south about a half mile. Though designated as New, they have been worked for upwards of twenty years, and many of the shafts have caved in and have now small trees growing over them. Some three or four shafts were worked at the time of my visit, in last October, the average depth of which, was twenty feet. They were sunk through clay and tumbling rock; and much annoyance is caused here by water.

The mineral is found in caves, or openings, some of which were represented as being ten feet wide and twenty feet deep. They are, most generally, on the same level, and filled with clay, and tumbling rock, and mineral, and heavy spar. Most of the mineral obtained here was found within twenty feet of the surface. Out of the above three or four shafts, I was informed that about 60,000 pounds of mineral had been obtained, and that from the whole diggings, during the past year, 100,000 pounds of ore had been procured. South-west of this, and on the same tract (which belongs to Col. F. Kennett), are represented to be other diggings; and, also, one mile north, on land belonging to John Evens.

LUPTON DIGGINGS.

Town. 38 N., R. 2 E., Sec. 17.

These diggings extend nearly north and south, over an area of half a mile in length, and 150 yards in width. The deepest shaft ever sunk was seventy-nine feet; the deepest now worked is sixty feet. The number of shafts now worked is twelve, and they lie on the side of an elevated ridge. The reddish clay, that overlies the rock, has a thickness of from twenty-five to thirty feet, and is intermixed, in the lower part, with tumbling rock.

The mineral has been found here, principally, in the rock, and in caves that communicate one with the other, and are, generally, on the same level. There is but little heavy spar found accompanying the mineral. The average number of persons mining here is from twenty to twenty-five, and the average working time of each, about three months during the year.

SIXTEENTH SECTION.—Town. 38 N., R. 2 E.

Adjoining the above, on the east side, is the sixteenth section, on which there has been considerable mining at several points. On that now worked by Mr. Lynch, seven shafts have been sunk, and much drifting between them. The mineral has been found here, in caves, at three different levels. On the same level the caves communicate one with the other, and contain, in addition to mineral, much clay, with some loose rock. The work done here has been more extensive than at most points in Washington county, the average depth of the shafts being about sixty-four feet, and the drifting extending between 200 and 300 feet.

In the center of the section, at which point the discovery of lead ore was first made, are other diggings, and, also, at some other points in this section; but the character of all of them is pretty much the same.

CASEY AND CLANCEY'S DIGGINGS.

Town. 38 N., R. 2 E., Sec. 7.

These diggings extend over an area of a half mile east and west, and a quarter of a mile north and south. They lie on the side of a hill. Ten years ago, at this place, two shafts, each ninety feet, were sunk; but the shafts now open vary from thirty to sixty feet. The average depth at which mineral has been found here, is from twenty to thirty feet, though it is not unfrequently found within four feet of the surface.

At the lower diggings, on the hill, there are now six shafts worked, the deepest of which is thirty feet. At a more elevated point of the hill, and 200 yards west of the former, there is a shaft fifty or sixty feet deep. The mineral was found here, both in the clay and in the rock, at two different levels, in caves, which, as usual, were found filled with clay and tumbling rock and galena.

At these diggings the mineral seems to be found in three belts, the course of which is north-west and south-east.

COOK'S DIGGINGS.

These diggings lie east of Casey and Clancey's, and have been confined principally to the clay, the shafts being about twenty feet. During the last year they have been very productive; 200,000 pounds of mineral, according to Mr. Casey, having been obtained with about three hands.

BROCK DIGGINGS.

Town. 38 N., R. 1 E., Sec. 4, N. W. ¼.

These diggings cover an area of about ten acres, but have not been worked since 1841. The mineral was obtained from the gravel and clay, and the deepest shaft was not over thirty feet. No digging was done here in the solid rock.

SHORE'S DIGGINGS.

Town. 38 N., R. 2 E., Sec. 18, S. W. ¼.

These diggings are situated on a high ridge. The principal shaft is about 100 feet deep, the first ten feet of which was through clay, and the remainder through the solid magnesian limestone of the country. At this depth (100 feet), a series of openings were found on the same level. Through these, drifts have been run, south-east, 160 feet. These are filled with tumbling rock, a glistening reddish clay, and mineral, accompanied by heavy spar. North-east from this principal shaft, are five others; one, ninety feet; two, seventy-five feet each; and one, eighty feet: all of these are connected by driftings, on nearly the same level.

Below the level of the openings, a shaft has been sunk forty feet, without finding any caves beneath.

Mr. Shore has been working here, at intervals, for three years; and, though prevented by water from working during one year, he reports that he has, during this period, obtained 250,000 pounds of mineral.

Along both sides of Fourche à Renault, for three miles, there are diggings. Section seven and eight are covered with shafts. In this vicinity are the following diggings, which were not visited:—

Du Cloe's, or Moreau's	Diggings,	town. 38 N., R. 2 E., sec. 4, N. E. ¼ of S. W. ¼.
Hinkson's	"	town. 38 N., R. 2 E., sec. 29, S. W. ¼.
Buzzard-Roost	"	town. 38 N., R. 2 E., sec. 31, N. W. ¼, E. ½.
Dry-Hollow	"	town. 38 N., R. 2 E., sec. 7, north part.
Crawfish	"	town. 38 N., R. 2 E., sec 4, S. E. ¼.

PRAIRIE DIGGINGS.

Town. 38 N., R. 3 E., Sec. 4.

These diggings are situated on the side of a hill. Five or six shafts have been sunk, varying in depth from twenty-eight to forty feet. The mineral was found at two different levels in the rock, but the mining has been, principally, limited to that found at the first level, the working of the lower being more laborious, on account of the water.

WET AND ELLIOT DIGGINGS.

Town. 39 N., R. 2 E., Sec. 26.

At the Elliot Diggings, seven shafts have been sunk, varying in depth from twenty-two to sixty feet. The mineral is found at two different levels, and yielded well, until the miners were incommoded by water. At the Wet Diggings, the shafts vary from twenty to twenty-five feet; and these, also, well repaid the labor expended on them. At both of these, the mineral is found in the rock; and the only obstacle to uninterrupted mining, is the water, which could easily be removed with suitable machinery. From these last three mines, I am informed by Mr. Johnson, President of Mammoth Company, to which all of them belong, there has, during the last two years, been obtained about 300,000 pounds of mineral, with some five or six hands. On what is denominated the Becquette tract, belonging to this Company, there is every indication of a vertical lode. It has been traced on the surface of the ground for about 110 yards, with a course N., 82 W. The thickness of the vein varies from a quarter to nine inches. No work has been done here, excepting at points uncovering the fissure, and it is to be regretted, as it is well worthy of being tested. It is situated, I believe, in Town. 39 N., R. 3 E., Sec. 30.

In Town. 36 N., R. 3 E., are many diggings, among which may be enumerated, Rocky Diggings. These are shallow, and the deepest mineral taken out, was from a depth of not over twelve feet beneath the surface.

Bunker Hill	Diggings,	not worked	now.
Nigger	"	"	"
Brickey	"	"	"
Sand	"	"	"
Tan Yard	"	"	"
Le Clair	"	"	"
Haefner	"	one shaft sunk twenty-eight feet, some fourteen or eighteen of which was through clay.	

FAQUAHER DIGGINGS.

At these, acres of ground are perforated by numerous shallow shafts, the deepest I measured being only twenty-six feet, and most of them, were not over twelve feet. The mining here has been mostly confined to the clay; though some few shafts have been sunk a short distance into the rock. That portion of them, called the Flint Diggings, lies higher up on the hill; at which point the mineral was found in openings in the rock, at about the depth of twenty feet below the surface. The magnesian limestone is intermixed here with flint and chert.

FOURCHE A COURTOIS MINES.

These mines are situated in the south-eastern part of the county, and are almost entirely confined to the two townships, thirty-six, east and west of the fifth principal meridian. For the names and location of the more important of them, I am indebted to Major Manning, of Webster. They are as follows: —

Pigeon-Roost and Strawberry Diggings,		Town. 36 N., R. 1 W., Sec. 1.
Ismael	"	" 36 N., R. 1 E., Sec. 8, E. ½ of S. E. ¼.
Madden-Hill	"	" 36 N., R. 1 W., Sec. 2, S. E. ¼.
Flint-Hill	"	" 36 N., R. 1 W., Sec. 12, S. W. ¼.
Bit	"	" 36 N., R. 1 W., Sec. 12, S. W. ¼.
Bluff	"	" 36 N., R. 1 W., Sec. 14, E. ½ of N. W. ¼. Not worked.
Water-Hill	"	" 36 N., R. 1 W., Sec. 15, E. ½ of N. W. ¼. Not worked.
Coffee-Pot	"	" 36 N., R. 1 W., Sec. 34, W. ½ of N. W. ¼.
English	"	" 36 N., R. 1 W., Sec. 2, N. E. ¼. Not worked.
Cochran	"	" 36 N., R. 1 W., Sec. 12, W. ½ of N. E. ¼.
Picayune	"	" 37 N., R. 1 W., Sec. 34, W. ½ of S. E. ¼.
Polecat	"	" 36 N., R. 1 W., Sec. 14, W. ½ of S. W. ¼. Not worked.
Tarkey	"	" 36 N., R. 1 E., Sec. 15.
Gopher	"	" 36 N., R. 1 E., Sec. 22, E. ½ of S. W. ¼. Not worked.
Peru	"	" 36 N., R. 1 E., Sec. 19, W. ½ of N. E. ¼. Not worked.
Clemins	"	" 36 N., R. 1 E., Sec. 17, W. ½ of N. W. ¼.
Trash	"	" 36 N., R. 1 E., Sec. 6, E. ½ of S. W. ¼.
Sweassey	"	" 36 N., R. 1 E., Sec. 18, E. ½ of S. E. ¼.
Montgomery	"	" 36 N., R. 1 E., Sec. 7, S. W. ¼.
Hypocrite	"	" 36 N., R. 1 E., Sec. 22, E. ½ of N. W. ¼. Not worked.
Grave-Yard	"	" 36 N., R. 1 E., Sec. 8, E. ½ of N. E. ¼.
Turkey-Hill	"	" 36 N., R. 1 E., Sec. 7, W. ½ of N. E. ¼.

Of all these diggings, the Ismael, in past years, has been the most productive, and most worked; having, during a period, furnished more mineral than all the rest. But, during the present year, Pigeon-Roost and Trash Diggings have yielded the most mineral. The country, in this section, is very broken, and many of the hills are between 150 and 200 feet high. The rock is the magnesian limestone. The deepest shaft sunk on these mines is not over eighty-five feet, and the average depth of all of them is not over forty feet.

The Flint and the Bit Diggings lie, principally, upon the top of a ridge, and cover about fifteen acres of land. The deepest shaft I measured was thirty-one feet, from the bottom of which a hard quatzose magnesian limestone, intermixed with decomposing chert, had been thrown out.

The Pigeon-Roost, the Strawberry and the Trash Diggings, cover about fifty acres; all of them being on the same ridge, and the Trash nearest the summit; the Pigeon is less elevated, and more on the side of the ridge; the Strawberry lies nearest the adjacent ravine.

At the Trash Diggings, the shafts are about fifty feet deep; the depth of the clay is about thirty feet, and below it is the magnesian limestone. The mineral found here is small (hence the name of the diggings), and has been obtained from both the clay and the rock.

At Pigeon-Roost, the shafts are between fifty and sixty feet deep, and the mineral is found, principally, in the clay, and in the loose, tumbling rock beneath it. At the Strawberry, the shafts are from twenty-five to thirty feet, and the rock is found nearer the surface face of the ground. The mineral has been, principally, obtained from openings and caves, in the rock.

The Bluff Diggings lie on the East side of a high and steep ridge. The shafts are all shallow, and none, perhaps, over twenty-five feet.

The Polecat Diggings lie on the top of a ridge, that runs nearly north-east and south-west. The diggings run nearly parallel with the top of it, and have been principally confined to clay, excepting at the southern extremity, where the mineral has been found principally in the rock, accompanied with tiff. The shafts, at this point, range from eighteen to twenty-three feet in depth.

The Coffee-Pot Diggings are on the east side of a ridge, and cover about two acres of ground. The shafts measured varied from thirty-four to fifty feet in depth. The mineral here has been obtained from the clay alone. On the west of the same ridge are the Maury Diggings, in which, also, the mining has been confined to the clay.

The Ismael and Grave-Yard Diggings lie close together, and cover about fifty acres. The average depth of the shafts is about forty feet. The mineral found here is in openings in the rock, and the depth of it is, generally, about sixteen feet.

None of the other diggings, at the Fourche à Courtois, were visited, as our time was limited and the mining suspended at them.

These mines have been worked for the last forty years, but now nothing like the number of miners are engaged that formerly were. About 1831 there were as many as 200 persons engaged; but, during the present year, there have not been over thirty miners employed, and these not constantly. Of their yield, anterior to 1837, though very great, it is now impossible to obtain any reliable statement. For the succeeding years, I am enabled to present a very accurate statement, furnished me by Major Manning, at whose furnace all the mineral, obtained from the above diggings since 1837, was smelted, and for which I refer you to the remarks under the heading, "Furnaces of Washington county."

RICHWOODS.

At this point, there has been more or less mining for the last forty years; though, at present, there is but comparatively little. The points at which mining has been carried on are very many, and the success has, certainly, been such as to justify farther and deeper exploration; while the geological formation is such, as gives still stronger guaranty that abundant stores of mineral will yet be found at other points. Among the more important points may be enumerated—

THE OLD LA BEAUME MINES.

Town. 40 N., R. 2 E., Sec. 32.

These mines cover, in all, an area of some thirty acres. The principal diggings are confined to the two sides of a ridge, running north-east and south-west, and extend from the spur to the top of the hill, which is, probably, not over seventy-five feet in height.

The greatest depth which has ever been reached, is eighty feet, though most of the digging has been limited to depths of from six to twenty feet; at which depth, either rock or water interferes, that are, in Missouri, so often regarded as the insuperable obstacles to farther and deeper mining; though, often, a pickaxe can remove the one, and a windlass and bucket bail out the other.

The mineral is represented as occurring in horizontal sheets, accompanied by heavy spar, and running down to different levels. This mine, according to Mr. P. E. Blow, who has been smelting for many years, at Richwood, has yielded, for the last forty years, a large amount of mineral, varying from 200,000 to 600,000 pounds of mineral per annum. It has lately been purchased by Mr. Wm. Skewes, who is now preparing to explore them; and, I doubt not, it will be done with the same skill and ability which he has displayed at the Vallé, the Cove, and the Mount Hope Mines.

FRENCH DIGGINGS.

Town. 40 N., R. 2 E., Secs. 21 and 28.

These mines have been but little worked for the last four years. Previous to 1843, they had yielded abundantly, from superficial diggings, of from three to twelve feet. They were, afterwards, in 1843, worked by Mr. Thos. M. Taylor, when the average depth of the mining was not deeper than sixteen feet. At an average depth of twenty feet beneath the surface, rock or water was encountered, and this was the limit beyond which the mining did not extend. These have yielded, according to Mr. Blow, from 1844 to 1850, from 300,000 to 500,000 pounds of mineral per annum.

East of the above, and on the confirmation to F. M. Benoist, there have also been some shallow diggings, from six to twelve feet deep, and which have yielded from 100,000 to 200,000 pounds of mineral per annum. In addition to the above, are the following, in this neighborhood:—

Ben. Hornie's	Diggings,	1½ miles N. E. of old La Beaume Mines.	Not worked.
Goddard	"	1¾ miles N. E. " " " "	" "
Rogers'	"	3 miles N. " " " "	" "
Charboneau	"	the mining on which was confined to the clay, and yielded, according to report, not less than 100,000 pounds of mineral.	

The Old Dutch, or East-Wood Diggings, lie on the side of a hill, and have been worked, in a south-west direction, for 200 yards. The mineral is represented as being found here in a vertical fissure, and having a thickness of from one-quarter of an inch to six inches. in width. For the only returns of the produce of the Richwood Mines, that I have been able to obtain, in addition to the above, I refer you to the remarks on Furnaces.

The above are all the mining points, in Washington county, that I could visit, or of which I could obtain reliable information, from responsible persons. I endeavored to visit all at which I could learn that persons were then actually engaged in mining; but I am well satisfied that the above embraces but a small list of the localities, at which, during some period or other, mining has been carried on.

LEAD FURNACES OF WASHINGTON COUNTY.

There are now fourteen furnaces in operation in Washington county, during a greater or less portion of the year.

HIGGINBOTHAM'S FURNACE.

Town. 39 N., R. 3. E., Sec. 27.

This is the only point in the south-eastern part of the State, known to me, at which the old log and ash furnaces are still used. Mr. H. reports, that, with the log furnace, he obtains an average yield of fifty per cent.; and from the ashes, by means of the ash furnace, twenty per cent. more. Most of the mineral smelted here comes from within half a mile of the furnace; and all has been obtained from Washington county, excepting 7,000 or 8,000 pounds, that was procured from Lee's Diggings, in Jefferson county. He has been smelting for seventeen years; but, unfortunately, could give no more minute and accurate statement of the ore smelted, than that the total amount, during this period, was between three and four millions of pounds. His lead was sent to Selma and Plattin Rock; and from the books of these shipping points, I copied the following amounts, received from him, during the annexed years, which were all that I could find:—

1841,	95,882 lbs. of lead.		1847,	70,480 lbs. of lead.	
1842,	6,294	"	1848,	51,128	"
1843,	63,462	"	1849,	86,281	"
1844,	61,804	"	1851,	43,680	"
1845,	71,838	"	1853,	14,624	"
1846,	133,810	"	1854,	2,968	"

T. & W. MURPHREY'S FURNACE.

Town. 39 N., R. 3 E., Sec. 28, S. W. ¼.

This furnace was built in 1848; it is a Scotch hearth; and the blast is produced by water power. Most of the mineral smelted here, has been obtained from the neighborhood, within six or seven miles. The amount of mineral, belonging to the proprietors, smelted here since the commencement of operations, as given me, by Mr. Murphrey, is 1,209,278 pounds. In addition to this, there was a quantity smelted here for other persons; and he places the average amount at 220,000 pounds per annum:—

YEAR.	ORE.			LEAD.
1848, ...	220,000	yielding 70	per cent.	154,000
1849, ...	220,000	"	"	154,000
1850, ...	220,000	"	"	154,000
1851, ...	220,000	"	"	154,000
1852, ...	220,000	"	"	154,000
1853, ...	220,000	"	"	154,000
1854, ...	220,000	"	"	154,000
	1,540,000			1,078,000

LONG'S FURNACE—OLD MINES.

This furnace has been in operation since February, 1853. It is a Scotch hearth, and the blast is produced by horse power. The greater portion of the mineral smelted here, comes from the Shore, Arquait, Mud-Town, Camp, Rowdy and Block Diggings. The amount of mineral smelted was furnished me by Mr. Long:—

From Feb., 1853, to Oct. 14, '53, 178,000 lbs. of ore. 127,600 lbs. of lead.
From Oct. 14, '53, to Oct. 14, '54, 350,000 " 245,000 "

WHITE'S FURNACE—OLD MINES.

This is a double Scotch furnace, one of which was used by Mr. C. White, and the other, by Mr. La Marque; the blast produced by water power. It was, probably, built in 1838, and was used by John C. Reed & Co., up to 1840, when it came into the possession of Mr. C. White, who had the control of one of the furnaces; the other was in charge of Mr. La Marque up to 1849, when he died. A statement of the amount of ore smelted, by Mr. C. White, has been kindly furnished me by Mr. Thomas White; and of that smelted, by Mr. La Marque, I have been able to obtain no more minute and accurate statement, than that furnished me by Mr. Boldue, who had the kindness to make inquiries of Mrs. La Marque, and reported, that Mr. La Marque, for the thirty years previous to his death, had smelted not less than an average of half a million pounds of mineral per annum. The lead of Mr. White was sent mostly to Selma, while that of Mr. La Marque was sent to Herculaneum, Selma, Plattin Rock and Rush Tower.

For the purpose of showing the amount of lead, made at this furnace, I shall double the amounts, reported to me to have been smelted by C. White, and which will be rather under than above the true amount of lead made.

The ore smelted by C. White, was obtained from Mud-Town, New Shibboleth, Bee Mine, Masson, Tarpley, and others, in the neighborhood of the old mines; while that, smelted by Mr. La Marque, came from the Bluff, Masson, and the immediate neighborhood of the old mines. Statement of mineral, smelted by Mr. C. White: —

YEAR.	ORE.	LEAD—CALCULATED.	TOTAL AM'T. OF LEAD MADE AT THE FURNACE.
1842,	441,536	309,075	618,150
1843,	618,396	432,877	865,754
1844,	764,162	534,914	1,069,828
1845,	573,112	401,179	802,358
1846,	613,707	429,595	859,190
1847.	596,067	417,247	834,494
1848,	506,213	354,349	718,698
1849,	597,821	418,475	836,950
1850,	431,438	302,007	302,007
1851,	230,554	161,388	161,388
1852,	338,698	237,089	237,089
1853,	215,000	150,500	150,500
1854,	65,000	45,500	45,500

Mr. C. White died in 1853, since which, comparatively little has been done at this furnace, and this will satisfactorily explain the obvious falling off in the produce of this furnace.

McILVAINE'S FURNACE.

Town. 37 N., R. 2 E., Sec. 15.

This furnace is a Scotch hearth, blast produced by water power, and was first in the hands of S. T. Dunklin; and, in 1851, passed into the hands of Col. McIlvaine. To Mr. Daly, and to Col. McIlvaine, I am indebted for the following statement of mineral smelted here, from 1842, to November, 1854:—

YEAR.	ORE SMELTED.	LEAD — MADE FROM CALCULATION.
1843,	617,143	432,000
1844,	484,440	339,108
1845,	404,032	282,823
1846,	525,702	367,992
1847,	448,228	313,760
1848,	484,548	339,184
1849,	223,339	156,337
1850,	240,000	168,000
1851, 1st of March to 1st Sept.,	169,356	118,549
From 1st Sept., 1851, to 1st Sept., '52,	580,235	406,164
" 1st Sept., 1852, to 1st Sept., '53,	517,614	362,330
" 1st Sept., 1853, to 1st Sept., '54,	602,172	421,520

Much of the ore, smelted at this furnace, came from the lands of the late John Perry, in Washington county: viz., Lupton, Brushy Run, Burt Diggings, Sixteenth Section and Old Citadel; and from these, from 1st March, 1851, was obtained 1,302,785 pounds of mineral.

DEANE'S FURNACE.

This furnace is, also, in the neighborhood of Potosi, and is a Scotch hearth, the blast being produced by water power. Most of the mineral smelted here, came, in all probability, from the immediate vicinity of Potosi. I obtained from the Selma books, the following amounts of lead, sent by the different proprietors of this furnace, during the several years:—

YEAR.	LEAD — LBS.
1843, from May,	128,316
1844, "	108,902
1845, "	284,446

YEAR.	LEAD — LBS.
1846, from May,	210,378
1847, "	186,267
1848, "	115,224
1849, "	93,234
1850, "	166,297
1851, "	147,098
1852, "	71,312
1853, "	87,498
1854, "	111,728

KENNETT'S FURNACE, AT SHIBBOLETH.

This furnace was built in 1848, and commenced smelting in June, of that year. The mineral smelted here, came from Cannon, Liberty, Neasson, New Diggings, Shibboleth and Bellefontaine.

The amount smelted, as given me by Mr. John Latty, was:—

From June, 1848, to March, 1850,	594,895 lbs. of ore.
" March, 1850, to December, 1852,	1,053,367 " "
" December, 1852, to May, 1854,	495,595 " "
" May, 1854, to October, 1854.	186,482 " "

Giving an average for—

YEAR.	ORE.	LEAD.
1848, from June,	198,298	138,809 lbs.
1849, "	339,940	237,958 "
1850, "	375,857	263,100 "
1851, "	383,040	268,128 "
1852, "	380,273	266,191 "
1853, "	349,836	244,885 "
1854, "	303,094	212,166 "

BOASE'S FURNACE, ON MILL CREEK.

Mr. Boase has been smelting for twenty-five years; and, during the last twelve or fourteen years, has been using the Scotch hearth and slag furnace. The only returns of the amount of lead made by him, was:—

	LEAD — LBS.
For 1852,	100,000
" 1853,	84,000

HOPEWELL FURNACE, BELONGING TO MR. JOHN EVENS.

Mr. Evens has been smelting for thirty years; and, for the last eighteen, at Hopewell. He has both a Scotch hearth and slag furnace. His present furnace was built in 1839. Of the amount made each year, he was unable to give me a full statement; and I subjoin the following table, copied from the Selma books, although confident it does not represent the full amount made:—

YEAR.	LEAD—LBS.
1841,	388,222
1842,	465,748
1843,	520,400
1844,	517,482
1845,	706,596
1846,	411,496
1847,	313,663
1848,	440,296
1849,	354,072
1850,	273,008
1851,	389,125
1852,	399,654
1853,	272,234
1854, to October,	205,074

WALTON'S FURNACE.

This furnace has been in operation fourteen years; and the greater portion of the lead made there, was from slag. The mineral smelted was, principally, from Fourche à Courtois. As Mr. Walton was unable to give accurate returns, I subjoin the following amounts, copied from the Selma books:—

YEAR.	LEAD—LBS.
1841,	35,828
1842,	63,344
1843,	91,180
1844,	19,236
1845,	30,974
1846,	37,034
1847,	6,940
1848,	83,002
1850,	3,104
1851,	11,422
1852,	48,266
1853,	16,140

MANNING'S FURNACE, WEBSTER.

Major Manning has been smelting since 1831. His present furnace is a Scotch hearth, built in 1836; previous to which, only the log and ash furnaces were used at this point. Previous to 1837, there were three other smelters at Webster. All the mineral smelted by him was obtained from the Fourche à Courtois mines, excepting a small quantity, which would not exceed 100,000 pounds, that came from Crawford county; so that the following statement, furnished by him, not only represents the amount made by his furnace, but gives nearly the yield of the Fourche à Courtois mines:—

YEAR.	LEAD — LBS.
1837,	64,684
1838,	337,386
1839,	237,416
1840,	247,179
1841,	147,804
1842,	199,270
1843,	312,604
1844,	273,259
1845,	374,968
1846,	365,809

In addition to the above, there was made, during the above period, 450,069 pounds.

YEAR.	MINERAL.		LEAD — LBS.
1847,	537,487	calculated	376,241
1848,	546,820	"	382,774
1849,	295,189	"	206,632
1850,	309,823	"	216,876
1851,	352,203	"	246,542
1852,	210,385	"	147,270
1853,	190,132	"	133,093
1854,	303,375	"	212,363
Total amount of lead made, from 1837, to October, 1854,			4,952,239

CRESWELL'S FURNACE.

Town. 38 N., R. 2 E., Sec. 5, S. E. ¼ of S. W. ¼.

Mr. George Creswell commenced smelting, in 1828, on the Fourche à Renault, where he remained two or three years. He removed to Cold-Spring Hollow, where he smelted for seven years. Thence, he removed to his present place, where he now uses a Scotch hearth, the blast for which is produced by water power. The mineral smelted by him, comes mostly from his immediate neighborhood, and all, I believe, is obtained from Washington county. I subjoin the following amounts of lead, sent by him to Plattin Rock and Selma, which were copied from the books of these shipping points:—

YEAR.	LEAD — LBS.
1841,	292,570
1842,	233,671

YEAR.	LEAD — LBS.
1843,	274,205
1844,	274,665
1845,	205,418
1846,	211,888
1847,	211,078
1848,	210,659
1849,	277,954
1850,	215,194
1851,	128,874
1852,	116,407
1853,	170,462
1854,	61,788

CASEY AND CLANCEY'S FURNACE.

This furnace is a Scotch hearth; blast produced by water power. The ore smelted here, comes from their own mines; some from Potosi; and, since August, 1853, perhaps, one-eighth from Crawford county. The amount of lead made here, as furnished by Mr. Casey, is as follows: —

YEAR.	LEAD — LBS.
1849,	250,000
1850,	380,000
1851,	420,000
1852,	375,000
1853,	250,000
1854,	400,000

RICHWOOD'S FURNACES.

At this point, there have been two furnaces operating for a number of years; one, formerly belonging to Mr. Roussin, and the other, for ten years, to Mr. P. E. Blow. From these, I have been unable to obtain any more definite statement than that given me by Mr. Blow, who believes that the amount of mineral smelted here, for the last ten years, has been not less than 1,000,000 pounds per annum.

Though the returns from the furnaces of Washington county are incomplete, I shall add the following statement, made from these, as something like an approximation of the true amount of lead produced from the mines of this county. Of the ore smelted, at the furnaces of Mr. Higginbotham, of Mr. Boase and of Mr. Evens, I feel confident I have not given the full amounts, but have made use of the best data I could get.

In table 1, will be found a statement of the lead obtained from Franklin, Washington and St. François counties.

The lead made in Jefferson, Washington, St. François, Ste. Genevieve and Madison counties, has, most of it, been sent to some one of the shipping points on the Mississippi river. In past years, Herculaneum and Ste. Genevieve were the points to which most of the lead was sent. Latterly, other points have received far greater quantities. I have made efforts to obtain full statements of all the lead shipped from Salt Point, Herculaneum, Selma, Rush Tower, Ste. Genevieve and St. Mary's Landing; but, from most of them, have, as yet, been unable to obtain any returns. For the full statement of the amount received at Selma, I am indebted to the kindness of Mr. Foster, who furnished it to Dr. Shumard; and for that of Plattin Rock, I am indebted to Mr. I. Wilkinson, for the amount for 1845; and the amounts, for the remaining years, were taken from the receipt book, kept there by Geiger, Boise & Co. These will be found in the annexed table, No. 2.

Much mineral has been taken directly by land to St. Louis, in addition to that sent to the shipping points on the river.

A STATEMENT OF THE AMOUNT OF LEAD, MADE IN WASHINGTON COUNTY, FROM 1841 TO NOVEMBER, 1854, BASED UPON RETURNS (SO FAR AS OBTAINED) FROM THE FURNACES.

FURNACES.	1841.	1842.	1843.	1844.	1845.	1846.	1847.	1848.	1849.	1850.	1851.	1852.	1853.	1854.
Higginbotham's, .	95,882	6,294	63,462	61,804	71,838	133,810	70,480	51,128	86,281	......	43,680	......	14,624	2,968
T.&W. Murphrey's	......	......	......	......	......	......	......	154,000	154,000	154,000	154,000	154,000	154,000	154,000
S. C. White's, . .	......	618,150	865,754	1,069,828	802,358	859,190	834,494	718,698	836,950	302,007	161,388	237,089	150,500	45,500
A. Long's, . . .	......	......	......	......	......	......	......	......	......	......	......	......	127,600	245,000
F. Kennett's, . .	......	......	......	......	......	......	......	138,809	237,958	263,100	268,128	266,191	244,885	212,166
I. Deane's, . . .	......	......	128,316	108,902	284,446	210,378	186,267	115,224	93,234	166,297	147,098	71,312	50,112	69,350
John Evens', . .	388,222	465,748	520,400	517,482	706,596	411,496	313,663	440,296	354,072	273,008	389,125	399,654	272,234	205,074
George Walton's, .	35,828	63,344	91,180	19,236	30,974	37,034	6,940	83,002	......	3,104	11,422	48,266	16,140	......
Manning's, . . .	192,811	244,277	357,611	318,266	419,975	410,816	376,241	382,774	206,632	216,876	246,542	147,270	133,093	212,363
Casey & Clancey's,	......	......	......	......	......	......	......	......	250,000	380,000	420,000	375,000	250,000	400,000
George Creswell's,	292,570	233,671	274,205	274,665	205,418	211,888	211,078	210,659	177,954	215,194	128,874	116,407	170,462	61,788
Richwood's, . .	......	......	......	......	70,000	70,000	70,000	70,000	70,000	70,000	70,000	70,000	70,000	70,000
McIlvaine's, . .	......	......	432,000	339,108	282,823	367,992	313,760	339,184	156,337	168,000	253,937	391,553	361,988	301,086
Boase's, ...	......	......	......	......	......	......	......	......	......	......	......	100,000	84,000	......
	1,005,513	1,632,484	2,731,928	2,709,291	2,874,428	2,712,604	2,382,923	2,703,774	2,623,418	2,211,586	2,294,194	2,376,742	2,099,638	1,979,295

TABLE I.—AN INCOMPLETE STATEMENT OF THE AMOUNT OF LEAD, MADE ANNUALLY IN FRANKLIN, ST. FRANCOIS AND WASHINGTON COUNTIES, FROM 1841, TO OCTOBER, 1854

	1841.	1842.	1843.	1844.	1845.	1846.	1847.	1848.	1849.	1850.	1851.	1852.	1853.	1854.
Franklin county, .	......	......	......	......	......	......	......	......	......	496,744	380,606	378,630	658,169	461,557
St. François co., .	1,877,268	1,420,338	1,266,126	1,486,302	1,364,321	1,210,653	1,221,919	1,368,019	1,175,991	1,350,395	1,270,334	1,281,068	1,311,275	1,347,363
Washington co., .	1,005,313	1,632,484	2.731.928	2,709.291	2,874,428	2.712,604	2,382,923	2,703,774	2,623,418	2,211,586	2,294,194	2.376.742	2.099.638	1,979,295
Total amount, .	2,882,581	3,052,822	3,998,054	4,195,593	4,238,749	3,923,257	3,604,842	4,071,793	3,799,409	4,058,725	3,945 134	4,036.440	4,069.082	3,788.215

The total amount, from 1841, to October, 1854, is 53,663,696 pounds of lead, and, consequently, the average amount of lead made each year, for the same period, was 3,833,121 pounds.

TABLE II.—STATEMENT OF AMOUNT OF LEAD, RECEIVED AT SELMA AND PLATTIN ROCK.

Year.	Selma.	Plattin Rock.	*Rush Tower.	Total Am't.
1824, ...	219,003	....	....	219,003
1825, ...	864,364	....	....	864,364
1826, ...	1,392,766	....	....	1,392,766
1827, ...	1,674,169	....	....	1,674,169
1828, ...	2,962,831	....	....	2,962,831
1829, ...	1,936,632	....	....	1,936,632
1830, ...	1,899,951	....	....	1,899,951
1831, ...	1,323,902	....	....	1,323,902
1832, ...	3,615,952	....	....	3,615,952
1833, ...	3,835,878	....	....	3,835,878
1834, ...	2,958,897	....	....	2,958,897
1835, ...	3,346,347	....	....	3,346,347
1836, ...	2,930,516	....	....	2,930,516
1837, ...	2,560,812	....	....	2,560,812
1838, ...	3,025,085	....	....	3,025,085
1839, ...	3,990,814	....	....	3,990,814
1840, ...	3,127,877	....	....	3,127,877
1841, ...	3,715,448	....	....	3,715,448
1842, ...	2,290,178	....	849,092	3,139,270
1843, ...	2,829,780	....	694,880	3,524,660
1844, ...	2,694,730	....	915,056	3,609,786
1845, ...	2,906,580	556,414	923,025	4,386,019
1846, ...	2,015,375	722,005	839,755	3,577,135
1847, ...	2,169,674	486,085	885,987	3,541,746
1848, ...	1,877,469	386,826	915,269	3,179,564
1849, ...	1,531,220	795,541	727,967	3,054,728
1850, ...	1,759,338	55,887	857,218	2,672,443
1851, ...	2,354,253	157,541	632,867	3,144,661
1852, ...	2,084,574	....	653,561	2,738,134
1853, ...	1,940,793	....	687,058	2,627,851
1854, to October, .	1,465,428	....	666,936	2,132,364
				86,709,605

From the preceding tables, it will be seen, that, from the incomplete returns received from the furnaces, there have been, from 1848 to 1854, obtained from a portion of the mining country of Missouri, 53,663,696 pounds of lead; and that, from only three shipping points, at least, 86,709,605 pounds have been forwarded, from 1824 up to October of the present year. If to this last be added the 19,483,382

* Rush Tower became a shipping point in November, 1841, and to it was sent all the lead, made at Perry's Mine, and, doubtless, much more. I have placed here the amount made at Perry's Furnace, of which, an accurate statement will be obtained, by adding the yield of Perry's Big Lode, and half of that from Tarpley's Mine.

pounds, made at Vallé's Mine, in St. François county, and all of which was sent to Ste. Genevieve, we would have for the least total amount, shipped from four points on the river, 106,193,382 pounds during this period, giving, for the average annual amount, 3,425,593 pounds. But, that it was far greater, will be evident to you, from an examination of the above data. How much greater, I leave for others to show; my object being now, only to present facts, to which, by farther explorations, others can be added, until all the materials can be gathered for a full and complete description of the Missouri mining region.

Have we any evidence, in the above statistics, that there has been a falling off in the produce of the Missouri mines? The amount produced this year will fully equal that of the last, and the produce of 1853 was greater than that of 1852. Compared with reliable statistics, which have been published, I cannot, from the above, see any evident indication of a decline. Schoolcraft, in 1819, found forty-five lead mines actually worked in Missouri, giving employment to 1,100 hands; and he, from the returns obtained, from the few shipping points that then existed, and to which all the lead then obtained was sent, gave, as the annual yield of the mines, a little over three million pounds. At present, I do not believe that there are even forty-five lead mines actually worked; and were I to leave out of consideration Perry's, Vallé's and Skewes' mines (which are worked regularly and constantly, with a nearly uniform number of hands, most of which are the slaves of the proprietors), I should consider, after my observations and inquiries, that it would be a large estimate to place the number, actually engaged in mining, at 200 persons. And, nevertheless, we find that the average annual produce of the mines, for the last fourteen years, has been over 3,833,121 pounds. There will be, as there have been, fluctuations in the yield of particular mines; but this affects but little the total yield of the whole. There are many rich mines lying now entirely idle, for reasons that are altogether personal; and during the last two years, some valuable mining tracts have remained almost entirely, if not quite unworked, simply, because they were soon to be put up to the highest bidders; and miners were, in general, unwilling to invest their labor, while uncertain how long the right of mining would be secured to them; when no assurance could be given that they should continue to reap the advantage of any discoveries they might make, and when there was every possibility that their labors and discoveries would only be for the advantage of some unknown party.

But, even did full and accurate returns show an evident decline, I should not then view it as an indication that our mineral treasures were beginning to be exhausted; for, after visiting most of the scenes of mining operations, I inferred that the statistics would show an evident decline in the annual produce, as compared with former years. This inference was drawn entirely from the general character of the mining.

That fully three-fourths of all the mineral obtained in Missouri, has been from clay diggings, that overlie the rock, I think not an unfair nor unreasonable estimate. Such diggings have been every where, in certain counties, very abundant; and as any one could secure, by the payment of a reasonable rent, the privilege of mining on them, there was every inducement for persons, not proprietors, to flock from one digging to another. As a general rule, the proprietors of the land are not actually engaged in mining, but the wealth of their property is developed by those, whose other occupations give them some leisure, and who follow mining, not constantly, but irregularly, and at intervals. Consequently, most of the mining has been without system, and conducted on the most economical scale. Neither the means of the miners, nor the mining right secured to such persons, would justify any great outlay of capital in the improvement of property, to which they have no permanent title, and of which they are liable, at any moment, to be dispossessed, by a change of proprietors. As a necessary consequence, shafts are sunk, only where the least labor is required, and the least time demanded. Frequently, they are driven no deeper than the earth can be thrown out with the spade. Should, however, perseverance and the prospects induce them to go deeper, an offset is made a few feet below the surface, on which the clay, obtained from a still lower depth, can be thrown; and below this, they are not often willing to descend, unless mineral is in sight. When, however, encouraged by success, and by the daily returns for their labor, they descend still deeper; a temporary windlass is put up, that can be carried from shaft to shaft; and should they, aided by this, excavate the rock, it is an exception to the general rule, that they go deeper than they can penetrate with the pick and gad, driven by muscular strength. In general, cribbing is an outlay of labor and time, not justified by their temporary proprietorship. Thus, everything is done on the most economical scale, and in a manner often injurious to the reputation of the mines; for the object is immediate and daily returns for their labor.

That the clay diggings may be nearly exhausted, on the well-known localities, is not improbable; for, most certainly, they are sufficiently riddled with shallow shafts, to have obtained all the mineral. But, the mineral is found not alone in the clay, but, also, in the rock. Many points, at which it has been thus found, and which have been explored for a few feet only, have been already noticed. But, that not a tithe of the places, at which it has been thus desposited, has been discovered, I feel confident. It is, principally, from the explorations there, that must be obtained, in future, a great portion of the produce of the Missouri mines. This will, however, require capital, the erection of proper machinery, systematic and uninterrupted mining, and increased facilities by railroads for transportation; and with such aid, we have every assurance, from the success of the Vallé, the Perry, the Skewes and the Shore mines, that Missouri will continue, for years, to contribute to commerce a not less annual produce of lead, than she has, in past years, for the use of arts and manufactures.

COPPER.

Though the ores of this metal have been found at several points, in this State, but little has been done towards developing and mining, this element of State wealth. About 1830, a large quantity of copper ore was obtained in Washington county, five or six miles east of Caledonia, at Walden's mine. It was worked by Capt. Hughes and Elisha Walden. The mining was on the side of a low hill, on which no rock in place is visible. Nothing has been done, for ten or twelve years; and the only indication of former mining operations, is slight excavations, and the mass of red ferruginous earth, lying on the hill side. From the best information I could get, the digging was shallow, probably not extending deeper than fifteen feet, and the ore seems to have been found in a fissure, the course of which was north-west and south-east. Of the exact character of the ore, I cannot speak positively, not having seen any specimens; but, from descriptions, presume they were green carbonates and sulphurets. By Col. McIlvaine, I am informed, that about fifteen tons of pig copper were made from the ore of this mine, which was smelted at a furnace on Big river, and of which, in 1832, he took with him to Pittsburgh, two tons, that were afterwards sold in Baltimore for sixteen cents per pound.

Probably, the next mining of copper ores, was by Messrs. Bredell and Gamble, at Copper Hill, in Crawford county, in Town. 40 N., R. 2 W., Sec. 24, where it was carried on during 1848 and 1849, with much success. This hill, the summit of which is capped with sandstone, is, according to a barometrical observation, 233 feet high. Below this, wherever the rock is exposed, it is magnesian limestone. The deepest shaft sunk was 103 feet, besides which, there were several others, varying from seventy to eighty feet in depth. Two levels were run from different points, near the base of the hill; one, 150 feet, and the other 500 feet in length, communicating with the main body of the works.

At the time of my visit, it was impossible to enter the old works; for, several years ago, the proprietors, having become so engaged with other occupations, that they could not give it their attention, suspended operations, and it was, consequently, unsafe to enter the mines.

From Mr. Bredell, I learn that the discovery was made here by the depression observed on the hill side; that all their shafts were sunk through tumbling rock; that the mineral was amid this loose rock, and that there were, in all their excavations, no well-defined walls ever found. The ores obtained here, were gray sulphuret, red oxide and blue carbonate. These ores, together with the small proportion obtained from the Silver Hollow and the Phillips mine, were smelted at their furnace on the Meramec, and the pig metal made, was sold for $31,366; which, on the supposition that it was sold for sixteen cents per pound, would give, for the total amount of pig copper made, 195,038 pounds, or nearly eighty-eight tons. But the most extensive explorations for copper ore in the State, and those most energetically and systematically carried on, have been at the

STANTON COPPER MINE,
Town. 40 N., R. 2 W., Sec. 2,

where mining was commenced by the present Company, in 1851, and has been continued to the present date, without interruption.

This mine is in the spur of a ridge, the course of which is about N., 70° E., terminating, at its eastern extremity, in a valley. In most places, this ridge is covered with soil, with now and then, on its top and sides, an exposure of rock. As we pass from its eastern extremity, along the top of it, we find no other rock than magnesian limestone, in place, until within 300 yards of the range of the shafts, where sandstone is found both on the top and sides. At the eastern extremity of the ridge, the magnesian limestone is almost perfectly horizontal, with no perceptible dip, until it approaches the sandstone, when it is seen dipping down for a short distance, at an angle of ten or fifteen degrees, to the west. This sandstone continues west for about 600 feet, visible at points, both on the top and sides of the ridge; but no other rock was seen (excepting on the south side, and near its base, where Dr. Shumard measured a brecciated mass, eighteen feet high, consisting of chert and magnesian limestone), until passing a short distance west of the range of shafts, where the magnesian limestone was again visible, with, at first, a dip of ten or fifteen degrees to the east; but a short distance further west, on the same ridge, it was horizontal. In the sandstone, whether exposed on the ridge, or examined in the driftings, I found no appearance of stratification. The surface of the ridge is so covered with soil, that it is impossible to examine the eastern and western junctions of the sandstone, with the magnesian limestone; but I infer, from examination of the driftings in the mine, that the western junction is irregular, with a general course across the ridge, of about N., 20° W.; and that along this line, there is, in all probability, a space, for some distance beneath the surface, filled with the debris of the two rocks.

Plate 11.

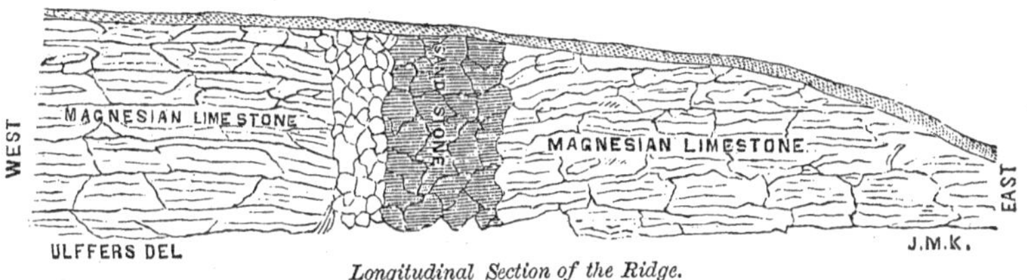

Longitudinal Section of the Ridge.

STANTON COPPER MINE, FRANKLIN COUNTY.

On plate 11, is represented a longitudinal section of the ridge, which will, probably, illustrate, better than a written description, the dip and position of the rocks. According to Dr. Shumard, the magnesian limestone is the third of the Missouri series; and I have no doubt that the sandstone, seen here, is that which overlies this magnesian rock.

Most of the mining done has been in a space, irregular, so far as explorations have shown, the direction of which is across and extending below the base of the ridge, and with a general course of about north, twenty degrees west, and of an estimated width of from forty to sixty feet, bounded on the east by sandstone, and on the west by magnesian limestone. This, so far as explored, is found filled with tumbling rock, clay, chert, calc spar (semi-crystalline, and colored red by peroxide of iron), masses of iron ore and copper ores.

Plate 12.

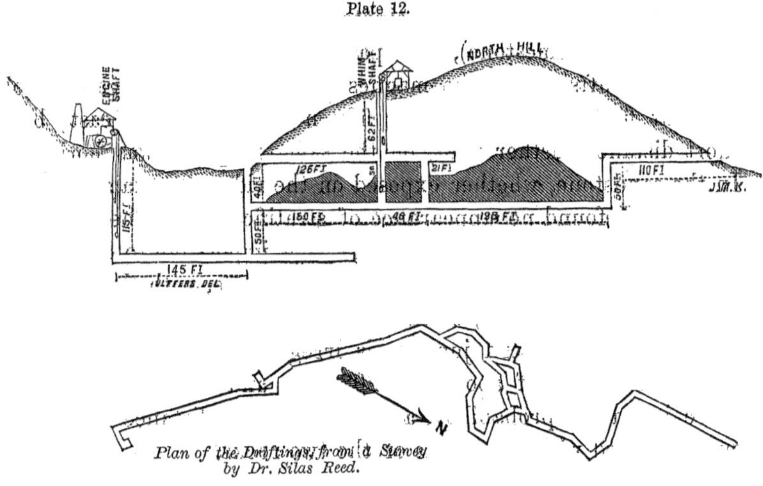

Plan of the Driftings, from a Survey by Dr. Silas Reed.

STANTON COPPER MINES, FRANKLIN COUNTY.

Scale—200 feet to inch.

On plate 12 is a vertical section of this mine, and below it, projected on the same plane, are the drifts, from a survey of them made by Dr. Reed.

From the vertical section, it will be seen that there are five shafts, the deepest of which (engine shaft) is 115 feet, and in which is the pump, worked by a steam engine. In sinking it, tumbling rock, of a magnesian character, was found through its entire depth, and it is cribbed from top to bottom. This shaft is connected by a level, 145 feet in length, with a shaft ninety feet deep, north of it, and thus connecting with the main works in the north hill. At the time of my last visit this level extended no farther than this shaft; but, since then, it has been run northwardly, the depth of about fifty feet below all preceding driftings; and, as I am informed by one of the Company, with good success and fine prospects. Levels have been run into the north hill, from both the north and south sides; but most of the driftings have been fifty feet below these, and above which driftings, only (as represented on the vertical section), the ground has been stopped away.

The copper ores found here are a mixture of the gray sulphuret and the green carbonate. Two analyses of a specimen, which was richer than the average run, gave the following results: —

	1	2
Silica,	1.16	1.29
Sulphur,	2.02	2.10
Peroxide of iron,	12.85	12.20
Oxide of copper,	61.16	60.16
Carbonic acid, water and loss,	22.81	24.25

Giving, as the mean of the two determinations, 48.41 per cent. of copper.

The furnace for smelting the ore is distant from the mine about one mile, where there is an abundance of water, during the whole year, for washing the ores, and for supplying a blast for the furnace during eight months in the year. For this last purpose, however, the Company have lately erected, at this point, a steam engine, and are now enabled to continue, at all seasons, their smelting operations. They are now engaged in smelting the large quantity of copper ore that has accumulated during the present year, and which, it is estimated, will produce thirty tons of copper; that, added to the twenty or thirty tons previously made, will make the total amount of copper made here, since the commencement of operations, in 1851, about fifty tons.

During the first year of the operations by the Company, there was but little mining, most of the labor having been expended in erecting the furnace; and the average number of hands was not over six. During 1852, the average number of hands was about ten; and, at present, there are, probably, twenty or twenty-five in the employ of the Company.

In Washington county, copper ores have been found at several points, only one of which was visited. This was Jordan's copper diggings, Town. 36 N., R. 3 and 4 W., secs. 1 and 6. It has not been worked for three years; and the only shaft sunk, which was sixteen feet deep, was found filled with water. Quite a number of specimens of sulphuret and green carbonate were found near the shaft, and the ore obtained was neither sold nor smelted. I infer that the water stopped mining operations here.

IRON.

This metal, being the main lever of civilization, its ores are, consequently, of the first importance and utility. When abundant, and accompanied by facilities for smelting and transportation, they have ever been the surest and most certain sources of individual and national wealth, and the most potent agent in securing that greatness which certain nations have obtained. These ores, Nature has scattered, with a lavish hand, over the territory of Missouri, and, at some points, has treasured them up in an abundance that seems inexhaustible. While the number of localities, at which they are found, is numerous, at some of them the quantity seems incredible, and can, undoubtedly, furnish occupation for labor and capital for centuries to come. The inland position of these, the necessarily heavy expenses of transportation, the absence of railroads and the scarcity of capital, have been the only barriers to the successful mining of this most durable element of our State wealth; for, at present, there are but four points in Missouri at which iron ores are smelted; and at two of these, there is such an abundance of ore, that it is almost impossible to make any correct estimate of the number of furnaces that could be kept in constant, successful and profitable operation. These points, as they have been, will continue to be the wonder of the illiterate, and the admiration of the educated.

Metallic iron is seldom, if ever, found pure in the mineral kingdom. It is from the compounds of this metal, with other substances, that all the iron, employed by man, is obtained.

The compounds, or ores of iron, that are principally used for smelting, are—the magnetic iron ore; the specular iron ore; brown hematite, and the spathic iron ore.

1. The magnetic iron ore gives a black powder; when pure, has a specific gravity of five; is strongly attracted by the magnet; found amorphous and crystallized; its color is black, and its lustre metallic. When pure, it contains 72.4 per cent. of iron, and 27.6 per cent. of oxygen. For the manufacture of iron, it is not inferior to any of the other ores, and is found at the Shepherd Mount, intermixed with specular iron.

2. Specular iron ore, iron glance, red hematite, micaceous iron ore, iron foam, and red-clay ironstone, are varieties of the same species. The first two names are generally restricted to specimens with a metallic lustre; when it has a foliated, or scaly appearance, it is denominated micaceous; while those possessing a non-metallic lustre are denominated red hematite. If, however, they be intermixed with clay, they are generally denominated red ochre. Its lustre is sometimes metallic, sometimes earthy; its color is a dark steel gray, or iron black, or red, if earthy, and, when pulverized, gives a brown-red or red powder. When pure, it contains seventy per cent. of iron,

and thirty of oxygen. It is found at the Iron Mountain, Pilot-Knob, and many other localities in Missouri. It does not yield so much iron as the magnetic ore, and is difficult to smelt, though this difficulty is frequently overcome by a judicious intermixture with other ores. It is, also, frequently accompanied with titanic acid.

3. Brown hematite, limonite, brown iron ore, brown ochre, hydrous peroxide of iron, iron-stone, and yellow clay iron-stone, are names for varieties of the same chemical compound. The name of brown hematite is mostly restricted to the purer and more compact varieties, that sometimes are found in mammillary, stalactitic and reniform masses. This ore, as generally found, contains some clay and lime. All of these varieties contain water, and, when pulverized, give a yellow powder. When pure, it contains about fourteen per cent. of water and sixty per cent. of metallic iron. It sometimes contains phosphoric acid, when the pig iron made from it is liable to contain phosphorus, and, though useful for casting, is unfit for the manufacture of sheet iron and iron wire.

This variety of iron ore is found at many points. On the hills of Franklin county it is frequently found in such quantities as to give indications of extensive deposits of it.

4. Spathic iron ore, sparry iron, carbonate of iron. This, when crystallized, is generally found in rhombohedrons, and might be easily mistaken for carbonate of lime, though its specific weight is greater. As used for metallurgic purposes, it is in a less pure form; and when found in the coal measures, is generally intermixed with some sesquioxide of iron, clay and silica.

Though iron ore is universally, in some form or other, distributed throughout Nature, constituting an essential element to both the organic and the inorganic kingdoms, and presented under forms no less various than it is abundant, it is almost entirely out of the above four ores that all the iron is made; and all of these, with the exception of the spathic iron ore (which, it is not improbable, may yet be discovered in the coal measures), have been found in Missouri. Though there are many points in Missouri at which these ores are sufficiently abundant to justify the erection of furnaces, there are now but four at which they have been erected.

The earliest attempt in Missouri, and, in all probability, in any of the States west of the Ohio, to smelt iron ore, was in 1823 or '24; when a blast furnace was erected in Washington county, by Eversol, Perry & Ruggles, between Potosi and Caledonia. This furnace was afterwards known as Perry's old iron furnace; and from Col. McIlvaine, who was well acquainted with all the operations there, I learn that the ore first smelted was obtained from Clear creek, which, however, was soon discontinued, because it was believed to contain copper; and that, afterwards, four-fifths of that smelted came from near Absalom Eaton's place, and was mixed with ore brought from the Iron Mountain. The ore near Mr. Eaton's is a brown hematite, apparently of a most excellent quality, and excavated from a bank on the hill side. In connection with this blast furnace, were two forges. The first bar of iron made out of pig metal in Missouri, Col. McIlvaine says, was made on Cedar creek, in May, 1825, and the first blooms were made in 1832. Though ore was abundant and easily smelted, the great expense of transportation, however, in a new and thinly-settled country, soon induced the abandonment of the enterprise. The next blast furnace was, probably, erected in 1828, by Mr. Massey, in Crawford, which has been in successful operation up to the present time; but not having been able to visit this, I defer any report upon it.

In Franklin county there is but one iron furnace, though there is, doubtless, such an abundance of iron ore there, that many furnaces could be kept constantly supplied. This furnace was formerly known by the name of the Moselle, but is now designated as the Furnace of the Franklin Iron Mining Company, and is in Town. 42 N., R. 1 E., Sec. 14, S. E. ¼.

The furnace is thirty-three feet high, and the blast is produced by a steam engine. The ore is found in banks, of which there are four or five now opened on the lands of the Company. One of them is about fifty feet wide and twenty-seven feet high. These ridge-shaped masses, presenting no appearance of stratification, are, in general, opened, or quarried, from the side of the hill, and are found, on the other three sides, to be surrounded with magnesian limestone. The ore obtained from these banks is a brown hematite, intermixed with yellow ochre, and found, often, in mammillary and stalactitic masses. In specimens from only one of the banks did I find any iron pyrites; and, in general, the ore is very pure.

These banks are in the second magnesian limestone, beneath which, on the creek, is visible the sandstone that underlies this member of the lower Silurian series.

The flux used is the magnesian limestone, separated from the chert which accompanies it; and the qualities of pig metal made, are numbers one, two and three, of the gray variety.

An analysis of a specimen from one of these banks, gave —

Silica,	1.36
Alumina,	1.04
Peroxide of iron,	82.94
Water,	13.54

In this specimen I could not find a trace of sulphur or phosphoric acid.

At this furnace has, also, been used some of the hematite ore, obtained from a deposit on Mrs. Farrar's land; and an analysis of a specimen of this, gave —

Silica,	8.03
Alumina,	0.79
Peroxide of iron,	80.44
Water,	11.39
	100.65

Another specimen of a compact, massive, brown hematite, covering the hill sides in Town. 42 N., R. 2 W., Sec. 17, N. E. ½, gave —

Silica,	8.27
Alumina,	0.70
Peroxide of iron,	80,15
Water,	11.11
	100.23

The excess in the two last analyses is, probably, owing to a portion of the iron being in combination with silica as a peroxide.

IRON MOUNTAIN.

Few, if any, localities in Missouri are more widely known than the Iron Mountain. The land on which it lies, was a grant to Jos. Pratte, that was confirmed in 1836; but, on account of the difficulty of transportation, and of the impression that the ore could not be smelted, this inexhaustible supply was permitted to remain unproductive until 1845, when the Iron Mountain Company was formed, and proceeded to the erection of furnaces.

The Iron Mountain is the south-western termination of a ridge, some portions of which, near the Mountain, attain to an elevation of between 300 and 400 feet; and the rocks of this ridge, near its junction with the Mountain, are porphyritic, containing a large portion of a reddish feldspar. The Mountain is a flattened, conical-shaped hill, with an average elevation above the surrounding valleys of 228 feet, the base of which covers an area of not less than 500 acres. To the west, it gradually slopes off, and this part is called the Little Iron Mountain.

South of the Iron Mountain is Miller's Knob, the height of which is about 300 feet; and its principal peak is distant from the summit of the Mountain, about one and a half miles. Buford Mountain, a hill not quite so high as Miller's Knob, lies south-west, and distant from the Iron Mountain, a little more than two miles. Both these hills are porphyritic; but, in the valleys along the streams, the only rock seen exposed was the magnesian limestone, which has little, if any, dip.

For the accompanying maps, number thirteen and fourteen, of the country in the immediate vicinity of the Iron Mountain and Pilot-Knob, I am indebted to the kindness of Mr. A. H. Ulffers, who, at my request, visited these localities, and made the necessary surveys for their construction. As specimens of art, they are not less beautiful than, I am confident, they are correct; and they will give a better idea of these interesting regions than any written description could.

As we ascend the south-western termination of the Little Iron Mountain, we find it covered with soil and clay, with, now and then, the iron ore lying loose on the surface. In passing over the ridge, connecting it with the Iron Mountain proper, we find these angular, and partially weather-worn, pebbles and masses increasing in size, even until we reach its summit, where we find disconnected masses, many tons in weight, and, often, six or eight feet in diameter. These are, sometimes, almost totally uncovered; but, at other points, are seen projecting out from the soil and clay, with which they are partially covered. Nowhere, on the Iron Mountain, can we find any rock; and the masses of iron ore cannot be seen in place on the surface, but seem scattered, irregularly, in confused masses.

It is not until we leave the Iron Mountain, and begin to ascend the ridge of higher hills, with which it is connected on the east, and the course of which is about north-east and south-west, that we could find any thing else than iron ore, and where we find the hill composed of feldspathic porphyry. According to Mr. Mersch, who had opportunities to examine, at the most favorable seasons, this locality, there is a narrow wall connecting the mountain on the east

Section 20

No.		thickness	depth
1	Clay and Iron	16	16
2	Coarse Sandstone	25	41
3	Fine white Sandstone	5½	46½
4	Fine yellow Sandstone	3½	50
5	Quartz, gravel and clay	1½	51½
6	Magnesian Limestone	7/12	
7	Gray Sandstone	7/12	53
8	Hard blue rock	37	90
9	Pure Iron Ore	5	95
10	Porphyritic rock	7	102
11	Iron Ore	50	152

Mrs. S. del. Schaerff & Bro. Lith. St. Louis.

ARTESIAN WELL AT THE IRON MOUNTAIN

with the main ridge, along the line of which wall, the iron ore and the porphyry are intermixed for a short distance; but, to the east of which, the porphyry, and, to the west of it, the iron ore, are each found perfectly pure and unmixed.

In sinking in the valleys around the Mountain, the iron ore is found extending out to considerable distances from the base; and, so far as explorations have been made, continuing down beneath the surface. Between the furnaces, two and three, the Company commenced boring an artesian well; and, from the journal kept, it seems that they have penetrated 150 feet. The first sixteen feet was through iron ore and clay; the next thirty-four was through beds of sandrock, beneath which was a bed of magnesian limestone, seven and a half inches thick, which seems to overlie another thin bed (seven and a half inches) of sandrock.

At the depth of eighty-nine feet, a bed of pure ore, five feet thick, was found, beneath which was seven feet of a porphyritic rock; when, again, at about 112 feet below the surface, ore was found, and into which they sunk fifty feet, without passing through it, when the boring ceased. From the journal of Mr. A. E. Leftwich, who had charge of the boring, has been constructed the annexed section, which shows the thickness of the different beds passed through.

From surface indications, and from all explorations made, the whole Iron Mountain seems to be a mass of iron ore. The elevation of its summit above the valley, varies according to the point at which the measurement is made; and, from the survey of the railroad, I take for its height, 228 feet; and at this depth, below its summit, its base cannot cover a smaller area than 500 acres. Considered as a cone, with a base of 500 acres, and a height of 228 feet, the solid contents of that portion *above the surface*, is 1,655,280,000 cubic feet. One cubic foot of water weighs 16.3 pounds, avoirdupois; and were this mass, water, its total weight would be 103,123,944,000 pounds. But the determination of the specific gravity of two specimens of the ore has shown, that it is between 5.05 and 5.23 times heavier than water. Considering it, however, as only five times heavier, it would give for the total weight of the iron ore, above the surface, 1,515,619,720,000 pounds, or 230,187,375 tons. The ore is the specular iron ore, and is remarkably pure; and in all the specimens examined, I have not yet discovered any other impurity than quartz. Its average yield in the furnace is fifty-six per cent. The analysis of a specimen gave —

Silica,	0.66
Peroxide of iron,	99.33 = 69.55 iron

and in which I could not discover a trace of titanic or phosphoric acid, or lime, or alumina, for each of which I searched in this specimen.

The excavation of the ore has been limited to the western termination of the Little Mountain, where it has been carried on along a course of S., 40 E., and extending over a line of 377 feet. At no point at this excavation have they descended deeper than eighteen feet, and to this, only in a very limited space. Near the surface, the ore is found in pebbles or lumps, varying in size; their edges are frequently rounded, and the surfaces apparently water worn; and the interstices between them are filled with a ferruginous clay, that is used as a flux. Below it, becomes more compact and massive. Up to the present time, the Company has had but two furnaces in operation. No. 1, thirty-one feet, and No. 2, thirty-two feet in height, and each nine feet across the boshes; but a third is now completed, having a height of thirty-eight feet, and width across the boshes of nine feet, and will be immediately put into operation. The large lumps of ore are roasted, that they may be the more easily crushed.

An average charge is 425 pounds of ore and clay, with sixty pounds of a magnesian limestone; and the average number of charges per diem, about 140. It is estimated that about 160 bushels of coal are consumed in the production of one ton of pig metal, weighing 2,268 pounds. The average amount of pig metal, made by each furnace per day, is six and a half tons; and the greatest product obtained from one furnace, during a day, has been eight tons.*

The quality of the metal made is principally No. 2, of the gray variety of pig metal. The total amount of metal made, from the commencement of operations to December 10th, 1854, is 24,500 tons, equal to 56,166,000 pounds.

The flux is obtained from a quarry of magnesian limestone, about half a mile from the furnaces. The rock has a light gray, and, sometimes, almost a buff color, and with, perhaps, a very slight dip to the south-west.

The analysis of a specimen, from this quarry, gave—

Residue, insoluble in dilute hydrochloric acid, ...	6.97
Alumina, with peroxide of iron, ...	1.11
Carbonate of lime, ...	50.38
Carbonate of magnesia, ...	41.74

* One furnace has since yielded fifteen tons per diem.

PLATE XV.

R. E. PRICE. DEL. J. M. KERSHAW, ENGRAVER.

TOP OF PILOT KNOB, SHOWING THE EXCAVATION IN THE IRON ORE.

PILOT-KNOB AND SHEPHERD MOUNTAIN.

About six miles south, and a little to the east of the Iron Mountain, are other deposits of iron ore, not less rich, and, in all probability, not less extensive. One of these, the Pilot-Knob, with an almost perpendicular peak, and a nearly isolated position, has, from the earliest settlement of the country, served as a land-mark to the pioneer and the traveler.

According to the measurement of Mr. Ulffers, the height of the Pilot-Knob is 581 feet above the level on which the bloomery stands (this point, according to the railroad survey, is 11,537 feet above St. Louis); its base covers an area of 360 acres. It is, as will be seen by reference to the accompanying topographical map, No. 14, an almost isolated, nearly conical hill, connected at its eastern base with a range of lower hills (the first of which is called Little Pilot-Knob), that gradually rise in height as they pass off to the east.

The rocks, near the base of the Pilot-Knob, are seldom seen in place; but when so, are of a dark gray color, present quite a silicious, and shaly or slaty character, and offer strong indications of stratification. They are not, however, horizontal, but dip at an angle of twenty-five or thirty degrees to the south-west. After ascending about 300 feet, the rock assumes more of a ferruginous character; and at the height of 440 feet, we find, on the north side of the Mountain, an exposure of a heavy bed, or rather stratum, of pure iron ore, about 273 feet in length, and nineteen to twenty-four feet in height, or thickness, apparently passing parallel with the lower slaty rocks, and with the same dip, through the Mountain to the south-west. It is said that, at still lower points than the above stratum, and beneath it, are other beds, interstratified with the silicious rock; but, at the time of my visit, the sides of the Mountain were so covered with debris and undergrowth, that I did not find these in place.

Above the heavy stratum of iron ore, which is now quarried for smelting, the iron ore seems to be interstratified with the silicious rock, even to the summit of the Mountain.

The ore differs much, in its appearance, from that of the Iron Mountain. It has a more slaty character, and a finer grain; and, in some specimens, assumes almost a micaceous appearance. The specimens vary in richness. An analysis of one, gave—

Silica,	12.03	
Alumina,	1.61	
Peroxide of iron,	86.07	equal. 60.27 per cent. of iron.

An analysis of a specimen of the ore, made several years ago, gave—

Silica, ...	23.12
Alumina, ...	2.78
Peroxide of iron, . . .	73.74 equal. 51.13 per cent. of iron.

The quantity of pure iron ore at the Pilot-Knob, is not, probably, less than all that portion of the Mountain, above the elevation of 440 feet above its base; for, beneath this point, there are large masses above the base of the hill. A section of the Pilot-Knob, 440 feet above, and parallel with its base, would cover an area of not less than fifty-three acres. Considering the upper 141 feet, as composed entirely of iron ore, and as a cone, with a base of fifty-three acres, it would make 108,507,960 cubic feet of iron ore; which volume, if water, would weigh 6,760,045,900 pounds. The specific gravity of three different specimens of the Pilot-Knob ore, was found to be 4.75, 4.49 and 4.66, the mean of which, is 4.63; and taking this last as the average specific weight of the ore, it would give for the total weight of the ore, upon the above supposition, in the upper 141 feet of the Pilot-Knob, 31,299,012,554 pounds, or 13,972,773 tons. The surface of the Little Pilot-Knob is covered with small fragments of iron ore, apparently much water worn, and the interstices between them are filled with a ferruginous clay. Beneath this, at one point, an excavation has been made, and there are exposed strata of a magnesian limestone, which has been quarried for a flux; a specimen of which, gave, upon analysis—

Silica, ...	5.62
Alumina and peroxide of iron, ...	0.82
Carbonate of lime, ...	50.10
Carbonate of magnesia, ...	43.24

SHEPHERD MOUNTAIN.

This Mountain lies S., 51° W. of the Pilot-Knob, and their summits are distant from each other 6,987 feet, or about one and a third miles. Its height, according to Ulffers' measurement, is 660 feet, and it is, consequently, seventy-nine feet higher than the Pilot-Knob. Its greatest length is one and three-quarter miles north-west and south-east; its breadth, north-east and south-west, about one mile; and its base covers an area of 800 acres. All the rocks, exposed on this hill, and in place, are porphyritic. This hill seems to be penetrated with veins or dikes of iron ore, running in different directions, four or five of which have been already discovered; only three of them, however, have been but partially explored. The principal explorations have been at two points; one, on the north-eastern slope, and the other, at the Janis vein, on the south-western slope of the hill. At the first, about 460 feet above the base of the hill, there is an open cut of 307 feet in length, running west of south, and the width from five to eight feet. The greatest depth of this cut is twenty-five feet. The walls are well defined, but present strong indications that the porphyritic rock has undergone partial decomposition.

The exploration of the Janis vein, the course of which is nearly east and west, has been commenced at nearly the same elevation, above the base of the hill, as the former vein, and by an open cut running east. This cut has been extended east 160 feet, and seems to widen as it enters the hill, for, at its eastern termination, its width is fourteen feet. Its greatest depth is twenty-five feet, and the wall rock presents exactly the same appearance as the vein on the northern slope.

The ores obtained from Shepherd Mountain, are the magnetic, the specular, and a mixture of the two. In a specimen of the last variety, from which the magnetic portion was carefully separated by a magnet, there was found twenty per cent. of magnetic iron ore.

Two specimens of ore, from different parts of the Janis vein, were analyzed, and gave the following results. Both were compact, and the second was taken from the greater depth:—

1 gave—	Silica,	1.04
	Alumina,	0.60
	Peroxide of iron,	98.30 = 68.83 iron.
2 gave—	Silica,	1.81
	Alumina,	Trace.
	Peroxide of iron,	99.18

In the vein, on the northern slope, some few specimens of sulphuret of iron were seen.

These two invaluable deposits of iron ore, the Pilot-Knob and the Shepherd Mountain, belong to the Madison Iron and Mining Company, which commenced operations in November, 1847. Up to the present time, they have had but one blast furnace in operation, at which has been principally used the ore obtained from the Pilot-Knob. The ore is fluxed with a magnesian limestone, and with ferruginous clay; and, for each charge of 400 pounds of ore, there is added, about twenty-five pounds of the clay (moist), and sixty-three of the lime. It is estimated, that 214 bushels of charcoal are employed in producing one ton (2,268 pounds) of pig metal.

The limestone, used for a flux, is brought some two or three miles, from a quarry that lies in Town. 34., R. 3 E., Sec. 35, E. ½, where there is an exposure of some twenty feet of limestone, consisting of several beds, with little or no dip, some of which (particularly the upper ones) are very pure. An analysis of a specimen, from one of these upper beds, which was compact, semi-crystalline, and almost white, gave —

Silica,	1.05
Alumina,	Trace.
Carbonate of lime,	97.06
Carbonate of magnesia,	1.70

Another specimen, from a lower bed, gave, for carbonate of magnesia, fifteen per cent., and in this the silica and alumina were more abundant; but both together did not exceed four per cent.

In 1850, near the Pilot-Knob, a bloomery was started, with six fires, at which the ore obtained from the Shepherd Mountain, is principally employed. It is estimated that there are consumed 367 bushels of charcoal, in the production and re-heating of one ton (2,464 pounds) of blooms.

This Company has commenced, and nearly completed, another blast furnace, which will soon be in operation. The blast furnace was started on August 11, 1846; and, for the following products of this and the bloomery, I am indebted to Col. Bogy: —

1st Blast, from	August 11, 1848, to October 19, 1848,	73 tons.
2d " "	February 4, 1849, to April 4, 1849,	300 "
3d " "	May 1, 1849, to June 31, 1849,	250 "
4th " "	July 11, 1849, to September 29, 1849,	580 "
5th " "	November 8, 1849, to February 18, 1850,	593 "
6th " "	March 22, 1850, to August 22, 1850,	829 "
7th " "	January 11, 1851, to March 12, 1851,	213 "
8th " "	March 19, 1851, to July 8, 1851,	573 "
9th " "	June 22, 1852, to November 12, 1852,	432 "
10th " "	July 6, 1853, to August 10, 1854,	2,167 "
11th " "	September 18, 1854, yet going on,	200 "
		6,210 tons

of pig metal, equal to 14,084,280 pounds, from the 11th August, 1848, up to the 15th November, 1854.

At the forge has been made 3,000 tons of blooms, from the commencement of operations in October, 1850, to November 15, 1854.

The hearth-stone of the furnaces, at the Iron Mountain and Pilot-Knob, is a sandrock, brought from near Cedar creek, where there is an exposure of thirty or forty feet of it, and the upper strata are from two to three feet thick. It is excellent, durable in quality, and answers well the purposes to which it is here applied.

The analyses of two specimens of this, gave—

	1	2
Silica,	96.35	95.40
Alumina,	3.50	2.90
Lime,	Trace.	Trace.

In the neighborhood of the Pilot-Knob are several other very valuable deposits of iron ore; and though, for the want of time, but one of them was visited, I subjoin the analyses of specimens brought from them.

The Bogy, or Buford ore bank, lies about five miles south of Pilot-Knob, in Town. 33, R. 3 E., Sec. 24, N. E. ¼. An analysis of a specimen from this mountain, made by me in 1852, for Colonel Bogy, gave—

Silica,	3.81
Peroxide of iron,	95.16
Alumina, and lime,	Traces.

Specimens from other deposits in this mountain, that were obtained at the furnace, and had been roasted, were found to contain a considerable portion of manganese.

A specimen, from the Big Bogy Mountain, in Town. 33, R. 3, Sec. 13, S. E. ¼, analyzed at the same time as the above, gave—

Silica,	0.21
Alumina,	0.51
Peroxide of iron,	99.08

The Russell ore bank lies south-west of the Pilot-Knob, and in Town. 33, R. 3 E., Sec. 3, E. ½. The ore exists in a porphyritic hill, and, probably, in a vein. It is a fine-grained peroxide, and remarkably pure. A specimen gave, by analysis—

Silica,	1.16
Peroxide of iron,	98.81

The Shut-in lies in Town. 33, R. 4 E., Sec. 2, N. ½. The ore is found here in veins, running through a porphyritic hill. The one which has been principally explored, is nearly vertical; has a nearly north and south course, and a width of about one foot; and the ore is a compact specular variety. It is very rich, and is said to work easily.

A brown hematite ore, of a pure and most excellent quality, has been found in Town. 34, R. 3 E., Sec. 21.

ZINC.

As yet, no attention has been paid to the mining of zinc ores in Missouri. Most of those found have been obtained from the lead mines; and at Perry's Mine, considerable quantities of the silicates and carbonates accompany the galena. At Mount Hope Mine, a considerable portion of the carbonate might be procured.

Should, however, the recently-discovered application of the oxide of zinc for a pigment, or other discoveries of the use of zinc and its compounds, create a still greater demand for this metal, I doubt not Missouri will be able to supply a considerable amount; for there are many points at which the ores of zinc seem to be the most abundant of the mineral deposits.

A little north of west, and about one and a half miles from Potosi, on land belonging to Messrs. Dunklin and Anderson, there has been traced, on the surface of the ground, for 170 yards in length, a ledge of rocks, from four to six feet wide, slightly projecting above the surface of the ground. They seem as though they were rocks standing on their edges; but are, in all probability, the filling up of a fissure, that has been better able to withstand disintegration. The course of the exposure is nearly north and south. This rock is sulphate of baryta, intermixed with chert and carbonate of zinc. It has been explored only superficially, and at no point has the excavation been deeper than two or three feet. It is well worthy of being tried still farther, to show if it be a lode of zinc ore.

One specimen, from this locality, gave 5.73 per cent. of oxide of zinc; the remainder being sulphate of baryta, silica, lime, alumina, water and carbonic acid. Another specimen, gave —

Res., insoluble in acid,	4.04	
Oxide of zinc,	55.77	44.76 per cent. of zinc.
Peroxide of iron,	4.10	
Carbonic acid, water and loss,	36.09	

Large deposits of carbonate of zinc are said to exist in Town. 36 N., R. 3 E., Sec. 4, S. E. ¼, near Mr. John Jamieson's farm; and, also, in Sec. 7, of the same township; but not being able to speak from personal observation, I shall postpone, to another time, any remarks upon them.

Our State is rich in a variety of other substances, that have a great economical value, and which must, undoubtedly, at some future day, constitute a not unimportant item of its wealth. Among these may be enumerated, its coal, its materials for the manufacture of glass, its building materials, its limestones, its clays; some of which are suitable for fire brick, some for the manufacture of earthen-ware, and, not improbably, for the making of porcelain.

Among these, I mention now, as existing in the greatest abundance, and sufficient to supply the wants of the Union, a remarkably pure sandstone, found in the neighborhood of Ste. Genevieve, Plattin Rock, and other places. This constitutes what is denominated the Saccharoidal Sandstone, and is, in many places, almost snow white, in beds easily approached, and of variable thickness. This sandstone separates the upper from the second magnesian limestone; and about eight miles from Ste. Genevieve there is an exposure of it, from twenty to twenty-five feet high. It is remarkably white, crumbles easily upon a slight pressure, is made up of rounded grains, and has little, if any, cementing substance to unite the particles. It does not color, in the least, by heating; and, so far as I could discover, does not contain any material that, by oxidation, would color the glass made from it. It is, and has been, extensively quarried, and, packed in barrels, is shipped from Ste. Genevieve and Plattin Rock to various points. Two analyses of this — number one, by fusion with carbonate of soda, and number two, by treating with hydrofluoric acid, gave —

	1	2
Silica, ...	98.81	99.02
Lime, ...	0.92	0.98

In the neighborhood of Ste. Genevieve is an oolitic limestone, belonging to the Carboniferous series, and which is extensively quarried, both for building material and for making lime. This limestone is exposed, at some places, from eighteen to twenty-five feet in height. It is heavy-bedded, composed of small egg-like particles, in a paste of limestone. It works easily; large and massive blocks ore obtained with, comparatively, little labor; and, though it will not take a high polish, withstands pretty well, so far as it has been tried in St. Louis, the action of atmospheric agencies. It is extensively quarried and shipped at Ste. Genevieve, to points (I believe) both above and below, on the Mississippi river. An analysis of this gave, for silica and alumina, 00.14 per cent., and for carbonate of lime, 99.44 per cent.

In conclusion, I subjoin the results of the analyses of specimens, furnished by yourself and Dr. Shumard. The discussion of these results, so far as they may have an economical bearing, I must reserve for a future report; and, for more minute information as to the localities, and the character of the deposits, I must refer to your own report and that of Dr. Shumard, in which, doubtless, will be given all information on these points.

In the analyses of the limestones, the method, in general, followed, was to dry them at a given temperature; to dissolve them in either dilute muriatic or nitric acid; out of which solution, the alumina and oxide of iron were precipitated by ammonia, the lime by oxalate of ammonia, and the magnesia by phosphate of soda. When the insoluble residue was considerable, it was most frequently analyzed by fusing with the carbonate of soda. The quantity of iron present being very small, I did not separate it from the alumina, as the labor and time necessary for this would have been considerable, and the results of no economical value. In many, the presence of alkalies was established; but the determination of these, however interesting it might be for speculative geology, was, for the same reason, omitted; for, in every case, they were present, in very minute quantities.

The following are the analyses of specimens sent by yourself:—

No. 1.—A specimen of magnesian limestone, from the well of Mr. Winston Walker, in Cooper county, and belonging to the Vermicular Sandstone. Two analyses were made, and gave—

	1	2
Silica,	11.89	11.99
Alumina, with peroxide of iron,	4.16	2.61
Carbonate of lime,	54.07	55.54
Carbonate of magnesia,	28.94	29.09
	99.06	99.23

No. 2.—A magnesian limestone, from near Chouteau Springs, Cooper county, and belonging to the *Chouteau Limestone* formation, gave—

	1	2
Res., insoluble in hydrochloric acid,	13.90	13.38
Alumina and peroxide of iron,	2.01	1.95
Carbonate of lime,	48.23	48.09
Carbonate of magnesia,	34.93	36.38
	99.07	99.80

No. 3. — A compact, hard and variegated limestone, from La Mine river, and, geologically, belonging to the *Lithographic Limestone* of the Missouri series, gave, dried at 100°, C. —

Silica,	6.22
Alumina and peroxide of iron,	0.93
Carbonate of lime,	89.66
Carbonate of magnesia,	1.55
Water,	1.63
	99.99

No. 4. — Compact, bluish gray limestone, from Chouteau Springs, Cooper county, dried at 100°, C. —

Res., insoluble in hydrochloric acid,	1.51
Alumina and peroxide of iron,	0.38
Carbonate of lime,	96.38
HO.,	0.76
	99.03

No. 5. — Hard, semi-crystalline, bluish limestone, Cooper co. —

Res., insoluble in hydrochloric acid,	1.44
Alumina and peroxide of iron,	1.68
Carbonate of lime,	95.51
HO.,	0.47
	99.10

No. 6. — Hard, bluish, semi-crystalline limestone, dried at 100°, C., from the *Coal Measures* —

Res., insoluble in nitric acid,	5.11
Alumina and peroxide of iron,	1.72
Carbonate of lime,	91.29
Water,	0.72
	98.84

No. 7. — Impure, sandy limestone, Cooper county — *Vermicular Sandstone* —

Res., insoluble in hydrochloric acid,	10.97
Alumina and peroxide of iron,	1.32
Carbonate of lime,	60.47
Carbonate of magnesia,	25.93

No. 8. — Fine blue, sub-crystalline, ferruginous limestone, from one mile above Boonville — *Coal Measures* —

Res., insoluble in hydrochloric acid,	5.04
Alumina and peroxide of iron,	2.19
Carbonate of lime,	89.96
Carbonate of magnesia,	2.29
	99.48

No. 9.—Hard, gray and blue ferruginous limestone, used for building at Weston and Parkville—*Coal Measures*—

Res., insoluble in hydrochloric acid,	2.82
Alumina and peroxide of iron,	4.03
Carbonate of lime,	87.86
Carbonate of magnesia,	4.82
	99.53

No. 10.—Hard, bluish gray ferruginous limestone, dried at 100°, C.—*Coal Measures*—

Res., insoluble in hydrochlorie acid,	4.02
Alumina and peroxide of iron,	3.02
Carbonate of lime,	87.73
Carbonate of magnesia,	1.87
Water,	2.99
	99.63

No. 11.—Dark, impure concretionary limestone, from bluffs at Lexington—*Coal Measures*—

Res., insoluble in hydrochloric acid,	7.26
Alumina and peroxide of iron,	1.77
Carbonate of lime,	90.12
	99.15

No. 12.—Fine-grained, ferruginous limestone—*Coal Measures*—

Res., insoluble in nitric acid,	5.27
Alumina and peroxide of iron,	2.57
Carbonate of lime,	90.48
HO.,	0.74
	99.06

No. 13.—Dark, impure limestone, from bluff at Weston—*Coal Measures*—

Res., insoluble in nitric acid,	3.25
Alumina and peroxide of iron,	1.92
Carbonate of lime,	91.94
Carbonate of magnesia,	1.05
Water,	1.60
	99.76

No. 14.—Hard, blue and gray-mottled limestone—*Coal Measures*—

Silica,	31.40
Alumina and peroxide of iron,	3.42
Carbonate of lime,	64.45
	99.27

No. 15. — Cotton Rock, from Atkisson's well, Warsaw — *2d Magnesian Limestone* —

Silica,	13.27
Alumina and peroxide of iron,	0.52
Carbonate of lime,	47.01
Carbonate of magnesia,	38.86
	99.66

No. 16. — Finely-stratified portion of Cotton Rock, from Warsaw — *2d Magnesian Limestone* —

Silica,	63.44
Alumina and peroxide of iron,	10.72
Carbonate of lime,	13.59
Carbonate of magnesia,	10.75
Water,	0.41
	98.91

No. 17. — Obtained from near Ruby Walker's, dried at 100°, C. — *2d Magnesian Limestone* —

Two analyses made of this — one, by fusion with carbonate of soda; the other, by treating with hydrofluoric acid, gave —

	1	2
Silica,	89.18	......
Alumina,	7.37	6.08
Lime,	0.52	Trace.
HO.,	2.21	2.22
	99.28	

No. 18. — Cotton Rock, gave —

Res., insoluble in nitric acid,	6.21
Alumina and peroxide of iron,	1.07
Carbonate of lime,	50.80
Carbonate of magnesia,	40.56
Water,	0.21
	98.85

No. 19. — Magnesian limestone, from bluff above Warsaw.

The mass of this rock was filled with cavities, containing a soft, whitish substance, resembling, in its appearance, number seventeen. A portion of it, separated, as well as possible, from the adjacent rock, gave —

Silica,	91.14
Alumina, with a trace of oxide of iron,	1.63
Lime,	2.60
Magnesia,	1.56
Water, carbonic acid and loss,	3.07

The other portion, gave —

Silica,	6.08
Alumina,	0.60
Carbonate of lime,	52.16
Carbonate of magnesia,	40.39
	99.23

No. 20. — Fine-grained, gray compact limestone, Cooper county —

Res., insoluble in nitric acid,	5.60
Alumina and oxide of iron,	1.84
Carbonate of lime,	90.76
Carbonate of magnesia,	Trace.
Water,	0.45

No. 21. — Magnesian limestone —

Res., insoluble in nitric acid,	6.67
Alumina and peroxide of iron,	0.98
Carbonate of lime,	49.35
Carbonate of magnesia,	41.98
Water,	0.90
	99.88

No. 22. — Argillaceous Slate — *Coal Measures* —
Two analyses, gave —

	1	2
Silica,	28.47	28.50
Alumina and peroxide of iron,	17.96	16.83
Carbonate of lime,	46.52	47.04
Carbonate of magnesia,	2.91	3.70
Water,	3.04	Not determined.

No. 23. — Calcareous concretions, in *Bluff Formation* —

Res. insoluble in hydrochloric acid,	35.08, principally Silica.
Alumina and peroxide of iron,	5.29
Carbonate of lime,	58.33
Carbonate of magnesia,	0.77
	99.47

No. 24. — Gray, semi-crystalline limestone, from Missouri river — *Coal Measures* —

Res., insoluble in nitric acid,	3.24
Alumina and peroxide of iron,	1.46
Carbonate of lime,	93.10
Carbonate of magnesia,	Trace.
Water,	1.33
	99.13

No. 25. — Impure limestone, from Missouri river — *Coal Measures* —

Res., insoluble in nitric acid, ...	8.45
Alumina and peroxide of iron, ...	1.87
Carbonate of lime, ...	87.70
Carbonate of magnesia, ...	2.30
Water, ...	0.42
	100.74

No. 26. — Gray magnesian limestone, from Missouri river — *Coal Measures.*

Two analyses of this were made: —

	1	2
Res., insoluble in hydrochloric acid, ...	3.11	3.04
Alumina and peroxide of iron, ...	9.01	9.00
Carbonate of lime, ...	60.18	61.18
Carbonate of magnesia, ...	26.53	25.70
Water, ...	0.29	......
	99.12	98.92

No. 27. — Concretionary limestone, from Missouri river — *Coal Measures* —

Silica, ...	17.24
Alumina and peroxide of iron, ...	5.25
Carbonate of lime, ...	75.82
Carbonate of magnesia and loss, ...	1.69
	100.00

No. 28. — Dark, ferruginous limestone, from Missouri river — *Coal Measures* —

Res., insoluble in hydrochloric acid, ...	2.91
Alumina and peroxide of iron, ...	1.08
Carbonate of lime, ...	92.47
Carbonate of magnesia, ...	1.84
Water, ...	0.64
	98.94

No. 29.—Dark limestone, from Missouri river—*Coal Measures*—

Silica, ...	16.31
Alumina and peroxide of iron, ...	4.01
Carbonate of lime, ...	69.77
Carbonate of magnesia, ...	8.94
	99.03

No. 30.—Brown, ferruginous limestone, from Missouri river—*Coal Measures*—

Res., insoluble in nitric acid,	3.55
Alumina and peroxide of iron,	4.47
Carbonate of lime,	82.85
Carbonate of magnesia,	8.90
	99.77

No. 31.—Concretions in coal, from Missouri river—*Coal Measures*—consist of carbonaceous matter and sand, with some alumina and a small portion of sulphuret of iron.

No. 32.—Compact gray limestone, from Missouri river—

Res., insoluble in acid, with alumina and peroxide of iron,	1.15
Carbonate of lime,	98.56
Carbonate of magnesia,	Trace.
	99.71

No. 33.—Limestone, from Jenkins' lime kiln, near Fulton—

Res., insoluble in acid, with alumina and peroxide of iron,	0.51
Carbonate of lime,	98.93
Carbonate of magnesia,	Trace.

No. 34.—Talcose Mineral, from Ferruginous Sandstone. Two determinations of the silica were made. Substance dried at 100°, C.—

	1	2
Silica,	44.44	44.07
Alumina,	37.93	......
Lime,	0.75	......
Water,	16.75	......

No. 35.—Ore sent from Cassville. Is Peroxide of Manganese, with a small portion of oxide of iron.

No. 36.—Ore sent from Cassville. Is essentially Peroxide of Iron, with a considerable portion of silica, some alumina, and a trace of manganese.

No. 37.—Ore from Cedar Gap, near Frémont. Almost entirely Peroxide of Iron, with some silica and a trace of alumina, and contains neither manganese, phosphoric acid, earths nor alkalies.

No. 38.—Salt, from near Wilson's coal-bed. The greater portion of this, is soluble in water; this part is essentially sulphate of alumina, with a small quantity of peroxide of iron. The part insoluble in water, was silica, a small quantity of alumina and sulphuret of iron.

No. 39.—Sediment, from a chalybeate spring, west of Oseola, contained only a trace of silica, with some alumina and peroxide of iron.

No. 40.—Salt, from above Maston's bridge, on the La Mine. The portion soluble in water, was sulphate of the protoxide of iron or copperas, and the insoluble part was silica, alumina and lime.

No. 41.—Salt, on the rock from the same place as the above. The salt is Epsom salt, or sulphate of magnesia, and the rock a magnesian limestone.

Nos. 42 and 43.—Brown Hematite, from near Buffalo, are essentially the same. An analysis of 42, gave—

Silica,	2.88
Alumina,	0.64
Peroxide of iron,	84.80
Water,	11.62
Sulphur,	0.12
	100.06

No. 44.—Galena, from Mr. Glenn's mine, Cole Camp creek. Two determinations of sulphur, gave—

	1	2
Sulphur,	13.76	13.86
Lead,	......	85.43

No. 45.—Brown Hematite, from half a mile west of Warsaw—

Sulphur,	1.05
Silica,	2.11
Peroxide of iron,	88.85
Alumina,	0.87
Water,	10.01
	102.89

A portion of the iron in this specimen was in combination with the sulphur, and hence the excess.

No. 46.—Brown Hematite, from a large deposit, near the mouth of Niangua—

Silica,	4.36
Peroxide of iron,	83.27
Alumina,	1.08
Water,	11.11
	99.82

This specimen contained neither phosphoric acid nor lime, but a trace of manganese.

The following specimens were collected by Dr. Shumard.

No. 47.—Magnesian limestone, of a light gray, silicious appearance, belonging to the beds of the 2d Magnesian Limestone, from near A. F. Evans', Franklin county, gave—

Silica,	6.77
Alumina, with a trace of iron,	0,97
Carbonate of lime,	49.64
Carbonate of magnesia,	42.05
	99.43

No. 48.—Limestone, obtained from one mile below Vancil's landing, Mississippi river, gave—

Silica,	28,26
Alumina, with peroxide of iron,	4.45
Carbonate of lime,	58,86
Carbonate of magnesia,	7.96
	99.53

The quantities given of the last specimen, are the mean of the analyses of two different portions. The silica, from the analyses of the two last specimens, was dissolved in hydrofluoric, to test its purity.

As yet, I have made no analysis of the mineral waters. The specimens of these sent by you did not come to hand until last month; since which date, I have been unable to find the time requisite for their analysis. All of which is respectfully submitted.

A. LITTON.

MR. MEEK'S REPORT,

ON

MONITEAU COUNTY.

PROF. G. C. SWALLOW,

State Geologist.

SIR: The following report is respectfully submitted as the result of that portion of my labors of the past season, not prosecuted under your immediate supervision, nor hitherto verbally or otherwise made known to you.

Moniteau county, as may be seen by reference to a map of Missouri, occupies a position almost exactly in the center of the State; being bounded on the east, by the Missouri river and Cole county; on the south, by Cole, Miller and Morgan counties; on the west, by Morgan and Cooper counties; and on the north, by Cooper county and the Missouri river. It embraces a superficial area of about four hundred square miles, and presents every variety of elevation, from that of the low alluvial bottoms of the Missouri, to the high prairie districts of the south and west, which rise to an altitude varying from three hundred and fifty, to near five hundred feet above the Missouri river.* In general terms, the face of the country may be characterized as broken and hilly, though there are districts of considerable extent, possessing an excellent soil, and only sufficiently undulating to secure good drainage, whilst even in the more hilly portions there is much good arable land, in the small valleys, and along the gentler slopes.

---

* Many of the Barometrical observations made, with a view of determining approximately, the elevation of the country, were carefully calculated by Mr. Warwick Hough, of Jefferson city.

I am also under many obligations to Prof. Geo. C. Pratt, Assistant Engineer of the Pacific Railroad, for a profile of the country along the line of that road through the county, from which much useful information was obtained, in regard to the elevation of the country.

The supply of good timber is ample, especially in the northern and eastern portions; and even in the prairie districts, there is timber along the small streams, sufficient for the wants of the country. The growth in the valleys, is principally oak, maple, hickory, ash, walnut, hackberry, buttonwood, poplar, &c. On the higher country, the forest is almost entirely composed of oak and hickory.

In the valleys, and along most of the streams, good springs are frequently met with, but on the higher part of the country, especially in the magnesian limestone districts, springs are not so common, consequently the inhabitants generally depend upon what are termed "cistern wells;" that is, wells of ordinary depth and construction, into which rain water is carried by spouts from the housetops. Owing to the retentive nature of the superficial deposits of the country, it is rarely found necessary to cement these reservoirs, to make them retain water; and they are always sunk to a sufficient depth to preserve it fresh and cool.

The principal streams in Moniteau county, are the Little Saline, Little and Big Splice creeks, Moniteau and Moreau creeks, and their tributaries. As the first of these runs through only a small portion of the northern extremity of the county, and the two following are but small streams, they need receive no especial notice here. The Moniteau, which is about thirty yards wide near its mouth, heads in Cooper county, and traverses the northern part of Moniteau county, in a direction a little south of east. It has a considerable fall, and affords water enough, excepting in very dry weather, to furnish some good sites for mills. The Moreau is about twice as large as the Moniteau. It heads in Cooper and Morgan counties, and flows through the southern part of Moniteau, in a south-east direction. It is a crooked stream, and has numerous large branches, which spread out in various directions. Some of these branches, as well as the main stream, have sufficient fall, and are large enough to furnish valuable water-power.

QUATERNARY DEPOSITS.

Of the quaternary, or modern formations, which you have, in your vertical section of the strata of the State, divided into *Alluvium*, *Bottom Prairie*, *Bluff*, or *Loess*, and *Drift*, I have recognized the first two in the alluvial bottoms of the Missouri, along the north-eastern part of the county.

The following section of the banks of the Missouri, taken near the mouth of a small stream, known by the name of "Splice Creek," conveys a very correct idea of these beds, as seen in this part of the county: —

No. 1. — Twelve to eighteen inches soil and yellow sand.

No. 2. — Eight inches dark vegetable mould and sand.

No. 3. — Three feet light yellowish sand, irregularly stratified.

No. 4. — Three feet ash-colored sand and clay, interstratified with seams and thin beds of dark gray clay, and vegetable mould.

No. 5. — Fifteen feet regularly-stratified, fine dark bluish gray clay, or marl, with logs and whole trees embedded.

The entire thickness of No. 5 is not known, as it passes downwards to an unknown depth below low-water mark. This bed is very rich in calcareous matter, and closely resembles, in color and composition, the dark marly clays of the Cretaceous formation, far up the Missouri, in Nebraska Territory, from which it was, doubtless, derived.

Over the higher portions of the county, after leaving the river bluffs, beds of red and yellow clay, sometimes nearly free from admixture of other materials, but more frequently mingled with fragments of chert, &c., are everywhere met with beneath the soil and sub-soil. These deposits vary from four or five, to fifteen or twenty feet in depth, and rest directly upon the rocks composing the solid frame-work of the country. By whatever agency they may have been deposited, it appears clearly manifest, the loose masses of chert and other materials contained in them, have not been transported from any very great distance, as they show little or no marks of attrition, and all belong to formations immediately beneath, or which are known from remaining outliers to have extended over the localities where we now find them. As these clays differ somewhat, in color and composition, from the Bluff deposit, as seen along the Missouri, and are, so far as my observations go, destitute of the shells and other organic remains found in that formation, where it is well marked, I am not quite satisfied they are the same.

In the northern part of the county, especially near the bluffs of the Missouri, the clays, previously referred to, are sometimes overlaid by a fine ash-colored, somewhat arenaceous deposit, which I suppose to be the same as the Bluff formation; this, however, was not seen south of the Moniteau.

Of Drift, unless some of our superficial deposits of clay may be referred to that agency, I am not sure we have any, as no boulders or beds of sand and water-worn pebbles were anywhere met with in the county. In one of the southern townships a few partly-worn fragments were occasionally seen; but, as they all belong to sedimentary rocks which occur in that part of the county, and were always found along ravines and branches, their slightly-worn appearance may be due to other causes.

Exclusive of the recent or quaternary deposits, the formations of Moniteau county may all be referred to the Carboniferous, Devonian, and Silurian epochs, though we have nothing like an unbroken series of the various rocks composing either.

CARBONIFEROUS SYSTEM.

Aside from the isolated bodies of coal so common in this region of country, the next rock in the descending order, after leaving the quaternary deposits, is that part of the Carboniferous system, called, by Dr. D. D. Owen, in his Report on the Geology of Wisconsin, Iowa, and Minnesota,

ENCRINITAL LIMESTONE.

This rock — whether considered with regard to its thickness, its economical value as an inexhaustible store of material for the manufacture of quick-lime, or with regard to its influence on the topography of the country — is by far the most important limestone in the county. As seen here, it is a coarse, semi-crystalline limestone, containing more or less cherty masses in the form of concretions. It is everywhere easily recognized, as well by its strongly-marked lithological characters, as by its many characteristic organic remains — being, indeed, almost wholly composed of columns and other parts of *Crinoidea*, broken and mingled together with a great profusion of corals, shells, &c. The lower part has usually a yellowish hue, and is generally not very compact, being little else than a mass of *Crinoidal* remains, with barely enough inorganic calcareous matter to cement them together, whilst the upper part is more compact, and has, for the most part, a lighter color.

In districts immediately underlaid by heavy beds of this formation, especially near the bluffs of streams, numerous "sink holes" are met with. They have, usually, the form of a broad inverted cone, and are not confined to the surface materials, but always terminate in a fissure or cavern in the rocks beneath. Many instances of this kind may be seen near the Missouri bluffs, north of Mount Vernon, where they have been mistaken for ancient mines. Exactly similar sinks occur in districts, underlaid by heavy beds of Lower Carboniferous Limestones, in Kentucky, Illinois, Indiana, Tennessee and Alabama, where they have no connection with metalliferous dêposits.

The fossils most frequently met with in this rock, in Moniteau county, were the following: viz., ·One or two species *Zaphrentis, Orthis Michelini, Spirifer cuspidatus, S. Burlingtonensis, S. striatus, Productus semireticulatus, P. punctatus*, two species of *Capulus*, and two large species of *Euomphalus.*

This formation enters Moniteau from Cooper county, and underlies all that portion of the county north of Moniteau creek, excepting along the borders of that and other streams, where it has been denuded away, so as to expose the lower rocks. It is seen, however, in greatest force along the Missouri river, near Mount Vernon, and for five or six miles below that village, where it composes most of the upper part of those bold mural precipices, which form such a conspicuous feature in the topography of that region.

In this part of the county, it varies in thickness, from forty or fifty, to one hundred and thirty feet, in proportion as it has been more or less worn away by the erosive action of atmospheric agencies. As it is quite probable, however, that some of the upper part was covered by the slope, at the place where it measured one hundred and thirty feet, its maximum thickness, in this county, may be set down as about one hundred and fifty feet. On following it southward, and south-westward, it is found to diminish rapidly in thickness, partly in consequence of the denudation of the upper surface, and, to some extent, in consequence of the thinning out of the lower beds; so that, by the time we reach the neighborhood of Moniteau creek, it is found to be, as previously stated, either entirely worn away, or crowning the summits of the highest elevations, and only maintaining a thickness of from twenty to forty feet.

South of the Moniteau it again makes its appearance in the form of numerous local patches and small outliers, which are seen at intervals, even to within a short distance of the southern limits of the county. Some of these may be so connected with larger bodies of the same formation in the surrounding counties, the Geology of which is unknown to me, as to be improperly called outliers.

Judging from numerous exposures seen along the tributaries of Moniteau and Moreau creeks, a considerable portion of the divide between the head-waters of those streams, in Town. 45, Rs. 16 and 17, is underlaid by this formation, varying from ten to fifty feet in thickness, which may be connected with larger bodies of this rock in Cooper and Morgan counties. At any rate, it was met with in Town. 45, R. 16, at the following localities: viz., In the edge of Cooper county, on Upper Brush creek, near Mount Pleasant Meeting House, where it is seen in a bluff, exposing a thickness of about fifty feet; and on the farm of Mr. Solomon Kemp, in Sec. 24, where a bed twelve feet in thickness rests upon one of the oldest rocks in the country. In R. 17, of same Township, it was seen on land owned by Judge Brookling, in Sec. 10, exposing about fifty feet in thickness. About three miles south of last locality, it was again observed, on a stream known as Willow Fork of the Moreau, where it forms a bluff thirty or forty feet in height. On the south side of the same branch, in south-west corner of Sec. 26, on land owned by Mr. Robert Price, it again crops out, exposing in a bluff, a thickness of twenty-two feet. Some sixteen feet of the lower part of this last exposure are composed of the lower yellow beds so frequently met with, north of the Moniteau, but which were not recognized at any other locality south of that stream.

With the above exceptions, this rock only exists in this county, south of the Moniteau, as local outliers of comparatively limited extent. To refer to all of these in detail, would be exceedingly tedious, and serve no useful purpose. I would, therefore, merely remark, that they are found at various elevations, and rest sometimes on one, and sometimes on another of the older rocks. In many instances, they are seen in the valleys, along slopes, and on the tops of hills and ridges, dipping into the earth, at various angles below the horizon, without regard to the general dip or inclination of the older rocks upon which they rest. An instance of this kind may be seen on the left side of the Moreau, in Sec. 23, Town. 45, R. 16, which will be better understood by reference to the following figure: —

Fig. 1.

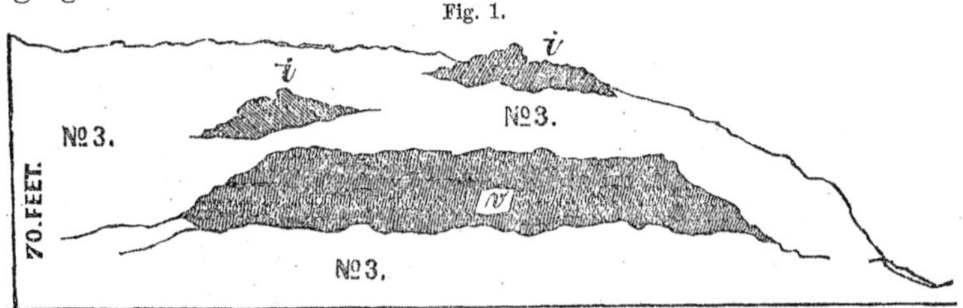

i i— represent huge masses of Encrinital Limestone, on the summit and slope of a ridge, seventy feet in height, plunging at different angles beneath the soil and loose chert, whilst undisturbed strata of magnesian limestone (*v*) are seen below. No. 3, 3, 3, represent slopes where no rocks are seen in place. Cases of this kind are so common, in this region, as to have attracted the attention of the people of the county, by whom these titled masses of limestone have been termed "Tumbling Rocks."

That these masses have not been thrown from their original horizontal position by forces, acting from beneath, is manifest from the undisturbed condition of the strata upon which they repose; consequently, their present anomalous condition must be due to some peculiarity of those denuding agencies, whatever they may have been, which have so strongly modified the physical features of the country.

CHEMUNG GROUP.

In the northern part of Moniteau, we have everywhere, immediately beneath Encrinital Limestone, the upper member of a series of rocks, apparently of the age of the Chemung Group of New York. Like the Encrinital Limestone, this upper member of the Chemung (Chouteau Limestone of the general section) is most extensively developed in the northern part of the county, along the Missouri river. Southward and south-westward, it diminishes in thickness, so that with, perhaps, only a few unimportant exceptions, it is met with on the south side of the Moniteau only, as outliers.

Along the Missouri, in the vicinity of Mount Vernon, it varies in thickness, from sixty to eighty feet, and forms a considerable portion of the lower part of the high bluffs seen near that place. Near the Moniteau, it is not generally well exposed, but is seen under circumstances indicating a thickness of from forty to fifty feet. South of the Moniteau, it is known to underlie the Encrinital Limestone mentioned as occurring in Sec. 25, Town. 46, R. 14, and is probably coextensive with that rock, thence into Cole county. Excepting at one other locality, on Willow Fork of the Moreau, some four miles from the county line on the west, and another in section 11 of same township and range, it was not met with south of the Moniteau, in this county. At the first of the latter two places, only a foot or two in thickness of the upper part is seen forming the bed of the creek, and passing beneath a bluff of Encrinital Limestone, previously referred to. As all the outliers of Encrinital Limestone seen south of the Moreau, appear to rest directly upon the older rocks, it is probably reduced here to a thickness of eight or ten feet.

Although there is everywhere a strongly-defined line of demarkation between this rock and the Encrinital Limestone, both as regards mineral and prevailing palæontological characters, the line separating its lower beds from the rocks beneath, is often so faint, in this county, as to be scarcely recognizable where no fossils are met with.

As seen in Moniteau county, the Chouteau Limestone usually presents the following characters: The upper part, perhaps about one-third of the whole formation, consists of a heavy-bedded, bluish gray, impure calcareous mass, with occasional concretionary bodies of calc spar embedded. This part of the formation is generally nearly destitute of organic remains; though in the upper part, near its junction with the Encrinital Limestone, we sometimes find a peculiar *Fucoid*, very nearly like the species so abundant in the *Cauda-galli* Grit, but perhaps more nearly related to some of those of the Hamilton and Chemung Groups of New York. The only other fossils found in it, were a *Crinoid*, a reticulated coral, and a small *Turbo-like Gasteropod.*

The lower beds are generally distinct enough from the upper though sometimes, near their junction, they alternate, and at others, shade almost imperceptibly into each other. In composition, color and other characters, the lower beds present a considerable variety, but are generally hard, compact limestones, of a gray or bluish gray color. For the most part, they are in rather thin layers; and, where much exposed, show a disposition to split into thin shelly pieces; though, at some places, the layers run together and form more massive beds.

Of all the rocks in this county, these lower beds of Chouteau Limestone are perhaps the most interesting to the Palæontologist; for, although not generally so highly charged with organic remains as portions of the Encrinital Limestone, their fossils are usually found in a better state of preservation. The species most frequently met with, were the same as those referred and named as follows by Dr. Shumard: *Orthis resupinata* (*Martin*), *Productus Murchisonianus?* (*Kon.*), *P. subaculeatus* (*Murch.*), *Spirifer striatus?* (*Martin*), *Rhynconella gregaria* (*Shumard*), *R. obscuraplicata* (*Shumard*), *Terebratula Fusiformis* (*Murch. and Vern.*), *and Avicula Cooperensis* (*Shumard*), together with a considerable variety of *Nuculas*, *Pectas*, *Avicula*, and other *Acephala*, closely allied to, if not identical with, Hamilton and Chemung species. I also found in these beds, at some localities, a peculiar *Canda-galli-like Fucoid*, apparently identical with that in the upper bed.

The best locality for the fossils of this rock, seen in the county, is at Mount Vernon, where I collected specimens of nearly all the species usually found in it, together with some new species not hitherto met with. As they, together with those collected from other rocks, will be thoroughly studied by Dr. Shumard, the able Palæontologist of the Survey, it would be going out of my province to attempt to characterize them here.

The stratigraphical position of this and the other two members of the same series (Lithographic Limestone and Vermicular Sandstone*), with relation to other well-marked geological horizons below them, taken in connection with their organic remains, leaves little room to doubt that they represent the Chemung Group of New York; though, as in the case with the Chemung in eastern New York, they also contain some Hamilton forms.

DEVONIAN SYSTEM.†

UPPER HELDERBURG—ONONDAGA LIMESTONE.

Immediately beneath the Chouteau Limestone, at some localities in Moniteau county, we have two rocks, which, although quite distinct in their mineral characters, evidently belong, judging from their organic remains, to the same group.

The upper of these two rocks consists of from ten to forty feet in thickness, of gray or bluish gray limestone, in layers and beds, which shade off upwards into the lower part of the Chouteau Limestone, in such a manner that it is not always easy, where fossils are not found, to say where the one ends, and the other begins. It is, however, generally more crystalline than the Chouteau Limestone.

These upper beds were only recognized in the bluffs along the Missouri river, though they may exist at other localities in the county, as it would be very difficult to distinguish them from the lower beds of the Chouteau Limestone, where fossils are not found. These beds were first observed in a bluff, a short distance above the mouth of Splice creek, near the residence of a gentleman, by the name of Shields, where they present a thickness of about thirty feet. The following is a natural section of the rocks seen at this place, and shows the relations between the beds under consideration, and the other rocks with which they are associated.

---

* Not represented in this county.

† I am far from considering it a settled question that we should not carry up the Devonian so as to take in the Chouteau Limestone. It is true, by so doing, we would include, along with many Devonian forms, a few, apparently identical with species hitherto regarded as peculiar to the Carboniferous system. Not so many, however, as there are of Carboniferous forms in the Hamilton and Chemung groups of New York, both of which are considered by Murchison and Vernenil as Devonian. After all, it must be admitted that in this country, where we have a complete series of the Palaeozoic rock, the limits of the Devonian system, both upwards and downwards, are not so strongly marked as would appear to be the case in the old world.

Fig. 2.

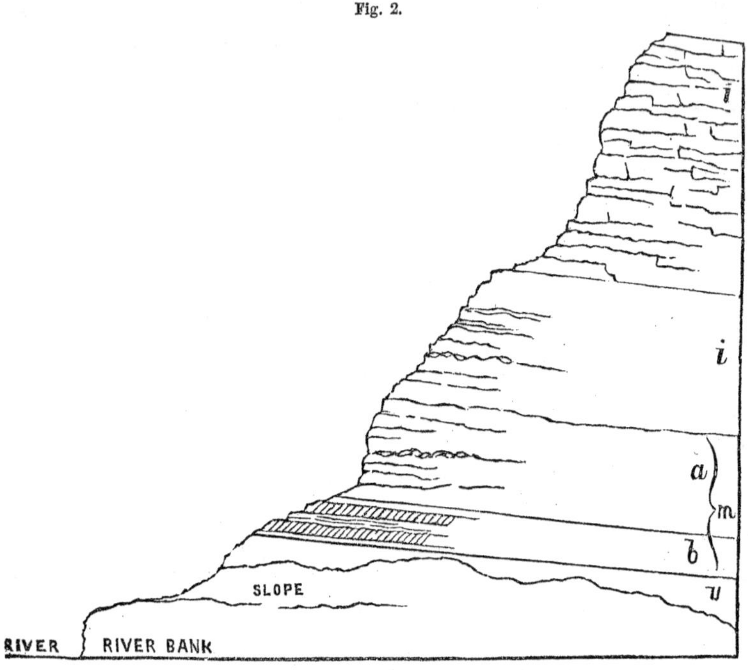

i—represents the Encrinital Limestone, eighty feet in thickness; *j*—the Chouteau Limestone; *m a* —some thirty feet of the beds above referred to; and *m b*—some eight feet in thickness of the lower member of the same group; *u*—is a bed of sandstone, hereafter to be mentioned.

At another locality, two miles and a half farther down the river, these upper beds are again seen in a bluff, beneath the Chouteau Limestone, and resting directly upon the 2d Magnesian Limestone, where they appear to be only ten feet in thickness. Some three-quarters of a mile lower down the river, the same beds are again seen holding the same position with relation to the Chouteau Limestone, but resting upon the Saccharoidal Sandstone, and presenting a thickness of twenty feet.

The most common fossils in these beds are the following: — One or more species of *Cyathophyllum*, *Favosites polymorpha*, *Terebratula reticularis*, an elongated *Brachiopod* of the type of *Pentamerus elongatus* of the Onondaga Limestone (New York), a small species of *Pentamerus* related to *P. galeatus*, but, perhaps, more closely allied to forms in the Onondaga and Corniferous Limestones, a *Leptaena* or *Strophodonta*, two species of *Spirifer*, and fragments of Trilobites.

Below the above-mentioned beds, we have at some places in Moniteau county, the lower member of the same group. This rock varies much in its composition, being at some places an arenaceous limestone, and at others a calcareous sandstone, and I even suspect it passes, in some instances, into a pure quartzose sandstone.

This formation was only met with at the following localities:— First, in a bluff on the Missouri, already referred to. (See *a b* of fig. 2.) At this place, it is a calcareous sandstone, whilst at another point, only a short distance along the same outcrop, it passes into layers of arenaceous limestone, containing its usual fossils, and alternating with beds of obliquely-laminated sandstone. It also occurs in the bed of a small branch of Little Splice creek, some mile and a quarter south of the above locality, where it is more calcareous, and contains many fossils, of a few species.

On the north side of the Moniteau, it was again seen at Mr. William Routon's place, in Sec. 27, Town. 46, R. 14. Here is only exposed about eight feet at the base of a hill, and it is made up of coarse, partly-rounded grains of quartz, cemented with calcareous matter.

The only organic remains seen in this part of the group were *Terebratula reticularis*, an *Orthis* like *O. resupinata*, a plicated *Spirifer* rather under medium size, and a small smooth *Spirifer*.*

LOWER SILURIAN STRATA.

The rocks in Moniteau county, referable to this epoch, appear to be the same as your Saccharoidal Sandstone, and 2d Magnesian Limestone. I would just here remark, however, that there is more difficulty and uncertainty in identifying the various members of the great series of magnesian limestones and sandstones, lying at the base of our palaeozoic rocks, than is met with in any of our other formations.

SACCHAROIDAL SANDSTONE.

The rock I have supposed to be identical with the above, is, everywhere in Moniteau, excepting in a few instances where it is very thin, a heavy-bedded more or less friable sandstone. It is usually

---

* This formation, and the last-mentioned beds, taken together, contain an assemblage of organic forms, limited in their range in the New York system to the Upper Helderburg group. (Corniferous and Onondaga Limestones, and Schoharie Grit.) This fact, together with their position above the Cape Girardeau limestone, which appears to represent the upper part of the Lower Helderburg group, fixes very definitely their position near the base of our Devonian rocks in the West. The Oriskany Sandstone, and, perhaps (as a distinct mass), the Cauda-galli Grit, having no representatives in the West.

indistinctly stratified, and varies in its color, from nearly a pure white, through various shades of yellow, to a kind of dusky brown. The darker colors being usually confined to, or near the weathered surfaces, whilst the interior, beyond the influence of atmospheric agencies, is lighter. Where it has nearly thinned out, it is more distinctly stratified, becomes harder, and is usually brown or brownish red. Sometimes it contains enough calcareous matter to cause feeble effervescence when acids are dropped upon it.

This rock appears to exist beneath the previously-mentioned formations, in nearly all the county north of Moniteau creek. South of the Moniteau, it is known to occur beneath the same formations, as far as they extend between the Little Moniteau and the eastern boundary of the county. From numerous exposures seen in the edge of Cooper county, along the head branches of Moniteau, it also appears to exist beneath the Chouteau and Encrinital Limestones, in portions of Town. 45, R. 16 and 17. As outliers, it is frequently met with over all that part of the county south of the Moniteau, where the 2d Magnesian Limestone forms the surface rock.

It was first seen in the northern part of the country on the Missouri river, in Town. 47, R. 14, at a locality previously referred to (see *u* of fig. 2), where, at an elevation of some twenty feet above the river, twelve or thirteen feet of its upper part is exposed beneath the Upper Helderburg limestone. To the south-west, owing to the general dip of the strata towards the north-east, it may be seen along the Moniteau, near the mouth of Howard's creek, at an elevation of nearly one hundred feet above the Missouri. South of the Moniteau, outliers of it are met with along near the eastern boundary of the county, in Town. 45, R. 14, as much as three hundred and fifty feet above the river; and at California, nearly four hundred feet above the same horizon.*

2D MAGNESIAN LIMESTONE.

As seen in this county, this formation presents a great diversity of appearances, not only in the thickness and arrangement of its layers, but in their color and composition. As a general thing it is distinctly, and for the most part thinly stratified; though some of the lower portions, seen on the Moreau, are more compact and heavy bedded. In color, it varies from a very light drab, through various shades of yellowish and bluish tints, to a light gray. In composition, some of the layers and beds appear to be a pure fine-grained, or compact magnesian limestone, whilst others contain a large proportion of silicious matter, both in the form of embedded angular fragments and concretions of flint, as well as in fine particles generally dissemi-

---

* With one exception, no organic remains were found in this rock, although careful search was made for them at numerous places. The exception alluded to, was in Sec. 29, Town. 46, R. 14, where masses of it are seen near the Moniteau, on the summit of a hill, at an elevation of some ninety feet above the creek. At this place, it is a little more distinctly stratified than usual, and contains occasional partly-worn fragments of flinty matter, along with a few dark silicious concretionary masses. On breaking open the latter, I found a few casts of small univalves, apparently of the genus *Murchisonia*, and a few impressions of small *Crinoid* columns.

nated through the whole mass. Alternating with these, there are often thin seams of bluish argillaceous matter, and sometimes, though rarely, we meet with thin layers and beds of sandstone. In a few instances, near the upper part, thin layers of very hard compact sandstone passing into a quartzite, were seen alternating with the other beds.

Some of the beds have a fragmentary structure, as though partly composed of broken-up materials of similar strata elsewhere, whilst others have a confused appearance, as though the layers had been bent and broken while in a yielding condition. Large concretionary masses are sometimes seen in some of the beds, around which the layers of the bed are variously bent and twisted, whilst those of the beds immediately above and below remain undisturbed.

In the more impure and porous layers and beds, as well as in the cherty masses embedded in them, the oolitic structure is often observed. Even in the most compact flinty masses, when a fresh fracture is examined with a magnifier, oolitic particles can be seen embedded in the translucent base; and on weathered surfaces, they often present beautiful examples of this structure in relief. Sometimes, these concretions, when broken, present an Agate-like structure, being composed of concentric layers or coats of various colors.

The upper part of the formation generally consists of the light drab-colored, fine-grained varieties of magnesian limestone, known amongst the country people by the appropriate local name of "Cotton Rock." The surfaces of these layers are almost always covered with *Fucoids*, very like those of the Calciferous Sandrock of New York. Sometimes, beds of considerable thickness are made up entirely of layers of these "Cotton Rocks," while, in other instances, they alternate with other varieties of magnesian limestone.

The lower part of the formation consists of the coarser varieties of magnesian limestone, which are usually in thicker beds, and sometimes alternate with sandy limestone, which often contain enough calcareous matter to make tolerably good lime.

Owing to the fact, that it is very difficult to identify the same beds at different localities, it is almost impossible to form any very correct estimate of the thickness of a formation like this, where no connected sections of all the beds are to be seen. Exposures seen in Cooper county, however, seem to indicate a thickness of from 160 or 170, to 200 feet, for this rock in this region.*

---

* The position below the Black-river and Birds-eye limestone of the entire series of magnesian limestones and sandstones to which this belongs, taken in connection with their organic remains and lithological characters, leaves little room to doubt that we have in them a representation of the Calciferous, and, perhaps, portions of the Chazy limestones of New York, and that they belong to the same epoch as Dr. Owens' Lower Magnesian Limestone of Iowa and Wisconsin. The Potsdam sandstone (F. No. 1, of Dr. Owen) will, doubtless, yet be found in Missouri at the base of this series.

The first exposure of this formation met with, on coming southward from the point where our explorations commenced at the northern extremity of the county, was on Splice creek, near the Missouri, where some forty feet of the upper beds are exposed along a slope beneath the Saccharoidal Sandstone, the base of the exposure being nearly on a level with the Missouri. About two miles a little north of west from this, on the same creek, it is again seen presenting the following section: —

No. 1. — Ten feet yellow porous magnesian limestone, made up of imperfectly formed oolitic particles.*

No. 2. — Eight feet slope — no rock seen.

No. 3 — Ten feet slope, with ledges of hard gray magnesian limestone, showing oolitic structure, exposed near the upper part.

No. 4. — Eight feet thin layers white magnesian limestone.

No. 5. — One foot hard sandy rock, passing into quartzite.

About four miles east of the above locality, this rock is seen in a bluff, near the Missouri, where it is immediately overlaid by the beds previously mentioned as occupying a position between the upper Helderburg and Chouteau Limestones. It would seem that the upper Helderburg Limestone, and Saccharoidal Sandstone, are wanting at this place.

Along the Moniteau, this formation is seen at numerous places beneath the other rocks, from thirty to eighty feet of the upper beds being exposed above the level of the creek. At one locality, not far from the mouth of Howard's creek, and near the residence of a gentleman by the name of Jesse Longan, I found, in one of the upper beds, several specimens of *Euomphalus*, and one of *Murchisonia*, of different species from those found at the locality previously mentioned.

The following section, taken on the North Moreau, near the eastern line of the county, will convey some idea of the nature of the lower beds, as seen along that stream: —

No. 1. — Twenty feet whitish magnesian limestone, "Cotton Rock."

No. 2. — Seven feet rough sandy magnesian limestone.

No. 3. — Seven feet same as No. 2, but in thinner layers.

No. 4. — Forty-five feet very hard sandy magnesian limestone† in heavy beds.

No. 5. — Ten feet very hard sandy layers, containing calcareous matter enough to make good lime.

On the South Moreau, near the south-east corner of the county, some beds were seen, which are, doubtless, the oldest rocks met with in the county; and I am by no means satisfied they may not even belong to the 3d magnesian limestone.

The section given below, from an exposure near the residence of Mr. Robert Morris, shows the nature of these beds.

No. 1. — Ten feet coarse breccia, composed of fragments of oolitic flint or hornstone and sand, firmly cemented with siliceous matter.

No. 2. — Twenty-eight inches hard sandstone, with white oolitic particles embedded.

No. 3. — Five feet breccia, like No. 1.

No. 4. — Five feet slope, no rocks seen.

No. 5. — Five feet rough, sandy, somewhat oolitic magnesian limestone.

---

* Here I collected some very interesting fossils, consisting of the following genera of Gasteropoda: viz., *Euomphalus*, *Murchisonia*, and *Pleurotomaria*.

† In the upper part of this stratum, a few specimens of a small species of *Euomphalus* were found. Owing to the oolitic structure of the material in which they occur, they are somewhat obscure, but appear to be closely allied to a species I have seen associated with *Ophileta levata* (*Vanuxem*), in the cherty portions of the "Lower Magnesian Limestone" of Dr. Owen, near Lake Pepin, in Minnesota; now, I believe, generally considered a western equivalent of the Calciferous Sandrock of the New York System.

Higher up the South Moreau, in Sec. 32, Town. 43, R. 15, an exposure of the same beds seen on the North Moreau (see section on page 108), near where it passes out of the eastern part of the county, were met with, in which two parallel vein-like masses eighteen, inches in thickness, of pure friable sandstone were seen cutting obliquely upwards through the beds, in all respects like dikes. In each instance, the beds on one side were thrown down about four feet. These were, doubtless, at first, fissures, which have by some means been filled by sand.

ECONOMICAL GEOLOGY.

SOIL.

The richest soil in the county, as might be expected, is to be found in the alluvial bottoms of the Missouri, along the north-eastern part of the county, and in the valleys of the Moniteau and Moreau, and their branches. There is, also, some very good land in the valley of Splice Creek, and a few other smaller streams. These bottom lands are, perhaps, not surpassed in fertility by those of any other part of the State — the soil being a rich, black, vegetable mould, which produces luxuriant crops of almost every kind usually cultivated in this latitude.

On the higher country, the soil is neither so rich nor so deep as in the valleys, though a considerable portion of the more elevated districts of the county may be ranked amongst the best quality of up-lands — the soil being a light loam, with a fair proportion of organic matter.*

The largest bodies of good, rich, arable land, are to be found in Town. 45, R. 15, 16 and 17, and Town. 44, R. 16 and 17, which contain much beautiful prairie. Town. 43, R. 15, and that portion of R. 16, in this county, contains much elevated, undulating prairie land, of fair quality, but not equal to that further north-west. The other townships are more or less broken and hilly; but the slopes are generally gentle, so that a considerable portion of the most broken districts is susceptible of cultivation; and the little valleys and slopes furnish much fine farming land.

It is almost always the case that northern slopes possess the richest and deepest soil; whilst those facing the south, have a thinner soil, and are often covered with loose masses of chert.

Wheat, I was informed, is an uncertain crop on prairie land in this part of the country, though the timber land produces excellent crops. Indian corn, oats, potatoes — in short, nearly all the various kinds of crops usually grown in this part of the State, excepting wheat and tobacco, do well on the prairies, and even tobacco would grow finely, but it is not cultivated, in consequence of its liability to be torn by the winds. I was informed, however, by an intelligent farmer who had made the experiment, that by planting alternate belts of corn and tobacco across his fields, at right angles to the course of the prevailing winds, he had raised good crops of both — the corn being tall enough to protect the tobacco from the force of the winds.

---

* Specimens of all the different varieties of soils in the county were collected for analysis.

BUILDING STONES.

No portion of the State is better supplied with rocks, for almost every kind of building purpose, than this. North of the Moniteau, the Encrinital Limestone, and the upper part of the Chouteau Limestone, are most generally used for these purposes. The Encrinital Limestone answers very well for all ordinary building purposes; but its coarse, semi-crystalline structure, and numerous suture joints, render much of it unfit for the finer kinds of masonry, especially where large blocks are required. The upper part of the Chouteau Limestone, where it is not in too heavy beds, is well adapted to almost all kinds of building purposes, excepting the construction of back walls and jambs of fire-places, for which it is unfit, in consequence of its liability to crack when heated.

Of all the various kinds of rocks found in this county, our magnesian limestones, especially those beds generally termed "Cotton Rock," furnish the most beautiful building material; and, should experience prove them to be durable, they will, doubtless, become the favorite rock for the construction of much of the better kinds of masonry. Their handsome light drab color would contrast beautifully with the green foliage of trees and shrubbery, whilst the facility with which they can be dressed into blocks of uniform size, would render them a very desirable material for such purposes.

I saw some handsome tombstones, made of this rock, by a stone-cutter at High Point, from which it would appear some of the more compact layers are well adapted to many ornamental purposes.

FIRE-STONES.

For the construction of back walls and jambs of common fire-places, the Encrinital Limestone, and many of our magnesian limestones, furnish a very good material. Some of the more porous and sandy beds of the latter, would, probably, answer very well for many kinds of furnaces where a much higher temperature is required, as they appear to have the composition and structure of some of the most refractory fire-stones. For purposes of this kind, selections should always be made from such beds as are entirely free from fragments of chert, as the presence of this subtance causes these rocks to break when heated. The "Cotton Rock," and other purer and more compact magnesian limestones, should never be used in this way, as they are wholly unfit for such purposes.

LIMESTONES, FOR LIME.

The upper whitish beds of Encrinital Limestone are more generally used for, and are perhaps better adapted to, this purpose than any other rock in the county. Some portions of the middle and lower beds of the Chouteau Limestone would make very good lime; but owing to the fact that they are, for the most part, overlaid by heavy beds of Encrinital Limestone, which is more accessible, they are not so much used. North of the Moniteau, and in some parts of the county south of that stream, the Encrinital Limestone is, of course, an inexhaustible source of material for this purpose. Numerous outliers of Encrinital Limestone will furnish an abundance in other parts of the county.

Some of the more calcareous of the lower sandy beds of magnesian limestones make good lime, and, at the same time, contain so much silicious matter as to require the addition of but a small proportion of sand in making mortar. In the manufacture of quick lime, however, to be applied as a fertilizer upon exhausted lands, they should be used with caution, as it is probable they contain so much magnesia as to be unfit for such purposes.

SAND, FOR MAKING MORTAR, &c.

In the north-eastern part of the county, the sand-bars of the Missouri river will always furnish a very pure sand for purposes of this kind; whilst in other districts, farther south-west, beds of Saccharoidal Sandstone are always to be found at convenient distances, and afford an abundant supply of good sand.

HYDRAULIC LIMESTONE.

There is little doubt that some of our various beds of magnesian limestones, and the upper Chouteau rocks, will furnish good materials for this purpose.

MILL-STONES.

Some of the beds of silicious breccia, previously referred to in the south-eastern corner of the county, I was informed, have furnished very good mill-stones. Judging from their extreme hardness, and cellular structure, it seems quite probable they would answer very well for such purpose.

MATERIALS, FOR THE CONSTRUCTION OF ROADS.

Of limestones, such as are frequently used in the construction of macadamized roads, there is an abundant supply, especially in the northern parts of the county. It is well known, however, that materials of this nature are so soft as to be soon crushed to powder, on roads much traveled. The purer kinds of flint, although exceedingly hard, are also, from their extreme brittleness, liable under such circumstances to be reduced to small fragments, and consequently soon worn out; so that the harder varieties of igneous rocks, possessing hornblende or other tough minerals in their composition, are generally preferred, where they can be had, for such purposes.

In passing through portions of Moniteau county, where great quantities of the impure varities of flint, we usually term *chert*, especially such as have been derived from our magnesian limestones, are strewed over the surface, I have always observed the roads at such places are exceedingly hard and firm, from which it seems probable this material may possess the requisite degree of toughness to make excellent roads. If so, its abundance will, doubtless, some day, bring it into general use for this purpose.

CLAYS, FOR THE MANUFACTURE OF BRICKS, &c.

As previously stated, when speaking of the surface deposits of the country, there are over all the higher portions of the county beneath the soil and sub-soil, beds of reddish and other colored clays, from ten to twenty feet in depth. These, where due care is taken to select such portions as are free from small fragments of chert, have been found, in the few instances where they have been tried, to make a very good article of bricks.

At a few places, beds of very pure light blue pipe-clay were seen beneath the other beds. The extent of these is not known, as they were only seen where wells and mining pits have been sunk. As a general thing, they appear to be associated with outliers of coal, and rest directly upon the surface rocks of the country. A bed of this kind, near Mr. T. Blackburn's place, in Sec. 24, Town. 43, R. 15, would probably answer a very good purpose for the manufacture of pottery.

COAL.

This highly-important mineral has been found in various parts of the county, and, doubtless, exists in sufficient quantities for the supply of all ordinary home consumption, for a long time to come. It is, nevertheless, a matter of some importance to the people of the county, that the nature of the coal-beds so frequently met with here, and their relations to the other formations of the country, should be rightly understood; as every one must know, over estimates of the value and extent of mineral deposits, have been more frequently the cause of loss to those interested, than anything else connected with mining operations.

Most observing persons who have frequented coal regions are aware of the fact, that beds of coal which crop out in valleys, and along slopes, where there are no considerable disturbances of the strata, usually extend horizontally beneath large areas of country. As general, however, as this law is, it is by no means applicable to the district under consideration; for instead of being spread out in continuous beds, as is usually the case, the coal of this county is found in widely-separated masses, which, although often of great thickness, are always very limited in their horizontal extent, being in every instance confined to shallow depression in the lower Carboniferous, and even Lower Silurian rocks. It is manifest these depressions must have been worn in the older rocks, previous to the depositions of the Coal Measures; though, in many instances, they appear to have been subsequently widened and deepened, in such a manner as to partly undermine the coal, and cause it to fall, or slide from its original horizontal position.

The first coal mine examined in the county, during the survey, is situated between two and three miles north-west of Jamestown, in Sec. 1, Town. 46, R. 15, on land owned by Mr. John Robertson. The mine is located partly in a small ravine on a north-eastern slope, some eighty or ninety feet below the summit level of the surrounding country, and near a small branch of Howard's creek. The ravine seems to be cut entirely through the coal, leaving only a small portion on the right hand, or south-east side; whilst the heavier body, on the other side, owing to the fact, that the bed dips some seven or eight degrees to the west or north-west, is, for the most part, below the level of the ravine, and has been opened by vertical shafts on that side, instead of drifting in from the ravine at a lower level.

Owing to the fact, that this coal seems to dip into the side of the hill so much below the summit of the country, one would naturally suppose a large portion of this hill must be composed of coal-bearing strata; yet numerous exposures show that not only this, but all the surrounding hills, from near their base up many feet above the level of the mine, consist of undisturbed strata of Encrinital Limestone.

The main bed of coal here varies much in thickness, in consequence of the irregularity of the floor upon which it rests; but, as near as could be ascertained, it appears to average about eight feet. As the coal and its accompanying beds of shale are not well exposed, no good section could be seen; though I was informed by a miner, who sunk several of the shafts, that there are one or two thinner beds of coal alternating with the shale above the main bed.

The eight-foot bed they are now working, rests directly upon irregular beds or heaps of chert, such as are now seen strewed over the surrounding hills. It does not, however, look as though originally deposited upon this floor, but is everywhere crushed and distorted near the chert, as if the latter had been violently forced up into it by some power acting from beneath; so that the coal appears to be much fractured, and often presents those peculiar polished surfaces, frequently seen in rocks which have been subjected to some kind of motion amongst themselves, while under powerful pressure.

This coal appears to be a fair quality of the common bituminous variety, and burns freely, though without producing as much flame as many of our western coals, and, I am told, is well adapted to blacksmiths' use. Its specific gravity appears to be rather less than an average, from which it seems probable it does not contain a large per cent. of ash. Some *pyrites* was seen in the bed; but as it usually occurs in isolated lumps and seams, which are easily separated as the coal is dug out, it is comparatively free from this impurity as sold to steamboats at the river. It is very much inclined to crumble in handling, so that the loss in moving it from place to place must be considerable.

There can be no doubt that this coal is an outlier, that has slidden down from a higher position, in consequence of some undermining process, connected with the denudation of the surface of the country.

Coal has, also, been found near the head of Upper Brush Creek, in Sec. 6, Town. 46, R. 15, on land belonging to Mr. L. L. Wood. This mine has been opened by three or four vertical shafts sunk in a ravine, near the base of a south or south-east slope, more than one hundred feet below the summit of the country. At the time this mine was examined, the openings were partly filled with water and loose earth, so that the coal could not be seen. Heaps of dark, shaly matter, and some decomposing coal, were lying about the mine, but no specimens from which anything could be learned in regard to the quality of the coal were seen. Amongst the loose materials about the mine, I found several fragments of the sulphurets of lead and zinc.

Judging from the few unsatisfactory exposures seen near this mine, the coal here rests in a depression in the Saccharoidal Sandstone, or the subjacent magnesian limestone; consequently, there is no probability that it passes beneath any of the strata of the surrounding hills.

From Mr. Wood, the proprietor, I learned that some 20,000 bushels of coal have been raised here, and that the bed is about nine feet in thickness. He, also, stated that it dips to the south, at an angle of four or five degrees, and that the fragments of lead and zinc, seen by me at the mine, were derived from veins of these ores in the coal.*

Some two miles a little south of east from the above locality, on land owned by Mr. John Jones, another coal-bed has been opened, near an outlier of Encrinital Limestone. The pits being all filled with water, the coal could not be examined in place, but some of it was seen near the mine, from which it would appear to be a compact variety, approaching cannel-coal, and of very good quality.

I was informed by Mr. John C. Balay, who assisted in opening this mine, that some twelve or fourteen inches in thickness of black slate overlies the coal-bed, which is fifteen feet in thickness; and that, after passing through the coal, they struck a bed of white clay, containing masses of chert. He, also, stated that the coal dips as much as 10° to the east.

It is probable, that this coal-bed rests either upon an outlier of Encrinital Limestone, or undisturbed strata of magnesian limestone.

In Sec. 26, Town. 45, R. 17, coal has been found in the Willow Fork of the Moreau. The coal here rests upon Encrinital Limestone, in the bottom of a valley, whilst in the hills on each side, undisturbed beds of the same rock are seen as much as forty or fifty feet above the coal. The mine has been opened directly in the bed of the branch, where the coal has been penetrated some four or five feet, without passing through it. In the bank of the little creek, a short distance above the opening, a bed some four or five feet in thickness, composed of thin layers of sandstone, is seen over-

* I saw thin, vein-like bodies of these ores cutting through a bed of cannel-coal, in an adjoining county.

lying the coal, whilst only eight or ten feet below the opening, the bottom of the creek is composed of horizontal layers of Encrinital Limestone. Both the sandstone and coal dip seven or eight degrees, a little north of west.

At the time this mine was visited, the pit or opening was partly filled with water, so that only three feet of the coal could be seen. It appears to consist of alternate layers of pure cannel-coal and black bituminous slaty matter, in about equal proportions. Below this, I was informed, a bed of common bituminous coal was struck, and penetrated one or two feet.

In the black shaly matter about this mine, some beautiful impressions of *Lepidodendron* and other coal plants were seen; but, owing to the crumbling condition of the shale, it was impossible to preserve specimens.

Some three or four hundred yards a little south of east from the above locality, on the summit of a hill composed of Encrinital Limestone, at an elevation of forty or fifty feet above the coal-mine, dark bituminous shale and a little coal have been dug out, on Mr. Benjamin Gilbert's land.

The following section will show the relation these beds of coal and shale bear to the Encrinital Limestone, on which they rest, and to the surface deposits of the country: —

Fig. 3.

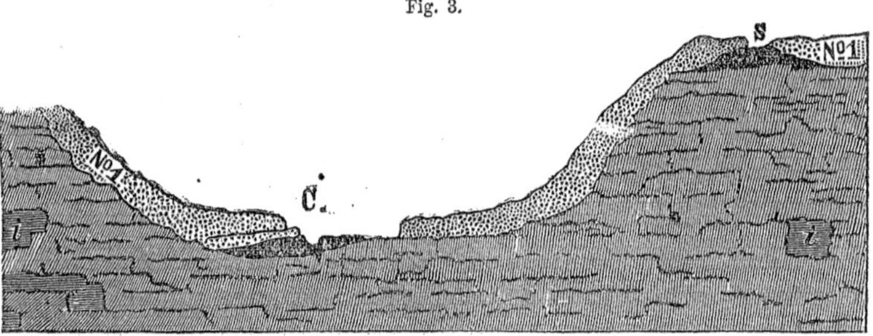

No. 1—represents the superficial deposits; *i i*—the Encrinital Limestone; *s*—the shale and coal on the hill; and *c*—the coal and sandstone in the valley.

On one of the small tributaries of the Moreau, in Sec. 24, Town. 44, R. 15, a coal-bed has been opened, which rests directly upon the 2nd Magnesian Limestone. The opening has been made at the base of a bluff, about fifteen feet in height, which is composed of "Cotton Rock." I did not see the coal in place, in consequence of the pit being partly filled with loose materials; but one of the gentlemen who opened the bed informed me it was penetrated about five feet, without passing through it; also, that the coal dips at a high angle to the east, or towards the bluff.

The specimens obtained here are impure cannel-coal, which burns freely, with a yellow flame, giving off at the same time a considerable quantity of black smoke, and leaving a large amount of ash. Portions of the magnesian limestone composing the bluff, at the base of which the coal is found, have fallen or slidden, so as to present the appearance of dipping down over the coal. In consequence of this disturbance, some of the coal has been subjected to so much pressure, that fragments of the magnesian limestone and chert have been forced into it.

A bed of impure cannel-coal has been discovered at a locality about two miles west of High-Point Lead Mine. It is situated in a valley, seventy or eighty feet below the highest portions of the surrounding country; whilst the hills on each side, are known to be composed of undisturbed strata of magnesian limestone, as much as forty or fifty feet above it.

The thickness of this bed is unknown, as it has been penetrated by a shaft to a depth of fifteen feet, without passing through it. No shale or fire-clay was seen, the coal being immediately overlaid by the usual surface materials of the country. It ends abruptly against loose materials at the west side, and dips gently towards the east. Its exact extent in other directions is unknown, though it is certainly circumscribed by the limits of the little valley in which it is found.

The following is a section across this valley, showing the coal, *c*, resting upon the 2d Magnesian Limestone, *v v*, and overlaid by the Quaternary Deposits, *No.* 1.

Fig 4.

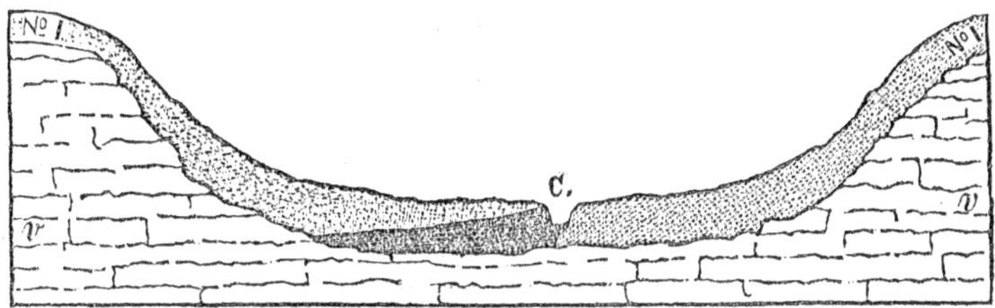

Coal will, doubtless, be found at other places in the county, as several openings have been made at other localities, where more or less dark shaly matter was found. If there is any coal at these localities, it certainly exists under circumstances, in all respects, like those already mentioned.

IRON ORE.

Loose masses of iron ore are occasionally seen amongst the chert and other rocks, scattered over the surface of the country, in various parts of the county. It was only seen at one locality, however, under circumstances indicating beds of even limited extent. This was in Sec. 34, Town. 46, R. 16, where irregular beds are seen along a slope, near Lower Brush Creek, composed of rugged cellular masses of the *Peroxide* of Iron. It would be difficult to come to any very definite conclusion in regard to the quantity of ore contained in an irregular deposit like this, but it appears to be of limited extent.

LEAD.

Lead ore has been found, at numerous localities, over all those portions of the county where magnesian limestone forms the surface rock. It is more frequently met with as loose fragments, such as miners term "Float Mineral," mingled with the surface deposits, than otherwise, though it is often found filling cavities, fissures, joints, &c., in the magnesian limestone, in the form of isolated masses or various vein-like expansions. In most cases, the cavities around the ore are filled with nothing but tough red clay, though sulphate of baryta (known amongst the miners by the name of "tiff") is often associated with it; and, sometimes, though rarely, calc spar and sulphate of zinc, in small quantities, are found in the same cavities.

The first mine, or lead locality, examined in the county, is in Sec. 24, Town. 47, R. 15, near a small branch of Howard's Creek. The ore was found amongst loose chert, on a slope some seventy feet below the summit of the country. As strata of Encrinital Limestone crop out of the slope below the openings, the lead must have been originally derived from that, or some of the newer rocks. No vein was discovered; and the probability is, only loose fragments of "Float Mineral" exist here. Much sulphate of baryta was, also, found amongst the loose chert. This is the only instance known to me where lead ore has been found in this county, in any position above the magnesian limestone.

In Sec. 25, Town. 46, R. 15, lead ore has been found on the land of Mr. Dickson. Some five or six openings have been made here, varying from three to ten feet in depth. Magnesian limestone was struck in some of the shafts, and penetrated a foot or two, but I could not ascertain whether any ore was found in this rock. I saw some sulphuret of lead about the mine, and many fragments of sulphate of baryta, both of which were probably found in the surface clay. "Float Mineral" has been found at numerous localities in this neighborhood.

In Sec. 5, Town. 45, R. 14, a lead mine has been found on the property of Judge James English and Mr. Powell. Some four or five shafts have been sunk here, on a ridge, but little below the summit level of the country. These openings vary from two or three, to thirty feet in depth, and usually struck magnesian limestone. In one of the shafts, a fissure was found in the rock, from three to six inches in width, bearing nearly north-east and south-west, in which a good deal of lead ore was found mingled with clay. In sinking these shafts, they also found a considerable quantity of ore in the surface clays. I could not ascertain the quantity of ore taken out here, but I was assured it paid well for the labor expended.

A lead mine has been opened, and worked to some extent, by Messrs. English, Sartan & Wells, in Sec. 17, Town. 45, R. 14. It is situated about one hundred feet below the summit of the surrounding country, on the slope of a small valley, which finds an outlet into a tributary of the Little Moniteau, known as "Pin-oak Branch." Some ten or eleven shafts, varying from thirty to sixty feet in depth, have been sunk, besides many shallow surface diggings. In the superficial deposits, a good deal of "Float Mineral" was found, some masses of which weighed as much as one hundred pounds. These deposits, as usual, consist of clay, with many fragments of chert and magnesian limestone, and vary from five to twenty feet in depth.

After passing through the surface materials, the lead-bearing strata, which here consist of the variety of magnesian limestone called "Cotton Rock," were struck and penetrated to various depths. No regular veins were discovered, the ore being found in isolated masses, and various flattened sheets or vein-like bodies, in cavities and joints of the rock, where it is often associated with red clay, and sometimes with masses of sulphate of baryta.

I was informed, the average yield per man here, while the mine was worked, was about one hundred, to one hundred and twenty-five pounds a day, though sometimes much larger quantities were taken out. In one instance, 10,000 pounds were raised by four men in one day. This mine was profitably worked, from the time it was opened, until the gold discoveries in California caused all the miners to leave the country. "Float Mineral" has been found, in considerable quantities, in many of the ravines and branches in this neighborhood.

In Sec. 10, Town. 45, R. 15, lead has been found on a small branch of Lower Brush Creek, on Mr. John English's land. Some twelve feet above the little branch, a shaft was sunk on the slope of a hill, to a depth of about ten or twelve feet, where, after passing through clay, &c., some four or five feet, light-colored magnesian limestone was struck, and penetrated six or seven feet. In this rock, a fissure, one or two inches in width, was found, filled with lead. It has much the appearance of a true vein, though no spars or gangue of any kind appear to be associated with it. As near as could be seen, the fissure bears nearly north and south, and is filled with lead as far as explored.

Near Burrows' Fork of the Moreau, in Sec. 33, Town. 44, R. 15, Mr. James Kelley discovered lead on government land. The openings were all partly filled up when examined; but I was informed by Mr. Kelley, that the lead fills a fissure or crack in magnesian limestone, about two inches in width, and bearing nearly east and west. Other smaller seams were, also, seen crossing this at nearly right angles. This mine is on a hill, some sixty feet above the level of the creek. Much loose mineral has also been found here.

In the bed of a stream, known as Straight Fork of the Moreau, in Sec. 12, Town.

44, R. 17, lead has been discovered on land belonging to Mr. Harrison Newkirk. The lead is seen here filling small cavities, seams and joints, from a quarter to a half an inch in thickness, in magnesian limestone. As far as could be seen, these seams have no general parallelism, and run in various directions. A shaft was sunk here on the slope of a hill, about twelve feet above the creek, where, after penetrating the usual surface materials, in which much "Float Mineral" was found, to a depth of ten or twelve feet, the same rock seen in the bed of the creek was struck, and the same vein-like bodies of mineral discovered.

At several places on Smith's Fork of the Moreau, in Sec. 24 and 25, of the same township and range as the last, a considerable quantity of loose lead ore has been found on the surface of the ground. I was informed by Judge Fulks, that after hard rains have washed the ground here, as much as half a bushel of loose lead ore can be gathered on the space of a few yards square.

In Sec. 3, Town. 43, R. 16, Mr. Charles Hart, of High-Point, discovered lead ore on a small branch of Burrows' Fork. He sunk three shafts, on a slope about fifteen feet above the creek, to a depth of nine or ten feet. After going through three or four feet of clay, he struck a soft, yellow magnesian limestone, two or three feet in thickness, in which lead ore was found, apparently in "bunches" or isolated pieces, associated with calc spar. Below this, he struck a soft, gray, porous magnesian limestone, in which no ore was found. In one of the pits, a fissure was found in the upper rock, eighteen inches in width, filled with red clay, containing loose pieces of lead ore.

Perhaps the most valuable discovery of lead yet made in this county, is what is known as High-Point Lead Mine. This mine is situated in Sec. 17, Town. 43, R. 15, about one mile a little west of south from, and near one hundred feet below, the highest point in the county. It was first discovered in 1841, and worked without much capital or skill, until about 1845, when, in consequence of bad management and the low price of lead, the Company was compelled to suspend operations. During the time this mine was worked, *two millions of pounds of lead ore* are known to have been raised and smelted.

More recently, this mine has passed into the hands of Messrs. Harrison, Berthoud & Co., of St. Louis, and is now under the management and direction of one of the Company, Mr. Wm. W. Prewett, who is preparing to reopen it. When once cleared of water, that has accumulated during the time operations have been suspended, comparatively little labor will be required to keep it free, as the mine was formerly kept dry by buckets, drawn up by a common horse whim, working two or three hours a day.

The explorations here have been prosecuted in such a manner as to form a circular pit, about three hundred and thirty feet in circumference at the upper part, and eighty feet in depth, which widens out gradually in every direction, from the top downwards. The middle of this excavation is occupied by an immense mass of rock, left by the miners, in the form of a depressed cone, the apex of which rises nearly to the top of the mine. The space thus worked out, I was informed by Mr. Prewitt, was occupied by masses of broken-up magnesian limestone of several varieties, confusedly mingled together in a softer material, apparently of the same composition as the masses themselves. Much of the lead ore was found embedded directly in this softer substance, but the larger bodies were found occupying cavities in it, such as miners term "pockets," where it was directly enveloped in a tough brownish red clay. To what depth this kind of mingling of materials may extend, is unknown, as no essential change was observed as far down as explorations were continued.

Not only that portion of the mine to which the attention of the miners was mainly directed, presents the peculiarities above mentioned, but the whole of the central conical mass has the same structure and composition, to an unknown depth, excepting that it appears not to be so rich in lead ore. It has, however, been perforated by the miners in various directions, and has yielded much ore, and is even supposed to contain enough to pay for working it entirely out.

Much of the mingled materials within the circumference of the mine, is so incoherent as to be worked out without blasting, whilst the surrounding wall is quite hard, and contains little or no ore. The richest nests of ore were found near the wall-rock, where the miners say it was usually found in a succession of bodies, forming almost continuous belts entirely round the mine; each belt being separated by a few feet of other materials.

When this mine was examined, it was still filled with water, to within sixteen or eighteen feet of the top, as far down as the wall-rock could be seen; however, with the exception of a thin bed of sandstone around the top, it consists of "Cotton Rock;" though I was informed by one of the old miners, that, lower down, it is composed of a gray, porous rock, which is, doubtless, correct, as much of the broken-up materials in the center of the mine is composed of that variety of magnesian limestone, and beds of that nature are known to occur beneath the "Cotton Rock" in this region. The wall-rock, though *comparatively* undisturbed, is, in places, fractured, and so traversed by cleavage-joints, as to partially obscure the planes of stratification; but, as far as could be ascertained, there is no perceptible dip in any direction. It appears probable, however, from exposures seen in the surrounding country, that there is a slight general dip of the strata in almost every direction, from a point somewhere near the mine.

The ore of this mine is a very pure sulphuret, and is generally found in large cubes. No other minerals appear to be associated with it, excepting, very rarely, a little calc spar and zinc blende.

Fig. 5.

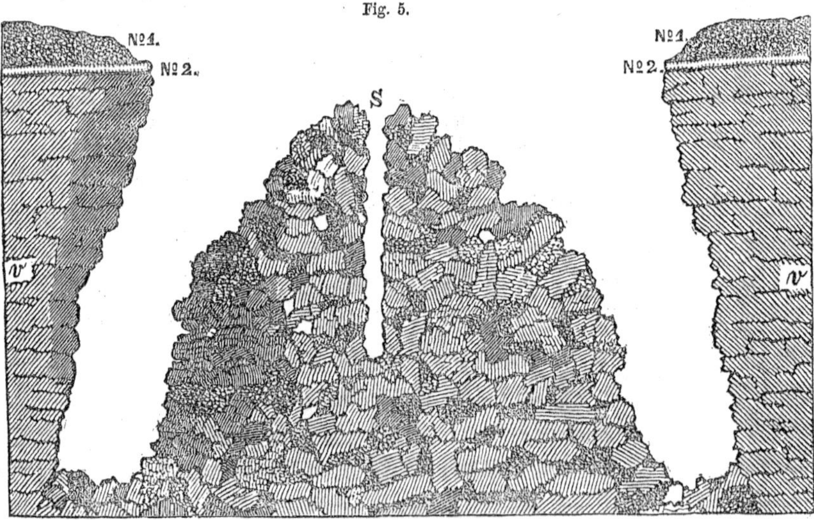

The above is a vertical section across this mine in an east and west direction. No. 1—represents the superficial clays; No. 2—a ten-inch layer of sandstone; *v v*—the surrounding wall-rock; and No. 4—the central mass of broken-up strata, with a sixty-foot shaft (S) in the center.

The phenomena connected with this interesting mine, as far as could be seen, are so peculiar, that it would be unsafe, in our present state of knowledge, to express any very decided opinion with regard to its probable extent and value. If it was originally a great vertical cavern in the strata, which has been filled from *above*, with broken rocks, clay, lead ore, &c.; or, if the lead ore has been subsequently deposited amongst the other materials, from a solution coming from *above*, it may be expected to terminate when the explorations are carried down to the original bottom of the cavern. On the contrary, if the lead and other materials have been raised to their present position, by forces acting from *beneath*, it seems highly probable, it will be found to continue to an indefinite distance below the surface, and may even increase in quantity at greater depths. It is much to be regretted that the condition of the mine was such, when examined (being nearly full of water), that most of the facts which would, probably, have thrown light upon this interesting and important question, were hidden from view.

With a few exceptions, mining, in this part of the State, has been confined to mere surface diggings; and as none of the mines have been recently worked, they were always found so filled with water and loose materials, that it was impossible to make sufficiently careful examinations, to have a clear and satisfactory understanding of the relations between the ore and the rocks of the country, or of its mode of occurrence in them. It would, therefore, be premature, at the present early period in the progress of the survey, to pronounce upon the probable value and extent of these metalliferous deposits. The general distribution, however, of galena, throughout all that portion of the country underlaid by magnesian limestone, both in this rock and mingled with the loose surface deposits of the country, taken in connection with the fact that extensive and valuable deposits of this mineral have already been discovered, seems to warrant the conclusion that the day is not far distant, when mining will form one of the important and profitable industrial pursuits of the county.

In conclusion, I would merely remark, that the citizens of Moniteau county manifested that lively interest in the objects of the survey, so characteristic of a liberal and enlightened community. I take pleasure in acknowledging, here, my indebtedness for many evidences of their kindness and hospitality, received at their hands during the progress of the Survey.

F. B. MEEK,
Assistant Geologist.

GEOLOGICAL ROOMS, UNIVERSITY OF MO.,
Columbia, December 1st, 1854.

MR. HAWN'S REPORT.

GEOLOGICAL ROOMS, STATE UNIVERSITY,
Columbia, February 1st, 1854.

PROF. G. C. SWALLOW,

State Geologist.

SIR: In carrying out your instructions, I commenced an examination of the country between the Missouri and Mississippi rivers, in November last, beginning at St. Joseph, and terminating at Hannibal.

I adopted the line of the Hannibal and St. Joseph Railroad as the base of my operations, and made lateral researches to a distance of fifteen miles, the extent of my district.

My examinations, then, were preliminary, having more in view general results than connected details, enabling me, subsequently, to conclude the survey with more accuracy and despatch. After being relieved from subsequent duties under your immediate supervision, I resumed the examinations, and concluded them a few days since, and herewith present you with my report.

In order to simplify detailed description, I have classified the vertical section into such sub-series of strata as are peculiar to extended localities; commencing with A, and noting in alphabetical and descending order.

It would be superfluous to dwell upon the geological or physical features of the valley proper of the Mississippi river, as that part of the field was examined by you in person.

In commencing my more detailed examinations, the first locality examined was at a point on Salt River, eight miles south south-west of Hannibal, where the Hannibal and New London Plank-road crosses that valley. At this place, the river has excavated a valley to the depth of some two hundred and forty feet, leaving exposed a mural escarpment on the north side, of one hundred and fifty feet of compact Trenton Limestone, which is fully described in your general section

It has occurred to me, that this rock would be admirably adapted to many kinds of structures in landscape gardening, such, for instance, as imitations of ancient views. The cavities would hold sufficient soil to support a luxuriant growth of cacti, as well as many kinds of vines, whilst the harder portions of the rock have solidity enough to sustain a structure that would be firm and lasting.

This formation may be traced along the northern slope of the valley for fifteen miles above, or west of the plank-road. Here, I observed several salt springs; the most important, is known by the appellation of "Muldrow Lick." The water of this spring was formerly used in the manufacture of salt, but is not of sufficient strength to make it profitable now.

On the south side of the valley, this formation (Trenton Limestone) is only traced for three miles above the plank-road, where it passes out of view by a dip towards the west. This dip is sufficient to bring down the lower portions of the Encrinital Limestone to the same level as the Trenton, in the short space of half a mile.

In a distance of five or six miles farther west, or up the river, the hills on the south side of the valley are wholly composed of Encrinital and Chouteau Limestone, supported by the Vermicular Sandstone; whilst the whole northern slope of the valley, immediately opposite, is composed of Trenton Limestone.

Here, then, we have an interesting example of the disturbances and upheaving of strata, by the operation of internal forces; by which, rocks belonging to entirely different systems, occupying, in their original undisturbed condition, widely different elevations, are brought upon the same horizon.

The above-mentioned dip, together with a similar one to the east, or towards the Mississippi river, forms an anticlinal axis, the trend of which is nearly north and south, extending beyond the southern limits of this district, as you have observed in your reconnoissance of the country, between Hannibal and Louisiana. On following this axis of elevation north, it is found to terminate on the north side of the valley of Salt River, by a northern dip of the strata; so that in going to Hannibal, on the Mississippi river, only eight miles north of Salt River, the Silurian rocks, which are seen in the bluffs on Salt River, two hundred and forty-five feet in thickness, are wholly submerged beneath the water at Hannibal. This fact will, also, be more clearly illustrated by your section along the south side of Marion county, which is situated nearly parallel with Salt River, and only six miles north of it.

In following up the valley of Salt River, I find that on the north side, at Cincinnati, on Sec. 8, Town. 56, R. 6, the Trenton Limestone is lost sight of, in consequence of a dip towards the west, under a similar condition to that mentioned as occurring on the south side of the valley, a few miles below. The upper portion of the bluff is here composed of Encrinital and Chouteau Limestone, one hundred and twenty feet in thickness. Beneath the base of the Chouteau Limestone, there is a slope of some eighty feet perpendicular height, in which is exposed broken fragments of shale, belonging to the Vermicular Sandstone.

At Newport, four miles above this, the section exposed is the same as at Cincinnati, except that shale is seen in place, under the Chouteau Limestone.

From Newport I crossed the river, and examined on S. E. ¼, Sec. 33, Town. 55, R. 7, for the first time, a locality of the Lick Creek coal-fields. The order of superposition of the beds composing this portion of the coal-bearing strata, will be better understood by examining the following sections:—

No. 1.— 5 feet bituminous shale, of a loose, thinly laminated structure, interstratified with fine ashy, silicious, earth-like matter, with small globular concretions of like material, and occasionally a large, dark blue, calcareous concretion, of a flattened ovoid form, of some 200 or 300 pounds in weight.
No. 2.— 1½ feet coal.
No. 3.— 26 " slide, with fragments of chert.
No. 4.—140 " white Encrinital Limestone.
No. 5.— 20 " gray Chouteau Limestone.
No. 6.— 15 " slide, to bottom of creek.

This section was overlaid by loess to the depth of fifteen feet, on the S. W. ¼, Sec. 22, Town. 54, R. 7. The following section was observed:—

No. 1.—13 feet loess.
No. 2.— 2 " blue impure limestone.
No. 3.— 8 " blue argillaceous shale.
No. 4.— 6 " bituminous shale, similar to the preceding section, No. 2.
No. 5.— 2 " coal.
No. 6.— 3 " yellow, or fire-clay.
No. 7.—22 " slide, with broken fragments of arenaceous shale.
No. 8.—60 " white Encrinital Limestone.
Bed of Lick Creek.

On the N. E. ¼, Sec. 12, Town. 54, R. 8, the following section is seen:—

No. 1.— 3 feet bituminous shale.
No. 2.— $1\frac{3}{4}$ " coal.
No. 3.— 2 " yellow clay.
No. 4.— 2 " bluish gray, concretionary impure limestone.
No. 5.— $3\frac{1}{2}$ " yellowish brown, impure limestone.
No. 6.—35 " Archimedes Limestone.
This section is overlaid by twenty-two feet of loess.

The foregoing sections embrace most of the strata belonging to the Lick Creek coal-fields, as observed in most of the area of the district, south of Salt River, west of Lick Creek, and North Fork of Salt River and the Grand Divide. At the latter point, this section is augmented by the interpolation of other beds, including one of coal.

The organic remains of this section, are Nos. 2, 3, 4, 9, 11, 12, 13, 15, 16, 19, 22, 23, 26, 29, 30, 33, 35 and 40, of the catalogue appended to this report.

The upper limestones of this series seem to possess hydraulic properties, and are found in the greatest abundance, near the surface, in the vicinity of Paris, Monroe county. Between Lick Creek and the South Fork of Salt River, the coal of this section is most available. Here, the stratum occupies nearly a horizontal position, near the surface, and is from twenty to twenty-four inches in thickness. It is of compact laminar structure; imperfect conchoidal fracture; a light lustrous black color; burns freely; and, when free from pyrites, is of excellent quality. Out-crops are so numerous that it is superfluous to mention localities. It is sufficient to say that it is found in every ravine, and on nearly every quarter section. The facilities for mining are superior, as the underlying stratum is of a consistency that will render excavation comparatively easy; whilst the small amount of superincumbent strata will not require expensive props to support the cap-rock.

Coal is found in small quantities north of Salt River, and east of the North Fork, on Sec. 27, Town. 56, R. 8, and a few other places; but their position is equivocal, being, probably, only outliers of beds farther west.

The coal of the Lick Creek section is also found on the North Fork of Salt River, on Sec. 5, Town. 56, R. 9, and vicinity. The stratum is about eighteen inches in thickness, and is overlaid by argillaceous shale, highly impregnated with alum. These are supported by ten feet of dark gray, impure limestone, interstratified with hard, compact, yellowish gray slate, chert, and small globular silicious geodes, the cavities of which are filled with crystals of quartz. The upper portion of this stratum merges into a yellow shale, upon which the coal rests, and the lower portion passes under the bed of the river.

About twelve miles up the river, at a point nearly due south of Shelbyville, coal is found in connection with a saccharoidal sandstone, highly quartzoze, and Archimedes Limestone. The stratum is about twenty inches in thickness, of medium quality, and, probably, also belongs to the Lick Creek series. In this vicinity, I observed a great number of geodes, filled with crystals, of quartz, of nearly every variety of form and size. They vary from two to fifteen inches in diameter; they are spheroidal.

No coal was found north of this point; but I see no good reason why it should not be found as far north as the northern limits of this district.

At, or near Sharpsburg, on Sec. 2, Town. 56, R. 8, the Encrinital Limestone is immediately overlaid by forty feet of brown micaceous sandstone; and frequent indications tend to the conclusion that this is the surface rock, between this and the Grand Divide, and for sixty or seventy miles beyond; but at that place (the Grand Divide) are interpolated, between it and the supporting rock, several strata, not represented in the section at Sharpsburg. Similar interpolations are repeated in going west, until this sandstone is found overlying nearly all the series of the Coal Measures. This rock will be noticed more fully hereafter.

The foundation of the lower coal-bearing rock, hitherto described, and represented in the different sections, consists of the Lower Carboniferous beds. This order is preserved along the valley of Salt River and its principal branches, to a meridian passing through Paris, Monroe county, and in some instances farther west, where they pass out of view by the superior elevation of the country.

These formations are found over nearly the entire county, east of the meridian indicated, and will become of great importance in furnishing excellent material for building purposes, including ornamental structures and monuments of a simple order of architecture. Rocks, for burning a superior article of lime, may be selected at most any locality. Organic remains, similar to those of your catalogue of Encrinital Limestone.

From the Grand Divide to Grand Chariton, the strata dip towards the west; and the section, hitherto under consideration, passes under, and is succeeded by other strata, in the ascending order, which are represented in the vertical section by Nos. 43, 44, 45, 46, 47, 48,

49, 50, 51, 52, 53, 54, 55 and 56. This section is found in the valley of Clay-Bank Creek, an eastern tributary of Middle Fork of the Chariton, three miles north of McGee College, in Macon county.

For organic remains, see catalogue Nos. 3, 11, 12, 16, 17, 18, 19, 20, 26, 30 and 32.

Vegetable impressions occur in the lower portions of stratum No. 46, of a flattened stem-like form, promiscuously intermingled with the rock, and forming about one-eighth of the entire mass. This sandstone is hard, and, generally, of a light yellowish brown color, changing in places to a dull, bluish gray. This is underlaid by about twelve feet of argillaceous shale, changing to an arenaceous slate, in some localities. These rest upon No. 49, the most important coal-bed in this district. At B. Powell's bank, on Sec. 14, Town. 56, R. 15, it is six feet in thickness, including a six-inch stratum of clay, and has a fine laminated structure, with a dull black, charcoal color and appearance. It is very light; burns freely, and contains but little pyrites. Judging by its lightness, I should suppose it would produce but a small proportion of ash or residuum. Its freedom from sulphuret of iron, renders it a valuable coal for steamboats and smiths. By accident, fire was communicated to this stratum, on the premises of E. S. Gibson, Esq., which revealed its existence at that point. After burning several weeks it was extinguished with much difficulty.

I traced this stratum west to Fish-trap Ford, on Grand Chariton, in the northeast corner of Chariton county, where I found it on a level with high-water mark. To the north, it soon passes under the bed of the river.

Stratum No. 52 burns into good lime, and may be used for underpinning.

Stratum No. 55 is an inferior article of coal, containing too much sulphuret of iron.

This stratum of coal is extensively available in the district between East and Grand Chariton rivers, and again in the valley of Grand River, west of the high grounds included in the Elk Knobs.

At some localities, stratum forty-nine, and the shale above it, were subjected to the denuding action of water, * by which the surface was cut into small ravines or cavities, resembling cross-sections of small hollows, which were subsequently filled up with different material. In one instance, it is composed of broken fragments of sandstone; at another point, the space is occupied by a hard, dark ferruginous conglomerate, composed of sand and gravel; and, at still another, the coal appears to be entirely cut away, and the interval filled with a brilliant red clay. This locality was formerly much visited by the aborigines, who made extensive use of this clay in painting their implements and decorating their persons.

On Rocky Branch, on the west side of the valley of Grand Chariton, two miles below the railroad, strata from No. 35 to 42 inclusive, are found cropping out.

No. 42 is a hard, compact, impure limestone, suitable for ordinary building purposes, but the available quantity is too limited to be of great importance.

---

*In the valley of East Chariton I observed a surface of smooth, hard limestone, marked with two courses of striæ; one bearing south, ten degrees east; and the other, south, twelve degrees west; and crossing each other. The lines of the working in each course are parallel, and one foot, or more, apart. Those bearing east are partially curved, with, occasionally, slight striæ between the principal parallels. The grooves are angular, remarkably smooth and regular, about three-fourths of an inch in depth, and some are twenty-five feet in length. The surface thus marked, includes an area of about four hundred square feet, and is so prominent that it attracts the attention of the most casual observers. This locality is in the bed of East Chariton River, three miles south-east of Bloomington, Macon county.

Stratum 46, in the preceding section, is here a compact sandstone, that weathers well, and may be used for some structures to a good advantage.

No. 38 is a coal similar in character to that of No. 49, hitherto described, and is two feet thick.

The Fossils obtained at this locality may be seen in catalogue, Nos. 8, 12, 16, 17, 18, 21, 26 and 30.

This section, and the preceding stratum, is very generally found in this valley, on Mush Fork, and strata Nos. 38 and 39 on Little Yellow, below Harvey's Mill.

Between Little Yellow Creek and Grand River, the strata, from 26 to 34 inclusive, crop out. Nos. 26 and 32, as observed on Little Yellow Creek, north of the railroad, and Utica, Livingston county, furnish good building materials; but, at most of the other localities, these rocks would not withstand the vicissitudes of the atmosphere.

The organic remains obtained are, Nos. 1, 3, 7, 9, 11, 12, 13, 16, 17, 18, 19, 21, 23, 26, 27, 29, 30, 33, and 39, of the catalogue.

Immediately above the section on Rocky Branch, and on Little Yellow, or east of Coulston's Mill, over the section last under consideration, we again meet with the micaceous sandstone of Sharpsburg, before mentioned. At the former point, and in the Elk Knobs, it appears to have attained a thickness of some hundred and fifty feet, and increases in thickness northward, probably in consequence of having been less exposed to denuding forces, in that direction. It, probably, constitutes the principal formation in the Elk Knobs, which constitute the peculiar topographical features of the country, north of the Hannibal and St. Joseph railroad, and west of Grand Chariton. They consist of short conical ridges, formed by irregular ravines. Two often head in a point common to both; and, after running in opposite directions, curve abruptly and unite again; thus forming, what is generally called, the "Knobs." Some of them are so regular in contour, that they resemble more the works of art than of Nature. The tendency to this peculiarity may be traced along the line of the railroad to Little Yellow Creek, and north of this, over the higher portions of Linn county, and west of Grand River, between Monroe's Bluff and the Blue Mounds, in Livingston county.

In the valley of Grand River this sandstone has been worn away, to give place to that stream. At Utica, in Livingston county, near the junction of the Forks of Grand River, it appears in a cliff, one hundred feet high, and there passes under the limestone of the overlying Coal Measures.

The strata, Nos. 21 to 25 inclusive, next appear, and are mostly composed of Sharpsburg sandstone, or that formation just under consideration, including two strata of coal. In this sandstone, at this locality, are many remains of plants and concretions, with nuclei of vegetable and other matter. *

---

* On Big Branch, seven miles west of Utica, the fossil stump of a tree is seen, that originally must have been two feet in diameter. It resembles a stump far advanced in decay; it is partially carbonized; has a brownish black color, and burns readily. The bark and roots are obvious; and its ligneous structure is observed at a glance. Its composition is entirely distinct from the rock in which it is embedded, though many small particles of a similar substance is found incorporated with the rock.

A few feet above this I observed many impressions of leaves of plants; and, still higher, a large shell, resembling some varieties of our fresh water *Unio.*

The lower stratum of coal, No. 24 in this section, is found cropping out in the cliff at Utica, about thirty feet above the water-line of the river. It is from fourteen to twenty inches in thickness, and of good quality. It is, also, found in Monroe's Bluff, at several points between that and the Blue Mounds, at the head of Brush Creek, and on Clear Creek, at the base of the Blue Mounds. It is, also, found on the East Fork, a few miles north of Chillicothe, the county town of Livingston, and on the premises of Dr. Gilbert, on Medicine Creek; and should be found in the valley of Shoal Creek, between Hixon's and Hahan's old mill.

The upper stratum, No. 22, is worked on the land of Mr. Joseph Clark, in the valley of the West Fork of Grand River, on the N. E. ¼, Sec. 8, Town. 56, R. 25 This stratum is about eighteen inches in thickness, and of medium quality. Unless it is confined to a small area, it should be found on or near the summit of the bluff at Utica; in the Blue Mounds, below the lower limestone, and along the two Forks of Grand River to the northern limits of this district.

With this series terminates that portion of the Coal Measures known to contain beds of workable coal; as no coal, in any useful quantities, is found in the series above.

It will be seen, from the preceding, that there are at least five beds of coal included in the Coal Measures of this district, with an aggregate thickness of eighteen feet. This will furnish an inexhaustible supply of one of the important elements of future wealth and prosperity. Though the quantity and value, according to present standards, may be expressed in numbers, yet the effects it will produce in the development of the great interests of social life cannot be foreseen or estimated.

The next strata in the ascending order, Nos. 11, 12, 13, 14, 15, 16, 17, 18, 19, and 20, are composed of limestones of various colors and grades of purity, with a few beds of shale, as the vertical section indicates. Their aggregate thickness is near one hundred feet, and they are the surface rock of nine-tenths of the district west of Grand River. At Utica, and White's Mill, on Shoal Creek, they are seen resting immediately upon the Sharpsburg Sandstone. At Jacob Hulser's, Sec. 19, Town. 56, R. 27, they are well exposed, and likewise in the valley of Grindstone Creek, DeKalb county, where they also overlie the Sharpsburg sandstone. From the extensive exposures of that formation, in the lower portions of the valley, the stream takes its name. The upper portions of the section are exposed at different points along the valley of Shoal Creek, to the head of the stream; on Brush and McDaniel's Creek, on Smith's Fork, near Plattsburg, on Castile, and Third Fork of Platte river; and it is wholly seen in the high rocky bluff of "Bond Town," above St. Joseph.

The fossils * observed in these strata are, Nos. 3, 5, 6, 8, 9, 10, 11, 12, 16, 17, 18, 19, 23, 24, 25, 33, 35, 36, 38, and 41 of the catalogue.

* Strata Nos. 10 and 12 of the vertical section abound in organic remains, which are most abundant at the heads of Smith's Branch, in the vicinity of Plattsburg. A good collection may be had at many localities in that vicinity.

In addition to these, there are some two or three varieties that are new.

Many of the strata of this section will answer a good purpose, for under-paving bridge abutments, and for rough stone buildings; while but few are capable of receiving a dressing, sufficient for fine work. No. 14 is composed of pure white limestone, of an oolitic structure, remarkably compact, and well adapted to fine work. It is massive, but may be quarried or split into any convenient form. It is available in the valley of Shoal Creek, in the vicinity of Kingston, in the valley of Castile, five miles below the Hannibal and St. Joseph Railroad, and, probably, in the valley of Grindstone. It would, also, make excellent lime.

No. 10 in the vertical section, as seen at Skinner's mill, is also an excellent building material, particularly for heavy abutments and arches; but it is too high in the series to be available, except at some high points on the Missouri river.

This series will furnish many localities, west of the East Fork of Grand River, with good and convenient rock for general purposes of building, and, at some few points, the common ornaments, such as window and door sills.

Stratum 11 is composed of disintegrated chert, of a dull, reddish brown color, varying from that to a creamy white; is a light porous substance; at some localities it has attained a considerable density, with portions of chert incorporated; at others, it is soft and friable. Where this has been subjected to disintegration, it leaves exposed many fragments of chert, as is seen at Flint Hill, two miles south of Kingston. This stratum furnished me a convenient guide in ascertaining the relative position of strata in the series.

In the valley of Grindstone, Sec. 8, Town. 57, R. 31, is found a red, chocolate-colored silicious clay, or shale, which, from its similarity in many respects to a material extensively used in Ohio, and other States, as a pigment, would, doubtless, furnish a cheap and abundant material for that purpose. When ground in oil, the color may be varied by adding a small quantity of white lead, lamp black, or other cheap paint, to suit the taste. This kind of paint is highly useful, not only for ornamental purposes, but, also, for rendering roofs fire-proof, by applying several heavy coats to the shingles. So soon as the oil evaporates, the strong coating of silicious matter left on the surface will prevent a roof from taking fire from sparks, or even large coals.

Strata 2, 3, 4, 5, 6, 7, 8 and 9, in the vertical section, are mostly composed of arenaceous matter, and constitute the formation of the upper portions of the Blue Mounds. The only stratum in this series worthy of particular note, is No. 5. This is composed of dark brown, variegated, and buff-colored sandstone, twenty-one feet in thickness. When first removed from its native bed, it is soft, and easily worked into any useful form; but, when exposed to the atmosphere, it hardens and is covered with a coating of white silica, that renders it comparatively impervious to water, and so hard and quartzose that it readily yields sparks with the steel. This will, undoubtedly, be found a cheap, durable, and convenient building stone, and, on that account, valuable. This stratum is seen at the heads of Clear and Mound Creeks.

The highest stratum, or No. 2, is a light gray limestone, that would, probably, burn into tolerably good lime.

Excepting the Quaternary deposits, this series is the highest in the vertical section; and the Blue Mounds, in which they occur, the highest point in the district; as no representative of any portion of the strata is found elsewhere. I observed the same formation in the high grounds west of Fort Leavenworth, Kansas Territory.

These Mounds are situated about ten miles south of the Forks of Grand River. On the north side, they rise rather abruptly to an elevation of some three hundred and fifty feet above Grand River valley, and gradually recede towards the south-east and north-west, and south of south-west, until they again merge into the common level of the country. Their area, I should judge to be equal to one and a half congressional townships.

Their topography, undoubtedly, gave rise to their name; for they have that peculiar regular contour of surface, and mound-like form, incident to districts where the frame-work of the country is composed of strata that disintegrate readily, or are easily worn away.

Notwithstanding the elevated and broken aspect of this Mound country, it is very productive, especially the northern portion. The reason of this will appear in the description of the next series, or the superficial deposits.

This section closes the vertical section, so far as relates to the stratified or sedimentary rocks. I shall, therefore, make a slight reference to their general position.

The distance across the State, between Hannibal and St. Joseph, is two hundred and ten miles, and the bearing varies but little from a due west course.

The bed of the Missouri river, at St. Joseph, is elevated three hundred and twenty-five feet above that of the Mississippi, at Hannibal; and the aggregate thickness of the strata between those points amounts to eight hundred and thirty feet.

The principal coal-beds, as observed in Macon county, are nearly on the same horizon with the bed of the Missouri river, at St. Joseph; but at the latter point the superincumbent strata, below the bed of the river, amounts to three hundred and fifty-five feet; and in no portion of the district can these coal strata be reached, in the valley of the Missouri river, in less than three hundred feet below the surface; premising, however, that the strata are constant in their thickness and horizontal position.

The strata generally increase in volume in going west, especially those of shale, which also become more arenaceous.

QUATERNARY.

The Loess, from ten to seventy feet in depth, is the principal deposit of this age, and extends from the Mississippi to the Missouri river. It is similar, in all its characteristics, to that you so extensively observed along the bluffs of the Missouri river, in the north-west part of the State, and is, probably, a continuation of the same formation.

Nearly every locality in the district gives evidence of identity, in the existence of small calcareous concretions and portions of shells.*

Little or no gravel was found, except in close proximity to the Mississippi and Missouri rivers; and but few transported boulders of any considerable magnitude. The largest, containing a cubic yard or more, lies on the surface near the railroad, on the summit between Castile Creek and Third Fork of Platte River.

The deposit of Loess exerts an important controlling influence in this district, for, without it, the coal-field, that extends over half the area, would be a barren waste; for the shales and sandstone members of the Coal Measures are developed in the usual degree, and would produce the usual deleterious effect upon the soils. But no such effects are produced here; for this Loess, rich in mineral fertilizing matters, covers those substances to such a depth as effectually to prevent them from mixing with the soil, except in limited localities.

It is not alone in the coal district that great advantages are derived from this deposit; but whatever preëminence this district, and, probably, North Missouri generally, enjoys in this respect, it is alone due to this deposit.

After the foregoing remarks, little is necessary to be said in relation to soils. The soil in all parts of the district is fertile in the highest degree, with slight modifications, requiring only a different mode of culture, and the products adapted to different localities, to produce equal results. Perhaps the preponderance may be in favor of the limestone district, west of Grand River, especially when we take into consideration, that the products best adapted to that region are those that now yield the greatest profit on the labor expended; but, should circumstances change, that preponderance will be lost.

At some few localities in the district, the soil is thin and heavy, in consequence of a superabundance of clay; but where it is properly tilled, and the subsoil is in reach of the plow, so as to be brought up and mixed with the surface, it becomes friable and produces well. Such a soil is remarkably well adapted to the cereal products, maturing those plants without the addition of artificial stimulants, so apt to produce a redundancy of straw at the expense of a proper development of grain.

The soil in Macon county is remarkably well adapted to the production of a superior article of tobacco; also, the upper portions of Chariton county, the higher

---

* The Hon. George Munroe, of Livingston county, a gentleman of intelligence and veracity, informed me that, in sinking a shaft for a well, near his residence, at Munroe's Bluff, elevated about three hundred feet above Grand River, a large quantity of shells, in a good state of preservation, were thrown up from a depth of forty feet below the surface, and with them a marl exceedingly rich in the elements of fertility. This locality rests upon the Sharpsburg sandstone.

portions of Linn, and the south-eastern portions of Livingston, and, also, the upper portions not included in the limestone district.

These regions will become as famous, for the production of superior tobacco, as were the most favored portions of Virginia in her palmiest days.

There is yet another variety of soil deserving attention — the alluvial deposits of the valleys, usually denominated "Bottoms," in the West. This soil is necessarily deep and of unbounded fertility, well adapted to the growth of Indian corn and hemp, but not to wheat and small grains, in consequence of its excessive fatness, or superabundance of organic matter.

In the valley of Grand River the bottoms vary from three to five miles in width, and are elevated from twenty to thirty feet above the bed, and above ordinary high-water mark. In the valley of Grand Chariton the bottom-lands are about equal in extent to those on Grand River, but not elevated so high above the bed of the stream, and are, consequently, more frequently inundated.

Timber usually exists in the valleys and along water courses, of the usual varieties found in this State, and the West generally. The most abundant and valuable varieties are the different kinds of white and black oaks, black and white walnut, and, occasionally, a grove of maples (*Acer Saccharinum*). The supply would be sufficient for domestic and agricultural purposes, if it were equally distributed; especially when we take into consideration the facilities the Hannibal and St. Joseph railroad will afford in distributing the products of the forest, and the coal-beds found along that line.

The Osage Orange, too, is under extensive experiment here, and, thus far, promises well; and, should success finally attend the rearing of hedges for fencing purposes, a small amount of timber will suffice this district.

It will be seen, by an inspection of the map, that this district is traversed by several rivers, with their branches diverging in every direction, and watering the country in an admirable manner. The largest of these is Grand River, running nearly north and south through the center of the district. This stream is navigable two months in the year for small steamboats (or those carrying eighty or a hundred tons), from its mouth up to the junction of the East and West Forks, and for keel boats thirty miles higher up the East Branch. The fall of the stream is less than a foot per mile. It runs over a muddy bed, except at Munroe's Bluff or Rapids, where it passes over a limestone bottom.

Grand Chariton is next in size. The volume of water is, perhaps, less than half that of Grand River, and, in almost all other respects, the same. Salt River discharges less water than Grand Chariton, and differs from it by being composed of alternate pools and rapids. These streams will afford no other facilities to the business of the country than in creating water-power, for which Salt River and its branches are well adapted. Several of the minor streams, too, are well suited to that purpose, particularly Medicine and Shoal Creeks. Many of the mill-sites on the streams are occupied by ordinary structures, with indifferent machinery; but on Platte river and its branches are a few mills, supplied with modern and improved appliances. At Utica, Livingston county, an establishment is now in course of construction on an extended scale; and, all things considered, I should suppose that a sufficient amount of water-power can be obtained to supply the domestic wants for many years to come.

There is but little waste land in this district. This circumstance, with the exceeding fertility and durability of the soil, and its adaptation to the various products of this climate; its exhaustless beds of coal, and its salubrious climate, renders this a favored district, and capable of sustaining a population as dense as any other portion of equal extent in the northern temperate zone. And I can but express a gratification for the trust you confided in me, in assigning so important and interesting a field to my charge, and thereby connecting me in an humble way with the development of its resources.

There are, probably, but few portions of equal extent, where the geological or natural advantages of the country and internal improvements will react upon each other with such important results. I have been frequently impressed, during the progress of my researches, with the great advantages that may accrue to the State, as well as to individual corporations, by conducting geological investigations with the various lines of public improvements now in progress, or that may hereafter be undertaken, in various parts of the State.

The science of Geology, which has of late shed such a brilliant flood of light upon mining, agriculture, and various other branches of industry, bids fair to furnish the civil engineer with one of the surest and [illegible] collateral aids in selecting and locating roads, canals, &c.

In consequence of your recent professional tour down the Missouri river, from the State line, I made no examinations in the immediate vicinity of that stream, save in relation to the supposed existence of rock in the bed of the river, near the city of St. Joseph; being assured that, formerly, rocks were visible at low water, which are now covered with sand, in consequence of a change of the channel. My examinations proved that these conjectures were founded on fact, though my preparations were not sufficient to ascertain their precise character. They are, probably, outliers of ledges in the vicinity.

I am indebted to your able and accomplished assistant, Mr. F. B. Meek, for many important suggestions, and other professional courtesies, of great value to me. All of which is respectfully submitted.

F. HAWN,

Assistant Geologist.

CATALOGUE OF FOSSILS,

FROM THE COAL MEASURES, ON THE LINE OF THE HANNIBAL AND ST. JOSEPH RAILROAD,

COLLECTED BY F. HAWN.

No. 1.—*Calamites*......................—2 sp. (Undt.), Locust Creek, Linn county, Chillicothe and Huntsville road.
No. 2.—*Chaetetes milleporaceus*......—Farrington's Mill, Sec. 30, Town. 58, R. 14.
No. 3.—*Zaphrentis*......................—(Undt.), N. E. ¼ Sec. 8, Town. 56, R. 25, immediately above the coal strata.
No. 4.—*Cyathophyllum*.................—Hoover's Creek, S. W. ¼ Sec. 35, Town. 56, R. 13.
No. 5.—*Syringopora*....................—(Undt.), on Smith's Branch, four miles east of Plattsburg.
No. 6.—*Retepora*.........................—Union Mills, Platte county, Grindstone Creek.
No. 7.—*Fenestella*.......................—Coulston's Mill, Little Yellow, E. ½ S. W. ¼ Sec. 19, Town. 58, R. 18.
No. 8.—*Arca*...............................—Four miles east of Plattsburg, Clinton co., and Sec. 9. Town. 57, R. 16.
No. 9.—*Orthis umbraculum*..........—Union Mills, Platte county, and N. W. corner N. E. ¼ Sec. 12, Town. 54, R. 8.
No. 10.—— *resupinata?*..........—Smith's Branch, four miles east of Plattsburg, Clinton county.
No. 11.—*Spirifer Meusebachanus*....—Generally diffused.
No. 12.—— *lineatus*...............—Ranges through the whole series.
No. 13.—— *striatus?*...............—S. E. ¼ Sec. 18, Town. 54, R. 7, and E. ½ S. W. ¼ Sec. 19, Town. 58, R. 18.
No. 14.—— *hemiplicata*...........—(Hall), Fort Leavenworth, K. T.
No. 15.—— *Kentuckensis*.........—(Shumard), *S. octopliaatus* (Hall), S. W. ¼ Sec. 22, Town. 54, R. 7.
No. 16.—*Productus Semireticulatus*.—Very generally diffused through the series.
No. 17.—— *costatus*................—Very generally diffused—abundant at Smith's Branch, Clinton co.
No. 18.—— *aequicostatus*.........—(Shumard), Union Mills and Platte county.
No. 19.—— *Wabashensis*.........—N. ½ E. ½ N. W. ¼ Sec. 9, Town. 54, R. 7, N. E. ¼ N. E. ¼ Sec. 24, Town. 56, R. 7.
No. 20.—— *cora*......................—Rutherford's Mill, East Chariton, Sec. 26, Town. 56, R. 15.
No. 21.—— *punctatus*.............—Smith's Branch, four miles east of Plattsburg.
No. 22.—— *splendens*..............—Four miles east of Plattsburg.
No. 23.—*Terebratula subtilita*.........—(Hall), Skinner's Mills, Platte River, Platte county.
No. 24.—— *plano-sulcata?*......—Joseph Clark's, West Fork, Grand River.
No. 25.—— ....—(Undt. large plicated, probably new), four miles east of Plattsburg.
No. 26.—*Chonetes mesoloba*............—(Norwood and Pratten), S. E. ¼ Sec. 18, Town. 54, R. 7, and lower coal-bearing rock.
No. 27.—— *granulifera*..........—Locust Creek, Linn county, Chillicothe and Huntsville road.
No. 28.—— (*Smithi*),...............—Coleiar's Mill, Medicine Creek, half a mile north of railroad.
No. 29.—*Orbiculoidea*....................—Three miles north of McGee College, on S. W. ¼ S. W. ¼, Town. 56, R. 15.
No. 30.—*Bellerophon*......................—(Undt.), Utica, Livingston county, Mussel Fork, half a mile below State road.
No. 31.—*Syringopora*......................—(Undt.), N. E. ¼ Sec. 8, Town. 56, R. 25, immediately above the coal strata.
No. 32.—*Lingula*............................—(Undt.), S. W. ¼ W. W. ¼ Sec. 22, Town. 56, R. 15, three miles north of McGee College.
No. 33.—*Allorisma*..........................—N. E. ¼ N. E. ¼ Sec. 24, Town. 56, R. 30.
No. 34.—— ....—(Undt.), Rutherford's Mill, East Chariton, Sec. 26, Town. 56, R. 15.
No. 35.—*Pecten*..............................—2 (Undt.) sp., on Smith's Branch, four miles east of Plattsburg.
No. 36.—*Myalina subquadrata*.......—(Shumard), Union Mills, Platte county.
No. 37.—*Cypricardia*.....................—On Smith's Branch, four miles east of Plattsburg.
No. 38.—*Pinna*...............................—(Undt.), N. E. ¼ N. E. ¼ Sec. 24, Town. 56, R. 30.
No. 39.—*Avicula*............................—(Undt.), Utica, Livingston county.
No. 40.—*Tellinomya?*.....................—S. W. ¼ S. E. ¼, Sec. 29, Town. 56, R. 13.
No. 41.—— ....—Small univalves, like Murchisonia, Skinner's Mill, Platte River.

VERTICAL SECTION OF STRATA,

SEEN IN MR. HAWN'S DISTRICT.

SERIES A.

No. 1... 70 feet, Bluff—everywhere.

SERIES B.

No. 2... 17 feet, Fine compact gray limestone—Bondtown.
No. 3... 9 " Hard, compact buff limestone—Fort Leavenworth.
No. 4... 3 " Bituminous shale—Fort Leavenworth.
No. 5... 21 " Fine, dark brown and pure sandstone.
No. 6... 3 " Dark blue, crystalline limestone, with zinc blende.
No. 7...120 " Argillaceous shale and shelly sandstone.
No. 8... 3 " Dark brown, impure limestone.
No. 9... 30 " Brown sand-slate and shelly sandstone.
206 " *Total thickness of Series B.*

SERIES C.

No 10... 22 feet, Blue and gray, hard, compact limestone—Platte.
No. 11... 3 " Decomposing chert.
No. 12... 20 " Dark blue and gray limestone—Shells abundant.
No. 13... 13 " Brown, thinly-laminated slate.
No. 14... 4 " White oolitic limestone.
No. 15... 6 " Brown, hard, compact impure limestone.
No. 16... 4 " Gray, compact limestone.
No. 17... 6 " Bluish gray, brittle limestone, breaking into angular fragments.
No. 18... 3 " Bituminous shale.
No. 19... 6 " Fine-grained limestone, with concretions of iron stone.
No. 20... 13 " Bluish gray, compact limestone.
94 " *Total thickness of Series C.*

SERIES D.

No. 21... 12 feet, Argillaceous shale—Grindstone Creek.
No. 22... 1½ "
No. 23... 82 " Brown and blue sandy shale and sandstone—Elk Knobs.
No. 24... 1½ " Coal—Utica, Livingston county.
No. 25... 42 " Brown, ferruginous sandstone—Monroe's Bluff.
139 " *Total thickness of Series D.*

SERIES E.

No. 26... 6 feet, Compact, gray and ferruginous limestone—Utica.
No. 27... 3 " Clay.
No. 28... 4 " Gray, irregularly-stratified limestone.
No. 29... 25 " Dark brown sandstone, with Calamites.
No. 30... 5 " Argillaceous shale.
No. 31... 15 " Black shale—Medicine Creek.
No. 32... 10 " Yellowish gray, impure limestone—fossils, abundant.
No. 33... 10 " Ferruginous clay.
No. 34... 3 " Yellowish brown limestone.
No. 35... 13 " Blue, arenaceous slate.
No. 36... 3 " Bituminous shale.
No. 37... 9 " Blue, argillaceous and sandy shale.
No. 38... 2 " Coal—valley of Grand Chariton.
No. 39... 13 " Brown sandy slate.
No. 40... 3 " Gray, concretionary limestone.
No. 41... 3 " Calcareous sandy slate.
No. 42... 6 " Blue and buff limestone.
133 " *Total thickness of Series E.*

SERIES F.

No. 43... 3 feet, Bituminous shale — valley of Grand Charito
No. 44... 3 " Blue and yellow, argillaceous shale.
No. 45... ½ " Coal.
No. 46... 25 " Brown, compact micaceous sandstone.
No. 47... 12 " Argillaceous shale.
No. 48... 3 " Bituminous shale.
No. 49... 6 " Coal — Town. 56, R. 15, Sec. 14, N. E. ¼.
No. 50... 6 " Gray, concretionary limestone.
No. 51... 6 " Buff and blue limestone.
No. 52... 7 " Gray, irregularly-stratified limestone.
No. 53... 2½ " Bituminous shale.
No. 54... 8 " Blue and yellow, argillaceous shale.
No. 55... 3 " Coal — E. S. Gibson's.
No. 56... 3 " Yellow clay
82 " *Total thickness of Series F.*

SERIES G.

No. 57... 10 feet, Hard, compact, brown impure limestone.
No. 58... 6 " Hydraulic limestone — Grand Divide.
No. 59... 8 " Bituminous shale — Grand Divide.
No. 60... 2 " Coal — Town. 56, R. 15, Sec. 24, S. W. ¼.
No. 61... 5 " Yellow clay.
No. 62... 15 " Hard, brown micaceous sandstone.
No. 63... 5 " Bituminous shale.
No. 64... 2 " Dark blue limestone.
No. 65... 8 " Alum shale — N. Fork of Salt River.
No. 66... 6 " Bituminous shale.
No. 67... 2 " Coal — Lick Creek Coal-Field.
No. 68... 5 " Yellow clay and slate.
No. 69... 10 " Gray, concretionary limestone.
No. 70... 3 " Hard, compact limestone.
85 " *Total thickness of Series G.*

SERIES H.

No. 71... 6 feet, St. Louis Limestone — Salt River.
No. 72... 2 " Brown, impure limestone.
No. 73... 80 " Archimedes Limestone — Salt River.
No. 74...145 " Encrinital Limestone — Hannibal.
234 " *Total thickness of Series H.*

SERIES I.

No. 75... 25 feet, Chouteau Limestone — Cincinnati.
No. 76... 80 " Vermicular Sandstone — Hannibal.
No. 77... 56 " Lithographic Limestone — Hannibal.
161 " *Total thickness of Series I.*

SERIES J.

No. 78... 50 feet, Blue, argillaceous shale — West of Hannibal.
No. 79... 45 " Hard, compact, blue limestone.
No. 80... 30 " Brown and red sandstone — Salt River.
No. 81...170 " Trenton Limestone — Salt River.
295 " *Total thickness of Series J.*

DR. B. F. SHUMARD'S REPORT.

ST. LOUIS, *November*, 1855.

PROF. G. C. SWALLOW,

State Geologist.

DEAR SIR: As Assistant Geologist, in the Survey under your direction, I herewith submit my report on the several districts entrusted to me for examination, comprising a description of a geological section on the Mississippi, from St. Louis to Commerce, and the results of my detailed surveys in Franklin and St. Louis counties, with maps and sections illustrating the same.

Agreeable to your instructions, I have prepared, and, also, submit, descriptions of some of the new organic remains discovered in the strata of our State; and a catalogue embracing nearly all the species that have been collected during the progress of the Survey, up to the present time, in which the fauna, occurring in each group of strata of your general vertical section, are arranged in separate lists.

It gives me pleasure to acknowledge here the assistance I have received, at different times, from my associates in the Survey, while engaged in the prosecution of the duties assigned to me. To Dr. A. LITTON I am under obligations for valuable aid in the preliminary examinations of St. Louis and Franklin counties. In the palæontology, I am indebted to Mr. F. B. MEEK for important suggestions, and for the beautiful and accurate delineations of the fossils described in my report. To Mr. R. B. PRICE for drawings of the maps, and for reducing and copying sections, which he has executed with neatness and accuracy.

I am, also, under obligations to Messrs. JOHN BRUERE and MONTROSE PALLEN, who accompanied me in the explorations on the Mississippi, and, without charge to the State, proved valuable assistants. To Mr. FORD, Engineer on the Pacific Railroad, for the use of maps, profiles, etc.; and to J. F. EVANS, Esq., Dr. LEWIS, Gen. JEFFRIES, and various other persons, residing in the districts examined, for aid and information.

With an earnest desire that the results of my labors may meet your approbation, and with grateful acknowledgments for your uniform courtesy and friendly assistance,

I remain,

Very truly, yours,

B. F. SHUMARD,

Palaeontologist and Assistant Geologist.

DESCRIPTION

OF A

GEOLOGICAL SECTION, ON THE MISSISSIPPI RIVER,

FROM ST. LOUIS TO COMMERCE.

In descending the Mississippi from St. Louis, the first rock exposure, immediately adjacent to the river, occurs a short distance above the United States Arsenal. At this place the St. Louis Limestone has been quarried extensively for curb-stones, window-sills, and the foundations of buildings. The rocks have been laid bare to the height of thirty feet, and consist of light and dark gray compact limestone, in strata, from a few inches to a foot and a half in thickness, with thin seams of chert interstratified. Some of the layers would burn into a good lime, but others contain too much silicious matter for this purpose. The characteristic fossils are—*Lithostrotian Canadense*, *Syringopora*, *Echinocidaris*, *Terebratula Roisyii*, *Terebratula*, *Spirifer*, and teeth and scales of fishes. These strata are overlaid by the Quaternary deposits, which extend to the level of the Carondelet road; its elevation being about ninety feet above the Mississippi.

Lower down the river, at LaBeaume's quarries, we find, reposing on the above-mentioned rocks, from eighteen to twenty feet of heavy-bedded gray limestone, rather softer and more argillaceous than the rocks of the preceding locality. The layers are from one to four feet thick, separated by thin partings of argillaceous shale. They break with an even, granular fracture, and are quarried quite easily. A stratum, about three feet thick, of a mottled gray color, and more crystalline than the others, is here burned for lime.*

From this place the hills gradually increase in elevation as we descend the river, and, in a little less than a mile, rise to the height of one hundred and forty feet. In this distance the St. Louis Limestone is constantly exposed, forming, at several points, perpendicu-

---

* An analysis of a pure variety of this rock, by Dr. Litton, yielded as follows:

Insol. residue, ...	0.50
Carbonate of lime, ...	99.40
Alumina, ...	A trace.
	99.90

lar walls, sixty feet high. About a mile and a half below the Arsenal, the following section of the strata is presented, which will convey a good general idea of the lithological features of the St. Louis Limestone. Commencing ten feet above the water level, and proceeding in the ascending series, there is —

1.	— Bluish gray, rather coarse textured, sub-crystalline limestone, in thin strata, filled with *Fenestella*, *Productus cora*, *Spirifer*, *Echinocrinus*, *Palæchinus*, and fish remains,	13 ft.
2.	— Light gray and bluish gray silico-calcareous rock, containing nodules and thin seams of chert,	5 ft.
3.	— Buff and bluish gray, hard, silicious limestone, of a finely-granular texture,	6 ft.
4.	— Same as the preceding, with a good deal of chert disseminated,	8 ft.
5.	— Compact, light gray silicious limestone, in thick beds, breaking with an even fracture,	7 ft.
6.	— Light drab, compact, brittle limestone, with a smooth, angular fracture (an excellent lime-rock),	3 ft.
7.	— Gray, mottled limestone, of a fine granular texture, with nodules and seams of chert,	44 ft.
8.	— Bluish gray, sub-crystalline limestone, containing cavities of brown calcareous spar; some layers beautifully ripple-marked,	10 ft.
9.	— Light drab, compact lithographic limestone, with a smooth, splintery fracture, containing Echinocidaris, Terebratula, and small columns of *Crinoidea*,	2 ft.
10.	— Earthy, decomposing, ferruginous limestone,	1 ft.
11.	— Gray, close-textured limestone, containing same fossils as No. 9,	4½ ft.
12.	— Earthy, decomposing, ferruginous limestone,	9 in.
13.	— Light drab and variegated, brittle, lithographic limestone,	1 ft. 8 "
14.	— Light drab, fine-textured, lithographic limestone, with a smooth, splintery fracture, traversed by fine spar veins, and delicately clouded with flesh color and reddish brown,	4 ft. 9 "
15.	— Strata like No. 9,	7 ft.

The strata included in No. 8 of this section are burned for lime, and make an article of excellent quality.

No. 14 appears to be a local bed. It is a remarkably fine variety of limestone, being nearly a pure carbonate. Some layers are, also, susceptible of a fine polish, the fine spar veins and delicate flesh-colored cloudings forming, with the light drab ground, a pleasing combination. I was not able, however, to satisfy myself whether slabs of a workable size could be got out, free from impurities and cracks. *

* The analysis of this rock, by Dr. Litton, resulted as follows: —

Insol. residue,	1.12
Alumina,	A Trace.
Carbonate of lime,	97.99
Water,	0.21
	99.32

A few hundred yards lower down the river, these rocks are overlaid with thick-bedded, finely-granular gray limestone, containing *Lithostrotian* and *Productus*, and these again are surmounted by thin strata of even-bedded, compact, sub-crystalline limestone, with *Palachinus multipora*, *Echinnocidaris*, *Poteriocrinus longidactylus*, *Spirigera Roisyii*, *Productus cora*, *Spirifer*, and *Fenestella.*

Several of these fossils are quite characteristic of the superior division of the *St. Louis Limestone.*

Continuing our section down the Mississippi, no marked change in the character of the rocks is observed before reaching Carondelet. The bluffs prevail along the river the whole distance, with an elevation of from 120 to 150 feet. The St. Louis Limestone is constantly exposed in nearly horizontal strata, the lower members projecting at intervals from the inferior slopes of the hills, while the superior beds appear in perpendicular walls near their summits.

At the quarry above Carondelet, a rapid inclination of the strata occurs, in a direction a little south of west; and the St. Louis Limestone dips beneath the water level of the Mississippi.

About two hundred and fifty yards below this place, is an exposure of nine feet of hard silicious limestone, in thin strata, with thin bands of fine-grained sandstone, interstratified, dipping at an angle of about eight degrees west south-west; and, near the center of the town, at an elevation of thirty-seven feet above the river, we find heavy-bedded, fine-grained micaceous sandstone, of white and ferruginous-brown colors, overlaid by dark and ash-gray, sandy, micaceous shale. These strata are much discolored with dark carbonaceous matter, which predominates in the shale. The latter, also, contains concretions, frequently of a branching form, probably the remains of coal-plants, although I was unable to detect any traces of organic structure in any of the specimens examined.

It is evident that we have here an outlier of the Missouri coal-field, occupying a narrow depression in the St. Louis Limestone, and constituting, I believe, the only example where strata belonging to the Coal Measures reach the west side of the Mississippi, south of St. Louis.

Towards the lower end of Carondelet I noticed some interesting sections, through the Quaternary deposits, which can be seen here to good advantage.

Just below the town, on the river, the upper part of the St. Louis Limestone, with its characteristic fossils, is quarried extensively, to be conveyed to St. Louis for harbor purposes. The strata are about sixty feet high, and dip to the north-east, at an angle of twenty degress. Some of the layers are quite cherty, but most of them would make a pure white lime.

Between this point and the mouth of Meramec river, no change occurs in the character of the geological formations; the St. Louis Limestone continues to be seen, at intervals, the whole distance, forming bluffs sometimes of 175 feet high, and appearing often, near their summits, in perpendicular escarpments, from sixty to eighty feet high.

Just above the Meramec, I observed a fine locality for fossil corals, chiefly *Lithostrotian, Canadense and Syringopora*, the former occurring in lenticular masses, some of them nearly five feet in diameter.

Below the Meramec, the hills recede from the Mississippi, and a bottom land sets in, which continues for two and a half miles, forming a bank from ten to twenty feet high. In Jefferson county, within half a mile of Rock Creek, we find for the first time, below the mouth of Missouri river, the Encrinital Limestone, Chemung and Trenton Groups. The hills are about 170 feet high, and exhibit the following section in the ascending order:—

1. — Perpendicular wall of heavy-bedded, yellowish and reddish subcrystalline limestone, traversed from base to summit by deep vertical fissures, and some of the layers containing cavities from one to five inches in diameter, frequently communicating with each other. The most common fossils of the mass are *Chaetetes lycoperdon, Leptena fillitexta, Leptena sericea, Orthis testudinaria*, and *Receptaculites*, . . .	thickness,	50 ft.
2. — Slope, covered by soil and debris, ...	"	15 ft.
3. — Reddish argillaceous limestone of a granular texture, with thin marly partings, containing *Cyathoxonia cynodon*, an *Orthis* nearly allied to *O. Michelini*, *Productus Murchisonianus, Platycrinus*, and *Poteriocrinus*, ...	"	15 ft.
4. — Slope with layers as above, projecting from the surface	"	30 ft.
5. — Encrinital Limestone, with chert bands interstratified, and filled with crinoids and other characteristic fossils of this group, ...	"	60 ft.

The lower beds of this section (No. 1) are Lower Silurian, and, probably, represent the "lead-bearing" or Galena Limestone of Iowa, Wisconsin and Illinois (Upper Magnesian Limestone, in part, of Dr. Owen), although the mass in the two districts differs essentially in lithological appearance, and in Missouri, so far as I know, it contains no productive deposits of lead.

The occurrence of the same species of *Receptaculites* in our strata, *R. sulcata* (*Coscinopora Sulcata, Owen*), leaves but little doubt with regard to the true parallelism, as this fossil in the north-west is never found below the galeniferous beds.

Nevertheless, while there is a marked lithological difference in Iowa and Wisconsin, as well as in Missouri, between the rocks of recognized Trenton age and the so-called Galena Limestone, we have, as yet, but little palæontological evidence for separating them into distinct groups. In fact, by far the greatest proportion of species found in the lead-bearing rocks of the north-west, are Trenton forms. Mr. Whitney states that, of forty-five species collected by Mr. A. Lapham and himself from the lead-bearing beds of Wisconsin, thirty-two were of Trenton age. (Metallic Wealth U. S., page 410.) And Prof. Hall mentions that he has found in the Galena Limestone, besides Receptaculites, the head of an *Illaenus*, *Leptena* not unlike *L. alternata*, *Orthis* (*Spirifer*) *lynx* and *Atrypa increvescens*. The three last-mentioned species are common to the Trenton Limestone and the Hudson river group, while the genus Receptaculites in New York, occurs in the Trenton Limestone, although Mr. Hall thinks the eastern species distinct from ours. For these reasons I have thought it best, for the present, to include our Receptaculite beds in the Trenton Limestone.

The slope, which is marked No. 2 in the above section, is, doubtless, occupied partly by sandstone, and partly by beds like No. 3; the former being exposed in this position a short distance lower down the river.

The fossils contained in the reddish, argillaceous limestone (Nos. 3 and 4), are a mixture of Chemung and Carboniferous forms. Some are identical with species which I have found in the argillaceous layers, interstratified with the fine-grained sandstone of the knobs of Kentucky, hitherto regarded as forming the base of the Carboniferous System in that State; others are species which, everywhere in Missouri, characterize the Chemung rocks. The last-mentioned group is here by no means so thick, or so highly fossiliferous as you found it in Cooper and the adjoining counties, on the Missouri river.

Continuing our way down the Mississippi, just below Rock Creek we find the Trenton Limestone forming low ledges on the river shore, from ten to twenty feet high. The lower strata are quite cherty, and contain but few fossils; the upper layers are filled with *Chaetetes lycoperdon*, *Leptena fillitexta*, and *Leptena sericea*, and other well-known species of the group.

Below this exposure, the bank of the river is twenty feet high, and composed of ash-colored loam, with terrestrial shells embedded.

The hills, removed a short distance from the river, are a hundred feet high, and exhibit, near their summits, perpendicular walls of Encrinital Limestone.

At the Sulphur Spring, just above Grand Glaize Creek, the following section occurs, counting from below, upwards: —

1.— Crystalline Trenton Limestone, with Receptaculites, forty-five feet.
2.— White and brown sandstone, made up of moderately fine quartz grains, loosely cemented, seven feet.
3.— Yellow, compact limestone (Chemung Group), eight feet.
4.— Red argillaceous and compact limestone (Chemung), twenty-five feet.
5.— Encrinital Limestone, highly fossiliferous, forty-five feet.

It will be perceived that, in this section, the Trenton rocks are separated from the Chemung and Carboniferous by only seven feet of sandstone; while the Hudson River Group, Upper Silurian and Devonian Systems, which are well represented in other parts of the State, are entirely wanting.

The water of the Sulphur Springs, at this place, contains a notable quantity of saline ingredients, and is strongly impregnated with sulphuretted hydrogen. In the bottom of the spring, a white deposit of sulphur is found. The water issues from beneath the sandstone, and its mineral properties are, probably, derived from the decomposition of pyrites in the reddish argillaceous limestone.

Between Grand Glaize and Rattlesnake Creeks, the formations of the above section continue the whole way, the Trenton Limestone forming perpendicular escarpments, from the water-level to the height of from sixty to eighty feet. The hills vary from 100 to 170 feet in height.

Just below Rattlesnake Creek, the Trenton Limestone, overlaid by sandstone, the Chemung and Encrinital Limestone, is exposed to the height of seventy-three feet, indicating a rise in the strata of twenty-eight feet in about a mile. It consists of heavy-bedded, white, crystalline limestone, with soft, chalky-looking, calcareous matter, and containing numerous cavities, lined with this substance, disseminated.

A stratum, near the top of it, furnishes the columns for the Court House, at St. Louis. This layer is six and a half feet thick, and is quarried quite easily. Beneath it, we find an apparently solid bed of nearly similar rock, twenty feet thick. The whole of the Trenton Limestone, at this place, would burn into a pure white lime. I found in these beds the following characteristic fossils: — *Chaetetes lycoperdon*, *Leptaena deltoidea*, *L. sericea*, *L. fillitexta*, *Atrypa capax*, *Lichas Trentonensis* and *Receptaculites.*

From this place, a rapid rise in the strata takes place, and the Chemung Group and Encrinital Limestone disappear from the tops of the hills. About a mile below Rattlesnake Creek, the lower Trenton beds emerge from beneath the crystalline portion above described; and in less than a mile further, we find them occupying the summits of the hills, which are elevated 150 feet above the bed of the Mississippi. This part of the Trenton Limestone is, in lithological appearance, quite different from the upper portion. It consists of bluish gray, or dove-colored, compact brittle limestone, breaking with a smooth conchoidal fracture. The beds vary in thickness from a few inches to several feet, the uppermost layers being the thinnest. The prevailing fossils are *Orthis tricenaria*, *O. subaequata*, *Leptaena deltoidea* *L. fillitexta*, *Murchisonia gracilis*, *Pleu-*

rotomaria subconica, *Chaetetes lycoperdon* and the columns of a small species of Crinoid.

Two miles below Rattlesnake Creek, we find these strata passing downwards, into beds containing *Gonioceras anceps*, and an *Ormoceras*, closely allied, if not identical with *O. tenuifilum* (Hall) species, which, in New York, are confined to the Black River Limestone. It is, therefore, certain that this group is represented in our State, although there is not, at least at the locality of which we are speaking, any difference in lithological characters between the beds containing Black River species and those with Trenton forms.

Beneath these beds, and just above the edge of the river, the strata assume a cellular character, and some layers are traversed in all directions by cylindrical cavities, varying from a fourth to half of an inch in diameter; many of them are filled with soft, yellow, argillaceous matter, while others are merely lined with this substance. These cavities, it is quite probable, were once filled with a fossil plant, very similar to *Phytopsis tubulosum* (Hall), from the Birds-Eye Limestone of New York; the substance of the fossil having been obliterated, its form is left in the more durable matrix. From the stratigraphical position of these perforated beds, I feel much inclined to the opinion that they will be found to represent the Birds-Eye Limestone of New York and Kentucky.

In the next two miles, there is no change in the formations; the Trenton and Black River Limestone continuing the whole distance, forming bold perpendicular escarpments, facing the river. At the "Old Shot Tower," just above Herculaneum, the bluffs are 170 feet high. The lower twenty feet consists of cellular limestone in thin layers, above which rises a perpendicular wall of heavy-bedded limestone, to the height of one hundred and ten feet. I found here, in addition to most of the species above enumerated, an *Illaenus*, very nearly allied to *I. crassicauda*, and an undescribed *Cythere*.

Below Herculaneum, the same rocks continue to escarp the river for upwards of a mile, and then the 1st Magnesian Limestone and Saccharoidal Sandstone of your general section appear at the base of the bluffs. These strata are best exposed at Plattin Rock, where we find, at the river margin, about fifteen feet of heavy-bedded Saccharoidal Sandstone, colored with oxide of iron. On this reposes 130 feet of buff magnesian limestone, in moderately thick beds, with thin partings of bluish argillaceous shale, passing upwards into thin-bedded magnesian limestone, with crystalline facets of calcspar disseminated. Then succeeds the Black River and Trenton

Limestones: the latter extending to the summits of the hills. This section indicates a rise in the strata of about one hundred and fifty feet in the distance of a mile.

Below Plattin Rock the hills recede from the river, and do not approach it again for a mile and a half. At two miles from Plattin Rock their altitude is 368 feet, ascertained by barometrical measurements.

At this place, the section in the ascending order is: —

1. — Heavy-bedded, white Saccharoidal Sandstone, . . . 15 ft.
2. — Thick beds of buff magnesian limestone, and thin partings of blue and green argillaceous marl, passing upward into lighter-colored magnesian limestone, in beds from an inch to a foot thick, containing crystalline particles of calc spar disseminated (1st Magnesian Limestone), ... 152 ft.
3. — Perpendicular bluff of compact, heavy-bedded, brittle limestone, containing Black River and Trenton fossils, . . 141 ft.
4. — Slope covered with soil and vegetation, ... 60 ft.

From this point to Selma, the general elevation of the hills does not vary much from 300 feet. A talus, covered with soil and masses of limestone, usually commences at the water margin, and extends to a height of from 100 to 150 feet; from which arises precipitous cliffs of rock, frequently cleft from base to summit by deep fissures.

At the upper end of Selma is an interesting section of the Silurian rocks, nearly all the beds being visible from the 1st Magnesian Limestone to the upper crystalline strata of the Trenton Limestone, inclusive. The elevation of this bluff is 413 feet, determined by several observations with the barometer.

The base consists of seventy feet of alternations of buff magnesian limestone, and compact, brittle, smooth-textured gray limestone, in layers from an inch to two feet thick. Then succeeds the limestones of Black River and Trenton age, presenting a thickness of more than 300 feet, the upper third being white crystalline limestone.

Selma has been for many years a prominent shipping point for lead, obtained chiefly from the mines of Washington county. Through the politeness of Mr. Foster, I was furnished with statistics of the amounts of lead received here during a period of twenty-eight years. These will be found in the Report of Dr. Litton.

Leaving Selma, we find a continuous line of bluffs extending to Rush Tower, the distance being about four miles. This portion of the river is remarkable for its picturesque scenery, which reminds one forcibly of the Mississippi above Prairie du Chien. The Silurian strata are constantly exposed in bold, perpendicular cliffs, towards the tops of the hills, while, below, are wooded slopes, covered with huge blocks of limestone, reaching to the margin of the water. In some instances the strata have been weathered in such a manner as to leave standing, isolated, tower-like masses, from twenty to thirty feet high, as represented in the cut.

BLUFFS ON THE MISSISSIPPI RIVER, BETWEEN SELMA AND RUSH TOWER.

Rush Tower is another shipping point for lead, most of which is brought from Perry's Mines, in St. François county.

At Rush Tower the bluffs again leave the Mississippi, and an alluvial bottom sets in and continues six miles, with a width of from one to three miles.

In this distance a considerable depression of the strata occurs, in a direction contrary to that observed at Selma. The Silurian rocks, which, between the latter place and Rush Tower, exhibit a thickness of from three to four hundred feet, here appear only as a low ledge, scarcely ten feet high, while the Carboniferous strata constitute the chief mass of the hills.

About four miles above Salt Point I found the elevation of the hills to be 274 feet, and obtained the following section, given in the ascending order: —

1. — Trenton Limestone, in thin layers, containing *Illaenus crassicauda*, *Receptaculites*, *etc.*, ... 10 ft.
2. — Dark bluish gray, argillaceous shale, containing a small species of *Lingula*, ... 30 ft.

3. — Reddish and yellowish argillaceous and sub-crystalline limestone, of Chemung Group, ... 34 ft.
4. — Encrinital Limestone, with *Pentremites Sayi*, *Productus punctatus*, and *Spirifer striatus*, ... 200 ft.

The dark argillaceous shale of this section is exposed in a ravine, a couple of hundred yards distant from the river, where it is seen immediately beneath the Chemung rocks and above the Trenton Limestone, which occurs in a low ledge, scarcely elevated above the water margin. This shale appears to replace the sandstone, which, at Sulphur Springs and below the mouth of Rattlesnake Creek, divides the Silurian rocks from the Chemung. It has been here penetrated twenty-five feet in search of coal, at which depth the workmen reached the Trenton Limestone, and further operations were abandoned. This labor and expense might have been saved, had the eye of a Geologist rested on the spot, for he would have seen at once that these strata lie several hundred feet below the coal formation. May not this slate represent the black, bituminons slate of Indiana and Kentucky, which, in those States, forms the line of separation between the Devonian strata and fine-grained micaceous sandstone, with its intercalated fossiliferous shales? It appears to occupy the same stratigraphical position, since we find it here directly under the Chemung rocks, in which we have found a number of fossils, identical with species that occur in the blue argillaceous limestone and marls, which lie a little above the black slate of Kentucky.

Continuing our way down the river, we find the rocks of the above section prevailing, uninterruptedly, to the mouth of Establishment Creek, and the hills varying from 120 to 180 feet in elevation. In the first three-quarters of a mile there is a pretty constant dip to the north-west, the rate being about eighty feet per mile. The dip then changes to a contrary direction, but is so gradual that it is barely perceptible.

On Establishment Creek, a couple of hundred yards above its confluence, dark argillaceous slate is again well exposed, in a ledge three feet high. It is precisely similar to that observed four miles above Salt Point, and contains a small undescribed species of *Lingula*.

The next good exposure occurs two miles and a half below the mouth of Establishment Creek; and here I observed, for the first time since leaving St. Louis, the Archimedes Limestone of your general vertical section, containing the usual fossils of this formation. The hills are 180 feet high, and the rocks project at intervals from various portions of the slopes, with a south-easterly dip. A mile below this place the hills decline in elevation to a hundred feet, and consist of alternations of quartzose sandstone and chert. Lower down, the Archimedes Limestone appears in perpendicular walls, facing the river, presenting a peculiar fluted appearance. A half of a mile still lower, the bluffs are 180 feet high, and the strata consist of sub-crystalline limestone, of a moderately coarse texture, and light gray and blue colors. Nearly all the beds here would make excellent lime. They, also, afford a good building material, being the same as are quarried on the Pacific Railroad, for the Custom-House at St. Louis. For the whole distance from this place to Ste. Genevieve, the Archimedes Limestone appears in perpendicular cliffs, near the tops of the hills.

Two miles above Ste. Genevieve the strata present a considerable local dip to the north-east; and just above the town they are to be seen in heavy massive beds, with a layer of calcareous oolite interstratified.

After passing Ste. Genevieve, no exposures of rock occur for a distance of nine miles. The river courses through alluvial bottoms, from one to five miles wide, and the banks vary from ten to twenty feet in height.

About one mile above St. Mary's we find, just above the water margin, an exposure of fifteen feet of quartzose sandstone, in thin layers, passing into gritstone and coarse conglomerate. The pebbles in the latter consist of milky and ferruginous quartz, jasper, and dark porphyry, varying from the size of a pea to that of a hen's egg. Above these beds is a slope of twenty-five feet, covered with soil and debris, and then succeeds the Archimedes Limestone, with its usual fossils.

Just above St. Mary's we find, at twenty feet above the Mississippi, alternations of yellow and purple clay, surmounted by compact and very hard Silicious Limestone, and, at a lower level, near the center of the town, the Archimedes Limestone.

At St. Mary's the bluffs again recede from the river on the Missouri shore, and do not approach it again for the distance of twenty-five miles. The banks are from ten to twenty feet high, and, beneath the soil and sub-soil, consist of ash-gray loam and sand, with the common terrestrial and fluriatile shells of this part of the Quaternary Group, embedded.

The point at which the hills reach the river again, is about a half of a mile above Bailey's Landing, in Perry county. Here their elevation is 150 feet, and they consist entirely of sandstone, resembling, very closely, the Saccharoidal Sandstone of the general section. The rock is exposed in massive rugged cliffs, and is composed of moderately fine grains, rather loosely cemented, with a silicious paste. Its color is white and reddish brown. Some portions of the mass crumble readily when exposed to the action of the weather; other beds are not so friable, and have the appearance of a good building rock.

Further down the river, a few hundred yards above Bailey's Landing, occurs a low ledge of thinly-stratified, blue silicious limestone, presenting a banded appearance on the weathered face, and traversed by vertical joints, which separate the layers into flattened quadrangular masses. These are surmounted by thick beds of the same lithological appearance, and the whole exhibits a dip of fifteen degrees north-east.

The mass contains remains of *encrinities*, and a small *Atrypa*, but fossils are scarce and badly preserved.

A quarter of a mile below Bailey's Landing, is a bluff 130 feet high, composed of heavy-bedded, gray magnesian limestone, very compact and fine-textured. Near the top I found a small species of *Atrypa*, an *Orthis*, like *O. subaequata*, and a *Leptaena*, very similar to *L. fillitexta*. I refer these strata, with some doubt, to the Trenton Limestone, as all the fossils I found, after a diligent search, were so badly weathered that their specific characters could not be determined. These bluffs continue along the river a quarter of a mile, presenting an irregular dip. At one point, about midway the exposure, the strata are inclined at an angle of twenty-five degrees to the east.

About a mile below Bailey's Landing, in fractional Sec. 11, Town. 35, R. 12, E., the hills are 130 feet high. On the river shore we find shaly layers of magnesio-calcareous limestone, containing silicious masses and a variety of interesting fossils. The rock is compact-textured, and has, evidently, been derived from fine sedimentary material. On the newly-fractured surfaces, it is of a light gray color, clouded with yellowish gray; but, after being exposed for some time to the air, it assumes a light buff color. The fossils are: *Leptaena depressa Leptaena*, several species; *Orthis*, two species, very similar to *O. hybrida* and *O. elegantula;* an *Atrypa*, allied to *A. camura* (Hall); *Platyostoma*, several species; *Dalmania tridentifera*, and *Phacops*, *Cheirurus* and *Haplocrinus*, of undescribed species.

Some of the fossils here enumerated cannot be distinguished from species which I found, several years since, in the Upper Silurian strata of the glades of Perry county, Tennessee, which, Mr. Meek informs me, have been found by Prof. Hall, in the Delthyris shaly Limestone of New York, and are regarded by him as quite characteristic of that group. And recently, through the kindness of Prof. Hall, I have been permitted to examine a number of the plates of his third volume on the Palæontology of New York; and, if we may be permitted to judge from excellent figures without descriptions, our collection from the locality now under notice contains several other Delthyris Shale species. Regarding, therefore, the parallelism as being pretty well established, I have, in my section, referred these rocks, and some others, presently to be noticed, to the age of the Delthyris Shale, in preference to giving them a new name.

The most characteristic fossil of the mass is the remarkable *trilobite*, which I have described in the Palæontology, under the name of *Dalmania tridentifera*. (Pl. B., fig. 8, a b.)

Above these fossiliferous layers, and at an elevation of 100 feet above the river, perpendicular ledges, presenting similar lithological characters, project from the slope of the hill to the height of thirty-five feet.

About three hundred yards lower down the river, is a massive cliff of yellowish gray limestone, sixty feet high, containing remains of Encrinites, and presenting on the weathered face no marks of stratification. These, probably, correspond in age to the rocks last described.

From this place the dip of the strata is very rapid, in a direction corresponding to the course of the river. In less than a half of a mile, we find the Archimedes Limestone, with its characteristic fossils, exposed at the margin of the river, while the Silurian strata above described, are far beneath the surface.

A quarter of a mile below this place, the Archimedes Limestone constitutes hills 200 feet high. At the base the strata consist of alternating beds of gray limestone, and bluish and ash-colored marl, abounding in fossils.

The fossils occur most abundantly in the marly layers, where, after heavy rains, they may be procured in great perfection. Above these fossiliferous layers, are massive beds of compact, earthy gray limestone, with thin partings of argillaceous shale interstratified, extending to the summits of the hills.

The Archimedes Limestone now preserves nearly a horizontal position for the distance of two miles, when it begins to dip, and at the same time receives a capping of sandstone, which increases in thickness as we descend the river; and, at three miles below the point where it first appears, occupies nearly the entire mass of hills, two hundred feet high.

The lower part of this sandstone occurs in heavy beds, but the upper strata are often quite schistose. The rock is sometimes very hard, but usually it is so loosely cemented, that a blow with the hammer reduces it to fine sand. The color varies from white to ferruginous brown. At this point there seems to be an abrupt synclinal axis, for, in a few hundred yards, we find the Archimedes Limestone rapidly rising again, and, in a little upwards of a mile, the line of junction between it and the sandstone, is seen near the tops of the hills.

These rocks now continue, uninterruptedly, to *Brazos Bottom;* and the Archimedes Limestone being frequently exposed, excellent opportunities were afforded for collecting its characteristic fossils. At Wittenburg, the bluffs are 150 feet high; and from the lower two-thirds, ledges of gray limestone, with Productus, Echinocrinus and fish-teeth, occasionally appear. These strata are highly inclined, and resemble the beds observed just above Ste. Genevieve. The upper third of the hills is covered with soil and loose masses of sandstone.

Nearly opposite this place, on the Illinois shore, is the "Devil's Bake-Oven"—an isolated mass of rock, sixty feet high, with a large opening on the southern face.

Opposite "The Oven," on the Missouri shore, the bluffs are 120 feet high, and exhibit, near the base, perpendicular cliffs of thin-bedded calcareo-magnesian limestone, containing a small *Atrypa* and fragments of an Encrinite, which I refer, with some doubt, to the genus *Heterocrinus* of Hall. These rocks bear a very close resemblance to the Delthyris Shale, noticed a mile below Bailey's Landing, and, doubtless, belong to the same geological period.

The Grand Tower rises from the bed of the Mississippi, about a mile and a half below Wittenburg. It is an isolated mass of rock, of a truncated-conical shape, crowned at the top with stunted cedars, and situated about fifty yards from the Missouri shore. It is eighty-five feet high, and four hundred yards in circumference at the base. During high water, the current rushes around its base with great velocity, and the passage on the Missouri side is regarded as being a very dangerous one. The rock of which the tower is composed, is a buff and bluish gray silicious limestone, very compact and thin-bedded, and it dips at an angle of twenty-five degrees to the south-east. I could not discover any fossils here; but, from the lithological character of the mass, I am disposed to place it with the Delthyris Shaly Limestone, and, consequently, beneath the rocks of the Devil's-Oven, which, as I am informed, by Dr. Norwood, State Geologist of Illinois, contain many characteristic species of the Devonian System.

About a half of a mile below the Tower, near the middle of the river, is a huge mass of chert, of a quadrangular shape, which, at an ordinary stage of water, rises several feet above the surface. In the next two miles the Missouri shore is bounded by hills from 75 to 200 feet in altitude.

These hills are mostly covered with soil and vegetation; but not unfrequently at their bases, on the side facing the river, we find exposures of ferruginous and white silicious clay, filled with fragments of chert, derived from the decomposition of Upper Silurian rocks, which, further down the river, are seen to present a marked cherty character. This white clay sometimes gives to the faces of the hills a peculiar chalky appearance; hence, they have received, from travelers, the name of "Chalk Bluffs."

Two miles above Birmingham, in Cape Girardeau county, Delthyris Shaly Limestone again appears, just above the water margin, containing the same fossils that characterize the silico-magnesian limestone, observed a mile below Bailey's Landing. It is constantly exposed for the distance of four miles, appearing in ledges at the base of the hills, from ten to fifty feet high. The strata along the line of this exposure consist of alternations of silicious and earthy gray limestone, and ferruginous chert in moderately thin layers. The limestone frequently contains rounded masses of hornstone, from the size of a hen's egg to that of a bushel-measure. These masses often exhibit a concentric structure, and impart to the weathered surfaces of the strata an exceedingly rough appearance.

Fossils are not abundant, except at Birmingham, where I procured most of the species that were observed at one mile below Bailey's Landing. Three miles and a half below Birmingham, the same rocks appear in a mural escarpment, extending from the water's edge to the height of seventy feet. The lower part of the mass consists of limestone and chert, the latter predominating and occurring in layers, from an inch to a foot thick: the upper layers have the appearance of hydraulic limestone, and contain a beautiful species of *Conularia.*

Below this place, the faces of the cliffs are cut into deep vertical fissures, presenting a rude castellated appearance; and this feature prevails to within a short distance of Neily's Landing, situated in Town. 33 N., R. 14 E., Sec. 33.

Three-quarters of a mile lower down the river, the Delthyris Shaly Limestone is visible to the height of 100 feet above the Mississippi, presenting the same characters as the beds last mentioned. At the upper end of the exposure, is the "Devil's Tea-Table," a curious mass of rock, of an inverted conical form, standing on a rocky base, sixty feet above the river. It is eight feet high, two yards wide at the top, but contracted below to two feet. It is composed of horizontal layers of limestone and chert, and has been formed from the removal by denudation of the regular strata, with which it was once continuous.

The Missouri shore now exhibits a constant succession of high bluffs, with precipitous escarpments, until we reach Bainbridge, the distance being about six miles. Near Vancil's Landing, they attain an altitude of 330 feet, with perpendicular faces to the river of 120 feet. Towards the tops of the cliffs, are bluish and ash-colored, earthy-looking layers, which have the appearance of hydraulic limestone. An analysis of this rock will be found in the report of Dr. Litton. It contains *Phacops*, *Spirifer Orthis* and *Conulana* of undescribed species. The lower part of the mass contains fossil of the Delthyris Shaly Limestone.

After leaving Bainbridge, bottom-land sets in, and no rocks are again seen on the river, for the distance of six or seven miles.

From one and a half to two miles above Cape Girardeau, is an exposure of about forty feet of bluish gray limestone, in layers from two to six inches thick, and traversed by numerous vertical joints. The rock is very compact, and breaks with a smooth, splintery fracture.* The weathered surfaces are frequently covered with a thin film of oxide of iron. In some portions of the mass, fossils occur in great variety and abundance.

They are *Cyphaspis Girardeauensis* (*new sp.*), *Acidaspis Halli* (*new sp.*), *Proetus depressus* (*new sp.*), *Encrinurus deltoideus* (*new sp.*), *Cheirurus* (*undt.*), *Homocrinus flexuosus* (*new sp.*), *Glyptocrinas fimbriatus* (*new sp.*), *Tentaculites*, *incurvus*, *Protaster?* (*new sp.*), *Atrypa*, *Leptena*, *Orthis*, *Pleurotomaria* and *Turbo*. In addition to these, I found forms of Crinoids, which will not admit of being placed in any known genera. All the fossils of this locality appear to be distinct from any hitherto described, and they, therefore, constitute an interesting feature in the palæontology of our State.

The trilobites are especially abundant, and usually finely preserved. In a specimen before me, not more than four inches square, I am able to count four species of these Crustaceans, belonging to as many different genera. The Tentaculite, which I have described as *T. incurvus*, is also quite numerous, some slabs being completely covered with them. I have referred these beds to the Upper Silurian system, from their stratigraphical position, and from the occurrence of genera of trilobites, which, according to Barrande, in his valuable work on the Silurian System of Bohemia, are types which exhibit the greatest development of species in the strata of that period.

These rocks we have designated, provisionally, under the name of Cape Girardeau Limestone. They constitute the lowermost beds of Upper Silurian age, yet found in the State.

At Cape Girardeau, the Trenton Limestone is again well exhibited; and here we find the following section from below, upwards: —

1.—Blue schistose limestone, highly fossiliferous. Some of the layers are almost completely made up of *Chaetetes lycoperdon*, *Leptena filitexta* and *Orthis subaequata*, ...	2 ft.
2.—White crystalline limestone, in moderately-heavy beds, with *Illaenus crassicauda*, *Leptaena alternata*, &c., ...	35 ft.

---

* The composition of this rock, as ascertained by Dr. Litton, is as follows: —

Insoluble residue, ...	8.60
Alumina, and peroxide of iron, ...	1.93
Carbonate of lime, ...	86.00
Carbonate of magnesia, ...	3.70
	100.23

3.—White and bluish white, massive-bedded crystalline limestone, of fine texture, containing characteristic Trenton fossils, . 60 ft.
4.—Fine-grained argillaceous sandstone, of a light ferruginous brown color, ... 10 ft.

The strata included in No. 3 of this section constitute the well-known Cape Girardeau marble. The principal quarries are situated about three-quarters of a mile from the river, where the marble has been wrought to the thickness of forty feet. We find here two distinct varieties: one of a bluish tinge, and somewhat coarse-textured, affords an excellent and durable building stone, and is burned on the spot for lime; the other, a purer white, and more compact variety, answers all the ordinary purposes of marble.* It is extensively cut for tomb-stones in the neighborhood; and, if judiciously selected, takes a tolerable polish. It has been extensively shipped to St. Louis and other points; and I am informed that it was employed for the construction of the State-House, at Baton Rouge, Louisiana. This marble is also quarried on the river shore, in front of the Convent. It occupies precisely the same geological position as the quarry at Rattlesnake Creek, which affords the columns for the Court-House, at St. Louis.

On the summits of the hills, in the vicinity of Cape Girardeau, we find a reddish brown argillaceous sandstone, in heavy and thin beds. It is soft when first quarried, but becomes hard on exposure to the air. It is employed for the outside work of lime-kilns, and for walling and flagging stones.† The position of this rock is immediately above the "Cape Girardeau marble," and beneath the Upper Silurian strata, observed two miles above Cape Girardeau, on the Mississippi.

Resuming our journey, the Trenton Limestone was found to prevail for about a half of a mile, forming low ledges along the river

---

* The proportions of the different constituents of this marble are, according to Dr. Litton's analysis, as follows: —

Carbonate of lime,	99.57
Silica,	*a trace.*
Alumina,	*a trace.*

† Dr. Litton's analysis of this rock resulted as follows: —

Silica,	87.58
Alumina, and peroxide of iron,	9.67
Lime, not determined,	
Water,	1.35
	98.60

shore; then, alluvial lands, from ten to twenty-five feet high, succeed, and continue to a small creek, five miles below Cape Girardeau.

Just below the mouth of this creek, the Trenton Limestone is again exposed, in bold escarpments, fifty-five feet high. The blue schistose layers present a thickness of fifteen feet, and are densely crowded with fossils, usually in a most perfect state of preservation. These are surmounted by the white crystalline beds of the last section, which exhibit a thickness of forty feet. The upper portion appears to present all the characters of the Cape Girardeau marble; and there is, in my opinion, no doubt but that a marble of good quality may also be quarried here. This exposure extends along the river for several hundred yards, the schistose layers disappearing towards the lower extremity, whilst the crystalline beds form cliffs ninety feet high. In the uppermost strata, I found *Receptaculites*, and good specimens of a prettily-sculptured crinoid, of the genus *Echinoencrinites.*

At the foot of the "Grand Chain," on Oerter's land, the Trenton Limestone is capped with sandstone, similar to that noticed on the higher elevations in the vicinity of Cape Girardeau. The hills are about a hundred feet high; and on the declivities of some of them, deposits of potter's clay occur, of good quality. The variety preferred by Mr. Oerter, who has a pottery at this place, is of a yellowish ash color, and contains masses of ochre disseminated. It is, however, generally mixed with a white clay, obtained three-quarters of a mile west of the pottery, the mixture forming a better quality of ware than when either is used separately.*

A mile below the Grand Chain, the river shore is covered with huge blocks of white and brown sandstone, some of them weighing many tons; and a half of a mile below this locality, it is seen in place, reposing on clay and shale, with a dip of twenty degrees south-east. The section here, in the ascending order, is: —

1.— Slope, covered with large blocks of sandstone, ten feet.
2.— Gray and purple shale, with thin laminations of sandstone, eight feet.
3.— Ferruginous, highly plastic, silicious clay, with fragments of decomposing chert, embedded, twenty feet.
4.— White and brown heavy-bedded sandstone, thirty to forty feet.

A short distance from this place, and three-quarters of a mile above Commerce, is a deposit of pure white silicious clay, contain-

---

* I am indebted to Dr. Litton for the following analyses of these clays: —

No. 49. — Clay, from a point on Mississippi river, three-quarters of a mile above Commerce, gave —

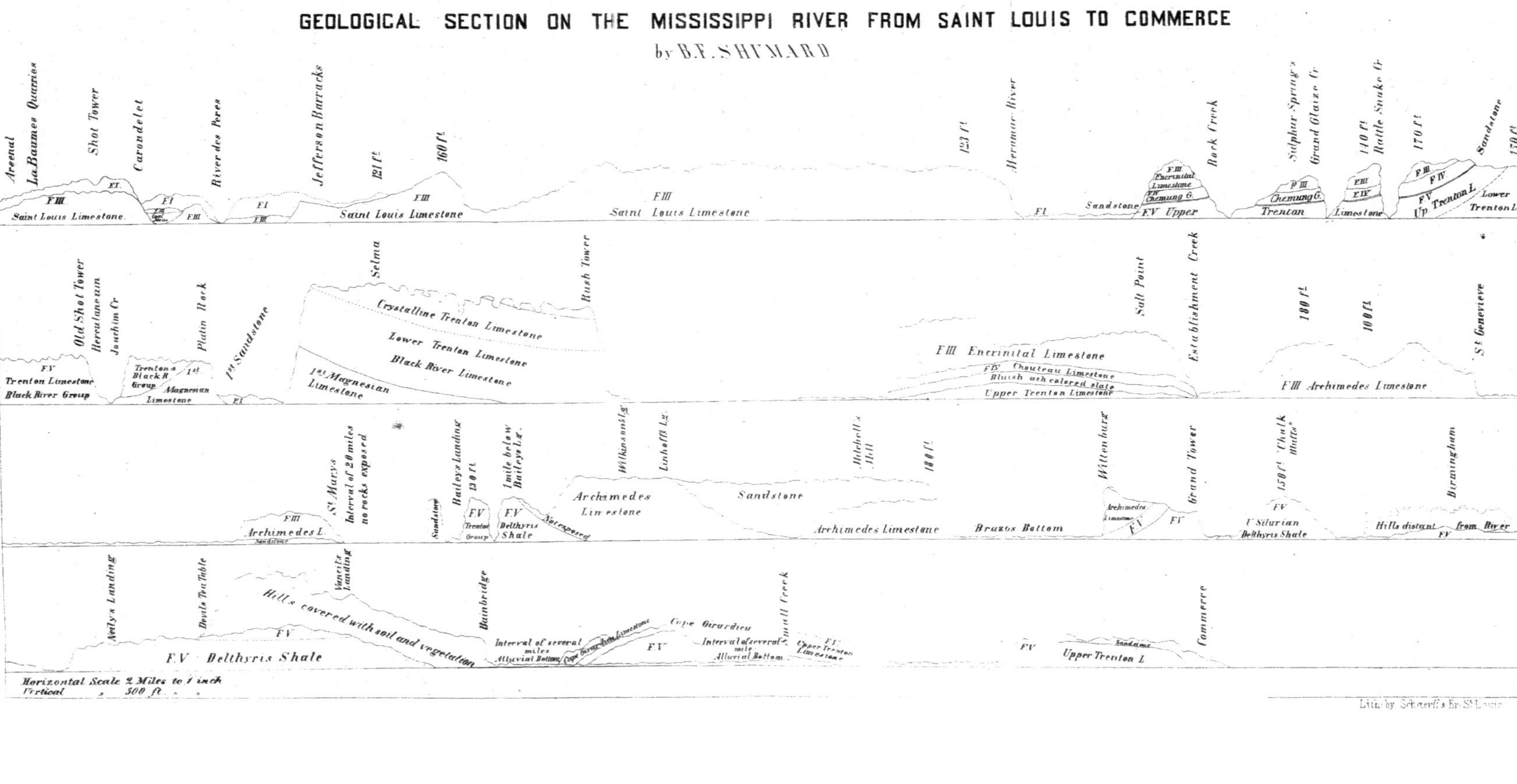
GEOLOGICAL SECTION ON THE MISSISSIPPI RIVER FROM SAINT LOUIS TO COMMERCE
by B.F. SHUMARD
Arsenal
LaBaumes Quarries
Shot Tower
Carondelet
River des Peres
Jefferson Barracks
121 ft
160 ft
Saint Louis Limestone
123 ft
Meramec River
Sandstone
Rock Creek
FV Upper
Chemung G.
Encrinital Limestone
Sulphur Springs
Grand Glaize Cr
Trenton
140 ft
Rattle Snake Cr
Limestone
170 ft
Up. Trenton L.
Lower Trenton L.
150 ft
Old Shot Tower
Herculaneum
Joachim Cr
Trenton Limestone
Black River Group
Trenton & Black R. Group
1st Magnesian Limestone
Platin Rock
1st Sandstone
Selma
Crystalline Trenton Limestone
Lower Trenton Limestone
Black River Limestone
Rush Tower
Salt Point
Establishment Creek
FIII Encrinital Limestone
FIV Chouteau Limestone
Bluish ash colored slate
Upper Trenton Limestone
180 ft
100 ft
FIII Archimedes Limestone
St Genevieve
Archimedes L.
St Marys
Interval of 20 miles no rocks exposed
Haileys Landing
130 ft
Trenton Group
1 mile below Haileys Lg.
Delthyris Shale
Not exposed
Wilkinsons Lg.
Linhoffs Lg.
Archimedes Limestone
Sandstone
Mitchells Hill
180 ft
Brazos Bottom
Wittenburg
Grand Tower
150 ft "Chalk Bluffs"
U Silurian Delthyris Shale
Birmingham
Hills distant from River
Neilys Landing
Devils Tea Table
Hills covered with soil and vegetation
Vancils Landing
Bainbridge
FV Delthyris Shale
Interval of several miles Alluvial Bottom
Cape Girardeau
Small Creek
Upper Trenton Limestone
Upper Trenton L.
Commerce
Horizontal Scale 2 Miles to 1 inch
Vertical 500 ft.
Lith. by Schaerff's Br. St Louis

ing masses of flint and ochre. It commences at the river margin, and extends to the height of twenty-five feet, where it is surmounted by sandstone.

Between this point and Commerce, the hills do not vary much from a hundred feet in height, and sandstone is the only rock to be seen. At the village, it reaches from the water level to the height of fifty feet. This rock exposure is the last to be seen on the Missouri shore in descending the Mississippi, and our section, therefore, terminates at this point.

FRANKLIN COUNTY.

This county embraces rather less than twenty-four townships, or an area of about eight hundred and sixty square miles.

By referring to the accompanying geological map, it will be seen that it is remarkably well watered by numerous streams, the most important of which, besides the Missouri, are the Meramec, Bourbeuse, St. John's, Bœuf and Berger. The three last-mentioned traverse the north-western portion of the county, receiving in their course a number of small tributaries, and flowing in a north-easterly direction to join the Missouri. The Meramec, a confluent of the Mississippi, is the largest stream that meanders through the county. It enters in Town. 40 N., R. 2 W., and, flowing in a north-easterly direction, leaves it in Town. 43 N., R. 2 E. It is exceedingly tortuous in its course, and its descent is often quite rapid. The valley through which it runs is very variable in width; it sometimes presents

---

Silica,	86.82
Alumina, with a trace of peroxide of iron,	9.09
Lime,	0.33
Water,	3.13
	99.37

The silica obtained was dissolved in hydrofluoric acid.

No. 50. — Clay, from creek on Oerter's place — whiter variety —

Silica,	80.50
Alumina, with some peroxide of iron,	14.05
Lime,	0.35
Magnesia,	0.44
Water,	3.71
	99.05

No. 51. — Clay, from the same place as the last, blue variety —

Silica,	62.73
Alumina, with some peroxide of iron,	23.17
Lime,	1.69
Magnesia,	1.42
Water,	10.49
	99.50

a broad valley, susceptible of a high state of cultivation, and at others confined between hills, which attain an altitude of 300 feet, with abrupt declivities down to the water level, and occasionally perpendicular escarpments 200 feet high.

The valley of the Bourbeuse, in its general features, resembles that of the Meramec. It enters Franklin from Gasconade county, in Town. 41 N., R. 4 W., and after a remarkably sinuous course, joins the Meramec in Town. 42 N., R. 1 E.

The surface of Franklin county consists chiefly of ranges of hills, elevated from 100 to 300 feet above the level of the adjacent streams, and often separated from each other by deep valleys, some of them very narrow, others wide. The general direction of the main ridges is pretty uniformly north-east and south-west. In the southern part, the country is very uneven, particularly in the mining districts. The soil throughout the county is, in general, of good quality, and well suited for cultivation. On the summits of the sandstone ridges, it is often too light and sandy, but, even here, we find some excellent farm sites. In the townships underlaid by the magnesian limestones, and in the valleys of the streams, the soil is generally remarkably productive, and well adapted to the culture of corn and different varieties of small grain.

The Quaternary deposits are pretty widely spread over the county. They consist of ash gray and light-colored clays, sandy clay and sand, in alternating layers, and lie immediately beneath the soil. At a few points, I have observed terrestrial and fluviatile shells embedded, belonging chiefly to the genera Helix, Lymnea, Physa and Planorbis, mostly of existing species. The greatest thickness that I have observed the formation to attain, in the county, is about thirty-five feet. It is often finely exhibited along the shores of the Missouri, Meramec and Bourbeuse. These deposits often furnish the very best materials in the county, for the manufacture of bricks.

All the rocks in Franklin county, beneath the soil and Quaternary deposits, belong to the Lower Silurian system. They represent the inferior part of this system, and are equivalent in age to the Trenton and Black River Limestones, and Calciferous Sandrock, of the New York series.

The general inclination of the strata is to the north-east, though there are frequent local variations from this direction. In many places, the beds appear to lie perfectly horizontal; sometimes they are inclined at angles, varying from one to thirty degrees; and at other, they exhibit an undulating dip.

In describing the several groups, we will commence with the uppermost, and proceed in the descending order.

Of the *Trenton Limestone*, we find only the inferior beds of the mass represented, and these confined to a limited portion of the county. It enters at the north-eastern corner, and makes its appearance at intervals, within a space about eight miles long, with an average breadth of about two miles. Over this area it constitutes the surface rock of all the higher elevations; but, in the valleys and on the inferior slopes of the hills, we find strata which belong to the inferior groups.

The best exposures that I have observed, occur on the Missouri river, at St. Albans, on Fox Creek, in the vicinity of Gray's Gap, and near the town of Franklin. At all these places it presents the usual characters of the lower part of the mass—a bluish gray, compact limestone, with a smooth angular fracture. The most characteristic fossils are *Leptaena filitexta*, *Leptaena sericea*, *Orthis disparilis*, *Orthis subaequata*, — *Orthis tricenaria* and *Chaetetes lycoperdon*.

The *Black River Limestone*, which underlies the last, may be seen at St. Albans, on Fox Creek, and in the vicinity of Franklin. The superior part cannot be separated from the Trenton Limestone, the lithological characters being precisely the same, and fossils are by no means abundant. The lower part is an exceedingly compact, brittle, pure limestone, of a pale drab color, and resembles very closely the upper beds of the St. Louis Limestone. In hand specimens, it would puzzle any one to perceive any difference between them. This rock is seen to advantage at Gray's Gap, near the summit of the hill.

The two groups we have described are the most valuable in the county for quicklime; nearly all the strata will answer for this purpose; but the light drab beds, at the base, will probably make the purest variety. The Trenton Group, also, affords some good materials for building purposes; and, if desirable, good quarries might be opened at points along the line of its exposure.

The 1*st Magnesian Limestone* of your general section is the next rock that appears in the descending order. This, also, occupies but a limited part of the county. It forms a narrow belt on the north side of Meramec river, in Town. 43, R. 2 E., its eastern limit being in Sec. 17. At several points on the Meramec it appears in perpendicular cliffs. It, also, shows itself beneath the Black River Limestone on the Missouri river, at St. Albans. Quarries have been opened in this rock at Gray's Gap, and on Keatley's farm, near Franklin.

At Gray's Gap it presents the following section, from above downwards:—

1. —	Buff-colored, ferruginous, magnesian limestone, in thin layers, separated by thin partings of soft argillaceous shale, banded with blue and yellow, ...	4½ ft.
2. —	Seam of bluish marl, ...	4 in.
3. —	Heavy-bedded, brown and buff magnesian limestone, with masses of calc spar disseminated, ...	12 ft.
4. —	Even-bedded, buff magnesian limestone, in thin layers, .	35 to 40 ft.

The strata marked 3 in this section have been selected for the construction of culverts and bridges on the Pacific Railroad, for which the rock answers a good purpose, having the appearance of durability, and being tolerably free from cherty intermixture.

The fossils of this formation are a small species of *Cythere*, which I have named *C. sublaevis*, and some small gasteropods, too imperfect for accurate determination. In this county, the fossils are invariably casts. It is difficult to decide whether this portion of the 1st Magnesian Limestone should be grouped with the Calciferous Sandrock, or with the Black River Limestone, or whether it is distinct from either, and representing the Chazy limestone of the New York Geologists. Regarding it lithologically, we would include it in the Calciferous group, with which it presents considerable analogy; but, on the other hand, the fossils are most like those of the Black River and Trenton Groups.

The next formation below is the *Calciferous Sandrock*, which occupies all the remainder of the county. It is a very important mass, not only on account of its extent and thickness, but as being the repository of valuable ores of lead, iron and copper. Its thickness is much greater than the same group in New York. It is the equivalent of the St. Peter's Sandstone, or Lower Magnesian Limestone of Iowa, Wisconsin and Minnesota, described by Dr. D. D. Owen, in his official reports to Congress; but its thickness is much greater.

In Franklin county, as elsewhere in Missouri, the mass consists of beds of magnesian limestone and sandstone, of greater or less thickness, which, for the sake of more easy reference, have been divided into several subordinate formations.

The first of these, beneath the 1st Magnesian Limestone, is the *Saccharoidal Sandstone*. By reference to the map, it will be seen that this division of the Calciferous Group (marked F. U.) prevails to a considerable extent in the county, and particularly in the northwestern quarter, where it occupies the summits of nearly all the highest ridges. It would be impossible to indicate, in this description, all the points where it appears. I shall, therefore, merely designate those places where it shows to the best advantage.

In the north-eastern portion of the county, we find it underlying the groups already described. On the Missouri river, in Town. 44 N., R. 2 E., it appears toward the base of the bluffs. It is, also, frequently exposed in the south-east quarter of this township, where it occupies the lower part of the hills, and constitutes the surface rocks of all the lower grounds. In Town. 43, of the same range, the sandstone occurs in all the sections, from five to thirteen inclusive; and, also, in sections 2, 3, 16, 17 and 18. In Wilhelm's field, north-west quarter of section 9, the junction of the sandstone with the 1st Magnesian Limestone may be seen to good advantage. On the south side of Meramec river, it forms the summit of the dividing ridge between the Little Meramec and Calva, occupying a narrow belt, scarcely a half of a mile in width, extending in a curve through the north-east corner of Town. 42 N., R. 2 E. Again, in the same township, it caps the ridges between the Meramec and Little Meramec rivers; thence, passes into Town. 41 of same range, and appears on all the higher elevations in that township. The sandstone again shows itself in Town. 43, and fractional township 44 N., R. 1 E., and 1 W., but here it occurs as mere outliers, of no great extent. The greatest development of the mass, as before stated, is in the north-west quarter of the county, where it occupies the summit of the dividing ridges between the St. John's, Bœuf and Berger rivers, and, also, between the heads of these streams and the waters of the Bourbeuse. As these ridges are separated from each other by valleys, often excavated through the sandstone, and deeply into the subjacent magnesian limestone, it frequently happens that the former occurs in bands, varying from a few yards to more than a mile in width, and several miles in length, along which we sometimes find the rock projecting above the general level, in the form of huge knobby cliffs, from sixty to eighty feet high.

On the accompanying geological map, I have represented, with as much accuracy as possible, the boundaries of the several areas in this district within which the sandstone prevails, from which a better idea of its extent can be gained than from any detailed description that could be written.

South of the Bourbeuse, the rock under consideration is again found capping the hills, in townships forty and forty-one, occupying a space from one to three miles wide on both sides of the line, between ranges two and three, west; it also occurs in Town. 40, Rs. 3 and 4 W.

The Saccharoid Sandstone usually occurs in thick beds, though it occasionally exists in thin layers, particularly near its junction with the formations that lie above and below it. The color varies from white to a dark ferruginous brown. Near the top it assumes, sometimes, a bluish tinge, from the presence of argillaceous matter. It is generally made up of quartzose grains, which often cohere so slightly, that, when struck with the hammer, it falls to fine sand. Sometimes the grains are firmly cemented with a silicious paste, and, at other times, though rarely, it passes into quartz rock.

The friable character of the mass renders it unfit, as a material, for the construction of buildings. The white variety is, from its pure quartzose character, well adapted for glass making, and for all purposes for which a fine quality of sand is required.

I have not been able to see its whole thickness at any point in Franklin county, but it may be estimated at not less than 175 feet.

Organic Remains.—No traces of fossils have been observed in the Saccharoid Sandstone in this county, although diligent search has been made, wherever the rock appeared likely to yield them. The absence of these remains, and the resemblance which portions of the mass bear to the sandstones beneath, have often rendered it difficult to recognize it with certainty.

2d Magnesian Limestone (F. v, of the general vertical section).—This formation, which underlies the sandstone we have just described, is generally known under the name of "Glade Rock," from the fact that barren places, termed glades, prevail, where certain portions approach the surface. Some layers are, also, frequently called "Cotton Rock," a name probably derived from their whitish appearance.

The mass is widely spread over the county, occupying rather more than half its entire extent. It frequently shows itself in perpendicular escarpments along the Missouri river, from the western limit of the county to within five or six miles of its eastern border. It occupies the valleys of all the streams flowing into the Missouri, except a few small branches in the eastern tier of townships, and it, also, exists on the dividing ridges between these streams.

East of St. John's river it underlies a wide district between the Missouri and Bourbeuse, limited on the east by the Saccharoidal Sandstone, already noticed. The two principal towns in the county, Washington and Union, are underlaid by this rock. From Union it may be traced in a narrow belt, running parallel with the Bourbeuse, but from a quarter to a half of a mile distant, as far as the western limit of the county.

The mass is again largely developed south of Meramec river, in Towns. 42 and 43, R. 2 E., and in the north half of Town. 41, of same range. It is, also, frequently visible in the south-west corner of the county, in the valley of the Red-Oak Creek, a small tributary of the Bourbeuse.

The thickness of this formation may be seen to good advantage on the Meramec, two or three miles below the mouth of the Bourbeuse. Here it rather exceeds, than falls short of, 300 feet. I have not observed so great a thickness elsewhere in the county.

In many cases we can readily distinguish the mass under consideration from the magnesian limestone, above and beneath, by its lithological appearance alone. It may be described, in general terms, as an even-bedded magnesian limestone, occurring on layers, from a couple of inches to two or three feet in thickness, with occasional intercalations of sandstone and silicious oolite.

At the top, we usually find thin alternations of magnesian limestone, sandstone and silicious oolite; the latter sometimes passing into hard chert. The thickness of these layers is from fifteen to thirty feet.

Below these, we have the "Cotton Rock," with thick beds of buff and gray magnesian limestone intercalated, the whole exhibiting a thickness of about 200 feet. The "Cotton Rock," which is by far the most important part of the 2d Magnesian Limestone, is usually of a light cream color, sometimes dull white, and sometimes light buff or gray. It breaks with an even fracture, has a dull earthy appearance, and, sometimes, contains crystalline particles of calc spar disseminated. Its texture is, in general, finely granular, and, owing to the presence of earthy matter, it is not susceptible of polish. The layers vary from a couple of inches to two feet in thickness, and are often separated by partings of argillaceous shale. Beneath these beds the strata assume a light gray, or buff hue, and contain more calcareous matter than any part of the mass; and, at the same time, resemble so closely some beds of the 3d Magnesian Limestone, that it is exceedingly difficult, if not impossible, to distinguish the one from the other. Below these again, we have alternations of sandstone, magnesian limestone and oolite, similar to the beds at the top of the formation.

Fossils are extremely rare in the 2d Magnesian Limestone. I have only noticed them at two localities, close together, on the Springfield road, not far from the point where it crosses the Bourbeuse. They are confined to the oolitic layers, near the base of the formation, and consist of *Pleurotomaria*, *Murchisonia* and *Straparollus*, but they are invariably casts, and good specimens of even these are not common. I have figured one of these shells in the third plate of the Palæontology, under the name of *Murchisonia melaniaformis*.

Economically considered, the mass is of great importance. All the workable ores of iron in the county are contained in this formation. It is, also, now known to contain productive deposits of lead, though by no means so extensive as occur in the 3d Magnesian Limestone. The Golconda Mines, situated about four miles northeast of Union, are in this formation; and I have received, through the politeness of Mr. Reese, Engineer on the Pacific Railroad, specimens of galena, which were obtained from this rock, on the Mississippi river, a short distance below Washington.

I do not purpose, however, to enter here into a description of the deposits of lead and iron that characterize the mass, since a particular account of these will be found in the report of Dr. A. Litton, on the mines.

Building Materials.—The 2d Magnesian Limestone furnishes some of the most beautiful rocks for buildings, in the county. The Cotton Rock is generally well adapted for this purpose. It is wrought easily, and many of the layers have the appearance of durability. Buildings constructed of this rock have a peculiarly neat and elegant appearance; and, as it frequently contains but a small proportion of iron, very little change in color takes place from exposure. Several quarries have been opened in the mass, near Washington and Franklin, and at various other localities in the county. It is not usually well suited for hearth-stones and fire-places, since it is liable to crack and fly to pieces when submitted to the action of much heat. The lower part of the formation will afford, perhaps, the best material for this purpose.

For *quicklime*, the mass is inferior to the rocks of the Trenton, and Black River Limestones; and some portions of it will not slake at all, after having been burned. However, throughout the district over which it prevails, beds may nearly always be found, that contain enough calcareous matter to make a tolerably strong lime. In the vicinity of Washington, and in other portions of the county, are kilns where some of the cream-colored layers are burned for lime, and furnish a good article for ordinary use.

Hydraulic Cement.—Some of the light-colored, earthy, granular varieties, resemble hydraulic limestone, but the rock has not yet been sufficiently tested to allow me to speak positively as to whether it really possesses such properties or not. For tomb-stones, fine selections may be made from the layers of the Cotton Rock; the light cream-colored and finely granular varieties being best adapted for this purpose.

The next sub-group of the Calciferous Sandrock, in the descending order, is the *2d Sandstone* (F. w, of the general section). This division of the formation lies mostly south of the line, between townships forty-two and forty-three. North of this line, we find it occupying merely a narrow strip, not exceeding a half of a mile wide, on both sides of the Bourbeuse, in Town. 43 N., R. 1 E., and a small space, a quarter of a mile north of this stream, in Town. 43, R. 1 W.

In the south-east corner of the county, it constitutes the prevailing surface rock of the high-lands, over an area of about twenty-two square miles, in townships forty and forty-one, of range two, east. It then enters into range one, east, of the same townships, where it occupies the summit levels of the ridges, between the small streams that traverse these townships, and extends in a narrow strip on the east side of the Meramec, passing in the vicinity of Messrs. Skewes and Vallé's, and Mr. Evans' lead mines.

Between the Meramec and Big Indian Creek, we find it overlying the 3d Magnesian Limestone on all the higher elevations; and between the former stream and its main tributary, the Bourbeuse, it occupies, for the most part, the summit of the divide, over which runs the surveyed route of the south-west branch of the Pacific Railroad; forming here an irregular belt, from one to six miles in width, and from sixteen to eighteen miles in length. Further west, it follows the valley of the Bourbeuse in a south-westerly course, from Voss Mill, in Town. 42 N., R. 2 W., Sec. 7, to Renick's Mill, in Town. 41 N., R. 4 W., Sec. 27, appearing frequently on the shores of the river, in bold perpendicular escarpments, sometimes capped with the 2d Magnesian Limestone.

Although the 2d Sandstone, as we have seen, is rather widely distributed, horizontally, in Franklin county, it, nevertheless, does not exhibit a great vertical thickness. In Town. 42 N., R. 3 W., near Mr. Park's farm, a half of a mile from the Bourbeuse, I saw an exposure of 120 feet; and on the dividing ridge, between the Bourbeuse and Big Indian Creek, and, also, near the Meramec, in Town. 41 N., R. 1 E., I estimated its thickness at 140 feet, but generally we do not find it to exceed eighty feet.

This sandstone may, in many cases, be readily distinguished from the Saccharoidal Sandstone. It generally occurs in thinner and more even beds, is not so friable, and is often most beautifully ripple-marked. Sometimes, however, we find it in heavy, massive beds, and tolerably friable. Its color varies from brick-red to light gray, and sometimes it is nearly white. The rock may be seen to good advantage at Cove and Evans' Mines, near the Meramec. At these places, we find about seventy feet exposed. The upper part consists of even layers, from a couple of inches to a foot thick, of a reddish color, often finely ripple-marked, and composed of moderately-fine grains of quartz, rather firmly cemented. The lower part consists of alternations of sandstone, magnesian limestone and chert. On Mr. Park's farm, near the Meramec, in Town. 42 N., R. 3 W., are fine exposures of this sandstone; the strata are in even layers, from three inches to a foot thick, and prettily variegated. On the ridges, between Indian Creek and the Meramec, it is frequently much indurated; and in the vicinity of Bredell's Copper Mine, it is an exceedingly hard quartz rock. On the Meramec, near Renick's Mill, it is a soft, brown, heavy-bedded, friable sandstone, scarcely distinguishable, lithologically, from the Saccharoidal Sandstone.

Lead Ore.—I have noticed the occurrence of lead in this sandstone at only one point in the county—at Skewes and Vallé's Mines, near the Meramec; for a detailed account of which, you are referred to the report of Dr. Litton.

For building, the sandstone of which we are speaking is a useful material, its texture being often quite uniform, and it usually contains but a small quantity of argillaceous matter. For paving and flagging stones, it is, also, well adapted; for, from the regularity of its stratification, slabs may often be obtained from six to eight feet square, and of a thickness varying from a couple of inches to a foot.

For *fire-stones*, this rock may be frequently employed to good advantage, taking care to select the purer varieties. The sandstone used for the hearths of Moselle Iron Furnace (now Franklin Mining Company) was obtained from a quarry in this rock, near Cove Mines, and it is said to have answered a good purpose. The hearths lasted about four months, when it was found necessary to substitute new ones. The cost of getting these stones out, I understood, did not exceed fifty dollars each time.

Organic Remains.—The upper part of the mass, as far as I know, is destitute of organic remains, but the lower cherty portion sometimes yields them. At Cove Mines, and at Evans', fragments of *Straparollus*, *Pleurotomaria* and *Orthoceratites* have been observed, which apparently differ from those of the other groups of the Calciferous sandrock.

The formation, underlying the sandstone just described, is the 3*d Magnesian Limestone*, or "Lead-bearing Rock," and represents the Lower Magnesian Limestone of Iowa, Wisconsin and Minnesota. It is the oldest formation in the county, and is a mass of great importance, as it contains nearly all the productive deposits of lead and copper.

This rock is almost entirely confined to the southern half of the county. North of the line, between townships 42 and 43, we find it occupying merely a small space of three or four miles, along the valley of the Bourbeuse, in Town. 43 N, R. 1 E.

To the south of this line, it first appears at a point near the confluence of the Bourbeuse, and follows in a south-westerly course the valley of the Meramec, to the southern line of the county. At first it occurs in a narrow belt, scarcely a mile wide, but it soon expands to five or six miles, forming the spurs of all the hills, and entering largely into the composition of the hills themselves.

Along the shores of the river it is frequently exposed in bold escarpments, from two to three hundred feet high, traversed by deep vertical fissures, and sometimes presenting perpendicular faces, of two hundred feet, to the stream. Its characteristic features are well exhibited in the vicinity of Stanton Copper Mines, Bredell's Mines, Gallagher's Mill, Virginia Mines, and at various other points along the course of the Meramec.

This formation, also, prevails along the valley of Big and Little Indian Creeks, throughout their entire course in the county, forming a strip from a half to a mile wide on either side of these streams, and affording many interesting exposures for the study of its characters.

Again, it may be traced on the Bourbeuse in a continuous band, somewhat crescent-shaped, for nearly its entire course through Town. 42 N., Rs. 1 and 2 W. On the north side of the stream it occupies but a very narrow strip of country; but on the south side it is much wider, and passes into the north-east portion of Town. 41 N., R. 2 W., where it forms, for the most part, the surface rock, over an area of about ten square miles.

By inspecting the accompanying map, it will be at once seen, that within the districts underlaid by the 3d Magnesian Limestone, occur nearly all the important mines of lead and copper in the county. If we except the Golconda Mines, which are, as already stated, in the 2d Magnesian Limestone, no productive mines of lead have been found in the county out of this division of the Calciferous sandrock. I have, therefore, on the geological map, endeavored to lay down, with as much accuracy as possible, its general boundaries; and these, I think, will, in the main, be found correct. I refer you to the report of Dr. Litton, for detailed descriptions of its ores and associated minerals, and an account of the most important mines.

Lithological appearance. — The beds now under notice, near their junction with the 2d Sandstone, consist usually of alternations of buff and gray magnesian limestone, chert and indurated sandstone, but sometimes of a rough cherty mass, with irregular-shaped cavities, occasionally lined with crystals of quartz. The magnesian layers are chiefly of a fine granular, earthy texture, varying very much in hardness, being sometimes so soft that they can be cut with a knife, and at other times very compact and tough. Below these, we have beds of magnesian limestone, varying from a couple of inches to several feet in thickness, with bands of chert interstratified. The magnesian beds consist chiefly of two distinct varieties. One is a compact, sub-crystalline, even-bedded calcareo-magnesian rock, breaking with an angular fracture, and of a light gray or delicate flesh-color; the other is a buff, earthy-looking magnesian limestone, of a finely-granular texture. Both varieties are finely exhibited in the vicinity of Stanton and Bredell's Copper Mines, Virginia, Cove, Hamilton and Darby's Lead Mines, and at Gallagher's Mill.

Fossils. — I have only noticed the occurrence of organic remains in these beds, in a few localities in the county. At Cove and Evans' Mines, Dr. Litton and myself found *Orthoceras primigenium* (*Vanuxem*), a species very characteristic of the Calciferous Sandrock of New York, and which I have, also, observed in the Lower Magnesian Limestone of Wisconsin. We observed here, also, a *Turbo* and *Pleurotomaria.* On Mitchell's Creek, near Mr. Generally's house, in Town. 41 N., R. 1 W., Sec. 13, we found *Straparollus* (*Ophileta*) *complanata* and *S. levata* (*Vanuxem*), which are both characteristic of the Calciferous Sandrock of New York and the North-western States. We observed the same species, also, at Stanton Copper Mine.

The 3d Magnesian Limestone affords some excellent materials for construction. The light gray or flesh-colored varieties are, perhaps, the best for this purpose. These beds contain a good deal of calcareous matter, and appear to be well calculated to withstand the influence of the weather. Structures in Europe, that have stood for centuries, with scarcely any perceptible alteration, were constructed of Calcareous Magnesian Limestone. Quarries of this rock may be opened at various points in the valleys of the Meramec and Bourbeuse. These beds may, also, be employed for burning into lime, if selected with care; the most crystalline varieties should, of course, be chosen.

ST. LOUIS COUNTY.

St. Louis county contains nearly fifteen townships, or an area of about 530 square miles; and, although not so large as the preceding, it embraces a much greater variety of geological formations. We find here, in addition to the Silurian rocks, the Chemung Group, Carboniferous Limestone, and Coal Measures.

I propose to commence my report on this county with a description of the geological section along the line of the Pacific Railroad. It begins at St. Louis, and, passing in a south-westerly direction, terminates in the south-west corner of the county. Along this route, excellent opportunities were afforded for studying the relative order and succession of the geological formations, at the numerous cuts that have been made through the rocks for the construction of the railroad.

The strata, underlying the Quaternary deposits, on which the city of St. Louis stands, belong to the superior division of the Carboniferous System, and is the St. Louis Limestone of western geologists. It is well characterized by its fossils, of which several are quite peculiar. These have been enumerated in my description of the Mississippi river section, where, also, the lithological characters of the mass have been minutely detailed.

On the line of our section, these rocks first appear at the eastern edge of Chouteau's Pond, near Poplar street, and they are again exposed at the quarries, a couple of hundred yards south of the railroad depôt, where they are overlaid by the Quaternary deposits, which here present a thickness of upwards of twenty feet. These deposits, or the Bluff Formation of your general vertical section, are also finely exhibited between Eleventh and Twelfth streets, at the cut recently made for the railroad.

The section at this place, from below, upwards, is —

No. 1. — Light, ash-colored, clay, with ferruginous bands, containing Lymnea, Physa and Helix, . . . 2 ft. 3 in.

No. 2. — Fine silicious sand, ...	6 in.
No. 3. — Ash-colored clay, ...	4 in.
No. 4. — Yellow and gray sandy clay, ...	2 ft. 9 in.
No. 5. — Fine sand, ...	5 ft.
No. 6. — Soil and sub-soil, ...	5 ft.

The St. Louis Limestone, overlaid by these deposits, prevails with a slight westerly dip, until we pass Rock Creek, when the Coal Measures succeed, and continue for a short distance beyond Cheltenham Sulphur Spring. At the spring, on the south side of the River des Peres, the hills are about seventy-five feet high, and consist chiefly of sandstone, with some beds of sandy shale. Just above the water level, we find a dark, ferruginous sandstone in thick beds; at forty feet, thin, shaly layers of argillaceous sandstone; and on the whole, rests fine-grained, soft, white sandstone. A hundred yards west of the spring, the St. Louis Limestone again appears underneath the Coal Measures, on the south side of the River des Peres, extending from the bed of the stream to the height of fourteen feet. It consists of light-colored, compact limestone, in layers, from an inch to a foot thick, with occasional bands of chert interstratified. These beds contain *Palaechinus* (*Melonites*) *multipora* and *Poteriocrinus longidactylus*, and other species of the upper beds of the St. Louis Limestone. The chert layers are highly fossiliferous, and contain *Avicula*, *Pecten*, *Arca* and *Cardiomorpha*.

The railroad now passes in gradual succession from the higher to the lower members of the St. Louis Limestone, and two miles beyond Kirkwood this group disappears altogether, and is succeeded by the Archimedes Limestone.

About a mile east of "Barrett's Station," is a cut through the Archimedes beds to the depth of twenty feet, and three hundred yards in length. The strata consist of bluish gray and buff limestone, in moderately thick beds, containing rounded masses of flint, which vary from an inch to a foot in diameter, and present often a concentric structure.

At the western extremity of the first tunnel ("Barrett's Station"), is an exposure of heavy-bedded, gray and blue, sub-crystalline and bluish argillaceous limestone. The section here, in the ascending order, is as follows: —

No. 1. — Dull, earthy-looking, argillaceous limestone, weathering in thin layers, ... 2 ft.

No. 2. — Heavy-bedded, compact, sub-crystalline limestone, highly charged with fossils. These strata have been chosen for the construction of the Custom-House, at St. Louis, and the selection appears to have been a good one; their texture being of a character to withstand the action of moisture and frost. The rock possesses uniformity of composition, is free from cherty intermixture, and, as it contains a large proportion of carbonate of lime, the refuse material can be advantageously employed for making quicklime.* The following are a few of the most characteristic fossils of these beds: —*Pentremites florealis*, *P. lateriformis*, *Productus punctatus*, *Euomphalus planorbis*, *Archimedipora archimedes*, and *Psammodus*. In some of the layers the fossils are elegantly preserved, the original shells being converted into pure white lime, which retains their most delicate markings, ... 21 ft.

No. 3. —Blue, argillaceous limestone, similar to that at the base of the section (No. 1), ... 10 ft.

No. 4. —Heavy-bedded, blue and gray fossiliferous limestone, presenting nearly the same characters as No. 2, . . . 12 ft.

No. 5. —Loose chert, ... 2 ft.

The second tunnel is, also, through Archimedes Limestone, very similar in lithological characters to that of the first tunnel. We find, first, heavy-bedded, bluish gray limestone, twelve feet; above this, bluish gray, argillaceous limestone, ten feet; and then, gray, sub-crystalline limestone, abounding in fossils, thirty-four feet.

At the heavy cut, seventeen miles from St. Louis, the Encrinital Limestone of the general vertical section first appears. The strata are exposed to the height of forty-three feet, and present a very perceptible dip to the north-east. The Archimedes Limestone forms the top of the exposure, and, beneath, occurs the Encrinital beds, consisting, here, as elsewhere in the State, of alternations of light-colored, crystalline limestone and chert, the former very rich in remains of encrinites.

This formation extends along the railroad for nearly five miles, the mass being readily distinguished from the formation directly above and beneath, by its cherty character alone. At some points it is represented by a mass of broken chert and reddish clay, the debris resulting from the destruction of its strata; and this is well seen just beyond the seventeenth mile post, where is a cut of upwards of twenty feet, through material of this kind. The limestone, which is often in beds three or four feet thick, is of good quality for quicklime, and preferable to the Archimedes beds.

---

* Dr. Litton's analysis of an average specimen gave—

Insoluble residue,	2.24
Alumina and peroxide of iron,	.57
Carbonate of lime,	87.20
Carbonate of magnesia,	10.07
	100.08

Near the nineteenth mile post is a fine locality for its fossils. Besides many others, I observed *Platycrinus Burlingtonensis*, *P. discoideus*, *Megistocrinus Evansi*, *Actinocrinus unicornus*, *Pentremites Sayi* and *Spirifer Burlingtonensis*, species which I have found quite characteristic of the same group, in Iowa and Illinois.

At the Sulphur Springs, twenty-one miles from St. Louis, the hills attain the height of 127 feet above the railroad grade, and 154 feet above Meramec River. The upper seventy-seven feet consists of alternations of gray Encrinital Limestone and chert, below which is a slope down to the water level, in which the strata are hidden from view by soil and debris of rocks that have fallen from above.

The Sulphur Spring issues from near the base of this slope, and only eight or ten feet above the bed of the river. The water, judging from its taste and the deposit formed in the bottom of the spring, appears to possess nearly the same properties as the Sulphur Spring on the Mississippi, in Jefferson county, mentioned in my description of the Mississippi river section, and it issues from beneath the same strata: *i. e.*, the argillaceous beds of the Chemung Group, which are seen in a short distance, and which, it is to be presumed, occupy the slope at this place.

The Chemung rocks are exposed, on the north side of the railroad, about a quarter of a mile west of Sulphur Spring.

The section here, in the ascending order, is: —

1. — Reddish brown and yellow limestone, in thick massive beds,	12 ft.
2. — Thin-bedded, reddish limestone and marl, ...	15 ft.
3. — Yellow marly limestone, ...	12 ft.
4. — Compact, light gray limestone, in thin strata, . .	8 ft.

The uppermost strata of this section contain but few fossils, but in the reddish beds they are quite abundant. The most common species are *Chonetes ornata*, *Orthis* allied to *O. Michelini*, *Spirifer striatus?* *Cyathoxonia cynodon*, *Amplexus*, and several species of *Crinoidea*.

The reddish beds (No. 1) at the base of this section have been employed for the piers of the bridge at Sulphur Spring, for which purpose they seem to be well adapted. The rock has the appearance of durability, the color is agreeable to the eye, and, being in thick beds, is suitable for heavy masonry. It forms, in my opinion, an excellent and durable building material. The same strata again show themselves about a quarter of a mile further on, where they are exposed to the height of eleven feet. The lower five feet consist of yellow limestone, on which rests six feet of reddish sub-crystalline limestone. At this place there is a considerable local dip of the strata to the south-west.

Twenty-one miles from St. Louis, the hills rise to a height of 120 feet above the railroad grade. The lower seventy-five feet is a slope, probably underlaid by the Chemung rocks, from which rise perpendicular cliffs of Encrinital Limestone, forty-five feet high.

The hills now continue of about the same elevation, with constant escarpments near their summits, for the distance of about one mile.

About a quarter of a mile beyond the twenty-second mile post is an out-crop of Lower Silurian strata, referable to the age of the Trenton Limestone.

The section here, in the ascending series, is as follows: —

1. — Light gray, highly crystalline limestone, passing upwards into buff and gray cherty magnesian limestone, containing *Leptaena alternata*, *Leptaena sericea*, *Leptaena filitexta*, *Orthis testudinaria?* *Illaenus crassicanda*, *Lichas Trentonensis*, *Asaphus Iowensis* and *Chaetetes lycoperdon*, . 34 ft.
2. — Slope, no strata exposed, ... 30 ft.
3. — Buff, sandy calcareo-magnesian limestone, . . . 11 ft.

To these, succeed thin-bedded buff and argillaceous limestone, with crinoids and other fossils of the Chemung Group.

The crystalline beds at the base of this section contain the same assemblage of fossils, and are identical with the rocks that are quarried near the mouth of Rattlesnake Creek, in Jefferson county, for the columns of the Court House at St. Louis, and at Cape Girardeau, to furnish the well-known Cape Girardeau marble. This part of the Trenton Limestone has supplied some of our choicest building rock, and, in fact, wherever it crops out, we are liable to find good materials for construction. It is, therefore, probable that valuable quarries will be found in the vicinity of the point of which we are now speaking.

A few hundred yards further, we find the lower division of the Trenton Group emerging from beneath the crystalline beds just mentioned. It is here composed of drab, compact, close-textured limestone, in thick beds, with thin seams of chert interstratified, and, towards the base, perforated in every direction by vermiform cavities. These strata continue to be seen along the railroad for the distance of a third of a mile, forming precipitous cliffs, from thirty to forty feet high.

The railway now passes through nearly level land, and no rock exposures are to be seen in its immediate vicinity, until we get beyond the 24th mile post from St. Louis. Here we again find the lower Trenton rocks, at first in perpendicular walls, twenty feet high, but soon afterwards they attain to the height of from fifty to seventy feet, forming bold and isolated cliffs, near the tops of the hills.

A quarter of a mile before we reached Hamilton Creek, the following section was observed, counting from below upwards: —

1. —Blue argillaceous limestone, in moderately thick beds, . 15 ft.
2. — Heavy-bedded, buff magnesian limestone, passing upwards into cream-colored layers of the same, ... 55 ft.
3. — Compact, close-textured, brittle limestone, of drab color, some of the layers containing vermiform cavities, . . . 45 ft.

The lower seventy feet of this rock is the 1st Magnesian Limestone of your general section; and some of the beds towards the upper part contain, in great profusion, the casts of a small *Cythere*, which I have described in the Palæontology under the name of *Cythere sublaevis*. Some layers, four feet thick, are composed almost entirely of this little Crustacean. The superior strata of this section contain *Orthis*, *Leptaena* and an *Ormoceras*, very similar to, if not identical with, a species of the Black River Limestone of New York; but, until we have found a greater variety of fossils for examination, it would, perhaps, be unsafe to pronounce the beds we are now noticing identical with that group.

Just beyond Hamilton Creek, the 1st Magnesian Limestone is exposed to the height of forty-three feet. It consists of grayish, buff magnesian limestone, in thick layers, with intercalations of argillo-magnesian limestone, and continues along the north side of the railroad for the distance of three miles, forming perpendicular walls, from five to twenty-five feet high, and frequently presenting a remarkably banded appearance. Near the 27th mile post they exhibit an undulating character.

In a ravine, on the north side of the railroad, about three-quarters of a mile east of Allenton, we first encountered the Saccharoidal Sandstone of your general section. It occurs in massive beds, of a ferruginous brown color, and is composed of moderately fine quartz grains, rather loosely cemented.

Near Allenton, the 1st Magnesian Limestone is quarried in the adjacent hills,* and on the west side of Fox Creek it again appears in a ledge, sixteen feet high. At the latter locality, I observed *Cythere sublaevis* and elongated cylindrical bodies, which appear to be casts of the columns of *Encrinites*.

The next exposure, near the railroad, is about a mile north-east of Franklin, where we find a cut through the sandstone to the depth of twenty-five feet. The rock lies in heavy beds, and consists of fine grains of colorless quartz, usually so loosely cemented, that, when struck with the hammer, it falls to fine sand. It occupies the same geological position, and in its lithological character resembles the white sandrock of Ste. Genevieve county, large quantities of which are shipped annually to Pittsburgh and other points for the manufacture of glass.

A short distance beyond this place are perpendicular escarp-

---

* Through the politeness of Dr. H. King, of St. Louis, I have been permitted to examine fragments of a straight-chambered shell, of huge dimensions, probably belonging to the genus Endoceras of Prof. Hall, which, when perfect, must have exceeded ten feet in length. He informs me that it was obtained from the quarry, near Allenton.

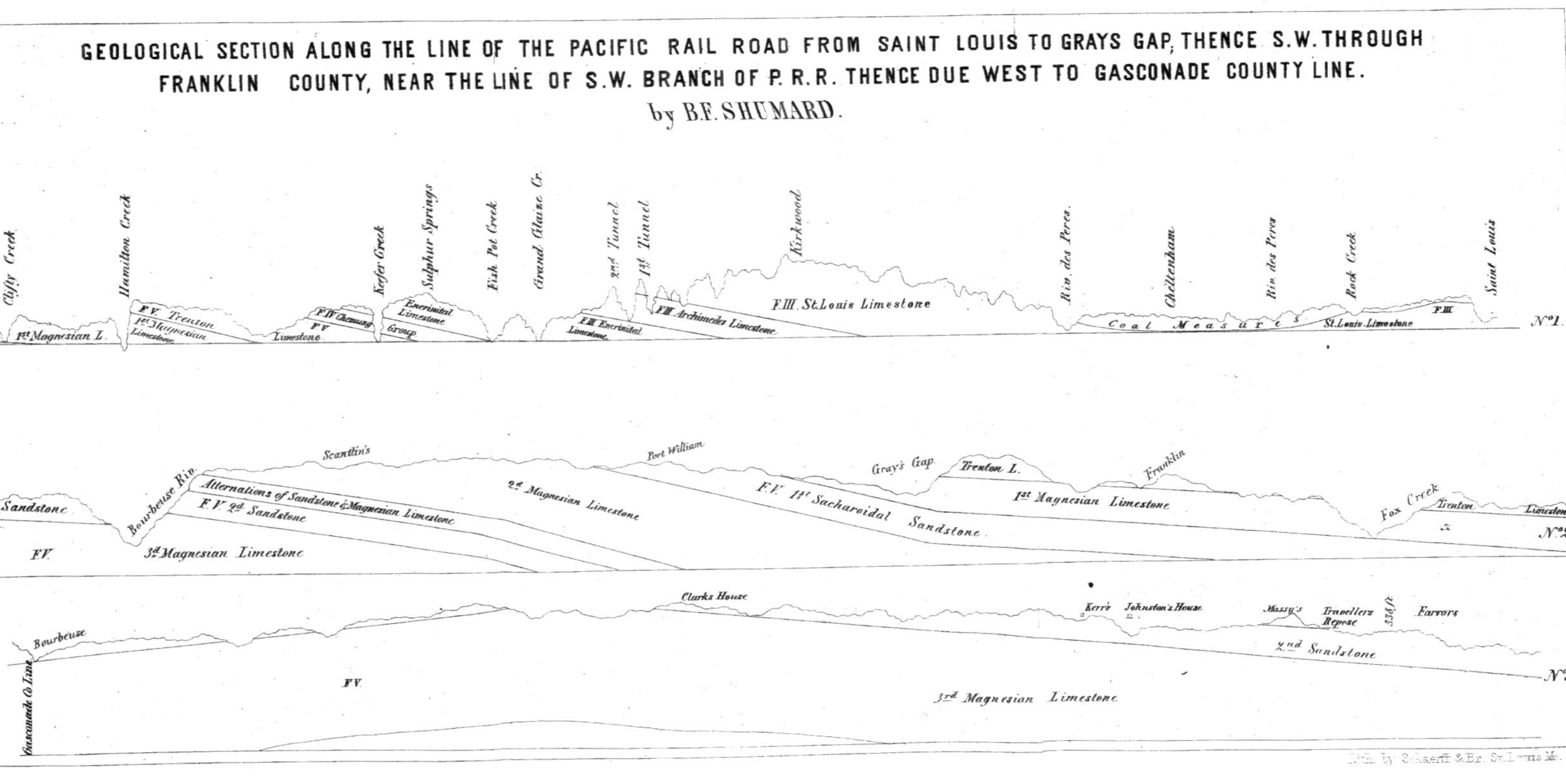

GEOLOGICAL SECTION ALONG THE LINE OF THE PACIFIC RAIL ROAD FROM SAINT LOUIS TO GRAYS GAP, THENCE S.W. THROUGH FRANKLIN COUNTY, NEAR THE LINE OF S.W. BRANCH OF P. R. R. THENCE DUE WEST TO GASCONADE COUNTY LINE.
by B.F. SHUMARD.
Clifty Creek
Hamilton Creek
Keefer Creek
Sulphur Springs
Fish Pot Creek
Grand Glaize Cr.
2nd Tunnel
1st Tunnel
Kirkwood
Riv. des Peres.
Cheltenham
Riv des Peres
Rock Creek
Saint Louis
1st Magnesian L.
F.V. Trenton
1st Magnesian Limestone
F.V Limestone
F.IV Chemung
Encrinital Limestone Group
F.III Encrinital Limestone
F.III Archimedes Limestone
F.III. St.Louis Limestone
Coal Measures
St.Louis Limestone
F.III
No. 1.
Scantlin's
Port William
Gray's Gap
Trenton L.
Franklin
Fox Creek
Trenton
Limestone
2d Sandstone
Bourbeuse Riv.
Alternations of Sandstone & Magnesian Limestone
F.V. 2d Sandstone
2d Magnesian Limestone
F.V. 1st Sacharoidal Sandstone
1st Magnesian Limestone
F.V.
3d Magnesian Limestone
No. 2.
Clarks House
Kerr's
Johnston's House
Massy's
Travellers Repose
338 ft
Farrors
Bourbeuse
Gasconade Co. Line
F.V.
2nd Sandstone
3rd Magnesian Limestone
No. 3.

ments of the Saccharoidal Sandstone, fifty feet high; then succeeds a talus of thirty-six feet, above which we find the 1st Magnesian Limestone, about twenty feet exposed, consisting of buff and gray magnesian rock, somewhat porous, and containing a good deal of calc spar. A large part of the sandstone at this place is colored with oxide of iron.

Within a quarter of a mile of Franklin, and a few hundred yards from the railroad, the hills are 250 feet high; and here we find the Saccharoidal Sandstone occupying their bases, above which is the 1st Magnesian Limestone, presenting the characters already noticed; and on the whole, rests the Black River and Trenton Limestones, with their characteristic fossils.

Having now completed an account of the geological formation along the line of the Pacific Railroad, I will next describe them as they appear in other parts of the county, beginning with the uppermost, and speaking of them in descending order.

Bluff, or Loess. — In sinking wells, and in excavations for roads and other purposes, we usually find between the soil and older stratified rocks of the county, the Bluff Formation of the general vertical section, varying in thickness from ten to forty feet, and consisting of clay, sand, sandy loam, and sometimes fine gravel. These deposits may, also, be frequently seen to good advantage along the courses of the streams, where they appear often in vertical cliffs.

At St. Louis, Carondelet, and other localities in the county, I have observed the characteristic terrestrial and fluviatile shells of the formation pertaining to the genera *Helix*, *Pupa*, *Physa*, *Limnea* and *Planorbis*. Fossil bones of the Mastodon (*M. giganteus*) have also recently been found in these deposits, at St. Louis, during an excavation for a sewer, near Flora Garden, in the southern part of the city. They were discovered at the depth of about sixteen feet beneath the surface, and consisted of two teeth, nearly perfect, and fragments of other bones, which crumbled on exposure to the air. This is the only locality in the county, known to me, where the remains of fossil quadrupeds have been encountered.

Referring to the section at the commencement of this report, and to your report, for further details with regard to the lithological character of this formation, I will here merely notice some points where it may be seen to the best advantage.

It is finely displayed at the Mound, in North St. Louis, where a cut has been made through it to the depth of nearly thirty feet. At the Bremen quarries, a thickness of twenty-five feet is exposed, passing downwards into a bed of gravel, about a foot thick, which rests on the St. Louis Limestone. Instructive sections of these deposits may also be seen in South St. Louis, near the Arsenal, in Carondelet, and at various points along the St. Charles and Bon Homme roads.

The clays of this formation are well fitted for the manufacture of bricks, for which purpose they are extensively employed in almost every part of the county. They, also, furnish materials for the coarser kinds of pottery.

CARBONIFEROUS SYSTEM.

This system is largely developed in St. Louis county. It forms the underlying rock over nearly four-fifths of its entire extent, reaching from the Mississippi river westward, to within from six to ten miles of the western boundary. All the formations of the system given in the general vertical section, from the Middle Coal Series to the Encrinital Limestone inclusive, are here represented; and I will now describe them, commencing with the highest, and proceeding in the descending order.

Coal Measures. — This formation, so important in an economical point of view, occupies an area of about one hundred and sixty square miles, and lies chiefly in the north-east portion of the county. In the accompanying geological map, I have laid down its boundaries, from which you will obtain a better idea of its range and extent, than from a written description.

Although its limits are quite extensive, I think I may safely assert that only the middle and inferior portions, observed by yourself, on the Missouri river, occur in the district under notice. And the former, I have been able to identify only in a single locality: viz., at Charbonniere, on the Missouri river. The section here, in the descending order, is —

No. 1.	— Slope, covered by soil and trees,	60 ft.
No. 2.	— Rough, light gray, compact limestone, in masses, embedded in clay,	6 ft.
No. 3.	— Light-colored, impure fire-clay?	6 ft.
No. 4.	— Hard, compact, light bluish gray, hydraulic limestone, in uneven masses,	2 ft.
No. 5.	— Yellow, argillaceous shale, with ochreous stains,	8 ft.
No. 6.	— Purple, sandy shale, with fine micaceous particles disseminated,	13 ft.
No. 7.	— Bluish, argillaceous shale,	46 ft.
No. 8.	— Dark greenish and reddish fossiliferous shale,	6 ft.
No. 9.	— Dark sandy shale,	8 ft.
No. 10.	— Seam of coal,	

The compact limestones of the above sections (Nos. 2 and 4) abound in fossils, and they are usually well preserved. The most common species are *Chonetes mesoloba*, *Productus costatus*, *P. punctatus*, *P. splendens*, *P. Wabashensis*, *Spirifer lineatus*, *Fusulina cylindrica*, and remains of *Crinoidea*. The dark shale, at the base of the section (No. 8), is also filled with fossils, chiefly *Chonetes*, of the following species, recently described by Drs. Norwood and Pratten, of the Illinois Geological Survey: *C. Verneuiliana*, *C. Smithi* and *C. mesoloba.*

At the time of my visit to this locality, the coal seam was beneath the surface of the Missouri, and could not be seen. I was informed, however, that its thickness is about eighteen inches.

The next rock we meet with in the descending order, is the *Micaceous Sandstone*, which constitutes the superior part of our

Lower Coal Series. If we commence at a point on the Natural Bridge Plank-road, about six and a half miles from St. Louis, and draw a line in a direction nearly north, to within a short distance of Cold-Water Creek, such a line will pretty nearly represent the western boundary of the principal sandstone district in the county. Within this line, it forms the prevailing rock over a space of from thirty to thirty-five square miles, or to within a short distance of the eastern limit of the coal formation.

A fine exhibition of this sandstone may be seen on the North Missouri Railroad, between seven and eight miles from St. Louis, where is a cut through it, of about five hundred yards in length, and twenty-two feet in depth. It consists of soft, brown, fine-grained micaceous sandstone, thick-bedded, and crumbling readily on exposure to the air. Some of the layers contain imperfect impressions of *Calamites*, *Lepidodendron*, and dark stains of carbonaceous matter. At the south-western extremity of the cut, the sandstone is seen resting on a stratum of fire-clay, about five feet thick.

This sandstone may, also, be seen in the bluffs that skirt the bottom lands of the Mississippi, in Town. 46, R. 7 E.

On the top of a high ridge, about seven and a half miles from St. Louis, on Mr. Claire's land, near the Natural Bridge Plank-road, a well was excavated to the depth of eighty feet, the lower fifty or sixty feet being through the Micaceous Sandstone, filled with remains of fossil plants.

A couple of miles beyond this place, in the north-east quarter of Sec. 14, Town. 46, R. 6, is a quarry in this sandstone, whence is obtained the rock used in the construction of bridges and culverts on the North Missouri Railroad, between the fourth and ninth sections. It consists, at its upper part, of soft, fine-grained ferruginous sandstone, and below of bluish gray sandstone, with nodules of argillaceous sandstone embedded. The beds are easily wrought, blocks of large size being obtained without much difficulty. The upper layers are regarded as being the best.

Another quarry of this sandstone is situated near the Old Bon Homme road, in the south-east quarter of Sec. 5, Town. 45, R. 6 E. It is very similar to the last, but is of a darker color, rather more compact, and occurs in thinner beds. This rock has been quarried and conveyed to St. Louis, a distance of about eleven miles, for building purposes. Near the quarry, on the same quarter section, a well has been sunk to the depth of seventy-five feet, and, I am informed, they first passed through about thirty-four feet of Quaternary Deposits; then forty feet of sandstone, and reached a hard, dark bluish gray limestone, in which I found *Chonetes mesoloba* and *Productus splendens*.

The sandstone we are noticing always contains a considerable proportion of mica and traces of coal plants, by which it can readily be distinguished from the older sandstones. The fossils, however, owing to the loose and crumbling character of the rock, are always badly preserved. The same quality, also, renders it, in general, unfit as a material for construction.

On the Hall's Ferry Plank-road the piers of bridges and culverts, constructed of this rock, are rapidly crumbling away. The strata, at the two quarries above mentioned, are the best that I have seen, but even these, in my opinion, are far inferior to many of the limestones of the county.

I have not been able to observe the total thickness of this sandstone, at any locality in the county, but it may be estimated at from sixty to seventy feet.

Beneath the sandstone I have just described, and above the St. Louis Limestone, we find those members of the Lower Coal Series in which, probably, occur all the important deposits of coal in the county. These prevail over about two-thirds of the whole area occupied by the Coal Formation, and consist of beds of clay, fire-clay, limestone, shale and coal. They are perfectly characterized by the fossils, which, in the limestone and the clays directly in contact with it, are sometimes exceedingly abundant. The most frequently occurring forms are *Chonetes mesoloba*, *Chonetes Smithi*, *Productus costatus*, *P. splendens*, *Spirifer lineatus* and *Fusulina cylindrica;* and so characteristic are these species, that I have not failed to detect them at a single locality. The Formation is often concealed from view by an extensive layer of Quaternary Deposits, so that, in general, the best sections of the different beds are to be found in shafts at the coal-mines.

The subjoined sections, obtained at several different localities, are examples representing the order of superposition most frequently observed in this county.

At Gartside's Coal-Mines, near the City Farm, three and a half miles south-west of St. Louis, the section is: —

1. — Soil and bluff deposit,	20 ft.
2. — Blue clay,	12 ft.
3. — Bluish gray, compact, fine-grained hydraulic limestone with? *Productus, Chonetes* and *Fusulina*,	7 ft.
4. — Dark indurated shale,	4 ft.
5. — Coal,	4 to 5 ft.
6. — Fire-clay,	0 ft.

At Mr. B. F. Buchanan's, on the west side of the River Des Peres, six miles west of St. Louis, the order observed is: —

1. — Yellow clay,	5 ft.
2. — Light-colored sandy clay,	4 ft.
3. — Masses of limestone embedded in red clay ("tumbling rock"),	6 ft.
4. — Red clay,	6 ft.
5. — Blue clay,	7 ft.
6. — Light gray earthy limestone,	3½ ft.
7. — Very compact, hard, dark gray limestone,	2½ ft.
8. — Dark blue shale,	2 ft.
9. — Coal,	5 ft.
10. — Slope (rocks unexposed),	80 ft.
11. — St. Louis Limestone,	26 ft.

At Watkins' coal-bank, near the Mississippi, in the south-east corner of Town. 47, R. 7 E., the section commencing beneath the Bluff Formation is: —

1. — Yellow and ash-colored tough clay,	8 inches.
2. — Ash-colored fire-clay,	2 ft. 6 "
3. — Blue clay with masses of dark hydraulic limestone, containing *Productus, Chonetes*, etc.,	1 ft.
4. — Seam of coal,	18 "

5.—Dark fire-clay, ...	2 ft.
6.—White fire-clay, ...	3 to 5 ft.
7.—White and brown, ferruginous, fine-grained sandstone, in thin layers,	10 to 15 ft.
8.—Archimedes Limestone, exposed in the bed of Watkins' Creek, .	0 ft.

At this place the St. Louis Limestone appears to be wanting, and the Coal Measures are separated from the Archimedes Limestone by merely a few feet of sandstone, which, doubtless, represents the Ferruginous Sandstone of the general section.

Coal.—This important mineral substance has been chiefly mined along the southern edge of the Formation. All the workings here are on the same stratum, which varies from two to five feet in thickness, and is nearly horizontal. At Gartside's Mines a number of shafts have been sunk, of an average depth of about forty feet, to the coal-bed. The latter consists of several layers, with thin partings of clay and iron pyrites interstratified, the aggregate thickness being about five feet. The average thickness of the workable coal is about three feet six inches. Sometimes it dwindles down, very suddenly, to two feet, for a few yards, and then as suddenly attains its usual thickness again.

On land belonging to Mr. Russell, a third of a mile south of Gartside's, coal crops out on the western slope of a hill fifty feet below the top. The bed is worked by Mr. Russell, by means of five shafts, sunk on the top of the hill.

The deepest of these is forty-five feet, the shallowest thirty feet, and the bed of coal varies from four feet eight inches to five feet in thickness. During the winter months about fifty hands are employed here in working the coal, and the average quantity extracted per day is about eighty bushels to the hand. The subjoined diagram exhibits a vertical section of the coal strata at this place. The first layer beneath the surface represents the Quaternary deposits, twenty-three feet; the second, "tumbling rock," consisting of masses of limestone embedded in clay; the third, main rock, or gray hydraulic limestone; the fourth, blue clay; the fifth, dark shale; the sixth, coal; and the seventh, gray fire-clay.

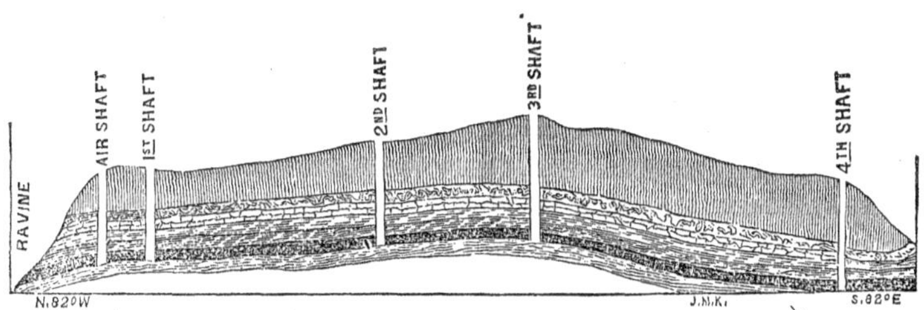

SECTION AT RUSSELL'S COAL MINE.

But the mines that have been, probably, worked most extensively in the county, are those of Messrs. Hunt & McDonald, situated in the Prairie des Noyers, on the west side of Grand Avenue, three miles from the Court-House. The land here is about of the same elevation as at Russell's Mines, and the coal is reached by a number of shafts, which vary from twenty-two to thirty-eight feet in depth. The bed is from three to six feet thick, but the common thickness of the workable coal is about five feet Mr. Hunt informed me that, during the summer months, he employs about sixty hands, and, during the winter, one hundred and fifty. Messrs. Hunt & McDonald sunk an Artesian well on their land to the depth of one hundred feet, and, at twenty feet below the bed now being worked, struck another stratum of coal, eighteen inches thick. This fact is of some importance, as showing the existence of more than one bed in this part of the coal district. It is very probable that this eighteen-inch stratum is coëxtensive with the thick bed above it.

South of Hunt's, are Morrow and McGreggor's coal mines, on the west side of the Gravois road; and a short distance further, in the same direction, is Peter Delore's, on the east side of the road. At both of these places, the bed of workable coal is about three and a half feet thick. I might mention numerous other points where coal is profitably mined in the southern part of the coal area; but, as all the workings are on the same bed, it would serve no good purpose.

About four miles west of the Court-House, on the Clayton road, a seam of impure coal, from eight to ten inches thick, shows itself at an elevation of fifty feet above the bed of the River des Peres. It is underlaid by fire-clay, beneath which is compact gray limestone, containing *Chonetes mesoloba*, *Productus Wabashensis*, and *Fusulina*. A third of a mile further west, on Chouteau's land, a bed of coal, thirty-one inches thick, is worked considerably below the level of the last-mentioned seam, the fossiliferous limestone being here about four feet above the coal. This bed is, doubtless, the same as that worked at Russell's, and other points in the Prairie des Noyers, while the eight-inch seam, seen in the road, is undoubtedly a distinct stratum lying above it. It is, therefore, pretty evident, that we have in St. Louis county, at least three beds of coal, beneath the ferruginous sandstone: viz., an eighteen-inch stratum below, and an eight-inch stratum above the main workable bed.

On land belonging to Mr. Shreve, four miles from the Court-House, a coal-bed, one foot thick, appears in the side of a hill, about ten feet above the bed of a small branch of Maline Creek.

On the St. Charles McAdamized road, a short distance beyond Prairie Place, I was informed that a thin seam of coal was struck in excavating a well.

South of the Clayton road, in Sec. 17 of Town. 45, R. 6 E., on Mrs. McCutchan's land, an eight-inch seam of coal crops out near the base of a hill. It is of inferior quality, and too light for blacksmiths' use. On Mr. Philip Litzinger's land, south-west quarter of north-west quarter, of Sec. 18, Town. 45, R. 6 E., in sinking a well on the top of a hill, the same bed was struck, thirty-eight feet below the surface. Coal, also, occurs on Mr. Fitzgerald's land, south of the Bon Homme road, about fifteen miles from St. Louis.

The coal of this county is all of the bituminous variety, burns with a good flame, and yields a gray ash. Sometimes it contains a good deal of sulphuret of iron, in the form of thin leaf-like laminæ, and at others, it is comparatively free from this substance. It, also, frequently contains very thin plates of crystalline carbonate of lime, generally vertical, but sometimes horizontal and oblique.

It is extremely rare to find fossil plants in the coal, sufficiently well preserved to enable one to make out, with any degree of satisfaction, even their generic characters. They are always converted into soft charcoal, that may frequently be seen along the planes of stratification. In a few instances, I have detected the structure of *Calamites* and *Equisetae*.

Fire-clay. — This highly useful substance may be said to occur in almost inexhaustible quantities in the Coal Measures of St. Louis county, as it forms the underlie of the workable coal-bed at nearly every locality that I have examined; and it, also, frequently exists between that bed and the thinner seams above and below it.

About four miles from the Court-House, between the Bellefontaine road and New Bremen Cemetery, it is extensively manufactured into fire-bricks, by Mr. Hambleton. The bank here presents the following section in descending order: —

1.—Yellow ferruginous impure fire-clay,	6 ft.
2.—Light gray fire-clay,	1 ft.
3.—Coarse ferruginous clay,	4 in.
4.—Variegated gray and purple fire-clay,	8 ft.

The bed at the base of the section is considered the purest variety;* that at the top does not answer a good purpose.† In the manufacture of fire-bricks, the former is generally mixed with a gray fire-clay that occurs directly under the coal-seam, on Mr. Shreve's land, a quarter of a mile west of the locality under notice. The mixture of the two clays makes an excellent quality of fire-bricks.

Hydraulic Lime. — The gray compact limestone, lying above the thick coal-bed, known at the coal-mines under the name of "Main Rock," exhibits frequently, the external characters of hydraulic limestone, and sometimes, also, the "Tumbling Rock," which lies above it. It will be necessary, however, to test them, to enable us to determine with certainty whether they are suitable for this purpose.

Ferruginous Sandstone. — This rock, which is the next below the Coal Measures, is to be seen only at a few points in the county. The best exhibition of it occurs at Emerson's quarry, near the Bon Homme road, about fourteen miles a little north of west from St. Louis. At this locality, it displays a thickness of twenty-five feet; and above it, we find the clays and limestones of the Coal Measures. It occurs in beds from four to five feet thick, and in its lithological appearance resembles very closely the Saccharoidal Sandstone. When first taken from the quarry it is quite soft, but it hardens somewhat after being exposed to the air. This sandstone, also, occurs at Cheltenham Sulphur Springs, where it is found directly above the St. Louis Limestone. Again, it is met with in the bed of a small branch of Maline Creek, near Hamilton's fire-clay bank. Here it is partly a white and partly a dirty ferruginous friable sandstone. The sandstone already mentioned as occurring beneath the coal-bed at Watkins', on the Mississippi river, also belongs to this formation. It here occurs in layers from a fourth to six inches in thickness, and is made up of fine quartzose particles, cemented with a silicious paste. Some of the beds are pure white, others are stained with oxide of iron.

The *St. Louis Limestone,* which in the descending series succeeds the Ferruginous Sandstone, is a highly important member of the Carboniferous System in St. Louis county, and its development here is greater than has been observed elsewhere in the State. Its lithological characters have been described at length in my account of the Mississippi river section. In the northern part of the county it forms a belt, estimated at from two to three miles in width, and about nine miles in length, lying be-

---

* According to Dr. Litton's analysis, a specimen, dried at 212° Fah., yielded—

Silica,	53.94
Alumina, with some peroxide of iron,	33.73
Lime,	1.17
Magnesia,	trace.
Water,	10.94
	99.78

† Dr. Litton's analysis of this clay resulted as follows, dried at 212° Fah.:—

Silica,	56.25
Alumina, with very little peroxide of iron,	29.85
Lime,	1.03
Magnesia,	trace.
Water.	11-11
Alkalies and carbonic acid?	not determined.
	98.24

tween the Coal Measures and the Missouri. Just below Belle-Fontaine, the upper part of the formation is exposed on the shore of the river to the height of forty feet. Opposite the site of the old fort, and for some distance above, it forms perpendicular walls on the river, from ten to twenty feet high.

It shows itself in an irregular patch, in Sec. 33 and 34, of Town. 46 N., R. 6 E. In Sec. 33, it has been quarried somewhat extensively on land belonging to Mr. Underwood, for macadamizing the St. Charles road. At the base of the quarry, is five feet of thick-bedded, brittle, compact, pure limestone, of fine texture, above which is a foot of hard, bluish gray magnesian limestone, and the whole is surmounted by five feet of buff, earthy-looking magnesian limestone, in beds two and a half feet thick. Watson's quarry, a half mile west of this place, is also in the upper part of the St. Louis Limestone. The rock here is very compact, of a gray color, and contains a good deal of chert. In the township in which St. Louis is situated (Town. 45 N., R. 7 E.), it occupies all the space between the Mississippi and the eastern boundary of the Coal Measures; and south of this township continues almost to the extremity of the county, forming a broad belt along the Mississippi, whose width from east to west is from six to nine miles. Again it skirts the south-western margin of the Coal Measures, in Town. 45 and 46, R. 5 and 6 E., appearing over a district from one to five miles in width; its greatest development here being in Town. 45, R. 6.

Excellent exposures of this formation are to be seen at the numerous quarries in and about St. Louis and Bremen, on the River des Peres and Gravois Creek.

The *Fossils* will be found in Catalogue No III., and all the species there enumerated were found in this county.

It has not been possible to see its entire thickness at one point; but, from careful observation on the different beds, at a number of places, I estimate it at about 250 feet.

As a *material for construction*, the St. Louis Limestone is, in my opinion, not surpassed by any rock in the county. It is durable, dresses well, and, save some of the very uppermost layers, is remarkably free from chert. The compact beds, near the top of the formation, containing *Palaechinus multipora* and *Poteriocrinus longidactylus*, are, perhaps, the best. At the quarries, near the river, and in the vicinity of the new reservoir in St. Louis, slabs may be obtained from two or three inches to as many feet in thickness, and of any required length and breadth.

Lime. — The numerous lime-kilns around St. Louis, and, in fact, wherever the formation occurs, sufficiently prove its value for making quicklime. In my Mississippi river section I have indicated the beds that are to be preferred.

Archimedes Limestone. — This formation is so extensively covered with superficial deposits in this county, that it has not been possible to trace out its boundaries with as much precision as could have been desired. On the State road, it first makes its appearance about sixteen miles from St. Louis, and from thence extends westward for the distance of about ten miles. Good exposures may be seen in the neighborhood of Manchester, particularly on the south side of Grand Glaize Creek, where several quarries have been opened in it. The strata here consist chiefly of white limestone, with some layers of chert interstratified.

From the State road it extends beyond Creve Cœur Lake, decreasing in width as we proceed northward. It has been quarried on the Bon Homme road, a few rods west of Creve Cœur Creek, and used for constructing the bridge over that stream. The beds here are the same as are being wrought for the Custom-House, at St. Louis. The lower strata are from three to four feet thick, but at the top of the quarry they are thin-bedded. Along Creve Cœur Creek the Archimedes Limestone may be seen at several points, presenting the characters observed on the Pacific Railroad at the two tunnels.

At the Big Bend of the Meramec, south of Barrett's Station, the hills are about one hundred and fifty feet high, and are composed entirely of this formation, abounding in many of its usual fossils.

On the west bank of Meramec River, at Fenton, it appears in fissile layers of a gray color, separated by thin marly partings. In addition to many characteristic species of the mass, I found here a beautiful variety of *Pentremite*, which I have described under the name of *P. curtus*, and a new species of *Capulus*. To the Palæontologist, these strata are very interesting, but their schistose character detracts from their value as a building material. A short distance from the river, the hills attain a height of about a hundred and twenty feet; and near the top, is a quarry in the Archimedes Limestone, which has furnished some of the rock for macadamizing the road leading from St. Louis to Hillsboro'. This rock consists of brown and gray subcrystalline and earthy limestone, containing cavities, lined with calc spar. The beds are from one to three feet thick, and have the appearance of a good building stone. Fossils are not so abundant as in the inferior beds of the river shore. The most characteristic are *Productus punctatus*, *Orthis umbraculum* and *Spirifer striatus*.

Both east and west of Fenton, the Archimedes Limestone forms the surface rock for two or three miles, and it also passes southward from this place into Jefferson county, forming, on the Meramec, hills upwards of a hundred feet high.

The qualities of this rock, as a building material and lime-rock, have been already mentioned in my description of the section along the Pacific Railroad; and its fossils are enumerated in Catalogue No. IV.

Encrinital Limestone. — This formation, which underlies the preceding, occupies an area of about forty-five square miles in St. Louis county, lying chiefly in Town. 44 N., Rs. 4 and 5 E., and Town. 45 N., R. 4 E. If we draw a line diagonally through the latter township, from the middle of the north line of Sec. 2, to the south line of Sec. 33, we shall find that nearly all the land in the township, west of such a line, is underlaid by the formation under notice. In Town. 44, R. 4, it occupies a district from one and a half to two miles wide on the north and east sides, and in Town. 44, R. 5, prevails in the two western tiers of sections.

The best exhibition of the Encrinital Limestone that I have seen in the county, is on the sides of a deep ravine, known under the name of "Stony Hollow," in Sec. 7, of Town. 44, R. 4 E. Here it is displayed to the height of about 250 feet, and is composed of buff-colored, earthy, granular limestone, white sub-crystalline limestone and chert, in beds from an inch to five feet thick. The sub-crystalline beds are a good and durable building stone, and have been quarried at two or three points in the ravine for the foundations of houses in the neighborhood, and for bridges on the State road. They will make a first-rate article of quicklime, and may at once be recognized by the abundance of Crinoid remains they contain, some beds being almost entirely composed of these beautiful "Lillies of the Ocean." I obtained here some good examples of *Pentremites Sayi Platycrinus planus*, and *Actinocrinus rotundus*. And among the Brachiopods, *Spirifer Burlingtonensis* and *Orthis Michelini.* Near the foot of the ravine, the Encrinital beds are found resting upon a compact bluish gray limestone in thin strata, which resembles very much portions of the Chemung Group.

At the point where the Howell's Ferry plank-road crosses Bon Homme Creek, there is an exposure of about thirty feet of the Encrinital Limestone, containing large elliptical spines of Encrinites and the usual characteristic fossils of the formation. It again appears at several points on Caulk's Creek, a small tributary of Bon Homme Creek, and also on both sides of the Meramec.

CHEMUNG GROUP.

This formation is but little developed in St. Louis county, being confined to a narrow band, scarcely more than a third of a mile wide, and which I have only observed in Town. 44 N., R. 4 E. The best and only good exhibition of it is to be seen on the Pacific Railroad, and its characters there have been described at sufficient length in the earlier part of this report. The boundary of its out-crop is represented on the geological map of the county by the light green color.

LOWER SILURIAN SYSTEM.

In this county, the Chemung rocks appear to repose directly on the Trenton Limestone; the Hudson River Group, Upper Silurian and Devonian systems having no representatives.

By reference to the geological map, it will be seen that the Lower Silurian Rocks occupy the whole of the western tier of townships, and also extend over a considerable district of country in Town'ps 43 and 44, R. 4 E.

The Trenton Limestone here, as on the Mississippi, may be separated into two well-marked divisions, an upper white sub-crystalline, and a lower bluish gray compact limestone. Both varieties have been already noticed to some extent in the description of the railroad section. The white limestone may be well seen along the valley of Hamilton Creek, between the railroad and State road, and about a mile and a half from the former. Here it exists in thick and thin layers, forming abrupt cliffs from forty to fifty feet high, and might be quarried to excellent advantage. It appears to me to be equal, if not superior, as a building rock, to that used for the columns of the Court-House. The bluish gray compact beds are exposed on the State road, where it crosses Fox Creek. They contain *Orthis disparilis*, *O. subaequata*, *Illaenus crassicanda* and an *Ambonychia.* These layers are near the top of the hill; at the base, the rock is perforated in all directions by vermiform cavities, sometimes lined with yellow argillaceous matter. At Melrose, similar beds occur on the declivities of the hills, and contain a great number of fossils.

Throughout the whole course of Wild-Horse Creek, the lower Trenton Limestone constitutes the entire mass of the hills, which are from one hundred to two hundred and fifty feet high. Near their bases, the limestone strata are occasionally separated by beds of blue and gray marl, abounding in fossils.

The 1*st Magnesian Limestone* and *Saccharoidal Sandstone* have been spoken of at sufficient length in my description of the railroad section.

PALÆONTOLOGY.

DESCRIPTION OF NEW SPECIES OF ORGANIC REMAINS.

The following descriptions and figures of new organic remains from the rocks of our State, embrace only such species as are characteristic of the formations in which they occur, none of them having been found to pass from one into another. The illustrations have been drawn with great care, by Mr. F. B. Meek, one of the principal assistants in the Survey, and are true portraits of the objects they are intended to represent. The examples we have selected form but a very small part of the new and interesting fossil forms that have been discovered in the strata of our State. Already, more than two hundred species, unknown to science, have been brought to light, and there is every reason to believe that many more will be added to the list, after our rocks have been more fully explored. The collections made by Professor Swallow from the upper palæozoic rocks, in North Missouri, would alone, if properly illustrated, occupy a large-sized volume; and such a volume would not only be an important contribution to science, but in the highest degree creditable to the State. I need not speak here of the value of fossil remains in the identification of strata, as this will, doubtless, be sufficiently dwelt upon by Professor Swallow.

CRINOIDEA.

GENUS PENTREMITES—SAY.

PENTREMITES SAYI*—SHUMARD.

Pl. B—Fig. 1—*a, b, c. d.*

Body subglobose; *base (pelvis,* Miller) small, concave, eight-sided, with five angles salient and three retreating; two of the pieces are broad pentagonal, and one is lozenge-shaped. *Fork pieces* short, forming rather more than one-fourth the length of the body, wider than long, enlarging rapidly from below upwards; upper edges arched on either side of the pseud-ambulacral fields; inferior edges of three, truncated and resting on the straight edges of the pentagonal plates of the base; the others terminating in obtuse angles, which rest in the retreating angles of the base, with their points corresponding to the basal sutures. These pieces are highest in the middle, and form five small projections around the base of the body. *Deltoid pieces* thicker than the fork-pieces, sub-triangular forming three fourths the

* In designating the shell pieces of this and the following species of Pentremites, I have, with some exceptions, availed myself of the terms employed by Dr. F. Roemer, in his valuable Monograph on the Blastoidea.

entire length of the body; lateral edges widely beveled, each beveled surface about as wide as one of the pseud-ambulacral fields; inferior edges excavated on each side of the median line, so as to form on every piece three obtusely salient angles. The surface at the summit bears a small deep pit, bounded below by a transverse ridge, and from the latter proceeds a distinct carina down the middle of the pieces to the base; a well-defined carina, also, surrounds the borders. The *pseud-ambulacral fields* are narrow, reach down to the base of the body, and their sides are nearly parallel. They consist of pore pieces, supplementary pore pieces, and lanceolate pieces. The pore pieces amount to about eighty in each field; they are transverse and wedge-shaped; supplementary pore pieces, small, triangular; lancet piece narrow, linear, forming not quite one-third the width of the field, and minutely crenulated. The ovarial apertures are very small, and situated on the sides of the deltoid pieces, which are notched at each of the openings. The anal opening is rather large, ovate, and situated on the upper extremity of one of the deltoid pieces. The central opening is closed by minute, usually pentagonal and hexagonal plates, arranged in a manner somewhat similar to those of *Pentremites* (*Elaeacrinus*) *Verneuili* (Roemer).

Dimensions. — Length, 7 lines; width, 7 lines; diameter of pelvis, 1⅝ lines; length of fork-pieces, 3 lines; length of deltoid pieces, 6 lines.

This fossil presents all the essential characters of the genus *Elaeacrinus*, founded by Dr. F. Roemer, on a species from the Devonian strata of the Falls of the Ohio. It possesses a circle of five pairs of ovarial apertures around the summit, and one large anal opening. A central opening is not visible in perfect specimens, this being perfectly closed by minute angular plates. The same structure occurs in *Pentremites Norwoodi* and *P. melo* (*Owen and Shumard*), of which I have fully satisfied myself from an attentive examination of many specimens. And I have but little hesitation in advancing the opinion, that all the *Pentremites* included at present in the group *Elliptici* of Dr. Roemer, will be found, like *Elaeacrinus*, deficient in a central summit opening.

Formation and Localities. — It occurs near the base of the Encrinital Limestone, in Boone, Marion, Jefferson, St. Louis and Ste. Genevieve counties.

Named in honor of Thomas Say, the founder of the family Blastoidea.

PENTREMITES ROEMERI. — SHUMARD.

Pl. B — Fig. 2 — *a, b, c, d.*

Body small, elliptical, a little flattened on the summit. *Base* small, pentagonal, slightly elongated, flattened convex or plane; edges slightly arcuated, composed of three pieces, two wide pentagonal and one quadrangular. *Fork pieces* (*radials*) sub-hexagonal, widest above, length a third greater than the width, and occupying about three-fourths the whole length of the body. Their branches are ornamented with crenulated ridges, longitudinal and transverse, the latter being usually most prominent towards the extremities of the pieces. Deltoid pieces rather small, a little longer than wide and sub-quadrangular. The pseud-ambulacral fields extend nearly to the base of the body. They are narrow, with sides nearly parallel. The disposition and form of the pore pieces cannot be seen.

The ovarial apertures are small, circular, and lie on either side of the extremity of the deltoid pieces. The *anal aperture* is large, and of an elliptical form. The central part of the summit, like the preceding species, is covered with small plates, but owing to the worn condition of the specimens, their form has not been ascertained.

Dimensions. — Length, 3½ lines; greatest width, 2⅞ lines; long diameter of base, 1½ lines.

The place of this handsome little Pentremite is in the group *Elliptici* of Dr. F. Roemer, and it is at once distinguished from all the species of this section, by its convex base.

Geological Position and Locality. — It occurs in the Chemung group, at Providence, Boone county, where it is associated with *Chonetes ornata* and *Rhynconella obscura-plicata.* It is very rare, only two examples having been discovered.

I am glad to be able to dedicate this species to Dr. Ferd. Roemer, of Bonn, Prussia, whose recent valuable researches have added so much to our knowledge of this interesting family.

PENTREMITES CURTUS. — SHUMARD.

Pl. B — Fig. 3 — *a*, *b*.

Body short, sub-globose. *Basal* pieces small, concave, not visible from a side view. *Fork pieces* hexagonal, arched, occupying nearly the entire height of the body; length and breadth about equal; bent inwards and upwards below to join the basal pieces; sides sub-parallel; upper edges oblique and slightly arcuated. Surface beautifully marked with granulose ridges, several of them uniting to form a broad band around the borders, within which the granules are not so distinctly collected in regular lines, but are diffused over the surface. Deltoid pieces sub-rhombic, about half as long as the fork pieces; a large portion of them lying on the summit plane; inferior edges rounded; surface granulose. The pseud-ambulacral fields are narrow, linear, and extend nearly the whole length of the body. The pore pieces are convex, and project beyond the edge of the fork pieces; they are moderately large, and very finely striated. The supplementary pore pieces, and lancet pieces cannot be made out. The structure of the summit, and characters of the ovarial and anal apertures, are, also, unknown.

Dimensions. — Height, about three lines; width, about four lines.

Formation and Locality. — I found this species at Fenton, on the Meramec River, in St. Louis county; where it occurs in the Archimedes Limestone, associated with *Pentremites florealis, Productus punctatus* and *Productus elegans.* The specimen figured is the only example we have found of this elegant *Pentremite.* It is considerably distorted, so that the figure represents it as being more transverse than natural.

PENTREMITES ELONGATUS. — SHUMARD.

Pl. B — Fig. 4.

Body much elongated, elliptical, usually more than twice as long as broad. *Base* small, short, truncated, sub-conical. *Fork pieces* much elongated, about one and a half times longer than wide, and occupying rather more than two-thirds the total length; their branches are long, narrow, and very obliquely truncated above; the surface is marked with very fine striæ, the direction of which is nearly parallel with the borders. *Deltoid* pieces elongate, quadrangular, the inferior edges being considerably shorter than the superior ones; surface striated in the same manner as the fork pieces. The *pseud-ambulacral fields* extend almost the entire length of the body, and gradually increase in width from below upwards. The pore and lanceolate pieces do not vary much from those of *P. floeralis,* except that the first are more numerous, and the second considerably longer.

Dimensions. — Length, 15½ lines; width, about 9 lines; diameter of base (*pelvis*), 3 lines; height of base, 1 line; length of fork pieces, 9 lines; width of ditto, 5 lines; length of deltoid pieces, 4 lines; greatest width of ditto, 1½ lines.

This *Pentremite* appertains to the section *Floreales* of Roemer, and is very nearly allied to *Pentremites florealis* and *P. pyriformis* of Say, and *P. sulcatus* (Roemer), from which species ours is distinguished by its greater proportionate length, and, consequently, increased number of plates in the pseud-ambulacral fields. Its form is, also, more regularly elliptical, and it invariably occupies a lower geological position.

Geological Formation and Localities. — We have found this species, but not abundantly, in the Encrinital Limestone, on the Mississippi, at Clarksville, Pike county. Professor Swallow found it near Columbia; and Dr. Litton showed me specimens of it from the same formation at Rocheport.

POTERIOCRINUS MEEKIANUS.* — SHUMARD.

Pl. A—Fig. 7—*a*, *b*.

Calyx inverted conical, expanding rapidly from below upwards; plates thick, smooth; sutures strongly defined. Basal plates five, pentagonal, as wide again as high, forming, united, a low cup, its under side deeply excavated, and presenting a wide funnel-shaped cavity to receive the last columnar joint. This facet is covered with numerous fine, radiating striæ, and contains a large pentagonal central perforation. The sub-radial pieces are hexagonal, their length and breadth about equal, and they are twice as high as the basal pieces. First radials (*Scapulae*, *Miller*) as wide again as high; upper edges excavated about one-third the length of the plates, and bearing a finely striated facet for articulating with the succeeding radial piece. This facet occupies about two-thirds the width of the piece. Of the second radial pieces, only one remains; this is very short, and scarcely fills one-third of the excavation of the large first radial. The upper radials, brachials and the column are unknown.

This encrinite is remarkable for the thickness of its shell pieces and its general robust appearance. It is distinguished from *Poteriocrinus impressus* (*Phillips*), to which it is most nearly related, by its more depressed form, the shortness of the basal pieces, and the greater proportionate width of the first radials. It cannot be mistaken for any other described species.

Dimensions. — Length of calyx, 8 lines; width of base, 5 lines; greatest width at summit, 14 lines; height of basal pieces, 2 lines; height of sub-radials, 4½ lines; height of radials, 4 lines.

A single specimen, only, has come under our observation. It was found by Mr. F. B. Meek, at Mount Vernon, in Moniteau county, and to him we have dedicated the species. Its geological position is probably near the base of the Encrinital Limestone, though this is somewhat doubtful, as Mr. Meek found it among loose debris, at the foot of bluffs, composed of both Chouteau and Encrinital Limestone.

POTERIOCRINUS LONGIDACTYLUS.— SHUMARD.

Pl. B—Fig. 5—*a*, *b*, *c*.

Body elongate-conical, surface of plates smooth. *Basal pieces* five, pentagonal, length and breadth nearly equal, uniting to form a little cup with a wide surface beneath, for the supra-columnar joint, and with sides expanding very gradually from below upwards; sutures not very apparent. *Sub-radial* pieces very slightly convex; three of them, regular, hexagonal, as broad as long; the two others, which are situated on the anal side of the body, are irregularly heptagonal, about equal in size, and a fourth larger than the regular pieces. *First radial pieces*, wider than long; articular surfaces occupying the whole width; four of them pentagonal, alternating with the sub-radials; the fifth is irregularly hexagonal, projects above the others, and rests on the upper straight edge of one of the large sub-radials; one of

---

* In the description of this and the following species of Crinoids, I have adopted the nomenclature recently submitted by MM. De Konninck and Le Hon, in their excellent work on the Crinoids of Belgium. (*Recherches sur les Crinoides des Terrain Carbonifere de la Belgique.*) By it each piece can be readily designated; and it appears to me to be founded on a more correct appreciation of the structure of these animals, than any hitherto offered by authors who have written on the subject.

its sides joins a regular radial, and three unite with the anal pieces; the upper edge is truncated obliquely. The *second radial pieces* are quadrangular, and rather wider than long. The remaining plates of the arms consist of rather short wedge-shaped pieces, obtusely angulated in the middle, of which the number to the first bifurcation varies from eight to twelve. Each arm appears to be thrice bifurcated. Of the *anal pieces*, the specimens under examination permit us to count eight, disposed as follows: one is pentagonal, and rests by its inferior angle between the two irregular sub-radials; a second is hexagonal, of the same size as the last, and rests on the upper truncated edge of an irregular sub-radial; above these, are three smaller hexagonal pieces, one with sides equal, the others unequal, and to these succeed three still smaller hexagonals, from which arises the proboscis. The *proboscis* (*trompe, Koninck*) is about two lines wide, and, in the specimen figured, about one inch remains, the upper part being, unfortunately, not preserved. The fragment preserved is composed of several longitudinal rows of small, transverse, invariably hexagonal plates. Five of these rows are to be seen in the specimen, each one consisting of about twenty-five pieces, which alternate with those of the adjoining rows. At the sutures of junction, between every two rows of plates, we may observe, with the aid of a strong lens, a series of minute pores extending their whole length, which remind one somewhat of the apertures in the ambulacral fields of Palæchinus. The *column* is cylindrical, very long and slender, and enlarges just before joining the body. It consists of short, alternate thin and thicker joints, and has a central opening of a pentagonal form; the exterior surface of each joint is surrounded by a line of small granules, which frequently coalesce and form a central carina.

Dimensions. — The column of this Poteriocrinus is upwards of two feet in length. Width of body at junction of free arms, 4½ lines; width at base, 2½ lines; height of anal side, 5½ lines; height of opposite side, 4½ lines; height of base, 2 lines; width of summit of base, 3 lines.

The remains of this *Poteriocrinus* are very common in the upper part of the St. Louis Limestone, in St. Louis county. It is associated with *Palaechinus* (*Melonites*) *multipora*. (Owen and Norwood.) The specimens figured, are from the Bremen quarries.

ACTINOCRINUS CONCINNUS. — Shumard.

Pl. A—Fig. 5.

The portion of the body of this species situated above the second radial pieces is unknown.

The inferior part of the calyx is nearly hemispherical, and the plates moderately thick. *Basal pieces*, three, nearly equal in size, forming a low cup with a nine-sided border, and presenting beneath a wide, circular, shallow depression for the column. *First radials*, moderately convex, length and breadth nearly equal, three hexagonal and two heptagonal; inferior angle of heptagonal pieces, corresponding with a basal suture. *Second radials*, wider than long, with the articular facets for third radials nearly perpendicular, large, reniform, occupying nearly half the length and two-thirds the width of each piece. *First interradials*, hexagonal, a little longer than wide, and rather larger than the second radials. *First anal pieces*, hexagonal, longer than wide, its inferior angle corresponding to a basal suture. Second anals, heptagonal, surface of the plates ornamented with prominent radiating ridges, which rise from near the center of the plates, and cross the sutures, so as to form several sets of double triangles around the body.

Dimensions. — Diameter at base, 4 lines; superior diameter, 13 lines; height of basal pieces, 1 line.

The specimen figured, is all that has been found of this beautiful species of Actinocrinus. It was discovered by Professor Swallow, in the Encrinital Limestone, on North River, in Marion county.

ACTINOCRINUS MISSOURIENSIS. — SHUMARD.

Pl. A—Fig. 4—*a*, *b*, *c*.

The body of this fine species has the form of an inverted truncated cone, with the truncated apex resting on a widened base. The plates are rather thick, many of them garnished with a central prominence, while others are plane or slightly convex. *Base* massive, moderately high, inferior border surrounded by a thick rim, which is notched at the sutures; articular facet for the column circular, slightly concave, occupying about one-third the diameter of the base, and usually surrounded by a shallow, but well-marked depression; two of the pieces are irregularly hexagonal, the third is sub-quadrangular. *Radial pieces* large, rather wider than long, three hexagonal and two heptagonal; upper oblique edges short, superior edges concave. The surface of each plate is marked with a prominent transverse ridge. The *second radials* are small, not more than a fourth as large as the first radials, quadrangular, as wide again as long, and raised in their centers. *The axillary pieces* (*third radials*) are pentagonal, twice as wide as high, and flattened convex; they usually support, on each of their oblique superior edges, two brachials; the first (sometimes not present) is small, short and often irregular in form; the second is comparatively large; its length and breadth being about equal, and in the upper edge is a small notch for the passage of the brachial vessels. The *first interradials* are rather large, as wide as long, and the number of their sides varies from six to nine; their surfaces bear a central mammillary projection. The *second interradials* are small, elongated, and irregular. The *anal pieces* are eight in number; the inferior one, a little longer and narrower than the *first radials*, is heptagonal, and bears on its upper edges three smaller anals, the middle one hexagonal and the others heptagonal; these again support the other and smallest anal pieces.

The pieces composing the vault have the following arrangement: Over every pair of second brachials is a rather large pentagonal piece, whose inferior angle corresponds to the axis of the radial pieces; and, on either side of this, is an elongated plate of an irregular form, which is situated over the interradials; these three form the inferior segment of a circle of seven pieces, in the center of which is a large wart-shaped plate, bearing a round articular facet; five such circles of plates surround the vertex, each enclosing wart-shaped platea. Near the center of the vault, but closer to the anal side, is a large tumid piece, encircled by eight or nine polygonal plates.

The *proboscis* is short and lies below the level of the vault-plane, and between two of the wart-shaped pieces that are wider apart than the others. It is of a semi-ovoid form, made up of small plates of various shapes; the aperture is heptagonal.

Dimensions. — Height of body, 1½ inches; diameter at vertex, 15 lines; inferior diameter of base, 9 lines; superior diameter of base, 7 lines; height of base, 3½ lines; height of first radials, 3 lines; width of base, about 4 lines.

This species, in the general arrangement of the plates, is very analagous to *Actiocrinus* (*Dorycrinus*), *Mississippiensis* of Dr. Roemer, but the general form of the body and pieces are quite different. Its summit, like that of *A. Mississippiensis*, was, doubtless, provided with spines or long thorns, since articular facets for such appendages are perfectly plain on our specimens; and detached spines, more than an inch long, occur in the strata which have yielded them.

Geological Position and Locality. — Found by Professor Swallow in the 6th Division of the Encrinital Limestone, on North River, near Palmyra, Marion county.

ACTINOCRINUS ROTUNDUS — YANDELL AND SHUMARD.

Pl. A—Fig. 2—*a, b.*

Synonym — *Actinocrinites*, Christy, 1848.— Letters on Geology, Pl. 1, fig. 3, 4.

General form ovate, sub-globose, surface of all the plates smooth. *Basal* pieces similar in form, rather small, pentagonal, forming united a low saucer, with a hexagonal rim; articular facet large, concave, central perforation very small. *1st radial pieces* hexagonal, as wide again as long; *2d radials* small, quadrangular, about half as wide as the 1st radials, width rather more than double the length; axillary pieces rather larger than the last, irregularly pentagonal, supporting on each of their oblique upper edges two brachials, and the upper ones of these, being axillary pieces, bear also two secondary brachials, from which arise the free arms. The interradial pieces, of which there are three between every two of the radial rows, are nearly equal in size; those of the first order are octagonal, moderately large, and their length and breadth is about equal; the pieces of the second order are elongated and irregular in form. The *anal* pieces amount to eight or ten in number; the first, which rests on the base, is regularly hexagonal; it is longer than the 1st radial, and bears three smaller pieces, one pentagonal, and two heptagonal.

The vault is elevated, regularly convex, and consists of numerous polygonal pieces, which are large at the summit and diminish in size as they approach the orifices of the arms. The proboscis is sub-central, and situated nearest the anal side of the body.

Arms. — The example we have figured, exhibits twenty-one arm openings.

Dimensions. — Height, 9 lines; greatest width, 9 lines.

Formation and Localities. — It occurs at Rocheport, in Boone county, and near Palmyra, in Marion county, near the base of the Encrinital Limestone, and is one of the most characteristic fossils of that formation.

ACTINOCRINUS CHRISTYI.

Pl. A—Fig. 3.

Synonym —*Actinocrinites*, Christy, 1848.—Letters on Geology, Pl. 1, Nos. 1, 2.

Body large, bell-shaped, plates thick, very slightly convex, surface smooth. *Base* cup-shaped, as wide again as high, pieces nearly equal in size; *1st radials* large, increasing slightly in width from below upwards, length and breadth about equal; *2d radials* small, short, quadrangular; *axillary* pieces pentagonal, as wide again as high; *1st brachials* much wider than long, irregular in form, and larger than the axillary radial pieces; *2d brachials* considerably larger than the 1st brachials, and, being axillary pieces, they support on their upper edges two large secondary brachials of an irregular form, each of which again bears a short sub-quadrangular piece, furnished with a facet for the articulation of the free arms. The *interradial* pieces amount to four in number, and are very variable in form. The first are large, longer than wide, and usually of an irregular octagonal form; the others are small. The *anal pieces* amount to seven; the first, which rests on the base, is of large size, heptagonal, longer than wide, and its sides are nearly parallel. It supports three small pieces: one, central, slightly elongated, and hexagonal; and two, heptagonal. These again are succeeded by three still smaller pieces, pentagonal and hexagonal. The proboscis is nearly central, but only the base of it is preserved in our specimen. In a specimen from Oquawka, Illinois, figured by Mr. D. Christy, in his letters on Geology, about one inch of the proboscis remains attached to the fossil. It is represented as being of a curved cylindrical form.

The *dimensions* of the specimen figured, are as follows: whole height, 14 lines; height from base to vault, 12 lines; greatest diameter, 17 lines; inferior diameter of base, 3 lines; superior diameter of base, 5 lines; height of base, 2½ lines.

I have dedicated this interesting species to Mr. David Christy, to whom we are indebted for the first notice of it. It was very properly placed by him in the genus *Actinocrinus*, but the figures were unaccompanied by either a description or a specific name.

This species was found by Professor Swallow, near Palmyra, Marion county, who regards it as being very characteristic of his division No. 6, of the Encrinital Limestone. It was, also, discovered by Dr. Litton, in similar geological position, at Rocheport, in Boone county.

ACTINOCRINUS PYRIFORMIS.—SHUMARD.

Pl. A—Fig. 6—*a, b.*

Body large, pyriform, plates moderately thick, often prominent in their centers; surface smooth, sutures not very evident.

Base sub-cylindrical; width greater than the length; inferior border slightly thickened, articular facet small, round, concave, central perforation minute, its form unknown; plates equal. *First radial pieces* large, elongated, about half as long again as wide, sides sub-parallel, upper edges very short. *Second radials* nearly square, very small, their length being only a fraction over a line, while the length of the first radials is four lines; third radials (axillary pieces) hexagonal, length and breadth about the same, and more than double the size of the second radials. *Brachial pieces* wide, hexagonal, and about equal in size to the axillary radials; their upper edges are nearly straight, and they are, also, longer than the others, and support a wide, pentagonal piece, on whose oblique upper edges rest the arm-bearing pieces; these are a little wider than long, and sometimes are hexagonal, and sometimes heptagonal. The upper edges are furnished with a semi-circular notch, which occupies about one-fourth the width of the piece, and leads into the interior of the body. The *interradials* are six in number; the first and largest heptagonal, on which rests two nearly regular pentagonal pieces; these are succeeded by one smaller pentagonal piece, which is surmounted by a larger piece of a heptagonal shape. *Anal pieces.* In neither of the specimens figured, can the number and form of these plates be made out.

The *vault* is very convex, and consists of rather large pieces, chiefly of hexagonal and heptagonal figures, of which the former are the most common.

Of the *proboscis*, only the base is preserved. Its position is sub-central and nearest the anal side. The number of arms vary in different specimens. In the larger specimen figured (Pl. A—Fig. 6,—*a*), the number of arms are indicated by nineteen apertures. In the smaller example (Pl. A—Fig. 6—*b*), there are twenty apertures.

The *dimensions* of the largest example we have figured, are as follows: Height, 23 lines; greatest diameter, about 15 lines; height, from base to arm openings, 13½ lines; height of base, 3½ lines; inferior diameter of base, 5½ lines; superior diameter of base, 5 lines.

Geological Position and Locality.—This is one of the finest species of Crinoids as yet found in the strata of our State, and is very characteristic of the Encrinital

Limestone. Both the specimens we have illustrated were discovered by Professor Swallow, near Palmyra, Marion county, associated with the preceding species.

ACTINOCRINUS PARVUS. — SHUMARD.

Pl. A — Fig. 9.

Of this elegant little Actinocrinus we possess only a fragment of the body, from which, however, we are able to characterize the species, so as to permit of its being easily identified. Its general form is globose; the surface is ornamented with very fine, somewhat flexuous striæ, which radiate from the center of each piece to the sides, where they unite with striæ from the adjacent pieces in such a manner as to form several series of isosceles triangles around the body; the plates are thick and very finely serrated at the sutures.

The *base* is moderately convex, and has nine angles, six of which are salient and three retreating; articular facet for the column small, concave, its border finely crenulated; central perforation, extremely small and pentalobate. *First radial pieces* wider than long, three of them hexagonal, and two pentagonal. *Second radial pieces* hexagonal, nearly as wide again as long, their superior lateral edges very short. *Axillary pieces* pentagonal, about as long as the second radials, but not as wide. Each row of radial pieces exhibits a slightly prominent longitudinal ridge, which becomes obsolete as it approaches the base. *First Brachial pieces* quadrangular, short, widest above, and crenulated on the superior articular border. The number of interradial pieces amounts to three, between every two radial rows. The first and largest is hexagonal, with sides nearly equal, the others are chiefly hexagonal, with sides unequal. *Anal pieces* unknown.

The vault consists of many small pieces, irregular in form. The situation of the proboscis is unknown.

Dimensions. — Length, 5 lines; greatest width, 5 lines; height from base to arm-openings, 3 lines; diameter of base, 2 lines.

Formation and Locality. — It was found at St. Louis, in the upper part of the St. Louis Limestone, associated with *Palaechinus multipora*, and *Poteriocrinus longidactylus*. It is very rare.

ACTINOCRINUS VERNEUILIANUS. — SHUMARD.

Pl. A — Fig. 1 — *a*, *b*.

General form obovate, surface of plates smooth.

Base, a low cup, widest above, slightly thickened at the inferior border, under surface gently convex; articular facet of moderate width, deeply concave; central perforation small. *First radials* large, as wide as long, three hexagonal, two heptagonal, all of them exhibiting a central prominence, which in some specimens is quite distinct, and in others obscure. *Second radial pieces* very small, quadrangular, about as wide again as long, their surfaces nearly plane. *Axillary pieces* wide pentagonal, supporting on each side a short first brachial, which on the same specimen is sometimes an axillary piece, and sometimes not; the form of the *second* and *third brachials* is very variable. Of the *interradials*, there usually exists but one between every two rows of regular radials; sometimes, however, there are two, in which case the second is quite small and irregular in form. The number of *anal pieces* amounts to seven or eight; the one resting on the base is hexagonal, equals in size the first radials, and bears on its oblique upper edges two hexagonal pieces, one wider than long, the other about as long as wide; these again, support three or four still smaller pieces.

The *vault* consists of numerous small pieces, united so as to form a nearly smooth convex surface. *Proboscis* sub-central. *Arms* unknown; the number of arm-openings in the specimens under examination varies from fourteen to fifteen.

Dimensions. — This species presents some variety in form, dependent on differences in age. The adult specimen we have figured (Pl. A, fig. 1, b), exhibits the following proportions: — Length, 9 lines; greatest diameter, 8½ lines; height of vault, 3 lines; inferior diameter of base, 3 lines; superior diameter of same, 3½ lines; height of same, 1 line. The young example (Pl. A, fig. 1, a) has the following dimensions: — Length, 8 lines; greatest diameter, 6 lines; height of vault, 3½ lines; inferior diameter of base, 2½ lines.

Geological Formation and Locality. — Dr. Litton found this species abundantly at Rocheport; and Prof. Swallow also obtained specimens of it in the Encrinital Limestone, near Palmyra, Marion county, associated with *Actinocrinus Missouriensis* and *A. pyriformis.*

ACTINOCRINUS KONINCKI.—SHUMARD.

Pl. A—Fig. 8—*a, b, c.*

Synonym—Actinocrinites, Christy, 1848.—Letters on Geology, Pl. 1, Figs. 5, 6.

The calyx of this elegant little species has somewhat the form of an ancient urn; the plates are thick, and nearly all of them are furnished with a central tubercle, which is very prominent on the pieces composing the inferior half of the calyx. *Base* about as wide again as high, decreasing rapidly in width from below upwards; inferior border trilobate; under surface nearly plane, articular facet small, deeply excavated, and circumscribed by a very slight prominence; central perforation very minute, round (?). *1st radial pieces,* three hexagonal and two heptagonal, rather higher than the base, length and breadth about equal, each one bearing a very prominent tubercle, the base of which is generally circular, but sometimes elliptical. *2d radial pieces,* small, quadrangular, rather wider than long, with or without a central tubercle. *Axillary pieces,* pentagonal as high as the first radials, and wider than long. *1st brachials* irregularly hexagonal and heptagonal, each supporting a 2d brachial of a transverse sub-hexagonal form, from which commences the free arms. The *interradial pieces* amount to only one between every two of the radial rows; this is of an octagonal shape. The *anal pieces* amount to ten; the first, which rests directly on the base, is heptagonal, longer than wide, and bears, like the 1st radials, a very large tubercle; on its upper edges rest three small pieces, the middle one hexagonal and the lateral ones heptagonal; these support three smaller pieces, one heptagonal and two pentagonal, to which succeed the remaining and still smaller pieces. The *vault* is of a depressed conical form, and consists of small polygonal plates. The *proboscis* is sub-central, and always situated nearest the anal side.

Dimensions. — Length, 7 lines; length, from base to arm openings, 5 lines; greatest diameter at summit, about 4 lines; height of base, about 1 line; inferior diameter of same, 3 lines; superior diameter of same, 2 lines.

Formation and Locality. — Occurs in the Encrinital Limestone, at Rocheport, Boone county, and near Palmyra, Marion county, where it is associated with the preceding species. Its vertical range in the strata is very limited.

GLYPTOCRINUS FIMBRIATUS.—SHUMARD.

Pl. A—Fig. 10—*a, b.*

The body of this little Crinoid, when the delicate arms, tentaculæ and column are attached, has the form of a broom.

The *column* is round, long, slender, and composed of thin joints, every third or fourth joint being enlarged; its surface is very finely crenulated. *Calyx* conical, expanding rapidly from base to summit. *Basal pieces* pentagonal; length and breadth about equal. *First radial pieces* hexagonal, alternating with and a little larger than the basals. To these succeed the second and third radials; and the latter, being axillary pieces, support the free arms. The remaining pieces comprising the cup are so worn, that their form and arrangement cannot be accurately made out. The *arms* are slender, twice or thrice bifurcated, and composed of numerous quadrangular joints, furnished with delicate tentaculæ; arms and tentaculæ, very finely and beautifully crenulated.

This little species, in its general appearance, and in the structure of the lower part of the cup, bears a strong resemblance to some of the species of Glyptocrinus of Professor Hall. I have, therefore, placed it in that genus, although the examination of more perfect specimens than we have at present may render it necessary to transfer it to some other.

Geological Position and Locality. — This species occurs in the Cape Girardeau Limestone, associated with *Tentaculites incurvus*, *Cyphaspis Girardeauensis*, and *Acidaspis Halli*, on the Mississippi river, in Cape Girardeau county.

TENTACULITES INCURVUS. — SHUMARD.

Pl. B — Fig. 6 — *a*, *b*.

Tube attenuated, curved, with prominent sharp annulations extending to the tip; at the large extremity there are from five to six rings in the space of an eighth of an inch, and the intervening spaces are about double the width; but near the tip the rings are much closer together, and there are from eighteen to twenty in the eighth of an inch; the whole number of rings amounts to about thirty-five. The surface is covered with fine longitudinal striæ, which cross the rings, as well as the spaces. In well-preserved specimens very fine transverse striæ can be perceived. The length of the tube varies from six to eight lines.

These little bodies occur on the Mississippi, two miles above Cape Girardeau, in Cape Girardeau Limestone. They occur in the greatest profusion, associated with *Encrinurus deltoideus*, *Cyphaspis Girardeauensis*, and *Proetus depressus*.

CRUSTACEA.

CYTHERE SUBLAEVIS. — SHUMARD.

Pl. B — Fig. 15.

Carapace small, sub-ovate, smooth, nearly as long again as high, moderately tumid, most prominent posteriorly; posterior end a little wider than the anterior, rounded; ventral margin straight, its anterior extremity extended into a minute pointed process. Just within the borders a faintly impressed line may be traced entirely around the valves. The surface is highly polished.

This little species is very analagous to *Cythere Phillipsiana*, Koninck, from the Carboniferous System of Belgium and Yorkshire. It differs in being proportionally longer, and the process on the ventral margin is much smaller and more acute.

Dimensions. — Length, two lines; height, $1\frac{1}{4}$ lines.

It occurs in the 1st Magnesian Limestone, near its junction with the Saccharoidal Sandstone, near Hamilton Creek, St. Louis county, and in Ste. Genevieve county. It is very abundant, beds several feet thick being composed almost entirely of the remains of this little crustacean. At these localities the fossil is always divested of its shell. Professor Swallow has, however, discovered some individuals on Spencer's Creek, Ralls county, in which the outer crust still remains, and from these the above description has been drawn.

TRILOBITES.

PROETUS SWALLOWI.* — Shumard.

Pl. B — Fig. 12 — *a, b.*

Head semicircular, swelled, exterior border narrow, slightly elevated and marked with four or five thread-like striæ; sinus of the border shallow and indistinct; posterior border of cheeks rather wide, and limited internally by a shallow, but distinct groove; genal angle short and rounded?; *glabella* tumid, elevated above the plane of the cheeks, occupying about four-fifths the entire length of the head, rather more than half as wide as long; front rounded; sides convex, in advance of the eyes; slightly concave in the middle, and expanding again posteriorly; lobation indistinctly marked by three very shallow depressions on each side, the anterior and middle ones being nearly obsolete; occipital segment wider than the base of the glabella; convex, and as high as the glabella; occipital furrow slightly arched towards the front, narrow, rather deeply impressed, widest at the extremities; the furrow which separates the globella from the cheeks (dorsal sinus) is narrow, flexuous and slightly impressed; *cheeks* elevated in the middle, declining rapidly towards the borders; *eyes* reniform, moderately developed, not as high as the glabella, palpebral lobes semi-oval, visual surface very minutely reticulated. *Thorax* with nine segments; axal lobe very elevated, width greater than the lateral lobes, rings rather wide, flattened in the direction of the axis; separated from each other by straight, narrow, but well-defined grooves; segments of lateral lobes flattened between the knee and axis; the two bands are of nearly equal width; extremities rounded. Pygidium parabolic, moderately convex; length about equal to the head, border rather wide; axal lobe elevated, as wide as lateral lobes; segments eleven, flattened, separated by straight and feebly-impressed grooves; lateral lobes about seven, indistinct.

The whole surface is minutely punctate; the punctæ sometimes disposed in quincunx and sometimes irregularly.

Dimensions. — Length of head, 3½ lines; greatest width, 6 lines.

Formation and Locality. — This pretty little species was found by Professor Swallow, in the lithographic limestone of the Chemung Group at Chouteau Springs, Cooper county; and by Mr. F. B. Meek, in Moniteau county.

Dedicated to its discoverer, Professor G. C. Swallow.

PROETUS MISSOURIENSIS. — Shumard.

Pl. B — Fig. 13. — *a, b.*

Glabella tumid, greatest height about the center, ovoid, obtusely rounded in front, truncated posteriorly, length a little greater than the width, widest behind, three furrows on either side, posterior pair strongly marked: these commence at the dorsal sinus, about one-third the distance from base to front, pass in a curve backwards, and bifurcate about midway between the center and sides of the glabella; one branch, very shallow, is continued for a short distance almost transversely; the other bends backwards nearly to the occipital sinus, and with the main branch partially encloses a large oval lobe on each side, the lobes separated by a space about half the width of the glabella; middle pair of furrows, shallow, curving backwards in a direction nearly parallel with the posterior ones, but considerably shorter; anterior pair feebly impressed, a little oblique; occipital sinus a little convex towards

* In the following description of Trilobites I have followed, with but little alteration, the nomenclature of Barrande.

the front, shallowest in the middle; occipital ring wide, flattened, much lower than the plane of the glabella. *Pygidium* semi-circular, flattened convex, width double the length, margin broad and slightly concave; axal lobe almost as wide as the lateral lobes, rounded at the extremity, segments ten, separated by strongly-marked furrows; lateral lobes flattened, with six or seven segments, separated by shallow, but well-marked furrows; surface thickly studded with granulæ, which are rather smaller than those of the glabella.

Dimensions. — Length of head, 8½ lines; greatest width of glabella, 7½ lines; length of pygidium, 6½ lines; width of ditto, 1 inch.

Checks and thorax unknown.

This is one of the most beautiful species found in our rocks. The test is of a light chesnut brown color.

Locality. — It was obtained by Prof. Swallow, from the Lithographic Limestone, at Hannibal, Louisiana and Chouteau Springs, Missouri, associated with *Productus Murchisonianus, Spirifer cuspidatus* and *Chonetes ornata.*

CYPHASPIS GIRARDEAUENSIS. — SHUMARD.

Pl. B — Fig. 11 — *a, b.*

Body ovate, depressed; *head* nearly semicircular, forming more than one-third the length of the body, very moderately convex, exterior border raised, narrow, prolonged posteriorly into slender, arched spines, which extend to the seventh thoracic articulation; within the border is a narrow well-defined groove, and between this and the furrow which passes round the front of the glabella is a slightly-raised surface. *Glabella* subovate, rounded before, truncated behind, occupying rather more than two-thirds the length of the head, greatest width a little in advance of the middle, surface moderately convex and but little elevated above the cheeks, when compared with other species of the genus; at the base on either side is a small ovate lobe, about half the length of the glabella, and entirely separated from it by a narrow, deeply-impressed groove; longitudinal furrows narrow, profound, uniting in front of the glabella; occipital furrow straight, narrow, deep; occipital ring about as high as the glabella, wide in the middle, narrowing towards the extremities, garnished with a minute central granule; cheeks depressed convex; eyes small, nearly circular, situated very near the glabella, and opposite the anterior half of its lateral lobes. *Thorax* with ten segments, trilobation strongly marked by the longitudinal furrows; *axal lobe* wider than the lateral lobes, slightly flattened in the middle, rings slightly arched towards the front, separated by strong furrows; seventh ring provided with a slender spine, a little flattened on the sides; it extends directly backwards, nearly two lines beyond the extremity of the pygidium. The entire length of this appendage is about four lines; it rises by a thickened base, and terminates in an acute point. *Pleuræ* rounded at extremities, each with a deep groove running nearly the entire length, bend of the knee nearest the axal extremities. *Pygidium* semicircular, twice as wide as long, border narrow, axal lobe about as wide as one lateral lobe, rings from five to eight (varying in different specimens), segments of lateral lobes tolerably distinct, grooved throughout their entire length. The surface of the crust appears perfectly smooth to the naked eye, but when examined with a strong lens, numerous minute granulæ are to be seen.

Dimensions. — Length, 7 lines; greatest breadth, 6 lines; length of head, 2½ lines.

The species described, as far as my observation extends, is the only example of the genus hitherto observed in American strata. The depressed form of the glabella and the large size of its basal lobes will distinguish it from its European congeners, with one exception, *Cyphaspis depressa* of Barrande, from the Upper Silurian strata of Bohemia, which, also, possesses these characters. In other respects, however, our fossil is widely different, and cannot be mistaken for that species.

The only perfect example of this trilobite we have found, is represented in plate B, Fig. 11, *a*. An interesting feature in this specimen is the remarkable spinal appendage, which rises from the seventh axal ring of the thorax, and which, notwithstanding its extreme delicacy, is beautifully preserved in nearly a normal position. Barrande has observed a similar appendage in a number of Bohemian species of Cyphaspis, and Salter figures a fine example from the Silurian rocks of Britain. In all the specimens mentioned by these authors, however, the spine arises from the sixth axal ring of the thorax, instead of from the seventh, as *Cyphaspis Girardeauensis*.

Formation and Locality. — It occurs in the Upper Silurian strata (Cape Girardeau Limestone), on the Mississippi river, two miles above Cape Girardeau, Missouri, where it is associated with *Proetus depressus*, *Encrinurus deltoideus*, and Homocrinus.

ENCRINURUS DELTOIDEUS. — SHUMARD.

Pl. B — Fig 10.

Head and *Thorax* unknown.

Pygidium subtriangular, width greater than the length, moderately convex, arched before, extremity rounded and bent slightly upward; *axal lobe* flattened convex, a little elevated above the convexity of the lateral lobes, from which it is well defined by the longitudinal furrows; rings about twenty-four, narrow; the first four or five only are entire, the others are interrupted by a longitudinal space, which runs down the middle of the axis, and bears several very small granules, which are indistinct, and, in the specimens before us, are only apparent on the anterior third of its length; on each side of this interval, the rings are separated by strong transverse furrows, nearly as wide as the rings; *lateral lobes*, each about one and a half times the width of axal lobe; ribs eight on each side, narrow at their origin, and becoming wider as they approach the border, curved downward and backwards, the last two or three being nearly parallel with a line drawn through the length of the axis; furrows deep, smooth, and about half as wide as the ribs. The surface of the test appears perfectly smooth to the unassisted eye, excepting the annulations of the axis, which show traces of granules. With the magnifier, minute granulæ are to be seen, particularly near the borders and posterior extremity. The shell is of a beautiful chestnut brown color.

Dimensions of largest specimen of the pygidium: length, 9 lines; width, 10½ lines.

It is nearly related to *Encrinurus sex-costatus*, Salter, from which it differs in the greater number of ribs of the axal and lateral lobes of the pygidium, and in its axis, which is longer and narrower. From the pygidium of *Encrinurus punctatus*, as figured by Murchison, McCoy and Hall, ours may be readily distinguished by its greater width, rounded posterior extremity, and the greater width of its ribs. It cannot be confounded with any other species of the genus.

Formation and Locality. — It occurs with the preceding species in the Cape Girardeau Limestone, on the Mississippi river, about two miles above Cape Girardeau. We have found several specimens of the pygidium, but, up to this time, no portions of the head or thorax have been discovered.

PHILLIPSIA MERAMECENSIS.—SHUMARD.

Pl. B—Fig. 9.

Pygidium semi-elliptical, rather wider than long, very convex; border moderately narrow; *axal lobe* not quite as wide as the lateral lobes, and considerably elevated above them; anterior extremity arched; posterior extremity obtusely rounded; rings thirteen, convex on the dorsum, flattened on the sides; transverse furrows rather deeply impressed on the dorsum, but shallow and narrow on the flattened sides; *lateral lobes* strongly arched downwards; ribs about twelve, distinct, except the two or three last, which are obscure; the first four from the thoracic margin marked with a shallow but distinct furrow, which is situated very near the posterior edge; furrows between the ribs rather deeply impressed. Surface very finely granulose.

Dimensions.—Length, 6 lines; greatest width, 6½ lines.

Geological Position and Locality.—Occurs in the Archimedes Limestone, on the Meramec River, at Fenton, St. Louis county.

DALMANIA TRIDENTIFERA.—SHUMARD.

Pl. B—Fig. 8—*a, b, c.*

Head sub-semicircular, but little elevated, granulose; external border wide, slightly raised, and with a broad shallow groove extending nearly the entire length; front extended into a remarkable three-lobed process, about four lines wide at the base, and three and a half lines long; the lobes angulated and bent slightly upwards; one, a little the largest, projects forward from the middle of the process, and occupies about half its length; the others arise from behind the central lobe, and project laterally one on either side, their extremities being about five lines apart. On each side of the process the border is notched about half its width. The genal angles are broad, flattened convex and slightly curved at the tip; their length about equal to the head, exclusive of the frontal process. *Glabella* very moderately convex; frontal lobe transverse, somewhat lozenge-shaped, with the angles rounded, occupying more than one-half the length of the glabella, including the occipital ring, and separated from the cheeks by a well-defined dorsal furrow, which becomes obsolete in front; lateral furrows well impressed, and extending rather more than one-third the distance across the glabella; anterior pair directed obliquely backwards, forming, with the axis, an angle of about seventy degrees; second pair directed forwards; posterior pair transverse. Eyes large, lunate, very close to the glabella, and extending from the occipital to the anterior lateral furrows. The visual surface of each eye contains about thirty-eight vertical rows of lenses, the maximum number in a row being ten, the whole number about 350. The cheeks are very slightly convex.

Pygidium sub-triangular, flattened convex; border from a half to a line wide, prolonged posteriorly into a pointed spine from one to two lines long. *Axis* but little raised above the lateral lobes, forming about one-fourth the entire width, tapering gradually, rounded and slightly prominent at the extremity, from which an obscure carina extends to the caudal spine; rings fourteen, flattened convex, separated by narrow grooves; *lateral lobes*, with nine or ten segments, gently curved, and their extremities coalescing with the border; furrows rather wide but shallow, each with two shallow pits near the border, separated by a slightly-raised carina.

Formation and Locality.—This species is quite characteristic of the Delthyris Shaly Limestone, on the Mississippi river, below Bailey's Landing, in Perry county, and at Birmingham, in Cape Girardeau county.

CALYMENE RUGOSA.—SHUMARD.

Pl. B—Fig. 14.

Of this handsome species we have found only the pygidium. It is much wider than long, and the posterior border is moderately rounded. The surface is thickly studded with granules, which are most numerous on the borders. *Axis* not as wide as one lateral lobe; rings eight, separated by rather deep furrows, scarcely half as wide as the rings; *lateral lobes* with about five segments, which continue to the exterior edge, each one divided into two nearly equal parts by a slight furrow, which extends nearly to the extremity; furrows between the ribs becoming nearly obsolete before attaining the edges.

Dimensions.—Length, 6½ lines; width, 10 lines.

The pygidium here described is very similar to that of *Calymene incerta*, Barrande, but the axis is narrower, and the lateral lobes wider.

Formation and Locality.—This species occurs on the Mississippi river, one mile below Birmingham, in the Delthyris Shaly Limestone.

ACIDASPIS HALLI.—SHUMARD.

Pl. B—Fig. 7—*a, b, c.*

This is, perhaps, the most beautiful of the American species of Acidaspis, and the only one known to me from western localities. We have not yet succeeded in obtaining an entire individual, but the specimens in the State collection are sufficient to enable us to illustrate most of the essential characters of the species.

The *glabella* is very moderately convex; its length is 2¼ lines, and its width, between the eyes, is about 3 lines; frontal border elevated, garnished with a row of closely-set granules, and limited internally by a deep furrow; dorsal sinuses rather deep and nearly parallel with each other; false sinuses well defined from their commencement at the middle lateral furrows, to the occipital furrow; mesial lobe of glabella slightly elevated above the lateral lobes, and bearing a wide frontal lobe, forming a little more than a fourth of its length, and behind which the sides are slightly arched; of the lateral lobes the middle one is nearly circular, the posterior one oval; no antero-lateral sinuses, the middle and posterior ones neatly defined and deep; occipital sinus distinctly marked, but rather shallow in its middle third; occipital ring very slightly elevated above the plane of the median lobe, rather wide in the middle, constricted at the extremities, posterior edge of constricted portion bearing a prominent granule on either side; area between the groove of the occular thread and dorsal sinus narrow, triangular, and ornamented with a double row of granules; occular thread very slender, bearing a single series of granules; eyes situated directly opposite the posterior lateral lobes; *movable cheeks* as wide as the median lobe of the glabella is long; border well defined, and terminating posteriorly in a slightly-curved acute spine, about two lines in length; exterior edge ornamented with about fourteen spines, increasing in length as they recede from the front, and two of them situated on the genal spine; the forward ones are blunt at their extremities, the others are drawn to a sharp point.

Thorax.—The number of segments composing the thorax is unknown. In the specimen figured, which is the most perfect one in our possession, eight are preserved; *axis* not so wide as one of the lateral lobes; *lateral segments* each bearing a *bourrelet* of a semi-cylindrical form, occupying about half its width, and garnished with a row of granules; posterior band very narrow and difficult to be seen; anterior band very slightly convex, narrow and granulose.

Pygidium minute, sub-semicircular; axal lobe occupying about one-third the entire width, consisting of two rings; lateral lobes very slightly convex; the single segment which arises from the first axal ring is narrow at its origin, but becomes rather broad before attaining the margin; it is prolonged into a primary spine, one on each side, about one and a half lines long, and between these are two secondary spines, about half as long as the former; the lateral borders are also furnished with two, and sometimes three secondary spines on either side.

Dimensions. — Length, about 7 lines; width of eighth rib of thorax, exclusive of spines, 6¼ lines; length of pygidium, 1 line.

Formation and Locality. — Fragments of this elegant little trilobite are quite common in the Cape Girardeau Limestone, on the Mississippi river, in Cape Girardeau county.

Dedicated to Prof. James Hall.

PRODUCTUS AEQUICOSTATUS. — SHUMARD.

Pl C — Fig. 10.

Synonyms — *Productus* — Christy, 1848, Letters on Geology, Pl. 5, Fig. 1. *Productus cora* — D. D. Owen, Geol. Rep., Iowa, Wisconsin and Minnesota, Tab. V., Fig. 1 (not *P. cora* of D'Orbigny).

Shell large, broad, hinge-line equal to the greatest width of the shell. Dorsal valve much elevated, arched, visceral portion slightly flattened on the middle, sides falling rather abruptly to the ears. Ears large, triangular, with three or four broad folds, which are not continued across the visceral portion. Just within the cardinal border is a range of four or five small tubes on either side of the beak. The beak is moderately obtuse, and passes a little beyond the cardinal border. The surface is covered with longitudinal rounded ribs, which, at about one-fourth of the distance from the beak, preserve nearly an uniform width to the front margin. Some of the ribs bifurcate near the beak, and then continue without further division, the spaces between being occasionally supplied with new ones; they are nearly straight on the back of the shell; on the sides, they are curved towards the lateral borders, and rendered flexuous by the folds. At ten lines from the beak there are fifteen ribs in the space of five lines; the whole number is from 150 to 160. The surface is studded with slender tubes, which in some specimens are separated from each other by pretty regular intervals, and arranged in oblique lines across the shell; in others, they are scattered promiscuously over the surface. In a specimen before us, we can count six ranges of these tubes separated from each other by regular distances of about four lines. In another example, they are more numerous and nearer together. They occupy rather more space than the width of the ribs. Ventral valve concave, visceral portion nearly plane, subquadrilateral, with several folds which continue across the shell; these are prominent on the ears and side, but as they approach the middle they become obscure.

Dr. Owen refers this species to *Productus cora*, D'Orbigny, from which, however, it differs in many respects. The cardinal line is much wider, ears larger, ribs coarser and fewer, and the spaces between the ribs are not more than half their width, the reverse of which is the case in the Productus Cora.

This fine species was found very abundantly by Professor Swallow, in the upper Coal Measures, on the Missouri river, at Iowa Point, Bondtown, Dallas, mouth of Platte river and Weston.

CHONETES PARVA. — SHUMARD.

Shell small, sub-semicircular, cardinal line straight, front and sides regularly rounded. Dorsal value convex, most prominent near the beak, sinus very shallow; ears short, slightly concave; surface marked with rounded, dichotomous ribs, separated by spaces not as wide as the ribs; the number on the border amounts to about forty-five. On the ears the ribs are not so prominent as on the vaulted portion of the shell. Ventral valve with a slight elevation in front, corresponding to the sinus of the dorsal valve. Area and spines unknown.

The specimens we have of this species are somewhat worn, so that all the characters cannot be determined. It is believed, however, that the above description will identify the species.

Locality.—Found by Professor Swallow, in the Coal Measures, in Boone county.

CHONETES ORNATA.—Shumard.

Pl. C—Fig. 1.—*a, b, c.*

Shell small, sub-semicircular, transverse, greatest width at the cardinal border. Dorsal valve moderately convex, hinge-line prolonged into small acute ears, which are smooth, slightly deflected and convex; cardinal border, with three or four minute spines on each side of the beak; surface, with from thirty to forty rounded ribs, separated by sulci not quite as wide as the ribs; some of the latter bifurcate twice or thrice, and others proceed from the beak to the border without division. They are crossed by fine concentric undulating lines of growth, which are barely visible to the naked eye. Ventral valve moderately concave, with a shallow transverse depression on the ears, corresponding to the convexity of the opposite valve.

Dimensions. — Length, 2½ lines; breadth, 5 lines. In the number and character of the ribs, the *C. ornata* is analagous to *C. nana,* but it differs in being proportionally wider and more depressed. From *C. convoluta* (Phillips' sp.), to which it, also, bears considerable resemblance, it may be readily distinguished by the ribs, many of which are dichotomous, whereas they are always simple in the former species.

This pretty Chonetes is one of the most characteristic fossils of the Chemung Group of Missouri. It was obtained by Professor Swallow, at Vandever's Falls, Cooper county, Louisiana and Hannibal, and by Mr. Meek, in Moniteau county. It is quite common, particularly in the Lithographic Limestone.

SPIRIFER PLANO-CONVEXA.—Shumard.

Shell small, plano-convex, semi-elliptical, greatest width near the middle, surface of valves smooth. Ventral valve nearly plane, presenting only a slight convexity near the beak, no mesial ridge; cardinal line straight, short, less than the width of the shell; lateral borders and front regularly rounded; area short, triangular, having a rather wide foramen, with the lateral edges raised. Dorsal valve gibbous, greatest convexity at the middle, a faint mesial sinus running from the beak to the front; beak produced and rather strongly incurved; deltoid foramen moderately wide, edges slightly raised; no deltidium in any of the specimens examined.

Dimensions. — Width, 3½ lines; length, 3 lines; height, 2 lines. The surface of this shell, to the naked eye, appears smooth, but some specimens under the magnifier exhibit faint longitudinal striæ and fine concentric lines of growth.

This species was found abundantly in the Upper Coal Measures, on the Missouri, near the mouth of Platte River, associated with *Productus Wabashensis, Chonetes granulifera,* etc. For other localities, refer to Prof. Swallow's Report, p. 79.

SPIRIFER? PECULIARIS.—Shumard.

Pl. C—Fig. 7—*a, b.*

Shell transverse, gibbous, length and breadth nearly equal, cardinal angles rounded. *Dorsal valve* more inflated than the ventral, greatest convexity near the beak; beak large, prolonged, elevated, incurved; hinge-line shorter than the width of the shell, flexuous; sinus shallow and narrow, extending from beak to front, not plicated; *ribs*, six or seven on each side of the sinus, simple, convex, rather broad, separated by narrow, slightly-impressed furrows; area very small, triangular, not very distinctly marked, equal to about one-third the width of the shell, aperture triangular, longer than wide; *ventral valve* convex, mesial ridge moderately elevated above the general convexity, simple, sometimes with a very slight linear longitudinal furrow; beak obtusely rounded, slightly incurved; area narrow; surface of the valves marked by very fine concentric undulating lines of growth.

Dimensions. — Length, 7½ lines; width, 9 lines.

This shell is placed with doubt in the genus Spirifer, as it presents some characters at variance with the species now included in that genus. In some of its characters it resembles the species for which the genus *Martinia* has been proposed by Prof. McCoy.

Formation and Locality. — This species is characteristic of the Chemung Group, at Chouteau Springs, Cooper county.

SPIRIFER KENTUCKENSIS. — SHUMARD.

Synonym — Spirifer octoplicatus? Hall, Stansb. Exped. to Salt Lake, p. 409 — Pl. XI. — Fig. 4 — *a, b* (not S. octoplicatus of Sowerby).

Mr. Hall refers with doubt the shell we have named as above, to *Spir. octoplicatus* of Sowerby, from which it differs in several respects. Mr. Sowerby's description, in the sixth volume of his Mineral Conchology, reads thus: "Transversely elongated, gibbous, semicircular, plaited; plaits eight or ten, deep and angular; central elevation, plain; beaks remote, incurved; area triangular curved." In some specimens procured by Professor Swallow, on the Missouri river, not far from Weston, we notice the following characters: Transversely elongate, gibbous, sub-semicircular, with from six to nine plaits on each side of the mesial sinus (the number varying with the age of the shell); plaits rounded, crossed by concentric, undulating, sharp lines of growth, thickly studded with minute granulae.

I found this shell, several years since, in the Coal Measures of Grayson county, Kentucky, and retain for it the name by which I have ever since known it. It is associated with *Terebratula subtilita, Productus splendens*, and *Chonetes mesoloba.*

SPIRIFER MARIONENSIS. — SHUMARD.

Pl. C — Fig. 8 — *a, b, c, d.*

Shell transverse, sub-semicircular, rather gibbous; hinge-line extended into acute ears, and equal to twice the length of the shell. Area narrow; borders sub-parallel, marked with very fine transverse striæ, and more apparent longitudinal striæ. Dorsal valve more gibbous than the ventral valve; aperture rather broadly triangular, and not closed by a deltidium; beak pointed, incurved; sinus commencing at apex of the beak, narrow, shallow, with three or four plications, which do not vary in size from those on the sides of the valve. Ventral valve regularly convex; mesial ridge scarcely elevated above the general convexity of the shell, being only a little prominent towards the front. The surface of the shell is marked with about fifty rounded ribs, mostly simple, except on the mesial fold and sinus, which are dichotomous; ribs crossed by fine undulating lines of growth.

This beautiful shell is easily recognized by its narrow area, and the slight elevation of its mesial fold, which, in young examples, is sometimes even concave. In young specimens, the cardinal border is produced into long mucronate points,

One of the most characteristic and abundant fossils of the Chemung rocks of our State. It was found by Professor Swallow, at Chouteau Springs, Cooper county; at Hannibal, Marion county, and Louisiana, Pike county. Mr. Meek, also, observed it in Moniteau county.

CYRTIA ACUTIROSTRIS.—SHUMARD.

Pl. C—Fig. 3—*a, b, c.*

Shell small; area very high, nearly an equilateral triangle; greatest width at the cardinal margin. Beak of dorsal valve very slightly incurved in most specimens, sometimes straight; deltoid aperture narrow, becoming abruptly dilated near the base; lateral edges slightly elevated; the elevation most prominent at the dilated portion; mesial sinus commencing at the tip of the beak, rather deeply impressed and destitute of ribs. Ventral valve semi-elliptical, flattened convex; mesial ridge elevated above the general convexity of the valve, and well defined by a wide concave space on either side. Some specimens exhibit a faint longitudinal sinus running the whole length of the mesial fold. Valves with four or five simple rounded ribs on each side of the mesial fold and sinus, crossed by fine undulating subimbricating lines of growth.

This shell is very nearly related to *Cyrtia* (*Spirifer*) *pyramidalis*, *Hall*, from the Niagara Group of New York; but it differs in the form of the aperture, which is wider, the ventral valve is more convex, and the mesial ridge and sinus, larger.

Occurs in the Lithographic Limestone of the Chemung Group on the Mississippi, at Hannibal and Louisiana.

RHYNCONELLA MISSOURIENSIS.—SHUMARD.

Pl. C—Fig. 5—*a, b, c.*

Shell gibbous, subtriangular; beaks sharp; greatest width usually near the front, but very variable in different ages of the shell. *Ventral valve* much more elevated than the dorsal valve; degree of elevation varying according to the age of the shell; beak incurved, pointed; mesial ridge obscure, with from two to three obscure rounded folds, commencing a short distance in advance of the beak, and becoming more prominent towards the front, where the valve is emarginate, and presents two or three deep indentations. Dorsal valve slightly convex near the beak, nearly plane anteriorly; sinus broad and shallow in young examples, becoming deeper in the more advanced ages of the shell; it has two or three wide obscure plaits, sometimes reaching the beak. Tongue of sinus quadrangular, bent upwards at nearly right angles to the plane of the valve, and in most specimens equal in length to one-third the length of the shell. The cardinal line is sinuous. The surface of the valves is covered with very fine, concentric, imbricating, waved lines of growth.

Professor Swallow found this species quite common in the Chouteau Limestone of the Chemung Group, at Vandever's Falls, Cooper county. It also occurs at Providence, Boone county.

RHYNCONELLA COOPERENSIS.—SHUMARD.

Pl. C—Fig. 4—*a, b, c, d.*

Shell sub-pentagonal, transverse; surface covered by prominent, simple ribs, increasing in size from beak to front. Dorsal valve moderately convex near the beak and on the lateral lobes; sinus shallow at first, but profound and very wide at the front, with seven rounded equal ribs, the last somewhat angular; lateral lobes with seven ribs, rounded at their origin, but becoming angular at the front; tongue of the sinus very wide, equal to nearly one-third the length of the shell.

Ventral valve more convex than the dorsal valve, and more regularly rounded; median ridge corresponding in width to the sinus, and very moderately elevated. Beak of dorsal valve pointed and entire; cardinal border longer than sides; anterior and lateral commissure denticulated; surface covered with numerous fine filiform striæ.

This shell is very variable in its proportions; some specimens are very gibbous; the tongue of the sinus is quadrangular and bent at nearly right angles to the plane of the ventral valve, while the opposite valve is profoundly emarginate.

This species was discovered by Professor Swallow, in the Chouteau Limestone, associated with the preceding.

It resembles very closely some of the varieties of *Rhynconella* (*Terebratula*) *pentatoma.*

RHYNCONELLA BOONENSIS. — Shumard.

Pl. C — Fig. 6 — *a*, *b*.

Shell sub-triangular, length and breadth about equal, greatest width at the cardinal border, and diminishing rapidly to the front, where it terminates in an obtuse angle; cardinal border sinuous, terminating exteriorly in small salient ears; dorsal valve longitudinally convex, concave from side to side, furnished with two folds which are very obscure at the beak, but become rather prominent and broadly angular as they approach the front; sinus indistinct near the beak, large and moderately deep in front; tongue of sinus triangular; beak rather obtuse and strongly incurved; hinge-line sinuous and situated some distance within the cardinal border; ventral valve shorter than dorsal valve, convex on the middle, sides nearly perpendicular; mesial fold indistinct near the beak, becoming broad and somewhat prominent in front.

Dimensions. — Length, 11 lines; height, 6 lines.

Formation and Locality. — This shell occurs in the middle division of the Encrinital Limestone, near Columbia, Boone county. It is rare, only one specimen having been found.

ORTHIS MISSOURIENSIS. — Shumard.

Pl. C — Fig. 9 — *a*, *b*.

Shell transverse, semi-elliptical, depressed convex; cardinal margin equal to the greatest width of the shell; dorsal valve very gently convex, with a broad and very shallow sinus; beak pointed, flattened, and not extending beyond the cardinal border; surface covered with fine, sharp, rounded, simple ribs, with interstitial ribs often planted between, which, before reaching the border, attain the same size as the regular ones; the number on the border amounts to fifty or sixty. With the assistance of the lens we can perceive numerous very fine concentric striæ, which give to the surface a very elegant appearance.

Formation and Locality. — Occurs in the Cape Girardeau Limestone, on the Mississippi river, two miles above Cape Girardeau.

LEPTAENA MESACOSTA. — Shumard.

Pl. C — Fig. 2.

Shell small, subquadrangular, transverse; greatest width at the cardinal border, which is extended into small triangular ears; dorsal valve gently convex; beak pointed, slightly prominent, and passing slightly beyond the cardinal border; a single longitudinal rib extends from beak to front, on either side of which the surface is thickly covered with fine dichotomous longitudinal striæ, of which the number, two lines from the beak, is about twelve in the space of one line; longitudinal striæ, crossed by very fine concentric striæ of growth.

Ventral valve and area unknown.

Dimensions. — Length, 4 lines; greatest width, 6 lines.

Formation and Locality. — This species is characteristic of the Cape Girardeau Limestone, on the Mississippi river, in Cape Girardeau county.

AVICULA CIRCULUS. — SHUMARD.

Pl. C — Fig. 14. — *a b.*

Shell suborbicular, slightly convex; cardinal line about equal to two-thirds the width of the shell; length and width about equal; ears small and angulated; beak rather pointed, elevated slightly above the cardinal line; posterio-superior edge of visceral portion gently concave; sides and front regularly rounded; surface marked with sharp concentric striæ, crossed by longitudinal undulating striæ; near the beak two or three obscure folds are occasionally seen.

The *Avicula circulus* is very nearly related to *Avicula* (*Pecten*) *dolabraeformis*, from the Chemung Group in New York, described by Professor Hall in the Geological Report of the 4th District. Our specimens, however, are constantly more orbicular, and less oblique.

Geological Position and Locality. — It was found very abundantly by Professor Swallow, in the Chouteau Limestone of the Chemung Group at Vandever's Falls, Cooper county, and by Mr. Meek, in Moniteau county.

AVICULA COOPERENSIS. — SHUMARD.

Pl. C — Fig. 15.

Shell flattened, convex, sub-orbicular, slightly oblique, length and width about equal; beak pointed; hinge-line short, equal to about one-third the length of the shell; wings small, subrectangular; surface of the shell covered with fine, concentric, crowded striæ, crossed by six or seven slightly elevated longitudinal ribs.

Dimensions. — Length and width, about nine lines.

In its surface markings, this shell resembles *Avicula Kanzanensis*, *Verneuil* (*Geol. de la Russie et Ural Mont.*, Tome 2, page 320, pl. xx., fig. 14), but it is neither so gibbous or oblique, and the longitudinal ribs are not spinous, as in that species.

Formation and Locality. — Very abundant and characteristic of the Chouteau Limestone at Vandever's Falls, Cooper county.

ALLORISMA HANNIBALENSIS. — SHUMARD.

Pl. C — Fig. 19.

Shell transverse, subovate, rather depressed; anterior extremity rounded, posterior extremity obliquely truncated and obtusely angulated; basal margin gently rounded; hinge margin slightly concave; beaks obtuse, situated at about one-third the distance from the anterior to the posterior extremity; surface marked with about eighteen concentric ribs, the lower ones broad and angulated, those near the beak rounded and very close together.

Dimensions. — Length, 18 lines; height, 9 lines.

It is associated with *Chonetes ornata*, *Cyrtia* (*Spirifer*) *cuspidatus*, and *Proetus Missouriensis*, in the Lithographic Limestone of the Chemung Group at Hannibal, in Marion county.

PECTEN MISSOURIENSIS.

Pl. C — Fig. 16.

Shell small, inequilateral, oval, regularly convex, sides falling rather abruptly to the ears; surface with numerous fine, radiating, unequal, rounded ribs, which usually bifurcate once or twice before reaching the border, intervening spaces not as wide as the ribs; posterior wing triangular, pointed; lateral border arcuated; anterior wing larger than the posterior; posterior border sinuous, surface with nine or ten ribs, beak projecting slightly beyond the cardinal border, its angle about 65°. The specimens we have seen of this species are all casts.

Formation and Locality. — This species is characteristic of the upper cherty portion of the St. Louis Limestone, in St. Louis county.

PECTEN OCCIDENTALIS. — SHUMARD.

Pl. C — Fig. 18.

Shell inequilateral, rather large, ovate, subtrigonal, length and breadth nearly equal; valves convex; surface marked with radiating, slender, rounded, bifurcating and somewhat flexuous ribs, separated by spaces double their width; ribs and spaces crossed by numerous very fine concentric striæ, and several imbricating lines of growth; wings triangular, ribbed; anterior one larger than the posterior and separated from the body of the shell by a broad groove, border sinuous; posterior wing terminating in a point, its border arcuated; beak projecting slightly beyond the cardinal edge; apicial angle about 80°. It was found by Mr. Hawn, in the Coal Measures, near Plattsburg, in Clinton county.

MYALINA SUB-QUADRATA. — SHUMARD.

Pl. C — Fig. 17.

Shell very large, inequilateral, thick, elongated, subquadrate, cardinal border very slightly arched, posterior border a little sinuous, anterior border deeply excavated; beaks terminal, pointed, a little incurved; umbones rather prominent, from which there is a gradual slope to the posterior border; anterior umbonial slope nearly perpendicular to the plane of the surface of the valves; surface covered with numerous imbricating lamellæ, marked with fine concentric striæ. The facet for the ligament is very broad and covered with numerous fine grooves, parallel and extending its whole length.

Dimensions. — Length, 3 inches; width at cardinal border, 21 lines; greatest width, about 2 inches.

Formation and Locality. — Discovered by Professor Swallow, in the Upper Coal Measures, of which it is quite characteristic. Its locality is on the Missouri river, two miles below the mouth of the Little Nemaha.

CHEMNITZIA TENUILINEATA. — SHUMARD.

Pl. C — Fig. 12.

Shell elongate, conical; spiral angle about 26°; aperture longer than wide, volutions regularly rounded, covered with numerous fine longitudinal thread-like striæ, slightly arched posteriorly, which again are crossed by rather obscure, revolving carinæ, of which about fifteen can be counted on the body volution. The specimen we have of this shell is a fragment, consisting of about four volutions.

Formation and Locality. — This species was found in the Chouteau Limestone, in Cooper county.

MURCHISONIA MELANIAFORMIS.—SHUMARD.

Pl. C—Fig. 13.

Shell slender, elongated; volutions about nine, slightly convex, flattened, the last one obtusely carinated and angulated beneath; sutures distinct; form of aperture unknown; spiral angle, about 18°; length, 8½ lines; width of body whorl, 3 lines. The specimens of this shell that we have seen are all casts, and the surface markings gone.

It occurs in the silicious oolitic strata of the 2d Magnesian Limestone (*Calciferous Sandstone*), in Franklin county, near the junction of the Bourbeuse with the Meramec river.

GONIATITES PLANORBIFORMIS.—SHUMARD.

Pl. C—Fig. 11—*a, b*.

Shell small; umbilicus broad and profound; whorls about six, transverse, moderately convex on the dorsum; surface covered with narrow, transverse, small, sub-imbricating bands, bearing very minute transverse striæ; bands flexuous on the dorsum; aperture transverse, and constricted just within the edge; dorsal lobe wider than high, bifurcated, superior lateral lobes wider than long, angulated at their extremities, and about as long as the dorsal lobe; dorsal saddle somewhat linguæform, and about equal in length and width to the dorsal lobe.

Dimensions. — Greatest diameter, 3 lines; width at aperture, 2½ lines.

Formation and Locality. — Found by Prof. Swallow, in the Coal Measures, on the Missouri river, above Dover Landing.

FILICITES GRACILIS.—SHUMARD.

Pl. A—Fig. 11.

This curious fossil, in its general appearance, bears considerable resemblance to the fimbriated tentaculæ of some of the Crinoids. As it appears on the surface of the rock it consists of a central bifurcating axis, very slender, from which proceeds, at nearly right angles on either side, a series of very thin leaf-like plates, about four lines in length; these laminæ rise directly opposite each other, and they appear to be directed obliquely backwards and downwards.

It has a more slender and delicate appearance than the species figured by Prof. Hall.

Formation and Locality. — It was found by Prof. Swallow, in the Lithographic Limestone, at Louisiana and Elk Spring, Pike county; and on North River, in Marion county.

EXPLANATIONS OF PLATE A.

Fig. 1. — ACTINOCRINUS VERNEUILIANUS, *Shumard.* Part II., p. 193.

a and *b*. — Side view of two extreme varieties.

Fig. 2. — ACTINOCRINUS ROTUNDUS, *Yandell* and *Shumard.* Part II., p. 191.

a. — Side view of a specimen from Boone county; natural size.

b. — Basal view of the same individual.

Fig. 3. — ACTINOCRINUS CHRISTYI, *Shumard.* Part II., p. 191.

Fig. 4. — ACTINOCRINUS MISSOURIENSIS, *Shumard.* Part II., p. 190.

a. — Specimen, natural size; view of the anal side.

b. — Another individual; view of the opposite side.

c. — View of the summit, representing the spines restored.

Fig. 5. — ACTINOCRINUS CONCINNUS, *Shumard.* Part II., p. 189.
Basal view.

Fig. 6. — ACTINOCRINUS PYRIFORMIS, *Shumard.* Part II., p. 192.

a. — An adult individual; natural size.

b. — A young individual.

Fig. 7. — POTERIOCRINUS MEEKIANUS, *Shumard.* Part II., p. 188.

a. — Specimen, natural size; view of the side.

b. — The same; basal view.

Fig. 8. — ACTINOCRINUS KONINCKI, *Shumard.* Part II., p. 194.

a. — View of the anal side of a specimen, four times enlarged.

b. — View of the opposite side.

c. — Basal view of the same; natural size.

Fig. 9. — ACTINOCRINUS PARVUS; specimen, four times enlarged. Part II., p. 193.

Fig. 10. — GLYPTOCRINUS FIMBRIATUS, *Shumard.* Part II., p. 194.

a. — A specimen, with the arms and column attached to the body; four times enlarged.

b. — Fragment of the column; much enlarged.

Fig. 11. — FILICITES GRACILIS, *Shumard.* Part II., p. 208.

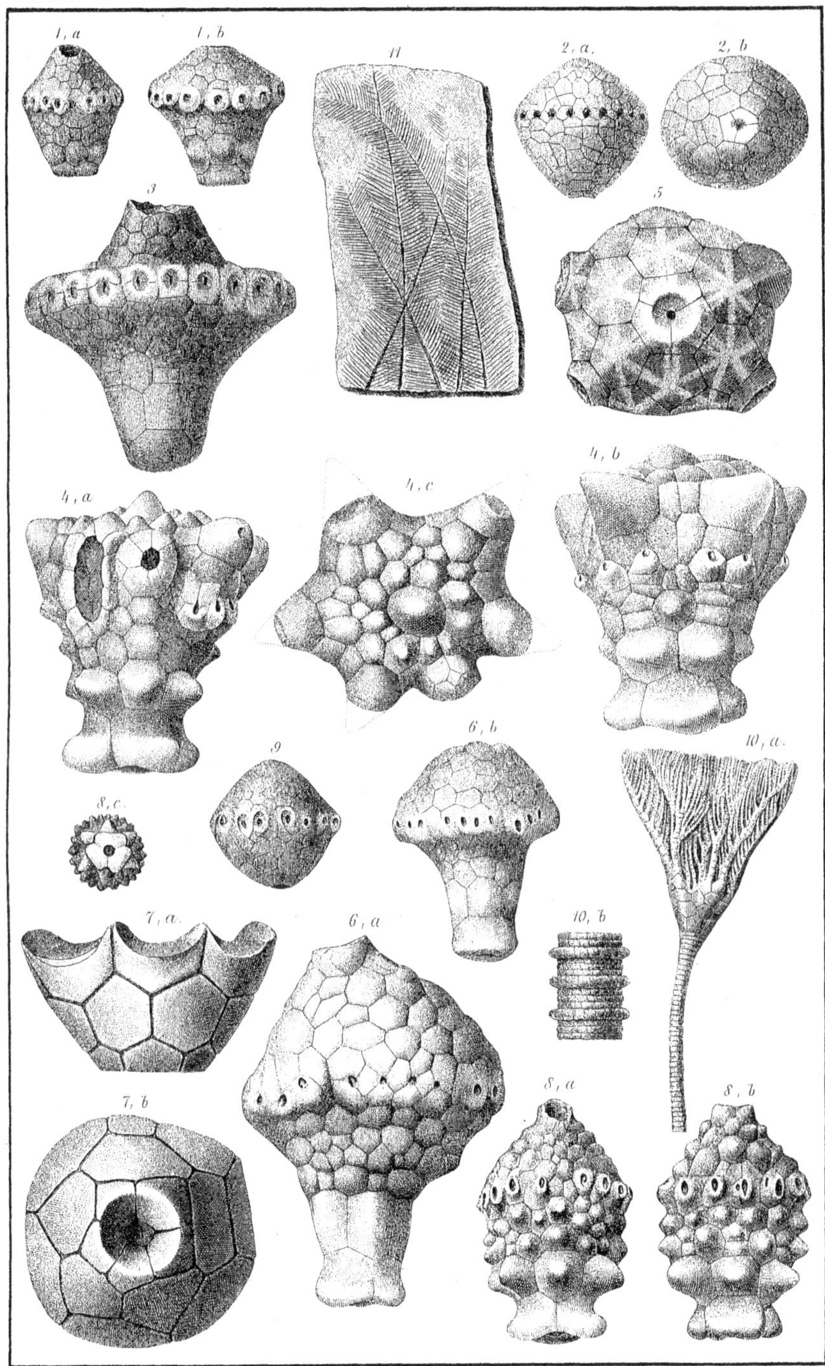

F. B. Meek del.

L. Gast & Bro. lith. St. Louis.

EXPLANATIONS OF PLATE C.

Fig. 1. — CHONETES ORNATA, *Shumard.* Part II., p. 202.
a. — Dorsal valve. The spines on the cardinal border are larger than natural.
b. — Surface enlarged.
c. — Profile view.

Fig. 2. — LEPTÆNA MESACOSTA, *Shumard.* Part II., p. 205.

Fig. 3. — CYRTIA ACUTIROSTRIS, *Shumard.* Part II., p. 204.
a. — Specimen nat. size view of the area.
b. — The same, profile view.
c. — View of the dorsal valve.

Fig. 4. — RHYNCONELLA COOPERENSIS, *Shumard.* Part II., p. 204.
a. — Gibbous variety; view of the ventral valve.
b. — The same; view of the front.
c. — Flattened variety; view of the dorsal valve.
d. — Tongue of sinus enlarged, showing the character of the striæ.

Fig. 5. — RHYNCONELLA MISSOURIENSIS, *Shumard.* Part II., p. 204.
a. — Young individual; view of dorsal valve.
b. — Adult specimen; view of dorsal valve.
c. — The same; view of the front, showing the large quadrangular tongue of the sinus.

Fig. 6. — RHYNCONELLA BOONENSIS, *Shumard.* Part II., p. 205.
a. — Ventral valve.
b. — Profile view.

Fig. 7. — SPIRIFER? PECULIARIS, *Shumard.* Part II., p. 202.
a. — View of the ventral valve.
b. — Profile view.

Fig. 8. — SPIRIFER MARIONENSIS, *Shumard.* Part II., p. 203.
a. — Ventral valve.
b. — Dorsal valve.
c. — Young example, showing a mesian sinus in the ventral valve.

Fig. 9. — ORTHIS MISSOURIENSIS, *Shumard.* Part II., p. 205.
a. — Specimen, natural size.
b. — Surface enlarged.

Fig. 10. — PRODUCTUS AEQUICOSTATUS, *Shumard.* Part II., p. 201.

Fig. 11. — GONIATITES PLANORBIFORMIS, *Shumard.* Part II., p. 208.
a. — Specimen, about sixteen times enlarged; view of the side.
b. — The same; ventral view.

Fig. 12. — CHEMNITZIA TENUILINEATA, *Shumard.* Part II., p. 207.

Fig. 13. — MURCHISONIA MELANIAFORMIS, *Shumard.* Part II., p. 208.

Fig. 14. — AVICULA CIRCULUS, *Shumard.* Part II., p. 206.
a. — Specimen enlarged.
b. — Surface very much enlarged, showing the character of the striæ.

Fig. 15. — AVICULA COOPERENSIS, *Shumard.* Part II., p. 206.

Fig. 16. — PECTEN MISSOURIENSIS, *Shumard.* Part II., p. 207.

Fig. 17. — MYALINA SUBQUADRATA, *Shumard.* Part II., p. 207.
a. — Specimen reduced four times.
b. — Fragment, showing a part of the hinge.

Fig. 18. — PECTEN OCCIDENTALIS, *Shumard.* Part II., p. 207.

Fig. 19. — ALLORISMA HANNIBALENSIS, *Shumard.* Part II., p. 206.

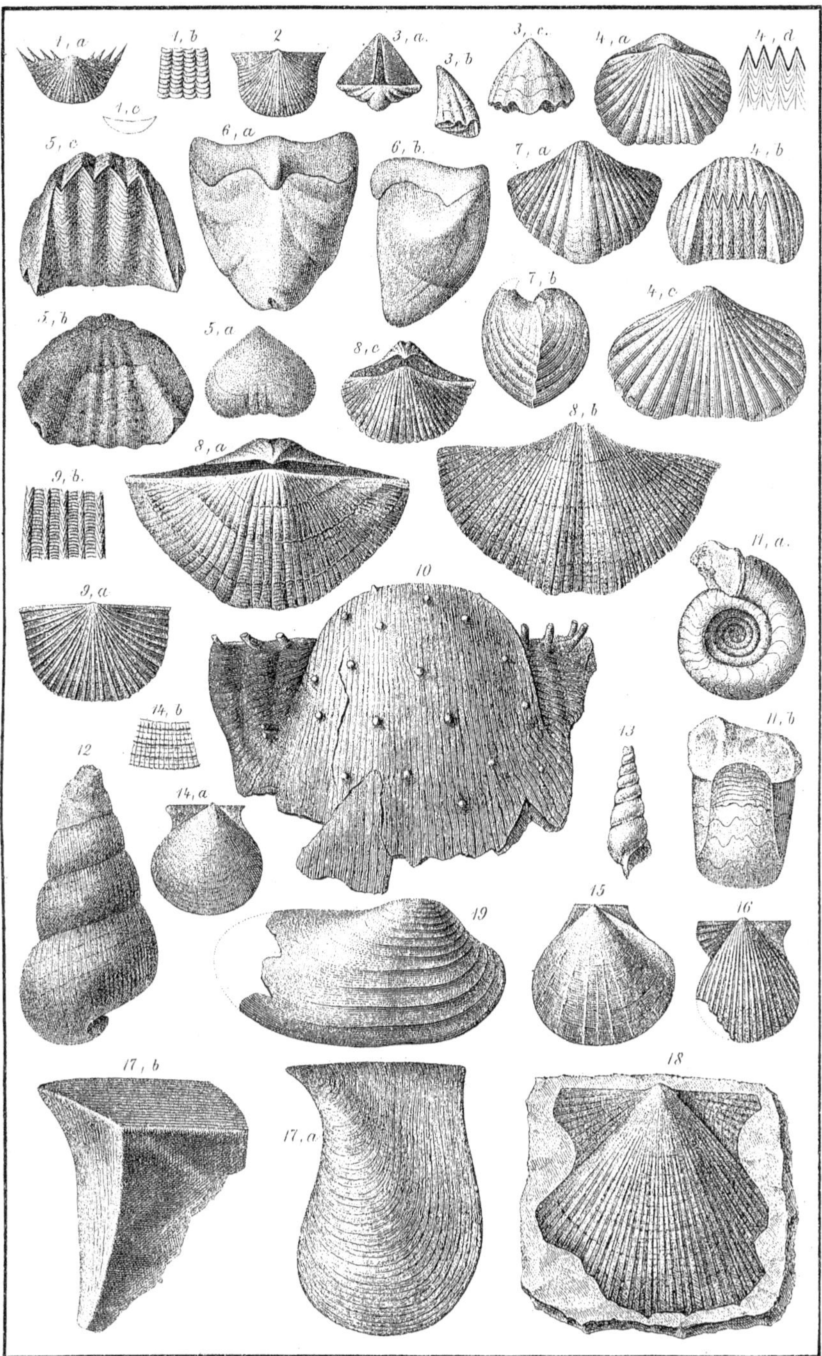

F. B. Meek del. L. Gast & Bro. lith. St. Louis.

APPENDIX.

A.

WHAT WAS KNOWN OF OUR GEOLOGY.

In justice to those who have, anterior to this Survey, investigated the Geology of Missouri, I have compiled the following Catalogue of such Books and Papers, treating upon that subject, as have come to my knowledge. Some, doubtless, have been omitted; if so, they will be added to the list when known.

Though much has been published on our Geology, yet little had been made out in detail. Nearly all that has been written is general in its character; but our information respecting the ores and other useful minerals, is more abundant and accurate.

Still, the pioneers in this great work deserve much praise; and we most cheerfully call attention to what they have published.

CAPTS. LEWIS AND CLARK.

"*The Travels of Capts. Lewis and Clark.*" — Philadelphia, 1809.

This work gives us the following estimate of the annual yield of the Mines of Missouri. It will be interesting for future comparison: —

"*An Estimate of the Produce of the several Mines.*"

" Mine a Burton, 550,000 lbs. mineral, estimated to produce 66⅔, is 366,666⅔ lbs. lead, at $5 ₱ cwt., is, ...	$18,333 33
To which add $30 (on 120,000 lbs. manufactured) to each thousand, is,	3,600 00
" Old Mines, 200,000 lbs. mineral, estimated to produce 66⅔, is 133,333⅓ lbs. lead, at $5 ₱ cwt., is, ...	6,666 67
" Mine a la Motte, 200,000 lbs. lead at $5 ₱ cwt., is, ...	10,000 00
" Suppose at all the other mines 30,000 lbs. lead at $5, is, ...	1,500 00
" Total amount is, ...	$40,100 00 "

We give this table as we find it, save a few errors in the carrying out of the numbers.

These explorers, also, mention the existence of Clays, Iron, Copper, and Coal, and the probable discovery of Tin, Silver, and Gold.

They speak in most flattering terms of the agricultural and commercial prospects of the Territory.

HENRY R. SCHOOLCRAFT, Esq.

View of the Lead Mines of Missouri — New York, 1819.
Thirty Years with the Indian Tribes. — Philadelphia, 1851.

Mr. Schoolcraft gives a Geographical, Topographical and Geological view of the mineral region; a list of the mines, and a catalogue of the minerals then known to exist in the State.

He gives a glowing account of the agricultural wealth of the State, and the commercial advantages of St. Louis. But the progress of our noble city, has more than realized his expectations.

HENRY KING, M.D.

Report of a Reconnoissance of that part of the State adjacent to the Osage River, to the Board of Internal Improvement. — Senate Journal, 1840.

Report on the Rives, Hinch, Bleeding-Hill, and Blanton Copper Mines. — St. Louis, 1853.

Report on the Lands of the "Birmingham Iron Mining Company." — St. Louis, 1853.

Papers: —

A Geological Survey of the State of Missouri.—Wes. Jour. and Civ., vol. iii., p. 12, 1850.

A Geological Survey of the State of Missouri.—Wes. Jour. and Civ., vol. iii., p. 76, 1850.

A Letter to the Representatives of Missouri in Congress, advocating a School of Mines. — Western Journal and Civilian, vol. iii., p. 226, 1850.

A Paper before the American Association. — 1851.

In these papers, Dr. King has given the most accurate view of our lower stratified rocks, I have yet seen published.

In the Second Report is given a section of the strata, from St. Louis to Massey's Iron Works.

These papers contain much valuable information and many important suggestions.

M. M. MAUGHAS, M. D.

Paper before the Missouri Historical and Philosophical Society. — 1853.

Geological Researches in Missouri. — Western Journal and Civilian, vol. ix., p. 382.

This paper gives us a somewhat detailed description of the rocks in those portions of Callaway and Montgomery counties drained by the Loutre and Au Vases rivers.

G. W. FEATHERSTONHAUGH, *U. S. Geologist.*

Report on the Elevated Country between the Missouri and Red Rivers. — 1835.

Report of a Geological Reconnoissance of Couteau de Prairie, etc. — 1836.

Canoe Voyage up the Minnay Sotor. — London, 1847.

Excursion through the Slave States.

Mr. Featherstonhaugh spends much *learning* upon the Geology of Missouri, Illinois and Wisconsin, and particularly upon the Galeniferous Limestones of these States. He considered them all *identical* and *Carboniferous.* He makes many other statements with about the same regard to scientific truth. But we could expect nothing better from a pompous, dogmatic, censorious pretender, who discourses more frequently upon his "tea" and the Entomology of his bed, than upon the fossil Flora and Fauna entombed in the geological formations he was commissioned to examine.

J. N. NICOLETT, Esq.

Report to Illustrate a Map of the Hydraulic Basin of the Upper Mississippi. — Washington, 1845.

This valuable document gives us some interesting information respecting the rocks of the Mississippi and Missouri rivers.

H. A. PROUT, M. D.

Papers: —

The Geology and Mineral Resources of the State of Missouri. — Western Journal and Civilian, vol. i., p. 6.

Classification of the Mineral Masses Composing the Earth. — Western Journal and Civilian, vol. i., p. 115.

Geology of the Valley of the Mississippi. — Western Journal and Civilian, vol. i., p. 243.

Economical Geology of Missouri. — Western Journal and Civilian, vol. i., p. 429.

In these and other papers, the titles of which have passed from my memory, Dr. Prout has described a portion of our Geology, and has called attention to our mineral resources.

PROF. JAMES HALL,

In his *Final Report on the Geology of New York*, has a map representing the Geology of our State along the Mississippi, and a short letter-press description of the rocks therein represented.

In *Capt. Stansbury's Report*, he, also, figures and describes some fossils from the Upper Coal Measures, near Weston and Fort Leavenworth.

DAVID CHRISTY, Esq.

"*Letters on Geology.*" — Oxford, Ohio, 1848.

In these letters to Dr. Locke, Mr. Christy has embodied many important geological facts respecting the mineral region of Missouri. He, also, gives a Geological Section from "Pilot Knob, Missouri, to Hollidaysburg, Pennsylvania."

PROF. W. R. JOHNSON.

Report on American Coals. — Washington, 1844.

An analysis of the Cannel-Coal of Missouri is given in this valuable Report.

F. WOODFORD, Esq.

Papers: —

Mineral Resources of Washington county, Missouri. — Wes. Jour. and Civ., v. i., p. 168.
Clays and Minerals of Missouri. — Western Journal and Civilian, vol. i., p. 193.

Mr. Woodford, in these papers, mentions the existence of Kaolin, and other minerals, in Missouri.

PROF. SHEPARD.

Description of Iron Mountain, Pilot Knob and the surrounding country. — Western Journal and Civilian, vol. viii., p. 140.

This paper gives a fine view of those wonderful mountains of iron and the adjacent country.

SIR CHARLES LYELL.

Second Visit to the United States.

In this work, the learned author has given a very instructive description of the "*Earthquake Region,*" about New Madrid.

WM. R. SINGLETON, *Principal Engineer.*

Report on Ste. Genevieve, Iron Mountain and Pilot Knob Plank-road.

If memory serves us correctly, this Report adds much statistical information to our knowledge of the Iron Mountain, Pilot Knob, and other iron deposits in that part of the State.

JAMES M. BUCKLIN, *Chief Engineer.*

Report of the Preliminary Surveys and Location of the Hannibal and St. Joseph Railroad.

This document gives us a view of an extensive coal-bed along the line of this road.

WM. S. MOSELEY, Esq.

Paper on the Lead Mines of the South-West. — West. Jour. and Civilian, vol. iv., p. 412.

This paper gives a historical account of the lead-mines and mining operations of South-Western Missouri, up to that date.

J. JAMISON, Esq.

Report on the Coal-fields and Coal-mines on the Western Waters — Washington, 1852.

This Report merely alludes to the coal of Missouri, and presents some facts respecting the cannel-coal of Callaway county.

DR. G. ENGELMANN.

Carboniferous Rocks of St. Louis and Vicinity.—Amer. Jour. of Science and Arts, 1847.

This paper gives a brief sketch of our Carboniferous rocks.

JOSHUA BARNEY, Esq.

Report of a Survey from St. Louis to the Big Bend of Red River. — Washington, 1852.

Mr. Barney, in this Report, mentions many of the rocks and trees observed on the line of this Survey.

R. C. TAYLOR, Esq.

Statistics of Coal. — Philadelphia, 1855.

This valuable work gives a very imperfect account of the coal deposits of this State.

D. D. OWEN, M. D., *U. S. Geologist.*

Geological Survey of Wisconsin, Iowa and Minnesota. — Philadelphia, 1852.

In his Geological Map, Dr. Owen lays down the whole of Missouri, north of the Osage and Missouri rivers, and St. Louis county, on the south, as Carboniferous, except the south-east part of Boone county, the south of Callaway, Montgomery and Warren; the south-west of St. Charles, and a narrow zone in the western part of Pike, which he makes Lower Silurian. He, also, excepts a small crescent-shaped zone, in Callaway, extending from Fulton some ten miles to the south-west, which is marked Devonian. His Report gives a detailed description of the rocks on the Missouri river.

FOSTER AND WHITNEY, *U. S. Geologists.*

Report on the Geology of the Lake Superior Land District. — Washington, 1851.

A description of the Iron deposits in and about Iron Mountain, is given in Part II. of this Report.

J. D. WHITNEY.

Report on the Lands of the "Birmingham Iron Mining Company." — St. Louis, 1853.
Metallic Wealth of the United States. — Philadelphia, 1854.

Mr. Whitney has given the world a large amount of important information respecting the *minerals* and *mines* of Missouri; but he has not magnified our 'Metallic Wealth.'

"Prospectus of the Stanton Copper Mining Company." — St. Louis, 1855.

In this pamphlet, we have an interesting description of the Stanton Copper Mine and its Geological position.

Contributions to the Geology of Missouri have been made by Capt. Pike, 1805; Mr. Bradbury, 1809; Mr. Breckenridge, 1814; Major Long, 1820; Dr. James, 1820; Professor H. D. Rogers, 1834; Dr. Daubeny, 1838; Mr. T. G. Clemson, 1838; Mr. J. T. Hodge, 1842; T. Nuttall, 1819; Major Cass, 1820; Mr. E. Harris, 1845; Lieut. A. R. Johnston, 1845, and Dr. A. Wislizenus, 1848; but I am unable, at present, to refer to their papers and works.

WESTERN JOURNAL.

Scarcely a number of the Western Journal and Civilian, from the first to the last, has been issued without some one or more papers, which have given to the world facts more or less in detail, respecting the vast mineral wealth of Missouri. This Journal has ever occupied the first rank in this great work.

B.

USE OF FOSSILS.

We are often requested to explain the use of so many fossils. A few facts will show their great value.

It should be kept in mind that the earth's crust is made up of certain strata of rocks, which always occupy the same position relative to each other. (See Sec. 1, Chap. I., the Rocks of Missouri.) In this State, coal is found in those strata called the *Coal Measures*. The lead, copper and cobalt, are generally found in the magnesian limestones of the *Calciferous Sandrock* and in the *Carboniferous Limestone*. Now, in searching for coal, it is of the highest importance to be able to detect the rocks in which it exists, and determine in what part of them it lies. These coal-rocks are made up of shales, clays, sandstones and limestones. The coal, shales, clays and sandstones readily crumble and fall down on exposure, and are usually covered up by the soil and debris; but the limestones are more generally exposed above the surface. Take, for example, the section from the Hinkston, in Boone county, represented in Fig. I.

Fig. 1.

1	SOIL AND DEBRIS	2
2	BLUFF OR LOESS	4
3	BITUMINOUS SHALE AND MOTTLED BLUE AND YELLOW CLAY	5
4	COAL	2¾
5	BITUMINOUS SHALE AND CLAY	2
6	BLUE AND YELLOW CLAY AND MARLITE	6
7	SANDY SHALE	2
8	HYDRAULIC LIMESTONE	6
9	YELLOW CLAY AND SHALE	3
10	COAL	1⅙
11	BITUMINOUS SHALE AND FIRE CLAY	2

All these strata, save No. 8, are usually covered with soil; while this is a hard blue limestone, which withstands the action of frost and water, and crops out in almost every place where it exists. Since the other strata of this section always hold the same relative position, it is evident, when this limestone is found, the position of the coal-beds, both above and below it, is easily determined. But this limestone is a fine blue rock, like eight or ten others in the Coal Measures, and cannot be distinguished by its lithological characters or general appearance. But on close examination, I found a delicate filiform coral, called *Chaetetes milleporaceus*, and three beautiful little bivalves, the *Spirifer lineatus*, *Chonetes mesoloba*, and *Productus splendens*, all well preserved and retaining the delicate markings of the living shells. These fossils are abundant in this rock, and are found together in no other similar limestone yet examined ; so that whenever we find these four fossils in a hard, blue, compact limestone, we know it to be this rock ; and we further know that immediately below it, is one bed of excellent coal, and that eight feet above it, is another bed, three feet thick. What better divining-rod than these four fossils? Persons not understanding these facts have often been greatly surprised at the accuracy with which we have pointed out the position of those coal strata, where they could see no indications of their presence. So it is with various other rocks and minerals ; the fossils are the guides which lead us with certainty through the apparently confused mazes of our Geological Strata. With them, all is certainty; without them, doubt and confusion often prevail. Every rock, in which fossils exist, can be distinguished by them from all the other rocks.

They have been of the utmost importance to us in the Survey, often enabling us to point out with certainty the age and geological position of those rocks in the State, in which they have been found; to give their true positions in the adopted classification of the strata of the earth; to point out their equivalents in other parts of the country; and to determine the identity of those in different parts of the State, though their physical properties are as distinct as those of a white Saccharoidal Sandstone and of a blue compact limestone, or a pure Oolite. They have, also, enabled us to determine the existence of coal over an area of more than two thousand square miles, where it was not supposed to exist in workable quantities.

These facts prove the wisdom of the framers of the law, which makes it our duty to collect the fossils, and arrange them, with the rocks and minerals, in the cabinets, to be deposited in the different parts of the State, where they will be open to the inspection of all, who may desire to examine or study them, and treasure up their wonderful history.

These petrified remains of the myriads of beings who lived and perished before Adam, are the history, and I had almost said, the only history, the Creator has left us of those countless cycles of the Pre-Adamite Earth. When every fossil is a chapter in this wonderful history, when every one aids us in our search for the precious treasures of earth, shall we not study them, read their history of the past, and follow their guidance in our search for mineral wealth ?

Still it should not be supposed, that we have spent much time in collecting the many thousands already in our possession; for they have been obtained during the progress of the work, in such a manner as not to retard, materially, our other labors. They have, indeed, accelerated rather than delayed the progress of the Survey.

Subjoined is a catalogue of the fossils thus far discovered and identified. Among them are many new ones, which are described in this Report. There are, at least, one hundred other undescribed species in our collection.

CATALOGUES OF THE FOSSILS OF MISSOURI.

THE FOLLOWING CATALOGUES COMPRISE, SO FAR AS DETERMINED, THE FOSSILS THAT HAVE BEEN COLLECTED DURING THE PROGRESS OF THE SURVEY, ARRANGED UNDER THE HEADS OF THE RESPECTIVE FORMATIONS IN WHICH THEY OCCUR.

CATALOGUE I.* — BLUFF, OR LOESS.

No. 1...*Cyclas* — Species undt.......Near mouth of Wolf River.
No. 2...*Amnicola lapidaria*, Say....Near St. Louis.
No. 3...*Helix rufa*, De Kay..........St. Joseph Landing.
No. 4...*Helix albolabris*, Say........Half mile below Great Nemaha.
No. 5...*Helix alternata*, Say.........Bellevue, Bluff City Landing, mouth Wolf River and Lexington.
No. 6...*Helix concava*, Say...........Bluff City Landing and near St. Louis.
No. 7...*Helix thyroideus*, Say.......Bluff City Landing.
No. 8...*Helix profunda*, Say ....Lexington, mouth Little Nemaha, Bluff City Landing, &c.
No. 9...*Helix multilineata*, Say......Near mouth Big Nemaha, Little Nemaha, and Platte River.
No. 10...*Helix clausa?* Say...........
No. 11...*Helix striatella*, Anthony...St. Louis, Boonville, below mouth Platte River, and Big Nemaha.
No. 12...*Helix monodon*, Rackett,...St. Louis.
No. 13...*Helix electrina*, Gould........St. Louis and Boonville.
No. 14...*Helix arborea*, Say ....St. Louis.
No. 15...*Helix indentata*, Say.........Below mouth Platte River.
No. 16...*Helix hirsuta*, Say.............Bluff near St. Louis.
No. 17...*Helix lineata*, Say.............Bluff City Landing, below mouth Platte, near mouth Big Nemaha.
No. 18...*Helix minuta*, Say.............Bluff City Landing, below mouth Platte, Boonville, &c.
No. 19...*Helix labyrinthica*, Say......St. Louis.
No. 20...*Helicina occulta*, Say........Boonville and near St. Louis.
No. 21...*Limnea fragilis*, Lin.......Bluff City Landing, below mouth Platte, Bellevue and Lexington.
No. 22...*Limnea reflexa*, Say.........Bluff City Landing.
No. 23...*Limnea umbrosa?* Say......Near mouth Great Nemaha.
No. 24...*Limnea* — Five or six sp......Bluff City Landing, mouth Wolf River, below mouth Platte, &c.
No. 25...*Physa plicata*, De Kay......Bluff City Landing, near mouth Wolf River.
No. 26...*Physa heterostropha*, Say...Below mouth Platte and mouth Little Nemaha.
No. 27...*Physa elongata*, Say..........Below mouth of Platte River.
No. 28...*Physa gyrinea*, Say...........Bluff City Landing and below mouth Platte.
No. 29...*Physa* — Several undt. sp...Most of the above localities.
No. 30...*Planorbis trivolvis*, Say......Bluff City Landing, below mouth Platte, and at Big Nemaha, &c.
No. 31...*Planorbis trivolvis*, (var.) ...Same as above.
No. 32...*Planorbis armigerus*, Say...Mouth Wolf River and below mouth Platte.
No. 33...*Planorbis* (undet.)............Below mouth of Platte River.
No. 34...*Pupa armifera*, Say..........Bluff near St. Louis, Bluff City Landing, mouth Platte, &c.
No. 35...*Pupa* (undet.)...................Near St. Louis.
No. 36...*Succinea obliqua*, Say.........Bluff City Landing and below mouth of Platte River.
No. 37...*Succinea campestris*, Say....Bluff City Landing.
No. 38...*Succinea ovalis?* Say........Below mouth of Platte, Bluff City Landing, &c.
No. 39...*Succinea*—3 or 4 undet sp. Same localities as above.
No. 40...*Valvata tricarinata*, Say.....Bluff City Landing.

PLANTS.

No. 41...*Seeds of Lithospermum*.......Nine miles below Bethlehem.

MAMMALIA.

No. 42...*Castor Fiber-Americana*.....Near mouth Big Nemaha.
No. 43...*Elephas primigenius* ....Bonne Femme Creek, Boone county.
No. 44...*Mastodon giganteus*............St. Louis.
No. 45...*Molar of Ruminant*..........Near mouth Big Nemaha.
No. 46...*Incisors of small Rodent*....Near mouth Big Nemaha and mouth Wolf River.

*I am indebted to Mr. Meek for the arrangement of this Catalogue.

CATALOGUE II.* — COAL MEASURES.

CRINOIDEA.

No. 1....*Echinocrinus* (new species.)
No. 2....*Poteriocrinus crateriformis*, Troost Mss.
No. 3....*Poteriocrinus* (new species.)
No. 4....*Actinocrinus?*

ZOOPHYTES.

No. 5....*Chaetetes milleporaceus.*
No. 6....*Zaphrentis* (3 or 4 undet. species.)
No. 7....*Campophyllum torquium.*
No. 8....*Ceripora* (undet. species.)

BRACHIOPODA.

No. 9...*Productus costatus*, Sowerby.
No. 10...*Productus punctatus*, Sowerby.
No. 11...*Productus semireticulatus*, Fleming.
No. 12...*Productus muricatus*, Norwood and Pratten.
No. 13...*Productus Nebrascensis*, Owen.
No. 14...*Productus Wabashensis*, Norwood & Pratten.
No. 15...*Productus splendens*, Norwood and Pratten.
No. 16...*Productus cora*, D'Orbig.
No. 17...*Productus aequicostatus*, Shumard.
No. 18...*Chonetes granulifera*, Owen.
No. 19...*Chonetes Smithi*, Norwood and Pratten.
No. 20...*Chonetes mesoloba*, Norwood and Pratten.
No. 21...*Chonetes Verneuiliana*, Norwood & Pratten.
No. 22...*Chonetes parva*, Shumard.
No. 23...*Orthis umbraculum*, Buch.
No. 24...*Orthis resupinata?* Phillips.
No. 25...*Orthis* (species undet.)
No. 26...*Spirifer Meusebachanus* (Roemer); *Sp. triplicata*, Hall, (non Kutorga.)
No. 27...*Spirifer lineatus*, Martin.
No. 28...*Spirifer Kentuckensis*, Shumard.
No. 29...*Spirifer hemiplicata*, Hall.
No. 30...*Spirifer plano-convexa*, Shumard.
No. 31...*Spirifer* (several undet. species.)
No. 32...*Terebratula subtilita*, Hall.
No. 33...*T. sulcata*, Phillips.
No. 34...*Terebratula* (sp. undet.)
No. 35...*Discina* (new sp.)

ACEPHALA.

No. 36...*Allorisma terminalis*, Hall.
No. 37....*Allorisma regularis*, King.
No. 38...*Allorisma* (sp. undet.)
No. 39...*Myalina subquadrata*, Shumard.

ACEPHALA.

No. 40...*Avicula subpapyracea?* Verneuil.
No. 41...*Avicula* (2 species undet.)
No. 42...*Pecten.*
No. 43...*Pecten* (2 sp. undet.)
No. 44...*Leda arata*, Hall.
No. 45...*Leda* (new sp.)
No. 46...*Tellinomya protensa*, Hall.
No. 47...*Cardiomorpha* (sp. undet.)
No. 48...*Cardinia* (sp. undet.)
No. 49...*Cypricardia occidentalis*, Hall.
No. 50...*Arca* (2 sp. undet.)
No. 51...*Pinna* (new sp.)

GASTEROPODA.

No. 52...*Straparollus* (*Inachus*) *catilloides*, Conrad.
No. 53...*Bellerophon Urii?*
No. 54...*Bellerophon* (sp. undet.)
No. 55...*Bellerophon hiulcus.*
No. 56...*Bellerophon percarinatus*, Conrad.
No. 57...*Turbo* (sp. undet.)
No. 58...*Pleurotomaria sphaerulata*, Conrad (*P. coronula*), Hall.
No. 59...*Loxonema* (sp. undet.)
No. 60...*Murchisonia* (sp. undet.)
No. 61...*Nerita* (sp. undet.)
No. 62...*Fusulina cylindrica*, Fischer.
No. 63...*Fusulina* (new sp.)

CEPHALOPODA.

No. 64...*Nautilus tuberculatus?* Sowerby.
No. 65...*Nautilus* (sp. undet.)
No. 66...*Goniatites planorbiformis*, Shumard.
No. 67...*Goniatites* (2 new species.)
No. 68...*Orthoceratites* (new sp.)

CRUSTACEA.

No. 69...*Phillipsia* (new sp.)

FISHES.

No. 70...Teeth and bones of undet. genera.

PLANTS.

No. 71...*Calamites* (sp. undet.)
No. 72...*Sphaereda* (sp. undet.)
No. 73...*Sigillaria* (2 sp. undet.)
No. 74...*Lepidodendron* (sp. undet.)

CATALOGUE III. — ST. LOUIS LIMESTONE.

CRINOIDEA.

No. 1...*Palaechinus* (*Melonites*) *multipora*, Owen and Norwood.
No. 2...*Echinocrinus* (*Cidaris*) *Nerei?* Desor and Agassiz.
No. 3...*Echinocrinus* (new sp.)
No. 4...*Poteriocrinus longidactylus*, Shumard.

CRINOIDEA.

No. 5...*Poteriocrinus magnoliaformis?* Troost Mss.
No. 6...*Platycrinus angulatus*, Shumard.

ZOOPHYTES.

No. 7...*Lithostrotian Canadense*, Castelnau.
No. 8...*Zaphrentis* (2 or 3 species.)
No. 9...*Syringopora* (sp. undet.)

---

* I am indebted to Dr. Shumard for the following Catalogues of Fossils.

BRACHIOPODA.

No. 10...*Productus cora*, D'Orbig.
No. 11...*Productus Altonensis*, Norwood & Pratten.
No. 12...*Productus muricatus?* Norwood & Pratten.
No. 13...*Atrypa? lingulata*, Nicollet.
No. 14...*Atrypa?* (several new species.)
No. 15...*Spirigera* (*Terebratula*) *Roissyi*, L'Eveille.
No. 16...*Orthis umbraculum*, Buch.
No. 17...*Spirifer* (several new species.)

ACEPHALA.

No. 18...*Pecten Missouriensis.*
No. 19...*Avicula.*
No. 20...*Arca.*

GASTEROPODA.

No. 21...*Straparollus.*
No. 22...*Natica.*
No. 23...*Loxonema.*

FISHES.

No. 24...*Cladodus* and *Cochliodus.*

MOLLUSCA BRYOZOA.

No. 25...*Fenestella* (several undet. species.)

TRILOBITES.

No. 26...*Phillipsia* (new species.)

CATALOGUE IV. — ARCHIMEDES LIMESTONE.

CRINOIDEA.

No. 1...*Echinocrinus* (2 new sp.)
No. 2...*Pentremites florealis*, Say.
No. 3...*Pentremites pyriformis*, Say.
No. 4...*Pentremites sulcatus*, Roemer.
No. 5...*Pentremites laterniformis*, Owen and Shumard (*P. obliquatus Roemer.*)
No. 6...*Pentremites curtus*, Shumard.
No. 7...*Poteriocrinus florealis*, Yandell and Shumard.
No. 8...*Poteriocrinus maniformis*, Yandell and Shumard.
No. 9...*Acrocrinus Shumardi*, Yandell.
No. 10...*Agassizocrinus dactyliformis*, Troost MSS.

CORALS.

No. 11...*Zaphrentis spinulosa*, Edw. and Haime.
No. 12...*Cyathophyllum* (new sp.)
No. 13...*Cyathoxonia* (new sp.)
No. 14...*Chaetetes* (new sp.)

BRACHIOPODA.

No. 15...*Productus punctatus*, Martin.
No. 16...*Productus semireticulatus*, Martin.
No. 17...*Productus elegans*, Norwood and Pratten.
No. 18...*Productus Flemingi*, Sowerby.
No. 19...*Spirigera* (*Terebratula*) *Roissyi*, L'Eveille.
No. 20...*Spirigera* (new sp.)
No. 21...*Atrypa* (several new species.)
No. 22...*Spirifer striatus*, Sowerby.
No. 23...*Spirifer incrassatus?* Eichwald.
No. 24...*Spirifer Leidyi*, Norwood and Pratten.
No. 25...*Spirifer spinosus*, Norwood and Pratten.
No. 26...*Orthis umbraculum*, Buch.
No. 27...*Orthis* (new sp.)

GASTEROPODA.

No. 28...*Capulus* (new sp.)
No. 29...*Pleurotomaria* (2 species.)

ACEPHALA.

No. 30...*Pinna* (new sp.)
No. 31...*Modiola* (new sp.)

MOLLUSCA BRYOZOA.

No. 32...*Archimedipora archimedes*, Lesueur.
No. 33...*Fenestella* (2 or more species.)

TRILOBITES.

No. 34...*Phillipsia Meramecensis*, Shumard.
No. 35...*Phillipsia* (new sp.)

FISHES.

No. 36...*Cochliodus* (sp. undet.)

CATALOGUE V. — ENCRINITAL LIMESTONE.

CRINOIDEA.

No. 1...*Platycrinus planus*, Owen and Shumard.
No. 2...*Platycrinus discoideus*, Owen and Shumard.
No. 3...*Platycrinus Americanus*, Owen & Shumard.
No. 4...*Platycrinus corrugatus*, Owen & Shumard.
No. 5...*Platycrinus* (undet.)
No. 6...*Dichocrinus ovatus*, Owen and Shumard.
No. 7...*Agaricocrinus tubaerosus*, Troost MSS.
No. 8...*Actinocrinus unicornus*, Owen and Shumard.
No. 9...*Actinocrinus rotundus*, Shumard.
No. 10...*Actinocrinus Christyi*, Shumard.
No. 11...*Actinocrinus Konincki*, Shumard.
No. 12...*Actinocrinus Missouriensis*, Shumard.
No. 13...*Actinocrinus Verneuilianus*, Shumard.
No. 14...*Actinocrinus concinnus*, Shumard.
No. 15...*Megistocrinus* (new sp.)
No. 16...*Poteriocrinus Meekianus*, Shumard.
No. 17...*Pentremites elongatus*, Shumard.
No. 18...*Pentremites Sayi*, Shumard.
No. 19...*Pentremites Norwoodi*, Owen and Shumard.
No. 20...*Pentremites melo*, Owen and Shumard.
No. 21...*Crinoids* (several undet. genera.)

BRACHIOPODA.

No. 22...*Productus punctatus*, Martin.
No. 23...*Productus cora*, D'Orbigny.
No. 24...*Productus semireticulatus*, Martin.
No. 25...*Productus Altonensis*, Norwood and Pratten.
No. 26...*Chonetes Shumardiana?* Koninck.
No. 27...*Chonetes Logani*, Norwood and Pratten.
No. 28...*Spirifer striatus*, Sowerby (*Large var.*)
No. 29...*Spirifer cuspidatus*, Sowerby.
No. 30...*Spirifer lineatus*, Martin.
No. 31...*Spirifer rotundatus*, Sowerby.
No. 32...*Spirifer Burlingtonensis*, Norwood & Pratten.
No. 33...*Spirifer* (new sp.)
No. 34...*Orthis* (*Orthisina*) *umbraculum*, Buch.
No. 35...*Orthis Michelini*, L'Eveille.
No. 36...*Terebratula? lamellosa*.
No. 37...*Terebratula* (a large smooth species.)
No. 38...*Spirigera* (*Terebratula*) *Roissyi*, L'Eveille.

BRACHIOPODA.

No. 39...*Atrypa* (2 new species.)
No. 40...*Rhynconella Missouriensis*, Shumard.

GASTEROPODA.

No. 41...*Euomphalus catillus*, Sowerby.
No. 42...*Euomphalus Missouriensis*, Shumard.
No. 43...*Loxonema* (sp. undet.)
No. 44...*Pleurotomaria* (sp. undet.)

BRYOZOA AND ZOOPHYTES.

No. 45...*Gorgonia* (new sp.)
No. 46...*Retepora? lyra*, Norwood and Pratten.
No. 47...*Fenestella* (2 or more species.)
No. 48...*Polypora* (new sp.)
No. 49...*Cyathophyllum* (new sp.)

TRILOBITES.

No. 50...*Phillipsia* (2 sp. undet.)

CATALOGUE VI. — CHEMUNG GROUP.

CRINOIDEA.

No. 1...*Actinocrinus?* (2 sp. undet.)
No. 2...*Crinoid* (undet. genus.)
No. 3...*Platycrinus* (sp. undet.)
No. 4...*Pentremites Roemeri*, Shumard.

ZOOPHYTES.

No. 5...*Alveolites vermicularis?* McCoy.
No. 6...*Fenestella rhombifera*, Phillips.
No. 7...*Fenestella* (sp. undet.)
No. 8...*Ceriopora* (sp. undet.)

BRACHIOPODA.

No. 9...*Productus crenulatus*, Shumard.
No. 10...*Productus Murchisonianus*, Koninck.
No. 11...*Productus subaculeatus*, Murchison.
No. 12...*Productus minutus*, Shumard.
No. 13...*Chonetes ornata*, Shumard.
No. 14...*Spirifer striatus?* Sowerby (small var.)
No. 15...*Spirifer mucronatus?* Conrad.
No. 16...*Spirifer Marionensis*, Shumard.
No. 17...*Spirifer* (*Cyrtia*) *cuspidatus*, Sowerby.
No. 18...*Spirifer lineatus?* Martin.
No. 19...*Spirifer* (*Martinia?*) *peculiaris*, Shumard.
No. 20...*Cyrtia acutirostris*, Shumard.
No. 21...*Rhynconella* (*Atrypa*) *occidentalis*, Shum'rd.
No. 22...*Rhynconella obscura-plicata*, Shumard.
No. 23...*Rhynconella* (*Atrypa*) *gregaria*, Shumard.
No. 24...*Atrypa* (sp. undet.)
No. 25...*Terebratula fusiformis?* Murch. and Vern.
No. 26...*Leptaena depressa*, Dalman.
No. 27...*Orthis umbraculum*, Buch.
No. 28...*Orthis Michelini?* L'Eveille.
No. 29...*Orthis resupinata*, Phillips.
No. 30...*Orbiculoidea* (new sp.)

ACEPHALA.

No. 31...*Avicula circula*, Hall.
No. 32...*Avicula Cooperensis*, Shumard.

ACEPHALA.

No. 33...*Avicula subduplicata*, D'Orb. (*Avicula duplicata*, Hall, not Sowerby.)
No. 34...*Mytilus elongatus*, Shumard.
No. 35...*Cardiomorpha sulcata*, Koninck.
No. 36...*Arca arguta?* Phillips.
No. 37...*Arca Missouriensis*, Shumard.
No. 38...*Arca* (new sp.)
No. 39...*Nucula bellatula*, Hall.
No. 40...*Lyonsia*, (new sp.)
No. 41...*Allorisma? Hannibalensis*, Shumard.
No. 42...*Isocardia* (new sp.)

CEPHALOPODA.

No. 43...*Nautilus* (sp. undet.)
No. 44...*Cyrtoceras* (new sp.)
No. 45...*Gomphoceras* (2 undet. sp.)
No. 46...*Orthoceras* (sp. undet.)

GASTEROPODA.

No. 47...*Chemnitzia tenuilineata*, Shumard.
No. 48...*Conularia* (new sp.)
No. 49...*Straparollus* (2 new sp.)

CRUSTACEA.

No. 50...*Proetus Swallowi*, Shumard.
No. 51...*Proetus Missouriensis*, Shumard.
No. 52...*Phillipsia* (sp. undet.)

MOLLUSCA BRYOZOA.

No. 53...Several undetermined species.

PLANTS.

No. 54...*Fucoides cauda-galli?*

INCERTÆ SEDIS.

No. 55...*Filicites gracilis*, Shumard.

CATALOGUE VII. — HAMILTON GROUP.

No. 1...*Atrypa reticularis.*
No. 2...*Spirifer* (a common species at Falls of Ohio, in beds equivalent to Hamilton Group, of New York).
No. 3...*Cyathophyllum* (a species characteristic of the Hamilton Group, at Louisville, Ky).

CATALOGUE VIII. — ONONDAGA LIMESTONE.

ZOOPHYTES.

No. 1...*Syringopora tubiporoides.*
No. 2...*Zaphrentis cornicula*, Lesueur.
No. 3...*Cyathophyllum rugosum*, Hall.
No. 4...*Favosites basaltica*, Goldfuss.
No. 5...*Favosites polymorpha*, Hisinger.
No. 6...*Favosites* (sp. undet.)
No. 7...*Alveolites suborbicularis?* Lamarck.
No. 8...*Emmonsia hemispherica.*

ZOOPHYTES.

No. 9...*Acervularia Davidsoni?* Edw. and Haine.

BRACHIOPODA.

No. 10...*Atrypa reticularis.*
No. 11...*Atrypa* (sp. undet.)
No. 12...*Pentamerus* (2 sp. undet.)
No. 13...*Strophodonta* (a species, like one of the shell beds at the Falls of Ohio.)
No. 14...*Chonetes* (new sp.)

CATALOGUE IX. — DELTHYRIS SHALY LIMESTONE.

CRINOIDEA.

No. 1...*Haplocrinus* (new sp.)
No. 2...*Crinoids* (several undet. species.)

BRACHIOPODA.

No. 3...*Spirifer* (sp. undet.)
No. 4...*Leptaena depressa*, Dalman.
No. 5...*Leptaena* (new sp.)
No. 6...*Orthis* (very nearly allied to *O. hybrida*.)
No. 7...*Orthis elegantula?*
No. 8...*Atrypa* (new sp.)

BRACHIOPODA.

No. 9...*Capulus* (*Acroculia*) *angulata*, Hall.
No. 10...*Platyostoma* (similar to *P. Niagarensis* of Niagara Group.)
No. 11...*Turbo* (new sp.)

TRILOBITES.

No. 12...*Dalmania tridentifera*, Shumard.
No. 13...*Phacops* (sp. undet.)
No. 14...*Cheirurus* (new sp.)

CATALOGUE X. — CAPE GIRARDEAU LIMESTONE (*Lower Helderberg Group.*)

CRINOIDEA.

No. 1...*Glyptocrinus fimbriatus*, Shumard.
No. 2...*Homocrinus flexuosus*, Shumard.
No. 3...*Tentaculites incurvus*, Shumard.
No. 4...*Palaeaster?* (new sp.)
No. 5...*Crinoids* (several undet. genera and species.)

CORALS.

No. 6...*Trematopora* (2 or 3 species.)

BRACHIOPODA.

No. 7...*Leptaena mesacosta*, Shumard.
No. 8...*Leptaena* (new sp.)
No. 9...*Orthis* (2 or 3 species undescribed.)
No. 10...*Orthis Missouriensis*, Shumard.

ACEPHALA.

No. 11...*Avicula* (new sp.)

GASTEROPODA.

No. 12...*Platyostoma* (2 or 3 species.)
No. 13...*Turbo?* (new sp.)
No. 14...*Pleurotomaria* (new sp.)

TRILOBITES.

No. 15...*Cyphaspis Girardeauensis*, Shumard.
No. 16...*Acidaspis Halli*, Shumard.
No. 17...*Asaphus* (sp. undet.)
No. 18...*Proetus depressus*, Shumard.
No. 19...*Encrinurus deltoideus*, Shumard.
No. 20...*Cheirurus* (sp. undet.)

CATALOGUE XI. — HUDSON RIVER GROUP.

No. 1...*Chaetetes lycoperdon.*
No. 2...*Orthis jugosa*, Carley and James' MSS.
No. 3...*Orthis subquadrata*, Hall.
No. 4...*Leptaena sericea*, Sowerby.
No. 5...*Leptaena alternata*, Conrad.
No. 6...*Leptaena planumbona*, Hall.
No. 7...*Atrypa capax*, Conrad.
No. 8...*Lingula quadrata*, Hall.

No. 9...*Lingula fragilis*, Shumard.
No. 10...*Lingula* (sp. undet.)
No. 11...*Lingula ancyloidea.*
No. 12...*Asaphus* (*Isotelus*) *megistos*, Locke.
No. 13...*Dalmania* (new sp.)
No. 14...*Calymene senaria.*

CATALOGUE XII. — TRENTON LIMESTONE.

CRINOIDEA.

No. 1...*Homocrinus* (sp. undet.)
No. 2...*Crinoid* (undet.)

ZOOPHYTES.

No. 3...*Chaetetes lycoperdon*, Say.
No. 4...*Streptolasma cornicula*, Hall.
No. 5...*Receptaculites sulcata*, Owen (*Coscinopora sulcata*, Owen, not Goldfuss.)

MOLLUSCA BRYOZOA.

No. 6...*Ptylodicta acuta* (*Escharapora acuta*, Hall.)
No. 7...*Ptylodicta recta* (*Escharapora recta*, Hall.)

BRACHIOPODA.

No. 8...*Orthis lynx*, Eichwald.
No. 9...*Orthis disparilis*, Conrad.
No. 10...*Orthis tricenaria*, Conrad.
No. 11...*Orthis subaequata*, Conrad.
No. 12...*Orthis pectinella*, Hall.
No. 13...*Orthis testudinaria?* Dalman.
No. 14...*Orthis* (new species.)
No. 15...*Leptaena sericea*, Sowerby.
No. 16...*Leptaena alternata*, Conrad.
No. 17...*Leptaena deltoidea*, Conrad.
No. 18...*Leptaena filitexta*, Hall.
No. 19...*Atrypa recurvirostra*, Hall.
No. 20...*Atrypa increbescens*, Hall.

ACEPHALA.

No. 21...*Cardiomorpha vetusta*, Hall.
No. 22...*Edmondia subtruncata*, Hall.

GASTEROPODA.

No. 23...*Murchisonia bellicincta*, Hall.
No. 24...*Murchisonia bicincta*, Hall.
No. 25...*Murchisonia gracilis*, Hall.
No. 26...*Subulites elongata*, Conrad.
No. 27...*Pleurotomaria? lenticularis*, Sowerby.
No. 28...*Pleurotomaria umbilicata*, Hall.
No. 29...*Pleurotomaria subtilistriata*, Hall.
No. 30...*Pleurotomaria* (sp. undet.)
No. 31...*Bellerophon bilobatus*, Sowerby.
No. 32...*Loxonema* (new sp.)

CEPHALOPODA.

No. 33...*Orthoceras junceum*, Hall.
No. 34...*Orthoceras vertebrale*, Hall.
No. 35...*Orthoceras* (undet. sp.)

TRILOBITES.

No. 36...*Illaenus crassicauda*, Wahl.
No. 37...*Dalmania* (*Phacops*) *callicephalus*, Hall.
No. 38...*Cheirurus pleurexanthemus*, Green.
No. 39...*Asaphus Iowensis*, Owen.
No. 40...*Cythere* (sp. undet.)

CATALOGUE XIII. — BLACK-RIVER LIMESTONE.

No. 1...*Gonioceras anceps*, Hall.
No. 2...*Ormoceras tenuifilum*, Hall.
No. 3...*Cythere sublaevis*, Shumard.

CATALOGUE XIV. — CALCIFEROUS SANDROCK.

No. 1...*Pleurotomaria* (2 or 3 species.)
No. 2...*Murchisonia melaniaformis*, Shumard.
No. 3...*Straparollus* (*Ophileta*) *levata*, Vanuxem.
No. 4...*Straparollus* (*Ophileta*) *complanata*, Vanux.
No. 5...*Loxonema* (new sp.)
No. 6...*Turbo* (new sp.)
No. 7...*Orthoceras primigenium*, Vanuxem.
No. 8...*Orthis* (sp. undet.)

C.

TREES AND SHRUBS.

It is deemed expedient to give a catalogue of such trees and shrubs as are mentioned in the Report, to avoid the necessity of repeating their scientific names, and still enable all to determine with certainty, from the common name used, what tree is referred to. I have followed the nomenclature of the *North American Sylva*, by Michaux and Nuttall, for scientific and popular names, except where other common names are more prevalent in Missouri. This is not given as a catalogue of all the trees of Missouri, but of the most common in the parts of the State examined. There may be some mistakes in one or two of the less important species, as I am compelled to depend upon my field-notes alone, while making the catalogue, not having access to the collection.

I am indebted to Mr. Frederic Pech, of Louisiana, for the privilege of examining his large and valuable collection of herbaceous phænogamous and cryptogamous plants of Missouri.

ALDER.

Alnus serulata, Common Alder — On streams in Newton and Lawrence counties.
Prinos laevigatus, Black Alder, Winter-Berry — In wet land, and wooded bottoms.*

APPLE.

Malus coronaria, Crab Apple — Bordering rich prairies and in open forests.

ASH.

Fraxinus Americana, White Ash — Common in good dry soil.
Fraxinus sambucifolia, Black Ash — Not so abundant as the foregoing species.
Fraxinus quadrangulata, Blue Ash — On good soil, quite abundant.
Zanthoxylum Americanum, Prickly Ash — In bottoms and moist places.

BASSWOOD.

Tilia Americana, American Linden or Lime — In rich soils, not very abundant.
Tilia Heterophylla ?† Large-leaved Linden or Lime — Very common in rich soil.

BIRCH.

Betula rubra, Red Birch, River Birch — On the borders of nearly all our streams.

BLACKBERRY.

Rubus Canadensis, Low Blackberry or Dewberry — In open forests.
Rubus cuneifolius, Wedge-leaved Blackberry — In forests and on the borders of prairies and fields.

BLADDER-NUT.

Staphylea trifolia (Gray), American Bladder-Nut — Under bluffs and in ravines.

---

* When no localities are given, the species is generally diffused through the State, wherever appropriate soils occur.

† This tree agrees very nearly with Nuttall's, but the leaves are less tomentose; it also differs from Michaux's *alba*, in having the peduncles subdivided.

BUCKEYE.

Aesculus Ohioensis? Ohio Buckeye — On the borders of streams, in middle counties.
Aesculus lutea, Large Buckeye — In low rich soil, in middle and northern counties.

BLUEBERRY.

Vaccinium — Several species; not common.

BOX-ELDER.

Negundo aceroides, Box-Elder or Ash-leaved Maple — In rich bottoms; abundant.

BURNING BUSH.

Euonymus atropurpureus (Gray), Burning Bush — On Little Pomme de Terre; very beautiful when in fruit.

BUTTONWOOD.

Platanus occidentalis, Sycamore — In the bottoms of all our principal streams.

BUTTON-BUSH.

Cephalanthus occidentalis, Button-Bush — In wet places and beside streams.

CEDAR.

*Juniperus Virginiana,** Red Cedar — On dry limestone bluffs and on the sands of the Missouri bottom.

CHERRY.

Cerasus serotina (D. C.), Black or Wild Cherry — On the best soils in the State.

COFFEE TREE.

Gymnocladus Canadensis, Coffee tree — In rich soil, bottom and high land.

COTTON-WOOD.

Populus Canadensis, Cotton-Wood — In the bottoms of all our large rivers.

CORAL BERRY.

Symphoricarpus vulgaris (Gray), Coral Berry or Indian Currant — Everywhere.

CURRANT.

Ribes — Several species, but none are abundant.

DOGWOOD.

Cornus florida, Flowering Dogwood — On bluffs and ridges; generally very sparse.

ELDER.

Sambucus Canadensis, Common Elder — Very large in rich bottoms.

ELM.

Ulmus Americana, White or American Elm — Abundant on the best soils in the State.
Ulmus rubra, Red or Slippery Elm — On good soils; but not so common as the last.
Ulmus alata, Wahoo Elm — Very common in the region of the Iron Mountain.

GRAPE.

Vitis aestivalis, Summer Grape — Abundant on good soils.

---

*There are several marked varieties of this tree in Missouri.

Vitis labrusca, Fox Grape — On good soil in the Missouri valley and on high lands.
Vitis cordifolia, Frost Grape — On good soil, on high land and in bottoms.

Several other species are abundant in the State; one is called Slough Grape

GREEN BRIER.

Smilax rotundifolia, Green Brier — Very common in thickets and beside fields.
Smilax glauca, Glaucus Green Brier — In thickets, in ravines and beside roads.

GOOSEBERRY.

Ribes Cynosbati, Prickly Gooseberry — In the central counties.
Ribes rotundifolium, Wild Gooseberry — In woods and on borders of prairies.

GUM.

Nyssa sylvatica, Black Gum — In the neighborhood of the Iron Mountain.
Liquidambar styraciflua, Sweet Gum — Southern Missouri.

HACK-BERRY.

Celtis occidentalis, American Nettle-Tree or Hack-berry — In low rich soil.
Celtis crassifolia, Hackberry — In rick soils and low grounds.

HAZEL.

Corylus Americana, American Hazel — In rich prairies and on the borders of forests.

HAW.

Viburnum prunifolium, Black Haw — In forests, on good soil.

RED HAW. (See Thorn.)

HICKORY.

Carya tomentosa, Common or Mockernut Hickory — On rich soils.
Carya pecan, Pecan — In the Missouri bottom and on the Marais des Cygnes.
Carya squamosa, Shellbark Hickory — Abundant on dry rich soil.
Carya sulcata (Nutt.), Thick Shellbark Hickory — In rich bottoms; nut very large.
Carya porcina, Pignut Hickory — Rich soils, particularly on high land.
Carya microcarpa? Black or Bullnut Hickory — With Post and Black-Jack Oak, on poor soil.
Carga amara, Bitternut Hickory — On Caps' Creek, in Newton county.

HONEYSUCKLE.

Lonicera parviflora, Small-flowered Honeysuckle — Marion county.

HORNBEAM.

Ostrya Virginica (Willd.), Hop-Hornbeam — Near streams and rocky branches.
Carpinus Americana, American Hornbeam or Iron-Wood — Sparsely diffused.

IRON-WOOD. (See Hornbeam.)

JUDAS TREE.

Cercis Canadensis, Red Bud or Judas Tree — Abundant on good soil.

LOCUST.

Gleditschia triacanthos, Sweet or Honey Locust — In the richest soils of the State.
Robinia pseudo-acacia, Common Locust — Naturalized in the older parts of the State.

LINDEN. (See Basswood.)

MAPLE.

Acer eriocarpum, White Maple — In the river bottoms, very common.
Acer nigrum? Sugar Tree — On good soil, most abundant where moist.

MULBERRY.

Morus rubra, Red Mulberry — On rich lands; generally diffused, not very abundant.

NETTLETREE. (See Hack-Berry.)

OAK.

First division — leaves lobed, lobes rounded.

Quercus alba, White Oak * — Dry soil; excellent timber.
Quercus macrocarpa, Over-Cup White Oak, or Bur Oak—Low rich soils; good timber.
Quercus obtusiloba, Post Oak — Dry, poor soils; timber most durable of all our oaks.

Second division — leaves coarsely toothed.

Quercus bicolor, Swamp White Oak, often called Bur Oak — On low, rich and damp soil.
Quercus prinus, Chesnut White Oak — Wet rich soil, in shaded places.
Quercus monticola, Rock Chesnut Oak — Dry soil on rocky bluffs and ridges.
Quercus acuminata, Chesnut Oak, Yellow Oak — On limestone bluffs and in dry bottoms.
Quercus prinoides, ? Chinquapin or Dwarf Chesnut Oak — In the South-West larger than usual; acorns often peduncled.

Third division — leaves entire.

Quercus imbricaria, Laurel Oak, erroneously called Pin Oak — On borders of prairies and fields.

Fourth division — leaves lobed, lobes mucronate.

Quercus heterophylla,† Bartram's Oak — In Cooper and Pettis counties.
Quercus nigra (Lin.), Black-Jack Oak — On the poorest soil in the State.
Quercus tinctoria, Black Oak — On good and medium soil; excellent timber.
Quercus coccinea, Scarlet Oak — On good soil; in the northern and central counties.
Quercus rubra, Red Oak — On damp rich soil; very large in the northern counties.
Quercus palustris, Pin Oak — On low wet soil, in swamps and bordering wet prairies.
Quercus ambigua, Gray Oak — Very rare in Boone, Howard and Cooper counties.
Quercus falcata, Spanish Oak — Rare in the South-West.

OSAGE ORANGE.

Maclura aurantiaca, Osage Orange — I saw a single stalk of this tree in the valley of Spring River.

PAPAW.

Anona triloba, Papaw — In rich soils, particularly under limestone bluffs.

PERSIMMON.

Diospyros Virginiana, Persimmon — In good soil on the borders of prairies and fields.

---

* In Pettis I found a single full-grown tree, which was very similar to the *Q. pedunculata* of Europe.

† This rare tree was discovered in the forest of Pettis, and in Cooper, at Pleasant Green. Mr. Meek saw it south of Round Hill. We could find but one tree in each place. The largest was two feet in diameter.

PINE.

Pinus mitis, Yellow Pine — In the neighborhood of the Iron Mountain, and in the South-West.

PLUM.

Prunus Americana, Red Plum — In rich bottoms, and on the borders of the prairies.

POPLAR (see Cotton Wood).

PRICKLY ASH.

Zanthoxylum Americanum, Prickly Ash — In wet places on the borders of prairies and forests.

ROSE.

Rosa setigera, Prairie Rose — Very showy on the borders of prairies, and in open forests.

Several other species were observed in the State.

RASPBERRY.

Rubus strigosus, Red Raspberry — Common on the borders of fields and forests.

Rubus occidentalis, Black Raspberry or Thimble-berry — In open forests, and beside roads and fields.

SYCAMORE.

Platanus occidentalis, Buttonwood or American Plane Tree — In the bottoms of all the principal streams.

SUMACHS.

Rhus copallina, Dwarf Sumach — Common by the borders of fields, roads and prairies.

Rhus glabra, Smooth Sumach — This is abundant by the road-side and in open forests.

Rhus typhina, Stag-horn Sumach — Often in clusters in prairies.

Rhus toxicodendron, Poison Ivy or Poison Oak — On rich soils, large and abundant.

Rhus aromatica, Fragrant Sumach — Abundant in forests, and by roads and fields.

SPIRAEA.

Spiraea opulifolia, L., Flowering Spiraea or Nine-bark — On limestone bluffs, bordering streams.

SASSAFRAS.

Laurus sassafras, Sassafras — Common on medium soil, very large in Marion.

SERVICE-BERRY.

Amelanchier Canadensis, T. and G., Wild Service-Berry or Shad-Bush — On bluffs and in forests.

STAFF-TREE.

Celastrus scandens, Staff Tree — On river-banks and broken bluffs.

THORN.

Crataegus tomentosa, Black Thorn — In forests in the central counties.

Crataegus coccinea (Gray), Red Haw or White Thorn — Abundant in open forests.

Crataegus punctata, Dotted Thorn — On bluffs and ridges and high lands generally.

There are several other species of Thorn in Missouri.

TRUMPET CREEPER.

Tecoma radicans, Trumpet Creeper — This magnificent plant is seen climbing over the bluffs and trees in all parts of the State.

WALNUT.

Juglans nigra, Black Walnut — Large in bottoms, and common on high rich soil.
Juglans cathartica, White Walnut or Butternut — In low rich soil, and under bluffs.

WILLOW.

Salix — There are numerous species of willow in Missouri, which grow on the borders of our streams and lakes.

WINTER BERRY.

Prinos laevigatus, Winter Berry — In low wet forests and thickets.

The Tulip Tree (*Liriodendron tulipifera*), the Chestnut (*Castanea Americana*), and the Beech, grow in Southern Missouri, according to Dr. Engelmann; but I have not seen them.

E.

GLOSSARY

OF GEOLOGICAL AND OTHER SCIENTIFIC TERMS.

SOME OF WHICH WERE TAKEN FROM LYELL'S PRINCIPLES OF GEOLOGY.

Acephalous. The Acephala are that division of molluscous animals, which, like the oyster and scallop, are without heads. The class Acephala of Cuvier comprehends many genera of animals with bivalve shells, and a few which are devoid of shells.

Algæ. An order or division of the cryptogamic class of plants. The whole of the sea-weeds are comprehended under this division, and many fresh-water species.

Alluvial. The adjective of alluvium, which see.

Alluvion. Synonymous with alluvium, which see.

Alluvium. This formation consists of sands, clays, marls, humus and various animal remains, which are accumulating in our rivers, lakes and oceans.

Alum-Stone, Alumina, Aluminous. Alumina is the base of pure clay, and strata of clay are often met with containing much iron pyrites. When the latter substance decomposes, sulphuric acid is produced, which unites with the aluminous earth of the clay to form alum. Where manufactories are established for obtaining the alum, the indurated beds of clay employed are called Alum-Stone.

Ammonite. An extinct and very numerous genus of the order of molluscous animals called Cephalopoda, allied to the modern genus Nautilus, which inhabited a chambered shell, curved like a coiled snake. Species of it are found in al geological periods of the secondary strata; but they have not been seen in the tertiary beds. They are named from their resemblance to the horns on the statues of Jupiter Ammon.

Amorphous. Bodies devoid of regular form

Amygdaloid. One of the forms of the Trap-rocks, in which agates and simple minerals appear like almonds in a cake.

Analogue. A body that resembles or corresponds with another body. A recent shell of the same species as a fossil shell, is the Analogue of the latter.

Anthracite. A shining substance like black-lead; a species of mineral charcoal.

Anticlinal Axis. If a range of hills, or a valley, be composed of strata, which on the two opposite sides dip in opposite directions, the imaginary line that lies between them, towards which the strata on each side rise, is called the Anticlinal Axis. Plate XIV., No. 1, shows an Anticlinal Axis where the Magnesian Limestone comes to the Surface.

Archimedes Limestone. The name of the formation on which rests the St. Louis Limestone, and derives its name from its most characteristic fossil. See page 95.

Arenaceous. Sandy.

Argillaceous. Clayey, composed of clay. *Etym.*, *argilla*, clay.

Basalt. One of the most common varieties of the Trap-rocks.

"*Basin*" of Paris, "*Basin*" of London. Deposits lying in a hollow or trough, formed of older rocks, sometimes used in geology almost synonymously with "formations" to express the deposits lying in a certain cavity or depression in older rocks. Oseola is in a geological basin. See Pl. XIV., No. 4.

Bed or Stratum. A layer of rock, the whole of which exhibits some common character.

Belemnite. An extinct genus of the order of molluscous animals called Cephalopoda, having a long, straight and chambered conical shell.

Bird's-Eye Limestone. This is the name of a formation in the New York System. See page 114.

Bitumen. Mineral pitch, of which the tar-like substance which is often seen to ooze out of bituminous coal, when on the fire, and which makes it cake, is a good example.

Bituminous Shale. An argillaceous shale, much impregnated with bitumen, which is very common in the Coal Measures.

Black-River Limestone. A member of the New York System. See page 114.

Blende. A metallic ore, a compound of metallic zinc with sulphur.

Bluff. A name given to the lacustrine formation which forms Council Bluffs, and gives character to nearly all the bluff scenery on the lower Missouri.

Bluffs. High banks which present a precipitous front to the sea or a river. A term used in the United States.

Bottom Prairie. The formation on which rests the prairies in our river bottoms, which is usually called "Bottom Prairie," to distinguish it from the high-land prairie.

Botryoidal. Resembling a bunch of grapes.

Boulders. A term for large rounded blocks of stone lying on the surface of the ground, or sometimes imbedded in loose soil, different in composition from the rocks in their vicinity, and which have been, therefore, transported from a distance.

Breccia. A rock composed of angular fragments connected together by lime or other mineral substance.

Calcareous. Containing lime.

Calciferous Sandrock. A member of the New York System, which rests upon the Potsdam Sandstone. See page 114.

Calc Sinter. A German name for the deposits from springs holding carbonate of lime in solution — petrifying springs.

Calcareous Spar. Crystallized carbonate of lime.

Chalcedony. A silicious simple mineral, uncrystallized. Agates are partly composed of Chalcedony.

Cambrian System. Is a name suggested by Mr. Sedgwick, to designate part of the Silurian series of North Wales.

Cape Girardeau Limestone. A name given to a member of the Sylurian System from Cape Girardeau, where it was first observed. See page 109.

Carbon. An inflammable substance, one of the simple elementary bodies. Charcoal is almost entirely composed of it.

Carbonate of Lime. Lime combines with great avidity with carbonic acid, a gaseous acid only obtained fluid when united with water, — and the compounds of it with other substances, are called *Carbonates.*

Carboniferous. A term usually applied, in a technical sense, to an ancient group of secondary strata, but any bed containing coal may be said to be Carboniferous.

Carbonated Springs. Springs of water, containing carbonic acid gas. They are very common, especially in volcanic countries; and sometimes contain so much gas, that if a little sugar be thrown into the water, it effervesces like soda-water.

Carbonic Acid Gas. A natural gas which often issues from the ground, especially in volcanic countries.

Cephalopoda. A class of molluscous animals, having their organs of motion arranged round the head.

Cetacea. An order of vertebrated mammiferous animals inhabiting the sea. The whale, dolphin and narwal are examples.

Chalk. A white earthy limestone.

Chalybeate. Water holding iron in solution.

Chert. A silicious mineral, nearly allied to chalcedony and flint, but less homogeneous and simple in texture.

Chemung. The name of a member of the New York System. See page 101.

Chloritic Sand. Sand colored green by an admixture of the simple mineral chlorite.

Chouteau Limestone. Is the name of the formation immediately below the Encrinital Limestone; it is so called from the Chouteau Springs, where it was first observed. See page 101.

Cleavage. Certain rocks, usually called Slate-rocks, may be cleaved into an indefinite number of thin laminæ which are parallel to each other, but which are generally not parallel to the planes of the true strata or layers of deposition. The planes of cleavage, therefore, are distinguishable from those of stratification.

Coal Formation. This term is generally understood to mean the same as Coal Measures. There are, however, "coal formations" in all the geological periods, wherever any of the varieties of coal form a principal constituent part of a group of strata.

Conformable. When the planes of one set of strata are generally parallel to those of another set, which are in contact, they are said to be conformable, but when the planes are not parallel they are non-conformable. In Fig. 6, p. 90, the Soil and Bluff are conformable, while the Drift rests unconformably upon the lower strata.

Conchoidal. Resembling a shell; used in mineralogy, to designate a particular kind of fracture like the surface of a shell.

Congeners. Species which belong to the same genus.

Conglomerate or *Puddingstone.* Rounded water-worn fragments of rock or pebbles, cemented together by another mineral substance, which may be of a silicious, calcareous or argillaceous nature.

Cosmogony, Cosmology. Words synonymous in meaning, applied to speculations respecting the first origin or mode of creation of the earth.

Crater. The circular cavity at the summit of a volcano, from which the volcanic matter is ejected.

Cretaceous. Belonging to chalk.

Crop Out. A term to express the rising up or exposure at the surface of a stratum or series of strata.

Crustacea. Animals having a shelly coating or crust, which they cast periodically. Crabs, shrimps and lobsters, are examples.

Crust of the Earth. See "Earth's crust."

Crustaceous. Animals having a shelly coating or crust, which they cast periodically. Crabs, shrimps, craw-fish and lobsters, are examples.

Cryptogamic. A name applied to a class of plants, such as ferns, mosses, sea-weeds. and fungi, in which the fructification or organs of reproduction are concealed.

Crystals. Simple minerals are frequently found in regular forms, with facets like the cut-glass drops of chandeliers. Quartz being often met with in rocks in such forms, and beautifully transparent like ice, was called *rock-crystal, crystallos*, being Greek for ice. Hence the regular *forms* of other minerals are called Crystals, whether they be clear or opaque.

Crystalline. The internal texture which regular crystals exhibit when broken, or a confused assemblage of ill-defined Crystals. Loaf-sugar and statuary-marble have a *Crystalline* texture. Sugar-candy and calcareous spar are crystallized.

Cycadeæ. A small and very anomalous order of flowering plants, chiefly found in Mexico, the East Indian Islands, South Africa and Australia. They are Gymnogens as to ovules, and neither Exogens nor Endogens in the wood of their short, simple or branched trunks, and they have dicotyledonous seeds. The leaves are pinnated (like those of cocoa-nut palms), and when young are rolled inwards as in Ferns. The wood fibres are curiously perforated, and marked, by which they are recognised in a fossil state as well as by the trunk and foliage, and the cones, which contain the male flowers.

Debris. Fragments of rocks removed by the action of water or frost.

Debacle. A great rush of waters, which, breaking down all opposing barriers, carries forward the broken fragments of rocks, and spreads them in its course.

Delta. When a great river, before it enters the sea, divides into separate streams, they often diverge and form two sides of a triangle, the sea being the base. The land included by the three lines, and which is invariably alluvial, was first called, in the case of the Nile, a dela, from its resemblance to the letter of the Greek alphabet which goes by that name. Geologists apply the term to alluvial land formed by a river at its mouth, without reference to its precise shape.

Delthyris Shaly Limestone. A name given to a formation of the New York System. See page 109.

Denudation. The carrying away, by the action of running water, of a portion of the solid materials of the land, by which inferior rocks are laid bare.

Detritus. Matter worn or rubbed off from rocks.

Dicotyledonous. A grand division of the vegetable kingdom, founded on the plant having two *cotyledons*, or seed-lobes.

Diluvium. Those accumulations of gravel and loose materials which, by some geologists, are said to have been produced by the action of a diluvian wave or deluge sweeping over the earth.

Dip. When a stratum does not lie horizontally, but is inclined, the greatest inclination to the point of the compass towards which it sinks is called the dip of the stratum, and the angle it makes with the horizon is called the angle or dip of inclination.

Dolomite. A crystalline limestone, containing magnesia as a constituent part.

Drift or Diluvium. A formation of the Recent period, made up of sands, clays and boulders, which some geologists have supposed was formed by the waters of the Deluge.

Dunes. Low hills of blown sand that skirt the shores of Holland, England, Spain and other countries.

Dykes. When a mass of the unstratified or igneous rocks, such as granite, trap and lava, appears as if injected into a great rent in the stratified rocks, cutting across the strata, it forms a dyke; and as they are sometimes seen running along the ground, and projecting, like a wall, from the softer strata on both sides of them having wasted away, they are called, in the north of England and Scotland, *Dykes*, the provincial name for wall. It is not easy to draw the line between dykes and veins. The former are generally of larger dimensions, and have their sides parallel for considerable distances ; while veins have, generally, many ramifications, and these often thin away into slender threads.

Earth's Crust. Such superficial parts of our planet as are accessible to human observation.

Encrinital Limestone. The name of the lowest division of the Carboniferous System; and derives its name from its numerous Encrinites. See page 97.

Endogens. A class of flowering plants, whose stems present no distinction of wood, pith and bark. The wood is disposed in bundles, placed nearer the axis than those of the previous year, as in palm trunks. This class answers to the Monocotyledons of Jussieu.

Eocene. The great tertiary era is divided into four periods, the first of which is called *Eocene*, indicating that in the beds of this division, we see the first traces or *dawn* of the present order of things. The class of fossils most serviceable in determining the relations of the existing to the extinct species, are *shells*, and it is between these, more particularly, that the comparison has been made. Out of about 1,200 shells discovered in Europe in this lower division of the tertiary rocks, thirty-eight only are identical with species known to be living. This small proportion (about three per cent.) varies a little, of course, with the deposits of different regions; and the deposits of this formation, like those of any other, are characterised less by the *precise* proportion of their extinct fossils, than by possessing a number of shells peculiar to the particular era, and found in no other tertiary groups.

Escarpment. The abrupt face of a ridge of high land.

Exogens. A class of flowering plants whose stems have bark, wood and pith. The bark is increased by layers deposited within the previously formed layers and the wood, of layers or rings placed outside of those of the previous year. This class answers to the Dicotyledons of Jussieu, and includes all common English trees except pines, &c. (See *Gymnogens.*)

Exuviæ. Properly speaking, the transient parts of certain animals which they put off or lay down to assume new ones, as serpents and caterpillars shift their skin; but in geology it refers not only to the cast-off coverings of animals, but to fossil shells and other remains, which animals have left in the strata of the earth.

Faluns. A French provincial name for some tertiary strata abounding in shells in Touraine, which resembles in lithological characters the "Crag" of Norfolk and Suffolk.

Fauna. The various kinds of animals peculiar to a country constitute its *Fauna*, as the various kinds of plants constitute its *Flora*. The term is derived from the *Fauni*, or rural deities, in Roman Mythology.

Fault, in the language of miners, is the sudden interruption of the continuity of strata in the same plane, accompanied by a crack or fissure varying in width from a mere line to several feet, which is generally filled with broken stone, clay, etc.

Felspar. A simple mineral, which, next to quartz, constitutes the chief material of rocks.

Felspathic. Of or belonging to felspar.

Ferruginous. Anything containing iron.

Ferruginous Sandstone. The name given to the formation which immediately underlies the Coal Measures and contains an important Stratum of Hematite. See page 91.

Fissile. Easily cleft, dividing readily into an indefinite number of parallel laminæ, like slate.

Flora. The various kinds of trees and plants found in any country, constitute the *Flora* of that country, in the language of botanists.

Fluviatile. Belonging to a river.

Formation. A group, whether of alluvial deposits, sedimentary strata, or igneous rocks, referred to a common origin or period.

Fossil. All minerals used to be called fossils, but geologists now use the word only to express the remains of animals and plants found buried in the earth.

Fossiliferous. Containing organic remains.

Fucoid. What resembles a fucus or sea-weed.

Galena. A metallic ore, a compound of lead and sulphur.

Gasteropods. A division of the Testacea, in which, as in the limpet, the foot is attached to the body.

Geode. A spherical hollow stone, whose cavity is usually filled with crystals.

Glacier. Vast accumulations of ice and hardened snow in the Alps and other lofty mountains.

Gneiss. A stratified primary rock, composed of the same materials as granite, but having usually a larger proportion of mica, and a laminated texture. The word is a German miner's term.

Granite. An unstratified or igneous rock, generally found inferior to or associated with the oldest of the stratified rocks, and sometimes penetrating them in the form of dykes and veins. It is usually composed of three simple minerals, felspar, quartz and mica. Granite Knob* is made up of solid granite. See p. 134.

Graywacke. *Grauwacke,* a German name, formerly used by geologists for the lowest members of the secondary strata. The rock is very often of a gray color, hence the name; *grau,* being German for gray, and *wacke* being a provincial miner's term.

Greenstone. A variety of trap, composed of hornblende and felspar.

Green Manure. When green crops, as clover, are plowed in for improving the soil, they are called green manure.

Greensand. Beds of sand, sandstone, limestone, belonging to the Cretaceous Period. The name is given to these beds because they often, but not always, contain an abundance of green earth or chlorite scattered through the substance of the sandstone and limestone.

Grit. A provincial name for a coarse-grained sandstone.

Gypsum. A mineral composed of lime and sulphuric acid; hence called, also, *sulphate of lime.* Plaster and stucco are obtained by exposing gypsum to a strong heat.

Hamilton Group. The name of one member of the New York System. See page 106.

HO. The chemical symbol for water.

---

* It would give us great pleasure to comply with the suggestion of the *Republican,* and use the name "Granite Mount," as it was christened by the party at Pilot Knob, had we not used this name in several places where it can not be changed. A party christened it Granite Knob, in the early part of the summer.

Hornblende. A simple mineral of a dark green or black color, which enters largely into the composition of several varieties of the trap rocks.

Hornstone. A silicious mineral substance sometimes nearly approaching to flint, or common quartz. It has a conchoidal fracture, and is infusible, which distinguishes it from compact felspar.

Hudson River Group. The name of a formation in the New York System. See page 110.

Humus or Vegetable Mould. A dark brown substance, formed by the decomposition of vegetable matter. It is very abundant in the bottom prairies and alluviums.

Iceberg. Great masses of ice, often the size of hills, which float in the polar and adjacent seas.

Igneous Rocks. All rocks, such as lava, trap and granite, known or supposed to have been melted by volcanic heat.

Inorganic. Not produced by vital action.

In Situ. In the place where they were formed.

Joints. Fissures or lines of parting in rocks, often at right angles to the planes of stratification. The partings which divide columnar basalt into prisms are joints.

Laminæ. Latin for plates; used in geology, for the smaller layers of which a stratum is frequently composed.

Lamelliferous. Having a structure consisting of thin plates or leaves like paper.

Lava. The stone which flows in a melted state from a volcano.

Lias. A provincial name, adopted in scientific language, for a particular kind of limestone, which, being characterised together with its associated beds, by peculiar fossils, forms a particular group of the secondary strata.

Lignite. Wood converted into a kind of coal.

Lithological. A term expressing the stony structure or character of a mineral mass. We speak of the lithological character of a stratum as distinguished from its zoological character.

Lithographic Stone. A slaty compact limestone, of a yellowish color and fine grain, used in lithography, which is the art of drawing upon and printing from stone.

Lithophites. The animals which form stone-coral.

Lithographic Sandstone. This formation derives its name from the lithographic properties of the beds. Section 2, page 63, was engraved upon it. See page 105.

Littoral. Belonging to the shore.

Loam. A mixture of sand and clay.

Loess. A recent formation on the Rhine.

Madrepore. A genus of corals, but generally applied to all the corals distinguished by superficial star-shaped cavities. There are several fossil species.

Magnesian Limestone. A limestone which contains Carbonate of Magnesia. It is also used to designate some of the older formations of the West. The Magnesian Limestone Series of Section 1, comprises the Calciferous Sandrock and Potsdam Sandstone of the New York System.

Mammoth. An extinct species of the elephant (*E. primigenius*), of which the fossil bones are frequently met with in various countries. The name is of Tartar origin, and is used in Siberia for animals that burrow under ground.

Mammillary. A surface which is studded over with rounded projections.

Marl. A mixture of clay and lime; usually soft, but sometimes hard, in which case it is called indurated marl.

Mastodon. A genus of fossil extinct quadrupeds allied to the elephant. So called from the form of the hind teeth or grinders, which have their surface covered with conical mammillary crests.

Matrix. If a simple mineral or shell, in place of being detached, be still fixed in a portion of rock, it is said to be in its matrix.

Mechanical Origin, Rocks of. Rocks composed of sand, pebbles or fragments, are so called, to distinguish them from those of a uniform crystalline texture, which are of chemical origin.

Metamorphic Rocks. A stratified division of hypogene rocks, highly crystalline, such as gneiss and mica-schist, and so named because they have been *altered* by plutonic action.

Mica. A simple mineral, having a shining silvery surface, and capable of being split into very thin elastic leaves or scales. It is often called *talc* in common life, but mineralogists apply the term talc to a different mineral. The brilliant scales in granite are mica.

Mica-slate, Mica-schist. One of the metamorphic or crystalline stratified rocks of the hypogene class, which is characterized by being composed of a large proportion of mica united with quartz.

Miocene. A division of tertiary strata intervening between the Eocene and Pliocene formations; so called, because a minority of its fossil shells are referable to living species.

Mollusca, Molluscous Animals. Animals, such as shell-fish, which, being devoid of bones, have soft bodies.

Moraine. A Swiss term for the débris of rocks brought into the valleys by glaciers.

Mountain Limestone. A series of limestone strata, of which the geological position is immediately below the Coal Measures.

Muriate of Soda. The scientific name for common culinary salt, because it is composed of muriatic acid and the alkali soda.

Muschelkalk. A limestone, belonging to the Upper New Red Sandstone group. Its position is between the Magnesian Limestone and the Lias. This formation has not yet been found in England or America, and the German name is adopted by English geologists. The word means shell limestone.

New Red Sandstone. A formation so named, because it consists chiefly of sandy and argillaceous strata, the predominant color of which is brick-red, but it contains portions which are of a greenish-grey. These occur often in spots and stripes, so that the series has sometimes been called the variegated sandstone. This formation is divided into the Upper New Red, in which the Muschelkalk is included, and the Lower New Red, of which the Magnesian Limestone is a member.

Nodule. A rounded irregular-shaped lump or mass. *Etym.*, diminutive of *nodus,* knot.

Non-conformable. See *conformable.*

Old Red Sandstone. A formation immediately below the Carboniferous Group. The term Devonian has been recently proposed for strata of this age, because in Devonshire they are largely developed, and contain many organic remains.

Oolite, Its. A limestone, so named because it is composed of rounded particles, like the roe or eggs of a fish. The name is also applied to a large group of strata, characterized by peculiar fossils, because limestone of this kind occurs in this group in England, France, &c.

Organic. Produced by vital action.

Organic Remains. The remains of animals and plants (*organized* bodies) found in a fossil state.

Orthocerata, Orthoceratites. An extinct genus of the order of Molluscous animals, called Cephalopoda, that inhabited a long-chambered conical shell, like a straight horn.

Osteology. That division of anatomy which treats of the bones.

Onondaga Limestone. A member of the New York System. See page 107.

Outliers. When a portion of stratum occurs at some distance, detached from the general mass of the formation to which it belongs, some practical mineral surveyors call it an *outlier*, and the term is adopted in geological language. In Plate XIV., No. 5, the Chouteau Limestone between Buffalo and Bolivar, is an *outlier*.

Ovate. The shape of an egg.

Oxide. The combination of a metal with oxygen; rust is oxide of iron.

Oxygen. One of the constituent parts of the atmosphere; that part which supports life. For a further explanation of the word, consult elementary works on chemistry.

Palæozoic. A name given to the older fossiliferous rocks.

Palæontology. The science which treats of fossil remains, both animal and vegetable.

Pelagian, Pelagic. Belonging to the *deep* sea.

Petroleum. A liquid mineral pitch, so called because it is seen to ooze like oil out of the rock.

Phænogamous, or *Phanerogamic Plants.* A name given by Linnæus to those plants, in which the productive organs are apparent.

Pit Coal. Ordinary coal; called so because it is obtained by sinking pits in the ground.

Plastic Clay. One of the beds of the Eocene Tertiary Period; so called, because it is used for making pottery. All clays of a similar character are *plastic.*

Pliocene. This is derived from *more,* and *recent,* and is founded upon the existence, in the beds which it embraces, of a *greater* number of recent than extinct species. The Pliocene rocks are referred to two periods, the Older Pliocene and Newer Pliocene. In the Newer Pliocene, the number of extinct species is extremely small.

Plutonic Rocks. Granite, porphyry and other igneous rocks, supposed to have consolidated from a melted state.

Porphyry. An unstratified or igneous rock. The term is as old as the time of Pliny, and was applied to a red rock, with small angular white bodies diffused through it, which are crystallized felspar, brought from Egypt. The term is hence applied to every species of unstratified rock, in which detached crystals of felspar are diffused through a base of other mineral composition.

Potsdam Sandstone is the name of the lowest member of the New York System. See page 129.

Precipitate. Substances, which having been dissolved in a fluid, are separated from it by combining chemically and forming a solid, that usually falls to the bottom of the fluid. This process is the opposite to that of chemical solution.

Puddingstone. See "Conglomerate."

Pumice. A light spongy lava, chiefly felspathic, of a white color, produced by gases or watery vapor getting access to the particular kind of glassy lava called obsidian, when in a state of fusion; it may be called the froth of melted volcanic glass.

Purbeck Limestone, Purbeck Beds. Limestone strata, belonging to the Wealden Group, which intervenes between the Green-sand and the Oolite.

Pyrites. (Iron.) A compound of sulphur and iron, found usually in yellow shining crystals like brass, and in almost every rock stratified and unstratified.

Qua-qua-versal Dip. The dip of beds to all points of the compass around a center, as in the case of beds of lava round the crater of a volcano.

Quartz. A German provincial term, universally adopted in scientific language, for a simple mineral composed of pure silex, or earth of flints: rock-crystal is an example.

Quartzite or *Quartz Rock.* An aggregate of grains of quartz, sometimes passing into compact quartz.

Roth-todt-liegendes. A name given to a part of the New Red Sandstone by German Miners.

Rubble. A term applied by quarry-men to the upper fragmentary and decomposed portion of a mass of stone.

Ruminantia. Animals which ruminate or chew the cud, such as the ox, deer, &c.

Saccharoidal Sandstone. A member of the Magnesian Limestone series, which very much resembles loaf-sugar in appearance. See page 117.

Saccharoid, Saccharine When a stone has a texture resembling that of loaf-sugar.

Sandstone. Any stone which is composed of an agglutination of grains of sand.

Schist is often used as synonymous with slate; but it may be very useful to distinguish between a schistose and a slaty structure. The hypogene or primary *schists,* as they are termed, such as gneiss, mica-schist and others, cannot be split into an indefinite number of parallel laminæ, like rocks which have a true slaty cleavage. The uneven schistose layers mica-schist and gneiss are probably layers of deposition, which have assumed a crystalline texture. See "Cleavage."

Seams. Thin layers which separate two strata of greater magnitude.

Secondary Strata. An extensive series of the stratified rocks which compose the crust of the globe, with certain characters in common, which distinguish them from another series below them, called *primary,* and from a third series above them called *tertiary.*

Sedimentary Rocks, are those which have been formed by their materials having been thrown down from a state of suspension or solution in water.

Septaria. Flattened balls of stone, generally a kind of iron-stone, or Marlite, which, on being split, are seen to be separated in their interior into irregular masses.

Shale. A provincial term, adopted by geologists, to express an indurated slaty clay.

Shell Marl. A deposit of clay, and other substances mixed with shells, which collects at the bottom of lakes.

Shingle. The loose and completely water-worn gravel on the sea-shore.

Silex, Silica. The name of one of the pure earths, being the Latin word for *flint,* which is wholly composed of that earth. French geologists have applied it as a generic name for all minerals composed entirely of that earth, of which there are many of different external forms.

Silicious. Of or belonging to the earth silica. *Etym., silex,* which see. A Silicious rock is one mainly composed of silex.

Silt. The more comminuted sand, clay and earth, which is transported by running water. It is often accumulated by currents in banks. Thus the mouth of a river is silted up when its entrance into the sea is impeded by such accumulation of loose materials.

Silurian. A name given by Murchison to the older members of the Palæozoic Rocks.

Simple Mineral. Individual mineral substances, as distinguished from the rocks, which last are usually an aggregation of simple minerals. They are not simple in regard to their nature, for, when subjected to chemical analysis, they are found to consist of a variety of different substances. Pyrites is a simple mineral in the sense we use the term, but it is a chemical compound of sulphur and iron.

Sinter, Calcareous or *Silicious.* A German name for a rock precipitated from mineral waters.

Slate. See "Cleavage" and "Schist."

Soil. See page 61.

St. Louis Limestone. The name given to the limestone formation upon which St. Louis stands. See page 93.

Stalactite. When water holding lime in solution deposits it in drops from the roof of a cavern, long rods of stone are formed, which hang down like icicles, and these are called *stalactites.*

Stalagmite. When water holding lime in solution drops on the floor of a cavern, the water evaporating leaves a crust composed of layers of limestone: such a crust is called *stalagmite.* The Stalactite from the top and the Stalagmite from the bottom often unite and form a pillar.

Strata, Stratum. When several rocks lie like the leaves of a book, one upon another, each individual forms a *stratum;* — strata is the plural of stratum.

Stratified. Rocks arranged in the form of *strata,* which see.

Stratification. An arrangement of rocks in *strata,* which see.

Strike. The direction or line of bearing of strata, which is always at right angles to their prevailing dip.

Syenite. A kind of granite, so called because it was brought from Syene in Egypt.

Synclinal Axis. When the strata dip in opposite directions towards a common central imaginary line, it is called a synclinal line or axis.

Talus. When fragments are broken off by the action of the weather from the face of a steep rock, as they accumulate at its foot, they form a sloping heap, called a talus. The term is borrowed from the language of fortification, where *talus* means the outside of a wall of which the thickness is diminished by degrees, as it rises in height, to make it the firmer.

Tertiary Strata. A series of sedimentary rocks, with characters which distinguish them from the two other great series of strata, — the secondary and primary, which lie *beneath* them.

Testacea. Molluscous animals, having a shelly covering.

Thin out. When a stratum, in the course of its prolongation in any direction, becomes gradually less in thickness, the two surfaces approach nearer and nearer.

Trap and *Trappean Rocks.* Volcanic rocks composed of felspar, augite and hornblende. The various proportions and state of aggregation of these simple minerals, and differences in external forms, give rise to varieties, which have received distinct appellations, such as basalt, amygdaloid, dolorite, greenstone and others. The term is derived from *trappa,* a Swedish word for stair, because the rocks of this class often occur in large tabular masses, rising one above another, like the steps of a staircase.

Travertin. A limestone, usually hard and semi-crystalline, deposited from the water of springs holding lime in solution.

Trenton Limestone, is the name of an important formation in the New York System. See page 112.

Trilobite. A common fossil so named from the characteristic species having the body divided into three lobes.

Tuff or *Tufa.* An Italian name for a variety of volcanic rock of an earthy texture, seldom very compact, and composed of an agglutination of fragments of scoriæ, and loose matter ejected from a volcano.

Tufa, Calcareous. A porous rock deposited by calcareous waters, on their exposure to the air, and usually containing portions of plants and other organic substances incrusted with carbonate of lime. The more solid form of the same deposit is called "travertin," into which it passes.

Unconformable. See Conformable.

Vegetable Mould. See Humus.

Veins, Mineral. Cracks in rocks filled up by substances different from the rock, which may either be earthy or metallic. Veins are sometimes many yards wide; and they ramify or branch off into innumerable smaller parts, often as slender as threads, like the veins in an animal, and hence their name.

Vermicular Sandstone and Shales. A formation below the Chouteau Limestone, which derives its name from the vermicular markings of the rock. See page 103.

Vitrification. The conversion of a body into glass by heat.

Zoophites. Corals, sponges, and other aquatic animals allied to them; so called because, while they are the habitation of animals, they are fixed to the ground, and have the forms of plants.

E.

The following analysis, by Dr. Litton, of water from the upper spring of Col. Williams, at Paris, Monroe county, was omitted in the proper place.

Specific gravity at temperature of 72½° F., 1.0009.

In 1,000 grains of the water were found the following constituents : —

Silica,	.01298
Carbonic acid,	.38565
Sulphuric acid,	.23459
Chlorine,	.01678
Peroxide of iron,*	.00599
Lime,	.27854
Magnesia,	.03556
Potassa,	.01998
Soda,	.05535

The ingredients may be combined to give the following composition of 1,000 grains of the water : —

Carbonate of protoxide of iron,	.00579
Carbonate of lime,	.29973
Carbonate of magnesia,	.02418
Sulphate of lime,	.35568
Sulphate of magnesia,	.03696
Chloride of magnesia,	.02278
Sulphate of potassa,	.03696
Sulphate of soda,	.06514
Silica,	.01298
Carbonic acid,	.23938
Total weight of salts and carbonic acid,	1.09958
Water,	998.90042
	1000.00000

In the above analysis, there is a slight excess of bases above what is necessary to combine with the chlorine and acids

The water from the lower spring of Mr. Williams was found to contain essentially the same salts, but, in general, in a less proportion.

---

* This does not represent all of the iron in this water, for some had fallen as a sediment before analysis.

ERRATA.

Page 93—Twentieth line, for Pomme de Terre, &c., read Turkey Creek.
" 98—Third line from bottom, for III., read V.

DR. LITTON'S REPORT.*

Page 6—Seventh line from top; for natural, read rational.
" 6—Sixth line from bottom; for Halfner, read Haefner.
" 9—Tenth line from bottom; for or, read and.
" 15—Fifteenth line from bottom; for examination, read enumeration.
" 17—Sixteenth line from top, and in other places; for stopping, read stoping.
" 18—Fifth line from top, and in other places; for stopped, read stoped.
" 18—Fifth line from top; for ladder, read Scott.
" 18—Sixth line from top; for second, read third.
" 18—Eleventh line from top; for part, read fact.
" 19—Tenth line from bottom; for are three, read are, then, three.
" 22—Fourth line from top; for continued, read connected.
" 23—Twelfth line from bottom; for more, read here.
" 23—Eighth line from bottom; for fifteen, read five.
" 29—Ninth line from top; for Hebbler, read Hibbler.
" 29—Sixteenth line from bottom; omit all the inverted commas under, "from 20th June."
" 29—Seventh line from bottom; for 61 lbs., read 60 lbs.
" 31—Sixth line from bottom; for Boldur, read Bolduc.
" 32—Second line from bottom; for Lead, read Lode.
" 33—Twenty-third line from bottom; read: After passing into this, when successful, openings or cavities are reached from which almost all the mineral has been obtained, and which are filled with clay, mineral and tiff. There have, &c.
" 40—Fourth line from top; for Potosi, read Poston.
" 41—Nineteenth line from bottom; for Argnait, read Arquait.
" 43—Seventh and thirteenth lines from bottom, and in other places, for Bee, read Kee.
" 52—Tenth line from top; omit face.
" 54—Eleventh line from top; for Hornie's, read Horine's.
" 55—Second line from bottom; for Camp, Rowdy, read Camp-Rowdy.
" 56—Thirteenth line from top; for Boldue, read Bolduc.
" 57—Second line from bottom; omit the inverted commas under 1842.
" 58—First line from top; omit, "from May," and all inverted commas under these words.
" 58—Thirteenth line from top; for Neasson, read Masson.
" 58—Seventeenth line from bottom; omit all inverted commas under, "from June."
" 66—Eighth line from bottom; for excavate, read reach.
" 72—Third line from top; for obtained, read attained.
" 74—Twelfth line from bottom; for ridge, read wedge.
" 77—Eleventh line from bottom; for 16.3 pounds, read 62.3 pounds.
" 77—Fifth line from bottom; for 1,515,619,720,000, read 515,619,720,000.
" 78—Fourteenth line from top; for below it, becomes, read below, it becomes.
" 79—Tenth line from top; for 11,537, read 537.
" 85—Fourth line from bottom; for ore, read are.
" 94—Eighth line from bottom; the sentence commencing, "The quantities given," &c., applies to analyses, Nos. 50 and 51, given on page 157 of Dr. Shumard's Report.

Dr. SHUMARD'S REPORT.

Page 137—For 1855, read 1854.
" 141—Fifth line from top; for Palachinus and Echinnocidaris, read Palaechinus and Echinocidaris.
" 175—Twelfth line from top; for formation, read formations.

---

* *Dr. Litton did not have an opportunity of reading the proofs of his Report.*

www.ingramcontent.com/pod-product-compliance
Lightning Source LLC
LaVergne TN
LVHW020912110826
845150LV00004B/655
* 9 7 8 1 4 2 5 5 5 7 1 1 9 *